Python 2.1 Bible

Python 2.1 Bible

Dave Brueck and Stephen Tanner

WILEY

Wiley Publishing, Inc.

Python 2.1 Bible

Published by

Wiley Publishing, Inc.

111 River Street

Hoboken, NJ 07030

www.wiley.com

Copyright ©2000 by Wiley Publishing, Inc.,
Indianapolis, Indiana

Published simultaneously in Canada

For general information on our other products and
services or to obtain technical support, please
contact our Customer Care Department within the
U.S. at 800-762-2974, outside the U.S. at 317-572-3993,
or fax 317-572-4002.

Wiley also publishes its books in a variety of
electronic formats. Some content that appears in
print may not be available in electronic books.

*Library of Congress Cataloging-in-Publication
Data:*

Library of Congress Control Number: 2001090703

ISBN: 0-7645-4807-7

10 9 8 7 6 5 4 3 2 1

1B/RS/QW/QR/IN

About the Authors

Dave Brueck is a professional software developer who loves to use Python whenever possible. His current projects include developing networked games, developing Python interfaces to his stockbroker's C SDK, and plotting to overturn various world governments. Previously Dave was a contributing author to *3D Studio Max R3 Bible* by Kelly Murdock, published by Wiley (formerly IDG Books Worldwide).

Stephen Tanner is currently using Python to build a black-box software testing framework. His side projects include Python tools to perform probabilistic derivatives-trading analysis, and to download mass quantities of .mp3s.

Aside from their "real" jobs, Dave and Stephen enjoy convincing people to pay them big bucks for consulting jobs.

Credits

Acquisitions Editor
Debra Williams Cauley

Project Editor
Barbra Guerra

Technical Editor
Joseph Traub

Copy Editors
Lisa Blake
Luann Rouff

Editorial Manager
Colleen Totz

Project Coordinator
Regina Snyder

Graphics and Production Specialists
Brian Torwelle

Quality Control Technicians
Laura Albert, Carl Pierce, Nancy Price,
Charles Spencer

Book Designer
Drew R. Moore

Proofreading and Indexing
TECHBOOKS Production Services

To Jennie, Rachael, and Jacob — thanks for being patient.
To Pokey the Penguin — NOW who is going to the restaurant?
To the weeds in my unfinished back yard — playtime is over.
— Dave

For great justice!
— Stephen

Preface

Python is an object-oriented, interpreted programming language useful for a wide range of tasks, from small scripts to entire applications. It is freely available in binary or source code form and can be used royalty-free on all major platforms including Windows, Macintosh, Linux, FreeBSD, and Solaris.

Compared with most programming languages, Python is very easy to learn and is considered by many to be the language of choice for beginning programmers. Instead of outgrowing the language, however, experienced developers enjoy lower maintenance costs without missing out on any features found in other major languages such as C++, Java, or Perl.

Python is well known for its usefulness as a rapid application development tool, and we often hear of Python projects that finish in hours or days instead of the weeks or months that would have been required with traditional programming languages. It boasts a rich, full-featured set of standard libraries as well as the ability to interface with libraries in other languages like C++.

Despite being incredibly powerful and enabling very rapid application development, the real reason we love to use Python is that it's just plain *fun*. Python is like a lever — with it, you can do some pretty heavy lifting with very little effort. It frees you from lots of annoying, mundane work, and before long you begin to wonder how you endured your pre-Python days.

About This Book

Although Python is a great first programming language, in this book we do assume that you already have some programming experience.

The first section of the book introduces you to Python and tells you everything you need to know to get started. If you're new to Python, then that section is definitely the place to start; otherwise, it serves as a useful language reference with many examples.

We've worked hard to ensure that the book works well as a quick reference. Often the quickest way to understand a feature is to see it in use: Flip through the book's pages and you'll see that they are dripping with code examples.

All the examples in the book work and are things you can try on your own. Where possible, the chapters also build complete applications that have useful and interesting purposes. We've gone to great lengths to explain not only *how* to use each module or feature but also *why* such a feature is useful.

What You Need

Besides the book, all you need is a properly installed copy of Python. Appendix A lists some Python resources available online, but a good place to start is www.python.org; it has prebuilt versions of Python for all major platforms as well as the Python source code itself. Once you've downloaded Python you'll be underway in a matter of minutes.

If you're a user of Microsoft Windows, you can download an excellent distribution of Python from www.activestate.com. ActiveState provides a single download that includes Python, a free development environment and debugger, and Win32 extensions.

PythonWare (www.pythonware.com) also offers a distribution of Python that comes bundled with popular third-party Python modules. PythonWare's version peacefully coexists with older versions of Python, and the small distribution size makes for a quick download.

No matter which site you choose, Python is free, so go download it and get started.

How the Book Is Organized

We've tried to organize the book so that related topics are close together. If you find the topic of one chapter particularly interesting, chances are that the chapters before and after it will pique your interest too.

Part I: The Python Language

The first chapter in this section is a crash course in Python programming. If you have many programming languages under your belt or just want to whet your appetite, try out the examples in that chapter to get a feel for Python's syntax and powerful features.

The remaining chapters in this first section cover the same material as Chapter 1 but in much greater detail. They work equally well as an initial tutorial of the Python language and as a language reference for seasoned Pythonistas.

Part II: Files, Data Storage, and Operating System Services

This part covers Python's powerful string and regular expression handling features and shows you how to access files and directories. In this section we also cover how Python enables you to easily write objects to disk or send them across network connections, and how to access relational databases from your programs.

Part III: Networking and the Internet

Python is an ideal tool for XML processing, CGI scripting, and many other networking tasks. This part guides you through Internet programming with Python, whether you need to send e-mail, run a Web site, or just amass the world's largest .mp3 collection.

Part IV: User Interfaces and Multimedia

This part covers Tkinter and wxPython, two excellent tools for building a GUI in Python. In this part, we also cover Python's text interface tools, including support for Curses. This section also delves into Python's support for graphics and sound.

Part V: Advanced Python Programming

This part answers the questions that come up in larger projects: How do I create multithreaded Python applications? How can I optimize my code, or glue it to C libraries? How can I make my program behave correctly in other countries? We also cover Python's support for number crunching and security.

Part VI: Deploying Python Applications

This part covers what you need to know to deploy your Python programs quickly and painlessly. Python's distribution utilities are great for bundling and distributing applications on many platforms.

Part VII: Platform-Specific Support

Sometimes it's nice to take advantage of an operating system's strengths. This part addresses some Windows-specific topics (like accessing the registry), and some UNIX-specific topics (like file descriptors).

Appendixes

Appendix A is a guide to online Python resources. Appendix B introduces you to IDLE and PythonWin — two great IDEs for developing Python programs. It also explains how to make Emacs handle Python code.

Conventions Used in This Book

Source code, function definitions, and interactive sessions appear in monospaced font. Comments appear in **bold monospaced font** preceded by a hash mark for easy reading. For example, this quick interpreter session checks the version of the Python interpreter. The >>> at the start of a line is the Python interpreter prompt and the text after the prompt is what you would type:

```
>>> import sys # This is a comment.
>>> print sys.version
2.0 (#8, Oct 16 2000, 17:27:58) [MSC 32 bit (Intel)]
```

References to variables in function definitions appear in italics. For example, the function random.choice(*seq*) chooses a random element from the sequence *seq* and returns it.

We divided up the writing of this book's chapters between ourselves. So, throughout the book's body, we use "I" (not "we") to relate our individual opinions and experiences.

What the Icons Mean

Throughout the book, we've used icons in the left margin to call your attention to points that are particularly important.

New Feature   This icon indicates that the material discussed is new to Python 2.0 or Python 2.1.

Note   The Note icons tell you that something is important — perhaps a concept that may help you master the task at hand or something fundamental for understanding subsequent material.

Tip   Tip icons indicate a more efficient way of doing something or a technique that may not be obvious.

Caution icons mean that the operation we're describing can cause problems if you're not careful.

We use the Cross-Reference icon to refer you to other sections or chapters that have more to say on a subject.

Visit Us!

We've set up a Web site for the book at www.pythonapocrypha.com. On the site you'll find additional information, links to Python Web sites, and all the code samples from the book (so you can be lazy and not type them in). The Web site also has a section where you can give feedback on the book, and we post answers to common questions.

Have fun and enjoy the book!

Acknowledgments

Although this book represents many hours of work on our part, there are many others without whom we would have failed.

First and foremost is Guido van Rossum, Python's creator and Benevolent Dictator for Life. We're glad he created such a cool language and that many others have joined him along the way.

Many thanks go to the good people at Wiley: Debra Williams Cauley, our acquisitions editor, for making it all possible; Barb Guerra, our project editor, for keeping everything on track; Joseph Traub, our technical editor, for clarifying exposition and squashing bugs; and Lisa Blake and Luann Rouff, our copy editors, who fixed more broken grammar and passive-voice constructions than a stick could be shaken at.

Contents at a Glance

Preface ix
Acknowledgments xiv

Part I: The Python Language 1
Chapter 1: Python in an Hour 3
Chapter 2: Identifiers, Variables, and Numeric Types 19
Chapter 3: Expressions and Strings 29
Chapter 4: Advanced Data Types 49
Chapter 5: Control Flow 73
Chapter 6: Program Organization 87
Chapter 7: Object-Oriented Python 99
Chapter 8: Input and Output 119

Part II: Files, Data Storage, and Operating System Services 131
Chapter 9: Processing Strings and Regular Expressions 133
Chapter 10: Working with Files and Directories 155
Chapter 11: Using Other Operating System Services 179
Chapter 12: Storing Data and Objects 195
Chapter 13: Accessing Date and Time 219
Chapter 14: Using Databases 229

Part III: Networking and the Internet 245
Chapter 15: Networking 247
Chapter 16: Speaking Internet Protocols 275
Chapter 17: Handling Internet Data 303
Chapter 18: Parsing XML and Other Markup Languages 325

Part IV: User Interfaces and Multimedia 345
Chapter 19: Tinkering with Tkinter 347
Chapter 20: Using Advanced Tkinter Widgets 371
Chapter 21: Building User Interfaces with wxPython 391
Chapter 22: Using Curses 415
Chapter 23: Building Simple Command Interpreters 433
Chapter 24: Playing Sound 453

Part V: Advanced Python Programming **465**

Chapter 25: Processing Images 467
Chapter 26: Multithreading 481
Chapter 27: Debugging, Profiling, and Optimization 497
Chapter 28: Security and Encryption 515
Chapter 29: Writing Extension Modules 527
Chapter 30: Embedding the Python Interpreter 553
Chapter 31: Number Crunching 581
Chapter 32: Using NumPy 589
Chapter 33: Parsing and Interpreting Python Code 605

Part VI: Deploying Python Applications **617**

Chapter 34: Creating Worldwide Applications 619
Chapter 35: Customizing Import Behavior 629
Chapter 36: Distributing Modules and Applications 643

Part VII: Platform-Specific Support **659**

Chapter 37: Windows 661
Chapter 38: UNIX-Compatible Modules 671

Appendix A: Online Resources **685**
Appendix B: Python Development Environments **689**

Index **701**

Contents

Preface ix

Acknowledgments xiv

Part I: The Python Language   1

Chapter 1: Python in an Hour 3

Jumping In: Starting the Python Interpreter 3
Experimenting with Variables and Expressions 4
    Pocket calculator 4
    Variables 5
Defining a Function 5
Running a Python Program 6
Looping and Control 6
    Integer division 7
    Looping 8
    Branching with if-statements 8
    Breaking and continuing 8
Lists and Tuples 9
    Tuples 9
    Slicing and dicing 9
Dictionaries 10
Reading and Writing Files 11
Sample Program: Word Frequencies 11
Loading and Using Modules 14
Creating a Class 14
    Some quick object jargon 14
    Object orientation, Python style 15
    Keep off the grass — Accessing class members 15
    Example: the point class 15
Recommended Reading 17

Chapter 2: Identifiers, Variables, and Numeric Types 19

Identifiers and Operators 19
    Reserved words 20
    Operators 20
Numeric Types 21
    Integers 21
    Long integers 21

Floating point numbers 22
Imaginary numbers 22
Manipulating numeric types 23
Assigning Values to Variables 26
Simple assignment statements 26
Multiple assignment 27
Augmented assignment 27

Chapter 3: Expressions and Strings **29**

Expressions 29
Comparing numeric types 29
Compound expressions. 31
Complex expressions 32
Operator precedence 33
Strings 34
String literals 35
Manipulating strings 37
Comparing strings 42
Unicode string literals 43
Converting Between Simple Types 43
Converting to numerical types 44
Converting to strings 45

Chapter 4: Advanced Data Types **49**

Grouping Data with Sequences 49
Creating lists 50
Creating tuples 52
Working with Sequences 52
Joining and repeating with arithmetic operators 52
Comparing and membership testing 53
Accessing parts of sequences 53
Iterating with for...in 55
Using sequence utility functions 55
Using Additional List Object Features 57
Additional operations 57
List object methods 58
Mapping Information with Dictionaries 60
Creating and adding to dictionaries 61
Accessing and updating dictionary mappings 61
Additional dictionary operations 62
Understanding References 63
Object identity 63
Counting references 64
Copying Complex Objects 65
Shallow copies 65
Deep copies 66

Identifying Data Types 67
Working with Array Objects 68
    Creating arrays 68
    Converting between types 69
    Array methods and operations 71

Chapter 5: Control Flow **73**
Making Decisions with If-Statements 73
Using For-Loops 74
    Anatomy of a for-loop 74
    Looping example: encoding strings 75
    Ranges and xranges 76
    Breaking, continuing, and else-clauses 77
    Changing horses in midstream 78
Using While-Loops 79
Throwing and Catching Exceptions 79
    Passing the buck: propagating exceptions 80
    Handling an exception 80
    More on exceptions 81
    Defining and raising exceptions 82
    Cleaning up with finally 82
Debugging with Assertions 83
    Assertions in Python 83
    Toggling assertions 84
Example: Game of Life 84

Chapter 6: Program Organization **87**
Defining Functions 87
    Pass by object reference 88
    All about parameters 88
    Arbitrary arguments 89
    Apply: passing arguments from a tuple 90
    A bit of functional programming 90
Grouping Code with Modules 91
    Laying out a module 91
    Taking inventory of a module 92
Importing Modules 92
    What else happens upon import? 93
    Reimporting modules 93
    Exotic imports 94
Locating Modules 94
    Python path 94
    Compiled files 95
Understanding Scope Rules 95
    Is it local or global? 95
    Listing namespace contents 96
Grouping Modules into Packages 96
Compiling and Running Programmatically 97

Chapter 7: Object-Oriented Python **99**

   Overview of Object-Oriented Python 99
   Creating Classes and Instance Objects 100
      Creating instance objects 101
      More on accessing attributes 101
   Deriving New Classes from Other Classes 102
      Multiple inheritance 103
      Creating a custom list class 104
      Creating a custom string class 105
      Creating a custom dictionary class 106
   Hiding Private Data 106
   Identifying Class Membership 107
   Overloading Standard Behaviors 108
      Overloading basic functionality 109
      Overloading numeric operators 111
      Overloading sequence and dictionary operators 112
      Overloading bitwise operators 114
      Overloading type conversions 115
   Using Weak References 115
      Creating weak references 116
      Creating proxy objects 117

Chapter 8: Input and Output **119**

   Printing to the Screen 119
   Accessing Keyboard Input 120
      raw_input 120
      input 121
   Opening, Closing, and Positioning Files 121
      open 122
      File object information 123
      close 123
      File position 123
   Writing Files 124
   Reading Files 125
   Accessing Standard I/O 126
   Using Filelike Objects 127

Part II: Files, Data Storage, and Operating System Services   **131**

Chapter 9: Processing Strings and Regular Expressions **133**

   Using String Objects 133
      String formatting methods 134
      String case-changing methods 134
      String format tests (the is-methods) 135

String searching methods 135
String manipulation methods 137
Using the String Module 138
Character categories 138
Miscellaneous functions 139
Defining Regular Expressions 140
Regular expression syntax 140
Backslashes and raw strings 142
Character groups and other backslash magic 142
Nongreedy matching 143
Extensions 143
Creating and Using Regular Expression Objects 144
Using regular expression objects 145
Applying regular expressions without compiling 147
Using Match Objects 147
group([groupid,...]) 148
groups([nomatch]) 148
groupdict([nomatch]) 148
start([groupid]), end([groupid]), span([groupid]) 148
re,string,pos,endpos, ... 149
Treating Strings as Files 149
Encoding Text 151
Using Unicode strings 151
Reading and writing non-ASCII strings 151
Using the Unicode database 153
Formatting Floating Point Numbers 154
fix(number,precision) 154
sci(number,precision) 154

Chapter 10: Working with Files and Directories **155**

Retrieving File and Directory Information 155
The piecemeal approach 156
The I-want-it-all approach 159
Building and Dissecting Paths 161
Joining path parts 161
Breaking paths into pieces 162
Other path modifiers 162
Listing Directories and Matching File Names 163
Obtaining Environment and Argument Information 165
Environment variables 165
Current working directory 165
Command-line parameters 166
Example: Recursive Grep Utility 166
Copying, Renaming, and Removing Paths 168
Copying and linking 168
Renaming 168
Removing 169

Creating Directories and Temporary Files 169
Comparing Files and Directories 171
Working with File Descriptors 173
    General file descriptor functions 173
    Pipes 174
Other File Processing Techniques 174
    Randomly accessing lines in text files 174
    Using memory-mapped files 175
    Iterating over several files 176

Chapter 11: Using Other Operating System Services 179

Executing Shell Commands and Other Programs 179
Spawning Child Processes 181
    popen functions 181
    spawn functions 182
    fork 183
    Process management and termination 183
Handling Process Information 185
Retrieving System Information 187
Managing Configuration Files 188
Understanding Error Names 190
Handling Asynchronous Signals 191

Chapter 12: Storing Data and Objects 195

Data Storage Overview 195
    Text versus binary 195
    Compression 196
    Byte order ("Endianness") 196
    Object state 196
    Destination 196
    On the receiving end 196
Loading and Saving Objects 197
    Pickling with pickle 197
    The marshal module 200
Example: Moving Objects Across a Network 200
Using Database-Like Storage 203
Converting to and from C Structures 204
Converting Data to Standard Formats 208
    Sun's XDR format 208
    Other formats 210
Compressing Data 210
    zlib 211
    gzip 213
    zipfile 214

Chapter 13: Accessing Date and Time **219**

　Telling Time in Python 219
　　Ticks 219
　　TimeTuple 220
　　Stopwatch time 220
　Converting Between Time Formats 221
　Parsing and Printing Dates and Times 222
　　Fancy formatting 222
　　Parsing time 223
　　Localization 223
　Accessing the Calendar 224
　　Printing monthly and yearly calendars 224
　　Calendar information 225
　　Leap years 226
　Using Time Zones 226
　Allowing Two-Digit Years 227

Chapter 14: Using Databases **229**

　Using Disk-Based Dictionaries 229
　DBM Example: Tracking Telephone Numbers 231
　Advanced Disk-Based Dictionaries 232
　　dbm 232
　　gdbm 232
　　dbhash 233
　　Using BSD database objects 233
　Accessing Relational Databases 234
　　Connection objects 234
　　Transactions 234
　　Cursor objects 235
　Example: "Sounds-Like" Queries 235
　Examining Relational Metadata 237
　Example: Creating Auditing Tables 238
　Advanced Features of the DB API 240
　　Input and output sizes 241
　　Reusable SQL statements 242
　　Database library information 242
　　Error hierarchy 243

Part III: Networking and the Internet　　　　　　**245**

Chapter 15: Networking **247**

　Networking Background 247
　Working with Addresses and Host Names 248

Communicating with Low-Level Sockets 250
    Creating and destroying sockets 250
    Connecting sockets 251
    Sending and receiving data 252
    Using socket options 253
    Converting numbers 256
Example: A Multicast Chat Application 256
Using SocketServers 261
    The SocketServer family 261
    Request handlers 263
Processing Web Browser Requests 264
    BaseHTTPRequestHandler 265
    SimpleHTTPRequestHandler 266
    CGIHTTPRequestHandler 267
    Example: form handler CGI script 267
Handling Multiple Requests Without Threads 269
    asyncore 271

Chapter 16: Speaking Internet Protocols **275**
Python's Internet Protocol Support 275
Retrieving Internet Resources 276
    Manipulating URLs 276
    Treating a URL as a file 277
    URLopeners 277
    Extended URL opening 278
Sending HTTP Requests 279
    Building and using request objects 279
Sending and Receiving E-Mail 281
    Accessing POP3 accounts 281
    Accessing SMTP accounts 283
    Accessing IMAP accounts 285
Transferring Files via FTP 289
Retrieving Resources Using Gopher 291
Working with Newsgroups 292
Using the Telnet Protocol 296
    Connecting 296
    Reading and writing 296
    Watching and waiting 297
    Other methods 297
Writing CGI Scripts 298
    Setting up CGI scripts 298
    Accessing form fields 299
    Advanced CGI functions 301
    A note on debugging 301
    A note on security 302

Chapter 17: Handling Internet Data **303**

Manipulating URLs 303
Formatting Text 304
    Formatter interface 304
    Writer interface 305
    Other module resources 306
Reading Web Spider Robot Files 307
Viewing Files in a Web Browser 308
Dissecting E-Mail Messages 309
    Parsing a message 309
    Retrieving header values 309
    Other members 310
    Address lists 310
    rfc822 utility functions 311
    MIME messages 311
Working with MIME Encoding 312
    Encoding and decoding MIME messages 312
    Parsing multipart MIME messages 313
    Writing out multipart MIME messages 313
    Handling document types 316
Encoding and Decoding Message Data 317
    Uuencode 317
    Base64 318
    Quoted-printable 319
Working with UNIX Mailboxes 320
    Working with MH mailboxes 320
Using Web Cookies 321
    Cookies 322
    Morsels 322
    Example: a cookie importer 323

Chapter 18: Parsing XML and Other Markup Languages **325**

Markup Language Basics 325
    Tags are for metatext 326
    Tag rules 326
    Namespaces 327
    Processing XML 327
Parsing HTML Files 327
    HTMLParser methods 328
    Handling tags 328
    Other parsing methods 328
    Handling unknown or bogus elements 329
Example: Bold Only 330
Example: Web Robot 331

Parsing XML with SAX 334
    Using a ContentHandler 334
    Example: blood-type extractor 335
    Using parser (XMLReader) objects 336
    SAX exceptions 337
Parsing XML with DOM 338
    DOM nodes 338
    Elements, attributes, and text 338
    The document node (DOM) 339
    Example: data import and export with DOM 339
Parsing XML with xmllib 341
    Elements and attributes 342
    XML handlers 343
    Other XMLParser members 343

Part IV: User Interfaces and Multimedia   345

Chapter 19: Tinkering with Tkinter 347

Getting Your Feet Wet 347
Creating a GUI 348
    Building an interface with widgets 348
    Widget options 349
Laying Out Widgets 349
    Packer options 350
    Grid options 351
Example: Breakfast Buttons 352
Using Common Options 354
    Color options 354
    Size options 355
    Appearance options 355
    Behavior options 355
Gathering User Input 356
Example: Printing Fancy Text 357
Using Text Widgets 359
Building Menus 360
Using Tkinter Dialogs 361
    File dialogs 362
Example: Text Editor 362
Handling Colors and Fonts 365
    Colors 365
    Fonts 366
Drawing Graphics 366
    The canvas widget 366
    Manipulating canvas items 367
Using Timers 368
Example: A Bouncing Picture 368

Chapter 20: Using Advanced Tkinter Widgets 371

Handling Events 371
    Creating event handlers 371
    Binding mouse events 372
    Binding keyboard events 372
    Event objects 373
Example: A Drawing Canvas 373
Advanced Widgets 375
    Listbox 375
    Scale 376
    Scrollbar 376
Example: Color Scheme Customizer 377
Creating Dialogs 381
Supporting Drag-and-Drop Operations 382
Using Cursors 385
Designing New Widgets 387
Further Tkinter Adventures 389
    Additional widgets 389
    Learning more 389

Chapter 21: Building User Interfaces with wxPython 391

Introducing wxPython 391
Creating Simple wxPython Programs 392
Choosing Different Window Types 394
    Managed windows 394
    Nonmanaged windows 395
Using wxPython Controls 399
    Common controls 399
    Tree controls 400
    Editor controls 401
Controlling Layout 401
    Specifying coordinates 402
    Sizers 403
    Layout constraints 406
    Layout algorithms 407
Using Built-in Dialogs 407
Drawing with Device Contexts 408
Adding Menus and Keyboard Shortcuts 411
Accessing Mouse and Keyboard Input 412
Other wxPython Features 412
    Clipboard, drag and drop, and cursors 413
    Graphics 413
    Date and time 413
    Fonts 413
    HTML 414
    Printing 414
    Other 414

Chapter 22: Using Curses **415**

A Curses Overview 415
Starting Up and Shutting Down 416
Displaying and Erasing Text 416
    Reading from the window (screen-scraping) 417
    Erasing 418
    Refreshing 418
    Boxes and lines 418
    The window background 418
    Example: masking a box 419
Moving the Cursor 420
Getting User Input 421
    Reading keys 422
    Other keyboard-related functions 422
    Fancy characters 422
    Reading mouse input 423
    Example: yes, no, or maybe 424
Managing Windows 425
    Pads 425
    Stacking windows 426
Editing Text 426
Using Color 427
    Numbering 427
    Setting colors 428
    Tweaking the colors 428
Example: A Simple Maze Game 428

Chapter 23: Building Simple Command Interpreters **433**

Beginning with the End in Mind 433
Understanding the Lepto Language 435
Creating a Lepto Lexical Analyzer 436
    The shlex module 436
    Putting shlex to work 437
Adding Interactive-Mode Features 440
    Using the cmd module 440
    Subclassing cmd.Cmd 442
Executing Lepto Commands 445

Chapter 24: Playing Sound **453**

Sound File Basics 453
Playing Sounds 454
    Playing sound on Windows 454
    Playing and recording sound on SunOS 455
Examining Audio Files 456

Reading and Writing Audio Files 456
    Reading and writing AIFF files with aifc 457
    Reading and writing AU files with sunau 458
    Reading and writing WAV files with wave 458
    Example: Reversing an audio file 458
    Reading IFF chunked data 460
Handling Raw Audio Data 461
    Examining a fragment 461
    Searching and matching 462
    Translating between storage formats 462
    Manipulating fragments 463

Part V: Advanced Python Programming   465

Chapter 25: Processing Images 467

Image Basics 467
Identifying Image File Types 468
Converting Between Color Systems 469
    Color systems 469
    Converting from one system to another 470
Handling Raw Image Data 472
Using the Python Imaging Library 472
    Retrieving image information 473
    Copying and converting images 474
    Using PIL with Tkinter 475
    Cropping and resizing images 476
    Modifying pixel data 476
    Other PIL features 480

Chapter 26: Multithreading 481

Understanding Threads 481
Spawning, Tracking, and Killing Threads 482
    Creating threads with the thread module 482
    Starting and stopping threads with the threading module 483
    Thread status and information under threading 484
    Finding threads under threading 484
    Waiting for a thread to finish 484
Avoiding Concurrency Issues 485
    Locking with thread 485
    Locking with threading 486
Preventing Deadlock 488
Example: Downloading from Multiple URLs 489
Porting Threaded Code 494
Weaving Threads Together with Queues 495
Technical Note: How Simultaneous Is Simultaneous? 495
For More Information 496

Chapter 27: Debugging, Profiling, and Optimization 497

Debugging Python Code 497
  Starting and stopping the debugger 497
  Examining the state of things 498
  Setting breakpoints 499
  Running 500
  Aliases 500
  Debugging tips 500
Working with docstrings 501
Automating Tests 502
  Synching docstrings with code 502
  Unit testing 503
Finding Bottlenecks 505
  Profiling code 505
  Using Profile objects 506
  Calibrating the profiler 507
  Customizing statistics 507
Common Optimization Tricks 509
  Sorting 509
  Looping 510
  I/O 510
  Strings 511
  Threads 511
Taking out the Trash — the Garbage Collector 512
  Reference counts and Python code 512
  Reference counts and C/C++ code 513

Chapter 28: Security and Encryption 515

Checking Passwords 515
Running in a Restricted Environment 516
  The rexec sandbox 517
  Using a class fortress 520
Creating Message Fingerprints 521
  MD5 522
  SHA 522
  Other uses 523
Using 1940s-Era Encryption 523

Chapter 29: Writing Extension Modules 527

Extending and Embedding Overview 527
Writing a Simple Extension Module 528
Building and Linking 531
Converting Python Data to C 532
  Unpacking normal arguments 532
  Using special format characters 535
  Unpacking keyword arguments 537
  Unpacking zero arguments 538

Converting C Data to Python 538
    Creating simple Python objects 539
    Creating complex Python objects 540
Embedding the Interpreter 541
    A simple example 541
    Shutting down 541
    Other setup functions 542
    System information functions 542
Running Python Code from C 543
Using Extension Tools 546
    SWIG 546
    CXX 549
    Extension classes 550

Chapter 30: Embedding the Python Interpreter **553**

Tracking Reference Counts 553
    Types of reference ownership 553
    Reference conventions 554
    Common pitfalls 555
Using the Abstract and Concrete Object Layers 555
    Object layers 556
    Working with generic objects 556
Working with Number Objects 558
    Any numerical type 558
    Integers 560
    Longs 560
    Floating-point numbers 561
    Complex numbers 561
Working with Sequence Objects 561
    Any sequence type 562
    Strings 563
    Lists 564
    Tuples 565
    Buffers 566
    Unicode strings 567
Working with Mapping Objects 569
    Functions for any mapping type 569
    Dictionaries 570
Using Other Object Types 571
    Type 571
    None 571
    File 571
    Module 572
    CObjects 574
Creating Threads and Sub-Interpreters 574
    Threads 575
    Sub-interpreters 576

Handling Errors and Exceptions 576
    Checking for errors 577
    Signaling error conditions 577
    Creating custom exceptions 578
    Raising warnings 578
Managing Memory 579

Chapter 31: Number Crunching **581**

Using Math Routines 581
    Rounding and fractional parts 581
    General math routines 582
    Logarithms and exponentiation 582
    Trigonometric functions 582
Computing with Complex Numbers 583
Generating Random Numbers 583
    Random numbers 583
    Example: shuffling a deck 585
    Random distributions 585
    Example: plotting distributions using Monte Carlo sampling 586
Using Arbitrary-Precision Numbers 587

Chapter 32: Using NumPy **589**

Introducing Numeric Python 589
    Installing NumPy 589
    Some quick definitions 590
    Meet the array 590
Accessing and Slicing Arrays 590
    Contiguous arrays 592
    Converting arrays to lists and strings 592
Calling Universal Functions 593
    Ufunc destinations 594
    Example: editing an audio stream 594
    Repeating ufuncs 595
Creating Arrays 597
    Array creation functions 597
    Seeding arrays with functions 598
Using Element Types 600
Reshaping and Resizing Arrays 600
Using Other Array Functions 601
    sort(array,[axis=-1]) 601
    where(condition,X,Y) 602
    swapaxes(array,axis1,axis2) 602
    Matrix operations 602
Array Example: Analyzing Price Trends 603

Chapter 33: Parsing and Interpreting Python Code 605

Examining Tracebacks 605
    Printing a traceback — print_exc and friends 605
    Extracting and formatting exceptions 606
    Example: reporting exceptions in a GUI 607
    Eating arbitrary exceptions is bad for you 607
Introspection 608
    Review: basic introspection 608
    Browsing classes 609
    Browsing function information 609
Checking Indentation 611
Tokenizing Python Code 611
Example: Syntax-Highlighting Printer 612
Inspecting Python Parse Trees 613
    Creating an AST 613
    ASTs and sequences 614
    Using ASTs 614
Low-Level Object Creation 614
Disassembling Python Code 615

Part VI: Deploying Python Applications   617

Chapter 34: Creating Worldwide Applications 619

Internationalization and Localization 619
Preparing Applications for Multiple Languages 620
    An NLS example 620
    What it all means 623
Formatting Locale-Specific Output 624
    Changing the locale 624
    Locale-specific formatting 625
    Properties of locales 626

Chapter 35: Customizing Import Behavior 629

Understanding Module Importing 629
Finding and Loading Modules with imp 631
Importing Encrypted Modules 633
Retrieving Modules from a Remote Source 636
    Subclassing Importer 636
    Creating the remote Importer 637
    Testing the remote Importer 640

Chapter 36: Distributing Modules and Applications **643**

Understanding distutils 643
Creating a simple distribution 644
Installing the simple distribution 645
Other distutils Features 647
Distributing packages 647
Including other files 648
Customizing setup 650
Distributing Extension Modules 650
Creating Source and Binary Distributions 651
Source distributions 652
Binary distributions 653
Installers 653
Building Standalone Executables 655
py2exe 655
Freeze 656
Other tools 657

Part VII: Platform-Specific Support **659**

Chapter 37: Windows **661**

Using win32all 661
Data types 661
Error handling 662
Finding what you need 662
Example: Using Some Windows APIs 662
Accessing the Windows Registry 664
Accessing the registry with win32all 664
Example: setting the Internet Explorer home page 666
Creating, deleting, and navigating keys 666
Example: recursive deletion of a key 667
Other registry functions 668
Accessing the registry with _winreg 668
Using msvcrt Goodies 669
Console I/O 669
Other functions 670

Chapter 38: UNIX-Compatible Modules **671**

Checking UNIX Passwords and Groups 671
Accessing the System Logger 673
Calling Shared Library Functions 675
Providing Identifier and Keyword Completion 675

Retrieving File System and Resource Information 677
    File system information 678
    Resource usage 678
    Resource limits 679
Controlling File Descriptors 680
Handling Terminals and Pseudo-Terminals 681
Interfacing with Sun's NIS "Yellow Pages" 682

Appendix A: Online Resources 685

Appendix B: Python Development Environments 689

Index 701

The Python Language

P A R T

Chapter 1
Python in an Hour

Chapter 2
Identifiers, Variables,
and Numeric Types

Chapter 3
Expressions and
Strings

Chapter 4
Advanced Data
Types

Chapter 5
Control Flow

Chapter 6
Program
Organization

Chapter 7
Object-Oriented
Python

Chapter 8
Input and Output

Python in an Hour

◆ ◆ ◆ ◆

In This Chapter

Jumping in: Starting the Python interpreter

Experimenting with variables and expressions

Defining a function

Running a Python program

Looping and control

Lists and tuples

Dictionaries

Reading and writing files

Loading and using modules

Creating a class

Python is a rich and powerful language, but also one that is easy to learn. This chapter gives an overview of Python's syntax, its useful data-types, and its unique features.

As you read, please fire up the Python interpreter, and try out some of the examples. Feel free to experiment, tinker, and wander away from the rest of the tour group. Everything in this chapter is repeated, in greater detail, in later chapters, so don't worry too much about absorbing everything at once. Try some things out, get your feet wet, and have fun!

Jumping In: Starting the Python Interpreter

The first thing to do, if you haven't already, is to install Python. You can download Python from `www.python.org`. As of this writing, the latest versions of Python are 2.0 (stable) and 2.1 (still in beta).

You can start the Python interpreter from the command line. Change to the directory where the interpreter lives, or add the directory to your path. Then type:

```
python
```

On UNIX, Python typically lives in `/usr/local/bin`; on Windows, Python probably lives in `c:\python20`.

On Windows, you can also bring the interpreter up from Start ⇨ Programs ⇨ Python 2.0 ⇨ Python (command line).

Once you start the interpreter, Python displays something like this:

```
Python 2.0 (#8, Oct 16 2000, 17:27:58) [MSC 32 bit (Intel)] on win32
Type "copyright", "credits" or "license" for more information.
>>>
```

The interpreter displays the >>> prompt to show that it's ready for you to type in some Python. And so, in the grand tradition of programming books everywhere, we proceed to the "Hello world" example:

```
>>> print "Hello world!"
Hello world!
```

To exit the interpreter, type the end-of-file character (Ctrl-Z on Windows, or Ctrl-D on Linux) and press Enter.

Note   You may prefer to interact with the interpreter in IDLE, the standard Python IDE. IDLE features syntax coloring, a class browser, and other handy features. See Appendix B for tips on starting and using IDLE.

Experimenting with Variables and Expressions

Python's syntax for variables and expressions is close to what you would see in C or Java, so you can skim this section if it starts looking familiar. However, you should take note of Python's loose typing (see below).

Pocket calculator

Python understands the standard arithmetic operators, including +, -, / (division), and * (multiplication). The Python interpreter makes a handy calculator:

```
>>> 8/2
4
>>> 5+4*6
29
```

Note that the second example evaluates 29 (and not 54); the interpreter multiplies 4 by 6 before adding 5. Python uses operator precedence rules to decide what to do first. You can control order explicitly by using parentheses:

```
>>> (5+4)*6
54
```

In practice, it's often easiest to use parentheses (even when they aren't required) to make code more readable.

Variables

You can use variables to hold values over time. For example, this code computes how long it takes to watch every episode of *Monty Python's Flying Circus* (including the two German episodes of *Monty Python's Fliegende Zirkus*):

```
>>> NumberOfEpisodes=47
>>> EpisodeLength=0.5
>>> PythonMarathonLength=(NumberOfEpisodes*EpisodeLength)
>>> PythonMarathonLength
23.5
```

A variable is always a reference to a value. Variables do not have types, but objects do. (Python is *loosely typed;* the same variable may refer to an integer value in the morning and a string value in the afternoon.)

Python does not require variable declarations. However, you cannot access a variable until you have assigned it a value. If you try to access an undefined variable, the interpreter will complain (the wording of the error may be different in your version of Python):

```
>>> print Scrumptious
Traceback (most recent call last):
  File "<stdin>", line 1, in ?
NameError: There is no variable named 'Scrumptious'
```

This example raised an *exception*. In Python, most errors are represented by exception objects that the surrounding code can handle. Chapter 5 describes Python's exception-handling abilities.

 Note   Python is *case-sensitive*. This means that names that are capitalized differently refer to different variables:

```
>>> FavoriteColor="blue"
>>> favoritecolor="yellow"
>>> print FavoriteColor,favoritecolor
blue yellow
```

Defining a Function

Assume you and some friends go out to dinner and decide to split the bill evenly. How much should each person pay? Here is a function that calculates each person's share:

```
>>> def SplitBill(Bill,NumberOfPeople):
...     # The hash character (#) starts a comment. Python
...     # ignores everything from # to the end of the line.
...     TotalWithTip = Bill * (1.15) # Add a 15% tip.
```

```
...      return (TotalWithTip / NumberOfPeople)
...
>>> SplitBill(23.35,3)
8.9508333333333336
```

The statement def FunctionName (parameter,...): starts a function definition. I indented the following four lines to indicate that they are a *control block*—a sequence of statements grouped by a common level of indentation. Together, they make up the body of the function definition.

Python statements with the same level of indentation are grouped together. In this example, Python knows the function definition ends when it sees a non-indented line. Grouping statements by indentation-level is common practice in most programming languages; in Python it is actually part of the syntax. Normally, one indentation level equals four spaces, and eight spaces equals one tab.

Running a Python Program

A text file consisting of Python code is called a *program,* or a *script,* or a *module.* There is little distinction between the three terms—generally a script is smaller than a program, and a file designed to be imported (rather than executed directly) is called a module. Normally, you name Python code files with a .py extension.

To run a program named spam.py, type the following at a command prompt:

```
python spam.py
```

In Windows, you can run a program by double-clicking it. (If the file association for the .py extension is not set up at installation time, you can configure it by right-clicking the script, choosing "Open With..." and then choosing python.exe.)

In UNIX, you can run a script directly by using the "pound-bang hack." Add this line at the top of the Python script (replacing the path with the path to env if it's different on your system):

```
#!/usr/bin/python
```

Then make the file executable (by running chmod +x <filename>), and you can run it directly.

Looping and Control

Listing 1-1 illustrates Python's looping and conditional statements. It prints out all the prime numbers less than 500.

Listing 1-1: PrimeFinder.py

```python
print 1
# Loop over the numbers from 2 to 499:
for PrimeTest in range(2,500):
    # Assume PrimeTest prime until proven otherwise:
    IsPrime = 1 # 0 is false, nonzero is true
    # Loop over the numbers from 2 to (PrimeTest-1):
    for TestFactor in range(2,PrimeTest):
        # a % b equals the remainder of a/b:
        if (PrimeTest % TestFactor == 0):
            # PrimeTest divides TestFactor (remainder is 0).
            IsPrime=0
            break # Jump out of the innermost for-loop.

    if (IsPrime):
        print PrimeTest
```

Integer division

The modulo operator, %, returns the remainder when the first number is divided by the second. (For instance, 8 % 5 is equal to 3.) If PrimeTest is zero modulo TestFactor, then this remainder is zero, so TestFactor is one of PrimeTest's divisors.

In Python, dividing one integer by another returns another integer — the quotient, rounded down:

```python
>>> 8/3 # I want an integer, not the "right answer."
2
```

So, here is a sneaky replacement to line 7 of PrimeFinder.py. If TestFactor does not divide PrimeTest evenly, then the quotient is rounded off, and so the comparison will fail:

```python
if ((PrimeTest/TestFactor)*TestFactor == PrimeTest)
```

Python uses the float class for floating-point (decimal) numbers. The float function transforms a value into a float:

```python
>>> 8.0/3.0
2.6666666666666665
>>> float(8)/float(3) # Give me the "real" quotient.
2.6666666666666665
```

Looping

The `for` statement sets up a loop — a block of code that is executed many times. The function `range(startnum,endnum)` provides a list of integers starting with `startnum` and ending just before `endnum`.

In the example, `PrimeTest` takes on each value in the range in order, and the outer loop executes once for each value of `PrimeTest`. The inner loop iterates over the "possible factors" of PrimeTest, starting at 2 and continuing until (PrimeTest-1).

Branching with if-statements

The statement `if expression:` begins a control block that executes only if `expression` is true. You can enclose the expression in parentheses. As far as Python is concerned, the number 0 is false, and any other number is true.

Note that in a condition, we use the `==` operator to test for equality. The `=` operator is used only for assignments, and assignments are forbidden within a condition. (Here Python differs from C/C++, which allows assignments inside an if-condition, even though they are usually a horrible mistake.)

In an `if` statement, an else-clause executes when the condition is not true. For example:

```
if (MyNumber % 2 == 0):
    print "MyNumber is even!"
else:
    print "MyNumber is odd!"
```

Breaking and continuing

The `break` statement jumps out of a loop. It exits the innermost loop in the current context. In Listing 1-1, the `break` statement exits the inner `TestFactor` loop, and continues on line 11. The `continue` statement jumps to the next iteration of a loop.

Loops can also be set up using the `while` statement. The syntax `while (expression)` sets up a control block that executes as long as `expression` is true. For example:

```
# print out powers of 2 less than 2000
X=2
while (X<2000):
    print X
    X=X*2
```

Lists and Tuples

A *list* is an ordered collection of zero or more elements. An element of a list can be any sort of object. You can write lists as a comma-separated collection of values enclosed in square brackets. For example:

```
FibonacciList=[1,1,2,3,5,8]
FishList=[1,2,"Fish"] # Lists can contain various types.
AnotherList=[1,2,FishList] # Lists can include other lists.
YetAnotherList=[1,2,3,] # Trailing commas are ok.
RevengeOfTheList=[] # The empty list
```

Tuples

A tuple is similar to a list. The difference is that a tuple is immutable — it cannot be modified. You enclose tuples in parentheses instead of brackets. For example:

```
FirstTuple=("spam","spam","bacon","spam")
SecondTuple=() # The empty tuple
LonelyTuple=(5,) # Trailing comma is *required*, since (5) is
                 # just a number-in-parens, not a tuple.
```

Slicing and dicing

Lists are ordered, so each list element has an index. You can access an element with the syntax listname[index]. Note that index numbering begins with zero:

```
>>> FoodList=["Spam","Egg","Sausage"]
>>> FoodList[0]
'Spam'
>>> FoodList[2]
'Sausage'
>>> FoodList[2]="Spam" # Modifying list elements in place
>>> FoodList
['Spam', 'Egg', 'Spam']
```

Sometimes it's easier to count from the end of the list backwards. You can access the last item of a list with listname[-1], the second-to-last item with listname[-2], and so on.

You can access a sublist of a list via the syntax listname[start:end]. The sublist contains the original list elements, starting with index *start*, up to (but not including) index *end*. Both *start* and *end* are optional; omitting them makes Python go all the way to the beginning (or end) of the list. For example:

```
>>>WordList=["And","now","for","something","completely",
"different"]
>>> WordList[0:2] # From index 0 to 2 (not including 2)
['And', 'now']
```

```
>>> WordList[2:5]
['for', 'something', 'completely']
>>> WordList[:-1]  # All except the last
['And', 'now', 'for', 'something', 'completely']
```

Substrings

Lists, tuples, and strings are all *sequence types*. Sequence types all support indexed access. So, taking a substring in Python is easy:

```
>>> Word="pig"
>>> PigLatinWord=Word[1:]+Word[0]+"ay"
>>> PigLatinWord
'igpay'
```

Immutable types

Tuples and strings are immutable types. Modifying them in place is not allowed:

```
FirstTuple[0]="Egg"  # Object does not support item assignment.
```

You can switch between tuples and lists using the `tuple` and `list` functions. So, although you cannot edit a tuple directly, you can create a new-and-improved tuple:

```
>>> FoodTuple=("Spam","Egg","Sausage")
>>> FoodList=list(FoodTuple)
>>> FoodList
['Spam', 'Egg', 'Sausage']
>>> FoodList[2]="Spam"
>>> NewFoodTuple=tuple(FoodList)
>>> NewFoodTuple
('Spam', 'Egg', 'Spam')
```

Dictionaries

A *dictionary* is a Python object that cross-references keys to values. A *key* is an immutable object, such as a string. A *value* can be any object. A dictionary has a canonical string representation: a comma-separated list of key-value pairs, enclosed in curly braces: {*key:value, key:value*}. For example:

```
>>> PhoneDict={"bob":"555-1212","fred":"555-3345"}
>>> EmptyDict={}  # Initialize a new dictionary.
>>> PhoneDict["bob"]  # Find bob's phone number.
'555-1212'
>>> PhoneDict["cindy"]="867-5309"  # Add an entry.
>>> print "Phone list:",PhoneDict
Phone list: {'fred': '555-3345', 'bob': '555-1212', 'cindy':
'867-5309'}
```

Looking up a value raises an exception if the dictionary holds no value for the key. The function `dictionary.get(key,defaultValue)` performs a "safe get"; it looks up the value corresponding to key, but if there is no such entry, returns *defaultValue*.

```
>>> PhoneDict["luke"] # May raise an exception.
Traceback (most recent call last):
  File "<stdin>", line 1, in ?
KeyError: luke
>>> PhoneDict.get("joe","unknown")
'unknown'
```

Often a good default value is the built-in value None. The value None represents nothing (it is a little Zen-like). The value None is similar to NULL in C (or null in Java). It evaluates to false.

```
>>> DialAJoe=PhoneDict.get("joe",None)
>>> print DialAJoe
None
```

Reading and Writing Files

To create a file object, use the function `open(filename,mode)`. The *mode* argument is a string explaining what you intend to do with the file — typical values are "w" to write and "r" to read. Once you have a file object, you can read() from it or write() to it, then close() it. This example creates a simple file on disk:

```
>>> fred = open("hello","w")
>>> fred.write("Hello world!")
>>> fred.close()
>>> barney = open("hello","r")
>>> FileText = barney.read()
>>> barney.close()
>>> print FileText
Hello world!
```

Sample Program: Word Frequencies

Different authors use different words. Patterns of word use form a kind of "author fingerprint" that is sometimes used as a test of a document's authenticity.

Listing 1-2 counts occurrences of a word in a body of text, and illustrates some more Python power in the process. (Don't be intimidated by all the comments — it's actually only 26 lines of code.)

Listing 1-2: **WordCount.py**

```python
# Import the string module, so we can call Python's standard
# string-related functions.
import string

def CountWords(Text):
    "Count how many times each word occurs in Text."
    # A string immediately after a def statement is a
    # "docstring" - a comment intended for documentation.
    WordCount={}
    # We will build up (and return) a dictionary whose keys
    # are the words, and whose values are the corresponding
    # number of occurrences.

    CurrentWord=""
    # To make the job cleaner, add a period at the end of the
    # text; that way, we are guaranteed to be finished with
    # the current word when we run out of letters:
    Text=Text+"."

    # We assume that ' and - don't break words, but any other
    # nonalphabetic character does. This assumption isn't
    # entirely accurate, but it's close enough for us.
    # string.letters is a string of all alphabetic characters.
    PiecesOfWords = string.letters + "'-"

    # Iterate over each character in the text. The
    # function len () returns the length of a sequence,
    # such as a string:
    for CharacterIndex in range(0,len(Text)):
        CurrentCharacter=Text[CharacterIndex]

        # The find() method of a string finds
        # the starting index of the first occurrence of a
        # substring within a string, or returns -1
        # if it doesn't find the substring. The next
        # line of code tests to see whether CurrentCharacter
        # is part of a word:
        if (PiecesOfWords.find(CurrentCharacter)!=-1):
            # Append this letter to the current word.
            CurrentWord=CurrentWord+CurrentCharacter
        else:
            # This character is not a letter.
            if (CurrentWord!=""):
                # We just finished off a word.
                # Convert to lowercase, so "The" and "the"
                # fall in the same bucket.
                CurrentWord = string.lower(CurrentWord)

                # Now increment this word's count.
                CurrentCount=WordCount.get(CurrentWord,0)
                WordCount[CurrentWord]=CurrentCount+1
```

```
                        # Start a new word.
                        CurrentWord=""
            return (WordCount)

    if (__name__=="__main__"):
        # Read the text from the file song.txt.
        TextFile=open("poem.txt","r")
        Text=TextFile.read()
        TextFile.close()

        # Count the words in the text.
        WordCount=CountWords(Text)
        # Alphabetize the word list, and print them all out.
        SortedWords=WordCount.keys()
        SortedWords.sort()
        for Word in SortedWords:
            print Word,WordCount[Word]
```

Listing 1-3: **poem.txt**

```
Shall I compare thee to a summer's day?
Thou art more lovely and more temperate:
Rough winds do shake the darling buds of May,
And summer's lease hath all too short a date:
Sometime too hot the eye of heaven shines
And often is his gold complexion dimmed;
And every fair from fair sometimes declines,
By chance or nature's changing course untrimmed;
But thy eternal summer shall not fade,
Nor lose possession of that fair thou ow'st:
Nor shall Death brag thou wander'st in his shade,
When in eternal lines to time thou grow'st:
So long as men can breathe, or eyes can see,
So long lives this, and this gives life to thee.
```

Listing 1-4: **WordCount output**

```
all 1
and 5
art 1
as 1
brag 1
[. . .omitted for brevity. . .]
too 2
untrimmed 1
wander'st 1
when 1
winds 1
```

Loading and Using Modules

Python comes with a collection of libraries to do all manner of useful things. To use the functions, classes, and variables in another Python module, you must first import that module with the statement `import modulename`. (Note: No parentheses.) After importing a module, you can access any of its members using the syntax `moduleName.itemName`. For instance, this line (from the preceding example) calls the function `lower` in the module `string` to convert a string to lowercase.

```
CurrentWord = string.lower(CurrentWord)
```

When you import a module, any code at module level (that is, code that isn't part of a function or class definition) executes. To set aside code to execute only when someone runs your script from the command line, you can enclose it in an `if` (`__name__=="__main__"`) block, as in Listing 1-2 above.

As an alternative to "import foo," you can use the syntax `from foo import itemName` to import a function or variable all the way into the current namespace. For example, after you include the line `from math import sqrt` in a Python script, you can call the square-root function `sqrt` directly, instead of calling `math.sqrt`. You can even bring in everything from a module with `from foo import *`. However, although this technique does save typing, it can become confusing—especially if you import functions with the same name from several different modules!

Note   Python does not enforce "privacy" in modules; you can call any of a module's functions. It is generally a good idea to be polite and only call those you are supposed to.

Creating a Class

Python is an object-oriented language. In fact, every piece of Python data is an object. Working with objects in Python is easy, as you will soon see.

Some quick object jargon

A *class* is a mechanism for tying together data and behavior. An *instance* of a particular class is called an *object*. Class instances have certain *methods* (functions) and *attributes* (data values). In Python, all data items behave like objects, even though a few base types (like integers) are not actual instances of a class.

You can derive a class from a parent class; this relationship is called *inheritance*. Instances of the child (derived) class have the same attributes and methods of the parent class. The child class may add new methods and attributes, and override methods of the parent. A class may be derived from more than one parent class; this relationship is called *multiple inheritance*.

Object-oriented programming (OOP) is a mindset that may take some getting used to. When inheritance becomes natural, and you start talking about your data in anthropomorphic terms, you will know that your journey to the OO side is complete. See the References section for some resources that explain object-oriented programming in detail.

Object orientation, Python style

You define a new class with the syntax `class ClassName`. The control block following the class statement is the class declaration; it generally consists of several method definitions. You define a child class (using inheritance) via the syntax `class ClassName(ParentClass)`.

You create an object via the syntax `NewObject = ClassName()`. When you create an object, Python calls its *constructor*, if any. In Python, a constructor is a member function with the name `__init__`. A constructor may require extra parameters to create an object. If so, you provide them when creating the object: `NewObject = ClassName(param1,param2,...)`.

Every object method takes, as its first parameter, the argument `self`, which is a reference to the object. (Python `self` is similar to `this` in C++/Java, but `self` is always explicit.)

You do not explicitly declare attributes in Python. An object's attributes are not part of the local namespace — in other words, to access an object's attribute `foo` in one of its methods, you must type `self.foo`.

Keep off the grass — Accessing class members

Attributes and methods are all "public" — they are visible and available outside the object. However, to preserve encapsulation, many classes have some attributes or methods you should not access directly. The motivation for this is that an object should be something of a "black box" — code outside the object should only care *what* it does, not *how* it does it. This helps keep code easy-to-maintain, especially in big programs.

Example: the point class

Listing 1-5 defines a class representing a point in the plane (or on a computer screen):

Listing 1-5: **Point.py**

```
import math
# The next statement starts our class declaration; the
# function declarations inside the indented control block are
# the class's methods.
class Point:
    # The method __init__ is the class's constructor. It
    # executes when you create an instance of the class.
    # When __init__ takes extra parameters (as it does here),
    # you must supply parameter values in order to create an
    # instance of the class. Writing an __init__ method is
    # optional.
    def __init__(self,X,Y):
        # X and Y are the attributes of this class. You do not
        # have to declare attributes. I like to initialize
        # all my attributes in the constructor, to ensure that
        # the attributes will be available when I need them.
        self.X=X
        self.Y=Y

    def DistanceToPoint(self, OtherPoint):
        "Returns the distance from this point to another"
        SumOfSquares = ((self.X-OtherPoint.X)**2) +\
        ((self.Y-OtherPoint.Y)**2)
        return math.sqrt(SumOfSquares)

    def IsInsideCircle(self, Center, Radius):
        """Return 1 if this point is inside the circle,
0 otherwise"""
        if (self.DistanceToPoint(Center)<Radius):
            return 1
        else:
            return 0

# This code tests the point class.
PointA=Point(3,5) # Create a point with coordinates (3,5)
PointB=Point(-4,-4)

# How far is it from point A to point B?
print "A to B:",PointA.DistanceToPoint(PointB)

# What if I go backwards?
print "B to A:",PointB.DistanceToPoint(PointA)

# Who lives inside the circle of radius 5 centered at (3,3)?
CircleCenter=Point(3,3)
print "A in circle:",PointA.IsInsideCircle(CircleCenter,5)
print "B in circle:",PointB.IsInsideCircle(CircleCenter,5)
```

Recommended Reading

If you are new to computer programming, you may find this tutorial useful:
`http://www.honors.montana.edu/~jjc/easytut/easytut/`.

To learn all about the language on one (large!) page, see the Python Quick
Reference at `http://starship.python.net/quick-ref1_52.html`.

If you like to learn by tinkering with finished programs, you can download a
wide variety of source code at the Vaults of Parnassus: `http://www.vex.net/
parnassus/`.

Summary

This wraps up our quick tour of Python. We hope you enjoyed the trip. You now
know most of Python's notable features. In this chapter, you:

- ✦ Ran the Python interpreter for easy interaction.
- ✦ Grouped statements by indentation level.
- ✦ Wrote functions to count words in a body of text.
- ✦ Created a handy Point class.

The next chapter digs a little deeper and introduces all of Python's standard types
and operators.

✦   ✦   ✦

Identifiers, Variables, and Numeric Types

♦ ♦ ♦ ♦

In This Chapter

Identifiers and operators

Numeric types

Assigning values to variables

♦ ♦ ♦ ♦

One of the simplest forms of data on which your programs operate is numbers. This chapter introduces the numeric data types in Python, such as integers and floating point numbers, and shows you how to use them together in simple operations like assignment to variables.

As with Chapter 1, you'll find it helpful to have a Python interpreter up and running as you read this and the following chapters. Playing around with the examples in each section will pique your curiosity and help keep Python's features firmly rooted in your brain.

Identifiers and Operators

Variable names and other identifiers in Python are similar to those in many other languages: they start with a letter (A–Z or a–z) or an underscore ("_") and are followed by any number of letters, numbers, and underscores. Their length is limited only by your eagerness to type, and they are case-sensitive (that is, spam and Spam are different identifiers). Regardless of length, choose identifiers that are meaningful. (Having said that, I'll break that rule for the sake of conciseness in many of the examples in this chapter.)

The following are some examples of valid and invalid identifiers:

```
wordCount
y_axis
errorField2
_logFile
_2              # Technically valid, but not a
good idea
```

```
7Index          # Invalid, starts with a number
won't_work      # Invalid due to apostrophe character
```

Note   Python considers these forms to have special meaning:

_name — Not imported by "from x import *" (see Chapter 6)

__name__ — System name (see Chapter 6)

__name — Private class member (see Chapter 7)

When you're running the Python interpreter in interactive mode, a single underscore character (_) is a special identifier that holds the result of the last expression evaluated. This is especially handy when you're using Python as a desktop calculator:

```
>>> "Hello"
'Hello'
>>> _
'Hello'
>>> 5 + 2
7
>>> _ * 2
14
>>> _ + 5
19
>>>
```

Reserved words

Although it would make for some interesting source code, you can't use the following words as identifiers because they are reserved words in the Python language:

```
and        del        for        is         raise
assert     elif       from       lambda     return
break      else       global     not        try
class      except     if         or         while
continue   exec       import     pass
def        finally    in         print
```

Operators

Python has the following operators, each of which we'll discuss in context with the applicable data types they operate on:

```
  -     !=     %      &      *      **     /      ^      |      ~
  +     <      <<     <=     <>     ==     >      >=     >>
```

Numeric Types

Python has four built-in numeric data types: integers, long integers, floating point numbers, and imaginary numbers.

Integers

Integers are whole numbers in the range of -2147483648 to 2147483647 (that is, they are signed, 32-bit numbers).

Tip   For convenience, the `sys` module has a `maxint` member that holds the maximum positive value of an integer variable:

```
>>> import sys
>>> sys.maxint
2147483647
```

In addition to writing integers in the default decimal (base 10) notation, you can also write integer literals in hexadecimal (base 16) and octal (base 8) notation by preceding the number with a `0x` or `0`, respectively:

```
>>> 300        # 300 in decimal
300
>>> 0x12c      # 300 in hex
300
>>> 0454       # 300 in octal
300
```

Keep in mind that for decimal numbers, valid digits are 0 through 9. For hexadecimal, it's 0 through 9 and A through F, and for octal it's 0 through 7. If you're not familiar with hexadecimal and octal numbering systems, or if you are but they don't thrill you, just nod your head and keep moving.

Long integers

Long integers are similar to integers, except that the maximum and minimum values of long integers are restricted only by how much memory you have (yes, you really can have long integers with thousands of digits). To differentiate between the two types of integers, you append an "L" to the end of long integers:

```
>>> 200L        # A long integer literal with a value of 200
200L

>>> 11223344 * 55667788     # Too big for normal integers...
Traceback (innermost last):
  File "<interactive input>", line 1, in ?
OverflowError: integer multiplication

>>> 11223344L * 55667788L   # ...but works with long integers
624778734443072L
```

The "L" on long integers can be uppercase or lowercase, but do yourself a favor and always use the uppercase version. The lowercase "L" and the one digit look too similar, especially if you are tired, behind schedule on a project, or both.

Floating point numbers

Floating point numbers let you express fractional numeric values such as 3.14159. You can also include an optional exponent. If you include neither an exponent nor a decimal point, Python interprets the number as an integer, so to express "the floating point number two hundred," write it as 200.0 and not just 200. Here are a few examples of floating point numbers:

```
200.05
9.80665
.1
20005e-2
6.0221367E23
```

Occasionally you may notice what appear to be rounding errors in how Python displays floating point numbers:

```
>>> 0.3
0.29999999999999999
```

Don't worry; this display is not indicating a bug, but is just a friendly reminder that your digital computer just approximates real world numbers. See "Formatting strings" in Chapter 3 to learn about printing numbers in a less ugly format.

The valid values for floating point numbers and the accuracy with which Python uses them is implementation-dependent, although it is at least 64-bit, double-precision math and is often IEEE 754 compliant.

Imaginary numbers

Unlike many other languages, Python has language-level support for imaginary numbers, making it trivial to use them in your programs. You form an imaginary number by appending a "j" to a decimal number (integer or floating point):

```
3j
2.5e-3j
```

When you add a real and an imaginary number together, Python recognizes the result as a complex number and handles it accordingly:

```
>>> 2 + 5j
(2+5j)
>>> 2 * (2 + 5j)
(4+10j)
```

Manipulating numeric types

You can use most of Python's operators when working with numeric data types.

Numeric operators

Table 2-1 lists operators and how they behave with numeric types.

Operator	Description	Example Input	Example Output
Unary Operations			
+	Plus	+2	2
-	Minus	-2	2
		-(-2)	2
~	Inversion[1]	~5	6
Binary Operations			
+	Addition	5 + 7	12
		5 + 7.0	12.0
-	Subtraction	5 - 2	3
		5 - 2.0	3.0
*	Multiplication	2.5 * 2	5.0
/	Division	5 / 2	2
		5 / 2.0	2.5
%	Modulo (remainder)	5 % 2	1
		7.5 % 2.5	0.0
**	Power	5 ** 2	25
		1.2 ** 2.1	1.466...
Binary Bitwise Operations[2]			
&	AND	5 & 2	0
		11 & 3	3
|	OR	5 | 2	7
		11 | 3	11
^	XOR (exclusive-or)	5 ^ 2	7
		11 ^ 3	8

Continued

Table 2-1 *(continued)*			
Operator	*Description*	*Example Input*	*Example Output*
Shifting Operations[2]			
<<	Left bit-shift	5 << 2	20
>>	Right bit-shift	50 >> 3	6

1 Unary bitwise inversion of a number x is defined as –(x+1).

2 Numbers used in binary bitwise and shifting operations must be integers or long integers.

It is important to notice what happens when you mix standard numeric types (adding an integer and a floating point number, for example). If needed, Python first coerces (converts) either of the numbers according to these rules (stopping as soon as a rule is satisfied):

1. If one of the numbers is a complex number, convert the other to a complex number too.

2. If one of the numbers is a floating point number, convert the other to floating point.

3. If one of the numbers is a long integer, convert the other to a long integer.

4. No previous rule applies, so both are integers, and Python leaves them unchanged.

Other functions

Python has a few other built-in functions for working with numeric types, as described in the following sections.

Absolute value – abs

The abs(x) function takes the absolute value of any integer, long integer, or floating point number:

```
>>> abs(-5.0)
5.0
>>> abs(-20L)
20L
```

When applied to a complex number, this function returns the *magnitude* of the number, which is the distance from that point to the origin in the complex plane. Python calculates the magnitude just like the length of a line in two dimensions: for a complex number (a + bj), the magnitude is the square root of a squared plus b squared:

```
>>> abs(5 - 2j)
5.3851648071345037
```

Convert two numbers to a common type — coerce(x, y)

The coerce function applies the previously explained numeric conversion rules to two numbers and returns them to you as a tuple (we cover tuples in detail in the next chapter):

```
>>> coerce(5,2L)
(5L, 2L)
>>> coerce(5.5,2L)
(5.5, 2.0)
>>> coerce(5.5,5 + 2j)
((5.5+0j), (5+2j))
```

Quotient and remainder — divmod(a, b)

This function performs long division on two numbers and returns the quotient and the remainder:

```
>>> divmod(5,2)
(2, 1)
>>> divmod(5.5,2)
(2.0, 1.5)
```

Power — pow(x, y [, z])

The pow function is similar to the power (**) operator in Table 2-1:

```
>>> pow(5,2)
25
>>> pow(1.2,2.1)
1.4664951016517147
```

As usual, Python coerces the two numbers to a common type if needed. If the resulting type can't express the correct result, Python yells at you:

```
>>> pow(2.0,-1) # The coerced type is a floating point.
0.5
>>> pow(2,-1)    # The coerced type is an integer.
Traceback (innermost last):
  File "<interactive input>", line 1, in ?
ValueError: integer to the negative power
```

An optional third argument to pow specifies the modulo operation to perform on the result:

```
>>> pow(2,5)
32
>>> pow(2,5,10)
2
>>> (2 **5) % 10
2
```

The result is the same as using the power and modulo operators, but Python arrives at the result more efficiently. (Speedy power-and-modulo is useful in some types of cryptography.)

Round — round(x [, n])

This function rounds a floating point number x to the nearest whole number. Optionally, you can tell it to round to n digits after the decimal point:

```
>>> round(5.567)
6.0
>>> round(5.567,2)
5.57
```

Chapter 31, "Number Crunching," covers several Python modules that deal with math and numerical data types.

Assigning Values to Variables

With basic numeric types out of the way, we can take a break before moving on to other data types, and talk about variables and assignment statements. Python creates variables the first time you use them (you never need to explicitly declare them beforehand), and automatically cleans up the data they reference when they are no longer needed.

Refer back to "Identifiers and Operators" at the beginning of this chapter for the rules regarding valid variable names.

Simple assignment statements

The simplest form of assignment statements in Python are of the form *variable = value*:

```
>>> a = 5
>>> b = 10
>>> a
5
>>> b
10
>>> a + b
15
>>> a > b
0
```

"Understanding References" in Chapter 4 goes into more depth about how and when Python destroys unneeded data, and "Taking Out the Trash" in Chapter 26 covers the Python garbage collector.

A Python variable doesn't actually *contain* a piece of data but merely *references* a piece of data. The details and importance of this are covered in Chapter 4, but for now it's just important to note that the type of data that a variable refers to can change at any time:

```
>>> a = 10
>>> a                # First it refers to an integer.
10
>>> a = 5.0 + 2j
>>> a                # Now it refers to a complex number.
(5+2j)
```

Multiple assignment

Python provides a great shorthand method of assigning values to multiple variables at the same time:

```
>>> a,b,c = 5.5,2,10
>>> a
5.5
>>> b
2
>>> c
10
```

You can also use multiple assignment to swap any number of variables. Continuing the previous example:

```
>>> a,b,c = c,a,b
>>> a
10
>>> b
5.5
>>> c
2
```

Cross-Reference

Multiple assignment is really tuple packing and unpacking, covered in Chapter 4.

Augmented assignment

Another shorthand feature is *augmented assignment,* which enables you to combine an assignment and a binary operation into a single statement:

```
>>> a = 10
>>> a += 5
>>> a
15
```

New Feature   Augmented assignment was introduced in Python 2.0.

Python provides these augmented assignment operators:

```
+=        -=        *=        /=        %=        **=
>>=       <<=       &=        |=        ^=
```

The statement a += 5 is nearly identical to the longer form of a = a + 5 with two exceptions (neither of which you need to worry about too often, but are worth knowing):

1. In augmented assignment, Python evaluates a only once instead of the two times in the longhand version.

2. When possible, augmented assignment modifies the original object instead of creating a new object. In the longhand example above, Python evaluates the expression a + 5, creates a place in memory to hold the result, and then re-assigns a to reference the new data. With augmented assignment, however, Python places the result in the original object.

Summary

Python has several built-in data types and many features to help you work with them. In this chapter you:

✦ Learned the rules for valid Python variable names and other identifiers.

✦ Created variables using integer, floating point, and other numerical data.

✦ Used augmented assignment statements to combine basic operations such as addition with assignment.

In the next chapter you discover how to use expressions to compare data and you learn how character strings work in Python.

✦   ✦   ✦

Expressions and Strings

◆ ◆ ◆ ◆

In This Chapter

Expressions

Strings

Converting between
simple types

◆ ◆ ◆ ◆

Character strings can hold messages for users to read (a la "Hello, world!"), but in Python they can also hold a sequence of binary data. This chapter covers how you use strings in your programs, and how you can convert between strings, numbers, and other Python data types.

Before you leave this chapter, you'll also have a solid grasp of expressions and how your programs can use them to make decisions and compare data.

Expressions

Expressions are the core building blocks of decision making in Python and other programming languages, and Python evaluates each expression to see if it is true or false.

The most basic form of a Python expression is any value: if the value is nonzero, it is considered to be "true," and if it equals 0, it is considered to be "false."

Cross-
Reference

Chapter 4 goes on to explain that Python also considers any nonempty and non-None objects to be true.

More common, however, is the comparison of two or more values with some sort of operator:

```
>>> 12 > 5 # This expression is true.
1
>>> 2 < 1 # This expression is false.
0
```

Comparing numeric types

Python supplies a standard set of operators for comparing numerical data types. Table 3-1 lists these comparison operators with examples.

Table 3-1
Comparison Operators

Operator	Description	Sample Input	Sample Output
<	Less than	10 < 5	0
>	Greater than	10 > 5	1
<=	Less than or equal	3 <= 5	1
		3 <= 3	1
>=	Greater than or equal	3 >= 5	0
==	Equality	3 == 3	1
		3 == 5	0
!=	Inequality*	3 != 5	1

* Python also supports an outdated inequality operator: <>. It may not be supported in the future.

Before comparing two numbers, Python applies the usual coercion rules if necessary.

A comparison between two complex numbers involves only the real part of each number if they are different. Only if the real parts of both are the same does the comparison depend on the imaginary part:

```
>>> 3 + 10j < 2 + 1000j
0
>>> 3 + 10j < 3 + 1000j
1
```

Python doesn't restrict you to just two operands in a comparison; for example, you can use the common a < b < c notation common in mathematics:

```
>>> a,b,c = 10,20,30
>>> a < b < c
# True because 10 < 20 and 20 < 30
```

Note that a < b < c is the same as comparing a < b and then comparing b < c, except that b is evaluated only once (besides being nifty, this could really make a difference if evaluating b required a lot of processing time).

Expressions like a < b > c are legal but discouraged, because to the casual observer (for example, you, late at night, searching for a bug in your code) they appear to imply a comparison or relationship between a and c, which is not really the case.

Python has three additional functions that you can use when comparing data:

min (x[, y,z,...])

The min function takes two or more arguments of any type and returns the smallest:

```
>>> min(10,20.5,5,100L)
5
```

max (x[, y,z,...])

Similarly, max chooses the largest of the arguments passed in:

```
>>> max(10,20.5,5,100L)
100L
```

Both min and max can accept a sequence as an argument (See Chapter 4 for information on lists and tuples.):

```
>>> Ages=[42,37,26]
>>> min(Ages)
26
```

cmp (x,y)

The comparison function takes two arguments and returns a negative number, 0, or a positive number if the first argument is less than, equal to, or greater than the second:

```
>>> cmp(2,5)
-1
>>> cmp(5,5.0)
0
>>> cmp(5,2)
1
```

Do not rely on the values being strictly 1, -1, or 0, especially when calling cmp with other data types (for example, strings).

Compound expressions

A compound expression combines simple expressions using the Boolean operators and, or, and not. Python treats Boolean operators slightly differently than many other languages do.

and

When evaluating the expression a and b, Python evaluates a to see if it is false, and if so, the entire expression takes on the value of a. If a is true, Python evaluates b and the entire expression takes on the value of b. There are two important points here. First, the expression does *not* evaluate to just true or false (0 or 1):

```
>>> a,b = 10,20
>>> a and b          # a is true, so evaluate b
20
>>> a,b = 0,5
>>> a and b
0
```

Second, if a (the first expression) evaluates to false, then Python never bothers to evaluate b (the second expression):

```
>>> 0 and 2/0        # Doesn't cause division by zero error
0
```

or

With the expression a or b, Python evaluates a to see if it is true, and if so, the entire expression takes on the value of a. When a is false, the expression takes on the value of b:

```
>>> a,b = 10,20
>>> a or b
10
>>> a,b = 0,5
>>> a or b
5
```

Similar to the and operator, the expression takes on the value of either a or b instead of just 0 or 1, and Python evaluates b only if a is false.

not

Finally, not inverts the "truthfulness" of an expression: if the expression evaluates to true, not returns false, and vice versa:

```
>>> not 5
0
>>> not 0
1
>>> not (0 > 2)
1
```

Unlike the and and or operators, not always returns a value of 0 or 1.

Complex expressions

You can form arbitrarily complex expressions by grouping any number of expressions together using parentheses and Boolean operators. For example, if you just can't seem to remember if a number is one of the first few prime numbers, this expression will bail you out:

```
>>> i = 5
>>> (i == 2) or (i % 2 != 0 and 0 < i < 9)
1
>>> i = 2
>>> (i == 2) or (i % 2 != 0 and 0 < i < 9)
1
>>> i = 4
>>> (i == 2) or (i % 2 != 0 and 0 < i < 9)
0
```

If the number is 2, the first sub-expression (i == 2) evaluates to true and Python stops processing the expression and returns 1 for true. Otherwise, two remaining conditions must be met for the expression to evaluate to true. The number must not be evenly divisible by 2, and it must be between 0 and 9 (hey, I said the first *few* primes, remember?).

Parentheses let you explicitly control the order of what gets evaluated first. Without parentheses, the order of evaluation may be unclear and different than what you expect (and a great source of bugs):

```
>>> 4 or 1 * 2
4
```

A well-placed pair of parentheses clears up any ambiguity:

```
>>> (4 or 1) * 2
8
```

Operator precedence

Python uses the ordering in Table 3-2 to guide the evaluation of complex expressions. Expressions using operators higher up in the table get evaluated before those towards the bottom of the table. Operators on the same line of the table have equal priority or precedence. Python evaluates operators with the same precedence from left to right.

Table 3-2 Operator Precedence (from lowest to highest)	
Operators	**Description**
`x`	String conversion
{key:datum, ...}	Dictionary
[x,y,...]	List
(x,y,...)	Tuple

Continued

Table 3-2 *(continued)*	
Operators	**Description**
f(x,y,...)	Function call
x[j:k]	Slice
x[j]	Subscription
x.attribute	Attribute reference
~x	Bitwise negation (inversion)
+x, -x	Plus, minus
**	Power
*, /, %	Multiply, divide, modulo
+, -	Add, subtract
<<, >>	Shifting
&	Bitwise AND
^	Bitwise XOR
|	Bitwise OR
<, <=, ==, !=, >=, >	Comparisons
is, is not	Identity
in, not in	Membership
not x	Boolean NOT
and	Boolean AND
or	Boolean OR
lambda	Lambda expression

Cross-Reference   See Chapters 4 through 7 for more information on operators and data types such as lists and tuples that we have not yet covered.

Strings

A string is Python's data type for holding not only text but also "non-printable" or binary data. If you've done much work with strings in languages like C or C++, prepare to be liberated from mundane memory management tasks as well as a plethora of bugs lying in wait. Strings in Python were not added as an afterthought or tacked on via a third party library, but are part of the core language itself, and it shows!

String literals

A string literal is a sequence of characters enclosed by a matching pair of single or double quotes:

```
"Do you like green eggs and ham?"
'Amu vian najbaron'
"Tuesday'  # Illegal: quotes do not match.
```

Which of the two you use is more of a personal preference (in some nerdy way I find single-quoted strings more sexy and "cool"), but sometimes the text of the string makes one or the other more convenient:

```
'Quoth the Raven, _Nevermore._ '
_Monty Python's Flying Circus_
_Enter your age (I'll know if you're lying, so don't): _
```

Python automatically joins two or more string literals separated only by whitespace:

```
>>> "one" 'two' "three"
'onetwothree'
```

A single backslash character inside a string literal lets you break a string across multiple lines:

```
>>> 'Rubber baby \
... buggy bumpers'
'Rubber baby buggy bumpers'
```

If your string of text covers several lines and you want Python to preserve the exact formatting you used when typing it in, use triple-quoted strings (the string begins with three single or double quotes and ends with three more of the same type of quote). An example:

```
>>> s = """"Knock knock."
... "Who's there?"
... "Knock knock."
... "Who's there?"
... "Knock knock."
... "Who's there?"
... "Philip Glass."
... """
>>> print s
"Knock knock."
"Who's there?"
"Knock knock."
"Who's there?"
"Knock knock."
"Who's there?"
"Philip Glass."
```

String length

Regardless of the quoting method you use, string literals can be of any length. You can use the `len(x)` function to retrieve the length of a string:

```
>>> len('Pokey')
5
>>> s = 'Data:\x00\x01'
>>> len(s)
7
```

Escape sequences

You can also use *escape sequences* to include quotes or other characters inside a string (see Table 3-3):

```
>>> print "\"Never!\" shouted Skeptopotamus."
"Never!" shouted Skeptopotamus.
```

Table 3-3
Escape Sequences

Sequence	Description
\n	Newline (ASCII LF)
\'	Single quote
\"	Double quote
\\	Backslash
\t	Tab (ASCII TAB)
\b	Backspace (ASCII BS)
\r	Carriage return (ASCII CR)
\xhh	Character with ASCII value hh in hex
\ooo	Character with ASCII value ooo in octal
\f	Form feed (ASCII FF)*
\a	Bell (ASCII BEL)
\v	Vertical tab (ASCII VT)

* Not all output devices support all ASCII codes. You won't use \v very often, for example.

Table 3-3 lists the valid escape sequences. If you try to use an invalid escape sequence, Python leaves both the backslash and the character after it in the string:

```
>>> print 'Time \z for foosball!'
Time \z for foosball!
```

As shown in Table 3-3, you can specify the characters of a string using their ASCII value:

```
>>> '\x50\x79\x74\x68\x6f\x6e'
'Python'
```

See "Converting Between Simple Types" later in this chapter for more on the ASCII codes for characters.

The values can be in the range of 0 to 255 (the values that a single byte can have). Remember: a string in Python doesn't have to be printable text. A string could hold the raw data of an image file, a binary message received over a network, or anything else.

Raw strings

One final way to specify string literals is with *raw strings*, in which backslashes can still be used as escape characters, but Python leaves them in the string. You flag a string as a raw string with an r prefix. For example, on Windows systems the path separator character is a backslash, so to use it in a string you'd normally have to type '\\' (the escape sequence for the backslash). Alternatively, you could use a raw string:

```
>>> s = r"c:\games\half-life\hl.exe"
>>> s
'c:\\games\\half-life\\hl.exe'
>>> print s
c:\games\half-life\hl.exe
```

The os.path module provides easy, cross-platform path manipulation. See Chapter 10 for details.

Manipulating strings

You can use the plus and multiply operators to build strings. The plus operator concatenates strings together:

```
>>> a = 'ha '
>>> a + a + a
'ha ha ha '
```

The multiply operator repeats a string:

```
>>> '=' * 10
'=========='
```

Note that operator precedence rules apply, as always:

```
>>> 'Wh' + 'e' * 10 +'!'
'Wheeeeeeeeee!'
```

Augmented assignment works as well:

```
>>> a = 'Ah'
>>> a += ' Hah! '
>>> a
'Ah Hah! '
>>> a *= 2
>>> a
'Ah Hah! Ah Hah! '
```

Accessing individual characters and substrings

Because strings are sequences of characters, you can use on them the same operators that are common to all of Python's sequence types, among them, *subscription* and *slice*.

 See Chapter 4 for a discussion of Python sequence types.

Subscription lets you use an index number to retrieve a single character from a Python string, with 0 being the first character:

```
>>> s = 'Python'
>>> s[1]
'y'
```

Additionally, you can reference characters from the *end* of the string using negative numbers. An index of -1 means the last character, -2 the next to last, and so on:

```
>>> 'Hello'[-1]
'o'
>>> 'Hello'[-5]
'H'
```

Python strings are *immutable*, which means you can't directly change them or individual characters (you can, of course, assign the same variable to a new string):

```
>>> s = 'Bad'
>>> s[2] = 'c' # Can't modify the string value
Traceback (innermost last):
  File "<interactive input>", line 1, in ?
TypeError: object doesn't support item assignment
>>> s = 'Good' # Can reassign the variable
```

Strings Are Objects

Python strings are actually objects with many built-in methods:

```
>>> s = 'Dyn-o-mite!'
>>> s.upper()
'DYN-O-MITE!'
>>> '   text   '.strip()
'text'
```

Refer to Chapter 9 for a discussion of all the String methods and how to use them.

Slicing is similar to subscription except that with it you can retrieve entire substrings instead of single characters. The operator takes two arguments for the lower and upper bounds of the slice:

```
>>> 'Monty'[2:4]
'nt'
```

It's important to understand that the bounds are not referring to character indices (as with subscription), but really refer to the spots *between* characters:

```
M o n t y
| | | | | |
0 1 2 3 4 5
```

So the slice of 2:4 is like telling Python, "Give me everything from the right of 2 and to the left of 4," which is the substring "nt".

The lower and upper bounds of a slice are optional. If omitted, Python sticks in the beginning or ending bound of the string for you:

```
>>> s = 'Monty'
>>> s[:2]
'Mo'
>>> s[2:]
'nty'
>>> s[:]
'Monty'
```

Don't forget: Python doesn't care if you use negative numbers as bounds for the offset from the end of the string. Continuing the previous example:

```
>>> s[1:-1]
'ont'
>>> s[-3:-1]
'nt'
```

You can also access each character via tuple unpacking. This feature isn't used as often because you have to use exactly the same number of variables as characters in the string:

```
>>> a,b,c = 'YES'
>>> print a, b, c
Y E S
```

Note   Python does not have a separate 'character' data type; a character is just a string of length 1.

Formatting strings

The modulo operator (%) has special behavior when used with strings. You can use it like the C printf function for formatting data:

```
>>> "It's %d past %d, %s!" % (7,9,"Fred")
"It's 7 past 9, Fred!"
```

Python scans the string for conversion specifiers and replaces them with values from the list you supply. Table 3-4 lists the different characters you can use in a conversion and what they do; those in bold are more commonly useful.

Table 3-4 String Formatting Characters	
Character	*Description*
d **or** I	**Decimal (base 10) integer**
f	**Floating point number**
s	**String or any object**
c	Single character
u	Unsigned decimal integer
X or x	Hexadecimal integer (upper or lower case)
o	Octal integer
e or E	Floating point number in exponential form
g **or** G	Like %f unless exponent < -4 or greater than the precision. If so, acts like %e or %E
r	repr() version of the object*
%	Use %% to print the percentage character.

* %s prints the str() version, %r prints the repr() version. See "Converting Between Simple Types" in this chapter.

Here are a few more examples:

```
>>> '%x %X' % (57005,48879)
'dead BEEF'
>>> pi = 3.14159
>>> '%f %E %G' % (pi,pi,pi)
'3.141590 3.141590E+000 3.14159'
>>> print '%s %r' % ('Hello','Hello')
Hello 'Hello'
```

Beyond these features, Python has several other options, some of which are holdovers from C. Between the % character and the conversion character you choose, you can have any combination of the following (in this order):

Key name
Instead of a tuple, you can provide a dictionary of values to use (dictionaries are covered in Chapter 4). Place the key names (enclosed in parentheses) between the percent sign and the type code in the format string. This one is best explained with an example (although fans of Mad-Libs will be at home):

```
>>> d = {'name':'Sam', 'num':32, 'amt':10.12}
>>> '%(name)s is %(num)d years old. %(name)s has $%(amt).2f' %
d
'Sam is 32 years old. Sam has $10.12'
```

- or 0
A minus indicates that numbers should be left justified, and a 0 tells Python to pad the number with leading zeros. (This won't have much effect unless used with the minimum field modifier, explained below.)

+
A plus indicates that the number should always display its sign, even if the number is positive:

```
>>> '%+d %+d' % (5,-5)
'+5 -5'
```

Minimum field width number
A number indicates the minimum field this value should take up. If printing the value takes up less space, Python adds padding (either spaces or zeros, see above) to make up the difference:

```
>>> '%5d' % 2   # Don't need () if there's only one value
'    2'
>>> '%-5d, %05d' % (2,2)
'2    , 00002'
```

Additional precision-ish number

This final number is a period character followed by a number. For a string, the number is the maximum number of characters to print. For a floating-point number, it's the number of digits to print after the decimal point, and for integers it's the minimum number of digits to print. Got all that?

```
>>> '%.3s' % 'Python'
'Pyt'
>>> '%05.3f' % 3.5
'3.500'
>>> '%-8.5d' % 10
'00010   '
```

Last but not least, you can use an asterisk in place of any number in a width field. If you supply an asterisk, you also provide a list of values (instead of a single number). Python looks in the list of values for that width value:

```
>>> '%*.*f' % (6,3,1.41421356)
' 1.414'
```

Comparing strings

String comparison works much the same way numeric comparison does by using the standard comparison operators (<, <=, !=, ==, >=, >). The comparison is lexicographic ('A' < 'B') and case-sensitive:

```
>>> 'Fortran' > 'Pascal'
0
>>> 'Perl' < 'Python'
1
```

For a string in an expression, Python evaluates any nonempty string to true, and an empty string to false:

```
>>> 'OK' and 5
5
>>> not 'fun'
0
>>> not ''
1
```

This behavior provides a useful idiom for using a default value if a string is empty. For example, suppose that the variable s in the following example came from user input instead of you supplying the value. If the user chose something, name holds its value; otherwise name holds the default value of 'index.html'.

```
>>> s = ''; name = s or 'index.html'
>>> name
'index.html'
```

```
>>> s = 'page.html'; name = s or 'index.html'
>>> name
'page.html'
```

You can use the min, max, and cmp functions on strings:

```
>>> min('abstract') # Find the least character in the string.
'a'
>>> max('i','love','spam') # Find the greatest string.
'spam'
>>> cmp('Vader','Maul') # Vader is greater.
9
```

Strings (and other sequence types) also have the in (and not in) operator, which tests if a character is a member of a string:

```
>>> 'u' in 'there?'
0
>>> 'i' not in 'teamwork' # Cheesy
1
```

Cross-Reference   Chapter 9 covers advanced string searching and matching with regular expressions.

Unicode string literals

Many computer languages limit characters in a string to values in the range of 0 to 255 because they store each one as a single byte, making nearly impossible the support of non-ASCII characters used by so many other languages besides plain old English. Unicode characters are 16-bit values (0 to 65535) and can therefore handle just about any character set imaginable.

New Feature   Full support for Unicode strings was a new addition in Python 2.0.

You can specify a Unicode literal string by prefixing a string with a u:

```
>>> u'Rang'
u'Rang'
```

Cross-Reference   See Chapter 9 for more on using Unicode strings.

Converting Between Simple Types

Python provides many functions for converting between numerical and string data types in addition to the string formatting feature in the previous section.

Converting to numerical types

The `int`, `long`, `float`, `complex`, and `ord` functions convert data to numerical types.

int (x[, radix])

This function uses a string and an optional base to convert a number or string to an integer:

```
>>> int('15')
15
>>> int('15',16) # In hexadecimal, sixteen is written "10"
21
```

The string it converts from must be a valid integer (trying to convert the string 3.5 would fail). Alternatively, the `int` function can convert other numbers to integers:

```
>>> int(3.5)
3
>>> int(10L)
10
```

The `int` function drops the fractional part of a number. To find the "closest" integer, use the `round` function (below).

long (x[, radix])

The `long` function can convert a string or another number to a long integer (you can also include a base):

```
>>> long('125')
125L
>>> long(17.6)
17L
>>> long('1E',16)
30L
```

float (x)

You should be seeing a pattern by now:

```
>>> float(12.1)
12.1
>>> float(10L)
10.0
>>> int(float("3.5")) # int("3.5") is illegal.
3
```

The exception is with complex numbers; use the `abs` function to "convert" a complex number to a floating-point number.

round (num[, digits])

This function rounds a floating point number to a number having the specified number of fractional digits. If you omit the `digits` argument, the result is a whole number:

```
>>> round(123.5678,3)
123.568
>>> round(123.5678)
124.0
>>> round(123.4)
123.0
```

complex (real[, imaginary])

The `complex` function can convert a string or number to a complex number, and it also takes an optional imaginary part to use if none is supplied:

```
>>> complex('2+5j')
(2+5j)
>>> complex('2')
(2+0j)
>>> complex(6L,3)
(6+3j)
```

ord (ch)

This function takes a single character (a string of length 1) as its argument and returns the ASCII or Unicode value for that character:

```
>>> ord(u'a')
97
>>> ord('b')
98
```

Converting to strings

Going the other direction, the following functions take numbers and make them into strings.

chr (x) and unichr (x)

Inverses of the `ord` function, these functions take a number representing an ASCII or Unicode value and convert it to a character:

```
>>> chr(98)
'b'
```

oct (x) and hex (x)

These two functions take numbers and convert them to octal and hexadecimal string representations:

```
>>> oct(123)
'0173'
>>> hex(123)
'0x7b'
```

str (obj)

The `str` function takes *any* object and returns a printable string version of that object:

```
>>> str(5)
'5'
>>> str(5.5)
'5.5'
>>> str(3+2j)
'(3+2j)'
```

Python calls this function when you use the `print` statement.

repr (obj)

The `repr` function is similar to `str` except that it tries to return a string version of the object that is valid Python syntax. For simple data types, the outputs of `str` and `repr` are often identical. (See Chapter 9 for details.)

A popular shorthand for this function is to surround the object to convert in back ticks (above the Tab key on most PC keyboards):

```
>>> a = 5
>>> 'Give me ' + a # Can't add a string and an integer!
Traceback (innermost last):
  File "<interactive input>", line 1, in ?
TypeError: cannot add type "int" to string
>>> 'Give me ' + `a` # Convert to a string on-the-fly.
'Give me 5'
```

New Feature   As of Python 2.1, `str` and `repr` display newlines and other escape sequences the same way you type them (instead of displaying their ASCII code):

```
>>> 'Hello\nWorld'
'Hello\nWorld'
```

When you use the Python interpreter interactively, Python calls `repr` to display objects. You can have it use a different function by setting the value of `sys.displayhook`:

```
>>> 5.3
5.2999999999999998  # The standard representation is ugly.
>>> def printstr(s):
...    print str(s)
>>> import sys
>>> sys.displayhook = printstr
>>> 5.3
5.3  # A more human-friendly format
```

New Feature The `sys.displayhook` feature is new in Python 2.1.

Summary

Python has a complete set of operators for building expressions as complex as you need. Python's built-in string data type offers powerful but convenient control over text and binary strings, freeing you from many maintenance tasks you'd be stuck with in other programming languages. In this chapter you:

✦ Built string literals and formatted data in strings.

✦ Used Python's operators to modify and compare data.

✦ Learned to convert between various data types and strings.

In the next chapter you'll unleash the power of Python's other built-in data types including lists, tuples, and dictionaries.

✦　　✦　　✦

Advanced Data Types

◆ ◆ ◆ ◆

In This Chapter

Grouping data with sequences

Working with sequences

Using additional list object features

Mapping information with dictionaries

Understanding references

Copying complex objects

Identifying data types

Working with array objects

◆ ◆ ◆ ◆

The simple data types in the last few chapters are common to many programming languages, although often not so easily managed and out-of-the-box powerful. The data types in this chapter, however, set Python apart from languages such as C, C++, or even Java, because they are built-in, intuitive and easy to use, and incredibly powerful.

Grouping Data with Sequences

Strings, lists, and tuples are Python's built-in *sequence* data types. Each sequence type represents an ordered set of data elements. Unlike strings, where each piece of data is a single character, the elements that make up a list or a tuple can be anything, including other lists, tuples, strings, and so on. Though much of this section applies to strings, the focus here is on lists and tuples.

Cross-Reference

Go directly to Chapter 3 to learn more about strings. Do not pass Go.

The main difference between lists and tuples is one of mutability: you can change, add, or remove items of a list, but you cannot change a tuple. Beyond this, though, you will find a conceptual difference on where you apply each. You'd use a list as an array to hold the lines of text from a file, for example, and a tuple to represent a 3-D point in space (x,y,z). Put another way, lists are great for dealing with many items that you'd process similarly, while a tuple often represents different parts of a single item. (Don't worry — when you go to use either in a program it becomes pretty obvious which one you need.)

Creating lists

Creating a list is straightforward because you don't need to specify a particular data type or length. You can surround any piece of data in square brackets to create a list containing that data:

```
>>> x = [] # An empty list
>>> y = ['Strawberry','Peach']
>>> z = [10,'Howdy',y] # Mixed types and a list within a list
>>> z
[10, 'Howdy', ['Strawberry', 'Peach']]
```

You can call the list(seq) function to convert from one sequence type to a list:

```
>>> list((5,10)) # A tuple
[5, 10]
>>> list("The World")
['T', 'h', 'e', ' ', 'W', 'o', 'r', 'l', 'd']
```

If you call list on an object that is already a list, you get a copy of the original list back.

See "Copying Complex Objects" in this chapter for more on copying objects.

Ranges

You use the range([lower,] stop[, step]) function to generate a list whose members are some ordered progression of integers. Instead of idling away your time typing in the numbers from 0 to 10, you can do the same with a call to range:

```
>>> range(10)
[0, 1, 2, 3, 4, 5, 6, 7, 8, 9] # 10 items, starting at 0
```

You can also call the function with start and stop indices, and even a step to tell it how quickly to jump to the next item:

```
>>> range(6,12)
[6, 7, 8, 9, 10, 11] # Stops just before the stop index.
>>> range (2,20,3)
[2, 5, 8, 11, 14, 17]
>>> range (20,2,-3)  # Going down!
[20, 17, 14, 11, 8, 5]
```

You most commonly use the range function in looping (which we cover in the next chapter):

```
>>> for i in range(10):
...      print i,
0 1 2 3 4 5 6 7 8 9
```

The `xrange ([lower,] stop[, step])` function is similar to `range` except that instead of creating a list, it returns an *xrange object* that behaves like a list but doesn't calculate each list value until needed. This feature has the potential to save memory if the range is very large or to improve performance if you aren't likely to iterate through every single member of the equivalent list.

List comprehensions

One final way to create a list is through *list comprehensions*, which are great if you want to operate on each item in a list and store the result in a new list, or if you want to create a list that contains only items that meet certain criteria. For example, to generate a list containing x^2 for the numbers 1 through 10:

```
>>> [x*x for x in range(1,11)]
[1, 4, 9, 16, 25, 36, 49, 64, 81, 100]
```

New Feature   List comprehensions are new in Python 2.0.

Python uses the `range(1,11)` to generate a list containing the numbers 1 through 10. Then, for each number in that list, it evaluates the expression `x*x` and adds the result to the output list.

You can add an `if` to the list comprehension so that items get added to the new list only if they pass some test. For example, to generate the same list as above while weeding out odd numbers:

```
>>> [x*x for x in range(10) if x % 2 == 0]
[0, 4, 16, 36, 64]
```

But wait, there's more! You can list more than one `for` statement and Python evaluates each in order, processing the rest of the list comprehension each time:

```
>>> [a+b for a in 'ABC' for b in '123']
['A1', 'A2', 'A3', 'B1', 'B2', 'B3', 'C1', 'C2', 'C3']
```

Python loops through each character of `'ABC'` and for each one goes through the entire loop of each character in `'123'`.

See where this is going? You can have as many `for` statements as you want, and each one can have an `if` statement (but if you think you need five or six then you might want to break them into separate statements for sanity's sake):

```
>>> [a+b+c for a in "HI" for b in "JOE" if b != 'E'
...       for c in '123' if c!= '2']
['HJ1', 'HJ3', 'HO1', 'HO3', 'IJ1', 'IJ3', 'IO1', 'IO3']
```

Finally, the expression that Python evaluates to generate each item in the new list doesn't have to be a simple data type such as an integer. You can also have it be lists, tuples, and so forth:

```
>>> [(x,ord(x)) for x in 'Ouch']
[('O', 79), ('u', 117), ('c', 99), ('h', 104)]
```

Creating tuples

Creating a tuple is similar to creating a list, except that you use parentheses instead of square brackets:

```
>>> x = ()   # Any empty tuple
>>> y = 22407,'Fredericksburg' # ()'s are optional
>>> z = ('Mrs. White','Ballroom','Candlestick')
```

Parentheses can also enclose any expression, so Python has a special syntax to designate a tuple with only one item. To create a tuple containing the string 'lonely':

```
>>> x = ('lonely',)
```

Use the tuple(seq) function to convert one of the other sequence types to a tuple:

```
>>> tuple('tuple')
('t', 'u', 'p', 'l', 'e')
>>> tuple([1,2,3])
(1, 2, 3)
```

Working with Sequences

Now that you have your list or tuple, what do you do with it? This section shows you the operators and functions you can use to work on sequence data.

Joining and repeating with arithmetic operators

Of the arithmetic operators, Python defines addition and multiplication for working with sequences. As with strings, the addition operator concatenates sequences and the multiplication operator repeats them:

```
>>> [1,2] + [5] + ['EGBDF']
[1, 2, 5, 'EGBDF']
>>> ('FACEG',) + (17,88)
('FACEG', 17, 88)
>>> (1,3+4j) * 2
(1, (3+4j), 1, (3+4j))
```

The augmented assignment version of these operators works as well (although for strings and tuples Python doesn't perform the operation in place but instead creates a new object):

```
>>> z = ['bow','arrow']
>>> z *= 2
>>> z
['bow', 'arrow', 'bow', 'arrow']
>>> q = (1,2)
>>> q += (3,4)
>>> q
(1, 2, 3, 4)
```

Comparing and membership testing

You can use the normal comparison ($<$, $<=$, $>=$, $>$) and equality ($!=$, $==$) operators with sequence objects:

```
>>> ['five','two'] != [5,2]
1
>>> (0.5,2) < (0.5,1)
0
```

Python checks the corresponding element of each sequence until it can make a determination. When the items in two sequence objects are equal except that one has more items than the other, the longer is considered greater:

```
>>> [1,2,3] > [1,2]
1
```

You can use the in operator to test if something is in a list or tuple, and not in to test if it is not:

```
>>> trouble = ('Dan','Joe','Bob')
>>> 'Bob' in trouble
1
>>> 'Dave' not in trouble
1
```

Accessing parts of sequences

When you need to retrieve data from a sequence object, you have several alternatives.

Subscription

When you want to access a single element of a sequence object, you use the subscript or index of the element you want to reference, with the first element having an index of zero (For some reason I get strange looks when I say, "Back to square zero!"):

```
>>> num = ['dek','dudek','tridek']
>>> num[1]
'dudek'
>>> num[-1]  # A negative index starts from the other end.
'tridek'
```

Slices

Slices let you create a new sequence containing all or part of another sequence. You specify a slice in the form of [start:end] and for each element Python adds that element to the new sequence if its index i is start <= i < end.

Tip   Conceptually, thinking of the slice parameters as pointing *between* items in a sequence is helpful.

```
>>> meses = ['marzo','abril','mayo','junio']
>>> meses[1:3]
['abril', 'mayo']
>>> meses[0:-2]  # Parameters can count from the right, too.
['marzo', 'abril']
```

The start and end parameters are both optional, and Python silently corrects invalid input:

```
>>> meses[2:]
['mayo', 'junio']
>>> meses[:2]
['marzo', 'abril']
>>> meses[-2:5000]
['mayo', 'junio']
```

Cross-Reference   See "Accessing individual characters and substrings" in Chapter 3 for more examples of using slices.

Unpacking

Just as you can create a tuple by assigning a comma-separated list of items to a single variable, you can *unpack* a sequence object (not just tuples!) by doing the opposite:

```
>>> s = 801,435,804
>>> x,y,z = s
>>> print x,y,z
801 435 804
```

Keep in mind that the number of variables on the left must match the length of the sequence you're unpacking on the right.

Note   Multiple assignment (in Chapter 3) is really just a special case of tuple packing and unpacking: you pack the objects into a single tuple and then unpack them into the same number of original variables.

Iterating with for...in

A common task is to loop over all the elements of a list or tuple and operate on each one. One of the easiest ways to do this is with a `for...in` statement:

```
>>> for op in ['sin','cos','tan']:
...       print op
sin
cos
tan
```

Using sequence utility functions

Python provides a rich complement of sequence processing functions.

len (x), min (x[, y,z,...]), and max (x[, y,z,...])

These three aren't really specific to sequences, but they're quite useful nonetheless:

```
>>> data = [0.5, 12, 18, 2, -5]
>>> len(data) # Count of items in the sequence
5
>>> min(data) # The minimum item in the sequence
-5
>>> max(data) # The maximum item in the sequence
18
```

filter (function, list)

When you call `filter` it applies a function to each item in a sequence, and returns all items for which the function returns true, thus filtering out all items for which the function returns false. In the following example I create a tiny function, `nukeBad`, that returns false if the string passed in contains the word `'bad'`. Combining `filter` with `nukeBad` eliminates all those 'bad' words:

```
>>> def nukeBad(s):
...       return s.find('bad') == -1
>>> s = ['bad','good','Sinbad','bade','welcome']
>>> filter(nukeBad,s)
['good', 'welcome']
```

If you pass in `None` for the function argument, `filter` removes any 0 or empty items from the list:

```
>>> stuff = [12,0,'Hey',[],'',[1,2]]
>>> filter(None,stuff)
[12, 'Hey', [1, 2]]
```

The `filter` function returns the same sequence type as the one you passed in. The example below removes any number characters from a string and returns a new string:

```
>>> filter(lambda d:not d.isdigit(),"P6yth12on")
'Python'
```

 See Chapter 6 for more information on lambda expressions.

map (function, list[, list, ...])

The map function takes a function and a sequence and returns to you the result of applying the function to each item in the original sequence. Regardless of the type of sequence you pass in, map always returns a list:

```
>>> import string
>>> s = ['chile','canada','mexico']
>>> map(string.capitalize,s)
['Chile', 'Canada', 'Mexico']
```

You can pass in several multiple lists, too, as long as the function you supply takes the same number of arguments as the number of lists you pass in:

```
>>> import operator
>>> s = [2,3,4,5]; t = [5,6,7,8]
>>> map(operator.mul,s,t) # s[j] * t[j]
[10, 18, 28, 40]
```

 Chapter 7 covers the operator class, which contains function versions of the standard operators so you can pass them into functions like map.

If the lists you use are of different lengths, map uses empty (None) items to make up the difference. Also, if you pass in None instead of a function, map combines the corresponding elements from each sequence and returns them as tuples (compare this to the behavior of the zip function, later in this section):

```
>>> a = [1,2,3]; b = [4,5,6]; c = [7,8,9]
>>> map(None,a,b,c)
[(1, 4, 7), (2, 5, 8), (3, 6, 9)]
```

reduce (function, seq[, init])

This function takes the first two items in the sequence you pass in, passes them to the function you supply, takes the result and the next item in the list, passes them to the function, and so on until it has processed all the items:

```
>>> import operator
>>> reduce(operator.mul,[2,3,4,5])
120 # 120 = ((2*3)*4)*5
```

An optional third parameter is an initializer reduce uses in the very first calculation, or when the list is empty. The following example starts with the string "-" and adds each character of a word to the beginning and end of the string (because strings are sequences, reduce calls the function once for each letter in the string):

```
>>> reduce(lambda x,y: y+x+y, "Hello", "-")
'olleH-Hello'
```

zip (seq[, seq, ...])

The `zip` function combines corresponding items from two or more sequences and returns them as a list of tuples, stopping after it has processed all the items in the shortest sequence:

```
>>> zip([1,1,2,3,5],[8,13,21])
[(1, 8), (1, 13), (2, 21)]
```

You may find the `zip` function convenient when you want to iterate over several lists in parallel:

```
>>> names = ['Joe','Fred','Sam']
>>> exts = [116,120,100]
>>> ages = [26,34,28]
>>> for name,ext,age in zip(names,exts,ages):
...         print '%s (extension %d) is %d' % (name,ext,age)
Joe (extension 116) is 26
Fred (extension 120) is 34
Sam (extension 100) is 28
```

Passing in just one sequence to `zip` returns each item as a 1-tuple:

```
>>> zip((1,2,3,4))
[(1,), (2,), (3,), (4,)]
```

 New Feature   The `zip` function was introduced in Python 2.0.

Using Additional List Object Features

List objects have several methods that further facilitate their use, and because they are mutable they support a few extra operations.

Additional operations

You can replace the value of any item with an assignment statement:

```
>>> todo = ['dishes','garbage','sweep','mow lawn','dust']
>>> todo[1] = 'boogie'
>>> todo
['dishes', 'boogie', 'sweep', 'mow lawn', 'dust']
```

What gets replaced in the list doesn't need to be limited to a single item. You can choose to replace an entire slice with a new list:

```
>>> todo[1:3] = ['nap'] # Replace from 1 to before 3
>>> todo
['dishes', 'nap', 'mow lawn', 'dust']
>>> todo[2:] = ['eat','drink','be merry']
>>> todo
['dishes', 'nap', 'eat', 'drink', 'be merry']
```

And finally, you can delete items or slices using del:

```
>>> del z[0]
>>> z
['nap', 'eat', 'drink', 'be merry']
>>> del z[1:3]
>>> z
['nap', 'be merry']
```

List object methods

The following methods are available on all list objects.

append (obj) and extend (obj)

The append method adds an item to the end of a list like the += operator (Python modifies the original list in place) except that the item you pass to append is not a list. The extend method assumes the argument you pass it is a list:

```
>>> z = ['Nevada','Virginia']
>>> z.append('Utah')
>>> z
['Nevada', 'Virginia', 'Utah']
>>> z.extend(['North Carolina','Georgia'])
>>> z
['Nevada', 'Virginia', 'Utah', 'North Carolina', 'Georgia']
```

index (obj)

This method returns the index of the *first* matching item in the list, if present, and raises the ValueError exception if not. Continuing the previous example:

```
>>> x.index(12)
1
>>> try: print x.index('Farmer')
... except ValueError: print 'NOT ON LIST!'
NOT ON LIST!
```

Cross-Reference   See the next chapter for information on try...exception blocks.

count (obj)

You use the count method to find out how many items in the list match the one you pass in:

```
>>> x = [15,12,'Foo',16,12]
>>> x.count(12)
2
```

 Cross-Reference   String objects also have count and index methods. See Chapter 9 for details.

insert (j, obj)

Use the `insert` method to add a new item anywhere in the list. Pass in the index of the item you want the new one to come *before* and the item to insert:

```
>>> months = ['March','May','June']
>>> months.insert(1,'April')
>>> months
['March', 'April', 'May', 'June']
```

Notice that `insert` is pretty forgiving if you pass in a bogus index:

```
>>> months.insert(-1,'February') # Item added at start
>>> months.insert(5000,'July')   # Item added at end
>>> months
['February', 'March', 'April', 'May', 'June', 'July']
```

remove (obj)

This function locates the first occurrence of an item in the list and removes it, if present, and yells at you if not:

```
>>> months.remove('March')
>>> months
['February', 'February', 'April', 'May', 'June', 'July']
>>> months.remove('August')
Traceback (innermost last):
  File "<interactive input>", line 1, in ?
ValueError: list.remove(x): x not in list
```

pop([j])

If you specify an index, `pop` removes the item from that place in the list and returns it. Without an index, the `pop` function removes and returns the last item from the list:

```
>>> saludos = ['Hasta!','Ciao','Nos vemos']
>>> saludos.pop(1)
'Ciao'
>>> saludos
['Hasta!', 'Nos vemos']
>>> saludos.pop()
'Nos vemos'
```

Calling pop on an empty list causes it to raise IndexError.

reverse()

As named, the reverse function reverses the order of the list:

```
>>> names = ['Jacob','Hannah','Rachael','Jennie']
>>> names.reverse()
>>> names
['Jennie', 'Rachael', 'Hannah', 'Jacob']
```

sort([func])

This function orders the items in a list. Continuing the previous example:

```
>>> names.sort()
>>> names
['Hannah', 'Jacob', 'Jennie', 'Rachael']
```

Additionally, you can provide your own comparison function to use during the sort. This function accepts two arguments and returns a negative number, 0, or a positive number if the first argument is less than, equal to, or greater than the second. For example, to order a list by length of each item:

```
>>> names.sort(lambda a,b:len(a)-len(b))  # Ch 5 covers lambdas.
>>> names
['Jacob', 'Hannah', 'Jennie', 'Rachael']
```

Tip   If you want to add and remove items to a sorted list, use the bisect module. When you insert an item using the insort(list, item) function, it uses a bisection algorithm to inexpensively find the correct place to insert the item so that the resulting list remains sorted. The bisect(list, item) function in the same module finds the correct insertion point without actually adding the item to the list.

Mapping Information with Dictionaries

A dictionary contains a set of mappings between unique keys and their values; they are Python's only built-in mapping data type. The examples in this section use the following dictionary that maps login user names and passwords to Web site names (who can ever keep track of them all?):

```
>>> logins = {'yahoo':('john','jyahooohn'),
...            'hotmail':('jrf5','18thStreet')}
>>> logins['hotmail']  # What's my name/password for hotmail?
('jrf5', '18thStreet')
```

Creating and adding to dictionaries

You create a dictionary by listing zero or more key-value pairs within curly braces. The keys used in a dictionary must be unique and immutable, so strings, numbers, and tuples with immutable items in them can all be used as keys. The values in the key-value pair can be anything, even other dictionaries if you want.

Adding or replacing mappings is easy:

```
>>> logins['slashdot'] = ('juan','lemmein')
```

Accessing and updating dictionary mappings

If you try to use a key that doesn't exist in the dictionary, Python barks out a KeyError exception. When you don't want to worry about handling the exception, you can instead use the get(key[, obj]) method, which returns None if the mapping doesn't exist, and even lets you specify a default value for such cases:

```
>>> logins['sourceforge','No such login']
Traceback (innermost last):
  File "<interactive input>", line 1, in ?
KeyError: ('sourceforge', 'No such login')
>>> logins.get('sourceforge') == None
1
>>> logins.get('sourceforge','No such login')
'No such login'
```

The setdefault(key[, obj]) method works like get with the default parameter, except that if the key-value pair doesn't exist, Python adds it to the dictionary:

```
>>> logins.setdefault('slashdot',('jimmy','punk'))
('juan', 'lemmein') # Existing item returned
>>> logins.setdefault('justwhispers',('jimmy','punk'))
('jimmy', 'punk') # New item returned AND added to dictionary
```

If you just want to know if a dictionary has a particular key-value pair (or if you want to check before requesting it), you can use the has_key(key) method:

```
>>> logins.has_key('yahoo')
1
```

The del statement removes an item from a dictionary:

```
>>> del logins['yahoo']
>>> logins.has_key('yahoo')
0
```

"Hashability"

The more precise requirement of a dictionary key is that it must be *hashable*. An object's hash value is a semi-unique, internally generated number that can be used for quick comparisons. Consider comparing two strings, for example. To see if the strings are equal, you would have to compare each character until one differed. If you already had the hash value for each string, however, you could just compare the two and be done.

Python uses hash values in dictionary lookups for the same reason: so that dictionary lookups will not be too costly.

You can retrieve the hash value of any hashable object by using the hash(obj) function:

```
>>> hash('hash')
-1671425852
>>> hash(10)
10
>>> hash(10.0) # Numbers of different types have the same hash.
10
>>> hash((1,2,3))
-821448277
```

The hash function raises the TypeError exception on unhashable objects (lists, for example).

You can use the update(dict) method to add the items from one dictionary to another:

```
>>> z = {}
>>> z['slashdot'] = ('fred','fred')
>>> z.update (logins)
>>> z
{'justwhispers': ('jimmy', 'punk'),
 'slashdot': ('juan', 'lemmein'), # Duplicate key overwritten
 'hotmail': ('jrf5', '18thStreet')}
```

Additional dictionary operations

Here are a few other functions and methods of dictionaries that are straightforward and useful:

```
>>> len(logins) # How many items?
3
>>> logins.keys() # List the keys of the mappings
['justwhispers', 'slashdot', 'hotmail']
>>> logins.values() # List the other half of the mappings
[('jimmy', 'punk'), ('juan', 'lemmein'), ('jrf5',
'18thStreet')]
>>> logins.items() # Both pieces together as tuples
```

```
[('justwhispers', ('jimmy', 'punk')), ('slashdot', ('juan',
'lemmein')), ('hotmail', ('jrf5', '18thStreet'))]
>>> logins.clear() # Delete everything
>>> logins
{}
```

You can destructively iterate through a dictionary by calling its popitem() method, which removes a random key and its value from the dictionary:

```
>>> d = {'one':1, 'two':2, 'three':3}
>>> try:
...     while 1:
...         print d.popitem()
... except KeyError: # Raises KeyError when empty
...     pass
('one', 1)
('three', 3)
('two', 2)
```

New Feature   popitem is new in Python 2.1.

Dictionary objects also provide a copy() method that creates a shallow copy of the dictionary:

```
>>> a = {1:'one', 2:'two', 3:'three'}
>>> b = a.copy()
>>> b
{3: 'three', 2: 'two', 1: 'one'}
```

Cross-Reference   See "Copying Complex Objects" later in this chapter for a comparison of shallow and deep copies.

Understanding References

Python stores any piece of data in an object, and variables are merely references to an object; they are names for a particular spot in the computer's memory. All objects have a unique identity number, a type, and a value.

Object identity

Because the object, and not the variable, has the data type (for example, integer), a variable can reference a list at one moment and a floating-point number the next. An object's type can never change, but for lists and other mutable types its value can change.

Python provides the id(obj) function to retrieve an object's identity (which, in the current implementation, is just the object's address in memory):

```
>>> shoppingList = ['candy','cookies','ice cream']
>>> id(shoppingList)
17611492
>>> id(5)
3114676
```

The is operator compares the identities of two objects to see if they are the same:

```
>>> junkFood = shoppingList # Both reference the same object
>>> junkFood is shoppingList
1
>>> yummyStuff = ['candy','cookies','ice cream']
>>> junkFood is not yummyStuff # Different identity, but...
1
>>> junkFood == yummyStuff # ...same value
1
```

Because variables just reference objects, a change in a mutable object's value is visible to all variables referencing that object:

```
>>> a = [1,2,3,4]
>>> b = a
>>> a[2] = 5
>>> b
[1, 2, 5, 4]
>>> a = 6
>>> b = a       # Reference the same object for now.
>>> b
6
>>> a = a + 1 # Python creates a new object to hold (a+1)
>>> b         # so b still references the original object.
6
```

Counting references

Each object also contains a *reference count* that tells how many variables are currently referencing that object. When you assign a variable to an object or when you make an object a member of a list or other container, the reference count goes up. When you destroy, reassign, or remove an object from a container the reference count goes down. If the reference count reaches zero (no variables reference this object), Python's garbage collector destroys the object and reclaims the memory it was using.

The sys.getrefcount(obj) function returns the reference count for the given object.

See Chapter 26 for more on Python's garbage collector.

As of version 2.0, Python now also collects objects with only *circular* references. For example,

```
a = []; b = []
a.append(b); b.append(a)
a = 5; b = 10 # Reassign both variables to different
objects.
```

The two list objects still have a reference count of 1 because each is a member of the other's list. Python now recognizes such cases and reclaims the memory used by the list objects.

Keep in mind that the del statement deletes a variable and not an object, although if the variable you delete was the last to reference an object then Python may end up deleting the object too:

```
>>> a = [1,2,3]
>>> b = a # List object has 2 references now
>>> del a # Back to 1 reference
>>> b
[1, 2, 3]
```

You can also create *weak references* to objects, or references that do not affect an object's reference count. See Chapter 7 for more information.

Copying Complex Objects

Assigning a variable to a list object creates a reference to the list, but what if you want to create a copy of the list? Python enables you to make two different types of copies, depending on what you need to do.

Shallow copies

A *shallow* copy of a list or other container object makes a copy of the object itself but creates references to the objects contained by the list. An easy way to make a shallow copy of a sequence is by requesting a slice of the entire object:

```
>>> faceCards = ['A','K','Q','J']
>>> myHand = faceCards[:] # Create a copy, not a reference
>>> myHand is faceCards
0
>>> myHand == faceCards
1
```

You can also use the `copy(obj)` function of the `copy` module:

```
>>> import copy
>>> highCards = copy.copy(faceCards)
>>> highCards is faceCards, highCards == faceCards
(0, 1)
```

Deep copies

A *deep* copy makes a copy of the container object and recursively makes copies of all the children objects. For example, consider the case when a list contains a list. A shallow copy of the parent list would contain a reference to the child list, not a separate copy. As a result, changes to the inner list would be visible from both copies of the parent list:

```
>>> myAccount = [1000, ['Checking','Savings']]
>>> yourAccount = myAccount[:]
>>> myAccount[1].remove('Savings') # Modify the child list.
>>> myAccount
[1000, ['Checking']] # Different parent objects share a
>>> yourAccount       # reference to the same child list.
[1000, ['Checking']]
```

Now look at the same example by using the `deepcopy(obj)` function in the `copy` module:

```
>>> myAccount = [1000, ['Checking','Savings']]
>>> yourAccount = copy.deepcopy(myAccount)
>>> myAccount[1].remove('Savings')
>>> myAccount
[1000, ['Checking']] # deepcopy copied the child list too.
>>> yourAccount
[1000, ['Checking', 'Savings']]
```

The `deepcopy` function tracks which objects it copied so that if an object directly or indirectly references itself, `deepcopy` makes only one copy of that object.

Not all objects can be copied safely. For example, copying a socket that has an open connection to a remote computer won't work because part of the object's internal state (the open connection) is outside the realms of Python. File objects are another example of forbidden copy territory, and Python lets you know:

```
f = open('foo','wt')
>>> copy.deepcopy(f)
Traceback (innermost last):
  File "<interactive input>", line 1, in ?
  File "D:\Python20\lib\copy.py", line 147, in deepcopy
    raise error, \
Error: un-deep-copyable object of type <type 'file'>
```

Chapter 7 shows you how to override standard behaviors on classes you create. By defining your own __getstate__ and __setstate__ methods you can control how your objects respond to shallow and deep copy operations.

Identifying Data Types

You can check the data type of any object at runtime, enabling your programs to correctly handle different types of data (for example, think of the int function that works when you pass it an integer, a float, a string, and so on). You can retrieve the type of any object by passing the object to the type(obj) function:

```
>>> type(5)
<type 'int'>
>>> type('She sells seashells')
<type 'string'>
>>> type(operator)
<type 'module'>
```

The types module contains the type objects for Python's built-in data types. The following example creates a function that prints a list of words in uppercase. To make it more convenient to use, the function accepts either a single string or a list of strings:

```
>>> import types
>>> def upEm(words):
...     if type(words) != types.ListType:  # Not a list so
...         words = [words]                 # make it a list.
...     for word in words:
...         print word.upper()
>>> upEm('horse')
HORSE
>>> upEm(['horse','cow','sheep'])
HORSE
COW
SHEEP
```

The following list shows a few of the more common types you'll use.

```
BuiltinFunctionType

FunctionType

MethodType

BuiltinMethodType

InstanceType

ModuleType

ClassType
```

```
IntType
NoneType
DictType
LambdaType
StringType
FileType
ListType
TupleType
FloatType
LongType
```

Classes and instances of classes have the types `ClassType` and `InstanceType`, respectively. Python provides the `isinstance(obj)` and `issubclass(obj)` functions to test if an object is an instance or a subclass of a particular type:

```
>>> isinstance(5.1,types.FloatType)
1
>>> class Foo:
...        pass
...
>>> a = Foo()
>>> isinstance(a,Foo)
1
```

Cross-Reference   Chapter 7 covers creating and using classes and objects.

Working with Array Objects

While lists are flexible in that they let you store any type of data in them, that flexibility comes at a cost of more memory and a little less performance. In most cases, this isn't an issue, but in cases where you want to exchange a little flexibility for performance or low level access, you can use the `array` module to create an array object.

Creating arrays

An array object is similar to a list except that it can hold only certain types of simple data and only one type at any given time. When you create an array object, you specify which type of data it will hold:

```
>>> import array
>>> z = array.array ('B') # Create an array of bytes
>>> z.append(5)
```

```
>>> z[0]
5
>>> q = array.array('i',[5,10,-12,13]) # Optional initializer
>>> q
array('i', [5, 10, -12, 13])
```

Table 4-1 lists the type code you use to create each type of array. You can retrieve the size of items and the type code of an array object using its itemsize and typecode members.

Table 4-1
Array Type Codes

Code	Equivalent C Type	Minimum Size in Bytes*
c	char	1
b (B)	byte (unsigned byte)	1
h (H)	short (unsigned short)	2
i (I)	int (unsigned int)	2
l (L)	long (unsigned long)	4
f	float	4
d	double	8

* Actual size may be greater, depending on the implementation.

Converting between types

Array objects have built-in support for converting to and from lists and strings, and for reading and writing with files. The following examples all deal with an array object of two-byte short integers initially containing the numbers 10, 1000, and 500:

```
>>> z = array.array('h',[10,1000,500])
>>> z.itemsize
2
```

Lists

The tolist() method converts the array to an ordinary list:

```
>>> z.tolist()
[10, 1000, 500]
```

The `fromlist(list)` method appends items from a normal list to the end of the array:

```
>>> z.fromlist([2,4])
>>> z
array('h', [10, 1000, 500, 2, 4])
```

If any item in the list to add is of an incorrect type, `fromlist` adds none of the items to the array object.

Strings

You can convert an array to a sequence of bytes using the `tostring()` method:

```
>>> z.tostring()
' \n\x00\xe8\x03\xf4\x01\x02\x00\x04\x00'
>>> len(z.tostring())
6     # 3 items, 2 bytes each
```

The `fromstring(str)` method goes in the other direction, taking a string of bytes and converting them to values for the array:

```
>>> z.fromstring('\x10\x00\x00\x02') # x10 = 16, x0200 = 512
>>> z
array('h', [10, 1000, 500, 2, 4, 16, 512])
```

Files

The `tofile(file)` method converts the array to a sequence of bytes (just like `tostring`) and writes the resulting bytes to a file you pass in:

```
>>> z = array.array('h',[10,1000,500])
>>> f = open('myarray','wb') # Chapter 8 covers files.
>>> z.tofile(f)
>>> f.close()
```

The `fromfile(file, count)` method reads the specified number of items in from a file object and appends them to the array. Continuing the previous example:

```
>>> z.fromfile(open('myarray','rb'),3) # Read 3 items.
>>> z
array('h', [10, 1000, 500, 10, 1000, 500])
```

If the file ends before reading in the number of items you requested, `fromfile` raises the `EOFError` exception, but still adds as many valid items as it could to the array.

Cross-Reference

The `marshal`, `pickle`, and `struct` modules all provide additional — and often better — methods for converting to and from sequences of bytes for use in files and network messages. See Chapter 12 for more.

Array methods and operations

Array objects support many of the same functions and methods of lists: len, append, extend, count, index, insert, pop, remove, and reverse. You can access individual members with subscription, and you can use slicing to return a smaller portion of the array (although it returns another array object and not a list).

The buffer_info() method returns some low-level information about the current array. The returned tuple contains the memory address of the buffer and the length in bytes of the buffer. This information is valid until you destroy the array or it changes length.

You can use the byteswap() method to change the byte order of each item in the array, which is useful for converting between big-endian and little-endian data:

```
>>> z = array.array('I',[1,2,3])
>>> z.byteswap()
>>> z
array('I', [16777216L, 33554432L, 50331648L])
```

See Chapter 12 for information on cross-platform byte ordering.

NumPy (Numeric Python) is a Python extension that you can also use to create arrays, but it has much better support for using the resulting arrays in calculations. See Chapter 31 for more information on NumPy.

Summary

Python provides several powerful and easy-to-use data types that simplify working with different types of data. In this chapter you:

✦ Learned the differences between Python's sequence types.

✦ Organized data with lists, sequences, and dictionaries.

✦ Created shallow and deep copies of complex objects.

✦ Used an object's type to handle it appropriately.

✦ Built array objects to hold homogenous data.

The next chapter shows you how to expand your programs to include loops and decisions and how to catch errors with exceptions.

✦   ✦   ✦

Control Flow

♦ ♦ ♦ ♦

In This Chapter

Making decisions
with if-statements

Using for-loops

Using while-loops

Throwing and
catching exceptions

Debugging with
assertions

Example: Game
of Life

♦ ♦ ♦ ♦

A program is more than simply a list of actions. A program can perform an action several times (with for- and while-loops), handle various cases (with if-statements), and cope with problems along the way (with exceptions).

This chapter explains how to control the flow of execution in Python. A simple Game of Life program illustrates these techniques in practice.

Making Decisions with If-Statements

The if-statement evaluates a conditional expression. If the expression is true, the program executes the if-block. For example:

```
if (CustomerAge>55):
print "You get a senior citizen's discount!"
```

An if-statement may have an else-block. If the expression is false, the else-block (if any) executes. This code block prints one greeting for Bob, and another for everyone else:

```
if (UserName=="Bob"):
print "Greetings, O supreme commander!"
else:
print "Hello, humble peasant."
```

An if-statement may have one or more elif-blocks ("elif" is shorter to type than "else if" and has the same effect). When Python encounters such a statement, it evaluates the if-expression, then the first elif-expression, and so on, until one of the expressions evaluates to true. Then, Python executes the corresponding block of code.

When Python executes an if-statement, it executes no more than one block of code. (If there is an else-block, then *exactly* one block of code gets executed.)

Listing 5-1 is a sample script that uses an if-statement (shown in both italics and bold) in a simple number-guessing game.

Listing 5-1: **NumberGuess.py**

```
import random
import sys

# This line chooses a random integer >=1 and <=100.
# (See Chapter 15 for a proper explanation.)
SecretNumber=random.randint(1,100)

print "I'm thinking of a number between 1 and 100."
# Loop forever (at least until the user hits Ctrl-Break).
while (1):
    print "Guess my number."
    # The following line reads a line of input from
    # the command-line and converts it to an integer.
    NumberGuess=int(sys.stdin.readline())
    if (NumberGuess==SecretNumber):
        print "Correct!  Choosing a new number..."
        SecretNumber=random.randint(1,100)
    elif (NumberGuess > SecretNumber):
        print "Lower."
    else:
        print "Higher."
```

You can use many elif clauses; the usual way to write Python code that handles five different cases is with an if-elif-elif-elif-else statement. (Veterans of C and Java, take note: Python does not have a `switch` statement.)

Note   Python stops checking if-expressions as soon as it finds a true one. If you write an if-statement to handle several different cases, consider putting the most common and/or cheapest-to-check cases first in order to make your program faster.

Using For-Loops

For-loops let your program do something several times. In addition, you can iterate over elements of a sequence with a for-loop.

Anatomy of a for-loop

A simple `for` statement has the following syntax:

```
for <variable> in <sequence>:
(loop body)
```

The statement (or block) following the `for` statement forms the body of the loop. Python executes the body once for each element of the sequence. The loop variable takes on each element's value, in order, from first to last. For instance:

```
for Word in ["serious","silly","slinky"]:
    print "The minister's cat is a "+Word+" cat."
```

The body of a loop can be a single statement on the same line as the for-statement:

```
for Name in ["Tom","Dick","Harry"]: print Name
```

Some people (myself included) usually stick with the first style, because all-on-one-line loops can lead to long and tricky lines of code.

Python can loop over any sequence type — even a string. If the sequence is empty, the loop body never executes.

Looping example: encoding strings

Listing 5-2 uses for-loops to convert strings to a list of hexadecimal values, and back again. The encoded strings look somewhat similar to the "decoder rings" popular on old children's radio programs.

Listing 5-2: **DecoderRing.py**

```
import string

def Encode(MessageString):
    EncodedList=[]
    # Iterate over each character in the string
    for Char in MessageString:
        EncodedList.append("%x" % ord(Char))
    return EncodedList

def Decode(SecretMessage):
    DecodedList=[]
    # Iterate over each element in the list
    for HexValue in SecretMessage:
        # The following line converts HexValue from
        # a hex-string to an integer, then finds the ASCII
        # symbol for that integer, and finally adds that
        # character to the list.
        # Don't try this at home! :)
        DecodedList.append(chr(int(HexValue,16)))
```

Continued

Listing 5-2 *(continued)*

```
     # Join these strings together, with no separator.
     return string.join(DecodedList,"")

if (__name__=="__main__"):
     SecretMessage=Encode("Remember to drink your Ovaltine!")
     print SecretMessage
     print Decode(SecretMessage)
```

Listing 5-3: **DecoderRing.py output**

```
['52', '65', '6d', '65', '6d', '62', '65', '72', '20', '74',
'6f', '20', '64', '72', '69', '6e', '6b', '20', '79', '6f',
'75', '72', '20', '4f', '76', '61', '6c', '74', '69', '6e',
'65', '21']
Remember to drink your Ovaltine!
```

Ranges and xranges

Many loops do something a fixed number of times. To iterate over a range of numbers, use range. For example:

```
# print 10 numbers (from 0 to 9)
for X in range(10):
print X
```

The function range returns a list of numbers that you can use anywhere (not just in a loop). The syntax is: range(start[,end[,step]]). The numbers in the range begin with *start*, increment by *step* each time, and stop just before *end*. Both *start* and *step* are optional; by default, a range starts at 0 and increments by 1. For example:

```
>>> range(10,0,-1) # Countdown!
[10, 9, 8, 7, 6, 5, 4, 3, 2, 1]
>>> range(5,10)
[5, 6, 7, 8, 9]
```

Code that does something once for each element of a sequence sometimes loops over range(len(SequenceVariable)). This range contains the index of each element in the sequence. For example, this code prints the days of the week:

```
DaysOfWeek=["Monday", "Tuesday", "Wednesday", "Thursday",
"Friday", "Saturday", "Sunday"]
for X in range(len(DaysOfWeek)):
    print "Day",X,"is",DaysOfWeek[X]
```

An *xrange* is an object that represents a range of numbers. You can loop over an xrange instead of the list returned by range. The only real difference is that creating a large range involves creating a memory-hogging list, while creating an xrange of any size is cheap. Try checking your system's free memory while running these interpreter commands:

```
>>> MemoryHog=range(1000000) # There goes lots of RAM!
>>> BigXRange=xrange(1000000) # Only uses a little memory.
```

To see the contents of an xrange in convenient list form, use the tolist method:

```
>>> SmallXRange=xrange(10,110,10)
>>> SmallXRange.tolist()
[10, 20, 30, 40, 50, 60, 70, 80, 90, 100]
```

Breaking, continuing, and else-clauses

Python's continue statement jumps to the next iteration of a loop. The break statement jumps out of a loop entirely. These statements apply only to the innermost loop; if you are in a loop-within-a-loop-within-a-loop, break jumps out of only the innermost loop.

You can follow the body of a for-loop with an else-clause. The code in the else-clause executes after the loop finishes iterating, unless the program exits the loop due to a break statement. (If you have no break statement in the loop, the else-clause always executes, so you really have no need to put the code in an else-clause.)

Listing 5-4 illustrates break, continue, and an else-clause:

Listing 5-4: **ClosestPoint.py**

```
import math
def FindClosestPointAboveXAxis(PointList,TargetPoint):
""" Given a list of points and a target point, this function
returns the list's closest point, and its distance from the
target. It ignores all points with a negative y-coordinate. We
represent points in the plane (or on screen) as a two-valued
tuple of the form (x-coordinate,y-coordinate). """
    ClosestPoint=None # Initialize.
    ClosestDistance=None
    # Iterate over each point in the list.
    for Point in PointList:
        # Throw out any point below the X axis.
        if (Point[1]<0):
            # Skip to the next point in the list.
            continue
        # Compute the distance from this point to the target.
```

Continued

Listing 5-4 *(continued)*

```
# The following two lines are one statement;
# indentation for clarity is optional.
DistToPoint=math.sqrt((TargetPoint[0]-Point[0])**2 +
                        (TargetPoint[1]-Point[1])**2)
    if (ClosestDistance == None or
        DistToPoint < ClosestDistance):
        ClosestPoint=Point
        ClosestDistance = DistanceToPoint
    if (DistanceToPoint==0):
    print "Point found in list"
    # Exit the loop entirely, since no point will
    # be closer than this
    break
else:
    # This clause executes unless we hit the break above.
    print "Point not found in list"
return (ClosestPoint, ClosestDistance)
```

Here is the function in action:

```
>>> SomePoints=[(-1,-1),(4,5),(-5,7),(23,-2),(5,2)]
>>> ClosestPoint.FindClosestPointAboveXAxis(SomePoints,(1,1))
Point not found in list
((5, 2), 4.12310562561766606)
>>> ClosestPoint.FindClosestPointAboveXAxis(SomePoints,(-1,-1))
Point not found in list
((5, 2), 6.7082039324993694)
>>> ClosestPoint.FindClosestPointAboveXAxis(SomePoints,(4,5))
Point found in list
((4, 5), 0.0)
```

Changing horses in midstream

Modifying the sequence that you are in the process of looping over is *not recommended*—Python won't get confused, but any mere mortals reading your program will.

The loop variable keeps iterating over its reference sequence, even if you change a sequence variable. For example, this loop prints the numbers from 0 to 99; changing the value that MyRange points to does not affect control flow:

```
MyRange=range(100)
for X in MyRange:
    print X
    MyRange = range(30) # No change in looping behavior!
```

However, changing the reference sequence does affect the loop. After executing for the nth element in a sequence, the loop proceeds to the (n+1)th element, even if the sequence changes in the process. For example, this loop prints even numbers from 0 to 98:

```
MyRange=range(100)
for X in MyRange:
    print X
    del MyRange[0] # Changing the loop-sequence in place
```

Modifying the loop variable inside a for-loop is also inadvisable. It does not change looping behavior; Python will continue the next iteration of the loop as usual.

Using While-Loops

If you could crossbreed an if-statement and a for-loop, you would get a while-statement, Python's other looping construct.

A while-statement has the form:

```
while (<expression>):
    <block of code>
```

When Python encounters a while-statement, it evaluates the expression, and if the expression is true, it executes the corresponding block of code. Python keeps executing the block of code until the expression is no longer true. For example, this code counts down from 10 to 1:

```
X=10
while (X>0):
print X
X -= 1
```

Within a while-loop, you can use the `continue` statement to jump to the next iteration, or the `break` statement to jump out of the loop entirely. A while-loop can also have an else-block. Code in the else-block executes immediately after the last iteration, unless a `break` statement exits the loop. These statements work similarly for for-loops and while-loops. See the section on for-loops, above, for examples of `break`, `continue`, and `else`.

Throwing and Catching Exceptions

Imagine a Python program innocently going about its business, when suddenly . . .

[dramatic, scary music] something goes wrong.

In general, when a function or method encounters a situation that it can't cope with, it raises an exception. An *exception* is a Python object that represents an error.

Passing the buck: propagating exceptions

When a function raises an exception, the function must either handle the exception immediately or terminate. If the function doesn't handle the exception, the caller may handle it. If not, the caller also terminates immediately as well. The exception propagates up the call-stack until someone handles the error. If nobody catches the exception, the whole program terminates.

In general, functions that return a value should return None to indicate a "reasonable" failure, and only raise an exception for "unreasonable" problems. Just what is reasonable is open to debate, so it is generally a good idea to clearly document the exceptions your code raises, and to handle common exceptions raised by the code you call.

Handling an exception

If you have some "suspicious" code that may raise an exception, you can defend your program by placing the suspicious code in a `try:` block. After the `try:` block, include an `except` statement, followed by a block of code which handles the problem (as elegantly as possible).

For example, the guess-the-number program from earlier in this chapter crashes if you try to feed it something other than an integer. The error looks something like this:

```
Traceback (most recent call last):
  File "C:\Python20\NumberGuess.py", line 7, in ?
    NumberGuess=int(sys.stdin.readline())
ValueError: invalid literal for int(): whoops!
```

Listing 5-5 shows a new-and-improved script that handles the exception. The call to `sys.stdin.readline()` is now in a `try:` block:

Listing 5-5: **NumberGuess2.py**

```
import random
import sys

# This line chooses a random integer >=1 and <=100.
# (See Chapter 15 for a proper explanation.)
SecretNumber=random.randint(1,100)
```

```
print "I'm thinking of a number between 1 and 100."
# Loop forever (at least until the user hits Ctrl-Break).
while (1):
    print "Guess my number."
    # The following line reads a line of input from
    # the command line and converts it to an integer.
    try:
        NumberGuess=int(sys.stdin.readline())
    except ValueError:
        print "Please type a whole number."
        continue
    if (NumberGuess==SecretNumber):
        print "Correct!  Choosing a new number..."
        SecretNumber=random.randint(1,100)
    elif (NumberGuess > SecretNumber):
        print "Lower."
    else:
        print "Higher."
```

More on exceptions

An exception can have an *argument,* which is a value that gives additional information about the problem. The contents (and even the type) of the argument vary by
exception. You capture an exception's argument by supplying a variable in the
except clause: `except ExceptionType,ArgumentVariable`

You can supply several except clauses to handle various types of exceptions. In this
case, exceptions are handled by the first applicable `except` clause. You can also
provide a generic `except` clause, which handles *any* exception. If you do this, I
highly recommend that you do *something* with the exception. Code that silently
"swallows" exceptions may mask important bugs, like a NameError. Here is some
cookie-cutter code I use for quick-and-dirty error handling:

```
try:
    DoDangerousStuff()
except:
    # The show must go on!
    # Print the exception and the stack trace, and continue.
    (ErrorType,ErrorValue,ErrorTB)=sys.exc_info()
    print sys.exc_info()
    traceback.print_exc(ErrorTB)
```

After the `except` clause(s), you can include an else-clause. The code in the else-block
executes if the code in the `try:` block does *not* raise an exception. The else-block is a
good place for code that does not need the `try:` block's protection.

Python raises an `IOError` exception if you try to open a file that doesn't exist. Here
is a snippet of code that handles a missing file without crashing. (This code grabs
the exception argument — a tuple consisting of an error number and error string —
but doesn't do anything interesting with it.)

```
try:
    OptionsFile=open("SecretOptions.txt")
except IOError, (ErrorNumber,ErrorString):
    # Assume our default option values are all OK.
    # We need a statement here, but we have nothing
    # to do, so we pass.
    pass
else:
    # This executes if we opened it without an IOError.
    ParseOptionsFile(OptionsFile)
```

Defining and raising exceptions

You can raise exceptions with the statement `raise exceptionType,argument`. *ExceptionType* is the type of exception (for example, NameError). *Argument* is a value for the exception argument. Argument is optional; if not supplied, the exception argument is None.

An exception can be a string, a class, or an object. Most of the exceptions that the Python core raises are classes, with an argument that is an instance of the class. Defining new exceptions is quite easy, as this contrived example demonstrates:

```
def CalculateElfHitPoints(Level):
    if Level<1:
        raise "Invalid elf level!",Level
    # (The code below won't execute if we raise
    # the exception.)
    HitPoints=0
    for DieRoll in range(Level):
        HitPoints += random.randint(1,6)
```

Note   In order to catch an exception, an "except" clause must refer to the same exception thrown. Python compares string exceptions by reference identity (`is`, not `==`). So, if you have code to raise "BigProblem" and an except-clause for "BigProblem," the except clause may not catch the exception. (The strings are equivalent, but may not point to the same spot in memory.) To handle exceptions properly, use a named constant string, or a class. (See Listing 5-6 for an example.)

Cleaning up with finally

An alternative mechanism for coping with failure is the `finally` block. The `finally` block is a place to put any code that *must execute*, whether the try-block raised an exception or not. You can provide `except` clause(s), or a `finally` clause, but *not both*.

For example, multithreaded programs often use a lock to prevent threads from stomping on each other's data. If a thread acquires a lock and crashes without releasing it, the other threads may be kept waiting forever — an unpleasant situation called deadlock. This example is a perfect job for the finally clause:

```
try:
   DataLock.acquire()
   # ... do things with the data ...
finally:
   # This code *must* execute. The fate of the
   # free world hangs in the balance!
   DataLock.release()
```

Debugging with Assertions

An *assertion* is a sanity-check that you can turn on (for maximum paranoia) or turn off (to speed things up). Using an assertion can help make code self-documenting; raising an AssertionError implies that a problem is due to programmer error and not normal problems. Programmers often place assertions at the start of a function to check for valid input, and after a function call to check for valid output.

Assertions in Python

You can add assertions to your code with the syntax assert <Expression>. When it encounters an assert statement, Python evaluates the accompanying expression, which is hopefully true. If the expression is false, Python raises an AssertionError.

You can include an assertion argument, via the syntax assert Expression,ArgumentExpression. If the assertion fails, Python uses *ArgumentExpression* as the argument for the AssertionError.

For example, here is a function that converts a temperature from degrees Kelvin to degrees Fahrenheit. Since zero degrees Kelvin is as cold as it gets, the function bails out if it sees a negative temperature:

```
>>> def KelvinToFahrenheit(Temperature):
...     assert (Temperature >= 0),"Colder than absolute zero!"
...     return ((Temperature-273)*1.8)+32
>>> KelvinToFahrenheit(273)
32.0
>>> int(KelvinToFahrenheit(505.78))
451
>>> KelvinToFahrenheit(-5)
Traceback (innermost last):
  File "<pyshell#186>", line 1, in ?
    KelvinToFahrenheit(-5)
  File "<pyshell#178>", line 2, in KelvinToFahrenheit
    assert (Temperature >= 0),"Colder than absolute zero!"
AssertionError: Colder than absolute zero!
```

Toggling assertions

Normally, assertions are active. They are toggled by the internal variable __debug__. Turning on optimization (by running python with the -O command-line argument) turns assertions off. (Direct access to __debug__ is also possible, but not recommended.)

Tip

In assert statements, avoid using expressions with side effects. If the assertion expression affects the data, then the "release" and "debug" versions of your scripts may behave differently, leaving you with twice as much debugging to do.

Example: Game of Life

Listing 5-6 simulates John Conway's Game of Life, a simple, cellular automata. The game is played on a grid. Each cell of the grid can be "alive" or "dead." Each "generation," cells live or die based on the state of their eight neighboring cells. Cells with three living neighbors come to life. Live cells with two living neighbors stay alive. All other cells die (or stay dead).

Cross-
Reference

This example introduces a class to represent the playing field. For further information on classes, see Chapter 7.

Listing 5-6: **LifeGame.py**

```python
# We arbitrarily set the field size to 10x10. Naming the size
# in upper-case implies that we shouldn't change its value.
FIELD_SIZE=10

# Create two strings for use as exceptions. We raise and catch
# these variables, instead of raw strings (which would be ==-
# equivalent, but possibly not is-equivalent).
STEADY_STATE="Steady state"
EVERYONE_DEAD="Everyone dead"

class PlayField:
    # Constructor. When creating a PlayField, initialize the
    # grid to be all dead:
    def __init__(self):
        self.LifeGrid={}
        for Y in range(FIELD_SIZE):
            for X in range(FIELD_SIZE):
                self.LifeGrid[(X,Y)]=0
    def SetAlive(self,X,Y):
        self.LifeGrid[(X,Y)]=1
    def SetDead(self,X,Y):
        self.LifeGrid[(X,Y)]=0
    def PrintGrid(self,Number):
        print "Generation",Number
```

```
            for Y in range(FIELD_SIZE):
                for X in range(FIELD_SIZE):
                    # Trailing comma means don't print newline:
                    print self.LifeGrid[(X,Y)],
                # Print newline at end of row:
                print
        def GetLiveNeighbors(self,X,Y):
            # The playing field is a "donut world", where the
            # edge cells join to the opposite edge.
            LeftColumn=X-1
            if (LeftColumn<0): LeftColumn=FIELD_SIZE-1
            RightColumn=(X+1) % FIELD_SIZE
            UpRow=Y-1
            if (UpRow<0): UpRow=FIELD_SIZE-1
            DownRow=(Y+1) % FIELD_SIZE
            LiveCount=(self.LifeGrid[(LeftColumn,UpRow)]+
                self.LifeGrid[(X,UpRow)]+
                self.LifeGrid[(RightColumn,UpRow)]+
                self.LifeGrid[(LeftColumn,Y)]+
                self.LifeGrid[(RightColumn,Y)]+
                self.LifeGrid[(LeftColumn,DownRow)]+
                self.LifeGrid[(X,DownRow)]+
                self.LifeGrid[(RightColumn,DownRow)])
            return (LiveCount)
        def RunGeneration(self):
            NewGrid={}
            AllDeadFlag=1
            for Y in range(FIELD_SIZE):
                for X in range(FIELD_SIZE):
                    CurrentState=self.LifeGrid[(X,Y)]
                    LiveCount=self.GetLiveNeighbors(X,Y)
                    if ((LiveCount==2 and CurrentState)
                        or (LiveCount==3)):
                        NewGrid[(X,Y)]=1
                        AllDeadFlag=0
                    else:
                        NewGrid[(X,Y)]=0
            if (AllDeadFlag): raise EVERYONE_DEAD
            if self.LifeGrid==NewGrid: raise STEADY_STATE
            self.LifeGrid,OldGrid=NewGrid,self.LifeGrid
        def ShowManyGenerations(self,GenerationCount):
            try:
                for Cycle in range(GenerationCount):
                    self.PrintGrid(Cycle)
                    self.RunGeneration()
            except EVERYONE_DEAD:
                print "The population is now dead."
            except STEADY_STATE:
                print "The population is no longer changing."

if (__name__=="__main__"):
    # This first grid quickly settles into a pattern
    # that does not change.
```

Continued

Listing 5-6 *(continued)*

```
BoringGrid=PlayField()
BoringGrid.SetAlive(2,2)
BoringGrid.SetAlive(2,3)
BoringGrid.SetAlive(2,4)
BoringGrid.SetAlive(3,2)
BoringGrid.ShowManyGenerations(50)

# This grid contains a "glider" - a pattern of live
# cells which moves diagonally across the grid.
GliderGrid=PlayField()
GliderGrid.SetAlive(0,0)
GliderGrid.SetAlive(1,0)
GliderGrid.SetAlive(2,0)
GliderGrid.SetAlive(2,1)
GliderGrid.SetAlive(1,2)
GliderGrid.ShowManyGenerations(50)
```

Summary

Python has several tools for controlling the flow of execution. In this chapter you:

✦ Made decisions with if-statements.

✦ Set up repeating tasks with for-loops and while-loops.

✦ Built code that copes with problems by handling exceptions.

✦ Learned to add test scaffolding with assertions.

In the next chapter you'll learn how to organize all your Python code into functions, modules, and packages.

✦   ✦   ✦

Program Organization

In This Chapter

Defining functions

Grouping code with modules

Importing modules

Locating modules

Understanding scope rules

Grouping modules into packages

Compiling and running programmatically

Python lets you break code down into reusable functions and classes, then reassemble those components into modules and packages. The larger the project, the more useful this organization becomes.

This chapter explains function definition syntax, module and package structure, and Python's rules for visibility and scope.

Defining Functions

Here is a sample function definition:

```
def ReverseString(Forwards):
    """Convert a string to a list of
characters, reverse the
    list, and join the list back into a string
"""
    CharacterList=list(Forwards)
    CharacterList.reverse()
    return string.join(CharacterList,"");
```

The statement `def FunctionName([parameters,...])` begins the function. Calling the function executes the code within the following indented block.

A string following the `def` statement is a *docstring*. A docstring is a comment intended as documentation. Development environments like IDLE display a function's docstrings to show how to call the function. Also, tools like HappyDoc can extract docstrings from code to produce documentation. So, a docstring is a good place to describe a function's behavior, parameter requirements, and the like. Modules can also have a docstring—a string preceding any executable code is taken to be the module's description.

The statement `return [expression]` exits a function, optionally passing back an expression to the caller. A `return` statement with no arguments is the same as `return None`. A function also exits (returning `None`) when the last statement finishes, and execution "runs off the end of" the function code block.

Pass by object reference

A Python variable is a reference to an object. Python passes function parameters using call-by-value. If you change what a parameter refers to within a function, the change does not affect the function's caller. For example:

```
>>> def StupidFunction(InputList):
...     InputList=["I","Like","Cheese"]
...
>>> MyList=[1,2,3]
>>> StupidFunction(MyList)
>>> print MyList # MyList is unchanged!
[1, 2, 3]
```

The parameter InputList is local to the function StupidFunction. Changing InputList within the function does not affect MyList. The function accomplishes nothing.

However, a function can change the object that a parameter refers to. For example, this function removes duplicate elements from a list:

```
def RemoveDuplicates(InputList):
    ListIndex=-1
    # We iterate over the list from right to left, deleting
    # all duplicates of element -1, then -2, and so on. (Because
    # we are removing elements of the list, using negative
    # indices is convenient: element -3 is still element -3
    # after we delete some items preceding it.)
    while (-ListIndex<len(InputList)):
        # list.index() returns a positive index, so get the
        # positive equivalent of ListIndex and name it
        # CurrentIndex (same element, new index number).
        CurrentIndex=len(InputList)+ListIndex
        CurrentElement=InputList[ListIndex]
        # Keep removing duplicate elements as long as
        # an element precedes the current one.
        while (InputList.index(CurrentElement)<CurrentIndex):
            InputList.remove(CurrentElement)
            CurrentIndex=CurrentIndex-1
        ListIndex=ListIndex-1
```

All about parameters

A function parameter can have a default value. If a parameter has a default value, you do not need to supply a value to call the function.

When you call a function, you can supply its parameters by name. It is legal to name some parameters and not others — but after supplying the name for one parameter, you must name any other parameters you pass.

For example, this function simulates the rolling of dice. By default, it rolls ordinary 6-sided dice, one at a time:

```
>>> import whrandom
>>> def RollDice(Dice=1,Sides=6):
...     Total=0
...     for Die in range(Dice):
...         Total += whrandom.randint(1,Sides)
...     return Total
...
>>> RollDice()
5
>>> RollDice(2) # Come on, snake-eyes!
8
>>> RollDice(2,4) # Roll two four-sided dice.
5
>>> RollDice(Sides=20) # Named parameter
17
>>> # After naming one parameter, you must name the rest:
>>> RollDice(Sides=5,4)
SyntaxError: non-keyword arg after keyword arg
```

A function evaluates its argument defaults only once. We recommend avoiding dynamic (or mutable) default values. For example, if you do not pass a value to this function, it will always print the time that you *first* called it:

```
def PrintTime(TimeStamp=time.time()):
    # time.time() is the current time in milliseconds,
    # time.localtime() puts the time into the
    # canonical tuple-form, and time.asctime() converts
    # the time-tuple to a cute string format.
    # The function's default argument, TimeStamp, does
    # not change between calls!
print time.asctime(time.localtime(TimeStamp))
```

This improved version of the function prints the current time if another time is not provided:

```
def PrintTime(TimeStamp=None):
    if (TimeStamp==None): TimeStamp=time.time()
    print time.asctime(time.localtime(TimeStamp))
```

Arbitrary arguments

A function can accept an arbitrary sequence of parameters. The function collects these parameters into one tuple. This logging function shows the internal object IDs of a sequence of arguments:

```
def LogObjectIDs(LogString, *args):
    print LogString
    for arg in args: print id(arg)
```

A function can also accept an arbitrary collection of named parameters. The function collects these named parameters into one dictionary. This version of the logging function lets you give names to the objects passed in:

```
def LogObjectIDs(LogString, **kwargs):
    print LogString
    for (ParamName,ParamValue) in kwargs.items():
        print "Object:",ParamName,"ID:",id(ParamValue)
```

To make a truly omnivorous function, you can take a dictionary of arbitrary named parameters *and* a tuple of unnamed parameters.

Apply: passing arguments from a tuple

The function `apply(InvokeFunction,ArgumentSequence)` calls the function *InvokeFunction*, passing the elements of *ArgumentSequence* as arguments. The usefulness of `apply` is that it breaks arguments out of a tuple cleanly, for any length of tuple.

For example, assume you have a function SetColor(Red,Green,Blue), and a tuple representing a color:

```
>>> print MyColor
(255, 0, 255)
>>> SetColor(MyColor[0],MyColor[1],MyColor[2]) # Kludgy!
>>> apply(SetColor,MyColor) # Same as above, but cleaner.
```

A bit of functional programming

Python can define new functions on the fly, giving you some of the functional flexibility of languages like Lisp and Scheme.

You define an anonymous function with the lambda keyword. The syntax is `lambda [parameters,...]: <expression>`. For example, here is an anonymous function that filters list entries:

```
>>> SomeNumbers=[5,10,15,3,18,2]
>>> filter(lambda x:x>10, SomeNumbers)
[15, 18]
```

This code uses anonymous functions to test for primes:

```
def FindPrimes(EndNumber):
    NumList = range(2,EndNumber)
    Index=0
    while (Index<len(NumList)):
        NumList=filter(lambda y,x=NumList[Index]:
                    (y<=x or y%x!=0), NumList)
        Index += 1
    print NumList
```

Lambda functions can be helpful for event handling in programs with a GUI. For example, here is some code to add a button to a Tkinter frame.

```
def AddCosmeticButton(ButtonFrame,ButtonLabel):
    Button(ButtonFrame,text=ButtonLabel,command = lambda
    =ButtonLabel:LogUnimplemented(1)).pack()
```

Clicking the button causes it to call LogUnimplemented with the button label as an argument. Presumably, LogUnimplemented makes note of the fact that somebody is clicking a button that does nothing.

Note An anonymous function cannot be a direct call to `print` because `lambda` requires an expression.

Note Lambda functions have their own local namespace and cannot access variables other than those in their parameter list and those in the global namespace.

Grouping Code with Modules

A *module* is a file consisting of Python code. A module can define functions, classes, and variables. A module can also include runnable code.

A stand-alone module is often called a script or program. You can use whichever word you like, because Python makes no distinction between them.

Grouping related code into a module makes the code easier to understand and use. When writing a program, split off code into separate modules whenever a file starts becoming too large or performing too many different functions.

Laying out a module

The usual order for module elements is:

✦ Docstring and/or general comments (revision log or copyright information, and so on)

✦ Import statements (see below for more information on importing modules)

✦ Definitions of module-level variables ("constants")

✦ Definitions of classes and functions

✦ Main function, if any

This organization is not required, but it works well and is widely used.

 Note   People often store frequently used values in ALL_CAPS_VARIABLES to make later code easier to maintain, or simply more readable. For example, the standard library ftplib includes this definition:

```
FTP_PORT = 21 # The standard FTP server control port
```

Such a variable is "constant by convention"—Python does not forbid modifications, but callers should not change its value.

Taking inventory of a module

The function dir(module) returns a list of the variables, functions, and classes defined in module. With no arguments, dir returns a list of all currently defined names. dir(__builtin__) returns a list of all built-in names. For example:

```
>>> dir() # Just after starting Python
['__builtins__', '__doc__', '__name__']
>>> import sys
>>> dir()
['__builtins__', '__doc__', '__name__', 'sys']
```

You can pass any object (or class) to dir to get a list of class members.

Importing Modules

To use a module, you must first import it. Then, you can access the names in the module using dotted notation. For example:

```
>>> string.digits # Invalid, because I haven't imported string
Traceback (most recent call last):
  File "<stdin>", line 1, in ?
NameError: There is no variable named 'string'
>>> import string # Note: No parentheses around module name.
>>> string.digits
'0123456789'
```

Another option is to import names from the module into the current namespace, using the syntax from ModuleName import Name, Name2,.... For example:

```
>>> from string import digits
>>> digits # Without a dot
'0123456789'
```

```
>>> string.digits # I don't know about the module, only digits.
Traceback (most recent call last):
  File "<stdin>", line 1, in ?
NameError: There is no variable named 'string'
```

To bring every name from a module into the current namespace, use a blanket import: from module import *. Importing modules this way can make for confusing code, especially if two modules have functions with the same name. But it can also save a lot of typing.

The import statements for a script should appear at the beginning of the file. (This arrangement is not required, but importing halfway though a script is confusing.)

What else happens upon import?

Within a module, the special string variable __name__ is the name of the module. When you execute a stand-alone module, its __name__ is always __main__. This provides a handy way to set aside code that runs when you invoke a module, but not when you import it. Some modules use this code as a test driver. (See Listing 6-1.)

Listing 6-1: **Alpha.py**

```
import string

def Alphabetize(Str):
    "Alphabetize the letters in a string"
    CharList=list(Str)
    CharList.sort()
    return (string.join(CharList,""))

if (__name__=="__main__"):
    # This code runs when we execute the script, not when
    # we import it.
    X=string.upper("BritneySpears")
    Y=string.upper("Presbyterians")
    # Strange but true!
    print (Alphabetize(X)==Alphabetize(Y))
else:
    # This code runs when we import (not run) the module.
    print "Imported module Alpha"
```

Reimporting modules

Once Python has imported a module once, it doesn't import it again for subsequent import statements. You can force Python to "reimport" a module with a call to reload(LoadedModule). This procedure is useful for debugging—you can edit a module on disk, then reload it without having to restart an interactive interpreter session.

Exotic imports

A module can override standard import behavior by implementing the function __import__ (name[, globals[, locals[, fromlist]]]). Because a module is a class, defining __import__ in a module amounts to overriding the default version of __import__.

Caution   We don't recommend overriding __import__ as it is a very low-level operation for such a high-level language! See the libraries imp, ihooks, and rexec for examples of overridden import behavior.

Locating Modules

When you import a module, the Python interpreter searches for the module in the current directory. If the module isn't found, Python then searches each directory in the PythonPath. If all else fails, Python checks the default path. On Windows, the default path consists of c:\python20\lib\ and some subdirectories; on UNIX, this default path is normally /usr/local/lib/python/. (The code for Python's standard libraries is installed into the default path. Some modules, such as sys, are built into the Python interpreter, and have no corresponding .py files.)

Python stores a list of directories that it searches for modules in the variable sys.path.

Python path

The PythonPath is an environment variable, consisting of a list of directories. Here is a typical PythonPath from a Windows system:

```
set PYTHONPATH=c:\python20\lib;c:\python20\lib\proj1;c:\python20\lib\bob
```

And here is a typical PythonPath from a UNIX system:

```
set PYTHONPATH=/home/stanner/python;/usr/bin/python/lib
```

I generally use a scratch folder to hold modules I am working on; other files I put in the lib directory (or, if they are part of a package, in subdirectories). I find that setting the PythonPath explicitly is most useful for switching between different versions of a module.

Compiled files

You can compile a Python program into system-independent bytecodes. The interpreter stores the compiled version of a module in a corresponding file with a `.pyc` extension. This precompiled file runs at the same speed, but loads faster because Python need not parse the source code. Files compiled with the optimization flag on are named with a `.pyo` extension, and behave like .pyc files.

When you import a module foo, Python looks for a compiled version of foo. Python looks for a file named `foo.pyc` that is as new as `foo.py`. If so, Python loads `foo.pyc` instead of re-parsing `foo.py`. If not, Python parses `foo.py`, and writes out the compiled version to `foo.pyc`.

Note   When you run a script from the command line, Python does not create (or look for) a precompiled version. To save some parsing time, you can invoke a short "stub" script that imports the main module. Or, you can compile the main script by hand (by importing it, by calling `py_compile.compile(ScriptFileName)`, or by calling `compileall.compile_dir(ScriptDirectoryName)`), then invoke the `.pyc` file directly. However, be sure to precompile the script again when you change it!

Understanding Scope Rules

Variables are names (identifiers) that map to objects. A *namespace* is a dictionary of variable names (keys) and their corresponding objects (values). A Python statement can access variables in a *local namespace* and in the *global namespace*. If (heaven forfend!) a local and a global variable have the same name, the local variable shadows the global variable.

Each function has its own local namespace. Class methods follow the same scoping rule as ordinary functions. Python accesses object attributes via the `self` argument; attributes are not brought separately into the namespace.

At the module level, or in an interactive session, the local namespace is the same as the global namespace. For purposes of an `eval`, `exec`, `execfile`, or `input` statement, the local namespace is the same as the caller's.

Is it local or global?

Python makes educated guesses on whether variables are local or global. It assumes that any variable assigned a value in a function is local. Therefore, in order to assign a value to a global variable within a function, you must first use the *global* statement. The statement `global VarName` tells Python that *VarName* is a global variable. Python stops searching the local namespace for the variable.

For example, Listing 6-2 defines a variable NumberOfMonkeys in the global name-space. Within the function AddMonkey, we assign NumberOfMonkeys a value—therefore, Python assumes NumberOfMonkeys is a local variable. However, we access the value of the local variable NumberOfMonkeys before setting it, so an UnboundLocalError is the result. Uncommenting the global statement fixes the problem.

Listing 6-2: **Monkeys.py**

```
NumberOfMonkeys = 11

def AddMonkey():
    # Uncomment the following line to fix the code:
    #global NumberOfMonkeys
    NumberOfMonkeys = NumberOfMonkeys + 1

print NumberOfMonkeys
AddMonkey()
print NumberOfMonkeys
```

Listing namespace contents

The built-in functions locals and globals return local and global namespace contents in dictionary form. These operations are handy for debugging.

Grouping Modules into Packages

You can group related modules into a package. Packages can also contain subpackages, and sub-subpackages, and so on. You access modules inside a package using dotted notation—for example, seti.log.FlushLogFile() calls the function FlushLogFile in the module log in the package seti.

Python locates packages by looking for a directory containing a file named __init__.py. The directory can be a subdirectory of any directory in sys.path. The directory name is the package name.

The script __init__.py runs when the package is imported. It can be an empty file, but should probably at least contain a docstring. It may also define the special variable __all__, which governs the behavior of a blanket import of the form from PackageName import *. If defined, __all__ is a list of names of modules to bring into the current namespace. If the script __init__.py does not define __all__, then a blanket-import brings into the current namespace only the names defined and modules imported in __init__.py.

Cross-Reference See Chapter 36 for information on how to install new modules and packages, and how to distribute your own code.

Compiling and Running Programmatically

The *exec* statement can run an arbitrary chunk of Python code. The syntax is exec ExecuteObject [in GlobalDict[, LocalDict]]. *ExecuteObject* is a string, file object, or code object containing Python code. *GlobalDict* and *LocalDict* are dictionaries used for the global and local namespaces, respectively. Both *GlobalDict* and *LocalDict* are optional. If you omit LocalDict, it defaults to *GlobalDict*. If you omit both, the code runs using the current namespaces.

The *eval* function evaluates a Python expression. The syntax is eval (ExpressionObject[,GlobalDict[,LocalDict]]). *ExpressionObject* is a string or a code object; *GlobalDict* and *LocalDict* have the same semantics as for exec.

The execfile function has the same syntax as exec, except that it takes a file name instead of an execute object.

These functions raise an exception if they encounter a syntax error.

The *compile* function transforms a code string into a runnable code object. Python passes the code object to exec or eval. The syntax is compile(CodeString,FileName,Kind). *CodeString* is a string of Python code. *FileName* is a string describing the code's origin; if Python read the code from a file, *FileName* should be the name of that file. *Kind* is a string describing the code:

✦ "exec" — one or more executable statements

✦ "eval" — a single expression

✦ "single" — a single statement, which is printed upon evaluation if not None

Note Multiline expressions should have two trailing newlines in order for Python to pass them to compile or exec. (This requirement is a quirk of Python that may be fixed in a later version.)

Summary

Program organization helps make code reusable, as well as more easily compre-hended. In this chapter you:

✦ Defined functions with variable argument lists.

✦ Organized code into modules and packages.

✦ Compiled and ran Python code on-the-fly.

In the next chapter you'll harness the power of object-oriented programming in Python.

✦   ✦   ✦

Object-Oriented Python

♦   ♦   ♦   ♦

In This Chapter

Overview of object-oriented Python

Creating classes and instance objects

Deriving new classes from other classes

Hiding private data

Identifying class membership

Overloading standard behaviors

Using weak references

♦   ♦   ♦   ♦

Python has been an object-oriented language from day one. Because of this, creating and using classes and objects are downright easy. This chapter helps you become an expert in using Python's object-oriented programming support.

Overview of Object-Oriented Python

If you don't have any previous experience with object-oriented (OO) programming, you may want to consult an introductory course on it or at least a tutorial of some sort so that you have a grasp of the basic concepts.

Python's object-oriented programming support is very straightforward and easy: you create *classes* (which are something akin to blueprints), and you use them to create *instance objects* (which are like the usable and finished versions of what the blueprints represent).

An instance object (or just "object," for short) can have any number of *attributes*, which include *data members* (variables belonging to that object) and *methods* (functions belonging to that object that operate on that object's data).

You can create a new class by deriving it from one or more other classes. The new *child class,* or *subclass,* inherits the attributes of its parent classes, but it may override any of the parent's attributes as well as add additional attributes of its own.

Creating Classes and Instance Objects

Below is a sample class and an example of its use:

```
>>> class Wallet:
        "Where does my money go?"
        walletCnt = 0
        def __init__(self,balance=0):
            self.balance = balance
            Wallet.walletCnt += 1

        def getPaid(self,amnt):
            self.balance += amnt
            self.displayBalance()

        def spend(self,amnt):
            self.balance -= amnt
            self.displayBalance()

        def displayBalance(self):
            print 'New balance: $%.2f' % self.balance
```

The class statement creates a new class definition (which is itself also an object) called Wallet. The class has a documentation string (which you can access via Wallet.__doc__), a count of all the wallets in existence, and three methods.

You declare methods like normal functions with the exception that the first argument to each method is self, the conventional Python name for the instance of the object (it has the same role as the this object in Java or the this pointer in C++). Python adds the self argument to the list for you; you don't need to include it when you call the methods. The first method is a special constructor or initialization method that Python calls when you create a new instance of this class. Note that it accepts an initial balance as an optional parameter. The other two methods operate on the wallet's current balance.

> **Note** All methods must operate on an instance of the object (if you're coming from C++, there are no "static methods").

Objects can have two types of data members: walletCnt, which is outside of any method of the class, is a *class variable*, which means that all instances of the class share it. Changing its value in one instance (or in the class definition itself) changes it everywhere, so any wallet can use walletCnt to see how many wallets you've created:

```
>>> myWallet = Wallet(); yourWallet = Wallet()
>>> print myWallet.walletCnt, yourWallet.walletCnt
2,2
```

The other type of data member is an *instance variable*, which is one defined inside a method and belongs only to the current instance of the object. The balance member of Wallet is an instance variable. So that you're never confused as to what belongs to an object, you must use the self parameter to refer to its attributes whether they are methods or data members.

Creating instance objects

To create an instance of a class, you "call" the class and pass in whatever arguments its __init__ method accepts, and you access the object's attributes using the dot operator:

```
>>> w = Wallet(50.00)
>>> w.getPaid(100.00)
New balance $150.00
>>> w.spend(25.0)
New balance $125.00
>>> w.balance
125.0
```

An instance of a class uses a dictionary (named __dict__) to hold the attributes and values specific to that instance. Thus object.attribute is the same as object.__dict__['attribute']. Additionally, each object and class has a few other special members:

```
>>> Wallet.__name__      # Class name
'Wallet'
>>> Wallet.__module__    # Module in which class was defined
'__main__'
>>> w.__class__          # Class definition for this object
<class __main__.Wallet at 010C1CFC>
>>> w.__doc__            # Doc string
'Where does my money go?'
```

More on accessing attributes

You can add, remove, or modify attributes of classes and objects at any time:

```
>>> w.owner = 'Dave'  # Add an 'owner' attribute.
>>> w.owner = 'Bob'   # Bob stole my wallet.
>>> del w.owner       # Remove the 'owner' attribute.
```

Modifying a class definition affects all instances of that class:

```
>>> Wallet.color = 'blue'  # Add a class variable.
>>> w.color
'blue'
```

Note that when an instance modifies a class variable without naming the class, it's really only creating a new instance attribute and modifying it:

```
>>> w.color = 'red'  # You might think you're changing the
>>> Wallet.color     # class variable, but you're not!
'blue'
```

Tip   Because you can modify a class instance at any time, a class is a great way to mimic a more flexible version of a C struct:

```
class myStruct: pass
z = myStruct()
z.whatever = 'howdy'
```

Instead of using the normal statements to access attributes, you can use the getattr(obj, name[, default]), hasattr(obj,name), setattr(obj,name,value), and delattr(obj, name) functions:

```
>>> hasattr(w,'color')   # Does w.color exist?
1
>>> getattr(w,'color')   # Return w.color please.
'red'
>>> setattr(w,'size',10) # Same as 'w.size = 10'.
>>> delattr(w,'color')   # Same as 'del w.color'.
```

As with functions, methods can also have data attributes. The method of the following class, for example, includes an HTML docstring for use with a Web browser-based class browser:

```
>>> class SomeClass:
...    def deleteFiles(self, mask):
...        os.destroyFiles(mask)
...    deleteFiles.htmldoc = '<bold>Use with care!</bold>'
>>> hasattr(SomeClass.deleteFiles,'htmldoc')
1
>>> SomeClass.deleteFiles.htmldoc
'<bold>Use with care!</bold>'
```

Cross-Reference   You can read more about function attributes in Chapter 6.

New Feature   Method attributes are new in Python 2.1.

Deriving New Classes from Other Classes

Instead of starting from scratch, you can create a class by deriving it from a pre-existing class by listing the parent class in parentheses after the new class name:

```
>>> class GetAwayVehicle:
...     topSpeed = 200
...     def engageSmokeScreen(self):
...         print '<Cough!>'
...     def fire(self):
...         print 'Bang!'
>>> class SuperMotorcycle(GetAwayVehicle):
...     topSpeed = 250
...     def engageOilSlick(self):
...         print 'Enemies destroyed.'
...     def fire(self):
...         GetAwayVehicle.fire(self) # Use method in parent.
...         print 'Kapow!'
```

The child class (SuperMotorcycle) inherits the attributes of its parent class (GetAwayVehicle), and you can use those attributes as if they were defined in the child class:

```
>>> myBike = SuperMotorcycle()
>>> myBike.engageSmokeScreen()
<Cough!>
>>> myBike.engageOilSlick()
Enemies destroyed.
```

A child class can override data members and methods from the parent. For example, the value of topSpeed in child overrides the one in the parent:

```
>>> myBike.topSpeed
250
```

The fire method doesn't just override the original version in the parent, but it also calls the parent version too:

```
>>> myBike.fire()
Bang!
Kapow!
```

Multiple inheritance

When deriving a new child class, you aren't limited to a single parent class:

```
>>> class Glider:
...     def extendWings(self):
...         print 'Wings ready!'
...     def fire(self):
...         print 'Bombs away!'
>>> class FlyingBike(Glider,SuperMotorcycle):
...     pass
```

In this case a `FlyingBike` enjoys all the benefits of being both a `Glider` and a `SuperMotorcycle` (which is also a `GetAwayVehicle`). When searching for an attribute not defined in a child class, Python does a left-to-right, depth-first search on the base classes until it finds a match. If you `fire` with a `FlyingBike`, it drops bombs, because first and foremost, it's a `Glider`:

```
>>> betterBike = FlyingBike()
>>> betterBike.fire()
Bombs away!
```

You can get a list of base classes using the __bases__ member of the class definition object:

```
>>> for base in FlyingBike.__bases__:
...     print base
__main__.Glider             # __main__ is the module in
__main__.SuperMotorcycle    # which you defined the class.
```

Tip   Just because multiple inheritance lets you have child classes with many parents (and other strange class genealogies) doesn't always mean it's a good idea. If your design calls for more than a few direct parent classes, chances are you need a new design.

Multiple inheritance really shines with *mix-ins*, which are small classes that override a portion of another class to customize behavior. The `SocketServer` module, for example, defines a generic TCP socket server class called `TCPServer` that handles a single connection at a time. The module also provides several mix-ins, including `ForkingMixIn` and `ThreadingMixIn` that provide their own `process_request` method. This lets the `TCPServer` code remain simple while making it easy to create multi-threaded or multi-process socket server classes:

```
class ThreadingServer(ThreadingMixIn, TCPServer): pass
class ForkingServer(ForkingMixIn, TCPServer): pass
```

Furthermore, you can use the same threading and forking code to create other types of servers:

```
class ThreadingUDPServer(ThreadingMixIn, UDPServer): pass
```

Cross-Reference   See Chapter 15 for information on networking and socket servers.

Creating a custom list class

The `UserList` class (in the `UserList` module) provides a listlike base class that you can extend to suit your needs. `UserList` accepts a list to use as an initializer, and internally you can access the actual Python list via the `data` member. The following example creates an object that behaves like an ordinary list except that it also provides a method to randomly reorder the items in the list:

```
>>> import UserList, whrandom
>>> from whrandom import randint
>>> class MangleList(UserList.UserList):
...     def mangle(self):
...         data = self.data
...         count = len(data)
...         for i in range(count):
...             data.insert(randint(0,count-1),data.pop())
>>> z = MangleList([1,2,3,4,5])
>>> z.mangle() ; print z
[1, 3, 5, 4, 2]
>>> z.mangle() ; print z
[5, 4, 1, 2, 3]
```

Creating a custom string class

You can also create your own custom string behaviors using the UserString class in the UserString module. As with UserLists and lists, a UserString looks and acts a lot like a normal string object:

```
>>> from UserString import *
>>> s = UserString('Goal!')
>>> s.data # Access the underlying Python string.
'Goal!'
>>> s
'Goal!'
>>> s.upper()
'GOAL!'
>>> s[2]
'a'
```

Of course, the whole point of having the UserString class is so that you can sub-class it. As an example, the UserString module also provides the MutableString class:

```
>>> m = MutableString('2 + 2 is 5')
>>> m
'2 + 2 is 5'
>>> m[9] = '4'
>>> m
'2 + 2 is 4'
```

Cross-
Reference

MutableString does its magic by overriding (among other things) the __setitem__ method, which is a special method Python calls to handle the index-based assignment in the example above. We cover __setitem__ and other special methods in the "Overloading Standard Behaviors" section later in this chapter.

Creating a custom dictionary class

And finally, Python also has the `UserDict` class in the `UserDict` module so that you can create your own subclasses of dictionaries:

```
>>> from UserDict import *
>>> d = UserDict({1:'one',2:'two',3:'three'})
>>> d
{3: 'three', 2: 'two', 1: 'one'}
>>> d.data
{3: 'three', 2: 'two', 1: 'one'}
>>> d.has_key(3)
1
```

The following example creates a dictionary object that, instead of raising an exception, returns `None` if you try to use a nonexistent key:

```
>>> from UserDict import *
>>> class NoFailDict(UserDict):
...     def __getitem__(self,key):
...         try:
...             value = self.data[key]
...         except KeyError:
...             value = None
...         return value
>>> q = NoFailDict({'orange':'0xFF6432','yellow':'0xFFFF00'})
>>> print q['orange']
0xFF6432
>>> print q['blue']
None
```

Hiding Private Data

In other object-oriented languages such as C++ or Java, an object's attributes may or may not be visible outside the class definition (you can say a member is public, private, or protected). Such conventions help keep the implementation details hidden and force you to work with objects through well-defined interfaces.

Python, however, takes more of a minimalist approach and assumes you know what you're doing when you try to access attributes of an object. Python programs usually have smaller and more straightforward implementations than their C++ or Java counterparts, so private data members aren't as useful or necessary (although if you're accustomed to using them you may feel a little "overexposed" for awhile).

Having said that, there still may come a time when you really don't want users of an object to have access to the implementation, or maybe you have some members in a base class that you don't want children classes to access. For these cases, you can name attributes with a double underscore prefix, and those attributes will not be directly visible to outsiders:

```
>>> class FooCounter:
...      __secretCount = 0
...      def foo(self):
...            self.__secretCount += 1
...            print self.__secretCount
>>> foo = FooCounter()
>>> foo.foo()
1
>>> foo.foo()
2
>>> foo.__secretCount
Traceback (innermost last):
  File "<interactive input>", line 1, in ?
AttributeError: 'FooCounter' instance has no attribute
'__secretCount'
```

Python protects those members by internally changing the name to include the class name. You can be sneaky and thwart this convention (valid reasons for doing this are rare!) by referring to the attribute using its mangled name: _className__attrName:

```
>>> foo._FooCounter__secretCount
2
```

Identifying Class Membership

Class definitions and instance objects each have their own data type:

```
>>> class Tree:
...      pass
>>> class Oak(Tree):
...      pass
>>> seedling = Oak()
>>> type(seedling); type(Oak)
<type 'instance'>
<type 'class'>
```

Cross-Reference

Refer to Chapter 4 for more on identifying the data types of an object.

Because the type is instance or class, all class definitions have the same type and all instance objects have the same type. If you want to see if an object is an instance of a particular class, you can use the isinstance(obj,class) function:

```
>>> isinstance(seedling,Oak)
1
>>> isinstance(seedling,Tree) # True because an Oak is a Tree.
1
```

The issubclass(class,class) checks to see if one class is a descendent of another:

```
>>> issubclass(Oak,Tree)
1
>>> issubclass(Tree,Oak)
0
```

You can also retrieve the string name for a class using the __name__ member:

```
>>> seedling.__class__.__name__
'Oak'
>>> seedling.__class__.__bases__[0].__name__
'Tree'
```

Tip   Your programs will often be more flexible if, instead of depending on an object's type or class, they check to see if an object has a needed attribute. This enables you and others to use your code with data types that you didn't necessarily consider when you wrote it. For example, instead of checking to see if an object passed in is a file before you write to it, just check for a `write` method, and if present, use it. Later you may find it useful to call the same routine passing in some other object that also has a `write` method. "Using Filelike Objects" in Chapter 8 covers this theme in more detail.

Overloading Standard Behaviors

Suppose you've created a Vector class to represent two-dimensional vectors. What happens when you use the plus operator to add them? Most likely Python will yell at you. You could, however, define the __add__ method in your class to perform vector addition, and then the plus operator would behave:

```
>>> class Vector:
...     def __init__(self,a,b):
...         self.a = a
...         self.b = b
...     def __str__(self):
...         return 'Vector(%d,%d)' % (self.a,self.b)
...     def __add__(self,other):
...         return Vector(self.a+other.a,self.b+other.b)
>>> v1 = Vector(2,10)
>>> v2 = Vector(5,-2)
>>> print v1 + v2
Vector(7,8)
```

Not only do users now have an intuitive way to add two vectors (much better than having them call some clunky function directly), but vectors also display themselves nicely when converted to strings (thanks to the __str__ method).

The operator module defines many functions for which you can *overload* or define new behavior when used with your classes. The following sections describe these functions and how to use them.

Note that some functions have two or even three very similar versions. For example, in the numeric operators, you can create an __add__ function, an __iadd__ function, and an __radd__ function all for addition. The first is to implement normal addition (x + y), the second for in-place addition (x += y), and the third for x + y when x does not have an __add__ method (so Python calls y.__radd(x) instead). If you don't define in-place operator methods, Python checks for an overloaded version of the normal operator (for example, if you don't define __iadd__, x += y causes Python to still call __add__ if defined). For simplicity, it's best to leave the in-place operators undefined unless your class in some way benefits from special in-place processing (such as a huge matrix class that could save memory by performing addition in place).

Overloading basic functionality

Table 7-1 lists some generic functionality that you can override in your own classes.

Table 7-1 Base Overloading Methods	
Method	*Sample Call*
__init__ (self[, args...])	obj = className(args)
__del__ (self)	del obj
__call__ (self[, args...]), callable function	obj(5)
__getattr__ (self, name)	obj.foo
__setattr__ (self, name, value)	obj.foo = 5
__delattr__ (self, name)	del obj.foo
__repr__ (self)	`obj` or repr(obj)
__str__ (self)	str(obj)
__cmp__ (self, x)	cmp(obj,x)
__lt__(self, x)	obj < x
__le__(self,x)	obj <= x
__eq__(self,x)	obj == x
__ne__(self,x)	obj != x
__gt__(self, x)	obj > x
__ge__(self,x)	obj >= x
__hash__ (self)	hash(obj)
__nonzero__ (self)	nonzero(obj)

Note that with the del statement, Python won't call the __del__ method unless the object's reference count is finally 0.

Python invokes the __call__ method any time someone tries to treat an instance of your object as a function. Users can test for "callability" using the callable(obj) function, which tries to determine if the object is callable (callable may return true and be wrong, but if it returns false, the object really isn't callable).

Python calls the __getattr__ function only after a search through the instance dictionary and base classes comes up empty-handed. Your implementation should return the desired attribute or raise an AttributeError exception. If __setattr__ needs to assign a value to an instance variable, be sure to assign it to the instance dictionary instead (self.__dict__[name] = val) to prevent a recursive call to __setattr__. If your class has a __setattr__ method, Python always calls it to set member variable values, even if the instance dictionary already contains the variable being set.

The hash and cmp functions are closely related: if you do not implement __cmp__, you should not implement __hash__. If you provide a __cmp__ but no __hash__, then instances of your object can't act as dictionary keys (which is correct if your objects are mutable). Hash values are 32-bit integers, and two instances that are considered equal should also return the same hash value.

The nonzero function performs truth value testing, so your implementation should return 0 or 1. If not implemented, Python looks for a __len__ implementation to use, and if not found, then all instances of your object will be considered "true."

You use the __lt__, __gt__, and other methods to implement support for *rich comparisons* where you have more complete control over how objects behave during different types of comparisons. If present, Python calls any of these methods before looking for a __cmp__ method. The following example prints a message each time Python calls a comparison function so you can see what happens:

```
>>> class Simple:
...     def __cmp__(self, obj):
...         print '__cmp__'
...         return 1
...     def __lt__(self, obj):
...         print '__lt__'
...         return 0
>>> s = Simple()
>>> s < 5
__lt__    # Python uses rich comparisons first.
0
>>> s > 5
__cmp__   # Uses __cmp__ if there are no rich comparison methods.
1
```

Your rich comparison methods can return `NotImplemented` to tell Python that you don't want to handle a particular comparison. For example, the following class implements an equality method that works on integers. If the object to which it is comparing isn't an integer, it tells Python to figure out the comparison result on its own:

```
>>> class MyInt:
...     def __init__(self, val):
...         self.val = val
...     def __eq__(self, obj):
...         print '__eq__'
...         if type(obj) != type(0):
...             print 'Skipping'
...             return NotImplemented
...         return self.val == obj
>>> m = MyInt(16)
>>> m == 10
__eq__
0
>>> m == 'Hi'
__eq__
Skipping
0
```

Tip   Although `__cmp__` methods must return an integer to represent the result of the comparison, rich comparison methods can return data of any type or raise an exception if a particular comparison is invalid or meaningless.

New Feature   Rich comparisons are new in Python 2.1.

Overloading numeric operators

By overloading the numeric operators methods, your classes can correctly respond to operators like +, -, and so on. Note that Python calls the right-hand side version of operators (for example, `__radd__`) if the left-hand operator doesn't have a corresponding method defined (`__add__`):

```
>>> class Add:
...     def __init__(self,val):
...         self.val = val
...     def __add__(self,obj):
...         print 'add',obj
...         return self.val + obj
...     def __radd__(self,obj):
...         print 'radd',obj
...         return self.val + obj
>>> a = Add(10)
>>> a
<__main__.Add instance at 00E5D354>
>>> a + 5 # Calls a.__add__(5).
```

```
add 5
15
>>> 5 + a # Calls a.__radd__(5).
radd 5
15
```

Table 7-2 lists the mathematic operations (and the right-hand and in-place variants) that you can overload and examples of how to invoke them.

Table 7-2
Numeric Operator Methods

Method	Sample Call
__add__ (self, obj), __radd__, __iadd__	obj + 10.5
__sub__ (self, obj), __rsub__, __isub__	obj - 16
__mul__ (self, obj), __rmul__, __imul__	obj * 5.1
__div__ (self, obj), __rdiv__, __idiv__	obj / 15
__mod__ (self, obj), __rmod__, __imod__	obj % 2
__divmod__ (self, obj), __rdivmod__	divmod(obj,3)
__pow__ (self, obj[, modulo]), __rpow__(self,obj)	pow(obj,3)
__neg__ (self)	-obj
__pos__ (self)	+obj
__abs__ (self)	abs(obj)
__invert__ (self)	~obj

Overloading sequence and dictionary operators

If you create your own sequence or mapping data type, or if you just like those nifty bracket operators, you can overload the sequence operators with the methods listed in Table 7-3.

Table 7-3
Sequence and Dictionary Operator Methods

Method	Sample Call
__len__(self)	len(obj)
__getitem__(self, key)	obj['cheese']
__setitem__(self, key, value)	obj[5] = (2,5)
__delitem__(self, key)	del obj['no']
__setslice__(self, i, j, sequence)	obj[1:7] = 'Fellow'
__delslice__(self, i, j)	del obj[5:7]
__contains__(self,obj)	x in obj

This class overrides the slice operator to provide an inefficient way to create a list of numbers:

```
>>> class DumbRange:
...     def __getitem__(self,slice):
...         step = slice.step
...         if step is None:
...             step = 1
...         return range(slice.start,slice.stop+1,step)
>>> d = DumbRange()
>>> d[2:5]
[2, 3, 4, 5]
>>> d[2:10:2]    # Extended (step) slicing!
[2, 4, 6, 8, 10]
```

The argument to __getitem__ is either an integer or a *slice object*. Slice objects have start, stop, and step attributes, so your class can support the extended slicing shown in the example.

If the key passed to __getitem__ is of the wrong type, your implementation should raise the TypeError exception, and the slice methods should reject invalid indices by raising the IndexError exception.

If your __getitem__ method raises IndexError on an invalid index, Python can iterate over object instances as if they were sequences. The following class behaves like a range object with a user-supplied step, but it limits itself to only 6 iterations:

```
>>> class Stepper:
...     def __init__(self, step):
...         self.step = step
...     def __getitem__(self, index):
...         if index > 5:
...             raise IndexError
...         return self.step * index
>>> s = Stepper(3)
>>> for i in s:
...     print i
0  # Python calls __getitem__ with index=0
3
6
9
12
15 # Python stops after a __getitem__ call raises an exception
```

Overloading bitwise operators

The bitwise operators let your classes support operators such as << and xor:

```
>>> class Vector2D:
...     def __init__(self,i,j):
...         self.i = i
...         self.j = j
...     def __lshift__(self,x):
...         return Vector2D(self.i << x, self.j << x)
...     def __repr__(self):
...         return 'Vector2D(%s,%s)' % (`self.i`,`self.j`)
>>> v1 = Vector2D(5,2)
>>> v1 << 2
Vector2D(20,8)
```

Table 7-4 lists the methods you define to overload the bitwise operators.

Table 7-4	
Bitwise Operator Methods	
Method	**Sample Call**
__lshift__ (self, obj), __rlshift__, __ilshift__	obj << 3
__rshift__ (self, obj), __rrshift__, __irshift__	obj >> 1
__and__ (self, obj), __rand__, __iand__	obj & 17
__or__ (self, obj), __ror__, __ior__	obj	otherObj
__xor__ (self, obj), __rxor__, __ixor__	obj ^ 0xFE

Overloading type conversions

By overloading type conversion methods, you can convert your object to different data types as needed:

```
>>> class Five:
...      def __int__(self):
...            return 5
>>> f = Five()
>>> int(f)
5
```

Python calls these methods when you pass an object to one of the type conversion routines. Table 7-5 lists the methods, sample Python code that would invoke them, and sample output they might return.

Table 7-5
Type Conversion Methods

Method	Sample Call	Sample Output
__int__(self)	int(obj)	53
__long__(self)	long(obj)	12L
__float__(self)	float(obj)	3.5
__complex__(self)	complex(obj)	2 + 3j
__oct__(self)	oct(obj)	'012'
__hex__(self)	hex(obj)	'0xFE'

Python calls the __coerce__(self, obj) method, if present, to coerce two numerical types into a common type before applying an arithmetic operation. Your implementation should return a 2-item tuple containing self and obj converted to a common numerical type or None if you don't support that conversion.

Using Weak References

Like many other high-level languages, Python uses a form of garbage collection to automatically destroy objects that are no longer in use. Each Python object has a reference count that tracks how many references to that object exist; when the reference count is 0, then Python can safely destroy the object.

While reference counting saves you quite a bit of error-prone memory management work, there can be times when you want a *weak reference* to an object, or a reference that doesn't prevent Python from garbage collecting the object if no other references exist. With the `weakref` module, you can create weak references to objects, and Python will garbage collect an object if its reference count is 0 or if the only references that exist are weak references.

New Feature The `weakref` module is new in Python 2.1.

Creating weak references

You create a weak reference by calling `ref(obj[, callback])` in the `weakref` module, where `obj` is the object to which you want a weak reference and `callback` is an optional function to call when Python is about to destroy the object because no strong references to it remain. The callback function takes a single argument, the weak reference object.

Once you have a weak reference to an object, you can retrieve the referenced object by calling the weak reference. The following example creates a weak reference to a socket object:

```
>>> ref = weakref.ref(a)
>>> from socket import *
>>> import weakref
>>> s = socket(AF_INET,SOCK_STREAM)
>>> ref = weakref.ref(s)
>>> s
<socket._socketobject instance at 007B4A94>
>>> ref
<weakref at 0x81195c; to 'instance' at 0x7b4a94>
>>> ref() # Call it to access the referenced object.
<socket._socketobject instance at 007B4A94>
```

Once there are no more references to an object, calling the weak reference returns `None` because Python has destroyed the object.

Note Most objects are not accessible through weak references.

The `getweakrefcount(obj)` and `getweakrefs(obj)` functions in the `weakref` module return the number of weak references and a list of referents for the given object.

Weak references can be useful for creating caches of objects that are expensive to create. For example, suppose you are building a distributed application that sends messages between computers using connection-based network sockets. In order to reuse the socket connections without keeping unused connections open, you decide to keep a cache of open connections:

```
import weakref
from socket import *

socketCache = {}
def getSocket(addr):
    'Returns an open socket object'
    if socketCache.has_key(addr):
        sock = socketCache[addr]()
        if sock: # Return the cached socket.
            return sock

    # No socket found, so create and cache a new one.
    sock = socket(AF_INET,SOCK_STREAM)
    sock.connect(addr)
    socketCache[addr] = weakref.ref(sock)
    return sock
```

In order to send a message to a remote computer, your program calls getSocket to
obtain a socket object. If a connection to the given address doesn't already exist,
getSocket creates a new one and adds a weak reference to the cache. When all
strong references to a given socket are gone, Python destroys the socket object and
the next request for the same connection will cause getSocket to create a new one.

The mapping([dict[,weakkeys]]) function in the weakref module returns a
weak dictionary (initializing it with the values from the optional dictionary dict). If
weakkeys is 0 (the default), the dictionary automatically removes any entry whose
value no longer has any strong references to it. If weakkeys is nonzero, the dictionary automatically removes entries whose keys no longer have strong references.

Creating proxy objects

Proxy objects are weak reference objects that behave like the object they reference
so that you don't have to first call the weak reference to access the underlying
object. Create a proxy by calling weakref's proxy(obj[, callback]) function.
You use the proxy object as if it was the actual object it references:

```
>>> from socket import *
>>> import weakref
>>> s = socket(AF_INET,SOCK_STREAM)
>>> ref = weakref.proxy(s)
>>> s
<socket._socketobject instance at 007E4874>
>>> ref # It looks like the socket object.
<socket._socketobject instance at 007E4874>
>>> ref.close() # The object's methods work too.
```

The `callback` parameter has the same purpose as the `ref` function. After Python deletes the referenced object, using the proxy results in a `weakref.ReferenceError`:

```
>>> del s
>>> ref
Traceback (most recent call last):
  File "<stdin>", line 1, in ?
```

Note This example assumes that Python immediately destroys the object once the last string is gone. While true of the current garbage collector implementation, future versions may be different.

Summary

Python fully supports object-oriented programming while requiring minimal effort from you, the programmer. In this chapter you:

✦ Created your own custom classes.

✦ Derived new classes from other classes.

✦ Extended built-in data types like strings and lists.

✦ Defined custom behaviors for operations on your classes.

In the next chapter you learn to create programs that interact with the user and store and retrieve data.

✦   ✦   ✦

Input and Output

I n order to be useful, most programs must interact with the "outside world" in some way. This chapter introduces Python's functions for reading and writing files, printing to the screen, and retrieving keyboard input from the user.

Printing to the Screen

The simplest way to produce output is using the `print` statement, which converts the expressions you pass it to a string and writes the result to standard output, which by default is the screen or console. You can pass in zero or more expressions, separated by commas, between which `print` inserts a space:

```
>>> print 'It is',5+7,'past',3
It is 12 past 3
```

Before printing each expression, `print` converts any non-string expressions using the `str` function. If you don't want the spaces between expressions, you can do the conversions yourself:

```
>>> a = 5.1; z = (0,5,10)
>>> print '(%0.1f + %0.1f) = \n%0.1f' %
(a,a,a*2)
(5.1 + 5.1) =
10.2
>>> print 'Move to '+str(z)
Move to (0, 5, 10)
>>> print 'Two plus ten is '+`2+10` # `` is
the same as repr.
Two plus ten is 12
```

Cross-Reference   Chapter 3 covers converting different data types to strings.

In This Chapter

Printing to the screen

Accessing keyboard input

Opening, closing, and positioning files

Writing files

Reading files

Accessing standard I/O

Using filelike objects

If you append a trailing comma to the end of the statement, `print` won't move to the next line:

```
>>> def addEm(x,y):
...     print x,
...     print 'plus',
...     print y,
...     print 'is',
...     print x+y
>>> addEm(5,2)
5 plus 2 is 7
```

Python uses the `softspace` attribute of `stdout` (`stdout` is in the `sys` module) to track whether it needs to output a space before the next item to be printed. You can use this feature to manually shut off the space that would normally appear due to using a comma:

```
>>> import sys
>>> def joinEm(a,b):
...     print a,
...     sys.stdout.softspace = 0
...     print b
...
>>> joinEm('Thanks','giving')
Thanksgiving
```

An extended form of the `print` statement lets you redirect output to a file instead of standard output:

```
>>> print >> sys.stderr    ,"File not found"
File not found
```

 The extended form of `print` was introduced in Python 2.0.

Any filelike object will do, as you will see in the "Using Filelike Objects" section later in this chapter.

Accessing Keyboard Input

Going the other direction, Python provides two built-in functions to retrieve a line of text from standard input, which by default comes from the user's keyboard. The examples in this section use italics for text you enter in response to the prompts.

raw_input

The `raw_input([prompt])` function reads one line from standard input and returns it as a string (removing the trailing newline):

```
>>> s = raw_input()
Uncle Gomez
>>> print s
Uncle Gomez
```

You can also specify a prompt for raw_input to use while waiting for user input:

```
>>> s = raw_input('Command: ')
Command: launch missiles
>>> print 'Ignoring command to',s
Ignoring command to launch missiles
```

If raw_input encounters the end of file, it raises the EOFError exception.

input

The input([prompt]) function is equivalent to raw_input, except that it assumes the input is a valid Python expression and returns the evaluated result to you:

```
>>> input('Enter some Python: ')
Enter some Python: [x*5 for x in range(2,10,2)]
[10, 20, 30, 40]
```

Note that input isn't at all error-proof. If the expression passed in is bogus, input raises the appropriate exception, so be wary when using this function in your programs.

Chapter 38 covers the readline module for UNIX systems. If enabled, this module adds command history tracking and completion to these input routines (and Python's interactive mode as well).

You may have noticed that you can't read one character at a time (instead you have to wait until the user hits Enter). To read a single character on UNIX systems (or any system with curses support), you can use the getch function in the curses module (Chapter 22). For Windows systems, you can use the getch function in the msvcrt module (Chapter 37).

Opening, Closing, and Positioning Files

The remaining sections in this chapter show you how to use files in your programs.

Part II of this book — "Files, Data Storage, and Operating System Services" — covers many additional features you'll find useful when using files.

open

Before you can read or write a file, you have to open it using Python's built-in
`open(name[, mode[, bufsize]])` function:

```
>>> f = open('foo.txt','wt',1) # Open foo.txt for writing.
>>> f
<open file 'foo.txt', mode 'wt' at 010C0488>
```

The mode parameter is a string (similar to the mode parameter in C's `fopen`
function) and is explained in Table 8-1.

Table 8-1	
Mode Values for open	
Value	*Description*
R	Opens for reading.
W	Creates a file for writing, destroying any previous file with the same name.
A	Opens for appending to the end of the file, creating a new one if it does not already exist.
r+	Opens for reading and writing (the file must already exist).
w+	Creates a new file for reading and writing, destroying any previous file with the same name.
a+	Opens for reading and appending to the end of the file, creating a new file if it does not already exist.

If you do not specify a mode string, `open` uses the default of `'r'`. To the end of the
mode string you can append a 't' to open the file in text mode or a 'b' to open it in
binary mode:

```
>>> f = open('somepic.jpg','w+b') # Open/create binary file.
```

If you omit the optional buffer size parameter (or pass in a negative number), `open`
uses the system's default buffering. A value of 0 is for unbuffered reading and writing,
a value of 1 buffers data a line at a time, and any other number tells `open` to use a
buffer of that size (some systems round the number down to the nearest power of 2).

If for any reason the function call fails (file doesn't exist, you don't have permission), `open` raises the `IOError` exception.

Cross-
Reference

The `os` module (Chapter 10) provides the `fdopen`, `popen`, `popen2`, and `popen3`
functions as additional ways to obtain file objects. You can also create a filelike object
wrapping an open socket with the `socket.makefile` function (Chapter 15).

File object information

Once you have a file object, you can use the `name`, `fileno()`, `isatty()`, `mode`, and `closed` methods and attributes to get different information about the object's status:

```
>>> f = open('foo.txt','wt')
>>> f.mode # Get the mode used to create the file object.
'wt'
>>> f.closed # Boolean: has the file been closed already?
0
>>> f.name # Get the name of the file.
'foo.txt'
>>> f.isatty() # Is the file connected to a terminal?
0
>>> f.fileno() # Get the file descriptor number.
0
```

With the file descriptor returned by the `fileno` method you can call `read` and other functions in the `os` module (Chapter 10).

close

The `close()` method of a file object flushes any unwritten information and closes the file object, after which no more writing can occur:

```
>>> f = open('foo.txt','wt')
>>> f.write('Foo!!')
>>> f.close()
```

File position

The `tell()` method tells you the current position within the file (in other words, the next read or write will occur at that many bytes from the beginning of the file):

```
>>> f = open('tell.txt','w+') # Open for reading AND writing.
>>> f.write('BRAWN') # Write 5 characters.
>>> f.tell()
5 # Next operation will occur at offset 5 (starting from 0).
```

The `seek(offset[, from])` method changes the current file position. The following example continues the previous one by seeking to an earlier point in the file, overwriting some of the previous data, and then reading the entire file:

```
>>> f.seek(2) # Move to offset 2 from the start of the file.
>>> f.write('AI')
>>> f.seek(0) # Now move back to the beginning.
>>> f.read() # Read everything from here on.
'BRAIN'
```

You can pass an additional argument to seek to change how it interprets the first parameter. Use a value of 0 (which is the default) to seek from the beginning of the file, 1 to seek relative to the current position, and 2 to seek relative to the end of the file. Using the previous example:

```
>>> f.seek(-4,2) # Seek 4 bytes back from the end of the file.
>>> f.read()
'RAIN'
```

Caution   When you open a file in text mode on a Microsoft Windows system, Windows silently and automatically translates newline characters ('\n') into '\r\n' instead. In such cases use seek only with an offset of 0 (to seek to the beginning or the end of the file) or to seek from the beginning of the file with an offset returned from a previous call to tell.

Writing Files

The write(str) method writes any string to an open file (keep in mind that Python strings can have binary data and not just text). Notice that write does not add a newline character ('\n') to the end of the string:

```
>>> f = open('snow.txt','w+t')
>>> f.write('Once there was a snowman,\nsnowman, snowman.\n')
>>> f.seek(0) # Move to the beginning of the file.
>>> print f.read()
Once there was a snowman,
snowman, snowman.
```

The writelines(list) method takes a list of strings to write to a file (as with write, it does not append newline characters to the end of each string you pass in). Continuing the previous example:

```
>>> lines = ['Once there was a snowman ','tall, tall,','tall!']
>>> f.writelines(lines)
>>> f.seek(0)
>>> print f.read()
Once there was a snowman,
snowman, snowman.
Once there was a snowman tall, tall, tall!
```

Tip   Like stdout, all file objects have a softspace attribute (covered in the first section of this chapter) telling whether or not Python should insert a space before writing out the next piece of data. As with stdout, you can modify this attribute to shut off that extra space.

The truncate([offset]) method deletes the contents of the file from the current position until the end of the file:

```
>>> f.seek(10)
>>> f.truncate()
>>> f.seek(0)
>>> print f.read()
Once there
```

Optionally you can specify a file position at which to truncate instead of the current file position:

```
>>> f.seek(0)
>>> f.truncate(5)
>>> print f.read()
Once
```

You can also use the flush() method to commit any buffered writes to disk.

 See the pickle, shelve, and struct modules in Chapter 12 for information on writing Python objects to files in such a way that you can later read them back in as valid objects.

Reading Files

The read([count]) method returns the specified number of bytes from a file (or less if it reaches the end of the file):

```
>>> f = open('read.txt','w+t') # Create a file.
>>> for i in range(3):
...         f.write('Line #%d\n' % i)
>>> f.seek(0)
>>> f.read(3) # Read 3 bytes from the file.
'Lin'
```

If you don't ask for a specific number of bytes, read returns the remainder of the file:

```
>>> print f.read()
e #0
Line #1
Line #2
```

The readline([count]) method returns a single line, including the trailing newline character if present:

```
>>> f.seek(0)
>>> f.readline()
'Line #0\012'
```

You can have `readline` return a certain number of bytes or an entire line (whichever comes first) by passing in a size argument:

```
>>> f.readline(5)
'Line '
>>> f.readline()
'#1\012'
```

The `readlines([sizehint])` method repeatedly calls `readline` and returns a list of lines read:

```
>>> f.seek(0)
>>> f.readlines()
['Line #0\012', 'Line #1\012', 'Line #2\012']
```

Note   Once they reach the end of the file, the `read` and `readline` methods return empty strings, and the `readlines` method returns an empty list.

The optional `sizehint` parameter limits how much data `readlines` reads into memory instead of reading until the end of the file.

When you're processing the lines of text in a file, you often want to remove the newline characters along with any leading or trailing whitespace. Here's an easy way to open the file, read the lines, and remove the newlines all in a single step (this example assumes you have the read.txt file from above):

```
>>> [x.strip() for x in open('read.txt').readlines()]
['Line #0', 'Line #1', 'Line #2'] # Yay, Python!
```

One drawback to the `readlines` method is that it reads the entire file into memory before returning it to you as a list (unless you supply a `sizehints` parameter, in which case you have to call `readlines` over and over again until the end of the file). The `xreadlines` works like `readlines` but reads data into memory as needed:

```
>>> for line in open('read.txt').xreadlines():
...     print line.strip().upper() # Print uppercase version of
lines.
```

New Feature   The `xreadlines` function is new in Python 2.1.

Accessing Standard I/O

The `sys` module provides three file objects that you can always use: `stdin` (standard input), `stdout` (standard output), and `stderr` (standard error). Most often `stdin` holds input coming from the user's keyboard while `stdout` and `stderr` print messages to the user's screen.

Note Some IDEs like PythonWin implement their own version of `stdin`, `stdout`, `input`, and so on, so redirecting them may behave differently. When in doubt, try it out from the command line.

Routines like `input` and `raw_input` read from `stdin`, and routines like `print` write to `stdout`, so an easy way to redirect input and output is to put file objects of your own into `sys.stdin` and `sys.stdout`:

```
>>> import sys
>>> sys.stdout = open('fakeout.txt','wt')
>>> print "Now who's going to the restaurant?"
>>> sys.stdout.close()
>>> sys.stdout = sys.__stdout__
>>> open('fakeout.txt').read()
"Now who's going to the restaurant?\012"
```

As the example shows, the original values are in the __stdin__, __stdout__, and __stderr__ members of `sys`; be a good Pythonista and point the variables to their original values when you're done fiddling with them.

Note External programs started via `os.system` or `os.popen` do not look in `sys.stdin` or `sys.stdout`. As a result, their input and output come from the normal sources, regardless of changes you've made to Python's idea of `stdin` and `stdout`.

Using Filelike Objects

One of the great features of Python is its flexibility with data types, and a neat example of this is with file objects. Many functions or methods require that you pass in a file object, but more often than not you can get away with passing in an object that *acts* like a file instead.

The following example implements a *filelike object* that reverses the order of anything you write to it and then sends it to the original version of `stdout`:

```
>>> import sys,string
>>> class Reverse:
...     def write(self,s):
...         s = list(s)
...         s.reverse()
...         sys.__stdout__.write(string.join(s,''))
...         sys.__stdout__.flush()
```

Not much of a file object is it? But, you'd be surprised at how often it'll do the trick:

```
>>> sys.stdout = Reverse()
>>> print 'Python rocks!'
!skcor nohtyP
```

Detecting Redirected Input

Suppose you're writing a nifty utility program that would most often be used in a script where the input would come from piped or redirected input, but you also want to provide more of an interactive mode for other uses. Instead of having to pass in a command line parameter to choose the mode, your program could use the `isatty` method of sys.stdin to detect it for you.

To see this in action, save this tiny program to a file called myutil.py:

```
import sys
if sys.stdin.isatty():
    print 'Interactive mode!'
else:
    print 'Batch mode!'
```

Now run it from an MS-DOS or UNIX shell command prompt:

```
C:\temp>python myutil.py
Interactive mode!
```

Run it again, this time redirecting a file to `stdin` using the redirection character (any file works as input—in the example below I chose myutil.py because you're sure to have it in your directory):

```
C:\temp>python myutil.py < myutil.py
Batch mode!
```

Likewise, a more complex (and hopefully more useful) utility could automatically behave differently depending on whether a person or a file was supplying the input.

In fact, you can trick most of Python into using your new file object, even when printing error messages:

```
>>> sys.stderr = Reverse()
>>> Reverse.foo # This action causes an error.
:)tsal llac tnecer tsom( kcabecarT
? ni ,1 enil ,">nidts<" eliF  rorrEetubirttA :oof
```

The point here is that no part of the Python interpreter or the standard libraries has any knowledge of your special file class, nor does it need to. Sometimes a custom class can act like one of a different type even if it's not derived from a common base class (that is, files and Reverse do not share some common "generic file" superclass).

One instance in which this feature is useful is when you're building GUI-based applications (see Chapter 19) and you want text messages to go to a graphical window instead of to the console. Just write your own filelike class that sends a string to the window, replace sys.stdout (and probably sys.stderr), and magically output goes to the right place, even if some third-party module that is completely ignorant of your trickery generates the output.

This flexibility comes in handy at other times too. For example, map lets you pass in the function to apply. The ability to recognize cases where it is both useful and intuitive is a talent worth cultivating.

Tip

As of Python 2.1, you can create a xreadlines object around any filelike object that implements a readlines method:

```
import xreadlines
obj = SomeFileLikeObject()
for line in xreadlines.xreadlines(obj):
    ... do some work ...
```

Summary

Whether you're using files or standard I/O, Python makes handling input and output easy. In this chapter you:

✦ Printed information to the user's console.

✦ Retrieved input from the keyboard.

✦ Learned to read and write text and binary files.

✦ Used filelike objects in place of actual file objects.

In the next chapter you'll learn to use Python's powerful string handling features. With them you can easily search strings, match patterns, and manipulate strings in your programs.

✦　　✦　　✦

Files, Data Storage, and Operating System Services

P A R T

II

◆   ◆   ◆   ◆

Chapter 9
Processing Strings
and Regular
Expressions

Chapter 10
Working with Files
and Directories

Chapter 11
Using Other
Operating System
Services

Chapter 12
Storing Data and
Objects

Chapter 13
Accessing Date
and Time

Chapter 14
Using Databases

◆   ◆   ◆   ◆

Processing Strings and Regular Expressions

◆   ◆   ◆   ◆

In This Chapter

Using string objects

Using the string module

Defining regular expressions

Creating and using regular expression objects

Using match objects

Treating strings as files

Encoding text

Formatting floating point numbers

◆   ◆   ◆   ◆

Strings are a very common format for data display, input, and output. Python has several modules for manipulating strings. The most powerful of these is the regular expression module. Python also offers classes that can blur the separation between a string (in memory) and a file (on disk).

This chapter covers all of the things you can do with strings, ordered from the crucial to the seldom used.

Using String Objects

String objects provide methods to search, edit, and format the string. Because strings are immutable, these functions do not alter the original string. They return a new string:

```
>>> bob="hi there"
>>> bob.upper() # Say it LOUDER!
'HI THERE'
>>> bob # bob is immutable, so he didn't
mutate.
>>> 'hi there'
>>> string.upper(bob) # Module function, same
as bob.upper
'HI THERE'
```

String object methods are also available (except as noted below) as functions in the string module. The corresponding module functions take, as an extra first parameter, the string object to operate on.

Cross-Reference See Chapter 3 for an introduction to string syntax and formatting in Python.

String formatting methods

Several methods are available to format strings for printing or processing. You can justify the string within a column, strip whitespace, or expand tabs.ljust(*width*), center(*width*), or rjust(*width*). These methods right-justify, center, or left-justify a string within a column of a given *width*. They pad the string with spaces as necessary. If the string is longer than *width*, these methods return the original string.

This kind of formatting works in a *monospaced* font, such as Courier New, where all characters have the same width. In a *proportional* font, strings with the same length generally have different widths on the screen or printed page.

```
>>> "antici".ljust(10)+"pation".rjust(10)
'antici        pation'
```

lstrip, rstrip, strip

lstrip returns a string with leading whitespace removed, rstrip removes trailing whitespace, and strip removes both. "Whitespace" characters are defined in string.whitespace — whitespace characters include spaces, tabs, and newlines.

```
>>> " hello world ".lstrip()
'hello world '
>>> _.rstrip() # Interpreter trick: _ = last expression value
'hello world'
```

expandtab([tabsize])

This method replaces the tab characters in a string with *tabsize* spaces, and returns the result. The parameter *tabsize* is optional, defaulting to eight. This method is equivalent to replace("\t"," "*tabsize).

String case-changing methods

You can convert strings to UPPERCASE, lowercase, and more.

lower, upper

These methods return a string with all characters shifted to lowercase and uppercase, respectively. They are useful for comparing strings when case is not important.

capitalize, title, swapcase

The method *capitalize* returns a string with the first character shifted to uppercase.

The method *title* returns a string converted to "titlecase." Titlecase is similar to the way book titles are written: it places the first letter of each word in uppercase, and all other letters in lowercase. Python assumes that any group of adjacent letters constitutes one word.

The method *swapcase* returns a string where all lowercase characters changed to uppercase, and vice versa.

```
>>> "hello world".title()
'Hello World'
>>> "hello world".capitalize()
'Hello world'
>>> "hello world".upper()
'HELLO WORLD'
```

String format tests (the is-methods)

These methods do not have corresponding functions in the string module. Each returns false for an empty string. For instance, `""`.isalpha() returns 0.

✦ **isalpha**—Returns true if each character is alphabetic. Alphabetic characters are those in string.letters. Returns false otherwise.

✦ **isalnum**—Returns true if each character is alphanumeric. Alphanumeric characters are those in string.letters or string.digits. Returns false otherwise.

✦ **isdigit**—Returns true if each character is a digit (from string.digits). Returns false otherwise.

✦ **isspace**—Returns true if each character is whitespace (from string. whitespace). Returns false otherwise.

✦ **islower**—Returns true if each letter in the string is lowercase, and the string contains at least one letter. Returns false otherwise. For example:

```
>>> "2 + 2".islower() # No letters, so test fails!
0
>>> "2 plus 2".islower() # A-ok!
1
```

✦ **isupper**—Returns true if each letter in the string is uppercase, and the string contains at least one letter. Returns false otherwise.

✦ **istitle**—Returns true if the letters of the string are in titlecase, and the string contains at least one letter. Returns false otherwise. (See the `title` formatting method discussed previously for a description of titlecase.)

String searching methods

Strings offer various methods for simple searching. For more powerful searching, use the regular expressions module (covered later in this chapter).

find(substring[, firstindex[, lastindex]])

Search for *substring* within the string. If found, return the index where the first occurrence starts. If not found, return -1.

A call to `str.find` searches the slice `str[firstindex:lastindex]`. So, the default behavior is to search the whole string, but you can pass values for *firstindex* and *lastindex* to limit the search.

```
>>> str="the rest of the story"
>>> str.find("the")
0
>>> str.find("the",1) # Start search at index 1.
12
>>> str.find("futplex")
-1
```

Here are some relatives of `find`, which you may find useful:

✦ **index** — Same syntax and effect as `find`, but raises the exception `ValueError` if it doesn't find the substring .

✦ **rfind** — Same as `find`, but returns the index of the *last* occurrence of the substring.

✦ **rindex** — Same as `index`, but returns the index of the *last* occurrence of the substring.

startswith(substr[,firstindex[,lastindex]])

Returns true if the string starts with *substr*. A call to `str.startswith` compares *substr* against the slice `str[firstindex:lastindex]`. You can pass values for *firstindex* and *lastindex* to test whether a slice of your string with *substr*. No equivalent function in the string module.

endswith(substr[,firstindex[,lastindex]])

Same as *startswith*, but tests whether the string ends with *substr*. The string module contains no equivalent function.

count(substr[,firstindex[,lastindex]])

Counts the number of occurrences of *substr* within a string. If you pass indices, `count` searches within the slice [firstindex:lastindex].

This example gives the answer to an old riddle: "What happens once today, three times tomorrow, but never in three hundred years?"

```
>>> RiddleStrings=["today","tomorrow","three hundred years"]
>>> for str in RiddleStrings: print str.count("o")
...
1
3
0
```

String manipulation methods

Strings provide various methods to replace substrings, split the string on delimiters, or join a list of strings into a larger string.

translate(table[,deletestr])

Returns a string translated according to the translation string *table*. If you supply a string *deletestr*, `translate` removes all characters in that string *before* applying the translation table. The string *table* must have a length of 256; a character with ASCII value *n* is replaced with `table[n]`. The best way to create such a string is with a call to `string.maketrans`, as described below.

For example, this line of code converts a string to "Hungarian style," with words capitalized and concatenated. It also swaps exclamation points and question marks:

```
>>>ProductName="power smart report now?"
>>>ProductName.title().translate(string.maketrans("?!","!?"),string.whitespace)
'PowerSmartReportNow!'
```

replace(oldstr,newstr[,maxreplacements])

Returns a string with all occurrences of *oldstr* replaced by *newstr*. If you provide *maxreplacements*, `replace` replaces only the first *maxreplacements* occurrences of oldstr.

```
>>> "Siamese cat".replace("c","b")
'Siamese bat'
```

split([separators[,maxsplits]])

Breaks the string on any of the characters in the string *separators*, and returns a list of pieces. The default value of *separators* is `string.whitespace`. If you supply a value for *maxsplits*, then `split` performs up to *maxsplits* splits, and no more.

This method is useful for dealing with delimited data:

```
>>> StockQuoteLine = "24-Nov-00,45.9375,46.1875,44.6875,45.1875,3482500,45.1875"
>>> ClosingPrice=float(StockQuoteLine.split(",")[4])
>>> ClosingPrice
45.1875
```

splitlines([keepends])

Splits a string on line breaks (carriage return and/or line feed). If you set *keepends* to true, `splitlines` retains the terminating character on each line. The `string` module has no corresponding function. For example:

```
>>> "The\r\nEnd\n\n".splitlines()
['The', 'End', '']
>>> "The\r\nEnd\n\n".splitlines(1)
['The\015\012', 'End\012', '\012']
```

join(StringSequence)

Returns a string consisting of all the strings in *StringSequence* concatenated together, using the string as a delimiter.

This method in generally used in the corresponding function form: `string.join(StringSequence[, Delimiter])`. The default value of *Delimiter* is a single space.

```
>>> Words=["Ready","Set","Go"]
>>> "...".join(Words) # weird-looking
'Ready...Set...Go'
>>> string.join(Words,"...") # equivalent, and more intuitive
'Ready...Set...Go'
```

encode([scheme[,errorhandling]])

Returns the same string, encoded in the encoding scheme *scheme*. The parameter *scheme* defaults to the current encoding scheme. The parameter *errorhandling* defaults to "strict," indicating that encoding problems should raise a ValueError exception. Other values for errorhandling are "ignore" (do not raise any errors), and "replace" (replace un-encodable characters with a replacement marker). See the section "Encoding Text," for more information.

Using the String Module

Because strings have so many useful methods, it is often not necessary to import the `string` module. But, the string module does provide many useful members.

Character categories

The string module includes several constant strings that categorize characters as letters, digits, punctuation, and so forth. Avoid editing these strings, as it may break standard routines.

✦ **letters** — All characters considered to be letters; consists of **lowercase** + **uppercase**.

✦ **lowercase** — All lowercase letters.

✦ **uppercase** — All uppercase letters.

✦ **digits** — The string `'0123456789'`.

✦ **hexdigits** — The string `'0123456789abcdefABCDEF'`.

- ✦ **octdigits** — The string '01234567'.

- ✦ **punctuation** — String of all the characters considered to be punctuation.

- ✦ **printable** — All the characters that are considered printable. Consists of digits, letters, punctuation, and whitespace.

- ✦ **whitespace** — All characters that are considered whitespace. On most systems this string includes the characters space, tab, linefeed, return, formfeed, and vertical tab.

Miscellaneous functions

Most of the functions in the string module correspond to methods of a string object, and are covered in the section on string methods. The other functions, which have no equivalent object methods, are covered here.

atoi,atof,atol

The function `string.atoi(str)` returns an integer value of *str*, and raises a ValueError if `str` does not represent an integer. It is equivalent to the built-in function `int(str)`.

The function `atof(str)` converts a string to a float; it is equivalent to the `float` function.

The function `atol(str)` converts a string to a long integer; it is equivalent to the `long` function.

```
>>> print string.atof('3.5')+string.atol('2')
5.5
```

capwords(str)

Splits a string (on whitespace) into words, capitalizes each word, then joins the words together with one space between them:

```
>>> string.capwords("The end...or is it?")
'The End...or Is It?'
```

maketrans(fromstring,tostring)

Creates a translation table suitable for passing to `maketrans` (or to `regex.compile`). The translation table instructs `maketrans` to translate the nth character in *fromstring* into the nth character in *tostring*. The strings *fromstring* and *tostring* must have the same length.

The translation table is a string of length 256 representing all ASCII characters, but with `fromstring[n]` replaced by `tostring[n]`.

splitfields, joinfields

These functions have the same effect as `split` and `join`, respectively. (Before Version 2.0, `splitfields` and `joinfields` accepted a string of separators, and `split` and `join` did not.)

zfill(str,width)

Given a numeric string *str* and a desired width *width,* returns an equivalent numeric string padded on the left by zeroes. Similar to `rjust`. For example:

```
>>> string.zfill("-3",5)
'-0003'
```

Defining Regular Expressions

A *regular expression* is an object that matches some collection of strings. You can use regular expressions to search and transform strings in sophisticated ways. Regular expressions use their own special syntax to describe strings to match. They can be very efficient, but also very cryptic if taken to extremes. Regular expressions are widely used in UNIX world. The module `re` provides full support for Perl-like regular expressions in Python.

The `re` module raises the exception `re.error` if an error occurs while compiling or using a regular expression.

Prior to Version 1.5, the modules `regex` and `regsub` provided support for regular expressions. These modules are now deprecated.

Regular expression syntax

The definition of a regular expression is a string. In general, a character in the regular expression's definition matches a character in a target string. For example, the regular expression defined by `fred` matches the string "fred," and no others. Some characters have special meanings that permit more sophisticated matching.

. A period (dot) matches any character except a newline. For example, `b.g` matches "big," "bag," or "bqg," but not "b\ng." If the `DOTALL` flag is set, then dot matches any character, including a newline.

[] Brackets specify a set of characters to match. For example, `p[ie]n` matches "pin" or "pen" and nothing else. A set can include ranges: the set `[a-ex-z]` is equivalent to `[abcdexyz]`. Starting a set with ^ means "match any character *except* these." For example, `b[^ae]d` matches "bid" or "b%d," but not "bad" or "bed."

* An asterisk indicates that the preceding regular expression is optional, and may occur any number of times. For example, `ba*n*` matches "banana" or "baaaa" or "bn" or simply "b."

+	A plus sign indicates that the preceding regular expression *must* occur at least once, and may occur many times. For example, `[sweatrd]+` matches various words, the longest of which is "stewardesses." The regular expression `[0-9]+/[0-9]+` matches fractions like "13/64" or "2/3."
?	A question mark indicates that the preceding regular expression is optional, and can occur, at most, once. For example, `col?d` matches either "cod" or "cold," but not "colld." The question mark has other uses, explained below in the sections on "Nongreedy matching" and "Extensions."
{m,n}	The general notation for repetition is two numbers in curly-braces. This syntax indicates that the preceding regular expression must appear at least m times, but no more than n times. If *m* is omitted, it defaults to 0. If *n* is omitted, it defaults to infinity. For example, `[^a-zA-Z]{3,}` matches any sequence of at least three non-alphabetic characters.
^	A caret matches the beginning of the string. If the MULTILINE flag is set, it also matches the beginning of a new line. For example, `^bob` matches "bobsled" but not "discombobulate." Note that the caret has an unrelated meaning inside brackets [].
$	A dollar sign matches the end of the string. If the MULTILINE flag is set, it also matches the end of a line. For example, `is$` matches "this" but not "fish." It matches "This\nyear" only if the MULTILINE flag is set.
		A vertical slash splits a regular expression into two parts, and matches either the first half or the last half. For example, `ab|cd` matches the strings "ab" and "cd."
()	Enclosing part of a regular expression in parentheses does not change matching behavior. However, Python flags the regular expression enclosed in parentheses as a *group*. After the first match, you can match the group again using backslash notation. For instance, the regular expression `^[\w]*(\w)\1[\w]*$` matches a single word with double letters, like "pepper" or "narrow" but not "salt" or "wide." (The syntax \w, explained below, matches any letter.) A regular expression can have up to 99 groups, which are numbered starting from 1.
	Grouping is useful even if the group is only matched once. For example, `Ste(ph|v)en` matches "Stephen" or "Steven." Without parens, `Steph|ven` matches only the strings "Steph" and "ven."
	Python also uses parentheses in extensions (see "Extensions" later in this chapter).
\	Escape special characters. You can use a backslash to escape any special characters. For example, `ca\$h` matches the string "ca$h." Note that without the backslash, `ca$h` could never match anything (except in MULTILINE mode). The backslash also forms character groups, as described below.

Backslashes and raw strings

You should generally write the Python string defining a regular expression as a raw string. Otherwise, because you must escape backslashes in the regular expression's definition, the excessive backslashes become confusing:

```
>>> ThePath="c:\\temp\\download\\"
>>> print ThePath
c:\temp\download\
>>> re.search(r"c:\\temp",ThePath) # Raw. Reasonably clear.
<SRE_Match object at 007CC7A8>
>>> re.search("c:\\temp",ThePath) # no match!
>>> re.search("c:\\\\temp",ThePath) # Less clear than raw
<SRE_Match object at 007ACFD0>
```

The second search fails to find a match, because the regular expression defined by c:\temp matches only the string consisting of "c:," then a tab, then "emp"!

Character groups and other backslash magic

In addition to escaping special characters, you can also use the backslash in conjunction with a letter to match various things. A rule of thumb is that if backslash plus a lowercase letter matches something, backslash plus the uppercase letter matches the opposite.

\1, \2, etc.	Matches a numbered group. If part of a regular expression is enclosed in parentheses, Python flags it as a group. Python numbers groups, starting from 1 and proceeding to 99. You can match groups again by number. For example, (.+)\1 matches the names of 80's bands "The The," "Mister Mister," and "Duran Duran."
	Python interprets escaped three-digit numbers, or numbers starting with 0, as the octal value of a character. For example, \012 matches a newline.
	Inside set brackets [], Python treats all escaped numbers as characters.
\A	Matches the start of the string: equivalent to ^.
\b	Matches a word boundary. Here "word" means "sequence of alphanumeric characters." For example, snow\b matches "snow angel" but not "snowball." Note that \b in the middle of a word indicates backspace, just as it would in an ordinary string. For instance, "bozo\b\b\b\bgentleman" matches the string consisting of "bozo," four backspace characters, then "gentleman."
\B	Matches a non-word-boundary. For example, \Bne\B matches part of "planet," but not "nest" or "lane."
\d	Matches a digit: equivalent to [0–9].

\D	Matches a non-digit: equivalent to [^0–9].
\s	Matches a whitespace character: equivalent to [\t\n\r\f\v].
\S	Matches a non-whitespace character: equivalent to [^ \t\n\r\f\v].
\w	Matches an alphanumeric character: equivalent to [a–zA–Z0–9_]. If the LOCALE flag is set, \w matches [0–9_] or any character defined as alphabetic in the current locale. If the UNICODE flag is set, matches [0–9_] or any character marked as alphanumeric in the full Unicode character set.
\W	Matches a non-alphanumeric character.
\Z	Matches the end of the string: equivalent to $.
\\	Matches a backslash. (Similarly, \. matches a period, \? matches a question mark, and so forth.)

Nongreedy matching

The repetition operators ?,+,* and {m,n} normally match as much as the target string as possible. You can modify the operators with a question mark to be "nongreedy," and match as little of the target string as possible. For example, when matched against the string "over the top," \b.*\b would normally match the entire string. The corresponding non-greedy version, \b.*?\b, matches only the first word, "over."

Extensions

Syntax n of the form (?...) marks a regular expression *extension*. The meaning of the extension depends on the character after the question mark.

(?#...)	Is a comment. Python ignores this portion of the regular expression.
(?P<name>...)	Creates a named group. Named groups work like numbered groups. You can match them again using (?P=name). For example, this regular expression matches a single word that begins and ends with the same letter: ^(?P<letter>\w)\w*(?P=letter)$. A named group receives a number, and can be referred to by number or by name.
(?:...)	Are non-grouping parentheses. You can use these to enhance readability; they don't change the regular expression's behavior. For example, (?:\w+)(\d)\1 matches one or more letters followed by a repeated digit, such as "bob99" or "x22." The string (?:\w+) does not create a group, so \1 matches the first group, (\d).
(?i), (?L), (?m),(?s), (?u),(?x)	Are REs that set the flags re.I, re.L, re.M, re.S, re.U, and re.X respectively. Note that (?L) uses an uppercase letter; the others are lowercase.

(?=...)   Is a lookahead assertion. Python matches the enclosed regular
                       expression, but does not "consume" any of the target string. For
                       example, blue(?=berry) matches the string "blue," but only if
                       it is followed by "berry."

(?!...)   Is a negative lookahead assertion. The enclosed regular
                       expression must *not* match the target string. For example,
                       electron(?!ic\b) matches the string "electron" only when it
                       is not part of the word "electronic."

Creating and Using Regular Expression Objects

The function re.compile(pattern[, flags]) compiles the specified *pattern*
string and returns a new regular expression object. The optional parameter *flags*
tweak the behavior of the expression. Each flag value has a long name and an
equivalent short name.

You can combine flags using bitwise or. For example, this line returns a regular
expression that searches for two occurrences of the word "the," ignoring case, with
any character (including newline) in between.

```
re.compile("the.the",re.IGNORECASE | re.DOTALL)
```

re.IGNORECASE, re.I	Performs case-insensitive matching.
re.LOCALE, re.L	Interprets words according to the current locale. This interpretation affects the alphabetic group (\w and \W), as well as word boundary behavior (\b and \B).
re.MULTILINE, re.M	Makes $ match the end of a line (not just the end of the string) and makes ^ match the start of any line (not just the start of the string).
re.DOTALL, re.S	Makes a period (dot) match *any* character, including a newline.
re.UNICODE, re.U	Interprets letters according to the Unicode character set. This flag affects the behavior of \w, \W, \b, \B.
re.VERBOSE, re.X	Permits "cuter" regular expression syntax. It ignores whitespace (except inside a set [] or when escaped by a backslash), and treats unescaped # as a comment marker. For example, the following two lines of code are equivalent. They match a single word containing three consecutive pairs of doubled letters, such as "zrqqxxyy." (Finding an

English word matching this description is left as an exercise for the reader.) Note that the second VERBOSE form of the regular expression is a bit more readable.

```
NewRE = re.compile(r"^\w*(\w)\1(\w)\2(\w)\3\w*$")
NewRE = re.compile(r"^\w* (\w)\1 (\w)\2 (\w)\3 \w*$#three doubled letters",
                   re.VERBOSE)
```

Using regular expression objects

You can use regular expressions to search, replace, split strings, and more.

search(targetstring[,startindex[,endindex]])

The core use of a regular expression! The method search(targetstring) scans through *targetstring* looking for a match. If it finds one, it returns a MatchObject instance. If it finds no match, it returns None. (See below for MatchObject methods.) The search method searches the slice targetstring[startindex: endindex] — by default, the whole string.

The characters $ and ^ match the beginning and ending of the *entire* string, not necessarily the start or end of the substring. For example, ^friends$ does not match the string "are friends electric?" even if one takes the slice "friends" from index 4 to index 11.

match(targetstring[,startindex[,endindex]])

Attempts to match the regular expression against the first part of *targetstring*. The match method is more restrictive than search, as it must match the first zero or more characters of *targetstring*. It returns a MatchObject instance if it finds a match, None otherwise. The parameters *startindex* and *endindex* function here as they do in search.

findall(targetstring)

Matches against *targetstring* and returns a list of nonoverlapping matches. For example:

```
>>> re.compile(r"\w+").findall("the larch") # Greedy matching
['the', 'larch']
>>> re.compile(r"\w+?").findall("the larch") # Nongreedy
['t', 'h', 'e', 'l', 'a', 'r', 'c', 'h']
```

If the regular expression contains a group, the list returned is a list of group values (in tuple form, if it contains multiple groups). For example:

```
>>> re.compile(r"(\w+)(\w+)").findall("the larch")
[('th', 'e'), ('larc', 'h')]
```

split(targetstring[,maxsplit])

Breaks *targetstring* on each match of the regular expression, and returns a list of pieces. If the regular expression consists of a single large group, then the list of pieces includes the delimiting strings; otherwise, the list of pieces does not include the delimiters. If you specify a nonzero value for *maxsplit,* then `split` makes, at most, *maxsplit* cuts, and the remainder of the string remains intact.

For example, this regular expression removes all ifs, ands, and buts from a string:

```
>>> MyRE=re.compile(r"\bif\b|\band\b|\bbut\b",re.I)
>>> LongString="I would if I could, and I wish I could, but I
can't."""
>>> MyRE.split(LongString)
['I would ', ' I could, ', ' I wish I could, ', " I can't."]
>>> MyRE=re.compile(r"(\bif\b|\band\b|\bbut\b)",re.I)
>>> MyRE.split(LongString) # Keep the matches in the list.
['I would ', 'if', ' I could, ', 'and', ' I wish I could, ',
'but', " I can't."]
```

sub(replacement, targetstring[, count])

Search for the regular expression in *targetstring,* and perform a substitution at each match. The parameter *replacement* can be a string. It can also be a function that takes a MatchObject as an argument, and returns a string. If you specify a nonzero value for *count,* then `sub` makes, at most, *count* substitutions.

This example translates a string to "Pig Latin." (It moves any leading consonant cluster to the end of the word, then adds "ay" so that "chair" becomes "airchay.")

```
>>> def PigLatinify(thematch):
>>> ...     return thematch.group(2)+thematch.group(1)+"ay"
>>> ...
>>> WordRE=re.compile(r"\b([b-df-hj-np-tv-z]*)(\w+)\b",re.I)
>>> WordRE.sub(PigLatinify, "fetch a comfy chair")
'etchfay aay omfycay airchay'
```

If *replacement* is a string, it can contain references to groups from the regular expression. For example, `sub` replaces a `\1` or `\g<1>` in *replacement* with the first group from the regular expression. You can insert named groups with the syntax `\g<name>`.

The `sub` method replaces empty (length-0) matches only if they are not adjacent to another substitution.

subn(replacement, targetstring[, count])

Same as `sub`, but returns a two-tuple whose first element is the new string, and whose second element is the number of substitutions made.

Applying regular expressions without compiling

The methods of a regular expression object correspond to functions in the re module. If you call these functions directly, you don't need to call re.compile in your code. However, if you plan to use a regular expression several times, it is more efficient to compile and reuse it. The following module functions are available:

escape(str)

Returns a copy of *str* with all special characters escaped. This feature is useful for making a regular expression for an arbitrary string. For example, this function searches for a substring in a larger string, just like string.find, but case-insensitively:

```
def InsensitiveFind(BigString,SubString):
    TheMatch = re.search(re.escape(SubString),BigString,re.I)
    if (TheMatch):
        return TheMatch.start()
    else:
        return -1
```

search(pattern,targetstring[,flags])

Compiles *pattern* into a regular expression object with *flags* set, then uses it to perform a search against *targetstring*.

match(pattern,targetstring[,flags])

Compiles *pattern* into a regular expression object with *flags* set, then uses it to perform a match against *targetstring*.

split(pattern,targetstring[,maxsplit])

Compiles *pattern* into a regular expression object, then uses it to split *targetstring*.

findall(pattern,targetstring)

Compiles *pattern* into a regular expression object, then uses it to find all matches in *targetstring*.

sub(pattern,replacement,targetstring[,count])

Compiles *pattern* into a regular expression object, then calls its sub method with parameters *replacement*, *targetstring*, and *count*. The function subn is similar, but calls the subn method instead.

Using Match Objects

Searching with a regular expression object returns a MatchObject, or None if the search finds no matches. The match object has several methods, mostly to provide details on groups used in the match.

group([groupid,...])

Returns the substring matched by the specified group. For index 0, it returns the substring matched by the *entire* regular expression. If you specify several group identifiers, group returns a tuple of substrings for the corresponding groups. If the regular expression includes named groups, *groupid* can be a string.

groups([nomatch])

Returns a tuple of substrings matched by each group. If a group was not part of the match, its corresponding substring is *nomatch*. The parameter *nomatch* defaults to None.

groupdict([nomatch])

Returns a dictionary. Each entry's key is a group name, and the value is the substring matched by that named group. If a group was not part of the match, its corresponding value is *nomatch*, which defaults to None.

This example creates a regular expression with four named groups. The expression parses fractions of the form "1 1/3," splitting them into integer part, numerator, and denominator. Non-fractions are matched by the "plain" group.

```
>>> FractionRE=re.compile(
... r"(?P<plain>^\d+$)?(?P<int>\d+(?= ))?
?(?P<num>\d+(?=/))?/?(?P<den>\d+$)?")
>>> FractionRE.match("1 1/3").groupdict()
{'den': '3', 'num': '1', 'plain': None, 'int': '1'}
>>> FractionRE.match("42").groupdict("x")
{'den': 'x', 'num': 'x', 'plain': '42', 'int': 'x'}
```

start([groupid]), end([groupid]), span([groupid])

The methods start and end return the indices of the substring matched by the group identified by *groupid*. If the specified group didn't contribute to the match, they return -1.

The method span(groupid) returns both indices in tuple form: (start(groupid),end(groupid)).

By default, *groupid* is 0, indicating the entire regular expression.

re,string,pos,endpos,

These members hold the parameters passed to search or match:

- ✦ **re** — The regular expression object used in the match
- ✦ **string** — The string used in the match
- ✦ **pos** — First index of the substring searched against
- ✦ **endpos** — Last index of the substring searched against

Treating Strings as Files

The module *StringIO* defines a class named StringIO. This class wraps an in-memory string buffer, and supports standard file operations. Since a StringIO instance does not correspond to an actual file, calling its `close` method simply frees the buffer. The StringIO constructor takes, as a single optional parameter, an initial string for the buffer.

The method *getvalue* returns the contents of the buffer. It is equivalent to calling `seek(0)` and then `read()`.

 Cross-Reference See Chapter 8 for a description of the standard file operations.

The module cStringIO defines a similar class, also named StringIO. Because cStringIO.StringIO is implemented in C, it is faster than StringIO.StringIO; the one drawback is that you cannot subclass it. The module cStringIO defines two additional types: InputType is the type for StringIO objects constructed with a string parameter, and OutputType is the type for StringIO objects constructed without a string parameter.

The StringIO class is useful for building up long strings without having to do many small concatenations. For instance, the function demonstrated in Listing 9-1 builds up an HTTP request string, suitable for transmission to a Web server:

Listing 9-1: **httpreq.py**

```
import re
import urlparse
import cStringIO
import string
import socket
```

Continued

Listing 9-1 *(continued)*

```python
STANDARD_HEADERS = """HTTP/1.1
Accept: image/gif, image/x-xbitmap, image/jpeg, */*
Accept-Language: en-us
Accept-Encoding: gzip, deflate
User-Agent: Mozilla/4.0 (compatible)"""
def CreateHTTPRequest(URL, CookieDict):
    """ Create an HTTP request for a given URL (as returned by
    urlparse.urlparse) and a dictionary of cookies (where key
    is the host string, and the value is the cookie in the
    form "param=value". """
    Buffer = cStringIO.StringIO()
    Buffer.write("GET ")
    FileString = URL[2] # File name
    if URL[3]!="": # Posted values
        FileString = FileString + ";" + URL[3]
    if URL[4]!="": # Query parameters
        FileString = FileString + "?" + URL[4]
    FileString = string.replace(FileString," ","%20")
    Buffer.write(FileString+"\r\n")
    Buffer.write(STANDARD_HEADERS)
    # Add cookies to the request.
    GotCookies=0
    for HostString in CookieDict.keys():
        # Perform a case-insensitive search. (Call re.escape so
        # special characters like . are searched for normally.)
        if (re.search(re.escape(HostString),URL[1],re.I)):
            if (GotCookies==0):
                Buffer.write("\r\nCookie: ")
                GotCookies=1
            else:
                Buffer.write("; ")
            Buffer.write(CookieDict[HostString])
    if (GotCookies):
        Buffer.write("\r\n")
    Buffer.write("Host: "+URL[1])
    Buffer.write("\r\n\r\n")
    RequestString=Buffer.getvalue()
    Buffer.close()
    return RequestString

if (__name__=="__main__"):
    CookieDict={}
    CookieDict["python"]="cookie1=value1"
    CookieDict["python.ORG"]="cookie2=value2"
    CookieDict["amazon.com"]="cookie3=value3"
    URL = urlparse.urlparse("http://www.python.org/2.0/")
    print CreateHTTPRequest(URL,CookieDict)
```

Encoding Text

All digital data, including text, is ultimately represented as ones and zeroes. A *character set* is a way of encoding text as binary numbers. For example, the ASCII character set represents letters using a number from 0 to 255. The built-in function *ord* returns the number corresponding to an ASCII character; the function *chr* returns the ASCII character corresponding to a number:

```
>>> ord('a')
97
>>> chr(97)
'a'
```

The ASCII character set has limitations — it does not contain Cyrillic letters, Chinese ideograms, et cetera. And so, various character sets have been created to handle various collections of characters. The Unicode character set is the mother of all character sets. Unicode subsumes ASCII and Latin-1. It also includes all widely used alphabets, symbols of some ancient languages, and everything but the kitchen sink.

Using Unicode strings

A Unicode string behaves just like an ordinary string — it has the same methods. You can denote a string literal as Unicode by prefixing it with a u. You can denote Unicode characters with \u followed by four hexadecimal digits. For example:

```
>>> MyUnicodeString=u"Hello"
>>> MyString="Hello"
>>> MyUnicodeString==MyString # Legal comparison
1
>>> MyUnicodeString=u"\ucafe\ubabe"
>>> len(MyUnicodeString)
2
>>> MyString="\ucafe\ubabe" # No special processing!
>>> len(MyString)
12
```

For a reference on the Unicode character set, and its character categories, see `http://www.unicode.org/Public/UNIDATA/UnicodeData.html`.

Reading and writing non-ASCII strings

You cannot use Unicode characters with an ordinary file object created by the open function:

```
>>> MyUnicodeString=u"\ucafe\ubabe"
>>> ASCIIFile=open("test.txt","w") # This file can't handle
unicode!
>>> ASCIIFile.write(MyUnicodeString)
Traceback (innermost last):
  File "<pyshell#39>", line 1, in ?
    ASCIIFile.write(MyUnicodeString)
UnicodeError: ASCII encoding error: ordinal not in range(128)
```

The codecs module provides file objects to help read and write Unicode text.

open(filename,mode[,encoding[,errorhandler[,buffering]]])

The function codecs.open returns a file object that can handle the character set specified by *encoding*. The *encoding* parameter is a string specifying the desired encoding. The *errorhandler* parameter, which defaults to "strict," specifies what to do with errors. The "ignore" handler skips characters not in the character set; the "strict" handler raises a ValueError for unacceptable characters. The *mode* and *buffering* parameters have the same effect as for the built-in function open.

```
>>> Bob=codecs.open("test-uni.txt","w","unicode-escape")
>>> Bob.write(MyUnicodeString)
>>> Bob.close()
>>> Bob=codecs.open("test-utf16.txt","w","utf16")
>>> Bob.write(MyUnicodeString)
>>> Bob.close()
```

You should generally read and write files using the same character set, or extreme garbling can result. The function sys.getdefaultencoding returns the name of the current default encoding.

EncodedFile(fileobject,sourceencoding[,fileencoding[,errorhandler]])

The function codecs.EncodedFile returns a wrapper object for the file *fileobject* to handle character set translation. This function translates data written to the file from the *sourceencoding* character set to the *fileencoding* character set; data read from the file does the reverse. For example, this code writes a file using UTF-8 encoding, then translates from UTF-8 to escaped Unicode:

```
>>> UTFFile=codecs.open("utf8.txt","w","utf8")
>>> UTFFile.write(MyUnicodeString)
>>> UTFFile.close()
>>> MyFile=open("utf8.txt","r")
>>> Wrapper=codecs.EncodedFile(MyFile,"unicode-escape","utf8")
>>> Wrapper.read()
'\\uCAFE\\uBABE'
```

Using the Unicode database

The module `unicodedata` provides functions to check a character's meaning in the Unicode 3.0 character set.

Categorization

These functions give information about a character's general category:

category(unichr)	Returns a string denoting the category of *unichr*. For example, underscore has category "PC" for connector punctuation.
bidirectional(unichr)	Returns a string denoting the bidirectional category of *unichr*. For example, `unicode.bidirectional(u"e")` is "L," indicating that "e" is normally written left-to-right.
combining(unichr)	Returns an integer indicating the combining class of *unichr*. Returns 0 for non-combining characters.
mirrored(unichr)	Returns 1 if *unichr* is a mirrored character, 0 otherwise.
decomposition(unichr)	Returns the character-decomposition string corresponding to *unichr*, or a blank string if no decomposition exists.

Numeric characters

These functions give details about numeric characters:

decimal(unichr[,default])	Returns *unichr*'s decimal value as an integer. If *unichr* has no decimal value, returns *default* or (if *default* is unspecified) raises a `ValueError`.
numeric(unichr[,default])	Returns *unichr*'s numeric value as a float. If *unichr* has no decimal value, returns *default* or (if *default* is unspecified) raises a `ValueError`.
digit(unichr[,default])	Returns *unichr*'s digit value as an integer. If *unichr* has no digit value, returns *default* or (if *default* is unspecified) raises a `ValueError`.

Formatting Floating Point Numbers

The `fpformat` module provides convenience functions for displaying floating point numbers.

fix(number,precision)

Formats floating point value *number* with at least one digit before the decimal point, and at most *precision* digits after. The number is rounded to the specified precision as needed. If precision is zero, this function returns a string with the number rounded to the nearest integer. The parameter number can be either a float, or a string that can be passed to the function `float`.

sci(number,precision)

Formats floating point value number in scientific notation — one digit before the decimal point, and the exponent indicated afterwards. The parameters *number* and *precision* behave as they do for the function `fix`.

Here are some examples of formatting with `fpformat`:

```
>>> fpformat.fix(3.5,0)
'4'
>>> fpformat.fix(3.555,2)
'3.56'
>>> fpformat.sci(3.555,2)
'3.56e+000'
>>> fpformat.sci("0.03555",2)
'3.56e-002'
```

These functions raise the exception `fpformat.NotANumber` (a subclass of ValueError) if the parameter *number* is not a valid value. The exception argument is the value of *number*.

Summary

Python offers a full suite of string-manipulation functions. It also provides regular expressions, which enable even more powerful searching and replacing. In this chapter you:

   ✦ Searched, formatted, and modified string objects.

   ✦ Searched and parsed strings using regular expressions.

   ✦ Formatted floating point numbers cleanly and easily.

In the next chapter you'll learn how Python can handle files and directories.

✦   ✦   ✦

Working with Files and Directories

♦ ♦ ♦ ♦

In This Chapter

Retrieving file and directory information

Building and dissecting paths

Listing directories and matching file names

Obtaining environment and argument information

Example: Recursive Grep Utility

Copying, renaming, and removing paths

Creating directories and temporary files

Comparing files and directories

Working with file descriptors

Other file processing techniques

♦ ♦ ♦ ♦

Chapter 8 discussed the basics of file input and output in Python, but the routines covered there assume you know what file you want to read and write and where it's located. This chapter explains operating system features that Python supports such as finding a list of files that match a given search pattern, navigating directories, and renaming and copying files.

This chapter and the next cover many modules, primarily `os`, `os.path`, and `sys`. Instead of organizing the chapters around the functions provided in each module, we've tried to group them by feature so that you can find what you need quickly. For example, you can find a file's size with `os.stat(filename)` `[stat.ST_SIZE]` or with `os.path.getsize(filename)` (something you wouldn't know unless you read through both the `os` and `os.path` modules), so I cover them in the same section. Where this is not possible, I've added cross-references to help guide you.

Retrieving File and Directory Information

With the exception of a few oddballs, modern operating systems let you store files in *directories* (locations in a named hierarchy or tree) for better organization. (Just imagine the mess if everything was in one chaotic lump.) This and the following sections consider a *path* to be a directory or file name. You can refer to a path *relative* to another one (`..\temp\bob.txt` means go up the tree a step, down into the `temp` directory to the file called `bob.txt`) while others are *absolute* (`/usr/local/bin/destroystuff` tells how to go from the top of the tree all the way down to `destroystuff`).

The Secret Identities of os and os.path

The os module contains plenty of functions for performing operating system-ish stuff like changing directories and removing files, while os.path helps extract directory names, file names, and extensions from a given path.

The great thing is that these modules work on any Python-supported platform, making your programs much more portable. For example, to join a directory name with a file name, using os.path.join makes sure the result is correct for the current operating system:

```
>>> print os.path.join('maps','dungeon12.map')
maps\dungeon12.map      # Result when run on Windows
>>> print os.path.join('maps','dungeon12.map')
maps/dungeon12.map      # Result when run on UNIX
```

To make this happen, each platform defines two modules to do the platform-specific work. (On Macintosh systems they are mac and macpath; on Windows they're nt and ntpath, and so on.) When the os module is imported, it looks inside sys.builtin_module_names for the name of a platform-specific module (such as nt), loads its contents into the os namespace, and then loads the platform-specific path module and renames it to os.path.

You can check the os.name variable to see which operating system-specific module os loaded, but you should rarely need to use it. The whole point of os and os.path is to make your programs blissfully ignorant of the underlying operating system.

You can choose how you want to access path information: Python provides several functions to retrieve a single bit of information (does this path exist?) or all of it in one big glob (give me creation time, last access time, file size, and so forth).

Note   Please note that many of the examples in this chapter use file and directory names that may not exist in your system. Accept the examples on faith or substitute valid file names of your own (just don't go and erase something important, though).

The piecemeal approach

The access(path, mode) function tests to see that the current process has permission to read, write, or execute a given path. The mode parameter can be any combination of os.R_OK (read permission), os.W_OK (write permission), or os.X_OK (execute permission):

```
>>> os.access('/usr/local',os.R_OK | os.X_OK)
1           # I have read AND execute permissions...
>>> os.access('/usr/local',os.W_OK)
0           # ...but not write permissions.
```

You can also use a mode of os.F_OK to test if the given path exists. Or you can use the os.path.exists(path) function:

```
>>> os.path.exists('c:\\winnt') # '\\' to "escape" the slash
1
```

The inverse of access is os.chmod(path, mode) which lets you set the mode for the given path. The mode parameter is a number created by adding different octal values listed in Table 10-1. For example, to give the owner read/write permissions, group members read permissions, and others no access to a file:

```
os.chmod('secretPlans.txt',0640)
```

Tip

The first few times you use this function you may forget that the values in Table 10-1 are *octal* numbers. This is a convention held over from the underlying C chmod function; as octals, the different mode values combine in that cute way while making the implementation easier. Remember to stick in the leading zero on the mode so that Python sees it as an octal, and not a decimal, number.

Table 10-1	
Values for os.chmod	
Value	*Description*
0400	Owner can read the path.
0200	Owner can write the path.
0100	Owner can execute the file or search the directory.
0040	Group members can read the path.
0020	Group members can write the path.
0010	Group members can execute the file or search the directory.
0004	Others can read the path.
0002	Others can write the path.
0001	Others can execute the file or search the directory.

Note

Different operating systems handle permissions differently (Windows, for example, doesn't really manage file permissions with owners and groups). You should try a few tests out before relying on a particular behavior. Also, consult the UNIX chmod man page for additional mode values that vary by platform.

The os.path.isabs(path) function returns 1 if the given path is an absolute path. On UNIX systems, a path is absolute if it starts with '/'; on Windows, paths are absolute if they either start with a backlash or if they start with a drive letter followed by a colon and a backslash:

```
>>> os.path.isabs('c:\\temp')
1
>>> os.path.isabs('temp\\foo')
0
```

The following four functions in the os.path module, isdir(path), isfile(path), islink(path), and ismount(path), test what kind of file system entry the given path refers to:

```
>>> os.path.isdir('c:\\winnt') # Is it a directory?
1
>>> os.path.isfile('c:\\winnt') # Is it a normal file?
0
>>> os.path.islink('/usr/X11R6/bin/X') # Is it a symbolic link?
1
>>> os.path.ismount('c:\\') # It is a mount point?
1
```

On platforms that support symbolic links, isdir and isfile return true if the path is a link to a directory or file, and the os.readlink(path) function returns the actual path to which a symbolic link points.

A mounting point is essentially where two file systems connect. On UNIX, ismount returns true if path and path/.. have a different device or inode. On Windows, ismount returns true for paths like c:\ and \\endor\.

Note An *inode* is a UNIX file system data structure that holds information about a directory entry. Each directory entry is uniquely identified by a device number and an inode number. Some of the following routines may return inode numbers; for UNIX machines these are valid, but for other platforms they are just dummy values.

You can retrieve a file's size in bytes using os.path.getsize(path):

```
>>> os.path.getsize('c:\\winnt\\uninst.exe')
299520 # About 290K
```

The os.path.getatime(path) and os.path.getmtime(path) functions return the path's last access and modified times, respectively, in seconds since the *epoch* (you know, New Year's Eve 1969):

```
>>> os.path.getmtime('c:\\winnt\\readme.exe')
786178800
>>> os.path.getatime('c:\\winnt\\readme.exe')
956901600
>>> import time
>>> time.ctime(os.path.getatime('c:\\winnt\\readme.exe'))
'Fri Apr 28 00:00:00 2000'
```

Going the other direction, the `os.utime(path, (atime, mtime))` function sets the time values for the given path. The following example sets the last access and modification times of a file to noon on March 1, 1977:

```
>>> sec = time.mktime((1977,3,1,12,0,0,-1,-1,-1))
>>> os.utime('c:\\temp\\foo.txt',(sec,sec))
```

You can also "touch" a file's times so that they are set to the current time:

```
>>> os.utime('c:\\temp\\foo.txt',None) # Set to current time.
```

 See the `time` module in Chapter 13 for a discussion of its features and a better definition of the epoch.

UNIX-compatible systems have the `os.chown(path, userID, groupID)` that changes the ownership of a path to that of a different user and group:

```
os.chown('grumpy.png',os.getuid(),os.getgid())
```

 Chapter 11 covers functions to get and set group and user IDs.

Non-Windows systems include the `os.path.samefile(path1,path2)` and `os.path.sameopenfile(f1,f2)` functions that return true if the given paths or file objects refer to the same item on disk (they reside on the same device and have the same inode).

The I-want-it-all approach

If you want to know several pieces of information about a path (for example, you need to know a file's size as well as the time it was last modified), the previous functions are inefficient because each one results in a call to the operating system. The `os.stat(path)` function solves this problem by returning a tuple with ten pieces of information all at once (many of the previous section's functions quietly call os.stat behind the scenes and throw away the information you didn't request):

```
>>> os.stat('c:\\winnt\\uninst.exe')
(33279, 0, 2, 1, 0, 0, 299520, 974876400, 860551690, 955920365)
```

Don't worry too much if the numbers returned look useless! The `stat` module provides names (listed in Table 10-2) for indexes into the tuple:

```
>>> import stat
>>> os.stat('c:\\winnt\\uninst.exe')[stat.ST_SIZE] # File size
299520 # Hmm... still about 290K
```

Table 10-2
Index Names for os.stat Tuple

Name	Description
ST_SIZE	File size (in bytes)
ST_ATIME	Time of last access (in seconds since the epoch)
ST_MTIME	Time of last modification (in seconds since the epoch)
ST_MODE	Mode (see below for possible values)
ST_CTIME	Time of last status change (access, modify, chmod, chown, and so on)
ST_UID	Owner's user ID
ST_GID	Owner's group ID
ST_NLINK	Number of links to the inode
ST_INO	inode's number
ST_DEV	inode's device

Once you have a path's mode value (stat.ST_MODE), you can use other stat-provided functions to test for certain types of path entries (see Table 10-3 for the complete list):

```
>>> mode = os.stat('c:\\winnt')[stat.ST_MODE]
>>> stat.S_ISDIR(mode)  # Is it a directory?
1                       # Yes!
```

Table 10-3
Path Type Test Functions

Function	Returns true for
S_ISREG(mode)	Regular file
S_ISDIR(mode)	Directory
S_ISLNK(mode)	Symbolic link
S_ISFIFO(mode)	FIFO (named pipe)
S_ISSOCK(mode)	Socket
S_ISBLK(mode)	Special block device
S_ISCHR(mode)	Special character device

When you call `os.stat` with a path to a symbolic link, it returns information about the path that the link references. The `os.lstat(path)` function behaves just like `os.stat` except that on symbolic links it returns information about the link itself (although the OS still borrows much of the information from the file it references).

See "Working with File Descriptors" later in this chapter for coverage of the `os.fstat` function that returns stats for open file descriptors.

On UNIX-compatible systems you can call `os.samestat(stat1,stat2)` to see if two sets of stats refer to the same file (it compares the device and inode number).

The Python standard library also comes with the `statcache` module, which behaves just like `os.stat` but caches the results for later use:

```
>>> import statcache
>>> statcache.stat('c:\\temp')
(16895, 0, 2, 1, 0, 0, 0, 975999600, 969904112, 969904110)
```

You can call `forget(path)` to remove a particular cached entry, or `reset()` to remove them all. The `forget_prefix(prefix)` function removes all entries that start with a given prefix, and `forget_except_prefix(prefix)` removes all that do *not* start with the prefix (removing a cache entry means a call to `stat` will have to check with the operating system again). The `forget_dir(prefix)` function removes all entries in a directory, but not in its subdirectories.

Building and Dissecting Paths

The different path conventions that operating systems follow can make path manipulation a nuisance. Fortunately Python has plenty of routines to help.

Joining path parts

The `os.path.join(part[, part...])` joins any number of path components into a path valid for the current operating system:

```
>>> print os.path.join('c:','r2d2','c3po','r5d4')
c:\r2d2\c3po\r5d4
>>> print os.path.join(os.pardir,os.pardir,'tmp')
..\..\tmp
```

The separator character used is defined in `os.sep`. You can use `os.curdir` and `os.pardir` with join when you want to refer to the current and parent directories, respectively.

Breaking paths into pieces

Given a path, it's not too hard to separate it into its pieces (file name, extension, directory name, and so on) using one of the os.path.split functions:

```
>>> os.path.split(r'c:\temp\foo.txt') # Yay, raw strings!
('c:\\temp', 'foo.txt') # Split into path and filename.
>>> os.path.splitdrive(r'c:\temp\foo.txt')
('c:', '\\temp\\foo.txt') # Split off the drive.
>>> os.path.splitext(r'c:\temp\foo.txt')
('c:\\temp\\foo', '.txt') # Split off the extension.
>>> os.path.splitunc(r'\\endor\temp\foo.txt')
('\\\\endor\\temp', '\\foo.txt') # Split off machine and mount.
```

The splitdrive function is present on UNIX systems, but for any path just returns the tuple ('',path); the splitunc function is available only on Windows.

The os.path.dirname(path) and os.path.basename(path) functions are short-hand functions that together return the same information as split:

```
>>> os.path.dirname(r'c:\temp\foo.txt')
'c:\\temp'
>>> os.path.basename(r'c:\temp\foo.txt')
'foo.txt'
```

Other path modifiers

The os.path.normcase(path) function normalizes the case of a path (makes it all lowercase on case-insensitive platforms, leaves it unchanged on others) and replaces forward slashes with backwards slashes on Windows platforms:

```
>>> print os.path.normcase('kEwL/lAmeR/hAckUr/d00d')
kewl\lamer\hackur\d00d
```

The os.path.normpath(path) function normalizes a given path by removing redundant separator characters and collapsing references to the parent directory (it also fixes forward slashes for Windows systems):

```
>>> print os.path.normpath(r'c:\work\\\temp\..\..\games')
c:\games
```

The os.path.abspath(path) function normalizes the path and then converts it to an absolute path:

```
>>> os.getcwd()
'/export/home'
>>> os.path.abspath('fred/backup/../temp/cool.py')
'/export/home/fred/temp/cool.py'
```

The os.path.expandvars(path) function searches the given path for variable names of the form $varname and ${varname}. If the variables are defined in the environment, expandvars substitutes in their values, leaving undefined variable references in place (you can use $$ to print $):

```
>>> os.environ.update({'WORK':'work','BAKFILE':'kill.bak'})
>>> p = os.path.join('$WORK','${BAKFILE}')
>>> print os.path.expandvars(p)
work\kill.bak
```

The os.path.expanduser(path) function replaces "~" or "~*username*" at the beginning of a path with the path to the user's home directory. For "~" (meaning the current user), expanduser uses the value of the HOME environment variable if present. On Windows, if HOME is not defined, then it also tries to find and join HOMEDRIVE and HOMEPATH, returning the original path unchanged if it fails. For users other than the current user ("~*username*"), Windows always returns the original path and UNIX uses the pwd module to locate that user's home directory.

Cross-Reference   See Chapter 38 to learn more about the pwd module.

Listing Directories and Matching File Names

This section lists several ways to retrieve a list of file names, whether they are all the files in a particular directory or all the files that match a particular search pattern.

The os.listdir(dir) function returns a list containing all the files in the given directory:

```
>>> os.listdir('c:\\sierra')
['LAND', 'Half-Life', 'SETUP.EXE']
```

The dircache module provides its own listdir function that maintains a cache to increase the performance of repeated calls (and uses the modified time on the directory to detect when a cache entry needs to be tossed out):

```
>>> import dircache
>>> dircache.listdir('c:\\sierra')
['Half-Life', 'LAND', 'SETUP.EXE']
```

The list returned is a reference, not a copy, so modifying it means your modifications are returned to future callers too. The module also has an annotate(head,list) function that adds a slash to the end of any entry in the list that is a directory:

```
>>> x = dircache.listdir('c:\\sierra')[:]  # Make a copy
>>> dircache.annotate('c:\\sierra',x)
>>> x
['Half-Life/', 'LAND/', 'SETUP.EXE']
```

Use the head parameter to join to each item in the list so that annotate can then call os.path.isdir.

The os.path.commonprefix(list) function takes a list of paths and returns the longest prefix that all items have in common:

```
>>> l = ['c:\\ax\\nine.txt','c:\\ax\\ninja.txt','c:\\axle']
>>> os.path.commonprefix(l)
'c:\\ax'
```

The os.path.walk(top,func,arg) function walks a directory tree starting at top, calling func in each directory. The function func should take three arguments: arg (whatever you passed to arg in the call to walk), dirname (the name of the current directory being visited), and names (a list of directory entries in this directory). The following example prints the names of any executable files in the d:\games directory or any of its subdirectories:

```
>>> def walkfunc(ext,dir,files):
...     goodFiles = [x for x in files if x.find(ext) != -1]
...     if goodFiles:
...         print dir,goodFiles
...
>>> os.path.walk('d:\\games',walkfunc,'.exe')
d:\games\Half-Life ['10051013.exe']
d:\games\q3a ['quake3.exe']
d:\games\q3a\Extras\cs ['sysinfo.exe']
```

With the fnmatch module you can test to see if a file name matches a specific pattern. Asterisks match everything, question marks match any single character:

```
>>> import fnmatch
>>> fnmatch.fnmatch('python','p*n')
1   # It's a match!
>>> fnmatch.fnmatch('python','pyth?n')
1
```

You can also enclose in square brackets a sequence of characters to match:

```
>>> fnmatch.fnmatch('python','p[a,e,i,o,u,y,0-9]thon')
1   # Matches p + [any vowel or number] + thon
>>> fnmatch.fnmatch('p5thon','p[a,e,i,o,u,y,0-9]thon')
1
>>> fnmatch.fnmatch('p5thon','p[!0-9]thon')
0   # Doesn't match p + [any char EXCEPT a digit] + thon
>>> fnmatch.fnmatch('python','p[!0-9]thon')
1
```

The fnmatch module also has a fnmatchcase(filename,pattern) function that forces a case-sensitive comparison regardless of whether or not the filesystem is case-sensitive.

The `glob` module takes the `fnmatch` module a step further by returning all the paths matching a search pattern you provide:

```
>>> import glob
>>> for file in glob.glob('c:\\da*\\?ytrack\\s*.*[y,e]'):
...     print file
c:\dave\pytrack\sdaily.py
c:\dave\pytrack\std.py
c:\dave\pytrack\StkHistInfo.py
c:\dave\mytrack\sdkaccess1.exe
c:\dave\mytrack\sdkaccess2.exe
```

Obtaining Environment and Argument Information

It's often useful to know a little about the world around Python. This section explains how to get and set environment variables, how to discover and change the current working directory, and how to read in options from the command line.

Environment variables

When you import the `os` module, it populates a dictionary named `environ` with all the environment variables currently in existence. You can use normal dictionary access to get and set the variables, and child processes or shell commands your programs execute see any changes you make:

```
>>> os.environ['SHELL']
'/usr/local/bin/tcsh'
>>> os.environ['BOO'] = `2 + 2`  # Convert value to string.
>>> print os.popen('echo $BOO').read()  # Use %BOO% on Win32.
4
```

Cross-Reference See Chapter 11 for information on child processes and executing shell commands.

The dictionary used is actually a subclass of `UserDict`, and requires that the value you assign be a string.

Current working directory

The current working directory is initially the directory in which you started the Python interpreter. You can find out what the current directory is and change to another directory using the `os.getcwd()` and `os.chdir(path)` functions:

```
>>> os.chdir('/usr/home')
>>> os.chdir('..')
>>> os.getcwd()
'/usr'
```

Command-line parameters

The `sys.argv` variable is a list containing the command-line parameters passed to the program on startup. Save the tiny program in Listing 10-1 to a file called `args.py` and try the following example from a command prompt:

```
C:\temp>args.py pants beable
There are 3 arguments
['C:\\temp\\args.py', 'pants', 'beable']
```

Listing 10-1: **args.py – Display Command-Line Arguments**

```
#!/usr/bin/env python
# Prints out command-line arguments

import sys
print 'There are %d arguments' % len(sys.argv)
print sys.argv
```

The `sys.argv` list always has a length of at least one; as in C, the item at index zero is the name of the script that is running. If you're running the Python interpreter in interactive mode, however, that item is present but is the empty string.

Example: Recursive Grep Utility

Listing 10-2 combines several of the features covered so far in this chapter to create `rgrep`, a grep-like utility that searches for a string in a list of files in the current directory or any subdirectory. The sample output below shows searching for "def" in any file that matches the pattern "d*.py" or "h*":

```
D:\Dev\pytrack>\rgrep.py def d*.py h*
D:\Dev\pytrack\dataio.py 185    def __init__(self,sTick):
D:\Dev\pytrack\dataio.py 189    def getData(self):
D:\Dev\pytrack\histInfo.py 9    def sum(self,count,tups,index):
D:\Dev\pytrack\histInfo.py 16   def ave(self,count,tups,index):
D:\Dev\pytrack\old\dataio.py 12   def __init__(self,sTick):
D:\Dev\pytrack\old\dataio.py 16   def getData(self):
...
```

Listing 10-2: **rgrep.py – Recursive File Search Utility**

```python
#!/usr/bin/env python
# Recursively searches for a string in a file or list of files.

import sys, os, fnmatch

def walkFunc(arg,dir,files):
    "Called by os.path.walk to process each dir"
    pattern,masks = arg

    # Cycle through each mask on each file.
    for file in files:
        for mask in masks:
            if fnmatch.fnmatch(file,mask):

                # Filename matches!
                name = os.path.join(dir,file)
                try:
                    # Read the file and search.
                    data = open(name,'rb').read()

                    # Do a quick check.
                    if data.find(pattern) != -1:
                        i = 0
                        data = data.split('\n')

                        # Now a line-by-line check.
                        for line in data:
                            i += 1
                            if line.find(pattern) != -1:
                                print name,i,line
                except (OSError,IOError):
                    pass
                break # Stop checking masks.

if __name__ == '__main__':
    if len(sys.argv) < 3:
        print 'Usage: %s pattern file [files...]' % sys.argv[0]
    else:
        try:

os.path.walk(os.getcwd(),walkFunc,(sys.argv[1],sys.argv[2:]))
        except KeyboardInterrupt:
            print '** Halted **'
```

Tip

UNIX shells usually expand wildcards before your program gets them, so when running this on UNIX you'd have to enclose in quotes command-line parameters that contain asterisks:

```
/usr/bin> rgrep.py alligator "*.txt"
```

You can use rgrep as a starting point for a more powerful search tool. For example, you could make it accept true regular expressions (as seen in Chapter 9) or make it support case-insensitive searches too. Although performance is pretty decent, you could fix the fact that rgrep reads the entire file into memory by reading the files one piece at a time.

Copying, Renaming, and Removing Paths

The routines to copy, rename, and remove paths are in the os and shutil modules. The shutil module aims to provide features normally found in command shells.

Copying and linking

The shutil.copyfile(src, dest) function copies a file from src to dest; shutil.copy(src, dest) does about the same thing, except that if dest is a directory it copies the file *into* that directory (just like when you copy a file in an MS-DOS or UNIX shell). copy also copies the permission bits of the file. The shutil.copy2 (src, dest) function is identical to copy except that it also copies last access and last modification times of the original file. shutil.copyfileobj(src, dest[, buflen]) copies two file-like objects, passing the optional buflen parameter to the source object's read function.

Cross-Reference   See Chapter 8 for more information on filelike objects.

The shutil.copymode (src, dest) function copies the permission bits of a file (see os.chmod earlier in this chapter), as does shutil.copystat(src, dest), which also copies last access and last modification times.

The shutil.copytree (src, dest[, symlinks]) function uses copy2 to recursively copy an entire tree. copytree raises an exception if dest already exists. If the symlinks parameter is 1, any symbolic links in the source tree also become symbolic links in the new copy of the tree. If symlinks is omitted or equal to zero, the copy of the tree contains copies of the files referenced by symbolic links.

On platforms that support links, os.symlink(src,dest) creates a symbolic link to src and names it dest, and os.link(src,dest) creates a hard link to src named dest.

Renaming

The os.rename(old,new) function renames a path, and os.renames(old,new) renames an entire path from one thing to another, creating new directories as needed and removing empty ones to cleanup when done. For example:

```
os.renames('cache/logs','/usr/home/dave/backup/0105')
```

basically moves the logs directory in cache to /usr/home/dave/backup and calls it 0105. If the cache directory is empty after the move, the function deletes it. Before the move, renames creates any intermediate directories along the way to make /usr/home/dave/backup/0105 a valid path. The old and new parameters can be individual files and not just entire directories.

Removing

The os.remove(filename) function deletes a file, os.rmdir(dir) removes an empty directory, and os.removedirs(dir) removes an empty directory and all empty parent directories.

If a directory is not empty, neither rmdir nor removedirs removes it. That job is reserved for shutil.rmtree(path[, ignore_errors[, onerror]]), which recursively deletes all files in the given directory (including the directory itself) as well as any subdirectories and their files. ignore_errors is 0 by default, if you supply a value of 1 then rmtree attempts to continue processing despite any errors that occur, and won't bother to tell you about them. You can provide a function in the onerror parameter to handle any errors that occur. The function must take three arguments, as shown in this example:

```
>>> def errFunc(raiser,problemPath,excInfo):
...        print raiser.__name__,'had problems with',problemPath
>>> shutil.rmtree('c:\\temp\\foo',0,errFunc)
rmdir had problems with c:\temp\foo\bar\yeah
rmdir had problems with c:\temp\foo\bar
rmdir had problems with c:\temp\foo
```

The arguments passed to your error function are the function object that raised an exception, the particular path it had a problem on, and information about the exception, equivalent to a call to sys.exc_info().

Caution   Please be careful with rmtree; it assumes you're smart and trusts your judgment. If you tell it to erase all your files on your hard drive, it'll obediently do so and without hesitation.

Creating Directories and Temporary Files

The os.mkdir(dir[, mode]) function creates a new directory. The optional mode parameter is for the permissions on the new directory, and they follow the form of those listed for os.chmod in Table 10-1. (If you don't supply mode, the directory has read, write, and execute permissions for everyone.)

The os.makedirs(dir[, mode]) function creates a new directory and any intermediate directories needed along the way:

```
>>> os.makedirs(r'c:\a\b\c\d\e\f\g\h\i')
>>> os.removedirs(r'c:\a\b\c\d\e\f\g\h\i')
```

Even though my computer didn't have an a directory or an a\b directory, and so on, makedirs took care of creating them until at last it created i, a subdirectory of h (and then I used os.removedirs to clean up the mess).

The tempfile module helps when you need to use a file as a temporary storage area for data. In such cases you don't generally care about a file name or where the file lives on disk, so tempfile takes care of that for you. Temporary files can help conserve memory by storing temporary information on disk instead of keeping it all loaded in memory.

The tempfile.mktemp([suffix]) function returns the absolute path to a unique temporary file name that does not exist at the time of the call, and includes the suffix in the file name if you supply it. Although two calls to mktemp won't return the same file name, it doesn't create the file, so it's possible (although quite unlikely) that if you wait long enough someone else may create a file by the same name. While it's safe to use the file name as soon as you get it, it isn't as safe to save a copy of the name and then at a later date expect to create a file by that name, for example.

You can set the tempfile.tempdir variable to tell mktemp where to store temporary files. By default, it tries its best to find a good home for them, first checking the values of the environment variables $TMPDIR, $TEMP, and $TMP. If none of them are defined, it then checks if it can create temporary files in known temporary file safe-havens such as /var/temp, /usr/tmp, or /tmp on UNIX and c:\temp or \temp on Windows. If all these fail, it'll try to use the current working directory. tempfile.gettempprefix() returns the prefix of the temporary files you have (you can set this value via tempfile.template).

The ultimate in hassle-free temporary files comes from the tempfile.TemporaryFile class. It gives you a file or filelike object that you can read and write to without worrying about cleanup when you're done. You use tempfile.TemporaryFile([mode[, bufsize[, suffix]]]) to create a new instance object. The following example figures out how many digits it takes to write out the numbers from 1 to high. (Of the many better ways to do this, the simplest improvement is simply to add the length of each number to a counter instead of building the entire string and taking its length, but that wouldn't give me an opportunity to use TemporaryFile now would it?):

```
>>> def digitCount(high):
...     import tempfile
...     f = tempfile.TemporaryFile()
...     for i in range(1,high+1):
...         f.write(`i`)
...     f.flush()
...     f.seek(0)
...     return len(f.read())
>>> digitCount(12)
15 # len('123456789101112') = 15
>>> digitCount(100)
192
>>> digitCount(100000)
488895
```

By default, mode is 'w+b' so you can read and write data and not worry about the type of data you're writing (binary or text). The optional bufsize argument gets passed to the open function, and the optional suffix argument is passed to mktemp. On UNIX systems, the file doesn't even have a directory entry, making it more secure. Other systems delete the temporary file as soon as you call close or when Python garbage collects the object.

On UNIX systems, the os module has three functions for working with temporary files. os.tmpfile() creates a new file object that you can read and write to. As with tempfile's TemporaryFile class, the file has no directory entry and ceases to exist when you close the file.

The os.tmpnam() function returns an absolute path to a unique file name suitable for use as a temporary file (it doesn't create an actual file). os.tempnam([dir, [prefix]]) does the same as tmpnam except that it enables you to specify the directory in which the file name will live, as well as supplies an optional prefix to use in the temporary file's name.

Comparing Files and Directories

The filecmp module aids in comparing files and directories. To compare two files, call filecmp.cmp(f1,f2[,shallow[,use_statcache]]):

```
>>> import filecmp
>>> open('one','wt').write('Hey')
>>> open('two','wt').write('Hey')
>>> filecmp.cmp('one','two')
1  # Files match
```

The shallow parameter defaults to 1, which means that if both are regular files with the same size and modification time, the comparison returns true. If they differ (or if shallow=0), the function compares the contents of the two. The use_statcache parameter defaults to 0 and cmp calls os.stat for file info. If 1, cmp calls statcache.stat.

The filecmp.cmpfiles(a, b, common[, shallow[, use_statcache]]) function takes a list of file names located in two directories (each file is in both directory a and b) and returns a three-tuple containing a list of files that compared equal, a list of those that were different, and a list of files that weren't regular files and therefore weren't compared. The shallow and use_statcache parameters behave the same as for cmp.

The dircmp class in the filecmp module can help you generate that list of common files, as well as do some other comparison work for you. You use filecmp.dircmp(a, b[, ignore[, hide]]) to create a new instance:

```
>>> d = filecmp.dircmp('c:\\Program Files','d:\\Program Files')
>>> d.report()
diff c:\Program Files d:\Program Files
Only in c:\Program Files : ['Accessories', 'Adobe', ...<snip>
Only in d:\Program Files : ['AnalogX', 'Paint Shop Pro...<snip>
Common subdirectories : ['WinZip', 'Yahoo!','work']
```

The ignore function is a list of file names to ignore (it defaults to ['RCS', 'CVS', 'tags']) and hide is a list of file names not to show in the listings (it defaults to [os.curdir, os.pardir], the entries corresponding to the current and parent directories).

The dircmp.report() method prints to standard output a comparison between a and b. dircmp.report_partial_closure() does the same, but also compares common immediate subdirectories. dircmp.report_full_closure() goes the whole nine yards and compares all common subdirectories, no matter how deep.

After you create a dircmp object, you can access any of the attributes listed in Table 10-4 for more information about the comparison.

Table 10-4
Other dircmp Object Attributes

Attribute	Description
left_list	Items in a after being filtered through hide and ignore
right_list	Items in b after being filtered through hide and ignore
common	Items in both a and b
left_only	Items only in a
right_only	Items only in b
common_dirs	Subdirectories found in both a and b
common_files	Files found in both a and b
common_funny	Items found in both a and b, but either the type differs between a and b or os.stat reports an error for that item
same_files	Common_files that are identical
diff_files	Common_files that are different
funny_files	Common_files that couldn't be compared
subdirs	Dictionary of dircmp objects—keys are common_dirs

Tip The Python distribution comes with ndiff (Tools/Scripts/ndiff.py), a utility that provides the details of what differs between two files (similar to the UNIX diff and Windows windiff utilities).

Working with File Descriptors

An alternative to using Python's file objects is to use file descriptors, a somewhat lower level approach to working with files.

General file descriptor functions

You create a file descriptor with the os.open(file, flags[, mode]) function. You can combine various values from the next table, Table 10-5, for the flags parameter, and the mode values are those you pass to os.chmod:

```
>>> fd = os.open('fumble.txt',os.O_WRONLY|os.O_CREAT)
>>> os.write(fd,'I like fudge')
12  # Wrote 12 bytes.
>>> os.close(fd)
>>> open('fumble.txt').read() # Use the nice Python way.
'I like fudge'
```

The os.dup(fd) function returns a duplicate of the given descriptor, and os.dup2(fd1,fd2) makes fd2 a duplicate of fd1, but closes fd2 first if necessary.

Given a file descriptor, you can use os.fdopen(fd[, mode[, bufsize]]) to create an open Python file object connected to the same file. The optional mode and bufsize arguments are the same as those used for the normal Python open function.

Table 10-5 File Descriptor Open Flags	
Name	**Description**
O_RDONLY	Allow reading only
O_WRONLY	Allow writing only
O_RDWR	Allow reading and writing
O_BINARY	Open in binary mode
O_TEXT	Open in text mode
O_CREAT	Create file if it does not exist
O_EXCL	Return error if create and file exists
O_TRUNC	Truncate file size to 0
O_APPEND	Append to the end of the file on each write
O_NONBLOCK	Do not block

The os module also has other flags such as O_DSYNC, O_RSYNC, O_SYNC, and O_NOCTTY. Their behavior varies by platform so you should consult the UNIX open man page for your system for details.

 The os.openpty function returns two file descriptors for a new pseudo-terminal. See Chapter 38 for details.

The following os file descriptor functions closely mirror their file method counterparts covered mostly in Chapter 8, "Input and Output":

```
close(fd)       isatty(fd)  lseek(fd,pos,how)       read(fd,n)
write(str)      fstat(fd)   ftruncate(fd,len)
```

UNIX systems can use the os.ttyname(fd) to retrieve the name of the terminal device the file descriptor represents (if it is a terminal):

```
>>> os.ttyname(1) # 1 is stdout
'/dev/ttyv1'
```

Pipes

A pipe is a communications mechanism through which you can read or write data as if it were a file. You use os.pipe() to create two file descriptors connected via a pipe:

```
>>> r,w = os.pipe() # One for reading, one for writing
>>> os.write(r,'Pipe dream')
>>> os.write(w,'Pipe dream')
10
>>> os.read(r, 1000)
'Pipe dream'
```

On UNIX, the os.mkfifo(path[, mode]) function creates a named pipe (FIFO) that you can use to communicate between processes. The mode defaults to read and write permissions for everyone (0666). After you create the FIFO on disk, you open it and read or write to it just like any other file.

Other File Processing Techniques

The modules below provide alternative methods for operating on file contents.

Randomly accessing lines in text files

The linecache module returns to you any line in any file you want:

```
>>> import linecache
```

```
>>> linecache.getline('linecache.py',5)
'that name.\012'
```

The first time you request a line from a particular file, it reads the file and caches the lines, but future calls for lines from the same file won't have to go back to the disk. Line numbers are 1-based (yes, line one is line one).

If keeping too many files around makes you nervous, you can call linecache.clearcache() to empty the cache. Also, calling linecache.checkcache() tosses out cached entries that are no longer valid.

Note

> This module was designed to read lines from modules (Python uses it to print traceback information in exceptions), so if linecache can't find the file you named it also searches for the file in the module search path.

Using memory-mapped files

A memory-mapped file (in the mmap module) behaves like some sort of file-mutable string hybrid. You can access individual characters and slices as well as change them, and you can use memory-mapped files with many routines that expect strings. (The re module, for example, is quite happy to do regular expression searching and mapping on a memory-mapped file.) They also work well for routines that operate on files, and you can commit to disk any changes you make to their contents.

When you create a new mmap object, you supply a file descriptor to a file opened for reading and writing and a length parameter specifying the number of bytes from the file the memory map will use:

```
>>> f = open('mymap','w+b')
>>> f.write('And now for something completely different')
>>> f.flush()
>>> import mmap
>>> m = mmap.mmap(f.fileno(),45) # Use the open file mymap.
>>> m[5:10]   # It slices.
'ow fo'
>>> m[5:10] = 'ew fi' # It dices.
>>> m[5:10]
'ew fi'
>>> m.flush(); m.close() # But wait, there's more!
1
>>> open('mymap').read()
'And new fir something completely different\000\000\000'
```

The Windows version for creating a new mmap object accepts an optional third argument of a string that represents the tag name for the mapping (Windows lets you have many mappings for the same file). If you use a mapping that doesn't exist, Python creates a new one; otherwise the mapping by that name is opened.

The UNIX version optionally takes `flags` and `prot` arguments. `flags` can be either `MAP_PRIVATE` or `MAP_SHARED` (the default), signifying that changes are visible only to the current process or are visible to all processes mapping the same portions of the file. The `prot` argument is the logical OR of arguments specifying the type of protection that mapping has, such as `PROT_READ | PROT_WRITE` (the default).

Tip Avoid using the optional flags if possible so that your code will work on Windows or UNIX.

You can use `mmap.size()` to retrieve the size of a `mmap` object, and `mmap.resize(newsize)` to change it:

```
>>> m.size()
50
>>> m.resize(100)
```

Call `mmap.flush([offset, size])` to save changes to disk. Passing no arguments flushes all changes to disk, otherwise the memory map flushes only `size` bytes starting at `offset`.

Caution Don't forget to flush. If you don't call flush, you have no guarantee that your changes will make it to disk.

All `mmap` objects have the `close()`, `tell()`, `seek()`, `read(num)`, `write(str)`, `readline()`, and `find(str[, start])` methods which behave just like their file and string counterparts. The `mmap.read_byte()` and `mmap.write_byte(byte)` methods are useful for reading and writing one byte at a time (the bytes are passed and returned as strings of length 1). You can copy data from one location to another within the memory-mapped file using `mmap.move(dest, src, count)`. It copies `count` bytes from `src` to `dest`.

Iterating over several files

The `fileinput` class lets you iterate over several files as if they were a single file, eliminating a lot of the housekeeping involved. Its designed use is for iterating all files passed in on the command line, processing each line individually:

```
>>> import fileinput
>>> for line in fileinput.input():
...     print line
```

The above example iterates over the files listed in sys.argv[1:] and prints out each line. The `input(files,inplace,backup)` function uses the command-line arguments if you don't pass it a `files` list. Any file (or command-line argument) that is just '-' reads from `stdin` instead. If the `inplace` parameter is 1, `fileinput` copies each file to a backup and routes any output on `stdout` to the original file, thus enabling in-place modification or filtering of each file. If `inplace` is 1 and you supply a value for `backup` (in the form of '.ext'), fileinput uses `backup`'s value as an extension when creating backups of the original files, and it doesn't erase the backups when finished.

While iterating over the files, you can call `fileinput.filename()` to get the name of the current file, and `filename.isstdin()` to test if the current file is actually `stdin`.

The `fileinput.lineno()` function gives you the overall line number of the line just read, and `fileinput.filelineno()` returns the number of that line within the current file. You can also call `fileinput.isfirstline()` to see if it is the first line of that file.

The `fileinput.nextfile()` function skips the rest of the current file and moves to the next one in the sequence, and `fileinput.close()` closes the sequence and quits.

Tip You can customize the `fileinput` functionality by subclassing the `fileinput.FileInput` class.

Summary

Python gives you a full toolbox of high-level functions to manipulate files and paths. In this chapter you learned to:

✦ Manipulate paths and retrieve file and directory information.

✦ Traverse directory trees and match file names to search patterns.

✦ Create and destroy directories and temporary files.

✦ Use file descriptors.

The next chapter covers more of Python's operating system features. You'll learn to access process information, start child processes, and run shell commands.

✦　　✦　　✦

Using Other Operating System Services

In This Chapter

Executing shell
commands and other
programs

Spawning child
processes

Handling process
information

Retrieving system
information

Managing
configuration files

Understanding error
names

Handling
asynchronous signals

This chapter finishes coverage of Python's main operating system services. One of the main points of focus is working outside the boundaries in which the interpreter is running. After you're done with this chapter you'll be able to execute commands in a sub-shell or spawn off an entirely new process.

Executing Shell Commands and Other Programs

The simplest way to execute a shell command is with the `os.system(cmd)` function (which is just a wrapper for the C `system` function). The following example uses the shell command `echo` to write contents to a file, including an environment variable set from within the Python interpreter:

```
>>> import os
>>> os.environ['GRUB'] = 'spam!'
>>> os.system('echo Mmm, %GRUB% > mm.txt')  #
Use $GRUB on UNIX
0
>>> print open('mm.txt').read()
Mmm, spam!
```

The return values vary by system and command, but 0 generally means the command executed successfully.

Unfortunately, `os.system` has some limitations. On Windows, your command runs in a separate MS-DOS window that rears its ugly head until the command is done, and on all operating systems it's kind of a pain to retrieve the output from the command (especially if the output is on both `stdout` and stderr). The next section shows how to get around this using the much cleaner calls to os.popen and friends.

Windows systems can use os.startfile(path) to launch a program by sending a file to the program associated with its file type. For example, if the current directory has a file called yoddle.html, you can launch a Web browser to view that file like this:

```
>>> os.startfile('yoddle.html')
```

The os.exec family of functions executes another program, but in doing so replaces the current process — your program doesn't continue when the exec function returns. Instead, your program terminates and at the same time launches a different program. Each of the exec functions comes in two versions: one that accepts a variable number of arguments and one that takes all the program's arguments in a list or tuple. All arguments are strings, and you always need to provide argument 0, which is just the name of the program being executed.

The os.execv(path,args) and os.execl(path, arg0, arg1, ...) functions execute the program pointed to by path and pass it the arguments. The following example shuts down the Python interpreter and launches the Windows calculator (the location of the calc program may vary):

```
>>> os.execv('c:\\winnt\\system32\\calc',['calc'])
```

The os.execvp(file, args) and os.execlp(file, arg0, arg1, ...) functions work the same as execv, except they look in the PATH environment variable to find the executable, so you don't have to name its absolute path. This example calls another Python interpreter, telling it to just print out a message. Note the use of the variable-argument form (execlp) and that you still have to list the program twice, once for the file argument, and once as argument 0:

```
>>> os.execlp('python','python','-c','"print \'Goodbye!\'"')
```

Tip If you need to modify the PATH environment variable, you can use os.defpath to see the default PATH used if it isn't set in the environment. os.pathsep is the separator character used between each directory listed in the PATH variable.

The os.execve(path, args, env) and os.execle(path, arg0, arg1, ..., env) functions are also like execv, except that you pass in a dictionary containing all the environment variables to be defined for the new program. The dictionary should contain string keys mapping to string values.

The final exec functions, os.execvpe(file, args, env) and os.execlpe(file, arg0, arg1, ..., env), are like execve and execvp combined. You pass in a file name instead of an absolute path because the functions search through the path for you, and you also pass in a dictionary of environment variables to use.

Note You don't *really* have to name the program twice for the exec calls. When supplying a value for argument 0, you can actually use any value you want. Be advised, however, that some programs (like gzip and gunzip) may expect argument 0 to have certain values.

Spawning Child Processes

Depending on your needs, you can start child processes using the popen, spawn, and fork functions.

popen functions

The popen family of functions opens pipes to communicate with a child process.

The os.popen(cmd[, mode[, bufsize]]) function opens a single pipe to read or write to another process. You pass in the command to execute in the cmd parameter, followed by an optional mode parameter to tell whether you'll be reading ('r') or writing ('w') with the pipe. An optional third parameter is a buffer size like the one used in the built-in open function. popen returns a file object ready for use:

```
>>> a = os.popen('dir /w /ad e:\\') # Mode defaults to 'r'.
>>> print a.read()
 Volume in drive E has no label.
 Volume Serial Number is 2C40-1AF5

 Directory of e:\

[RACER]          [maxdev]        [VideoDub]
[FlaskMPEG]      [Diablo II]     [archive]
[VNC]            [dxsdk]         [VMware]
[AnalogX]        [Python20]
...
```

The close() method of the file object returns None if the command was successful, or an error code if the command was unsuccessful.

The os.popen2(cmd[, bufsize[, mode]]) function is a more flexible alternative to popen; it returns to you the two-tuple (stdin, stdout) containing the standard input and output of the child process (the mode parameter is 't' for text or 'b' for binary). The following example uses the external program grep to look through lines of text and print any that have a colon character in them:

```
>>> someText = """
... def printEvents():
...     for i in range(100):
...         if i % 2 == 0:
...             print i
```

```
...       """
>>> w,r = os.popen2('grep ":"') # Grep for lines with ':'
>>> w.write(someText)
>>> w.close()
>>> print r.read()
def printEvents():
  for i in range(100):
    if i % 2 == 0:
```

Tip

Depending on the program you execute, you often need to flush or even close `stdin` of the child process in order to have it produce its output.

The `os.popen3(cmd[, bufsize[, mode]])` function does the same work as `popen2` but instead returns the three-tuple (`stdin`, `stdout`, `stderr`) of the child process. `os.popen4(cmd[, bufsize[, mode]])` does the same except that it returns the output of `stdout` and `stderr` together in a single stream for convenience. This function is a great way to execute arbitrary shell commands cleanly because you have to look in only one place for the output, and no matter what the command is, your users won't see error output sneaking past you and onto the screen. And on Windows systems, you don't get the ugly MS-DOS window while your command executes:

```
>>> w,r = os.popen4('iblahblahasdfasdfr *.foo')
>>> print r.read()
'iblahblahasdfasdfr' is not recognized as an internal or
external command, operable program or batch file.
```

New Feature

The `popen2`, `popen3`, and `popen4` functions were new in Python 2.0.

spawn functions

The `spawn` functions start a child process that doesn't replace the current process (like the `exec` functions do) unless specifically asked to. For example, to start up another Python interpreter (assuming it lives in `D:\Python20`) without stopping the current one:

```
>>> os.spawnl(os.P_NOWAIT,'d:\\python20\\python','python')
400 # Process ID of new interpreter
```

Like the `exec` functions, the `spawn` functions have many variations, as shown in the following paragraphs.

`os.spawnv(mode, path, args)` and `os.spawnl(mode, path, arg0, arg1, ...)` start a new child process.

`os.spawnve(mode, path, args, env)` and `os.spawnle(mode, path, arg0, arg1, ..., env)` start a child process using the environment variables contained in the dictionary `env`.

On UNIX systems, variants of each of the above functions search the current path for the program to execute, and are named `spawnlp`, `spawnlpe`, `spawnvp`, and `spawnvpe`.

The arguments passed in should include the program name for argument 0. A mode of `os.P_WAIT` forces the current thread to wait until the child process ends. `os.P_NOWAIT` runs the child process concurrently, and `os.P_OVERLAY` terminates the calling process before running the child process (making it identical to the `exec` functions). `os.P_DETACH` also runs the process concurrently, but in the background where it has no access to the console or the keyboard.

When you start a child process concurrently, the spawn function returns the process ID of the child process. If you use `os.P_WAIT` instead, the function returns the exit code of the child once the child process finally quits.

fork

The `os.fork()` function (available on UNIX systems) creates a new process that is a duplicate of the current process. To distinguish between the two processes, `os.fork()` returns 0 in the child process, and in the parent process it returns the process ID of the child:

```
>>> def forkFunc():
...     pid = os.fork()
...     if pid == 0:
...         print 'I am the child!'
...         os._exit(0)
...     else:
...         print 'I am the parent. Child PID is',pid
>>> forkFunc()
I am the parent. Child PID is 1844
I am the child!
```

Notice that the child process can force itself to terminate by calling `os._exit(status)`, which terminates a process without the usual cleaning up (which is good because the parent and child processes access some of the same resources, such as open file descriptors).

Cross-Reference Chapter 38 has information on the `pty` (pseudo-terminal) module, its `fork` and `spawn` functions, and the `os.forkpty` function.

Process management and termination

When you call `os._exit()` to end a process, Python skips the normal cleanup operations. The normal way to end the current process is by calling `sys.exit([status])`. The status parameter can be a numerical status code that Python returns to the parent process (which by convention is 0 for success and nonzero for an error), or any other object. For non-numeric objects, `sys.exit` prints the object to `stderr` and then exits with a status code of 1, making it a useful way for programs to exit when users supply invalid command-line arguments:

```
>>> import sys
>>> sys.exit('Usage: zapper [-force]')
Usage: zapper [-force]

C:\>
```

Other ways to shut down

Another way to terminate the current process is by raising the SystemExit exception (which is what sys.exit does anyway). You can cause the process to terminate abnormally by calling os.abort(), causing it to receive a SIGABRT signal.

The atexit module provides a way for you to register cleanup functions for Python to call when the interpreter is shutting down normally. You can register multiple functions, and Python calls them in the reverse order of how you registered them. Use atexit.register(func [, args]) to register each function, where args are any arguments (normal or keyword) that you want sent to the function:

```
>>> import atexit
>>> def bye(msg):
...     print msg

>>> def allDone(*args):
...     print 'Here are my args:',args

>>> atexit.register(bye,"I'm melting!")
>>> atexit.register(allDone,1,2,3)
>>> raise SystemExit # Shut down.
Here are my args: (1, 2, 3)
I'm melting!
```

New Feature The atexit module was new in Python 2.0.

Waiting around

On UNIX systems, you can call os.wait([option]) to wait for any child process to stop or terminate, or os.waitpid(pid,option) to wait for a particular child process. The values available to use for the option parameter vary by system, but you can always use os.WNOHANG to tell wait to return immediately if no processes have a termination to report, or 0 to wait. The wait functions return a two-tuple (pid,status), and you can decipher the status using any of the os functions listed in Table 11-1. The following example forks off a child process that sleeps for five seconds and then exits. The parent waits until the child finishes and then prints the exit information for the child:

```
>>> import os,time
>>> def useless():
...    z = os.fork()
...    if z == 0:
...      for i in range(5):
...        time.sleep(1)
...      os._exit(5)
...    else:
...      print 'Waiting on ',z
...      status = os.waitpid(z,0)[1]
...      print 'Exited normally:',os.WIFEXITED(status)
...      print 'Exit code:',os.WEXITSTATUS(status)
>>> useless()
Waiting on 1915
Exited normally: 1
Exit code: 5
```

Table 11-1
Wait Status Interpretation Functions

Function	Value returned
WIFSTOPPED(status)	1 if process was stopped (and not terminated)
WSTOPSIG(status)	Signal that stopped the process if WIFSTOPPED was true
WIFSIGNALED(status)	1 if process was terminated due to a signal
WTERMSIG(status)	Signal that terminated the process if WIFSIGNALED was true
WIFEXITED(status)	1 if the process exited due to _exit() or exit()
WEXITSTATUS(status)	Status code if WIFEXITED was true

Cross-Reference Instead of spawning off separate processes to do your bidding, you may just need to use threads. Chapter 26 covers multithreaded Python programs.

Handling Process Information

Table 11-2 lists the plethora of functions in the os module for getting and setting information about the current process. Except where noted, the functions are available only on UNIX.

Table 11-2
Process Information Functions in os

Functions	Description
getpid()	Gets the current process ID (Windows and UNIX).
getppid()	Gets the parent process ID.
getegid() / setegid(id)	Gets/sets effective group ID.
getgid() / setgid(id)	Gets/sets group ID.
getuid() / setuid(id)	Gets/sets user ID.
geteuid() / seteuid(id)	Gets/sets effective user ID.
getprgrp() / setprgrp()	Gets/sets process group ID.
ctermid()	Gets the file name of the controlling terminal.
getgroups()	Gets list of group IDs for this process.
getlogin()	Gets actual login name for current process.
setpgid(pid, pgrp)	Sets the process group for process pid (or the current process if pid is 0).
setreuid(ruid, euid)	Sets real and effective user IDs for the current process.
setregid(rgid, egid)	Sets real and effective group IDs for the current process.
tcgetprgrp(fd)	Gets the process group ID associated with fd (an open file descriptor of a terminal device).
tcsetpgrp(fd, pg)	Sets the process group ID associated with fd (an open file descriptor of a terminal device).
setsid()	Creates a new session/process group and returns the process group ID. The calling process is the group leader of the new process group.
umask(mask)	Sets the process's file mode creation mask and returns the previous mask (Windows and UNIX).
Nice(inc)	Adds inc to the process's nice value. The more you add, the lower the scheduling priority of that process (nicer means less important to the task scheduler).

For example, the following gets the current process's ID:

```
>>> os.getpid()
1072 # Hi, I'm process 1072.
```

Retrieving System Information

Many programs don't need to know too much about the platform on which they run, but when they do need to know, there's plenty of information available to them:

```
>>> import os, sys
>>> os.name # Name of the os module implementation
'posix'
>>> sys.byteorder # Is the processor big or little endian?
'little'
>>> sys.platform # Platform identifier
'freebsd3'
>>> os.uname()   # UNIX only
('FreeBSD', '', '3.4-RELEASE', 'FreeBSD 3.4-RELEASE #0','i386')
```

The five-tuple returned by os.uname is (sysname, nodename, release, version, machine).

See Chapter 38 for coverage of the UNIX statvfs module, useful for retrieving file system information.

UNIX system configuration information is available through os.confstr, os.sysconf, os.pathconf, and os.fpathconf:

os.confstr(name)	Returns the string value for the specified configuration item; the list of items defined for the current platform is in os.confstr_names.
os.sysconf(name)	Similar to os.confstr(name) except that the values os.sysconf(name) returns are integers. It also lists the names of the items you can retrieve.
os.pathconf(path,name) and os.fpathconf(fd,name)	Return system configuration information relating to a specific path of an open file descriptor. os.pathconf_names lists valid names.

For example, to retrieve the system memory page size you can use the following:

```
>>> os.sysconf('SC_PAGESIZE')
8192
```

Chapter 37 covers the winreg module that lets you access system information stored in the Windows registry.

Managing Configuration Files

The ConfigParser module makes reading and writing configuration files simple. Users can simply edit the configuration files to set various run-time options to customize your program's behavior. The config files are normal text files, organized into sections that contain key-value pairs. The files can have comments and can contain variables that ConfigParser evaluates when your program accesses them. If you save the file shown in Listing 11-1 to your current working directory as sample.cfg, you can then follow along with the examples.

Listing 11-1: **sample.cfg – Sample Configuration File**

```
# This listing is a sample configuration file.
# Comment lines start with pound symbols or semicolons.
[Server]
Address=171.15.2.5
Port=50002

[Hoth]
ID: %(team)s-1
Team=gold
DefaultName=%(__name__)s_User
```

Notice that the file can contain blank and comment lines, and that key-value pairs can be separated by equal signs or colons. A value can be anything, and you can use variable substitution to create values from other values. For example, %(team)s evaluates to the value of the team variable, and %(__name__)s evaluates to the name of the current section. If ConfigParser does not find a variable name in the current section, it also looks in a section named DEFAULT. The variable name in parentheses should be lowercase.

You create a ConfigParser by calling ConfigParser.ConfigParser([defaults]), where defaults is an optional dictionary containing values for the DEFAULT section. The readfp(f[, filename]) method reads a config file from an open filelike object. If the filelike object has a filename attribute, ConfigParser uses that for the config file's name (some exceptions it raises include the file name). You can also pass in an optional file name to use. The read(filenames) method reads in the contents of one or more config files. It fails silently on nonexistent files, making it safe to pass in a list of potential config files that may or may not exist:

```
>>> import ConfigParser
>>> cfg = ConfigParser.ConfigParser()
>>> cfg.read('sample.cfg')
['Server', 'Hoth']
```

When `ConfigParser` encounters an error while reading a file or retrieving values, it raises one of the exceptions listed in Table 11-3.

Table 11-3
ConfigParser Exceptions

Exception	Raised when
NoSectionError	The specified section does not exist.
DuplicateSectionError	A section with the specified name already exists.
NoOptionError	An option with the specified name does not exist.
InterpolationError	A problem occurred while performing variable evaluation.
InterpolationDepthError	The variable evaluation required too many recursive substitutions.
MissingSectionHeaderError	A key-value pair is not part of any section.
ParsingError	ConfigParser encountered a syntactic problem not covered by any of the other exceptions.

Once you have a valid `ConfigParser` instance object, you can use its methods to get and set values or learn more about the configuration file. The `defaults()` method returns a dictionary containing the default key-value pairs for this instance. `sections()` returns a list of section names for this config file (not including DEFAULT), and `has_section(section)` is a quick way to see if a given section exists. For any section, the `options(section)` method returns a list of options in that section, and `has_option(section, option)` tests for the existence of a particular option in that section:

```
>>> cfg.has_option('Server','port')
1
>>> cfg.options('Server')
['address', 'port']
```

Use the `get(section, option[, raw[, vars]])` method to retrieve the value of an option in a given section. If `raw` is 1, no variable evaluation takes place. You can optionally pass in a dictionary of key-value pairs that `get` uses in the variable evaluation:

```
>>> cfg.get('Hoth','ID',1) # Raw version
'%(team)s-1'
>>> cfg.get('Hoth','ID') # After variable evaluation
'gold-1'
>>> cfg.get('Hoth','ID',vars={'team':'blue'})
'blue-1' # Override values in the file
```

ConfigParser has a few other get convenience methods. getint(section, option) coerces the value into an integer before returning it, getfloat(section, option) does the same for floats, and getboolean(section,option) makes sure the value is a 0 or a 1 and returns it as an integer.

You can create a new section using the add_section(section) method, and you can set the value for an option by calling set(section, option, value):

```
>>> cfg.get('Server','port')
'50002'
>>> cfg.set('Server','port','4000') # Use string values!
>>> cfg.get('Server','port')
'4000'
```

The write(file) method writes the configuration file out to the given filelike object. The output is guaranteed to be readable by a future call to read or readfp.

The remove_option(section, option) method removes the given option from the given section. If the option didn't exist, remove_option returns 0, otherwise 1. remove_section(section) removes the given section from the config file. As with remove_option, remove_section returns 0 if the section didn't even exist, 1 otherwise.

Understanding Error Names

When an error occurs in the os module, it usually raises the OSError exception (found in os.error). OSError is a class, and instances of this class have the errno and strerror members that you can access to learn more about the problem:

```
>>> try:
...     os.close(-1) # A bogus file descriptor
... except OSError, e:
...     print 'Blech! %s [Err #%d]' % (e.strerror,e.errno)
...
Blech! Bad file descriptor [Err #9]
```

The strerror member is the result of calling os.strerror(code) with the errno member of the exception:

```
>>> os.strerror(2)
'No such file or directory'
```

The errno module contains the textual message for each error code. The list of defined errors varies by system (for example, the Windows version includes some Winsock error messages), but you can access the whole list through the errno.errorcode dictionary.

For errors involving files or directories, the `filename` member of `OSError` has a non-empty value:

```
>>> try:
...     os.open('asdfsf',os.O_RDONLY)
... except OSError, e:
...     print e.errno, e.filename, e.strerror
...
2 asdfsf No such file or directory
```

Handling Asynchronous Signals

The `signal` module lets your programs handle asynchronous process signals. If you've used the underlying C equivalents, you'll find that the Python version is pretty similar. A signal is just a message sent from the operating system or a process to the current process; most signals aren't handled directly by the process but are handled by default behavior in the operating system.

The `signal` module lets you register handler functions that override the default behavior and let your process respond to the signal itself. To register a signal handler, call `signal.signal(num,handler)` where num is the signal to handle and `handler` is your handler function. A signal handler should take two arguments, the signal number and a frame object containing the current stack frame. Instead of a function, `handler` can also be `signal.SIG_DFL` (meaning that you want the default behavior to occur for that signal) or `signal.SIG_IGN` (meaning that you want that signal to be ignored). The `signal` function returns the previous value of `handler`.

The signals that you can process vary by platform and are defined in your platform's `signal.h` file, but Table 11-4 lists some of the most common signals.

Table 11-4 Common Signals	
Name	*Description*
SIGINT	Interrupt (Ctrl-C hit)
SIGQUIT	Quit the program
SIGTERM	Request program termination
SIGFPE	Floating point error occurred (for example, division by zero, overflow)
SIGALRM	Alarm signal (not supported on Windows)
SIGBUS	Bus error
SIGHUP	Terminal line hangup
SIGSEGV	Illegal storage access

The getsignal(signalnum) function returns the current handler for the specified signal. It returns a callable Python object, SIG_DFL, SIG_IGN, or None (for non-Python signal handlers). default_int_handler is the default Python signal handler.

Except for handlers for SIGCHD, all signal handlers ignore the underlying implementation and continue to work until they are reset. Even though the signal handling happens asynchronously, Python dispatches the signals between bytecode instructions, so a long call into a C extension module could delay the arrival of some signals.

On UNIX, you can call signal.pause() to wait until a signal arrives (at which time the correct handler receives it). signal.alarm(time) causes the system to send a SIGALRM signal to the current process after time seconds; it returns the number of seconds left until the previous alarm would have gone off (if any). alarm cancels any previous alarm, and a time of 0 removes any current alarm. You can also call os.kill(pid, sig) to send the given signal to the process with the ID of pid.

Caution Be careful when using threads and signals in the same program. In such cases you should call signal.signal *only* from the main thread (although other threads can call alarm, pause, and getsignal). Be aware that signals are always sent to the main thread, regardless of the underlying implementation.

The following example prompts the user for input, but times out if the user doesn't respond in the allotted time (it uses signal.alarm, so it works on UNIX systems):

```
import signal,sys

def handler(sig, frm):
    raise 'timeout'  # Raise an exception when time runs out.

signal.signal(signal.SIGALRM,handler)  # Set up the handler.
try:
    signal.alarm(2.5)  # Send ALARM signal in 2.5 seconds.
    while 1:
        print 'Enter code to halt detonation:',
        s = sys.stdin.readline()
        if s.strip() == 'stop':
            print 'You did it!'
            break
        print 'Sorry.'
    signal.alarm(0)  # Disable the alarm.
except:  # Handle all exceptions so Ctrl-C will blow you up too.
    print '\nSorry. Too late.\n*KABOOM*'
```

I saved the file as sig.py. Here's some sample output:

```
/work> python sig.py
Enter code to halt detonation:  [ Wait a few seconds. ]
Sorry. Too late.
*KABOOM*
```

```
/work> python sig.py
Enter code to halt detonation:  foo
 Sorry.
Enter code to halt detonation:  stop
 You did it!
```

Summary

Python's great support for executing shell commands makes it an ideal solution as a scripting language or as a glue that holds various technologies together. Python also has ample functionality for starting, controlling, and monitoring child processes. In this chapter you learned to:

✦ Launch other programs in the foreground or the background.

✦ Access process and system configuration information.

✦ Read and write human-readable configuration files.

✦ Used file descriptors.

✦ Interpret os error message codes.

In the next chapter you'll learn to covert data between various formats, compress it, and decompress it. You'll also learn to convert Python objects to byte streams that can be saved for later retrieval or transmitted across a network.

✦   ✦   ✦

Storing Data and Objects

◆ ◆ ◆ ◆

In This Chapter

Data storage overview

Loading and saving objects

Example: moving objects across a network

Using database-like storage

Converting to and from C structures

Converting data to standard formats

Compressing data

◆ ◆ ◆ ◆

This chapter covers the many ways that you can convert Python objects to some form suitable for storage. Storage, however, is not limited to just saving data to disk. By the end of this chapter you'll be able to take a Python object and stick it in a database, compress it, send it across a network connection, or even convert it to a format that a C program could understand.

Data Storage Overview

Python's data storage features are easy to use, but before you say, "Hey, store this stuff" (it really is that easy), you should put some thought into how you might use the data down the road. The issues listed below are merely some things you should keep in mind; don't worry too much yet about how actually to deal with them.

Text versus binary

If you're storing data to file, you have to choose whether to store it in text or binary mode. A configuration file, for example, is in text mode because humans have to be able to read it and edit it with a text editor. It's often easier to debug your program if the output is stored in some human-readable format, and you can easily pass such a file around and use it on different platforms. Of course, storing it in a human-readable format means you handle the details of parsing it back in if you need to load it.

A binary mode representation of data often takes up less space, and can be processed faster if it is stored in fixed-size blocks or records.

Compression

If the size of an object is an issue, compression may be something you want to consider. In return for some additional processing power, compression often significantly shrinks the size of your data, which could really help if you have a lot of data or are transferring it over slow network connections.

Byte order ("Endianness")

The way a processor stores multibyte numbers in memory is either big-endian or little-endian:

```
>>> import sys
>>> print '"...%s-endian", Gulliver said.' % sys.byteorder
"...little-endian", Gulliver said. # On my Intel box
```

Most Python programs wouldn't care about such a low-level detail, but if your data has the potential to end up on another platform (by copying a data file, for example), the program on the other end has to know the byte order of the data in order to understand the data.

Object state

Before you store an object, you need to remember that some objects have state "outside" the Python interpreter. If you tried to save an open socket connection to disk, you certainly couldn't expect the connection to be open once you reload the socket.

Destination

You should keep in mind the destination of your data, because knowing that may let you take advantage of features particular to that medium. Is it going to a file on disk? How about a network connection or a database?

On the receiving end

One last thing to consider is what the receiving end of your data will be (who will read it in the future?). If you are saving a file that your same program will read later, you can use just about whatever storage format you like. If a C program is on the other end, maybe you need to send it data in the form of a C structure. Or maybe you don't even know who will read the data, so an industry standard format such as XDR or XML may be the answer.

Loading and Saving Objects

To save an object to disk, you convert it to a string of bytes that the program can later read back in to recreate the original object. If you're coming from a Java or C++ background, then you recognize this process as *marshaling* or *serialization*, but Python refers to making preserves out of your objects as *pickling*.

Pickling with pickle

The `pickle` module converts most Python objects to and from a byte representation:

```
>>> import pickle
>>> stuff = [5,3.5,'Alfred']
>>> pstuff = pickle.dumps(stuff)
>>> pstuff
"(lp0\012I5\012aF3.5\012aS'Alfred'\012p1\012a."
>>> pickle.loads(pstuff)
[5, 3.5, 'Alfred']
```

The `pstuff` variable in the above example is a string of bytes, so it's easy to send it to another computer via a network connection or write it out to a file.

The `pickle.dumps(object[, bin])` function returns the serialized form of an object, and `pickle.dump(object, file[, bin])` sends the serialized form to an open filelike object. If the optional `bin` parameter is 0 (the default), the object is pickled in a text form. A value of 1 generates a slightly more compact but less readable binary form. Either form is platform-independent.

The `pickle.loads(str)` function unpickles an object, converting the given string to its original object form. `pickle.load(file)` reads a pickled object from the given filelike object and returns the original, unpickled object.

The `load` and `dump` methods are really shorthand ways of instantiating the `Pickle` and `Unpickler` classes:

```
>>> s = StringIO.StringIO()  # Create a temp filelike object.
>>> p = pickle.Pickler(s,1)  # 1 = binary
>>> p.dump([1,2,3])
>>> p.dump('Hello!')
>>> s.getvalue()             # See the pickled form.
']q\000(K\001K\002K\003e.U\006Hello!q\001.'
>>> s.seek(0)                # Reset the "file."
>>> u = pickle.Unpickler(s)
>>> u.load()
[1, 2, 3]
>>> u.load()
'Hello!'
```

Using the `Pickler` and `Unpickler` classes is convenient if you need to pickle many objects, or if you need to pass the picklers around to other functions. You can also subclass them to create a custom pickler.

The `cPickle` module is a C version of the `pickle` module, making it up to several orders of magnitude faster than the pure Python `pickle` module. Anytime you need to do lots of pickling, use `cPickle`. Objects pickled by `cPickle` are compatible with those pickled by `pickle`, and vice versa. The only drawback to the `cPickle` module is that you can't subclass `Pickler` and `Unpickler`.

```
>>> import cPickle,pickle
>>> s = cPickle.dumps({'one':1,'two':2})
>>> pickle.loads(s)
{'one': 1, 'two': 2}
```

As Python evolves, future versions could change the format of pickled objects. To prevent disasters, each version of the format has a version number, and `pickle` has a list of other versions (in addition to the current one) that it knows how to read:

```
>>> pickle.format_version
'1.3'
>>> pickle.compatible_formats
['1.0', '1.1', '1.2'] # It can read some pretty old objects.
```

If you try to unpickle an unsupported version, `pickle` raises an exception.

What can I pickle?

You can pickle numbers, strings, `None`, and containers (tuples, lists, and dictionaries) that contain "picklable" objects.

When you pickle built-in functions, your own functions, or class definitions, `pickle` stores its name along with the module name in which it was defined, but not its implementation. In order to unpickle such an object, `pickle` first imports its module, so you must define the function or class at the top level of that module.

To save an instance object, `pickle` calls its __getstate__ method, which should return whatever information you need to capture the state of the object. When Python loads the object, `pickle` instantiates a new object and calls its __setstate__ method, passing it the unpickled version of its state:

```
>>> class Point:
...       def __init__(self,x,y):
...             self.x = x; self.y = y
...       def __str__(self):
...             return '(%d,%d)' % (self.x,self.y)
...       def __getstate__(self):
...             print 'Get state called!'
...             return (self.x,self.y)
...       def __setstate__(self,state):
...             print 'Set state called!'
```

```
...          self.x,self.y = state
...
>>> p = Point(10,20)
>>> z = pickle.dumps(p)
Get state called!
>>> newp = pickle.loads(z)
Set state called!
>>> print newp
(10,20)
```

If an object doesn't have a __getstate__ member, pickle saves the contents of its __dict__ member. When unpickling an object, the load function doesn't normally call the object's constructor (__init__). If you really want load to call the constructor, implement a __getinitargs__ method. As it saves the object , pickle calls __getinitargs__ for a tuple of arguments that it should pass to __init__ when the object is later loaded.

You can add pickling support for data types in C extension modules using the copy_reg module. To add support, you register a reduction function and a constructor for the given type by calling copy_reg.pickle(type, reduction_func[, constructor_ob]). For example, imagine you're creating a C extension module that determines the right stocks to trade on the stock market, and that the module defines a new data type called StockType (representing a particular security). Your constructor object (such as a function) returns a new StockType object and takes as arguments whatever data needed to create such an object. Your reduction function takes a StockType object and returns a two-tuple containing a constructor object for creating a new StockType object (most likely the same constructor function mentioned above). The reduction function also takes a tuple containing arguments to pass to that constructor. After registering your functions for the new type, any serialized StockType objects can use them.

Cross-Reference   See Chapter 29 for information on writing your own extension modules.

Other pickling issues

Because pickling a class doesn't store the class implementation, you can usually change the class definition without breaking your pickled data (you can still unpickle instance objects that were saved previously).

Multiple references to a particular object also reference a single object once you unpickle it. In the following example, a list has two members that are both references to another list. After pickling and unpickling it, the two members still refer to a single object:

```
>>> z = [1,2,3]
>>> y = [z,z]
>>> y[0] is y[1] # Two references to the same object
1
>>> s = pickle.dumps(y)
```

```
>>> x = pickle.loads(s)
>>> x
[[1, 2, 3], [1, 2, 3]]
>>> x[0] is x[1] # Both members still reference one object.
1
```

Of course, if you pickle an object, modify it, and pickle it again, pickle saves only the first version of the object.

Caution   If, while pickling to a filelike object, an error occurs (for example, you try to serialize a module), pickle raises the PicklingError exception, but it may have already written bytes to the file. The contents of the file will be in an unknown state and not too trustworthy.

The marshal module

Under the covers, the pickle module calls the marshal module to do some of its work, but most programs should not use marshal at all. The one advantage of marshal is that, unlike pickle, it can handle code objects (the implementation itself):

```
>>> def adder(a,b):
...     return a+b
>>> adder(10,2)
12
>>> import marshal
>>> s = marshal.dumps(adder.func_code)
>>> def newadder():
...     pass
>>> newadder.func_code = marshal.loads(s)
>>> newadder(20,10)
30
```

Cross-Reference   Chapter 33 shows you how to access code objects and other attributes of Python objects such as functions.

Example: Moving Objects Across a Network

The example in this section puts all this pickling stuff to work for you. Listing 12-1 is the swap module that creates a background thread that sends objects between two Python interpreters running in interactive mode. Although it works on a single computer, you can also run it between two separate computers if you change the IP address it uses.

Cross-Reference Consider this example as a sneak preview. Chapter 15 covers networking and Chapter 26 covers threads.

Here is some sample output from the program in Listing 12-1 (I opened two separate MS-DOS Windows on the same computer). After the sample output is a short explanation of how the program works. The first half shows what is happening in the first window, and the second in the other window, although both programs are running at the same time and interacting:

```
C:\temp>python -i -c "import swap"
Listen thread started.
Use swap.send(obj) to send an object
Look in swap.obj to see a received object

>>> swap.send(['game','of','the','year']) # See Obj1 below.

Received new object
(5, 10)                # Obj2 from below
>>> swap.obj
(5, 10)
>>> swap.obj[1] # Yep, it's a real Python object!
10

C:\temp>python -i -c "import swap"
Listen thread started.
Use swap.send(obj) to send an object
Look in swap.obj to see a received object
Received new object
['game', 'of', 'the', 'year']  # Obj1 from above

>>> swap.obj[2] # Poke around a little
'the'
>>> swap.send((5,10)) # See Obj2 above
```

Once both interpreters are up and running, they connect to each other via a network socket. Anytime you call swap.send(obj) in one interpreter, swap sends your object to the other interpreter, which stores it in swap.obj. Either side can send any picklable object to the other.

Notice that I started the Python interpreter using the "-c" argument (telling it to execute the command import swap) and the "-i" argument (telling it to keep the interpreter running after it executes its command). This feature lets you start with the swap module already loaded and running.

Listing 12-1: **swap.py – Swap Objects Between Python Interpreters**

```python
from socket import *
import cPickle,threading

ADDR = '127.0.0.1' # '127.0.0.1' = localhost
PORT = 50000
bConnected = 0

def send(obj):
    "Sends an object to a remote listener"
    if bConnected:
        conn.send(cPickle.dumps(obj,1))
    else:
        print 'Not connected!'

def listenThread():
    "Receives objects from remote side"
    global bServer, conn, obj, bConnected

    while 1:
        # Try to be the server.
        s = socket(AF_INET,SOCK_STREAM)
        try:
            s.bind((ADDR,PORT))
            s.listen(1)
            bServer = 1
            conn = s.accept()[0]
        except Exception, e:
            # Probably already in use, so I'm the client.
            bServer = 0
            conn = socket(AF_INET,SOCK_STREAM)
            conn.connect((ADDR,PORT))

        # Now just accept objects forever.
        bConnected = 1
        while 1:
            o = conn.recv(8192)
            if not o: break;

            obj = cPickle.loads(o)
            print 'Received new object'
            print obj
        bConnected = 0

# Start up listen thread.
threading.Thread(target=listenThread).start()
print 'Listen thread started.'
print 'Use swap.send(obj) to send an object'
print 'Look in swap.obj to see a received object'
```

Note For the sake of simplicity, the example leaves out a lot of error checking that you'd want if you were to use this for something important.

This module has two functions: `send` and `listenThread`. `send` takes any object you pass in, pickles it, and sends it out through the socket that is connected to the other Python interpreter.

The `listenThread` function loops forever, waiting for objects to come in over the socket. When the function first starts, it tries to bind to the given IP address and port so it can act as the server side of the connection. If this attempt fails, it assumes that the bind failed because the other interpreter is already acting as the server, so `listenThread` tries to connect (thus becoming the client side of the connection). Once connected, `listenThread` receives each object, unpickles it, prints it out and also saves it to the global variable `obj` so that you can then fiddle with it in your interpreter.

At the module level, a call to `threading.Thread().start()` starts the listening thread. By placing the call there, the background thread starts up automatically as soon as you import the module.

After you've played around with this a little, sit back and relish the fact that all this power required a measly 50 lines of Python code!

Using Database-Like Storage

The `shelve` module enables you to save Python objects into persistent, database-like storage, similar to the `dbm` module.

Cross-Reference See Chapter 14 for information on `dbm` and other Python database modules.

The `shelve.open(file[, mode])` function opens and returns a `shelve` object. The `mode` parameter (which is the same as the mode parameter to `dbm.open`) defaults to 'c', which means that the function opens the database for reading and writing, and creates it if it doesn't already exist. Use the `close()` method of the `shelve` object when you are finished using it.

You access the data as if the database were a dictionary:

```
>>> import shelve
>>> db = shelve.open('objdb') # Don't use a file extension!
>>> db['secretCombination'] = [5,23,17]
>>> db['account'] = 5671012
>>> db['secretCombination']
[5, 23, 17]
>>> del db['account']
>>> db.has_key('account')
0
```

```
>>> db.keys()
['secretCombination']
>>> db.close()
```

The shelve module uses pickle, so you can store any objects that pickle can store. shelve has the same limitations as dbm. Among other things, you should not use it to store large Python objects.

Converting to and from C Structures

Although pickle makes converting Python objects to a byte stream easy, really only Python programs can convert them back to objects. The struct module, however, lets you create a string of bytes equivalent to a C structure, so you could read and write binary files generated by a non-Python program or send binary network messages to something besides a Python interpreter.

To use struct, you call struct.pack(format, v1, v2, ...) with a format string describing the layout of the data followed by the data itself. Construct the format string using format characters listed in Table 12-1.

Table 12-1 struct Format Characters		
Character	**C type**	**Python type**
c	Char	string of length 1
s	char[]	string
p	(Pascal string)	string
i	Int	integer
I	Unsigned int	integer or long*
b	Signed char	integer
B	unsigned char	integer
h	Short	integer
H	unsigned short	integer
l	Long	integer
L	unsigned long	long
f	Float	float
d	Double	float
x	(pad byte)	-
P	void *	integer or long*

* The type Python uses is based on whether a pointer for this platform is 32 or 64 bits.

For example, to create the equivalent of this C struct:

```
struct
{
    int a;
    int b;
    char c;
};
```

with the values 10, 20, and 'Z,' use:

```
>>> import struct
>>> z = struct.pack('iic',10,20,'Z')
>>> z
'\012\000\000\000\024\000\000\000Z'
```

Given a string of bytes in a particular format, you can convert them to Python objects by calling struct.unpack(format, data). It returns a tuple of the reconstructed data:

```
>>> struct.unpack('iic',z)
(10, 20, 'Z')
```

The format string you pass to unpack must account for all the data in the string you pass it, or struct raises an exception. Use the struct.calcsize(format) function to figure out how many bytes would be taken up by the given format string:

```
>>> struct.calcsize('iic')
9
>>> len(z) # The earlier example verifies this.
9
```

As a shortcut, you can put a number in front of any format character to repeat that data type that many times:

```
>>> struct.pack('3f',1.2,3.4,5.6) # '3f' is the same as 'fff'
'\232\231\231?\232\231Y@33\263@'
```

For clarity, you can put whitespace between format characters in your format string (but not between the format character and a repeater number):

```
>>> struct.pack('2i h 3c',5,6,7,'a','b','c')
'\005\000\000\000\006\000\000\000\007\000abc'
```

The repeater number works a little differently with the 's' (string) format character. The repeater tells the length of the string (5s means a 5 character string). 0s means an empty string, but 0c means zero characters.

The 'I' format character unpacks the given number to a Python long integer if the C int and long are the same size. If the C int is smaller than the C long, 'I' converts the number to a Python integer.

The 'p' format character is for a Pascal string. Pascal uses the first byte to store the length of the string (so Pascal first truncates strings longer than the maximum length of 255) and then the characters in the string follow. If you supply a repeater number with this format character, it represents the total number of bytes in the string including the length byte. If the string is less than the specified number of bytes, pack adds empty padding characters to bring it up to snuff.

By default, struct stores numbers using the native format for byte order and structure member alignment (whatever your current platform's C compiler would use). You can override this behavior by starting your format string with one of the modifiers listed in Table 12-2. For example, you can force struct to use network order, a standard byte ordering for network messages:

```
>>> struct.pack('ic',65535,'D') # Native is little-endian.
'\377\377\000\000D'
>>> struct.pack('!ic',65535,'D') # Force network order.
'\000\000\377\377D'
```

Table 12-2
Order, Alignment, and Size Modifiers

Modifier	Byte order	Alignment	Size
<	Little-endian	None	Standard
> or !	Big-endian (Network)	None	Standard
=	Native	None	Standard
@	Native	Native	Native

If you don't choose a modifier from Table 12-2, struct uses native byte ordering, alignment, and size. When you use a modifier whose size is "standard," a C short takes up 2 bytes, an int, long, or float uses 4, and a double uses 8.

If you need to have alignment but aren't using the '@' (native alignment) modifier, you can insert pad bytes using the 'x' format character from Table 12-1. If you need to force the end of a structure to be aligned according to the alignment rules for a particular type, you can end your format string with the format code for that type with a count of 0. The following example shows how to force a single-character structure to end on an integer boundary:

```
>>> struct.pack('c','A')
'A'
>>> struct.pack('c0i','A')
'A\000\000\000'
```

The 'P' (pointer) format character is available with native alignment only.

The struct module is very useful for reading and writing binary files. For example, if you read the first 36 bytes of a Windows WAV file, you can use struct to extract some information about the file. The header of a WAV file starts with:

```
'RIFF' (4 bytes)
little-endian length field (4 bytes)
'WAVE' (4 bytes)
'fmt ' (4 bytes)
format subchunk length (4 bytes)
format specifier (2 bytes)
number of channels (2 bytes)
sample rate in Hertz (4 bytes)
bytes per second (4 bytes)
bytes per sample (2 bytes)
bits per channel (2 bytes)
```

One way to represent this header would be with the format string

```
'<4s i 4s 4s ihhiihh'
```

The following code extracts this information from a WAV file:

```
>>> s = open('c:\\winnt\\media\\ringin.wav','rb').read(36)
>>> struct.unpack('<4si4s4sihhiihh',s)
('RIFF', 10018, 'WAVE', 'fmt ', 16, 1, 1, 11025, 11025, 1, 8)
```

Extending that example, the following function rates the sound quality of a given WAV file:

```
>>> def rateWAV(filename):
...      format = '<4si4s4sihhiihh'
...      fsize = struct.calcsize(format)
...      data = open(filename,'rb').read(fsize)
...      data = struct.unpack(format,data)
...      if data[0] != 'RIFF' or data[2] != 'WAVE':
...          print 'Not a WAV file!'
...      rate = data[7]
...      if rate == 11025:
...          print 'Telephone quality!'
...      elif rate == 22050:
...          print 'Radio quality!'
...      elif rate == 44100:
...          print 'Oooh, CD quality!'
...      else:
...          print 'Rate is %d Hz' % rate

>>> rateWAV(r'c:\winnt\media\notify.wav')
Radio quality!
>>> rateWAV('online.wav')
Oooh, CD quality!
```

Converting Data to Standard Formats

Now that you have the `struct` module under your belt, you can build on that knowledge to read and write just about any file format. If your data needs to be readable by your own programs only, then you can create your own convention for storing data. In other cases, however, you may find it useful to convert your data to an industry-wide standard.

Sun's XDR format

The XDR (eXternal Data Representation) format is a standard data format created by Sun Microsystems. RFC 1832 defines the format, and it's most common use is in NFS (Network File System). Storing data in a standard format like XDR makes sharing files easier for different hardware platforms and operating systems.

The `xdrlib` module implements a subset of the XDR format, leaving out some of the less-used data types. To convert data to XDR, you create an instance of the `xdrlib.Packer` class, and to convert from XDR, you create an instance of `xdrlib.Unpacker`.

Packer objects

The `Packer` constructor takes no arguments:

```
>>> import xdrlib
>>> p = xdrlib.Packer()
```

Once you have a `Packer` object you can use any of its `pack_<type>` methods to pack basic data types:

```
>>> p.pack_float(3.5)      # 32-bit floating point number
>>> p.pack_double(10.5)    # 64-bit floating point number
>>> p.pack_int(-15)          # Signed 32-bit integer
>>> p.pack_uint(15)          # Unsigned 32-bit integer
>>> p.pack_hyper(100)      # Signed 64-bit integer
>>> p.pack_uhyper(200)     # Unsigned 64-bit integer
>>> p.pack_enum(3)         # Enumerated type
>>> p.pack_bool(1)         # Booleans are 1 or 0
>>> p.pack_bool("Hi")      # Value is true, so stores a 1
```

The `pack_fstring(count, str)` method packs a fixed-length string `count` characters long. The function does not store the size of the string, so to unpack it you have to know how long it is beforehand. Better yet, use `pack_string(str)`, which lets you pack a variable-length string:

```
>>> p.pack_string('Lovely')
>>> p.pack_fstring(3,'day')
```

The `pack_string` function calls `pack_uint` with the size of the string and then `pack_fstring` with the string itself. To more fully follow the XDR specification, a `Packer` object also has `pack_bytes` and `pack_opaque` methods, but they are really just calls to `pack_string`. Likewise, a call to `pack_fopaque` is really just a call to `pack_fstring`.

The `pack_farray(count, list, packFunc)` function packs a fixed-length array (`count` items long) of homogenous data. Unfortunately, `pack_farray` requires that you pass in the count as well as the list itself, but it won't let you use a count that is different from the length of the list (go figure). As with `pack_fstring`, the function does not store the length of the array with the data, so you have to know the length when you unpack it. Or you can call `pack_array(list, packFunc)` to pack the size and then the list itself. The `packFunc` tells `Packer` which method to use to pack each item. For example, if each item in the list is an integer:

```
>>> p.pack_array([1,2,3,4],p.pack_int)
```

The pack_list(list,packFunc) method also packs an array of homogenous data, but it works with sequence objects whose size might not be known ahead of time. For example, you could create a class that defines its own __getitem__ method:

```
>>> class MySeq:
...     def __getitem__(self,i):
...         if i < 5:
...             return i
...         raise IndexError
>>> m = MySeq()
>>> for i in m:
...     print i
0
1
2
3
4
>>> p.pack_list(m,p.pack_int)
```

The `get_buffer()` method returns a string representing the packed form of all the data you've packed. `reset()` empties the buffer:

```
>>> p.reset()
>>> p.pack_int(10)
>>> p.get_buffer()
'\000\000\000\012'
>>> p.reset()
>>> p.get_buffer()
''
```

Unpacker objects

Not surprisingly, an Unpacker object has methods that closely mirror those of a Packer object. When you construct an Unpacker, you pass in a string of bytes for it to decode, and then begin calling its unpack_<type> methods (each pack_ method has a corresponding unpack_ method):

```
>>> import xdrlib
>>> p = xdrlib.Packer()
>>> p.pack_float(2.0)
>>> p.pack_fstring(4,'Dave')
>>> p.pack_string('/export/home')

>>> u = xdrlib.Unpacker(p.get_buffer())
>>> u.unpack_float()
2.0
>>> u.unpack_fstring(4)
'Dave'
>>> u.unpack_string()
'/export/home'
>>> u.done()
```

The done() method tells the Unpacker that you are finished decoding data. If Unpacker still has data left in its internal buffer, it raises an Error exception to inform you that the internal buffer has leftover data.

Calling the reset(str) method replaces the current buffer with the data in str. At any time, you can call the get_buffer() method to retrieve the string representation of the data stream.

You can use the get_position() and set_position(pos) methods to track and reposition where in the buffer the Unpacker decodes from next. To be safe, set a position to 0 or to a value returned from get_position.

Other formats

Of course, you might use many other data formats. XML is gaining popularity as a data storage markup language; see Chapter 18 for more information.

For any given file format, a quick search on a Web search engine locates many documents describing the details of that format (for example, try searching for "WAV spec"). Once you have that information, creating format strings that struct can understand is usually a straightforward process.

Compressing Data

This final section covers the use of the zlib, a module wrapping the free zlib compression library. The gzip and zipfile modules use zlib to manipulate GZIP and ZIP files, respectively.

zlib

You can use the zlib module to compress any sort of data; if you are transferring large messages over a network, it may be worthwhile to compress them first, for example.

The most straightforward use of zlib is through the compress(string[, level]) and decompress(string[, wbits[, bufsize]]) functions. The level used during compression is from 1 (fastest) to 9 (best compression), defaulting to 6. During decompression, the wbits argument controls the size of the history buffer, and should have a value between 8 and 15 (the default). A higher value consumes more memory but increases the chances of better compression. The bufsize argument determines the initial size of the buffer used to hold decompressed data. The library modifies this size as needed, so you never really *have* to change it from its default of 16384. Both compress and decompress take a string of bytes and return the compressed or decompressed equivalent:

```
>>> import zlib
>>> longString = 100 * 'That zlib module sure is fun!'
>>> compressed = zlib.compress(longString)
>>> len(longString); len(compressed)
2900
62                      # Yay, zlib!
>>> zlib.decompress(compressed)[:40]
'That zlib module sure is fun!That zlib m'
```

> **Tip**
>
> To learn more about zlib's features, visit the zlib Web site at http://www.info-zip.org/pub/infozip/zlib/.

The zlib module has two functions for computing the checksum of a string (useful in detecting changes and errors in data or as a way to warm your CPU), crc32(string[, value]) and adler32(string[, value]). If present, the optional value argument is the starting value of the checksum, so you can calculate the checksum of several pieces of input. The following example shows you how to use a checksum to detect data corruption:

```
>>> data = 'My dog has no fleas!'
>>> zlib.adler32(data)
1193871046
>>> data = data[:5]+'z'+data[6:]
>>> data
'My doz has no fleas!'   # A solar flare corrupts your data...
>>> zlib.adler32(data)
1212548825               # ...resulting in a different checksum.
```

The value returned from crc32 is more reliable than that returned from adler32, but it also requires much more computation. (More reliable means that the function is less likely to return the same checksum if the data changes at all.) Don't forget to dazzle your friends by informing them that Mark Adler wrote the decompression portion of zlib.

If you have more data than you can comfortably fit in memory, zlib lets you
create compression and decompression objects. Create a compression object by
calling compressobj([level]). Once you have your object, you can repeatedly call
its compress(string) method. Each call returns another portion of the compressed version of the data, although some is saved for later processing. Calling the
compression object's flush([mode]) method finishes the compression and
returns the remaining compressed data:

```
>>> c = zlib.compressobj(9)
>>> out = c.compress(1000 * 'I will not throw knives')
>>> out += c.compress(200 * 'or chairs')
>>> out += c.flush()
>>> len(out) # out holds the entire compressed stream.
115
```

If you call flush with a mode of Z_FULL_FLUSH or Z_SYNCH_FLUSH, all the currently
buffered compressed data is returned, but you can later compress more data with
the same object. Without those mode values, the compression object assumes
you're finished and doesn't allow any additional compression.

You create a decompression object by calling zlib's decompressobj([wbits])
function. A decompression object lets you decompress a stream of data one piece
at a time (for example, you could decompress a file by repeatedly reading a chunk
of data, decompressing that chunk, and writing the result to an output file).

Call the decompress(string) method of your decompression object to decompress the next chunk of data. decompress returns the largest amount of decompressed data that it can, although it may need to buffer some until you supply more
data to decompress. The following code decompresses the output from the previous example 20 bytes at a time:

```
>>> d = zlib.decompressobj() # Create a decompressor.
>>> msg = ''
>>> while out:
...     msg += d.decompress(out[:20]) # Decompress some.
...     out = out[20:]
>>> msg += d.flush() # Let it know that we're all done.
>>> len(msg)
24800
>>> 1000 * len('I will not throw knives') +\
... 200 * len('or chairs')
24800       # Length matches that of the original message.
>>> msg[:50] # Looks like the message itself matches too.
'I will not throw knivesI will not throw knivesI wi'
```

Call the decompression object's flush() method when you're done giving it more
data (after this you can't call decompress any more with that object).

Decompression objects also have an unused_data member that holds any leftover compressed data from the last call to decompress. A nonempty unused_data string means that the decompression object is still waiting on additional data to finish decompressing this particular piece of data.

gzip

The gzip module lets you read and write .gz (GNU gzip) files as if they were ordinary files (that is, your program can pretty much ignore the fact that compression/ decompression is taking place).

> **Note** The GNU gzip and gunzip programs support additional formats (for example, compress and pack), but the gzip Python module does not.

The gzip.GzipFile([filename[, mode[, compresslevel[, fileobj]]]]) function constructs a new GzipFile object. You must supply either the filename or the fileobj argument, although the file object can be anything that looks like a file such as a cStringIO object. The compresslevel parameter has the same values as for zlib module earlier in this section.

If you don't supply a mode, then gzip tries to use the mode of fileobj. If that's not possible, the mode defaults to 'rb' (open for reading). A GzipFile can't be open for both reading and writing, so you should use a mode of 'rb', 'wb', or 'ab'.

When you call the close() method of a GzipFile, the file object (if you supplied one) remains open.

To further the illusion of normal file I/O, you can call the open(filename[, mode[, level]]) function in the gzip module. The filename argument is required, so the call looks very similar to Python's built-in open function:

```
>>> f = gzip.open('small.gz','wb')
>>> f.write('''Old woman!
... Man!
... Old Man, sorry.  What knight lives in that castle over
there?
... I'm thirty-seven.
... What?
... I'm thirty-seven -- I'm not old!
... Well, I can't just call you 'Man'.
... Well, you could say 'Dennis'.
>>> f.close()

>>> f = gzip.open('small.gz')
>>> print f.read()

Old woman!
Man!
Old Man, sorry.  What knight lives in that castle over there?
I'm thirty-seven.
```

```
What?
I'm thirty-seven -- I'm not old!
Well, I can't just call you 'Man'.
Well, you could say 'Dennis'.
```

zipfile

The zipfile module lets you read, write, and get information about files stored in the common ZIP file format.

Note The zipfile module does not currently support ZIP files with appended comments or files that span multiple disks.

The ipfile.is_zipfile(filename) function returns true if the given file name appears to be a valid zip file.

The zipfile module defines the ZipFile, ZipInfo, and PyZipFile classes.

The ZipFile class

This class is the primary one used to read and write a ZIP file. You create a ZipFile instance object by calling the ZipFile(filename[, mode[, compression]]) constructor:

```
>>> import zipfile
>>> z = zipfile.ZipFile('room.zip')
>>> z.printdir()  # Print formatted summary of the archive
File Name                 Modified             Size
world                     2000-09-05 09:25:14  10919
cryst.cfg                 1999-03-07 06:14:34     27
```

The mode is 'r' (read, the default), 'w' (write), or 'a' (append). If you append to a ZIP file, Python adds new files to it. If you append to a non-ZIP file, however, Python adds a ZIP archive to the end of the file. Not all ZIP readers can understand this format. The compression argument is either ZIP_STORED (no compressed) or ZIP_DEFLATED (use compression).

The namelist() method of your ZipFile object returns the list of files the ZIP contains. You can get a ZipInfo object (described in the next section) for any file via the getinfo(name) method, or you can get a list of ZipInfos for the entire archive with the infolist() method:

```
>>> z.namelist()
['world', 'cryst.cfg'] # The ZIP contains two files.
>>> z.getinfo('world') # Get some info for file named 'world.'
<zipfile.ZipInfo instance at 010FD14C>
>>> z.getinfo('world').file_size
10919
```

```
>>> z.infolist()
[<zipfile.ZipInfo instance at 010FD14C>,
 <zipfile.ZipInfo instance at 010E116C>]
```

If you open the ZIP in read or append mode, `read(name)` decompresses the specified file and returns its contents:

```
>>> print z.read('cryst.cfg')
[World]
MIXLIGHTS=true_rgb
```

The `testzip()` method returns the name of the first corrupt file or `None` if all files are okay:

```
>>> z.testzip()
'world'  # The file called 'world' is corrupt.
```

For ZIPs opened in write or append mode, the `write(zipInfo, bytes)` method adds a new file to the archive. `bytes` contains the content of the file, and `zipInfo` is a `ZipInfo` object (see the next section) with the file's information. You don't have to fill in every attribute of `ZipInfo`, but at least fill in the file name and compression type.

The `write(filename[, arcname[, compress_type]])` function adds the contents of the file `filename` to the archive. If you supply a value for `arcname`, that is the name of the file stored in the archive. If you supply a value for `compress_type`, it overrides whatever compression type you used when you created the `ZipFile`.

After making any changes to a ZIP file, calling the `close()` method is essential to guaranteeing the integrity of the archive.

Tip   A `ZipFile` object has a `debug` attribute that you can use to change the level of debug output messages. Most output comes with a value of 3, the least (no output) is with a value of 0, the default.

The ZipInfo class

Information about each member of a ZIP archive is represented by a `ZipInfo` object. You can use the `ZipInfo([filename[, date_time]])` constructor to create one; `getinfo()` and `infolist()` also return `ZipInfo` objects. The `filename` should be the full path of the file and `date_time` is a six-tuple containing the last modification timestamp (see the `date_time` attribute in Table 12-3).

Each `ZipInfo` instance object has many attributes; the most useful are listed in Table 12-3.

Table 12-3
ZipInfo Instance Attributes

Name	Description
filename	Name of the archived file
compress_size	Size of the compressed file
file_size	Size of the original file
date_time	Last modification date and time, a six-tuple consisting of year, month (1–12), day (1–31), hour (0–23), minute (0–59), second (0–59)
compress_type	Type of compression (stored or deflated)
CRC	The CRC32 of the original file
comment	Comment for this entry
extract_version	Minimum software version needed to extract the archive
header_offset	Byte offset to the file's header
file_offset	Byte offset to the file's data

The PyZipFile class

The PyZipFile class is a utility class for creating ZIP files that contain Python modules and packages. PyZipFile is a subclass of ZipFile, so its constructor and methods are the same as for ZipFile.

The only method that PyZipFile adds is writepy(pathname), which searches for *.py files and adds their corresponding bytecode files to the ZIP file. For each Python module (for example, file.py), writepy archives file.pyo if it exists. If not, it adds file.pyc if it exists. If that doesn't exist either, writepy compiles the module to create file.pyc and adds it to the archive.

If pathname is the name of a package directory (a directory containing the __init__.py file), writepy searches that directory and all package subdirectories for all *.py files. If pathname is the name of an ordinary directory, it searches for *.py files in that directory only. Finally, if pathname is just a normal Python module (for example, file.py), writepy adds its bytecode to the ZIP file.

Cross-Reference   Refer to Chapter 6 for more information on Python packages.

Summary

Python makes a breeze of serializing or marshaling objects to disk or over a network, and its support for compression and data conversion only makes life easier. In this chapter you:

✦ Serialized objects.

✦ Transported objects across a network connection.

✦ Converted objects to formats readable by C programs.

✦ Stored objects in the standard XDR format.

✦ Compressed data to save space.

In the next chapter you'll learn to track how long parts of your program take to run, retrieve the date and time, and print the date and time in custom formats.

✦   ✦   ✦

Accessing Date and Time

In This Chapter

Telling time in Python

Converting between time formats

Parsing and printing dates and times

Accessing the calendar

Using time zones

Allowing two-digit years

Dates can be written in many ways. Converting between date formats is a common chore for computers. Date arithmetic — like finding the number of days between June 10 and December 13 — is another common task. Python's time and calendar modules help track dates and times. They even handle icky details like daylight savings time and leap years.

Telling Time in Python

Time is usually represented as either a number or a tuple. The `time` module provides functions for working with times, and for converting between representations.

Ticks

You can represent a point in time as a number of "ticks" — the number of seconds that have elapsed since the epoch. The *epoch* is an arbitrarily chosen "beginning of time." For UNIX and Windows systems, the epoch is 12:00am, 1/1/1970. For example, on my computer, my next birthday is 983347200 in ticks (which translates into February 28, 2001).

The function `time.time` returns the current system time in ticks. For example, here is the number of days from now until my birthday:

```
>>> 983347200 - time.time()
7186162.7339999676
```

Note that Python uses a floating-point value for ticks. Because time precision varies by operating system, `time.time` is always an integer on some systems.

Date arithmetic is easy to do with ticks. However, dates before the epoch *cannot* be represented in this form. Dates in the far future also cannot be represented this way — the cutoff point is sometime in 2038 for UNIX and Windows.

 Note   Third-party modules such as mxDateTime provide date/time classes that function outside the range 1970–2038.

TimeTuple

Many of Python's time functions handle time as a tuple of 9 numbers, as shown in Table 13-1:

	Table 13-1	
	Time Functions	
Index	*Field*	*Values*
0	4-digit year	1993
1	Month	1–12
2	Day	1–31
3	Hour	0–23 (0 is 12 a.m.)
4	Minute	0–59
5	Second	0–61 (60 or 61 are leap-seconds)
6	Day of week	0–6 (0 is Monday)
7	Day of year	1–366 (Julian day)
8	Daylight savings	-1,0,1

Note that the elements of the tuple proceed from broadest (year) to most granular (second). This means that one can do linear comparisons on TimeTuples:

```
>>> TimeA = (1972, 5, 15, 12, 55, 32, 0, 136, 1)
>>> TimeB = (1972, 5, 16, 7, 9, 10, 1, 137, 1)
>>> TimeA<TimeB # TimeA is a day before TimeB.
1
```

Note that a TimeTuple does not include a time zone. To pinpoint an actual time, one needs a time zone as well as a TimeTuple.

Stopwatch time

The *clock* function acts as a stopwatch for timing Python code — you call clock before doing something, call it again afterwards, and take the difference between numbers to get the elapsed seconds. The actual values returned by clock are system-dependent and generally don't translate into a time-of-day. This code checks how quickly Python counts to one million:

```
>>> def CountToOneMillion():
...     StartTime=time.clock()
...     for X in xrange(0,1000000): pass
...     EndTime=time.clock()
...     print EndTime-StartTime
...
>>> CountToOneMillion() # Elapsed time, in seconds
0.855862726726
```

Note   The proper way to pause execution is with time.sleep(n), where n is a floating point number of seconds. In a Tkinter application, once can call the after method on the root object to make a function execute after n seconds. (See Chapter 19 for more on Tkinter.)

Converting Between Time Formats

The function *localtime* converts from ticks to a TimeTuple for the local time zone. For example, this code gets the current time:

```
>>> time.localtime(time.time())
(2000, 12, 6, 20, 0, 9, 2, 341, 0)
```

Reading the fields of the TimeTuple, I can see that it is the year 2000, December 6, at 20:00 (8 p.m.) and 9 seconds. The day of the week is 2 (Wednesday), it is the 341st day of the year, and local clocks are not currently on Daylight Savings Time.

The function *gmtime* also converts from EpochSeconds to a TimeTuple. It returns the current TimeTuple for UTC (Universal Coordinated Time, formerly Greenwich Mean Time). This call to gmtime shows that it is 4 a.m. in England (a bad time to telephone):

```
>>> time.gmtime(time.time())
(2000, 12, 7, 4, 4, 9, 3, 342, 0)
```

The function *mktime* converts from a TimeTuple to EpochSeconds. It interprets the TimeTuple according to the local time zone. The function mktime is the inverse of localtime, and it is useful for doing date arithmetic. (The inverse function of gmtime is calendar.timegm.) This code finds the number of seconds between two points in time:

```
>>> TimeA = (1972, 5, 15, 12, 55, 32, 0, 136, 1)
>>> TimeB = (1972, 5, 16, 7, 9, 10, 1, 137, 1)
>>> time.mktime(TimeB)-time.mktime(TimeA)
65618.0
>>> _ / (60*60) # How many hours is that?
18.227222222222224
```

Parsing and Printing Dates and Times

The *asctime* function takes a TimeTuple, and returns a human-readable timestamp. It is especially useful in log files:

```
>>> Now=time.localtime(time.time()) # Now is a TimeTuple.
>>> time.asctime(Now)
'Sun Dec 10 10:09:41 2000'
>>> # In version 2.1, you can call asctime() and localtime()
>>> # with no arguments to use the current time:
>>> time.asctime()
'Sun Dec 10 10:09:41 2000'
```

The function *ctime* returns a timestamp for a time expressed in ticks:

```
>>> time.ctime(time.time())
'Sun Dec 10 10:11:29 2000'
```

Fancy formatting

The function `strftime(format,timetuple)` formats a TimeTuple in a format you specify. The function `strftime` returns the string *format* after performing substitutions on various codes marked with a percent sign, as shown in Table 13-2:

Table 13-2
Time Formatting Syntax

Code	Substitution	Example / Range
%a	Abbreviated day name	Thur
%A	Full day name	Thursday
%b	Abbreviated month name	Jan
%B	Full month name	January
%c	Date and time representation (equivalent to %x %X)	12/10/00 10:09:41
%d	Day of the month	01–31
%H	Hour (24-hour clock)	00–23
%h	Hour (12-hour clock)	01–12
%j	Julian day (day of the year)	001–366
%m	Month	01–12
%M	Minute	00–59
%p	A.M. or P.M.	AM

Code	Substitution	Example / Range
%S	Second	00–61
%U	Week number. Week starts with Sunday; days before the first Sunday of the year are in week 0.	00–53
%w	Weekday as a number (0=Sunday)	0–6
%W	Week number. Week starts with Monday; days before the first Monday of the year are in week 0.	00–53
%x	Date	12/10/00
%X	Time	10:09:41
%y	2-digit year	00–99
%Y	4-digit year	2000
%Z	Time-zone name	Pacific Standard Time
%%	Literal % sign	

For example, I can print the current week number:

```
>>> time.strftime("It's week %W!",Now)
"It's week 49!"
```

Here is the default formatting string (with the same results as calling `ctime`):

```
>>> time.strftime("%a %b %d %I:%M:%S %Y",Now)
'Sun Dec 10 10:09:41 2000'
```

Parsing time

The function `strptime(timestring[,format])` is the reverse of `strftime`; it parses a string and returns a TimeTuple. It guesses at any unspecified time components. It raises a ValueError if it cannot parse the string *timestring* using the format *format*. The default format is the one that `ctime` uses: "%a %b %d %I:%M:%S %Y".

Note   The `strptime` function is available on most UNIX systems; however, it is unavailable on Windows.

Localization

Different countries write dates differently — for example, the string "2/5" means "February 5" in the United States, but "May 2" in England. The function `strftime` refers to the current locale when performing each substitution. For example, the format string "%x" uses the correct day-month ordering for the current locale. However, you still need to take locale into account when writing code — for instance, the format string "%m/%d" is not correct for all locales.

Cross-Reference See Chapter 34 for an overview of the locale module and other information on internationalization.

Accessing the Calendar

The calendar module provides high-level functions and constants that complement the lower-level functions in the time module. Because calendar uses ticks internally to represent dates, it cannot provide calendars outside the epoch (usually 1970–2038).

Printing monthly and yearly calendars

The following sections show examples of printing monthly and yearly calendars.

monthcalendar(yearnum,monthnum)

The function monthcalendar returns a list of lists, representing a monthly calendar. Each entry in the main list represents a week. The sublists contain the seven dates in that week. A 0 (zero) in the sublist represents a day from the previous or next month:

```
>>> calendar.monthcalendar(2000,5) # 4 1/2 weeks in May, 2000
[[1, 2, 3, 4, 5, 6, 7], [8, 9, 10, 11, 12, 13, 14], [15, 16,
17, 18, 19, 20, 21], [22, 23, 24, 25, 26, 27, 28], [29, 30, 31,
0, 0, 0, 0]]
```

month(yearnum,monthnum[,width[,linesperweek]])

The month function returns a multiline string that looks like a monthly calendar for month *monthnum* of year *yearnum*. Months are numbered normally (from 1 for January up to 12 for December). The parameter *width* specifies how wide each column is; the minimum (and default) value is 2. The parameter *linesperweek* specifies how many rows to print for each week. It defaults to 1; setting it to a higher number like 5 leaves space to write on a printed calendar. Here are two examples:

```
>>> print calendar.month(2002,5)
      May 2002
Mo Tu We Th Fr Sa Su
       1  2  3  4  5
 6  7  8  9 10 11 12
13 14 15 16 17 18 19
20 21 22 23 24 25 26
27 28 29 30 31
```

```
>>> # 2 rows per week; 3 cols per day
>>> print calendar.month(2002,5,3,2)
        May 2002

Mon Tue Wed Thu Fri Sat Sun
             1   2   3   4   5

  6   7   8   9  10  11  12

 13  14  15  16  17  18  19

 20  21  22  23  24  25  26

 27  28  29  30  31
```

The function prmonth(yearnum,monthnum[,width[,linesperweek]]) prints the corresponding output of month.

calendar(yearnum[,width[,linesperweek[,columnpadding]]])

The function *calendar* prints a yearly calendar, with three months per row. The parameters *width* and *linesperweek* function as for month. The parameter *columnpadding* indicates how many spaces to add between month-columns; it defaults to 6. The function prcalendar prints the corresponding output of calendar.

Calendar information

The *weekday* function looks up the day of the week for a particular date. The syntax is weekday(year,month,day). Weekdays range from Monday (0) to Sunday (6). Constants for each day (in all-caps) are available, for convenience and code-clarity:

```
>>> # Is May 1, 2002 a Wednesday?
>>> calendar.weekday(2002,5,1)==calendar.WEDNESDAY
1
```

The function monthrange(yearnum,monthnum) returns a two-tuple: The weekday of the first day of month *monthnum* in year *yearnum*, and the length of the month.

```
>>> calendar.monthrange(2000,2) # 2000 was a leap year!
(1, 29)
```

By default, calendar starts its weeks on Monday, and ends them on Sunday. I like this setting best, because the week ends with the weekend. But you can start your calendar's weeks on another day by calling setfirstweekday(weekday). The function firstweekday tells you which day of the week is currently the first day of the week:

```
>>> calendar.setfirstweekday(calendar.WEDNESDAY)
>>> print calendar.month(2002,5)
      May 2002
We Th Fr Sa Su Mo Tu
 1  2  3  4  5  6  7
 8  9 10 11 12 13 14
15 16 17 18 19 20 21
22 23 24 25 26 27 28
29 30 31
>>> calendar.firstweekday()  # Weeks start with day #2 (Wed.)
2
```

Leap years

The function isleap(yearnum) returns true if year *yearnum* is a leap year. The function leapdays(firstyear,lastyear) returns the number of leap days from *firstyear* to *lastyear*, inclusive.

Using Time Zones

The value time.daylight indicates whether a local DST (Daylight Savings Time) time zone is defined. A value of 1 indicates that a DST time zone is available.

The value time.timezone is the offset, in seconds, from the local time zone to UTC. This makes it easy to convert between time zones. The value time.altzone is an offset from the local DST time zone to UTC. The offset altzone is more accurate, but it is available only if time.daylight is 1.

```
>>> Now=time.time()
>>> time.ctime(Now) # Time in Mountain time zone, USA
'Sun Dec 10 10:44:49 2000'
>>> time.ctime(Now+time.altzone) # Time in England
'Sun Dec 10 17:44:49 2000'
```

The value time.tzname is a tuple. The first entry is the name of the local time zone. The second entry, if available, is the name of the local Daylight Savings Time time zone. The second entry is available only if time.daylight is nonzero. For example:

```
>>> time.tzname
('Pacific Standard Time', 'Pacific Daylight Time')
```

Allowing Two-Digit Years

Two-digit dates are convenient, but they can be ambiguous. For example, the year "97" should precede the year "03" if the years are 1997 and 2003, but not if they are 1997 and 1903.

In 1999, programmers around the world began rooting through legacy code to solve *the Y2K Bug* — a blanket term for all bugs caused by indiscriminate use of two-digit years. Some people worried that the Y2K Bug would cause The End Of The World As We Know It on January 1, 2000. Fortunately, it didn't and we can all sleep safely at night — at least until 2038 when epoch-based time starts to overflow.

Normally, Python adds 2000 to a two-digit year from 00 to 68, and adds 1900 to two-digit years from 69 to 99. However, for paranoia's sake, the value `time.accept2dyear` can be set to 0; this setting causes all two-digit years to be rejected. If you set the environment variable `PYTHON2K`, the value `time.accept2dyear` is initialized to 0. For example:

```
>>> Y4=(2000, 12, 10, 10, 9, 41, 6, 345, 0)
>>> Y2=(00, 12, 10, 10, 9, 41, 6, 345, 0) # Same date
>>> time.mktime(Y4)
976471781.0
>>> time.mktime(Y2) # 2-digit year below 69; add 2000
976471781.0
>>> time.accept2dyear=0 # Zero tolerance for YY!
>>> time.mktime(Y2)
Traceback (most recent call last):
  File "<stdin>", line 1, in ?
ValueError: year >= 1900 required
```

Summary

Python includes standard libraries for telling time, doing date arithmetic, and converting between time zones. In this chapter, you:

- ✦ Converted time between tuple and ticks representations.

- ✦ Formatted and parsed times in human-readable formats.

- ✦ Checked months and days on a yearly calendar.

- ✦ Handled various time zones, as well as Daylight Savings Time.

In the next chapter you will learn how to use Python to store and retrieve data from databases.

✦   ✦   ✦

Using Databases

Databases support permanent storage of large amounts of data. You can easily perform CRUD (Create, Read, Update, and Delete) on database records. Relational databases divide data between tables and support sophisticated SQL operations.

Python's standard libraries include a simple disk-dictionary database. The Python DB API provides a standard way to access relational databases. Various third-party modules implement this API, providing easy access to many flavors of database, including Oracle and MySQL.

Using Disk-Based Dictionaries

Python's standard libraries provide a simple database that takes the form of a single disk-based dictionary (or *disktionary*). This functionality is based on the UNIX utility dbm — on UNIX, you can access databases created by the dbm utility. Several modules define such a database, as shown in Table 14-1.

In This Chapter

Using disk-based dictionaries

DBM example: tracking telephone numbers

Advanced disk-based dictionaries

Accessing relational databases

Example: "sounds-like" queries

Examining relational metadata

Example: creating auditing tables

Advanced features of the DB API

Table 14-1
Disk-Based Dictionary Modules

Module	Description
anydbm	Portable database; chooses the best module from among the others
dumbdbm	Slow and limited, but available on all platforms
dbm	Wraps the UNIX dbm utility; available on UNIX only
gdbm	Wraps GNU's improved dbm; available on UNIX only
dbhash	Wraps the BSD database library; available on UNIX and Windows

In general, it is recommended that you use `anydbm`, as it is available on any platform (even if it has to use `dumbdbm`!)

Each dbm module defines a dbm object and an exception named `error`. The features in this section are available from every flavor of dbm; the "Advanced Disk-Based Dictionaries" section describes extended features not available in `dumbdbm`.

The `open` function creates a new dbm object. The function's syntax is `open (filename[,flag[,mode]])`. The *filename* parameter is the path to the file used to store the data. The *flag* parameter is normally optional, but is required for `dbhash`. It has the following legal values:

r	[default] Opens the database for read-only access
w	Opens the database for read and write access
c	Same as *w*, but creates the database file if necessary
n	Same as *w*, but always creates a new, empty database file

> **Note** The flag parameter is required for `dbhash.open`.

> **Caution** Some flavors of dbm (including `dumbdbm`) permit modifications to a database opened read-only!

The optional parameter *mode* specifies the UNIX-style permissions to set on the database file.

Once you have opened a database, you can access it much like a standard dictionary:

```
>>> SimpleDB=anydbm.open("test","c") # create a new datafile
>>> SimpleDB["Terry"]="Gilliam" # add a record
>>> SimpleDB["John"]="Cleese"
>>> print SimpleDB["Terry"] # access a record
Gilliam
>>> del SimpleDB["John"] # delete a record
```

The keys and values in a dbm must all be strings. For example:

```
>>> SimpleDB["Eric"]=5 # illegal; value is not a string!
Traceback (most recent call last):
  File "<stdin>", line 1, in ?
TypeError: bsddb value type must be string
```

Attempting to access a key with no value raises a KeyError exception. You can use the `has_key` method to verify that a key exists, or call `keys` to get a list of keys. However, the safe `get` method from a dictionary is not available:

```
>>> SimpleDB.keys()
['Terry']
>>> SimpleDB.has_key("Eric")
0
```

When you are finished with a dbm object, call its close method to sync it to disk and free its used resources.

DBM Example: Tracking Telephone Numbers

The example shown in Listing 14-1 uses a dbm object to track telephone numbers. The dictionary key is a person's name; the value is his or her telephone number.

Listing 14-1: **Phone list**

```
import anydbm
import sys

def AddName(DB):
    print "Enter a name. (Null name to cancel)"
    # Take the [:-1] slice to remove the \n at the end
    NewName=sys.stdin.readline()[:-1]
    if (NewName==""): return
    print "Enter a phone number."
    PhoneNumber=sys.stdin.readline()[:-1]
    DB[NewName]=PhoneNumber # Poke value into database!

def PrintList(DB):
    # Note: A large database may have MANY keys (too many to
    # casually put into memory). See Listing 14-2 for a better
    # way to iterate over keys in dbhash.
    for Key in DB.keys():
        print Key,DB[Key]

if (__name__=="__main__"):
    PhoneDB= dbhash.open("phone","c")
    while (1):
        print "\nEnter a name to look up\n+ to add a name"
        print "* for a full listing\n. to exit"
        Command=sys.stdin.readline()[:-1]
        if (Command==""):
            continue # Nothing to do; prompt again
        if (Command=="+"):
            AddName(PhoneDB)
        elif (Command=="*"):
            PrintList(PhoneDB)
```

Continued

Listing 14-1 *(continued)*

```
        elif (Command=="."):
            break # quit!
        else:
            try:
                print PhoneDB[Command]
            except KeyError:
                print "Name not found."
print "Saving and closing..."
PhoneDB.close()
```

Advanced Disk-Based Dictionaries

The various flavors of dbm don't use compatible file formats — for example, a database created using dbhash cannot be read using gdbm. This means that the only database file-format available on all platforms is that used by dumbdbm. The whichdb module can examine a database to determine which flavor of dbm created it. The function whichdb.whichdb(filename) returns the name of the module that created the datafile *filename*, returns None if the file is unreadable or does not exist, and returns an empty string if it can't figure out the file's format. For example, the following code uses anydbm to create a database, and then queries the database to see what type it really is:

```
>>> MysteryDB=anydbm.open("Unknown","c")
>>> MysteryDB.close() # write file so we can check its db-type
>>> whichdb.whichdb("Unknown")
'dbhash'
```

dbm

The dbm module provides an extra string variable, library, which is the name of the underlying ndbm implementation.

gdbm

The gdbm module provides improved key navigation. The dbm method firstkey returns the first key in the database; the method nextkey(currentkey) returns the key after *currentkey*. After doing many deletions from a gdbm database, you can call reorganize to free up space used by the datafile. In addition, the method sync flushes any unwritten changes to disk.

dbhash

The dbhash module also provides key navigation. The dbm methods `first` and `last` return the first and last keys, respectively. The methods `next(currentkey)` and `previous(currentkey)` return the key before and after currentkey, respectively. In addition, the method `sync` flushes any unwritten changes to disk.

Databases can be very large, so accessing the list of all keys returned by the `keys` method of a database may eat a lot of memory. The key-navigation methods provided by `gdbm` and `dbhash` enable you to iterate over all keys without loading them all into memory. The code in Listing 14-2 is an improved replacement for the PrintList method in the previous telephone list example.

Listing 14-2: **Improved list iteration with dbhash**

```
def PrintList(DB):
    Record=None
    try:
        # first() raises a KeyError if there are no entries
        Record = DB.first()
    except KeyError:
        return # Zero entries
    while 1:
        print Record
        try:
            # next() raises a KeyError if no next entry
            Record = DB.next()
        except KeyError:
            return # all done!
```

Using BSD database objects

The bsddb module, available on UNIX and Windows, provides access to the Berkeley DB library. It provides hashtable, b-tree, and record objects for data storage. The three constructors — `hashopen`, `btopen`, and `rnopen` — take the same parameters (filename, flag, and mode) as the dbm constructor. The constructors take other optional parameters — they are passed directly to the underlying BSD code, and should generally not be used.

BSD data objects provide the same functionality as dbm objects, as well as some additional methods. The methods first, last, next, and previous navigate through (and return) the records in the database. The records are ordered by key value for a b-tree object; record order is undefined for a hashtable or record. In addition, the method `set_location(keyvalue)` jumps to the record with key *keyvalue*:

```
>>> bob=bsddb.btopen("names","c")
>>> bob["M"]="Martin"
>>> bob["E"]="Eric"
>>> bob["X"]="Xavier"
>>> bob.first() # E is first, since this is a b-tree
('E', 'Eric')
>>> bob.next()
('M', 'Martin')
>>> bob.next()
('X', 'Xavier')
>>> bob.next() # navigating "off the edge" raises KeyError
Traceback (most recent call last):
  File "<stdin>", line 1, in ?
KeyError
>>> bob.set_location("M")
('M', 'Martin')
```

The `sync` method of a BSD database object flushes any changes to the datafile.

Accessing Relational Databases

Relational databases are a powerful, flexible way to store and retrieve many kinds of data. There are many relational database implementations, which vary in scalability and richness of features. The standard libraries do not include relational database support; however, Python modules exist to access almost any relational database, including Oracle, MySQL, DB/2, and Sybase.

The Python Database API defines a standard interface for Python modules that access a relational database. Most third-party database modules conform to the API closely, though not perfectly. This chapter covers Version 2.0 of the API.

Connection objects

The connect method constructs a database connection. The connection is used in constructing cursors. When finished with a connection, call its close method to free it. Databases generally provide a limited pool of connections, so a program should not needlessly use them up.

The parameters of the connect method vary by module, but typically include *dsn* (data source name), *user*, *password*, *host*, and *database*.

Transactions

Connections oversee transactions. A *transaction* is a collection of actions that must execute atomically — completely, or not at all. For example, a bank transfer might debit one account and credit another; this should be done within a single transaction, as performing only one half of the transfer would obviously be unacceptable.

Calling the `commit` connection method completes the current transaction; calling `rollback` cancels the current transaction. Not all databases support transactions — for example, Oracle does, MySQL doesn't (yet). The `commit` method is always available; `rollback` is only available where transaction support is provided.

Cursor objects

A cursor can execute SQL statements and retrieve data. The connection method `cursor` creates and returns a new cursor. The cursor method `execute(command [,parameters])` executes the specified SQL statement *command*, passing any necessary parameters. After executing a command that affects row data, the cursor attribute `rowcount` indicates the number of rows altered or returned; and the `description` attribute (described in the "Examining Relational Metadata" section) describes the columns affected. After executing a command that selects data, the method `fetchone` returns the next row of data (as a sequence, with one entry for each column value). The method `fetchmany([size])` returns a sequence of rows — up to *size* of them. The method `fetchall` returns all the rows.

After using a cursor, call its `close` method to free it. Databases typically have a limited pool of available cursors, so it is important to free cursors after use.

Example: "Sounds-Like" Queries

The example shown in Listing 14-3 uses the mxODBC module to look up people whose names "sound like" another name. ODBC is a standard interface for relational databases; ODBC drivers are available for many databases, including Oracle and MySQL. Therefore, the mxODBC module can handle most of the databases you are likely to deal with. Listing 14-4 shows the output from the example.

Listing 14-3: **Soundex.py**

```
# Replace this import with the appropriate one for your system:
import ODBC.Windows

# Dictionary used for sounds-like coding
SoundexDict = {"B":"1","P":"1","F":"1","V":"1",
               "C":"2","S":"2","G":"2","J":"2",
               "K":"2","Q":"2","X":"2","Z":"2",
               "D":"3","T":"3",
               "L":"4",
               "M":"5","N":"5",
               "R":"6",
               "A":"7","E":"7","I":"7","O":"7","U":"7","Y":"7",
               "H":"8","W":"8"}
```

Continued

Listing 14-3 *(continued)*

```
# These SQL statements may need to be tweaked for your database
# (They work with MySQL)
CREATE_EMPLOYEE_SQL = """CREATE TABLE EMPLOYEE (
EMPLOYEE_ID INT NOT NULL,
FIRST_NAME VARCHAR(20) NOT NULL,
LAST_NAME VARCHAR(20) NOT NULL,
MANAGER_ID INT
)"""
DROP_EMPLOYEE_SQL="DROP TABLE EMPLOYEE"
INSERT_SQL = "INSERT INTO EMPLOYEE VALUES "

def SoundexEncoding(str):
    """Return the 4-character SOUNDEX code for a string. Take
    first letter, then encode subsequent consonants as numbers.
    Ignore repeated codes (e.g MM codes as 5, not 55), unless
    separated by a vowel (e.g. SOS codes as 22)"""
    if (str==None or str==""): return None
    str = str.upper() # ignore case!
    SoundexCode=str[0]
    LastCode=SoundexDict[str[0]]
    for char in str[1:]:
        CurrentCode=SoundexDict[char]
        if (CurrentCode=="8"):
            pass # Don't include, or separate used consonants
        elif (CurrentCode=="7"):
            LastCode=None # Include consonants after vowels
        elif (CurrentCode!=LastCode): # Skip doubled letters
            SoundexCode+=CurrentCode
        if len(SoundexCode)==4: break # limit to 4 characters
    # Pad with zeroes (e.g. Lee is L000):
    SoundexCode += "0"*(4-len(SoundexCode))
    return SoundexCode

# Create the EMPLOYEE table
def CreateTable(Conn):
    NewCursor=Conn.cursor()
    try:
        NewCursor.execute(DROP_EMPLOYEE_SQL)
        NewCursor.execute(CREATE_EMPLOYEE_SQL)
    finally:
        NewCursor.close()
# insert a new employee into the table
def CreateEmployee(Conn,DataValues):
    NewCursor=Conn.cursor()
    try:
        NewCursor.execute(INSERT_SQL+DataValues)
    finally:
        NewCursor.close()

# Do a sounds-like query on a name
def PrintUsersLike(Conn,Name):
```

```
    if (Name==None or Name==""): return
    print "Users with last name similar to",Name+":"
    SoundexName = SoundexEncoding(Name)
    QuerySQL = "SELECT EMPLOYEE_ID, FIRST_NAME, LAST_NAME FROM"
    QuerySQL+= " EMPLOYEE WHERE LAST_NAME LIKE '"+Name[0]+"%'"
    NewCursor=Conn.cursor()
    try:
        NewCursor.execute(QuerySQL)
        for EmployeeRow in NewCursor.fetchall():
            if (SoundexEncoding(EmployeeRow[2])==SoundexName):
                print EmployeeRow
    finally:
        NewCursor.close()

if (__name__=="__main__"):
    # pass clear_auto_commit=0, because MySQL doesn't support
    # transactions (yet) and can't handle autocommit flag
    # Replace "MyDB" with your datasource name!
    Conn=ODBC.Windows.Connect("MyDB",clear_auto_commit=0)
    CreateTable(Conn)
    CreateEmployee(Conn,'(1,"Bob","Hilbert",Null)')
    CreateEmployee(Conn,'(2,"Sarah","Pfizer",Null)')
    CreateEmployee(Conn,'(3,"Sandy","Lee",1)')
    CreateEmployee(Conn,'(4,"Pat","Labor",2)')
    CreateEmployee(Conn,'(5,"Larry","Helper",Null)')
    PrintUsersLike(Conn,"Heilbronn")
    PrintUsersLike(Conn,"Pfizer")
    PrintUsersLike(Conn,"Washington")
    PrintUsersLike(Conn,"Lieber")
```

Listing 14-4: **Soundex output**

```
Users with last name similar to Heilbronn:
(1.0, 'Bob', 'Hilbert')
(5.0, 'Larry', 'Helper')
Users with last name similar to Pfizer:
(2.0, 'Sarah', 'Pfizer')
Users with last name similar to Washington:
Users with last name similar to Lieber:
(4.0, 'Pat', 'Labor')
```

Examining Relational Metadata

When a cursor returns data, the cursor attribute description is metadata—
definitions of the columns involved. A column's definition is represented as a
seven-item sequence; description is a sequence of such definitions. The items in
the sequence are listed in Table 14-2.

	Table 14-2
	Metadata Sequence Pieces
Index	*Data*
0	Column name
1	Type code
2	Display size (in columns)
3	Internal size (in characters or bytes)
4	Numeric scale
5	Numeric precision
6	Nullable (if 0, no nulls are allowed)

For example, the following is metadata from the Employee table of the Soundex example:

```
>>> mc.execute("select FIRST_NAME, MANAGER_ID from EMPLOYEE")
>>> mc.description
(('FIRST_NAME', 12, None, None, 5, 0, 0), ('MANAGER_ID', 3,
None, None, 1, 0, 1))
```

Note   The mxODBC module does not return display size and internal size.

Example: Creating Auditing Tables

Sometimes, it is useful to view old versions of data. For example, you may want to know both someone's current address and his or her old address. Or, a medical database may track who changed a patient's record, and when. One way to capture this data is with a *mirror table* — whenever an insert or update or delete occurs in the main table, a corresponding row is written to the mirror table. The mirror rows contain data, a timestamp, and the ID of the editing user — therefore, they provide a full audit trail of all data changes. Ideally, mirror rows should be inserted in the same transaction as the data-manipulation, to ensure that the audit trail is accurate.

The script shown in Listing 14-5 uses metadata to write SQL that creates a mirror table for a data table. Listing 14-6 shows a sample of the script's output.

Listing 14-5: **MirrorMaker.py**

```python
import ODBC.Windows
""" MirrorMaker builds mirror tables, for purposes of auditing.
For a table TABLEX, we create SQL to add a mirror table
TABLEX_M. The mirror table tracks version numbers, update
times, and updating users. """
# Replace these constants with values for your database
SERVER_NAME = "MyDB"
USER_NAME = "eva"
PASSWORD = "destruction"
SAMPLE_TABLE = "EMPLOYEE"


# Metadata for the mirror table's special columns
VERSION_NUMBER_COLUMN=("VERSION_NUMBER",
    ODBC.Windows.NUMERIC,None,None,0,0,0)
LAST_UPDATE_COLUMN=("LAST_UPDATE",
    ODBC.Windows.TIMESTAMP,None,None,0,0,0)
UPDATE_USER_COLUMN=("UPDATE_USER_ID",
    ODBC.Windows.NUMERIC,None,None,0,0,0)

def CreateColumnDefSQL(ColumnTuple):
    ColumnSQL = ColumnTuple[0] #name
    ColumnSQL += " "
    # The mxODBC function sqltype returns the SQL name of a
    # (numeric) column type. (For a different database
    # module, you may need to code this translation yourself.)
    OracleColumnType = ODBC.Windows.sqltype[ColumnTuple[1]]
    ColumnSQL += OracleColumnType
    # width of character fields
    if (OracleColumnType == "VARCHAR2" or
        OracleColumnType == "VARCHAR"):
        # Internal size not returned by mxODBC; so, use scale
        ColumnSQL += "("+`ColumnTuple[4]`+")" # width
    if (OracleColumnType == "NUMBER"):
        if (ColumnTuple[4]): # precision+scale
        ColumnSQL += "(" + `ColumnTuple[4]` +
          ","+`ColumnTuple[5]`+")" #
    if (ColumnTuple[6]): # nullable
        ColumnSQL += " NULL"
    else:
        ColumnSQL += " NOT NULL"
    return ColumnSQL

def CreateMirrorTableDefSQL(MyConnection,TableName):
    MyCursor = MyConnection.cursor()
    # This query returns no rows (because 1!=2), but returns
    # metadata (the definitions of each column in the table).
```

Continued

Listing 14-5 *(continued)*

```
    # Analogous to the SQL command "describe TABLENAME".
    MyCursor.execute("SELECT * from "+TableName+" where 1=2");
    SQLString = "CREATE TABLE "+TableName+"_M ("
    # Loop through columns, and create DDL for each
    FirstColumn=1
    for ColumnInfo in MyCursor.description:
        if (FirstColumn!=1):
            SQLString=SQLString+","
        FirstColumn=0
        SQLString += "\n"+CreateColumnDefSQL(ColumnInfo)
    # Add SQL to create the special mirror-table columns
    SQLString +=  ",\n" +
      CreateColumnDefSQL(VERSION_NUMBER_COLUMN)
    SQLString +=  ",\n" +
      CreateColumnDefSQL(LAST_UPDATE_COLUMN)
    SQLString += ",\n" +
      CreateColumnDefSQL(UPDATE_USER_COLUMN)
        SQLString += "\n)\n"
    MyCursor.close()
    return SQLString

if (__name__=="__main__"):
    MyConnection =
        ODBC.Windows.Connect(SERVER_NAME,USER_NAME,PASSWORD)
    print CreateMirrorTableDefSQL(MyConnection,SAMPLE_TABLE)
```

Listing 14-6: MirrorMaker output

```
CREATE TABLE EMPLOYEE_M (
EMPLOYEE_ID DECIMAL NOT NULL,
FIRST_NAME VARCHAR(0) NOT NULL,
LAST_NAME VARCHAR(0) NOT NULL,
MANAGER_ID DECIMAL NULL,
VERSION_NUMBER NUMERIC NOT NULL,
LAST_UPDATE TIMESTAMP NOT NULL,
UPDATE_USER_ID NUMERIC NOT NULL
)
```

Advanced Features of the DB API

Relational databases feature various column types, such as INT and VARCHAR. A database module should export constants describing these datatypes; these constants are used in description metadata. For example, the following code checks a column type (12) against a module-level constant (VARCHAR):

```
>>> MyCursor.execute("SELECT EMPLOYEE_NAME from EMPLOYEE where
FIRST_NAME='Bob'")
>>> MyCursor.description[0]
('FIRST_NAME', 12, None, None, 3, 0, 0)
>>> MyCursor.description[0][1]==ODBC.Windows.VARCHAR
1
```

Some column types, such as dates, demand a particular kind of data. A database module should export functions to construct date, time, and timestamp values. For example, the function Date(year,month,day) constructs a date value (suitable for insertion into the database) corresponding to the given year, month, and day. The module mxDateTime provides the preferred implementation of date and time objects.

Input and output sizes

The cursor attribute arraysize specifies how many rows, by default, to return in each call to fetchmany. It defaults to 1, but you can increase it if desired. Manipulating arraysize is more efficient than passing a size parameter to fetchmany:

```
>>> MyCursor.execute("SELECT FIRST_NAME FROM EMPLOYEE")
>>> MyCursor.rowcount # total fetchable rows
5
>>> MyCursor.fetchmany() # default arraysize is 1
[('Bob',)]
>>> MyCursor.arraysize=5 # get up to 5 rows at once
>>> MyCursor.fetchmany() # (only 4 left, so I don't get 5)
[('Sarah',), ('Sandy',), ('Pat',), ('Larry',)]
```

The cursor methods setinputsizes(size) and setoutputsize(size [,columnindex]) let you set an "expected size" for columns before executing a SQL statement. These methods are optional, and exist to improve performance and memory usage.

The *size* parameter for setinputsizes is a sequence. Each entry in *size* should specify the maximum length for each parameter. If an entry in *size* is None, then no block of memory will be set aside for the corresponding parameter value (this is the default behavior).

The method setoutputsize sets a maximum buffer size for data read from large columns (LONG or BLOB). If *columnindex* is not specified, the buffer size is set for all large columns in the result sequence. For example, the following code limits the data read from the long DESCRIPTION column to 50 characters:

```
>>> MyCursor.setoutputsizes(1,50)
>>> MyCursor.execute("select GAME_NAME, DESCRIPTION from GAME")
>>> MyCursor.fetchone()
('005', ' You play a spy who must take a briefcase and suc')
```

Reusable SQL statements

Before a SQL statement can be executed, it must be parsed. Vendors such as Oracle cache recently parsed SQL commands so that the commands need not be re-parsed if they are used again. Therefore, you should build re-usable SQL statements with *marked parameters,* instead of hard-coded values. This way, the parameters can be passed into the execute method. The following example re-uses the same SQL statement to query a video game database twice:

```
>>> SQLQuery = "select GAME_NAME from GAME where GAME_ID = ?"
>>> MyCursor.execute(SQLQuery,(60,)) # tuple provides ID of 60
>>> MyCursor.fetchall()
[('Air Combat 22',)]
>>> MyCursor.execute(SQLQuery,(200,)) # no need to re-parse SQL
>>> MC.fetchall()
[('Badlands',)]
```

The syntax for parameter marking is described by the module variable paramstyle (see the next section, "Database library information"). The cursor method executemany(command,parametersequence) runs the same SQL statement *command* many times, once for each collection of parameters in *parametersequence.*

Database library information

The module variable apilevel is a string describing the supported DB API level. It should be either 1.0 or 2.0; if it is not available, assume the supported API level is 1.0.

The module variable threadsafety describes what level of concurrent access the module supports:

0	Threads may not share the module
1	Threads may share the module
2	Threads may share connections
3	Threads may share cursors

The module variable paramstyle describes which style of parameter marking the module expects to see in SQL statements. Following are the legal values of paramstyle and an example of such a marked parameter:

qmark	WHERE NAME=?
numeric	WHERE NAME=.1
named	WHERE NAME=.name
format	WHERE NAME=%s
pyformat	WHERE NAME=%(name)s

Error hierarchy

Database warnings and errors are subclasses of the class StandardError from the module exceptions. You can catch the Error class to do general error handling, or catch more specific exceptions. Figure 14-1 shows the inheritance hierarchy of database exceptions. See Table 14-3 for a description of each exception.

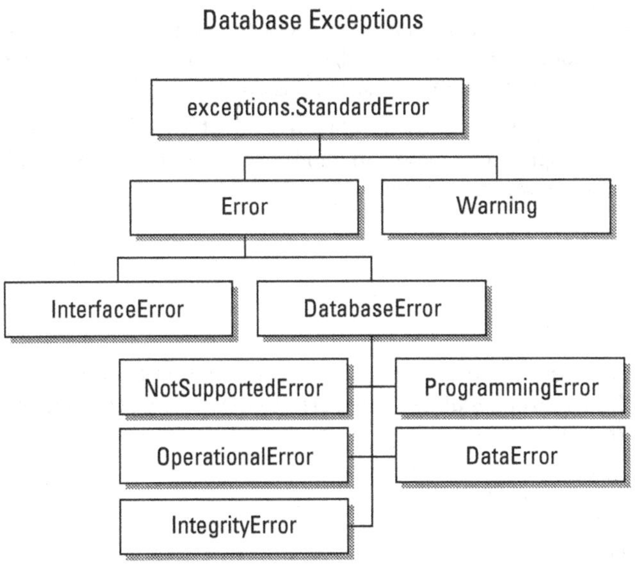

Database Exceptions

Figure 14-1: Database exception class hierarchy

<table>
<tr><td colspan="2" align="center">Table 14-3
Database Exceptions</td></tr>
<tr><td>*Type*</td><td>*Meaning*</td></tr>
<tr><td>Warning</td><td>Significant warnings, such as data-value truncation during insertion.</td></tr>
<tr><td>Error</td><td>Base class for other errors. Not raised directly.</td></tr>
<tr><td>InterfaceError</td><td>Raised when the database module encounters an internal error. An InterfaceError stems from the database module, not the database itself.</td></tr>
<tr><td>DatabaseError</td><td>Errors relating to the database itself. Mostly used as a base class for other errors.</td></tr>
<tr><td>DataError</td><td>Errors due to invalid data, such as an out-of-range numeric value.</td></tr>
</table>

Continued

	Table 14-3 *(continued)*	
Type	**Meaning**	
OperationalError	Operational errors, such as a failure to connect to the database.	
IntegrityError	Data integrity errors, such as a missing foreign key.	
InternalError	Internal database error, such as a cursor becoming disconnected.	
ProgrammingError	Invalid call to the database module; for example, trying to use a cursor that has been closed, or calling `fetch` on a cursor before executing a command that returns data.	
NotSupportedError	Some portions of the DB API are optional. A module that does not implement optional methods may raise NotSupportedError if you attempt to call them.	

Summary

Python's standard libraries include powerful tools for handling dictionaries on disk. Modules implementing the Python Database API permit easy access to relational databases. In this chapter, you:

✦ Learned about Python's flavors of dbm.

✦ Stored and retrieved dictionary data on disk.

✦ Looked up employees with a "sounds-like" query.

✦ Used table metadata to easily build new relational tables.

In the next chapter, you learn how to harness Python for networking.

✦　　✦　　✦

Networking and the Internet

P A R T

III

Chapter 15
Networking

Chapter 16
Speaking Internet
Protocols

Chapter 17
Handling Internet
Data

Chapter 18
Parsing XML and
Other Markup
Languages

Networking

T he modules covered in this chapter teach you everything you need to know to communicate between programs on a network. The networking topics covered here don't require more than one computer, however; you can use networking for interprocess communication on a single machine.

Networking Background

This section provides a brief introduction to some of the terms you'll encounter in the rest of this chapter.

A *socket* is a network connection endpoint. When your Web browser requests the main Web page of www.python.org, for example, your Web browser creates a socket and instructs it to connect to the Web server hosting the Python Web site, where the Web server is also listening on a socket for incoming requests. The two sides use the sockets to send messages and other data back and forth.

When in use, each socket is *bound* to a particular IP address and port. An IP address is a sequence of four numbers in the range of 0 to 255 (for example, 173.15.20.201); port numbers range from 0 to 65535. Port numbers less than 1024 are reserved for well-known networking services (a Web server, for example, uses port 80); the maximum reserved value is stored in the socket module's IPPORT_RESERVED variable. You can use other port numbers for your own programs, although technically, ports 1024 to 5000 (socket.IPPORT_USERRESERVED) are used for officially registered applications (although nobody will yell at you for using them).

Not all IP addresses are visible to the rest of the world. Some, in fact, are specifically reserved for addresses that are never public (such as addresses of the form 192.168.y.z or 10.x.y.z). The address 127.0.0.1 is the *localhost* address; it always refers to the current computer. Programs can use this address to connect to other programs running on the same machine.

In This Chapter

Networking background

Working with addresses and host names

Communicating with low-level sockets

Example: a multicast chat application

Using SocketServers

Processing Web browser requests

Handling multiple requests without threads

Remembering more than a handful of IP addresses can be tedious, so you can also pay a small fee and register a *host name* or *domain name* for a particular address (not surprisingly, more people visit your Web site if they can point their Web browser at www.threemeat.com instead of 208.114.27.12). *Domain Name Servers* (DNS) handle the task of mapping the names to the IP addresses. Every computer can have a host name, even if it isn't an officially registered one.

Exactly how messages are transmitted through a network is based on many factors, one of which is the different *protocols* that are in use. Many protocols build upon simpler, lower-level protocols to form a *protocol stack*. HTTP, for example, is the protocol used to communicate between Web browsers and Web servers, and it is built upon the TCP protocol, which is in turn built upon a protocol named IP.

When sending messages between two programs of your own, you usually choose between the TCP and UDP protocols. TCP creates a persistent connection between two endpoints, and the messages that you send are guaranteed to arrive at their destination and to arrive in order. UDP is connectionless, a bit faster, but less reliable. Messages you send may or may not make it to the other end; and if they do make it, they might arrive out of order. Occasionally, more than one copy of a message makes it to the receiver, even if you sent it only once.

You can find volumes full of additional information on networking; this section doesn't even scratch the surface. It does, however, give you a head start on understanding the following sections.

Working with Addresses and Host Names

The socket module provides several functions for working with host names and addresses.

Note   The socket module is a very close wrapper around the C socket library; and like the C version, it supports all sorts of options. This chapter covers the most common and useful features of sockets; consult the Winsock help file or the UNIX socket man pages for coverage of more arcane features. In many cases, the socket module defines variables that map directly to the C equivalent (for example, socket.IP_MAX_MEMBERSHIPS is equivalent to the C constant of the same name).

gethostname() returns the host name for the computer on which the program is running:

```
>>> import socket
>>> socket.gethostname()
'endor'
```

`gethostbyname(name)` tries to resolve the given host name to an IP address. First a check is made to determine whether the current computer can do the translation. If it doesn't know, a request is sent to a remote DNS server (which in turn may ask other DNS servers too). `gethostbyname` returns the name or raises an exception if the lookup fails:

```
>>> socket.gethostbyname('endor')
'10.0.0.6'
>>> socket.gethostbyname('www.python.org')
'132.151.1.90'
```

An extended form, `gethostbyname_ex(name)`, returns a 3-tuple consisting of the primary host name of the given address, a list of alternative host names for the same IP address, and a list of other IP addresses for the same interface on that same host (both lists may be empty):

```
>>> socket.gethostbyname('www.yahoo.com')
'64.58.76.178'
>>> socket.gethostbyname_ex('www.yahoo.com')
('www.yahoo.akadns.net', ['www.yahoo.com'],
['64.58.76.178', '64.58.76.176', '216.32.74.52',
 '216.32.74.50', '64.58.76.179', '216.32.74.53',
 '64.58.76.177', '216.32.74.51', '216.32.74.55'])
```

The `gethostbyaddr(address)` function does the same thing, except that you supply it an IP address string instead of a host name:

```
>>> socket.gethostbyaddr('132.151.1.90')
('parrot.python.org', ['www.python.org'], ['132.151.1.90'])
```

`getservbyname(service, protocol)` takes a service name (such as 'telnet' or 'ftp') and a protocol (such as 'tcp' or 'udp') and returns the port number used by that service:

```
>>> socket.getservbyname('http','tcp')
80
>>> socket.getservbyname('telnet','tcp')
23
>>> socket.getservbyname('doom','udp')
666   # id Software registered this for the game "Doom"
```

Often, non-Python programs store and use IP addresses in their 32-bit packed form. The `inet_aton(ip_addr)` and `inet_ntoa(packed)` functions convert back and forth between this form and an IP address string:

```
>>> socket.inet_aton('177.20.1.201')
'\261\024\001\311' # A 4-byte string
>>> socket.inet_ntoa('\x7F\x00\x00\x01')
'127.0.0.1'
```

socket also defines a few variables representing some reserved IP addresses. INADDR_ANY and INADDR_BROADCAST are reserved IP addresses referring to any IP address and the broadcast address, respectively; and INADDR_LOOPBACK refers to the loopback device, always at address 127.0.0.1. These variables are in the numeric 32-bit form.

The getfqdn([name]) function returns the fully qualified domain name for the given hostname (if omitted, it returns the fully qualified domain name of the local host):

```
>>> socket.getfqdn('')
'dialup84.lasal.net'
```

New Feature   getfqdn was new in Python 2.0.

Communicating with Low-Level Sockets

Although Python provides some wrappers that make using sockets easier (you'll see them later in this chapter), you can always work with sockets directly too.

Creating and destroying sockets

The socket(family, type[, proto]) function in the socket module creates a new socket object. The family is usually AF_INET, although others such as AF_IPX are sometimes available, depending on the platform. The type is most often SOCK_STREAM (for connection-oriented, reliable TCP connections) or SOCK_DGRAM (for connectionless UDP messages):

```
>>> from socket import *
>>> s = socket(AF_INET,SOCK_STREAM)
```

The combination of family and type usually implies a protocol, but you can specify it using the optional third parameter to socket using values such as IPPROTO_TCP or IPPROTO_RAW. Instead of using the IPPROTO_ variables, you can use the getprotobyname(proto) function:

```
>>> getprotobyname('tcp')
6
>>> IPPROTO_TCP
6
```

fromfd(fd, family, type[, proto]) is a rarely used function for creating a socket object from an open file descriptor (returned from a file's fileno() method). The descriptor should be connected to a real socket, and not to a file. The fileno() method of a socket object returns the file descriptor (an integer) for this socket. See the section "Handling Multiple Requests Without Threads" later in this chapter for an idea of where this might be useful.

When you are finished with a `socket` object, you call the `close()` method, after which no further operation on the object will succeed (sockets are automatically closed when they are garbage collected, but it's a good idea to explicitly close them when possible, both to free up resources sooner and to make your program clearer). Alternatively, you can use the `shutdown(how)` method to close one or both halves of a connection. Passing a value of 0 prevents the socket from receiving any more data, 1 prevents any additional sends, and 2 prevents additional transmission in either direction.

Connecting sockets

When two sockets *connect* (via TCP, for example), one side listens for and accepts an incoming connection, and the other side initiates that connection. The listening side creates a socket, calls `bind(address)` to bind it to a particular address and port, calls `listen(backlog)` to listen for incoming connections, and finally calls `accept()` to accept the new, incoming connection:

```
>>> s = socket(AF_INET,SOCK_STREAM)
>>> s.bind(('127.0.0.1',44444))
>>> s.listen(1)
>>> q,v = s.accept() # Returns socket q and address v
```

Note that the preceding code will *block* or appear to hang until a connection is present to be accepted. No problem; just initiate a connection from another Python interpreter. The connecting side creates a socket and calls `connect(address)`:

```
>>> s = socket(AF_INET,SOCK_STREAM)
>>> s.connect(('127.0.0.1',44444))
```

At this point, the first side of the connection uses socket q to communicate with the second side, using socket s. To verify that they are connected, enter the following line on the first, or server, side:

```
>>> q.send('Hello from Python!')
18 @code:# Number of bytes sent
```

On the other side, enter the following:

```
>>> s.recv(1024) # Receive up to 1024 bytes
'Hello from Python!'
```

The addresses you pass to `bind` and `connect` are 2-tuples of (`ipAddress,port`) for `AF_INET` sockets. Instead of `connect`, you can also call the `connect_ex(address)` method. If the underlying call to the C `connect` returns an error, `connect_ex` will also return an error (or 0 for success), instead of raising an exception.

When you call listen, you pass in a number specifying the maximum number of incoming connections that will be placed in a wait queue. If more connections arrive when the queue is full, the remote side is informed that the connection was refused. The SOMAXCONN variable in the socket module indicates the maximum size the wait queue can be.

The accept() method returns an address of the same form used by bind and connect, indicating the address of the remote socket. The following uses the v variable from the preceding example:

```
>>> v
('127.0.0.1', 1039)
```

UDP sockets are not connection-oriented, but you can still call connect to associate a socket with a given destination address and port (see the next section for details).

Sending and receiving data

send(string[, flags]) sends the given string of bytes to the remote socket. sendto(string[, flags], address) sends the given string to a particular address. Generally, the send method is used with connection-oriented sockets, and sendto is used with non-connection–oriented sockets, but if you call connect on a UDP socket to associate it with a particular destination, you can then call send instead of sendto.

Both send and sendto return the number of bytes that were actually sent. When sending large amounts of data quickly, you may want to ensure that the entire message was sent, using a function like the following:

```
def safeSend(sock,msg):
    sent = 0
    while msg:
        i = sock.send(msg)
        if i == -1: # Error
            return -1
        sent += i
        msg = msg[i:]
        time.sleep(25) # Wait a little while the queue empties
    return sent
```

This keeps resending part of the message as needed until the entire message has been sent.

Tip   An even better solution to this problem is to avoid sending data until you know at least some if it can be written. See "Handling Multiple Requests Without Threads" later in this chapter for details.

The recv(bufsize[,flags]) method receives an incoming message. If a lot of data is waiting, it returns only the first bufsize bytes that are waiting. recvfrom (bufsize[,flags]) does the same thing, except that with AF_INET sockets the return value is (data, (ipAddress, port)) so that you can see from where the message originated (this is useful for connectionless sockets).

The send, sendto, recv, and recvfrom methods all take an optional flags parameter that defaults to 0. You can use a bitwise-OR on any of the socket.MSG_* variables to create a value for flags. The values available vary by platform, but some of the most common are listed in Table 15-1.

Table 15-1
Flag Values for send and recv

Flag	Description
MSG_OOB	Process out-of-band data.
MSG_DONTROUTE	Don't use routing tables; send directly to the interface.
MSG_PEEK	Return the waiting data without removing it from the queue.

For example, if you have an open socket that has a message waiting to be received, you can take a peek at the message without actually removing it from the queue of incoming data:

```
>>> q.recv(1024,MSG_PEEK)
'Hello!'
>>> q.recv(1024,MSG_PEEK) # You could call this over and over.
'Hello!'
```

The makefile([mode[, bufsize]]) method returns a file-like object wrapping this socket, so that you can then pass it to code that expects a file argument (or maybe you prefer to use file methods instead of send and recv). The optional mode and bufsize parameters take the same values as the built-in open function.

Cross-Reference

Chapter 8 explains the use of files and filelike objects.

Using socket options

A socket object's getpeername() and getsockname() methods both return a 2-tuple containing an IP address and a port (just as you'd pass to connect or bind). getpeername returns the address and port of the remote socket to which it is connected, and getsockname returns the same information for the local socket.

By default, sockets are *blocking,* which means that socket method calls don't return until the action completes. For example, if the outgoing buffer is full and you try to send more data, the call to send will try to block until it can put more data into the buffer. You can change this behavior by calling the setblocking(flag) method with a value of 0. When a socket is nonblocking, it will raise the error exception if the requested action would cause it to block One useful application of this behavior is that you can create servers that shut down gracefully:

```
s = socket(AF_INET,SOCK_STREAM)
s.bind(('10.0.0.6',55555))
s.listen(5)
s.setblocking(0)
while bKeepGoing:
    try:
        q,v = s.accept()
    except error:
        q = None
    if q:
        processRequest(q,v)
    else:
        time.sleep(0.25)
```

This server continuously tries to accept a new connection and send it off to the fictional processRequest function. If a new connection isn't available, it sleeps for a quarter of a second and tries again. This means that some other part of your program can set the bKeepGoing variable to 0, and the preceding loop will exit.

Tip   Another approach is to call select or poll on your listen socket to detect when a new connection has arrived. See "Handling Multiple Requests Without Threads" later in this chapter for more information.

Other socket options can be set and retrieved with the setsockopt(level, name, value) and getsockopt(level, name[, buflen]) methods. Sockets represent several layers of a protocol stack, and the level parameter specifies at what level the option should be applied. (For example, the option may pertain to the socket itself, an intermediate protocol such as TCP, or a lower protocol such as IP.) The values for level start with SOL_ (SOL_SOCKET, SOL_TCP, and so on). The name of the option identifies exactly which option you're talking about, and the socket module defines whatever option names are available on your platform.

The C version of setsockopt requires that you pass in a buffer for the value parameter, but in Python you can just pass in a number if that particular option expects a numeric value. You can also pass in a buffer (a string), but it's up to you to make sure you use the proper format. With getsockopt, not specifying the buflen parameter means you're expecting a numeric value, and that's what it returns. If you do supply buflen, getsockopt returns a string representing a buffer, and its maximum length will be buflen bytes.

Although there's a ton of options in existence, Table 15-2 lists some of the more common ones you'll need, along with what type of data the value parameter is supposed to be. For example, use the following to set the send buffer size of a socket to about 64 KB:

```
>>> s = socket(AF_INET,SOCK_STREAM)
>>> s.setsockopt(SOL_SOCKET, SO_SNDBUF, 65535)
```

To get the time-to-live (TTL) value or number of hops a packet can make before being discarded by a router, use this:

```
>>> s.getsockopt(SOL_IP, IP_TTL)
32
```

See the sample chat application in the next section for more examples of using setsockopt.

Table 15-2
Common setsockopt and getsockopt Options

Option Name	Value	Description
Options for SOL_SOCKET		
SO_TYPE	(Get only)	Socket type (for example, SOCK_STREAM)
SO_ERROR	(Get only)	Socket's last error
SO_LINGER	Boolean	Linger on close if data present
SO_RCVBUF	Number	Input (receive) buffer size
SO_SNDBUF	Number	Output (send) buffer size
SO_RCVTIMEO	Time struct[1]	Input (receive) timeout delay
SO_SNDTIMEO	Time struct[1]	Output (send) timeout delay
SO_REUSEADDR	Boolean	Enable multiple users of a local address/port
Options for SOL_TCP		
TCP_NODELAY	Boolean	Send data immediately instead of waiting for minimum send amount
Options for SOL_IP		
IP_TTL	0–255	Maximum number of hops a packet can travel
IP_MULTICAST_TTL	0–255	Maximum number of hops a packet can travel
IP_MULTICAST_IF	inet_aton(ip)	Select interface over which to transmit
IP_MULTICAST_LOOP	Boolean	Enable sender to receive a copy of multicast packets it sends out
IP_ADD_MEMBERSHIP	ip_mreq[2]	Join a multicast group
IP_DROP_MEMBERSHIP	ip_mreq[2]	Leave a multicast group

1 The struct is two C long variables to hold seconds and microseconds.

2 The struct is the concatenation of two calls to inet_aton—one for multicast address and one for local address.

Converting numbers

Because the byte ordering can vary by platform, a *network order* specifies a standard ordering to use when transferring numbers across a network. The `nthol(x)` and `ntohs(x)` functions take a network number and convert it to the same number using the current host's byte ordering, and the `htonl(x)` and `htons(x)` functions convert in the other direction (if the current host has the same byte ordering as network order, the functions do nothing):

```
>>> import socket
>>> socket.htons(20000) # Convert a 16-bit value
8270
>>> socket.htonl(20000) # Convert a 32-bit value
541982720
>>> socket.ntohl(541982720)
20000
```

Example: A Multicast Chat Application

The example in this section combines material from several chapters to create a chat application that also enables you to draw on a shared whiteboard, as shown in Figure 15-1.

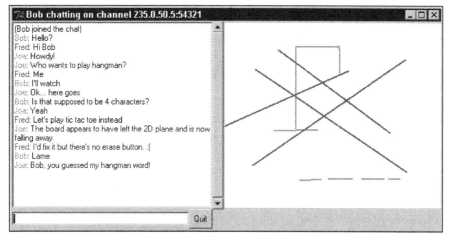

Figure 15-1: The chat/whiteboard application in action

Instead of using a client/server model, the program uses multicast sockets for its communication. When you send a message to a multicast address (those addresses in the range from 224.0.0.1 to 239.255.255.255, inclusive), the message is sent to all computers that have joined that particular multicast *group*. This provides a simple way to send messages to any number of other computers, without having to keep track of which computers are listening. (This could also be considered a security hole—were this a "real-world" application, you'd want to encrypt the messages or use some other means to prevent eavesdropping.)

Save the program in Listing 15-1 to a file named multichat.py. To start the application, specify on the command line your name or alias and your color. The color is passed to Tkinter (the module in charge of the user interface), so normal color names such as blue or red work, but you can also use any of Tkinter's niftier colors:

```
C:\temp> python multitest.py Bob SlateBlue4
```

You don't need several computers to try this program out; just start multiple copies and watch them interact.

This application uses Tkinter for its user interface. To learn more about Tkinter, see Chapters 19 and 20. It also uses threads, which you can learn about in Chapter 26. Finally, read Chapter 12 to learn about serializing Python objects with pickle and cPickle.

Listing 15-1: multichat – Multicast chat/ whiteboard application

```python
from Tkinter import *
from socket import *
import cPickle, threading, sys

# Each message is a command + data
CMD_JOINED,CMD_LEFT,CMD_MSG,CMD_LINE,CMD_JOINRESP = range(5)
people = {} # key = (ipaddr,port), value = (name,color)

def sendMsg(msg):
    sendSock.send(msg,0)

def onQuit():
    'User clicked Quit button'
    sendMsg(chr(CMD_LEFT)) # Notify others that I'm leaving
    root.quit()

def onMove(e):
    'Called when LButton is down and mouse moves'
    global lastLine,mx,my
    canvas.delete(lastLine) # Erase temp line
    mx,my = e.x,e.y

    # Draw a new temp line
    lastLine = \
            canvas.create_line(dx,dy,mx,my,width=2,fill='Black')
```

Continued

Listing 15-1 *(continued)*

```python
def onBDown(e):
    'User pressed left mouse button'
    global lastLine,dx,dy,mx,my
    canvas.bind('<Motion>',onMove) # Start receiving move msgs
    dx,dy = e.x,e.y
    mx,my = e.x,e.y

    # Draw a temporary line
    lastLine = \
        canvas.create_line(dx,dy,mx,my,width=2,fill='Black')

def onBUp(e):
    'User released left mouse button'
    canvas.delete(lastLine) # Erase the temporary line
    canvas.unbind('<Motion>') # No more move msgs, please!

    # Send out the draw-a-line command
    sendMsg(chr(CMD_LINE)+cPickle.dumps((dx,dy,e.x,e.y),1))

def onEnter(foo):
    'User hit the [Enter] key'
    sendMsg(chr(CMD_MSG)+entry.get())
    entry.delete(0,END) # Clear the entry widget

def setup(root):
    'Creates the user interface'
    global msgs,entry,canvas

    # The big window holding everybody's messages
    msgs = Text(root,width=60,height=20)
    msgs.grid(row=0,col=0,columnspan=3)

    # Hook up a scrollbar to see old messages
    s = Scrollbar(root,orient=VERTICAL)
    s.config(command=msgs.yview)
    msgs.config(yscrollcommand=s.set)
    s.grid(row=0,col=3,sticky=N+S)

    # Where you type your message
    entry = Entry(root)
    entry.grid(row=1,col=0,columnspan=2,sticky=W+E)
    entry.bind('<Return>',onEnter)
    entry.focus_set()

    b = Button(root,text='Quit',command=onQuit)
    b.grid(row=1,col=2)

    # A place to draw
    canvas = Canvas(root,bg='White')
    canvas.grid(row=0,col=5)
    # Notify me of button press and release messages
```

```
        canvas.bind('<ButtonPress-1>',onBDown)
        canvas.bind('<ButtonRelease-1>',onBUp)

    def msgThread(addr,port,name):
        'Listens for and processes messages'

        # Create a listen socket
        s = socket(AF_INET, SOCK_DGRAM)
        s.setsockopt(SOL_SOCKET,SO_REUSEADDR,1)
        s.bind(('',port))

        # Join the multicast group
        s.setsockopt(SOL_IP,IP_ADD_MEMBERSHIP,\
                    inet_aton(addr)+inet_aton(''))

        while 1:
            # Get a msg and strip off the command byte
            msg,msgFrom = s.recvfrom(2048)
            cmd,msg = ord(msg[0]),msg[1:]

            if cmd == CMD_JOINED: # New join
                msgs.insert(END,'(%s joined the chat)\n' % msg)

                # Introduce myself
                sendMsg(chr(CMD_JOINRESP)+ \
                        cPickle.dumps((name,myColor),1))

            elif cmd == CMD_LEFT: # Somebody left
                who = people[msgFrom][0]
                if who == name: # Hey, _I_ left, better quit
                    break
                msgs.insert(END,'(%s left the chat)\n' % \
                            who,'color_'+who)

            elif cmd == CMD_MSG: # New message to display
                who = people[msgFrom][0]
                msgs.insert(END,who,'color_%s' % who)
                msgs.insert(END,': %s\n' % msg)

            elif cmd == CMD_LINE: # Draw a line
                dx,dy,ex,ey = cPickle.loads(msg)
                canvas.create_line(dx,dy,ex,ey,width=2,\
                                fill=people[msgFrom][1])

            elif cmd == CMD_JOINRESP: # Introducing themselves
                people[msgFrom] = cPickle.loads(msg)
                who,color = people[msgFrom]

                # Create a tag to draw text in their color
                msgs.tag_configure('color_' + who,foreground=color)
```

Continued

Listing 15-1 *(continued)*

```
        # Leave the multicast group
        s.setsockopt(SOL_IP,IP_DROP_MEMBERSHIP,\
                    inet_aton(addr)+inet_aton(''))

if __name__ == '__main__':
    argv = sys.argv
    if len(argv) < 3:
        print 'Usage:',argv[0],'<name> <color> '\
              '[addr=<multicast address>] [port=<port>]'
        sys.exit(1)

    global name, addr, port, myColor
    addr = '235.0.50.5' # Default IP address
    port = 54321         # Default port
    name,myColor = argv[1:3]
    for arg in argv[3:]:
        if arg.startswith('addr='):
            addr = arg[len('addr='):]
        elif arg.startswith('port='):
            port = int(arg[len('port='):])

    # Start up a thread to process messages
    threading.Thread(target=msgThread,\
                    args=(addr,port,name)).start()

    # This is the socket over which we send out messages
    global sendSock
    sendSock = socket(AF_INET,SOCK_DGRAM)
    sendSock.setsockopt(SOL_SOCKET,SO_REUSEADDR,1)
    sendSock.connect((addr,port))

    # Don't let the packets die too soon
    sendSock.setsockopt(SOL_IP,IP_MULTICAST_TTL,2)

    # Create a Tk window and create the GUI
    root = Tk()
    root.title('%s chatting on channel %s:%d' % \
              (name,addr,port))
    setup(root)

    # Join the chat!
    sendMsg(chr(CMD_JOINED)+name)
    root.mainloop()
```

Note   Although this application will work on a local network, it may have trouble working between computers on the Internet. Some routers are configured to ignore
multicast data packets, and the time-to-live (TTL) setting for the packets must be
high enough to make the necessary number of *hops* between each computer.

As with most Python programs, this one packs a lot of punch in very few lines of code (it weighs in at about 120 lines, ignoring comments). The first thing to note is the msgThread function, which creates a socket to listen for incoming multicast messages. It uses the SO_REUSEADDR socket option to enable you to run multiple copies on one computer (otherwise, bind would complain that someone else was already bound to that address and port). It also uses IP_ADD_MEMBERSHIP to join a multicast group, and IP_DROP_MEMBERSHIP to leave it. The first byte of each message is a predefined command character, which msgThread uses to determine what to do with the message.

When you type a message into the text entry box at the bottom of the dialog box, onEnter sends the text from the entry box to the multicast channel. Likewise, pressing the left mouse button, dragging a line, and releasing it causes onBUp to send the message to draw a new line. Note that neither of these actually displays a message or draws a line — they just send a message to the multicast group, and all running copies, including the one that originated the message, receive the message and process it. The socket that sends these messages doesn't need to join the multicast group; anyone can send to a group, but only members can receive messages.

When msgThread calls recvFrom to get a new message, it also gets the IP address and port of the sender. The program uses this tuple as a dictionary key to map to the name and color of the sender (each line is drawn in the sender's color, as is that user's name when they send a text message).

One final thing to note is how the listening thread decides when to shut down. When you click the Quit button, the application notifies everyone that you are leaving the chat group. Your listener also hears this message, and recognizing that the sender is itself, it stops waiting for more messages.

Using SocketServers

The SocketServer module defines a base class for a group of socket server classes — classes that wrap up and hide the details of listening for, accepting, and handling incoming socket connections.

The SocketServer family

TCPServer and UDPServer are SocketServer subclasses that handle TCP and UDP messages, respectively.

Note   SocketServer also provides UnixStreamServer (a child class of TCPServer) and UnixDatagramServer (a child of UDPServer), which are the same as their parent classes except that the listening socket is created with a family of AF_UNIX instead of AF_INET.

By default, the socket servers handle connections one at a time, but you can use the ThreadingMixIn and ForkingMixIn classes to create threading or forking versions of any SocketServer. In fact, the SocketServer module helpfully provides the following classes to save you the trouble: ForkingUDPServer, ForkingTCPServer, ThreadingUDPServer, ThreadingTCPServer, ThreadingUnixStreamServer, and ThreadingUnixDatagramServer. Obviously, the threading versions work only on platforms that support threads, and the forking versions work on platforms that support os.fork.

Cross-Reference   See Chapter 7 for an overview of mix-in classes, Chapter 11 for forking, and Chapter 26 for threads.

SocketServers handle incoming connections in a generic way; to make them useful, you provide your own *request handler* class to which it passes a socket to handle. The BaseRequestHandler class in the SocketServer module is the parent class of all request handlers. Suppose, for example, that you need to write a multithreaded e-mail server. First you create MailRequestHandler, a subclass of BaseRequestHandler, and then you pass it to a newly created SocketServer:

```
import SocketServer

... # Create your MailRequestHandler class here

addr = ('175.15.30.2', 25) # Listen address and port
server = SocketServer.ThreadingTCPServer(addr,
                                         MailRequestHandler)
server.serve_forever()
```

Each time a new connection comes in, the server creates a new MailRequestHandler instance object and calls its handle() method so it can process the new request. Because the server is derived from ThreadingTCPServer, with each new request it starts a separate thread to handle the request, so that multiple requests will be processed simultaneously. Instead of calling server_forever, you can also call handle_request(), which waits for, accepts, and processes a single connection. server_forever merely calls handle_request in an infinite loop.

Don't worry too much about the details of the request handler just yet; the next section covers everything you need to know.

Normally, you can use one of the socket servers as is, but if you need to create your own subclass, you can override any of the following methods to customize it.

When the server is first created, the __init__ function calls the server_bind() method to bind the listen socket (self.socket) to the correct address (self.server_address). It then calls server_activate() to activate the server (by default, this calls the listen method of the socket).

The socket server doesn't do anything until the user calls either of the handle_request or serve_forever methods. handle_request calls get_request() to wait for and accept a new socket connection, and then calls verify_request(request, client_address) to see if the server should process the connection (you can use this for access control — by default, verify_request always returns true). If it's okay to process the request, handle_request then calls process_request(request, client_address), and then handle_error(request, client_address) if process_request raised an exception. By default, process_request simply calls finish_request(request, client_address); the forking and threading mix-in classes override this behavior to start a new process or thread, and then call finish_request. finish_request instantiates a new request handler, which in turn calls its handle() method. If you want to subclass a SocketServer, trace through this sequence of calls once or twice to make sure it makes sense to you, and review the source code of SocketServer for help.

When a SocketServer creates a new request handler, it passes to the handler's __init__ function the self variable, so that the handler can access information about the server.

The SocketServer's fileno() method returns the file descriptor of the listen socket. The address_family member variable specifies the socket family of the listen socket (for example, AF_INET), and server_address holds the address to which the listen socket is bound. The socket variable holds the listen socket itself.

Request handlers

Request handlers have setup(), handle(), and finish() methods (none of which do anything by default) that you can override to add your custom behavior. Normally, you need to override only the handle method. The BaseRequestHandler's __init__ function calls setup() for initialization work, handle() to service the request, and finish() to perform any cleanup, although finish isn't called if handle or setup raise an exception. Keep in mind that a new instance of your request handler is created for each request.

The request member variable has the newly accepted socket for stream (TCP) servers; for datagram (UDP) servers, it is a tuple containing the incoming message and the listen socket. client_address holds the address of the sender, and server has a reference to the SocketServer (through which you can access its members, such as server_address).

The following example implements EchoRequestHandler, a handler that repeats back to the remote side any data it sends:

```
>>> import SocketServer
>>> class EchoRequestHandler(SocketServer.BaseRequestHandler):
...     def handle(self):
...         print 'Got new connection!'
...         while 1:
...             msg = self.request.recv(1024)
...             if not msg:
...                 break
```

```
...              print '  Received :',msg
...              self.request.send(msg)
...          print 'Done with connection'
>>> server = SocketServer.ThreadingTCPServer(\
...                    ('127.0.0.1',12321),EchoRequestHandler)
>>> server.handle_request() # It'll wait here for a connection
Got new connection!
  Received : Hello!
  Received : I like Tuesdays!
Done with connection
```

In another Python interpreter, you can connect to the server and try it out:

```
>>> from socket import *
>>> s = socket(AF_INET,SOCK_STREAM)
>>> s.connect(('127.0.0.1',12321))
>>> s.send('Hello!')
6
>>> print s.recv(1024)
Hello!
>>> s.send('I like Tuesdays!')
16
>>> print s.recv(1024)
I like Tuesdays!
>>> s.close()
```

The SocketServer module also defines two subclasses of BaseRequestHandler:
StreamRequestHandler and DatagramRequestHandler. These override the setup
and finish methods and create two file objects, rfile and wfile, that you can use
for reading and writing data to the client, instead of using the usual socket methods.

Processing Web Browser Requests

Now that you have a SocketServer, what do you do with it? Why, extend it, of
course! The standard Python library comes with BaseHTTPServer,
SimpleHTTPServer, and CGIHTTPServer modules that implement increasingly
complex Web server request handlers.

Most likely, you would use them as starting points on which to build, but to some
extent they do work on their own as well. For example, how many lines does it take
to implement a multithreaded Web server that supports running CGI scripts? Well,
at a bare minimum, it takes the following:

```
import SocketServer,CGIHTTPServer
SocketServer.ThreadingTCPServer(('127.0.0.1',80),\
        CGIHTTPServer.CGIHTTPRequestHandler).serve_forever()
```

Point your Web browser to http://127.0.0.1/file (where file is the name of
some text file in your current directory) and verify that it really does work.

BaseHTTPRequestHandler

The starting class for a Web server request handler is `BaseHTTPRequestHandler` (in the `BaseHTTPServer` module), a child of `StreamRequestHandler`. This class accepts an HTTP connection (usually from a Web browser), reads and extracts the headers, and calls the appropriate method to handle the request.

Subclasses of `BaseHTTPRequestHandler` should not override the `__init__` or `handle` methods, but should instead implement a method for each HTTP command they need to handle. For each HTTP command (GET, POST, and so on), `BaseHTTPRequestHandler` calls its `do_<command>` method, if present. For example, if your subclass needs to support the HTTP PUT command, just add a `do_PUT()` method to your subclass and it will automatically be called for any HTTP PUT requests.

The request handler stores the original request line in its `raw_request` instance variable, and its parts in `command` (GET, POST, and so on), `path` (for example, / index.html), and `request_version` (for example, HTTP/1.0). `headers` is an instance of `mimetools.Message`, and contains the parsed version of the request headers.

Cross-Reference See Chapter 17 for more information about the `mimetools.Message` class. Alternatively, you can specify a different class to use for reading and parsing the headers by changing the value of the `BaseHTTPRequestHandler.MessageClass` class variable.

Use the `rfile` and `wfile` objects to read and write data. If the request has additional data beyond the request headers, `rfile` will be positioned at the beginning of that data by the time the handler calls the appropriate `do_<command>` method.

`BaseHTTPRequestHandler` uses the value in `server_version` when writing out a Server response header; you can customize this from its default of BaseHTTP/0.x. Additionally, the `protocol_version` variable defaults to HTTP/1.0, but you can set it to a different version if needed.

In your `do_<command>` method, the first output you send should be via the `send_response(code[, message])` method, where `code` is an HTTP code (such as 200) and `message` is an optional text message explaining the code. (If the request is invalid, you can instead call `send_error(code[, message])`, and then return from the command method.) When you call `send_response`, `BaseHTTPRequestHandler` adds in Date and Server headers.

After a call to `send_response`, you can call `send_header(key, value)` as needed to write out MIME headers; call `end_headers()` when you're done:

```
def do_GET(self):
    self.send_response(200)
    self.send_header('Content-type','text/html')
    self.send_header('Content-length',`len(data)`)
    self.end_headers()
    # send the rest of the data
```

Most Web servers generate logs for later analysis. Call the log_request([code[, size]]) method to log a successful request (including the size, if known, makes the logs more useful). log_message(format, arg0, arg1, ...) is a general-purpose logging method; the format and arguments are similar to normal Python string formatting:

```
self.log_message('%s : %d', 'Time taken',425)
```

Each request is automatically logged to stdout using the NCSA httpd logging format.

SimpleHTTPRequestHandler

Whereas the BaseHTTPRequestHandler doesn't actually handle any HTTP commands, SimpleHTTPRequestHandler (in the SimpleHTTPServer module) adds support for both HEAD and GET commands by sending back to the client requested files that reside in the current working directory or any of its subdirectories. If the requested file is actually a directory, SimpleHTTPRequestHandler generates, on the fly, a Web page containing a directory listing; and sends it back to the client.

Try the following example to see this in action. This code starts a Web server on port 8000, and then opens a Web browser and begins browsing in the current working directory. Because the server continuously loops to serve requests, the example starts the server on a separate thread so you can still launch a Web browser:

```
>>> import Webbrowser,threading,SimpleHTTPServer
>>> def go():
...     t = SimpleHTTPServer.test
...     threading.Thread(target=t).start()
...     Webbrowser.open('http://127.0.0.1:8000')
>>> go() # Below is the output after browsing around a little
Serving HTTP on port 8000 ...
endor - - [28/Dec/2000 18:00:48] "GET /3dsmax3/ HTTP/1.1" 200 -
endor - - [28/Dec/2000 18:00:50] "GET /3dsmax3/Maxsdk/
HTTP/1.1" 200 -
endor - - [28/Dec/2000 18:00:53] "GET /3dsmax3/Maxsdk/Include/
HTTP/1.1" 200 -
```

The test() function in the SimpleHTTPServer module simply starts a new server on port 8000.

In addition to the variables inherited from BaseHTTPRequestHandler, this class has an extensions_map dictionary that maps file extensions to MIME data types, so that the user's Web browser will correctly handle the file it receives. You can expand this list to add new types you want to support.

CGIHTTPRequestHandler

The `CGIHTTPRequestHandler` (in the `CGIHTTPServer` module) takes `SimpleHTTPRequestHandler` one step further and adds support for executing CGI scripts. The CGI (Common Gateway Interface) is a standard for executing server-side programs that can process input from the user's browser (saving data they entered in an HTML form, for example).

Caution

Before you ever make a Web server open to public use, take the time to learn about what security risks are involved. This warning is doubly strong for modules such as `CGIHTTPRequestHandler` that can execute arbitrary Python code; even the smallest security hole is an invitation for intruders.

For each GET or POST command that comes in, `CGIHTTPRequestHandler` checks whether the specified file is actually a CGI program and, if so, launches it as an external program. If it is not, the file contents are sent back to the browser normally. Note that the POST method is supported for CGI programs only.

To decide if a file is a valid CGI program, `CGIHTTPRequestHandler` checks the file's path against the `cgi_directories` member list, which, by default, contains the directories /cgi-bin and htbin (you can add other directories if you want). If the file is in one of those directories or any of their subdirectories and is either a Python module or an executable file, the file is executed and its output returned to the client.

Example: form handler CGI script

The example in this section shows `CGIHTTPRequestHandler` at work. Follow these steps to try it out:

1. Listing 15-2 is a tiny HTML form that asks you to enter your name. Save the file to disk (anywhere you want) as `form.html`. I saved it to `c:\temp`, so in the following steps, replace `c:\temp` with the directory you chose.

2. In the same directory, create a subdirectory called `cgi-bin`:

   `md c:\temp\cgi-bin`   **(from an MS-DOS prompt)**

3. Listing 15-3 is a small CGI script; save it to your new `cgi-bin` directory as `handleForm.py`.

4. Switch to your original directory (`c:\temp`), start up a Python interpreter, and enter the following lines to start a Web server:

   ```
   >>> import CGIHTTPServer
   >>> CGIHTTPServer.test()
   ```

5. Open a Web browser and point it to `http://127.0.0.1:8000/form.html` to display the simple Web page shown in Figure 15-2.

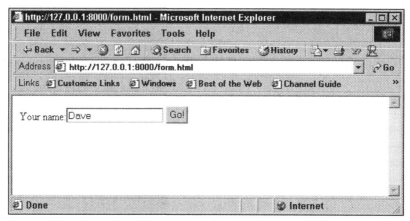

Figure 15-2: The Python Web server returned this page; clicking Go executes the CGI script.

6. Enter your name in the text box and click Go. The Web server executes the Python CGI script and displays the results shown in Figure 15-3.

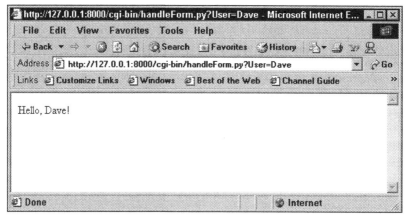

Figure 15-3: The Python Web server ran the CGI script and returned the results.

Listing 15-2: **form.html – A simple HTML form**

```
<html><body>
<form method=GET
 action="http://127.0.0.1:8000/cgi-bin/handleForm.py">
Your name:<input name="User">
<input type="Submit" value="Go!">
</form>
</body></html>
```

Listing 15-3: **handleForm.py – A Python CGI script**

```
import os
print "Content-type: text/html\r\n<html><body>"
name = os.environ.get('QUERY_STRING','')
print 'Hello, %s!<p>' % name[len('User='):]
print '</body></html>'
```

To make use of this functionality, you should read up on CGI (which is certainly not specific to Python). Although a complete discussion is outside the scope of this chapter, the following few hints will help get you started:

✦ CGIHTTPRequestHandler stores the user information (including form values) in environment variables. (Write a simple CGI script to print out all variables and their values to test this.)

✦ Anything you write to stdout (via print or sys.stdout.write) is returned to the client, and it can be text or binary data.

✦ CGIHTTPRequestHandler outputs some response headers for you, but you can add others if needed (such as the Content-type header in the example).

✦ After the headers, you must output a blank line before any data.

✦ On UNIX, external programs run with the nobody user ID.

Handling Multiple Requests Without Threads

Although threads can help the Web servers in the previous sections handle more than one connection simultaneously, the program usually sits around waiting for data to be transmitted across the network. (Instead of being CPU bound, the program is said to be I/O bound.) In situations where your program is I/O bound, a lot of CPU time is wasted switching between threads that are just waiting until they can read or write more data to a file or socket. In such cases, it may be better to use the select and asyncore modules. These modules still let you process multiple requests at a time, but avoid all the senseless thread switching.

The select(inList, outList, errList[, timeout]) function in the select module takes three lists of objects that are waiting to perform input or output (or want to be notified of errors). select returns three lists, subsets of the originals, containing only those objects that can now perform I/O without blocking. If the timeout parameter is given (a floating-point number indicating the number of seconds to wait) and is non-zero, select returns when an object can perform I/O or when the time limit is reached (whereupon empty lists are returned). A timeout value of 0 does a quick check without blocking.

The three lists hold input, output, and error objects, respectively (objects that are interested in reading data, writing data, or in being notified of errors that occurred). Any of the three lists can be empty, and the objects can be integer file descriptors or filelike objects with a fileno() method that returns a valid file descriptor.

See "Working with File Descriptors" in Chapter 10 for more information.

By using select, you can start several read or write operations and, instead of blocking until you can read or write more, you can continue to do other work. This way, your I/O-bound program spends as much time as possible being driven by its performance-limiting factor (I/O), instead of a more artificial factor (switching between threads). With select, it is possible to write reasonably high-performance servers in Python.

On Windows systems, select() works on socket objects only. On UNIX systems, however, it also works on other file descriptors, such as named pipes.

A slightly more efficient alternative to select is the select.poll() function, which returns a *polling* object (available on UNIX platforms). After you create a polling object, you call the register(fd[, eventmask]) method to register a particular file descriptor (or object with a fileno() method). The optional eventmask is constructed by bitwise OR-ing together any of the following: select.POLLIN (for input), select.POLLPRI (urgent input), select.POLLOUT (for output), or select.POLLERR.

You can register as many file descriptors as needed, and you can remove them from the object by calling the polling object's unregister(fd) method.

Call the polling object's poll([timeout]) method to see which file descriptors, if any, are ready to perform I/O without blocking. poll returns a possibly empty list of tuples of the form (fd, event), an entry for each file descriptor whose state has changed. The event will be a bitwise-OR of any of the eventmask flags as well as POLLHUP (hang up) or POLLNVAL (an invalid file descriptor).

asyncore

If you've never used select or poll before, it may seem complicated or confusing. To help in creating select-based socket clients and servers, the asyncore module takes care of a lot of the dirty work for you.

asyncore defines the dispatcher class, a wrapper around a normal socket object that you subclass to handle messages about when the socket can be read or written without blocking. Because it is a wrapper around a socket, you can often treat a dispatcher object like a normal socket (it has the usual connect(addr), send(data), recv(bufsize), listen([backlog]), bind(addr), accept(), and close() methods).

Although the dispatcher is a wrapper around a socket, you still need to create the underlying socket (either the caller needs to or you can create it in the dispatcher's constructor) by calling the create_socket(family, type) method:

```
d = myDispatcher()
d.create_socket(AF_INET,SOCK_STREAM)
```

create_socket creates the socket and sets it to nonblocking mode.

asyncore calls methods of a dispatcher object when different events occur. When the socket can be written to without blocking, for example, the handle_write() method is called. When data is available for reading, handle_read() is called. You can also implement handle_connect() for when a socket connects successfully, handle_close() for when it closes, and handle_accept() for when a call to socket.accept will not block (because an incoming connection is available and waiting).

asyncore calls the readable() and writable() methods of the dispatcher object to see if it is interested in reading or writing data, respectively (by default, both methods always return 1). You can override these so that, for example, asyncore doesn't waste time checking for data if you're not even trying to read any.

In order for asyncore to fire events off to any dispatcher objects, you need to call asyncore.poll([timeout]) (on UNIX, you can also call asyncore.poll2 ([timeout]) to use poll instead of select) or asyncore.loop([timeout]). These functions use the select module to check for a change in I/O state and then fire off the appropriate events to the corresponding dispatcher objects. poll checks once (with a default timeout of 0 seconds), but loop checks until there are no more dispatcher objects that return true for either readable or writable, or until the timeout is reached (a default of 30 seconds).

The best way to absorb all this is by looking at an example. Listing 15-4 is a very simple asynchronous Web page retrieval class that retrieves the index.html page from a Web site and writes it to disk (including the Web server's response headers).

**Listing 15-4: asyncget.py – Asynchronous
HTML page retriever**

```python
import asyncore, socket

class AsyncGet(asyncore.dispatcher):
    def __init__(self, host):
        asyncore.dispatcher.__init__(self)
        self.host = host

        self.create_socket(socket.AF_INET, socket.SOCK_STREAM)
        self.connect((host,80))

        self.request = 'GET /index.html HTTP/1.0\r\n\r\n'
        self.outf = None
        print 'Requesting index.html from',host

    def handle_connect(self):
        print 'Connect',self.host

    def handle_read(self):
        if not self.outf:
            print 'Creating',self.host
            self.outf = open(self.host,'wt')

        data = self.recv(8192)
        if data:
            self.outf.write(data)

    def writeable(self):
        return len(self.request) > 0

    def handle_write(self):
        # Not all data might be sent, so track what did make it
        num_sent = self.send(self.request)
        self.request = self.request[num_sent:]

    def handle_close(self):
        asyncore.dispatcher.close(self)
        print 'Socket closed for',self.host
        if self.outf:
            self.outf.close()

# Now retrieve some pages
AsyncGet('www.yahoo.com')
AsyncGet('www.cnn.com')
AsyncGet('www.python.org')
asyncore.loop() # Wait until all are done
```

Here's some sample output:

```
C:\temp>asyncget.py
Requesting index.html from www.yahoo.com
Requesting index.html from www.cnn.com
Requesting index.html from www.python.org
Connect www.yahoo.com
Connect www.cnn.com
Creating www.yahoo.com
Connect www.python.org
Creating www.cnn.com
Creating www.python.org
Socket closed for www.yahoo.com
Socket closed for www.python.org
Socket closed for www.cnn.com
```

Notice that the requests did not all finish in the same order they were started. Rather, they each made progress according to when data was available. By being event-driven, the I/O-bound program spends most of its time working on its greatest performance boundary (I/O), instead of wasting time with needless thread switching.

Summary

If you've done any networking programming in some other languages, you'll find that doing the same thing in Python can be done with a lot less effort and bugs. Python has full support for standard networking functionality, as well as utility classes that do much of the work for you. In this chapter, you:

- ✦ Converted IP addresses to registered names and back.

- ✦ Created sockets and sent messages between them.

- ✦ Used `SocketServers` to quickly build custom servers.

- ✦ Built a working Web server in only a few lines of Python code.

- ✦ Used `select` to process multiple socket requests without threads.

The next chapter looks at more of Python's higher-level support for Internet protocols, including modules that hide the nasty details of "speaking" protocols such as HTTP, FTP, and telnet.

✦   ✦   ✦

Speaking Internet Protocols

◆ ◆ ◆ ◆

In This Chapter

Python's Internet
protocol support

Retrieving Internet
resources

Sending HTTP
requests

Sending and
receiving e-mail

Transferring files via
FTP

Retrieving resources
using Gopher

Working with
newsgroups

Using the Telnet
protocol

Writing CGI scripts

◆ ◆ ◆ ◆

O n the Internet, people use various protocols to transfer files, send e-mail, and request resources from the World Wide Web. Python provides libraries to help work with Internet protocols. This chapter shows how you can write Internet programs without having to handle lower-level TCP/IP details such as sockets. Supported protocols include HTTP, POP3, SMTP, FTP, and Telnet. Python also provides useful CGI scripting abilities.

Python's Internet Protocol Support

Python's standard libraries make it easy to use standard Internet protocols such as HTTP, FTP, and Telnet. These libraries are built on top of the `socket` library, and enable you to program networked programs with a minimum of low-level code.

Each Internet protocol is documented in a numbered *request for comment* (RFC). The name is a bit misleading for established protocols such as POP and FTP, as these protocols are widely implemented, and are no longer under much discussion!

These protocols are quite feature-rich — the RFCs for the protocols discussed here would fill several hundred printed pages. The standard Python modules provide a high-level client for each protocol. However, you may need to know more about the protocols' syntax and meaning, and the RFCs are the best place to learn this information. One good online RFC repository is at `http://www.rfc-editor.org/`.

Cross-Reference Refer to Chapter 15 for more information about the `socket` module and a quick overview of TCP/IP.

Retrieving Internet Resources

The library urllib provides an easy mechanism for grabbing files from the Internet. It supports HTTP, FTP, and Gopher requests. Resource requests can take a long time to complete, so you may want to keep them out of the main thread in an interactive program.

The simplest way to retrieve a URL is with one line:

```
urlretrieve(url[,filename[,callback[,data]]])
```

The function urlretrieve retrieves the resource located at the address *url* and writes it to a file with name *filename*. For example:

```
>>> MyURL="http://www.pythonapocrypha.com"
>>> urllib.urlretrieve(MyURL, "pample2.swf")
>>> urllib.urlcleanup()  # clean the cache!
```

If you do not pass a filename to urlretrieve, a temporary filename will be magically generated for you. The function urlcleanup frees up resources used in calls to urlretrieve.

The optional parameter *callback* is a function to call after retrieving each block of a file. For example, you could use a callback function to update a progress bar showing download progress. The callback receives three arguments: the number of blocks already transferred, the size of each block (in bytes), and the total size of the file (in bytes). Some FTP servers do not return a file size; in this case, the third parameter is -1.

Normally, HTTP requests are sent as GET requests. To send a POST request, pass a value for the optional parameter *data*. This string should be encoded using urlencode.

To use a proxy on Windows or UNIX, set the environment variables http_proxy, ftp_proxy, and/or gopher_proxy to the URL of the proxy server. On a Macintosh, proxy information from Internet Config is used.

Manipulating URLs

Special characters are encoded in URLs to ensure they can be passed around easily. Encoded characters take the form %##, where ## is the ASCII value of the character in hexadecimal. Use the function quote to encode a string, and unquote to translate it back to normal, human-readable form:

```
>>> print urllib.quote("human:nature")
human%3anature
>>> print urllib.unquote("cello%23music")
cello#music
```

The function `quote_plus` does the encoding of `quote`, but also replaces spaces with plus signs, as required for form values. The corresponding function `unquote_plus` decodes such a string:

```
>>> print urllib.quote_plus("bob+alice forever")
bob%2balice+forever
>>> print urllib.unquote_plus("where+are+my+keys?")
where are my keys?
```

Data for an HTTP POST request must be encoded in this way. The function `urlencode` takes a dictionary of names and values, and returns a properly encoded string, suitable for HTTP requests:

```
>>> print urllib.urlencode(
        {"name":"Eric","species":"sea bass"})
species=sea+bass&name=Eric
```

See the module `urlparse`, covered in Chapter 17, for more functions to parse and process URLs.

Treating a URL as a file

The function `urlopen(url[,data])` creates and returns a filelike object for the corresponding address *url*. The source can be read like an ordinary file. For example, the following code reads a Web page and checks the length of the file (the full HTML text of the page):

```
>>> Page=urllib.urlopen("http://www.python.org")
>>> print len(Page.read())
339
```

The *data* parameter, as for `urlretrieve`, is used to pass urlencoded data for a POST request.

The filelike object returned by `urlopen` provides two bonus methods. The method `geturl` returns the real URL — usually the same as the URL you passed in, but possibly different if a Web page redirected you to another URL. The method `info` returns a `mimetools.Message` object describing the file.

Refer to Chapter 17 for more information about `mimetools`.

URLopeners

The classes `URLopener` and `FancyURLopener` are what you actually build and use with calls to `urlopen` and `urlretrieve`. You may want to subclass them to handle new addressing schemes. You will probably always use `FancyURLopener`. It is a subclass of `URLopener` that handles HTTP redirections (response code 301 and 302) and basic authentication (response code 401).

The opener constructor takes, as its first argument, a mapping of schemes (such as HTTP) to proxies. It also takes the keyword arguments `key_file` and `cert_file`, which, if supplied, allow you to request secure Web pages (using the HTTPS scheme).

Note   The default Python build does not currently include SSL support. You must edit Modules/Setup to include SSL, and then rebuild Python, in order to open https:// addresses with `urllib`.

Openers provide a method, `open(url[,data])`, that opens the resource with address *url*. The *data* parameter works as in `urllib.urlopen`. To open new url types, override the method `open_unknown(url[,data])` in your subclass. By default, this method returns an "unknown url type" IOError.

Openers also provide a method `retrieve(url[,filename[,hook[,data]]])`, which functions like `urllib.urlretrieve`.

The HTTP header `user-agent` identifies a piece of client software to a Web server. Normally, urllib tells the server that it is `Python-urllib/1.13` (where 1.13 is the current version of urllib). If you subclass the openers, you can override this by setting the `version` attribute *before* calling the parent class's constructor.

Extended URL opening

The module `urllib2` is a new and improved version of `urllib`. `urllib2` provides a wider array of features, and is easier to extend. The syntax for opening a URL is the same: `urlopen(url[,data])`. Here, *url* can be a string or a `Request` object.

The `Request` class gathers HTTP request information (it is very similar to the class `httplib.HTTP`). Its constructor has syntax `Request(url[,data[,headers]])`. Here, *headers* must be a dictionary. After constructing a `Request`, you can call `add_header(name,value)` to send additional headers, and `add_data(data)` to send data for a POST request. For example:

```
>>> # Request constructor is picky: "http://" and the
>>> # trailing slash are both required here:
>>> MyRequest=urllib2.Request("http://www.python.org/")
>>> MyRequest.add_header("user-agent","Testing 1 2 3")
>>> URL=urllib2.urlopen(MyRequest)
>>> print URL.readline() # read just a little bit
<HTML>
```

The module `urllib2` can handle some fancier HTTP requests, such as basic authentication. For further details, consult the module documentation.

New Feature   The module `urllib2` is new in Python Version 2.1.

Sending HTTP Requests

HyperText Transfer Protocol (HTTP) is a format for requests that a client (usually a browser) sends to a server on the World Wide Web. An HTTP request includes various *headers*. Headers include information such as the URL of a requested resource, file formats accepted by the client, and *cookies,* parameters used to cache user-specific information (see RFC 2616 for details).

The `httplib` module lets you build and send HTTP requests and receive server responses. Normally, you retrieve Web pages using the `urllib` module, which is simpler. However, `httplib` enables you to control headers, and it can handle POST requests.

Building and using request objects

The module method `HTTP([host[,port]])` constructs and returns an HTTP request object. The parameter *host* is the name of a host (such as `www.yahoo.com`). The port number can be passed via the *port* parameter, or parsed from the host name; otherwise, it defaults to 80. If you construct an HTTP object without providing a host, you must call its `connect(host[,port])` method to connect to a server before sending a request.

To start a Web request, call the method `putrequest(action,URL)`. Here, `action` is the request method, such as GET or POST, and *URL* is the requested resource, such as `/stuff/junk/index.html`.

After starting the request, you can (and usually will) send one or more headers, by calling `putheader(name, value[, anothervalue,...])`. Then, whether you sent headers or not, you call the `endheaders` method. For example, the following code informs the server that HTML files are accepted (something most Web servers will assume anyway), and then finishes off the headers:

```
MyHTTP.putheader('Accept', 'text/html')
MyHTTP.endheaders()
```

You can pass multiple values for a header in one call to `putheader`.

After setting up any headers, you may (usually on a POST request) send additional data to the server by calling `send(data)`.

Now that you have built the request, you can get the server's reply. The method `getreply` returns the server's response in a 3-tuple: (`replycode, message, headers`). Here, *replycode* is the HTTP status code (200 for success, or perhaps the infamous 404 for "resource not found").

The body of the server's reply is returned (as a file object with `read` and `close` methods) by the method `getfile`. This is where the request object finally receives what it asks for.

For example, the following code retrieves the front page from www.yahoo.com:

```
>>> Request=httplib.HTTP("www.yahoo.com")
>>> Request.putrequest("GET","/")
>>> Request.endheaders()
>>> Request.getreply()
(200, 'OK', <mimetools.Message instance at 0085EBD4>)
>>> ThePage=Request.getfile()
>>> print ThePage.readline()[:50]
<html><head><title>Yahoo!</title><base href=http:/
```

This example performs a Web search by sending a POST request. Data in a POST request must be properly encoded using urllib.urlencode (see Listing 16-1). This code uses an HTMLParser (from htmllib) to extract all links from the search results.

Cross-Reference   See Chapter 18 for complete information about htmllib.

Listing 16-1: WebSearch.py

```
import httplib
import htmllib
import urllib
import formatter
# Encode our search terms as a URL, by
# passing a dictionary to urlencode
SearchDict={"q":"Charles Dikkins",
    "kl":"XX","pg":"q","Translate":"on"}
SearchString=urllib.urlencode(SearchDict)
print "search:",SearchString
Request=httplib.HTTP("www.altavista.com")
Request.putrequest("POST","/cgi-bin/query")
Request.putheader('Accept', 'text/plain')
Request.putheader('Accept', 'text/html')
Request.putheader('Host', 'www.alta-vista.com')
Request.putheader("Content-length",`len(SearchString)`)
Request.endheaders()
Request.send(SearchString)
print Request.getreply()
# Read and parse the resulting HTML
HTML=Request.getfile().read()
MyParser=htmllib.HTMLParser(formatter.NullFormatter())
MyParser.feed(HTML)
# Print all the anchors from the results page
print MyParser.anchorlist
```

Sending and Receiving E-Mail

Python provides libraries that receive mail from, and send mail to, a mail server. Electronic mail is transmitted via various protocols. The most common mail protocols are POP3 (for receiving mail), SMTP (for sending mail), and IMAP4 (for reading mail and managing mail folders). They are supported by the Python modules poplib, smtplib, and imaplib, respectively.

Accessing POP3 accounts

To access a POP3 mail account, you construct a POP3 object. The POP3 object offers various methods to send and retrieve mail. It raises the exception poplib.error_proto if it encounters problems. See RFC 1939 for the full POP3 protocol.

Many of its methods return output as a 3-tuple: a server response string, response lines (as a list), and total response length (in bytes). In general, you can access the second tuple element and ignore the others.

Connecting and logging in

The POP3 constructor takes two arguments: *host* and *port number*. The port parameter is optional, and defaults to 110. For example:

```
Mailbox=poplib.POP3("mail.gianth.com")  # connect to mail server
```

After connecting, you can access the mail server's greeting by calling getwelcome. You normally sign in by calling user(name) and then pass(password). To sign on using APOP authentication, call apop(username, secret). To sign in using RPOP, call rpop(username). (Currently, rpop is not supported.)

Once you log in, the mailbox is locked until you call quit (or the session times out). To keep a session from timing out, you can call the method noop, which simply keeps the session alive.

Checking mail

The method stat checks the mailbox's status. It returns a tuple of two numbers: the number of messages and the total size of your messages (in bytes).

The method list([index]) lists the messages in your inbox. It returns a 3-tuple, where the second element is a list of message entries. A message entry is the message number, followed by its size in bytes. Passing a message index to list makes it return just that message's entry:

```
>>> Mailbox.list()
('+OK 2 messages (10012 octets)', ['1 9003', '2 1009'], 16)
>>> Mailbox.list(2)
+OK 2 1009
```

The method `uidl([index])` retrieves unique identifiers for the messages in a mailbox. Unique identifiers are unchanged by the addition and deletion of messages, and they are unique across sessions. The method returns a list of message indexes and corresponding unique IDs:

```
>>> Mailbox.uidl()
('+OK 2 messages (10012 octets)', ['1 2', '2 3'], 10)
>>> Mailbox.uidl(2)
+OK 2 3
```

Retrieving mail

The method `retr(index)` retrieves and returns message number *index* from your mailbox. What you get back is actually a tuple: the server response, a list of message lines (including headers), and the total response length (in bytes). To retrieve part of a message, call the method `top(index, lines)` — top is the same as `retr`, but stops after *lines* lines.

Deleting mail

Use the method `dele(index)` to delete message number *index*. If you change your mind, use the method `rset` to cancel all deletions you have done in the current session.

Signing off

When you finish accessing a mailbox, call the `quit` method to sign off.

Example: retrieving mail

The code in Listing 16-2 signs on to a mail server and retrieves the full text of the first message in the mailbox. It does no fancy error handling. It strips off all the message headers, printing only the body of the message.

Listing 16-2: **popmail.py**

```python
import poplib
# Replace server, user, and password with your
# mail server, user name, and password!
Mailbox=poplib.POP3("mail.seanbaby.com")
Mailbox.user("dumplechan@seanbaby.com")
Mailbox.pass_("secretpassword")
MyMessage=Mailbox.retr(1)
FullText="" # Build up the message body in FullText
PastHeaders=0
```

```
for MessageLine in MyMessage[1]:
    if PastHeaders==0:
        # A blank line marks the end of headers:
        if (len(MessageLine)==0):
            PastHeaders=1
    else:
        FullText+=MessageLine+"\n"
Mailbox.quit()
print FullText
```

Accessing SMTP accounts

The module `smtplib` defines an object, `SMTP`, that you use to send mail using the Simple Mail Transport Protocol (SMTP). An enhanced version of SMTP, called ESMTP, is also supported. See RFC 821 for the SMTP protocol, and RFC 1869 for information about extensions.

Connecting and disconnecting

You can pass a host name and a port number to the SMTP constructor. This connects you to the server immediately. The port number defaults to 25:

```
Outbox=smtplib.SMTP("mail.gianth.com")
```

If you do not supply a host name when you construct an SMTP object, you must call its `connect` method, passing it a host name and (optionally) a port number. The host name can specify a port number after a colon:

```
Outbox=smtplib.SMTP()
Outbox.connect("mail.gianth.com:25")
```

After you finish sending mail, you should call the `quit` method to close the connection.

Sending mail

The method `sendmail(sender, recipients, message[,options, rcpt_options])` sends e-mail. The parameter *sender* is the message author (usually your e-mail address!). The parameter *recipients* is a list of addresses that should receive the message. The parameter *message* is the message as one long string, including all its headers. For example:

```
>>> MyAddress=bob@myserver.com
>>> TargetAddress="earl@otherserver.com"
>>> HeaderText="From: "+MyAddress+"\r\n"
>>> HeaderText+="To: "+TargetAddress+"\r\n\r\n"
>>> Outbox.sendmail(MyAddress,[TargetAddress],HeaderText+"Hi!")
```

To use extended options, pass a list of ESMTP options in the *options* parameter. You can pass RCPT options in the *rcpt_options* parameter.

The method sendmail raises an exception if it could not send mail to any recipient. If at least one address succeeded, it returns a dictionary explaining any failures. In this dictionary, each key is an address. The corresponding value is a tuple: result code and error message.

Other methods

The method verify(address) checks an e-mail address *address* for validity. It returns a tuple: the first entry is the response code, the second is the server's response string. A response code of 250 is success; anything above 400 is failure:

```
>>> Outbox.verify("dumplechan@seanbaby.com")
(250, 'ok its for <dumplechan@seanbaby.com>')
>>> Outbox.verify("dimplechin@seanbaby.com")
(550, 'unknown user <dimplechin@seanbaby.com>')
```

An ESMTP server may support various extensions to SMTP, such as delivery service notification. The method has_extn(name) returns true if the server supports a particular extension:

```
>>> Outbox.has_extn("DSN") # is status-notification available?
1
```

To identify yourself to a server, you can call helo([host]) for an SMTP server; or ehlo([host]) for an ESMTP server. The optional parameter host defaults to the fully qualified domain name of the local host. The methods return a tuple: result code (250 for success) and server response string. Because the sendmail method can handle the HELO command, you do not normally need to call these methods directly.

Handling errors

Methods of an SMTP object may raise the following exceptions if they encounter an error:

SMTPException	Base exception class for all smtplib exceptions.
SMTPServerDisconnected	The server unexpectedly disconnected, or no connection has been made yet.
SMTPResponseException	Base class for all exceptions that include an SMTP error code. An SMTPResponseException has two attributes: smtp_code (the response code of the error, such as 550 for an invalid address) and smtp_error (the error message).
SMTPSenderRefused	Sender address refused. The exception attribute sender is the invalid sender.

SMTPRecipientsRefused	All recipient addresses refused. The errors for each recipient are accessible through the attribute `recipients`, which is a dictionary of exactly the same sort as `SMTP.sendmail()` returns.
SMTPDataError	The SMTP server refused to accept the message data.
SMTPConnectError	An error occurred during establishment of a connection with the server.
SMTPHeloError	The server refused a "HELO" message.

Accessing IMAP accounts

IMAP is a protocol for accessing mail. Like POP, it enables you to read and delete messages. IMAP offers additional features, such as searching for message text and organizing messages in separate mailboxes. However, IMAP is harder to use than POP, and is far less commonly used.

Cross-Reference   See RFC 2060 for the full description of IMAP4rev1.

The module `imaplib` provides a class, `IMAP4`, to serve as an IMAP client. The names of IMAP4 methods correspond to the commands of the IMAP protocol. Most methods return a tuple (code, data), where *code* is "OK" (good) or "NO" (bad), and *data* is the text of the server response.

The IMAP protocol includes various magical behaviors. For example, you can move all the messages from INBOX into a new mailbox by attempting to rename INBOX. (The INBOX folder isn't actually renamed, but its contents are moved to the other mailbox!) Not all the features of the protocol are covered here; consult RFC 2060 for more information.

Connection, logon, and logoff

The IMAP4 constructor takes host and port arguments, which function here just as they do for a POP3 object. If you construct an IMAP4 object without specifying a host, you must call `open(host,port)` to connect to a server before you can use other methods. The port number defaults to 143.

To log in, call the method `login(user,password)`. Call `logout` to log off. The method `noop` keeps an existing session alive. For example:

```
>>> imap=imaplib.IMAP4("mail.mundomail.net")
>>> imap.login("dumplechan","tacos")
('OK', ['LOGIN completed'])
>>> imap.noop()
('OK', ['NOOP completed'])
```

An IMAP server may use more advanced authentication methods. To authenticate in fancier ways, call the method authenticate(machanism,handler). Here, *mechanism* is the name of the authentication mechanism, and *handler* is a function that receives challenge strings from the server and returns response strings. (Base64 encoding is handled internally.)

Checking, reading, and deleting mail

Before you can do anything with messages, you must choose a mailbox. The mailbox INBOX is always available. To select a mailbox, call select([mailbox[, readonly]]). The parameter *mailbox* is the mailbox name, which defaults to INBOX. If *readonly* is present and true, then modifications to the mailbox are forbidden. The return value includes the number of messages in the mailbox. For example:

```
>>> imap.select("INBOX")
('OK', ['2'])
```

When finished with a mailbox, call close to close it.

The method search(charset,criteria...) searches the current mailbox for messages satisfying one or more criteria. The parameter charset, if not None, specifies a particular character set to use. One or more values can be passed as criteria; these are concatenated into one search string. A list of matching message indexes is returned. Note that text (other than keywords) in criteria should be quoted. For example, the following code checks for messages from the president (none today), and then checks for messages whose subject contains "Howdy!" (and finds message number 2):

```
>>> imap.search(None,"ALL","FROM",'"president@whitehouse.gov"')
('OK', [None])
>>> imap.search(None,"ALL","SUBJECT",'"Howdy!"')
('OK', ['2'])
```

To retrieve a message, call fetch(messages,parts). Here, *messages* is a string listing messages, such as "2", or "2,7", or "3:5" (for messages 3 through 5). The parameter *parts* should be a parenthesized list of what parts of the message(s) to retrieve—for instance, FULL for the entire message, BODY for just the body. For example:

```
>>> imap.fetch("2","(BODY[text])")
('OK', [('2 (BODY[text] {13}', 'Howdy cowboy!'), ')', '2 (FLAGS
(\\SEEN))'])
```

To change a message's status, call store(messages,command,flags). Here, *command* is the command to perform, such as "+FLAGS" or "-FLAGS". The parameter *flags* is a list of flags to set or remove. For example, the following line of code deletes message 2:

```
>>> imap.store("2","+FLAGS",["\Deleted"])
('OK', ['2 (FLAGS (\\SEEN \\DELETED))'])
```

The method `expunge` permanently removes all messages marked as deleted by a `\Deleted` flag. Such messages are automatically expunged when you `close` the current mailbox.

The method `copy(messages,newmailbox)` copies a set of messages to the mailbox named *newmailbox.*

The method `check` does a mailbox "checkpoint" operation; what this means depends on the server.

You normally operate on messages by index number. However, messages also have a *unique identifier,* or *uid.* To use uids to name messages, call the method `uid (commandname, [args...])`. This carries out the command *commandname* using uids instead of message indices.

Administering mailboxes

To create a new mailbox, call `create(name)`. To delete a mailbox, call `delete(name)`. Call `rename(oldname,newname)` to rename mailbox *oldname* to the name *newname.*

Mailboxes can contain other mailboxes. For example, the name "nudgenudge/winkwink" indicates a sub-box named "winkwink" inside a master mailbox "nudgenudge." The hierarchy separator character varies by server; some servers would name the mailbox "nudgenudge.winkwink."

A mailbox can be marked as *subscribed.* The effects of subscribing vary by server, but generally subscriptions are a way of flagging mailboxes of particular interest. Use `subscribe(name)` and `unsubscribe(name)` to toggle subscription status for the mailbox *name.*

The command `list([root[,pattern]])` finds mailbox names. The parameter *root* is the base of a mailbox hierarchy to list. It defaults to ""(not a blank string, but a string of two double-quotes) for the root level. The parameter *pattern* is a string to search for; *pattern* may contain the wildcards * (matching anything) and % (matching anything but a hierarchy delimiter). The output of `list` is a list of 3-tuples. Each tuple corresponds to a mailbox. The first element is a list of flags, such as \Noselect. The second element is the server's hierarchy separator character. The third is the mailbox name.

To list only subscribed mailboxes, use the command `lsub([root[,pattern]])`.

For example, the following code creates and lists some mailboxes:

```
>>> print imap.list()
('OK', ['() "/" "INBOX"'])
>>> imap.create("x1")
('OK', ['CREATE completed'])
>>> imap.create("x1/y1")
('OK', ['CREATE completed'])
```

```
>>> imap.create("x1/y2")
('OK', ['CREATE completed'])
>>> imap.rename("x1/y2","x1/y3")
('OK', ['RENAME completed'])
>>> imap.list()
('OK', ['() "/" "INBOX"', '() "/" "x1"', '() "/" "x1/y1"', '()
"/" "x1/y3"'])
>>> print imap.list('""',"*y*") # string "" for root
('OK', ['() "/" "x1/y1"', '() "/" "x1/y3"'])
>>> imap.list('""',"*foo*") # Nothing found: get list of "None"
('OK', [None])
>>> imap.list("x1","*3")
('OK', ['() "/" "x1/y3"'])
```

You can check the status of a mailbox by calling `status(mailbox,names)`. The parameter *mailbox* is the name of a mailbox. The parameter *names* is a parenthesized string of status items to check. For example:

```
>>> imap.status("INBOX","(MESSAGES UIDNEXT)")
('OK', ['"INBOX" (MESSAGES 1 UIDNEXT 3)'])
```

Other functions

You can add a message to a mailbox by calling the method `append(mailbox, flags, datetime, message)`. Here, *mailbox* is the name of the mailbox, *flags* is an optional list of message flags, *datetime* is a timestamp for the message, and *message* is the message text, including headers.

IMAP uses an INTERNALDATE representation for dates and times. Use the module function `Internaldate2tuple(date)` to translate an INTERNALDATE to a TimeTuple, and the function `Time2Internaldate(tuple)` to go from TimeTuple to INTERNALDATE.

Cross-Reference   See Chapter 13 for more information about the `time` module's tuple representation of time.

The function `ParseFlags(str)` splits an IMAP4 `FLAGS` response into a tuple of flags.

Handling errors

The class `IMAP4.error` is the exception raised by any errors using an IMAP4 object. The error argument is an error message string. It has subclasses IMAP4.abort (raised for server errors) and `IMAP4.readonly` (raised if the server changed a mailbox while you were reading mail, and you must re-open the mailbox).

Transferring Files via FTP

The module `ftplib` provides the class `FTP`, which serves as an FTP client. The Python source distribution includes a script, `Tools/script/ftpmirror.py`, that uses ftplib to mirror an FTP site.

See RFC 959 for more on the FTP protocol.

Logging in and out

The FTP constructor takes several optional parameters. A call to `FTP([host[, user[,password[,acct]]]])` constructs and returns an FTP object. The constructor also connects to the specified host if *host* is supplied. If *user* is supplied, the constructor logs in using the user *user*, the password *password*, and the account *acct*.

You can also connect to a host by calling the FTP method `connect(hostname [,port])`. The port number defaults to 21; you will probably never need to set it manually. You can log in by calling `login([user[,password[,acct]]])`. If *user* is not specified, anonymous login is performed. The following two examples demonstrate the long and short way to log on to a server:

```
>>> # long way:
>>> session=ftplib.FTP()
>>> session.connect("gianth.com")
'220 gianth Microsoft FTP Service (Version 5.0).'
>>> session.login() # anonymous login (login string returned)
'230-Niao!  Greetings from Giant H Laboratories!\015\012230
Anonymous user logged in.'
>>> # short way:
>>> session2=ftplib.FTP("gianth.com","anonymous","bob@aol.com")
```

The method `getwelcome` returns the server welcome string (the same string returned by `connect`).

When finished with an FTP connection, call `quit` or `close`. (The only difference between the two is that `quit` sends a "polite" response to the server.)

Navigating

The method `pwd` returns the current path on the server. The method `cwd(path)` sets the path on the server. You can call `mkd(path)` to create a new directory; call `rmd(dirname)` to delete an empty directory.

The method nlst([dir[,args]]) returns directory contents as a list of file names. By default, both functions list the current directory; pass a different path in *dir* to list a different one. Extra string arguments are passed along to the server. The function dir([dir[,args]]) gets a list of files for processing. If the last argument to dir is a function, that function is used as a callback when retrieving each line (see retrlines, in the next section); the default processor simply prints each line.

The method size(filename) returns the size of a particular file. You can delete a file with delete(filename), and rename a file by calling rename(oldname, newname).

Transferring files

To store (upload) a file, call storbinary(command,file,blocksize) for binary files, or storlines(command,file) for plain text files. The parameter *command* is the command passed to the server. The parameter *file* should be an opened file object. The *storbinary* parameter *blocksize* is the block size for data transfer. For example, the following code uploads a sound file to a server in 8K blocks, and then verifies that the file exists on the server:

```
>>> Source=open("c:\\SummerRain.mp3")
>>> Session.storbinary("STOR SummerRain.mp3",Source,8192)
'226 Transfer complete.'
>>> Session.nlst().index("SummerRain.mp3")
```

To retrieve (download) a file, call retrbinary(command,callback[,blocksize [,rest]]) or retrlines(command[,callback]). The parameter *command* is the command passed to the server. The parameter *callback* is a function to be called once for each block of data received. Python passes the block of data to the callback function. (The default callback for retrlines simply prints each line.) The parameter *blocksize* is the maximum size of each block. Supply a byte position for *rest* to continue a download part way through a file. For example, the following code retrieves a file from the server to a file:

```
>>> destination=open("foo.mp3","w")
>>> session.retrbinary("RETR SummerRain.mp3",dest.write)
'226 Transfer complete.'
>>> destination.close()
```

A lower-level method for file transfer is ntransfercmd(command[,rest]), which returns a 2-tuple: a socket object and the expected file size in bytes. The method transfercmd(command[,rest]) is the same as ntransfercmd, but returns only a socket object.

The method abort cancels a transfer in progress.

Other methods

The method set_pasv(value) sets passive mode to *value*. If *value* is true, the PASV command is sent to the server for file transfers; otherwise, the PORT command is used. (As of Python Version 2.1, passive mode is on by default; in previous versions, passive mode was not on by default.)

The method `set_debuglevel(level)` sets the level of debug output from ftplib — 0 (the default level) produces no debug output; 2 is the most verbose.

Handling errors

The module defines several exceptions: `error_reply` is raised when the server unexpectedly sends a response; `error_temp` is raised for "temporary errors" (with error codes in the range 400–499); `error_perm` is raised for "permanent errors" (with error codes in the range 500–599); and `error_proto` is raised for errors with unknown error codes.

Using netrc files

The supporting module `netrc` is used to parse .netrc files. These files cache user information for various FTP servers, so that you don't need to send it to the host by hand each time. They can also store macros.

The module provides a class, `netrc`, for accessing netrc contents. The constructor `netrc([filename])` builds a netrc object by parsing the specified file. If *filename* is not provided, it defaults to the file .netrc in your home directory.

The attribute `hosts` is a dictionary mapping from host names to authentication information of the form (username, account, password). If the parsed .netrc file includes a default entry, it is stored in `hosts["default"]`. The attribute `macros` is a dictionary, mapping macro names to string lists. The method `authenticators(hostname)` returns either the authentication tuple for *hostname*, the default tuple (if there is no tuple for *hostname*), or (if there is no default either) `None`.

The netrc class implements a __retr__ method that returns .netrc file contents. This means that you can edit an existing file. For example, the following code adds (or overrides) an entry on disk:

```
MyNetrc=netrc.netrc(".netrc")
MyNetrc.hosts["ftp.oracle.com"]=("stanner","","weeble")
NetrcFile=open(".netrc")
NetrcFile.write(repr(MyNetrc))
NetrcFile.close()
```

Retrieving Resources Using Gopher

Gopher is a protocol for transferring hypertext and multimedia over the Internet. With the rise of the World Wide Web, Gopher is no longer widely used. However, the urllib module supports it, and the `gopherlib` module supports gopher requests.

See RFC 1436 for the definition of the Gopher protocol.

The function `send_selector(selector,host[,port])` sends a *selector* (analogous to a URL) to the specified host. It returns an open file object that you can read from. The port-number parameter, *port*, defaults to 70. For example, the following code retrieves and prints the Gopher Manifesto:

```
Manifesto=gopherlib.send_selector(
"0/the gopher manifesto.txt","gopher.heatdeath.org")
print Manifesto.read()
```

The function `send_query(selector,query,host[,port])` is similar to send_selector, but sends the query string *query* to the server along with the selector.

Working with Newsgroups

Network News Transport Protocol, or *NNTP,* is used to carry the traffic of *newsgroups* such as comp.lang.python. The module `nntplib` provides a class, `NNTP`, which is a simple NNTP client. It can connect to a news server and search, retrieve, and post articles.

See RFC 977 for the full definition of NNTP.

Most methods of an NNTP object return a tuple, of which the first element is the server response string. The string begins with a three-digit status code.

Dates in `nntplib` are handled as strings of the form yymmdd, and times are handled as strings of the form hhmmss. The two-digit year is assumed to be the year closest to the present, and the time zone assumed is that of the news server.

Articles are identified in two ways. Articles are assigned numeric *article numbers* within a group in ascending order. Each article also has a unique *message-id*, a magic bracketed string unique across all articles in all newsgroups. For instance: An article cross-posted to rec.org.mensa and alt.religion.kibology might be article number 200 in rec.org.mensa, article number 500 in alt.religion.kibology, and have message-id `<mwb06.162488$e5.131709@newsfeeds.bigpond.com>`.

Some methods are not available on all news servers — the names of these methods begin with x (for "extension").

Connecting and logging in

The constructor syntax is `NNTP(host[,port[,user[,password [,readermode]]]])`. Here, *host* is the news server's host name. The port number, *port*, defaults to 119. If the server requires authentication, pass a username and password in the *user* and *password* parameters. If you are connecting to a news server on the local host, pass a non-null value for *readermode*.

Once connected, the getwelcome method returns the server's welcome message. When you are finished with the connection, call the quit method to disconnect from the server.

Browsing groups

To select a particular newsgroup, call the method group(name). The method returns a tuple of strings (response,count,first,last,name). Here, *count* is the approximate number of messages in the group, *first* and *last* are the first and last article numbers, and *name* is the group name.

The method list examines the newsgroups available on the server. It returns a tuple (response,grouplist), where *response* is the server response. The list *grouplist* has one element per newsgroup. Each entry is a tuple of the form (name,last,first,postable). Here, *name* is the name of the newsgroup, *last* is the last article number, and *first* is the first article number. The flag *postable* is either "y" if posting is allowed, "n" if posting is forbidden, or "m" if the group is moderated.

Caution   There are thousands of newsgroups out there. Retrieving a list usually takes several minutes. You may want to take a snack break when you call the list method!

The following code finds all newsgroups with "fish" in their name:

```
GroupList=news.list()[1]
print filter(lambda x:x[0].find("fish")!=-1,GroupList)
```

New newsgroups appear on USENET constantly. The method newgroups (date,time) returns all newsgroups created since the specified date and time, in the same format as the listing from list.

Browsing articles

New news is good news. The method newnews(name,date,time) finds articles posted after the specified moment on the group *name*. It returns a tuple of the form (response, idlist), where *idlist* is a list of message-ids.

Once you have entered a group by calling group, you are "pointing at" the first article. You can move through the articles in the group by calling the methods next and last. These navigate to the next and the previous article, respectively. They then return a tuple of the form (response,number,id), where *number* is the current article number, and *id* is its message-id.

The method stat(id) checks the status of an article. Here, *id* is either an article number (as a string) or a message-id. It returns the same output as next or last.

On most news servers, you can scan article headers to find the messages you want. Call the method `xhdr(header, articles)` to retrieve the values of a header specified by *header*. The parameter *articles* should specify an article range of the form *first-last*. The returned value is a tuple (response, headerlist). The entries in *headerlist* have the form (id, text), where *id* is the message-id of an article, and *text* is its value for the specified header. For instance, the following code retrieves subjects for articles 319000 through 319005, inclusive:

```
>>> news.xhdr("subject","319000-319005")
('221 subject fields follow', [('319000', 'Re: I heartily
endorse: Sinfest!'), ('319001', 'Re: Dr. Teg'), ('319002', 'Re:
If you be my bodyguard'), ('319003', 'Re: Culture shock'),
('319004', 'Re: Dr. Teg'), ('319005', 'Todays lesson')])
```

The method `xover(start,end)` gathers more detailed header information for articles in the range [start,end]. It returns a tuple of the form (response, articlelist). There is one element in the list *articlelist* for each article. Each such entry contains header values in a tuple of the form (article number, subject, poster, date, message-id, references, size, lines).

The method `xgtitle(name)` finds all the newsgroups matching the specified name *name*, which can include wildcards. It returns a tuple of the form (response, grouplist). Each element of *grouplist* takes the form (name, description). For example, here is another (much faster) way to search for groups that talk about fish:

```
print news.xgtitle("*fish*")
```

Reading articles

The method `article(id)` retrieves the article with the specified id. It returns a tuple of the form (response, number, id, linelist), where *number* is the article number, *id* is its message-id, and *linelist* is a list whose elements are the lines of text of the article. The text in *linelist* includes all its headers. The method `head(id)` and `body(id)` retrieve head and body, respectively.

For example, the simple code in Listing 16-3 dumps all articles by a particular poster on a newsgroup into one long file:

Listing 16-3: **NewsSlurp.py**

```
import nntplib
import sys
def dump_articles(news,TargetGroup,TargetPoster):
    GroupInfo=news.group(TargetGroup)
    ArticleList=news.xhdr("from",GroupInfo[2]+"-"+GroupInfo[3])

    dumpfile = open("newsfeed.txt","w")
    for ArticleTuple in ArticleList:
        (MessageID,Poster)=ArticleTuple
```

```
        if (Poster.find(TargetPoster)!=-1):
            ArticleText=news.body(MessageID)[3]
            for ArticleLine in ArticleText:
                dumpfile.write(ArticleLine+"\n")
            dumpfile.flush()
    dumpfile.close()

news=nntplib.NNTP("news.fastpointcom.com")
dump_articles(news,"alt.religion.kibology","kibo@world.std.com"
)
```

Posting articles

The method post(file) posts, as a new article, the text read from the file object *file*. The file text should include the appropriate headers.

The method ihave(id,file) informs the server that you have an article whose message-id is *id*. If the server requests the article, it is posted from the specified file.

Other functions

The helper method date returns a tuple of the form (response, date, time), where date and time are of the form yymmdd and mmhhss, respectively. It is not available on all news servers.

Call set_debug(level) to set the logging level for an NNTP object. The default, 0, is silent; 2 is the most verbose.

The method help returns a tuple of the form (response, helplines), where *helplines* is the server help text in the form of a list of strings. Server help is generally not especially helpful, but may list the extended commands that are available.

Call the slave method to inform the news server that your session is a helper (or "slave") news server, and return the response. This notification generally has no special effect.

Handling errors

An NNTP object raises various exceptions when things go horribly wrong. NNTPError is the base class for all exceptions raised by nntplib. NNTPReply is raised if the server unexpectedly sends a reply. For error codes in the range of 400–499 (for example, calling next without selecting a newsgroup), NNTPTemporaryError is raised. For error codes in the range of 500–599 (for example, passing a bogus header to xhdr), NNTPPermanentError is raised. For unknown error codes, NNTPProtocolError is raised. Finally, NNTPDataError is raised for bogus response data.

Using the Telnet Protocol

The Telnet protocol is used for remote access to a server. Telnet is quite low-level, only a little more abstract than using socket directly. For example, you can (if you are a masochistic) read USENET by telnetting to port 119 and entering NNTP commands by hand.

See RFC 854 for a definition of the Telnet protocol.

The module telnetlib defines a class, Telnet, which you can use to handle a Telnet connection to a remote host.

Connecting

The Telnet constructor has the syntax Telnet([host[,port]]). If you pass a host name in the parameter *host*, a session will be opened to the host. The port number, optionally passed via the parameter *port*, defaults to 23. If you don't connect when constructing the object, you can connect by calling open(host[,port]). Once you are finished with a session, call the close method to terminate it.

After establishing a connection, do not call the open method again for the same Telnet object.

Reading and writing

You can run a simple Telnet client (reading from stdin and printing server responses to stdout) by calling the interact method. The method mtinteract is a multithreaded version of interact. For example, the following lines would connect you to an online MUD (Multi-User Dungeon) game:

```
>>> link=telnetlib.Telnet("materiamagica.com",4000)
>>> link.interact()
```

Writing data is simple: To send data to the server, call the method write(string). Special IAC (Interpret As Command) characters such as chr(255) are escaped (doubled).

Reading data from the server is a bit more complicated. The Telnet object keeps a buffer of data read so far from the server; each read method accesses buffered (or "cooked") data before reading more from the server. Each returns data read as a (possibly empty) string. The following read methods are available:

✦ read_all — Read until EOF. Block until the server closes the connection.

✦ read_some — Read at least one character (unless EOF is reached). Block if data is not immediately available.

✦ read_very_eager — Read all available data, without blocking unless in the middle of a command sequence.

✦ read_eager — Same as read_very_eager, but does not read more from the server if cooked data is available.

✦ read_lazy — Reads all cooked data. Does not block unless in the middle of a command sequence.

✦ read_very_lazy — Reads all cooked data. Never blocks.

The read methods, except `read_all` and `read_some`, raise an `EOFError` if the connection is closed and no data is buffered. For example, if you use read_very_lazy exclusively for reading, the only way to be certain the server is finished is if an `EOFError` is raised. For most purposes, you can just call `read_some` and ignore the other methods.

For example, the following code connects to port 7 (the echo port) and talks to itself:

```
echo=telnetlib.Telnet("gianth.com",7)
echo.write("Hello!")
print echo.read_very_eager()
```

Watching and waiting

The method `read_until(expected[,timeout])` reads from the server until it encounters the string *expected*, or until *timeout* seconds have passed. If timeout is not supplied, it waits indefinitely. The method returns whatever data was read, possibly the empty string. It raises `EOFError` if the connection is closed and no data is buffered.

A more powerful method `expect(targets[,timeout])` watches for a list of strings or regular expression objects, provided in the parameter *targets*. It returns a tuple of the form (matchindex, match, text), where *matchindex* is the index (in *targets*) of the first matched item, *match* is a match object, and *text* is the text read up to and including the match. If no match was found, *matchindex* is -1, *match* is None, and *text* is the text read, if any.

Other methods

The method `set_debug(level)` sets the level of debug logging. A level of 0 (the default) is silent; level 2 is the most verbose.

The method `get_socket` returns the socket object used internally by a Telnet object. The method `fileno` returns the file descriptor of the socket object.

Writing CGI Scripts

Many Web pages respond to input from the user — these pages range from simple feedback forms to sophisticated shopping Web sites. *Common Gateway Interface (CGI)* is a standard way for the Web server to pass user input into a script. The module cgi enables you to build Python modules to handle user requests to your Web site.

Your CGI script should output headers, a blank line, and then content. The one required header is *Content-type,* and its usual value is "text/html." For example, Listing 16-4 is a very simple CGI script, which returns a static Web page:

Listing 16-4: **HelloWorld.py**

```
# (add #! line here under UNIX, or if using Apache on Windows)
import cgi
# Part 1: Content-Type header, followed by a blank line
# to indicate the end of the headers.
print "Content-Type: text/html\n"
# Part 2: A simple HTML page
print "<title>Gumby</title>"
print "<html><body>My brain hurts!</body></html>"
```

Setting up CGI scripts

Making your Web server run a script is half the battle. In general, you must do the following:

1. Put the script in the right place.

2. Make it executable.

3. Make it execute properly.

Configuration details vary by Web server and operating system, but the following sections provide information for some common cases.

Windows Internet Information Server (IIS)

First, create a directory (below your root Web directory) for CGI files. A common name is cgi-bin.

Next, bring up the Internet Services Manager — in Windows 2000, go to Start ➪ Control Panel ➪ Administrative Tools ➪ Internet Services Manager.

In Internet Services Manager, edit the properties of the CGI directory. In the Application section, click Configuration... (if Configuration is disabled, click

Add first). This brings up the Application Configuration dialog. On the App Mappings tab, add an entry mapping the extension .py to python.exe -u %s %s. The -u setting makes Python run in unbuffered binary mode. The %s %s ensures that IIS runs your script (and not just an instance of the interpreter!).

UNIX

Put your scripts in the appropriate CGI directory, probably cgi-bin. Make sure the script is executable by everyone (chmod 077 script.py). In addition, make sure any files it reads or writes are accessible by everyone. To make sure the script is executed *as a python script*, add a "pound-bang" line to the very top of the script, as follows:

```
#!/usr/local/bin/python
```

Apache (any operating system)

To set up a CGI directory under Apache, add a ScriptAlias line to httpd.conf that points at the directory. In addition, make sure there is a <Directory> entry for that folder, and that it permits execution. For example, my configuration file includes the following lines:

```
ScriptAlias /cgi-bin/ "C:/Webroot/cgi-bin/"
<Directory "C:/Webroot/cgi-bin">
    AllowOverride None
    Options None
</Directory>
```

Apache uses the "pound-bang hack" to decide how to execute CGI scripts, even on Windows. For example, I use the following simple test script to test CGI under Apache:

```
#!python
import cgi
cgi.test() # the test function exercises many CGI features
```

Accessing form fields

To access form fields, instantiate one (and only one) cgi.FieldStorage object. The master FieldStorage object can be used like a dictionary. Its keys are the submitted field names. Its values are also FieldStorage objects. (Actually, if there are multiple values for a field, then its corresponding value is a list of FieldStorage objects.)

The FieldStorage object for an individual field has a value attribute containing the field's value as a string. It also has a name attribute containing the field name (possibly None).

For example, the script in Listing 16-5 (and its corresponding Web page) gathers and e-mails site feedback. Listing 16-6 is a Web page that uses the script to handle form input.

Listing 16-5: **Feedback.py**

```python
#!python
import cgi
import smtplib
import sys
import traceback

# Set these e-mail addresses appropriately
SOURCE_ADDRESS="robot_form@gianth.com"
FEEDBACK_ADDRESS="dumplechan@seanbaby.com"

sys.stderr = sys.stdout
print "Content-Type: text/html\n"
try:
    fields=cgi.FieldStorage()
    if (fields.has_key("name") and fields.has_key("comments")):
        UserName=fields["name"].value
        Comments=fields["comments"].value
        # Mail the feedback:
        Mailbox=smtplib.SMTP("mail.seanbaby.com")
        MessageText="From: <"+SOURCE_ADDRESS+">\r\n"
        MessageText+="To: "+FEEDBACK_ADDRESS+"\r\n"
        MessageText+="Subject: Feedback\r\n\r\n"
        MessageText+="Feedback from "+UserName+":\r\n"+Comments
        Mailbox.sendmail(SOURCE_ADDRESS, FEEDBACK_ADDRESS,
            MessageText)
        # Print a simple thank-you page:
        print "<h1>Thanks!</h1>Thank you for your feedback!"
    else:
        # They must have left "name" and/or "comments" blank:
        print "<h1>Sorry...</h1>"
        print "You must provide a name and some comments too!"
except:
    # Print the traceback to the response page, for debugging!
    print "\n\n<PRE>"
    traceback.print_exc()
```

Listing 16-6: **Feedback.html**

```html
<html>
<title>Feedback form</title>
<h1>Submit your comments</h1>
<form action="cgi-bin/Feedback.py" method="POST">
Your name: <input type="text" size="35" name="name">
<br>
```

```
Comments: <br>
<textarea name="comments" rows="5" cols="35"></textarea>
<input type="submit" value="Send!">
<form>
</html>
```

Advanced CGI functions

You can retrieve field values directly from the master FieldStorage object by calling the method getvalue(fieldname[,default]). It returns the value of field *fieldname*, or (if no value is available) the value *default*. If not supplied, *default* is None. If there are multiple values for a field, getvalue returns a list of strings.

If a field value is actually a file, accessing the value attribute of the corresponding FieldStorage object returns the file's contents as one long string. In this case, the filename attribute is set to the file's name (as given by the client), and the file attribute is an opened file object.

A FieldStorage object provides some other attributes:

✦ type — Content-type as a string (or None if unspecified)

✦ type_options — Dictionary of options passed with the content-type header

✦ disposition — Content-disposition as a string (or None if unspecified)

✦ disposition_options — Dictionary of options passed with the content-disposition header

✦ headers — Map of all headers and their values

A note on debugging

Debugging CGI scripts can be difficult, because the traceback from a crashed script may be buried deep in the bowels of the Web server's logging. Listing 16-7 uses a trick to make debugging easier.

Listing 16-7: **CGIDebug.py**

```
import sys
import traceback
sys.stderr = sys.stdout
print "Content-Type: text/html\n"
try:
    # The script body goes here!
except:
    print "\n\n<PRE>"
    traceback.print_exc()
```

Pointing stderr at stdout means that the output of print_exc goes to the resulting Web page. The <PRE> tag ensures that the text is shown exactly as printed.

A note on security

Internet security is crucial, even for casual users and simple sites. A common vulnerability is a CGI script that executes a command string passed from a Web request. Therefore, avoid passing user-supplied values to os.system, or accessing file names derived from user data. Remember that hidden fields on forms are hidden for presentation purposes only — enterprising users can see and manipulate their values.

For a good introduction to Web security, see the World Wide Web Consortium's security FAQ at http://www.w3.org/Security/Faq/www-security-faq.html.

Summary

Python provides simple client implementations of many Internet protocols. Python also makes a great CGI scripting language. In this chapter, you:

✦ Sent and received e-mail.

✦ Retrieved Web pages and files in various ways.

✦ Created a Web page with a simple feedback form.

In the next chapter, you will meet various modules that help handle many flavors of Internet data.

✦   ✦   ✦

Handling Internet Data

In This Chapter

Manipulating URLs

Formatting text

Reading Web spider robot files

Viewing files in a Web browser

Dissecting e-mail messages

Working with MIME encoding

Encoding and decoding message data

Working with UNIX mailboxes

Using Web cookies

Internet data takes many forms. You may find yourself working with e-mail messages, mailboxes, cookies, URLs, and more. Python's libraries include helper modules for handling this data. This chapter introduces modules to help handle several common tasks in Internet programming — handling URLs, sending e-mail, handling cookies from the World Wide Web, and more.

Manipulating URLs

A Uniform Resource Locator (URL) is a string that serves as the address of a resource on the Internet. The module `urlparse` provides functions to make it easier to manipulate URLs.

The function
`urlparse(url[,default_scheme[,allow_fragments]])`
parses the string *url*, splitting the URL into a tuple of the form (scheme, host, path, parameters, query, fragment). For example:

```
>>> URLString="http://finance.yahoo.com/q?s=MWT&d=v1"
>>> print urlparse.urlparse(URLString)
('http', 'finance.yahoo.com', '/q', '', 's=MWT&d=v1', '')
```

The optional parameter *default_scheme* specifies an addressing scheme to use if none is specified. For example, the following code parses a URL with and without a default scheme:

```
>>> URLString="//gianth.com/stuff/junk/DestroyTheWorld.exe"
>>> print urlparse.urlparse(URLString) # no scheme!
('', 'gianth.com', ' /stuff/junk/DestroyTheWorld.exe', '', '', '')
>>> print urlparse.urlparse(URLString,"ftp")
('ftp', 'gianth.com', '/stuff/junk/DestroyTheWorld.exe', '', '', '')
```

The parameter *allow_fragments* defaults to true. If set to false, no fragments are permitted in the parsed URL:

```
>>> URLString="http://www.penny-arcade.com/#food"
>>> print urlparse.urlparse("URLString")
('http', 'www.penny-arcade.com', '/', '', '', 'food')
>>> print urlparse.urlparse("URLString",None,0)
('http', 'www.penny-arcade.com', '/#food', '', '', '')
```

The function `urlunparse(tuple)` unparses a tuple back into a URL string. Parsing and then unparsing yields a URL string that is equivalent (and quite possibly identical) to the original.

The function `urljoin(base, url[,allow_fragments])` merges a base URL (*base*) with a new URL (*url*) to create a new URL string. It is useful for processing anchors when parsing HTML. For example:

```
>>> CurrentPage="http://gianth.com/stuff/junk/index.html"
>>> print urlparse.urljoin(CurrentPage,"../../foo.html")
http://gianth.com/foo.html
```

The parameter allow_fragments has the same usage as `urlparse`.

 Cross-Reference   The module urllib includes functions to encode strings as valid URL components. See "Manipulating URLs" in Chapter 16.

Formatting Text

The `formatter` module defines interfaces for formatters and writers. A *formatter* handles requests for various kinds of text formatting, such as fonts and margins. It passes formatting requests along to a *writer*. In particular, it keeps a stack of fonts and margins, so that they know which settings to revert to after turning off the "current" font or margins. Formatters and writers are useful for translating text between formats, or for displaying formatted text. They are used by `htmllib.HTMLParser`.

Formatter interface

The formatter attribute `writer` is the writer object corresponding to the formatter.

Writing text

The methods `add_flowing_data(text)` and `add_literal_data(text)` both send text to the writer. The difference between the two is that `add_flowing_data` collapses extra whitespace; whitespace is held in the formatter before being passed to the writer. The method `flush_softspace` clears buffered whitespace from the formatter.

The method `add_label_data(format, counter)` sends label text (as used in a list) to the writer. If *format* is a string, it is used to format the numeric value *counter* (in a numbered list). Otherwise, *format* is passed along to the writer directly.

If you manipulate the writer directly, call `flush_softspace` beforehand, and call `assert_line_data([flag])` after adding any text. The parameter *flag*, which defaults to 1, should be true if the added data finished with a line break.

Spacing, margins, and alignment

The method `set_spacing(spaces)` sets the desired line spacing to *lines*.

The methods `push_alignment(align)` and `pop_alignment` set and restore alignment. Here, *align* is normally left, right, center, justify (full), or `None` (default).

The methods `push_margin(name)` and `pop_margin` increase and decrease the current level of indentation; the parameter *name* is a name for the new indentation level. The initial margin level is 0; all other margin levels must have names that evaluate to true.

The method `add_line_break` adds a line break (at most, one in succession), but does not finish the current paragraph. The method `end_paragraph(lines)` ends the current paragraph and inserts at least *lines* blank lines. Finally, the method `add_hor_rule` adds a horizontal rule; its parameters are formatter- and writer-dependent, and are passed along to the writer's method `send_line_break`.

Fonts and styles

The method `push_font(font)` pushes a new font definition, *font*, of the form (size,italics,bold,teletype). Values set to `formatter.AS_IS` are left unchanged. The new font is passed to the writer's `new_font` method. The method `pop_font` restores the previous font.

The method `push_style(*styles)` passes any number of style definitions. A tuple of all style definitions is passed to the writer's method `new_styles`. The method `pop_style([count])` pops *count* styles (by default, 1), and passes the revised stack to `new_styles`.

Writer interface

Writers provide various methods to print or display text. Normally, the formatter calls these methods, but a caller can access the writer directly.

Writing text

The methods `send_flowing_data(text)` and `send_literal_data(text)` both output text. The difference between the two is that `send_literal_data` sends pre-formatted text, whereas send_flowing_data sends text with redundant whitespace collapsed. The method send_label_data(text) sends text intended for a list label; it is called only at the beginning of a line.

The method flush is called to flush any buffered output.

Spacing, margins, and alignment

The method send_line_break breaks the current line. The method send_paragraph(lines) is called to end the current paragraph and send at least *lines* blank lines. The method set_spacing(lines) sets the level of line spacing to *lines*. The method send_hor_rule is called to add a horizontal rule; its arguments are formatter- and writer-dependent.

The method new_margin(name,level) sets the margin level to *level*, where the indentation level's name is *name*.

The method new_alignment(align) sets line alignment. Here, *align* is normally left, right, center, justify (full), or None (default).

Fonts and styles

The method new_font(font) sets the current font to *font*, where *font* is either None (indicating default font), or a tuple of the form (size,italic,bold,teletype).

The method new_styles(styles) is called to set new style(s); pass a tuple of new style values in *styles*.

Other module resources

The AbstractFormatter is a simple formatter that you can use for most applications. The NullFormatter is a trivial implementation of the formatter interface — it has all the available methods, but they do nothing. It is useful for creating an HTTPParser that does not format Web pages.

The NullWriter is a writer that does nothing. The AbstractWriter is useful for debugging formatters; method calls are simply logged. The DumbWriter is a simple writer that outputs word-wrapped text. Its constructor has the syntax DumbWriter ([file[,maxcol]]). Here, *file* is an open filelike object for output (if none is specified, text is written to standard output); and *maxcol* (which defaults to 72) is the maximum width, in characters, of a line. For example, this function prints a text-only version of a Web page:

```
import htmllib
import urllib
import formatter

def PrintTextPage(URL):
    URLFile = urllib.urlopen(URL)
    HTML = URLFile.read()
```

```
URLFile.close()
parser=htmllib.HTMLParser(
   formatter.AbstractFormatter(formatter.DumbWriter()))
parser.feed(HTML)
```

Reading Web Spider Robot Files

A *robot* is a program that automatically browses the Web. For example, a script could programmatically check CD prices at several online sites in order to find the best price. Some Webmasters would prefer that robots not visit their systems. Therefore, a well-behaved robot should check a host's Web root for a file named *robots.txt,* which specifies any URLs that are off-limits.

The module robotparser provides a class, RobotFileParser, which makes it easy to parse robots.txt. Once you instantiate a RobotFileParser, call its set_url(url) to point it at the robots.txt file at the specified URL *url.* Then, call its read method to parse the file. Before retrieving a URL, call can_fetch(useragent, url) to determine whether the specified URL is allowed. The parameter *useragent* should be the name of your robot program. For example, Listing 17-1 tests a "polite get" of a URL:

Listing 17-1: **PoliteGet.py**

```
import robotparser
import urlparse
import urllib

def PoliteGet(url):
    """Return an open url-file, or None if URL is forbidden"""
    RoboBuddy=robotparser.RobotFileParser()
    # Grab the host-name from the URL:
    URLTuple=urlparse.urlparse(url)
    RobotURL="http://"+URLTuple[1]+"/robots.txt"
    RoboBuddy.set_url(RobotURL)
    RoboBuddy.read()
    if RoboBuddy.can_fetch("I,Robot",url):
        return urllib.urlopen(url)
    else:
        return None

if (__name__=="__main__"):
    URL="http://www.nexor.com/cgi-bin/rfcsearch/location?2449"
    print "Forbidden:",(PoliteGet(URL)==None)
    URL="http://www.yahoo.com/r/sq"
    print "Allowed:",(PoliteGet(URL)==None)
```

You can manually pass a list of `robots.txt` lines to a `RobotFileParser` by calling the method `parse(lines)`.

If your parser runs for many days or weeks, you may want to re-read `robots.txt` periodically. `RobotFileParser` keeps a "last updated" timestamp. Call the method `modified` to set the timestamp to the current time. (This is done automatically when you call `read` or `parse`.) Call `mtime` to retrieve the timestamp, in ticks.

Viewing Files in a Web Browser

The module `webbrowser` provides a handy interface for opening URLs in a browser. The function `open(url[,new])` opens the specified URL using the default browser. If the parameter *new* is true, a new browser window is opened if possible. The function `open_new(url)` is a synonym for `open(url,1)`.

Normally, pages are displayed in their own window. However, on UNIX systems for which no graphical browser is available, a text browser will be opened (and the program will block until the browser session is closed).

If you want to open a particular browser, call the function `register(name, class[,instance])`. Here, *name* is one of the names shown in Table 17-1, and either *class* is the corresponding class, or *instance* is an instance of the corresponding class.

Table 17-1
Available Browsers

Name	Class	Platform
netscape	Netscape	All
kfm	Konquerer	UNIX
grail	Grail	All
windows-default	WindowsDefault	Windows
internet-config	InternetConfig	Macintosh
command-line	CommandLineBrowser	All

Once a browser is registered, you can call `get(name)` to retrieve a controller for it. The controller provides `open` and `open_new` methods similar to the functions of the same names. For example, the following code asks for the Grail browser by name, and then uses it to view a page:

```
>>> Webbrowser.register("grail",Webbrowser.Grail)
>>> Controller=Webbrowser.get("grail")
>>> Controller.open("www.python.org")
```

Dissecting E-Mail Messages

E-mail messages have *headers* with a standard syntax. The syntax, described in RFC 822, is a bit complicated. Fortunately, the module `rfc822` can parse these headers for you. It also provides a class to help handle lists of addresses.

Parsing a message

To parse a message, call the constructor `Message(file[,seekable])`. Here, *file* is an open file. The file is parsed, and all headers are matched case-insensitively.

The *file* parameter can be any filelike object with a `readlines` method; it must also have `seek` and `tell` methods in order for `Message.rewindbody` to work. If *file* is unseekable (for example, it wraps a socket), set *seekable* to 0 for maximum portability.

Retrieving header values

The method `get(name[,default])` returns the *last* value of header *name*, or *default* (by default, `None`) if no value was found. Leading and trailing whitespace is trimmed from the header; newlines are removed if the header takes up multiple lines. The method `getheader` is a synonym for `get`. The method `getrawheader(name)` returns the *first* header *name* with whitespace (including trailing linefeed) intact, or `None` if the header was not found.

If a header can have multiple values, you can use `getallmatchingheaders(name)` to retrieve a (raw) list of all header lines matching *name*. The method `getfirstmatchingheader(name)` returns a list of lines for the first match:

```
>>> MessageFile=open("msg1.txt")
>>> msg=rfc822.Message(MessageFile)
>>> msg.get("received") # The last value
'from 216.20.160.186 by lw8fd.law8.hotmail.msn.com with
HTTP;\011Thu, 28 Dec 2000 23:37:18 GMT'
>>> msg.getrawheader("RECEIVED") # the first value:
' from hotmail.com [216.33.241.22] by mail3.oldmanmurray.com
with ESMTP\012  (SMTPD32-6.05) id AB8884C01EE; Thu, 28 Dec 2000
18:23:52 -0500\012'
>>> msg.getallmatchingheaders("Received") # ALL values:
['Received: from hotmail.com [216.33.241.22] by
mail3.oldmanmurray.com with ESMTP\012', '  (SMTPD32-6.05) id
AB8884C01EE; Thu, 28 Dec 2000 18:23:52 -0500\012', 'Received:
from mail pickup service by hotmail.com with Microsoft
SMTPSVC;\012', '\011 Thu, 28 Dec 2000 15:37:19 -0800\012',
'Received: from 216.20.160.186 by lw8fd.law8.hotmail.msn.com
with HTTP;\011Thu, 28 Dec 2000 23:37:18 GMT\012']
```

Some headers are dates. Call getdate(name) to retrieve the value of header name as a TimeTuple. Alternatively, call getdate_tz(name) to retrieve a 10-tuple; its first nine entries form a TimeTuple, and the tenth is the time zone's offset (in ticks) from UTC. (Entries 6, 7, and 8 are unusable in each case.) For example:

```
>>> msg.getdate("date")
(2000, 12, 28, 16, 37, 18, 0, 0, 0)
>>> msg.getdate_tz("date")
(2000, 12, 28, 16, 37, 18, 0, 0, 0, -25200)
```

The method getaddr(name) helps parse To: and From: headers, returning their values in the form (full name, e-mail address). If the header *name* is not found, it returns (None,None). For example:

```
>>> msg.getaddr("From")
('Stephen Tanner', 'dumplechan@hotmail.com')
>>> msg.getaddr("PurpleHairySpiders")
(None, None)
```

Other members

The method rewindbody seeks to the start of the message body (if the filelike object parsed supports seeking).

A Message object supports the methods of a dictionary — for example, keys returns a list of headers found. The attribute fp is the original file parsed, and the attribute headers is a list of all header lines.

If you need to subclass Message, you may want to override some of its parsing methods. The method islast(line) returns true if *line* marks the end of header lines. By default, islast returns true when passed a blank line. The method iscomment(line) returns true if *line* is a comment that should be skipped. Finally, the method isheader(line) returns the header name if *line* is a valid header line, or None if it is not.

Address lists

The class AddressList holds a list of e-mail addresses. Its constructor takes a list of address strings; passing None results in an AddressList with no entries.

You can take the length of an AddressList, add (merge) two AddressLists, remove (subtract) one of AddressList's elements from another AddressList, and retrieve a canonical string representation:

```
>>> List1=rfc822.AddressList(msg.getheader("To"))
>>> List2=rfc822.AddressList(msg.getheader("From"))
>>> MergedList=List1+List2 # Merge lists
>>> len(MergedList) # access list length
2
```

```
>>> str(MergedList) # canonical representation
'dumplechan@seanbaby.com, "Stephen Tanner"
<dumplechan@hotmail.com>'
>>> str(MergedList-List1) # remove one list's elements
'"Stephen Tanner" <dumplechan@hotmail.com>'
```

An AddressList also provides the attribute addresslist, a list of tuples of the form (full name, e-mail address):

```
>>> MergedList.addresslist
[('', 'dumplechan@seanbaby.com'), ('Stephen Tanner',
'dumplechan@hotmail.com')]
```

rfc822 utility functions

The functions parsedata(str) and parsedata_tz(str) parse the string *str*, in the manner of the Message methods getdate and getdate_tz. The function mktime_tz(tuple) does the reverse — it converts a TimeTuple into a UTC timestamp.

MIME messages

The class mimetools.Message is a subclass of rfc822.Message. It provides some extra methods to help parse content-type and content-transfer-encoding headers.

The method gettype returns the message type (in lowercase) from the content-type header, or text/plain if no content-type header exists. The methods getmaintype and getsubtype get the main type and subtype, respectively.

The method getplist returns the parameters of the content-type header as a list of strings. For parameters of the form name=value, *name* is converted to lowercase but *value* is unchanged.

The method getparam(name) gets the first value (from the content-type header) for a given name; any quotes or brackets surrounding the value are removed.

The method getencoding returns the value of the content-transfer-encoding header, converted to lowercase. If not specified, it returns 7bit.

This example scrutinizes some headers from an e-mail message:

```
>>> MessageFile=open("message.txt","r")
>>> msg=mimetools.Message(MessageFile)
>>> msg.gettype()
'text/plain'
>>> msg.getmaintype()
'text'
>>> msg.getsubtype()
'plain'
```

```
>>> msg.getplist()
['format=flowed']
>>> msg.get("content-type")
'text/plain; format=flowed'
>>> msg.getparam("format")
'flowed'
>>> msg.getencoding()
'7bit'
```

Working with MIME Encoding

Multipurpose Internet Mail Extensions (MIME) are a mechanism for tagging the document type of a message — or for several parts of one message. (See RFC 1521 for a full description of MIME.) Several Python modules help handle MIME messages — most functions you need are there, though they may be spread across libraries.

The module `mimetools` provides functions to handle MIME encoding. The function `decode(input,output,encoding)` decodes from the filelike object *input* to *output*, using the specified encoding. The function `encode(input,output,encoding)` encodes. Legal values for *encoding* are base64, quoted-printable, and uuencode. These encodings use the modules `base64`, `quopri`, and `uu`, discussed in the section "Encoding and Decoding Message Data."

The function `choose_boundary` returns a unique string for use as a boundary between MIME message parts.

Encoding and decoding MIME messages

The module mimify provides functions to encode and decode messages in MIME format. The function `mimify(input, output)` encodes from the filelike object *input* into *output*. Non-ASCII characters are encoded using quoted-printable encoding, and MIME headers are added as necessary. The function `unmimify(input, output[,decode_base64)` decodes from input into output; if decode_base64 is true, then any portions of *input* encoded using base64 are also decoded. You can pass file names (instead of files) for *input* and *output*.

The functions `mime_encode_header(line)` and `mime_decode_header(line)` encode and decode a single string.

The `mimify` module assumes that any line longer than `mimify.MAXLEN` (by default, 200) characters needs to be encoded. Also, the variable `mimify.CHARSET` is a default character set to fill in if not specified in the content-type header; it defaults to ISO-8859-1 (Latin1).

Parsing multipart MIME messages

A MIME message can have several sections, each with a different content-type. The sections of a MIME message, in turn, can be divided into smaller subsections. The multifile module provides a class, MultiFile, to wrap multi-part messages. A MultiFile behaves like a file, and can treat section boundaries like an EOF.

The constructor has syntax MultiFile(file[,seekable]). Here, *file* is a filelike object, and *seekable* should be set to false for nonseekable objects such as sockets.

Call the method push(str) to set *str* as the current boundary string; call pop to remove the current boundary string from the stack. The MultiFile will raise an error if it encounters an invalid section boundary — for example, if you call push(X), and then push(Y), and the MultiFile encounters the string X before seeing Y. A call to next jumps to the next occurrence of the current boundary string. The attribute level is the current nesting depth.

The read, readline, readlines, seek, and tell methods of a MultiFile operate on only the current section. For example, seek indices are relative to the start of the current section, and readlines returns only the lines in the current section.

When you read to the end of a section, the attribute last is set to 1. At this point, it is not possible to read further, unless you call next or pop.

The method is_data(str) returns false if *str* might be a section boundary. It is used as a fast test for section boundaries. The method section_divider(str) converts *str* into a section-divider line, by prepending "–". The method end_marker(str) converts *str* into an end-marker line, by adding "–" at the beginning and end of *str*.

Writing out multipart MIME messages

The module MimeWriter provides the class MimeWriter to help write multipart MIME messages. The constructor takes one argument, an open file (or filelike object) to write the message to.

To add headers, call addheader(header, value[,prefix]). Here, *header* is the header to add, and *value* is its value. Set the parameter *prefix* to true to add the new header at the beginning of the message headers, or false (the default) to append it to the end. The method flushheaders writes out all accumulated headers; you should only call it for message parts with an empty body (which, in turn, shouldn't happen).

To write a single-part message, call startbody(content[,plist[,prefix]]) to construct a filelike object to hold the message body. Here, *content* is a value for the content-type header, and *plist* is a list of additional content-type parameter tuples of the form (name,value). The parameter *prefix* defaults to true, and functions as in addheader.

To write a multipart message, first call `startmultipartbody(subtype [,boundary[,plist[,prefix]]])`. The content-type header has main type "multipart," subtype *subtype*, and any extra parameters you pass in *plist*. For each part of the message, call `nextpart` to get a MimeWriter for that part. After finishing each part of the message, call `lastpart` to finish the message off. The call to `startmultipartbody` also returns a filelike object; it can be used to store a message for non-MIME-capable software.

Note You should not `close` the filelike objects provided by the MimeWriter, as each one is a wrapper for the same file.

For example, Listing 17-2 writes out a multipart message and then parses it back again.

Listing 17-2: **MimeTest.py**

```
import MimeWriter
import mimetools
import base64
import multifile

def TestWriting():
    # Write out a multi-part MIME message. The first part is
    # some plain text. The second part is an embedded
    # multi-part message; its two parts are an HTML document
    # and an image.
    MessageFile=open("BigMessage.txt","w")
    msg=MimeWriter.MimeWriter(MessageFile)
    msg.addheader("From","dumplechan@hotmail.com")
    msg.addheader("To","dave_brueck@hotmail.com")
    msg.addheader("Subject","Pen-pal greetings (good times!)")
    # Generate a unique section boundary:
    OuterBoundary=mimetools.choose_boundary()
    # Start the main message body. Write a brief message
    # for non-MIME-capable readers:
    DummyFile=msg.startmultipartbody("mixed",OuterBoundary)
    DummyFile.write("If you can read this, your mailreader\n")
    DummyFile.write("can't handle multi-part messages!\n")
    # Sub-part 1: Simple plain-text message
    submsg=msg.nextpart()
    FirstPartFile=submsg.startbody("text/plain")
    FirstPartFile.write("Hello!\nThis is a text part.\n")
    FirstPartFile.write("It was a dark and stormy night...\n")
    FirstPartFile.write("  * * TO BE CONTINUED * *\n")
    # Sub-part 2: Message with parallel html and image
    submsg2=msg.nextpart()
    # Generate boundary for sub-parts:
    InnerBoundary=mimetools.choose_boundary()
    submsg2.startmultipartbody("mixed",InnerBoundary)
```

```
    submsg2part1=submsg2.nextpart()
    # Sub-part 2.1: HTML page
    SubTextFile=submsg2part1.startbody("text/html")
    SubTextFile.write("<html><title>Hello!</title>\n")
    SubTextFile.write("<body>Hello world!</body></html>\n")
    # Sub-part 2.2: Picture, encoded with base64 encoding
    submsg2part2=submsg2.nextpart()
    submsg2part2.addheader("Content-Transfer-Encoding",
        "base64")
    ImageFile=submsg2part2.startbody("image/gif")
    SourceImage=open("pic.gif","rb")
    base64.encode(SourceImage,ImageFile)
    # Finish off the sub-message and the main message:
    submsg2.lastpart()
    msg.lastpart()
    MessageFile.close() # all done!

def TestReading():
    MessageFile=open("BigMessage.txt","r")
    # Parse the message boundary using mimetools:
    msg=mimetools.Message(MessageFile)
    OuterBoundary=msg.getparam("boundary")
    reader=multifile.MultiFile(MessageFile)
    reader.push(OuterBoundary)
    print "**Text for non-MIME-capable readers:"
    print reader.read()
    reader.next()
    print "**Text message:"
    print reader.read()
    reader.next()
    # Parse the inner boundary:
    msg=mimetools.Message(reader)
    InnerBoundary=msg.getparam("boundary")
    reader.seek(0) # rewind!
    reader.push(InnerBoundary)
    reader.next() # seek to part 2.1
    print "**HTML page:"
    print reader.read()
    reader.next()
    print "**Writing image to pic2.gif..."
    # seek to start of (encoded) body:
    msg=mimetools.Message(reader)
    msg.rewindbody()
    # decode the image:
    ImageFile=open("pic2.gif","wb")
    base64.decode(reader,ImageFile)

if (__name__=="__main__"):
    TestWriting()
    TestReading()
```

Handling document types

There is no official mapping between MIME types and file extensions. However, the module mimetypes can make reasonable guesses. The function guess_extension (type) returns a reasonable extension for files of content-type *type*, or None if it has no idea.

The function guess_type(filename) returns a tuple of the form (type, encoding). Here, *type* is a content-type that is probably valid, based on the file's extension. If guess_type doesn't have a good guess for type, it returns None. The value *encoding* is the name of the encoding program used on the file, or None:

```
>>> mimetypes.guess_extension("text/plain")
'.txt'
>>> mimetypes.guess_type("fred.txt")
('text/plain', None)
>>> mimetypes.guess_type("Spam.mp3")
(None, None)
```

You can customize the mapping between extensions and types. Many systems store files named mime.types to hold this mapping; the mimetools module keeps a list of common UNIX paths to such files in knownfiles. The function read_mime_types (filename) reads mappings from the specified file. Each line of the file should include a mime-type and then one or more extensions, separated by whitespace. Listing 17-3 shows a sample mime.types file:

Listing 17-3: **sample mime.types file**

```
plain/text txt
application/mp3 mp3 mp2
```

The function init([files]) reads mappings from the files in the list *files*, which defaults to knownfiles. Files later in the list override earlier files in the case of a conflict. The module variable inited is true if init has been called; calling init multiple times is allowed. The following shows an easy way to customize the mapping:

```
>>> MyPath="c:\\python20\\mime.types" # (customize this)
>>> mimetools.init([MyPath]) # old settings may be overridden
```

You can also directly access the mapping from extensions to encodings (encodings_map), and the mapping from extensions to MIME-types (types_map). The mapping suffix_map is used to map the extensions .tgz, .taz, and .tz to .tar.gz.

Parsing mailcap files

A mailcap (for "mail capability") file maps document MIME-types to commands appropriate for each type of document. Mailcap files are commonly used on UNIX systems. (On Windows, file associations are normally stored in the registry.)

 Cross-Reference   See RFC 1524 for a definition of the file format.

The module mailcap provides functions to help retrieve information from mailcap files. The function getcaps returns a dictionary of mailcap information. You use it by passing it to findmatch(caps,MIMEType[,key[,filename[,plist]]]). Here, *caps* is the dictionary returned by getcaps, and *MIMEType* is the type of document to access. The parameter *key* is the type of access (such as view, compose, or edit); it defaults to view. The return value of findmatch is the command line to execute (through os.system, for example). You can pass a list of extra parameters in *plist*. Each entry should take the form name=value—for example, colors=256.

The function getcaps parses /etc/mailcap, /usr/etc/mailcap, /usr/local/etc/mailcap, and $HOME/mailcap. The user mailcap file, if any, overrides the system mailcap settings.

Encoding and Decoding Message Data

E-mail messages must pass through various systems on their way from one person to another. Different computers handle data in different (sometimes incompatible) ways. Therefore, most e-mail programs encode binary data as 7-bit ASCII text. The encoded file is larger than the original, but is less likely to be mangled in transit. Python provides modules to help use three such encoding schemes—uuencode, base64, and quoted-printable.

Uuencode

The module uu provides functions to encode (binary-to-ASCII) and decode (ASCII-to-binary) binary files using uuencoding. The function encode(input, output[,name[,mode]]) uuencodes the file *input*, writing the resulting output to the file *output*. If passed, *name* and *mode* are put into the file header as the file name and permissions.

The function decode(input,output) decodes from the file *input* to the file *output*.

```
For example, the following lines encode a Flash animation
file.>>> source=open("pample2.swf","rb")
>>> destination=open("pample2.uu","w")
>>> uu.encode(source,destination)
```

Note   In this case, the file must be opened in binary mode ("rb") under Windows or Macintosh; this is not necessary on UNIX.

These lines decode the file, and then launch it in a browser window:

```
>>> source=open("pample2.uu","r")
>>> destination=open("pample.swf","wb")
>>> uu.decode(source,destination)
>>> destination.close()
>>> Webbrowser.open("pample.swf")
```

Note   It is possible to pass file names (instead of open files) to encode or decode. However, this usage is deprecated.

Base64

Base64 is another algorithm for encoding binary data as ASCII. The module base64 provides functions for working with MIME base64 encoding.

The function encodestring(data) encodes a string of binary data, *data*, and returns a string of base64-encoded data. The function encode(input, output) reads data from the filelike object *input*, and writes an encoded base64 string to the filelike object *output*.

To decode a base64 string, call decodestring(data). To decode from one filelike object to another, call decode(input,output).

Base64 is sometimes used to hide data from prying eyes. It is no substitute for encryption, but is better than nothing. The code in Listing 17-4 uses base64 to hide the files from one directory in another directory:

Listing 17-4: **Conceal.py**

```
import base64
import string
import os
""" Hide files by base64-encoding them. Use Conceal to hide
files, and Reveal to un-hide them. """

# not ok for filenames:
EvilChars="/\n"
# not Base64 characters, ok for filenames:
GoodChars="_ "
TranslateEvil = string.maketrans(EvilChars,GoodChars)
UnTranslateEvil = string.maketrans(GoodChars,EvilChars)
```

```
def GetEncodedName(OldName):
    MagicName = base64.encodestring(OldName)
    MagicName = string.translate(MagicName,TranslateEvil)
    return MagicName

def GetDecodedName(OldName):
    MagicName = string.translate(OldName,UnTranslateEvil)
    MagicName = base64.decodestring(OldName)
    return MagicName

def Conceal(SourceDir,DestDir):
    """ Encode the files in sourcedir as files in destdir """
    for FileName in os.listdir(SourceDir):
        FilePath = os.path.join(SourceDir,FileName)
        # Note: need "rb" here! (on UNIX, just "r" is ok)
        InFile=open(FilePath,"rb")
        OutputFilePath=os.path.join(
            DestDir,GetEncodedName(FileName))
        OutFile=open(OutputFilePath,"w")
        base64.encode(InFile,OutFile)
        InFile.close()
        OutFile.close()

def Reveal(SourceDir,DestDir):
    """ Decode the files in sourcedir into destdir """
    for FileName in os.listdir(SourceDir):
        FilePath = os.path.join(SourceDir,FileName)
        InFile=open(FilePath,"r")

OutputFilePath=os.path.join(DestDir,GetDecodedName(FileName))
        OutFile=open(OutputFilePath,"wb")
        base64.decode(InFile,OutFile)
        InFile.close()
        OutFile.close()
```

Quoted-printable

Quoted-printable encoding is another scheme for encoding binary data as ASCII text. It works best for strings with relatively few non-ASCII characters (such as German text, with occasional umlauts); for binary files such as images, base64 is more appropriate.

The module quopri provides functions to handle quoted-printable encoding. The function decode(input,output) decodes from the filelike object *input* to the filelike object *output*. The function encode(input,output,quotetabs) encodes from *input* to *output*. The parameter *quotetabs* indicates whether tabs should be quoted.

Working with UNIX Mailboxes

Many UNIX mail programs store all e-mail in one file or directory called a *mailbox*. The module mailbox provides utility classes for parsing such a mailbox. Each class provides a single method, next, which returns the next rfc822.Message object. Mailbox parser constructors each take either a file object or directory name as their only argument. Table 17-2 lists the available mailbox parser classes.

Table 17-2 Mailbox Parsers	
Class	**Mailbox Type**
UnixMailbox	Classic UNIX-style mailbox, as used by elm or pine
MmdfMailbox	MMDF mailbox
MHMailbox	MH mailbox (directory)
Maildir	Qmail mailbox (directory)
BabylMailbox	Babyl mailbox

Working with MH mailboxes

The module mhlib provides advanced features for managing MH mailboxes. It includes three classes: MH represents a collection of mail folders, Folder represents a single mail folder, and Message represents a single message.

MH objects

The constructor has the syntax MH([path[,profile]]). You can pass *path* and/or *profile* to override the default mailbox directory and profile.

The method openfolder(name) returns a Folder object for the folder *name*. The method setcontext(name) sets the current folder to *name*; getcontext retrieves the current folder (initially "inbox").

The method listfolders returns a sorted list of top-level folder names; listallfolders returns a list of all folder names. listsubfolders(name) returns a list of immediate child folders of the folder *name*; listallsubfolders(name) returns a list of all subfolders of the folder name.

The methods makefolder(name) and deletefolder(name) create and destroy a folder with the given name.

The method `getpath` returns the path to the mailbox. The method `getprofile(key)` returns the profile entry for key (or None, if none is set). And the method `error(format,arguments)` prints the error message (format % arguments) to stderr.

Folder objects

The methods `getcurrent` and `setcurrent(index)` are accessors for the current message number. `getlast` returns the index of the last message (or 0 if there are no messages). `listmessages` returns a list of message indices.

The method `getsequences` returns a dictionary of sequences, where each key is a sequence name and the corresponding value is a list of the sequence's message numbers. `putsequences(dict)` writes such a dictionary of sequences back to the sequence files. The method `parsesequence(str)` parses the string *str* into a list of message numbers.

You can delete messages with `removemessages(list)`, or move them to a new folder with `refilemessages(list, newfolder)`. Here, *list* is a list of message numbers on which to operate. You can move one message by calling `movemessage(index, newfolder,newindex)`, or copy one message by calling `copymessage(index,newfolder,newindex)`. Here, *newindex* is the desired message number in the new folder *newfolder*.

The path to the folder is accessible through `getfullname`, while `getsequencesfilename` returns the path to the sequences file, and `getmessagefilename(index)` returns the full path to message *index*. The method `error(format,arguments)` prints the error message (format % arguments) to stderr.

Message objects

The class `mh.Message` is a subclass of `mimetools.Message`. It provides one extra method, `openmessage(index)`, which returns a new Message object for message number *index*.

Using Web Cookies

A *cookie* is a token used to manage sessions on the World Wide Web. Web servers send cookie values to a browser; the browser then regurgitates cookie values when it sends a Web request. The module `Cookie` provides classes to handle cookies. It is especially useful for making a robot, as many Web sites require cookies to function properly.

Cookies

The class `SimpleCookie` is a dictionary mapping cookie names to cookie values. Each cookie value is stored as a `Cookie.Morsel`. You can pass a cookie string (as received from the Web server) to `SimpleCookie`'s constructor, or to its `load` method.

To retrieve cookie values in a format suitable for inclusion in an HTTP request, call the method `output([attributes[,header[,separator]]])`. To retrieve only some cookie attributes, pass a list of desired attributes in *attributes*. The parameter *header* is the header to use (by default, "Set-Cookie:"). Finally, *separator* is the separator to place between cookies (by default, a newline).

For example, the following lines capture cookies as returned from a Web request:

```
>>> Request=httplib.HTTP("www.mp3.com")
>>> Request.putrequest("GET",URLString)
>>> Request.endheaders()
>>> Response=Request.getreply()
>>> # Response[2] is the header dictionary
>>> CookieString=Response[2]["set-cookie"]
>>> print CookieString
LANG=eng; path=/; domain=.mp3.com
>>> CookieJar=Cookie.SimpleCookie()
>>> CookieJar.load(CookieString)
>>> print CookieJar.output()
'Set-Cookie: LANG=eng; Path=/; Domain=.mp3.com;'
>>> print CookieJar.output(["domain"])
'Set-Cookie: LANG=eng; Domain=.mp3.com;'
```

The method `js_output([attributes])` also outputs cookies, this time in the form of a JavaScript snippet to set their values.

Morsels

A morsel stores a cookie name in the attribute `key`, its value in the attribute `value`, and its coded value (suitable for sending) in the attribute `coded_value`. The convenience function `set(key, value, coded_value)` sets all three attributes.

Morsels provide `output` and `js_output` methods mirroring those of their owning cookie; they also provide an `OutputString([attributes])` method that returns the morsel as a human-readable string.

A morsel also functions as a dictionary, whose keys are cookie attributes (expires, path, comment, domain, max-age, secure, and version). The method `isReservedKey(key)` tests whether *key* is one of the reserved cookie attributes.

Caution When sending cookies in an HTTP request, you should only send cookies whose domain is a substring of the host's name. Otherwise, you might confuse the host. Or, you may send it information it shouldn't know about, such as passwords for an unrelated site. Moreover, be aware that the Cookie class only handles one value for a given name; setting a new value for that name overwrites the old one.

Example: a cookie importer

The code in Listing 17-5 provides functions to import cookies from Internet Explorer 5.0 or Netscape.

Listing 17-5: **CookieMonster.py**

```
import Cookie
import os

def AddMorsel(CookieJar,CookieName,CookieValue,HostString):
    # Cookie set expects a string, so CookieJar["name"]="value"
    # is ok, but CookieJar["name"]=Morsel is not ok.
    # But, cookie get returns a Morsel:
    CookieJar[CookieName]=CookieValue
    CookieJar[CookieName]["domain"]=HostString

def ParseNetscapeCookies(filename):
    # Netscape stores cookies in one tab-delimited file,
    # starting on the fourth line
    CookieFile=open(filename)
    CookieLines=CookieFile.readlines()[4:]
    CookieFile.close()
    CookieJar=Cookie.SimpleCookie()
    for CookieLine in CookieLines:
        CookieParts = CookieLine.strip().split('\t')
        AddMorsel(CookieJar,CookieParts[-2],
            CookieParts[-1],CookieParts[0])
    return CookieJar

def ParseIECookies(dir):
    CookieJar=Cookie.SimpleCookie()
    for FileName in os.listdir(dir):
        # Skip non-cookie files:
        if len(FileName)<3 or FileName[-3:].upper()!="TXT":
            continue
        CookieFile=open(os.path.join(dir,FileName))
        CookieLines=CookieFile.readlines()
        CookieFile.close()
        LineIndex=0
```

Continued

Listing 17-5 *(continued)*

```
        while (LineIndex+2)<len(CookieLines):
            # :-1 removes trailing newline
            CookieName=CookieLines[LineIndex][:-1]
            CookieValue=CookieLines[LineIndex+1][:-1]
            HostString=CookieLines[LineIndex+2][:-1]
            AddMorsel(CookieJar,CookieName,
                CookieValue,HostString)
            LineIndex+=9
    return CookieJar

def OutputForHost(CookieJar,Host,attr=None,
    header="Set-Cookie:",sep="\n"):
    # Return only cookie values matching the specified host.
    CookieHeader=""
    for OneMorsel in CookieJar.values():
        MorselHost=OneMorsel.get("domain",None)
        if (MorselHost==None or Host.find(MorselHost)!=-1):
            CookieHeader+=OneMorsel.output(attr,header)+sep
    return CookieHeader

if (__name__=="__main__"):
    Cookies=ParseIECookies(
"C:\\Documents and Settings\\Administrator\\Cookies\\")
    print OutputForHost(Cookies,"www.thestreet.com/")
```

Summary

Python's standard libraries help with many common tasks in Internet programming. In this chapter, you:

✦ Parsed `robots.txt` to create a well-behaved robo-browser.

✦ Handled various e-mail headers.

✦ Imported cookies from a browser cache.

In the next chapter, you learn simple, powerful ways to make your Python programs parse HTML and XML.

✦   ✦   ✦

Parsing XML and Other Markup Languages

◆   ◆   ◆   ◆

In This Chapter

Markup language
basics

Parsing HTML files

Example: bold only

Example: Web robot

Parsing XML with
SAX

Parsing XML with
DOM

Parsing XML with
xmllib

◆   ◆   ◆   ◆

Markup languages are a powerful way to store text, complete with formatting and metadata. HTML is the format for about half a billion pages on the World Wide Web. Extensible Markup Language (XML) promises to facilitate data exchange of all types.

Python includes standard libraries to parse HTML and XML. This chapter shows you how to use these libraries to create a Web robot, a data importer/exporter, and more.

Markup Language Basics

HyperText Markup Language, or HTML, is used for nearly all the pages on the World Wide Web. It defines tags to control the formatting of text, graphics, and so forth, by a browser.

Extensible Markup Language, or XML, is a tool for data exchange. It includes metadata tags to explain what text items mean. For instance, a person (or program) reading the number "120/80" might not know that it represents a blood pressure, but XML can include tags to make this clear:
`<blood-pressure>120/80</blood-pressure>`

Standard general markup language, or *SGML,* is very general and rarely used.

Tags are for metatext

Markup languages are a way to store text together with *tags*. Tags are *metatext* that govern the text's formatting or describe its meaning. Tags are enclosed in brackets <like this>. An opening tag has a corresponding closing tag, which includes a backslash </like this>. The text between (inside) the tags is the text they describe or modify. For example, the following HTML fragment formats a sentence:

```
Presentation tags can set <b>bold</b> type or <i>italics</i>
```

Tags may have *attributes* to refine their meanings. For example, in HTML, the font tag sets the font, and the color attribute specifies the desired font color:

```
<FONT COLOR=#FFFFFF>white text</FONT>
```

In XML, the information contained between a start tag and its end tag is called an *element*. Elements store data, and may contain sub-elements. Start and end tags may be collapsed into a single tag for the element:

```
<blood type="A" color="red" />
```

XML data can be stored in the element attributes, or in text. For example, these lines are both reasonable ways to store a person's name:

```
<Person name="Bob Hope" />
<Person>Bob Hope</Person>
```

Tag rules

In XML, each start tag must have a corresponding end tag. This is a good idea in HTML as well. Many HTML documents do not close all their tags; however, the World Wide Web Consortium (W3C) has proposed a new standard, XHTML, that requires an end tag for each start tag.

Tags may be nested within other tags. It is best to close a child tag before closing its parent tag. This is mandatory in XML. It is recommended in HTML, as bad testing may make a Web page render badly:

```
<b>I'm not dead <i>yet</b></i>    Bad!
<b>I'm not dead <i>yet</i></b>    Good!
```

The available tags in HTML are described in the HTML standard. The available tags in XML vary from file to file — because XML is Extensible Markup Language, one extends it by adding new tags. A *Document Type Descriptor,* or *DTD*, lists available tags for an XML document. A DTD also includes rules for tag placement — which tags are parents of other tags, and so on.

Namespaces

XML files can organize tag and attribute names into *namespaces*. A name within a namespace takes the form `NamespacePrefix:Name`. For example, this tag's local name is Name, and its namespace prefix is Patient:

```
<Patient:Name>Alfred</Patient:Name>
```

A namespace prefix maps to a particular URI, which is often the URL of a Web page explaining the namespace. In general, when parsing XML, you can ignore namespaces. But, they are a handy tool for designing a good XML DTD.

Processing XML

There are two main ways of processing XML. You can parse the entire document into memory, and navigate the tree of tags and attributes at your leisure. The Document Object Model (DOM) API is an interface for such a parser. Or, you can perform event-driven parsing, handling each tag as you read it from the file. The Simple API for XML (SAX) is an interface for such a parser. (The module `xmllib` is also an event-driven parser.)

Of the two interfaces, I find DOM to be the easiest. Also, DOM can change an XML file without doing direct string manipulation, which gives it big points in my book. One disadvantage of DOM is that it must read the entire XML file into memory upfront, so SAX may be a better choice if you must parse mammoth XML files. Both interfaces are very rich, offering more features than you are likely to need or want; this chapter covers only the core of the two parsing APIs.

In order to process XML with Python, you will need a third-party XML parser. The Python distribution for Windows currently includes the Expat non-validating parser. But on UNIX, you will need to build the Expat library, and make sure that the pyexpat module is built as well.

Parsing HTML Files

The module `htmllib` defines the HTMLParser class. You create a subclass of HTMLParser to build your own HTML parser. The HTMLParser class is itself a subclass of `sgmllib.SGMLParser`, but you will probably never use the superclass directly.

The HTMLParser constructor takes a formatter, as defined in the `formatter` module. (See Chapter 17 for information about `formatter`.) The formatter is used to output the text in the HTML stream. The member `formatter` is a reference to the parser's formatter. If you don't need to use a formatter, you can use a null formatter, as the following subclass does:

```
class SimpleHTMLParser(htmllib.HTMLParser):
    def __init__(self):
        # initialize the superclass
        htmllib.HTMLParser.__init__(self,
            formatter.NullFormatter())
    # ... override other methods here ...
```

HTMLParser methods

Call the method feed(text) to send the HTML string *text* into the parser. You can feed the parser an entire file at one time, or one piece at a time; its behavior is the same. The reset method causes the parser to forget everything it was doing and start over. The close method finishes off the current file; it has the same effect as feeding an end-of-file marker to the parser. If you override close, your subclass's close method should call the close method of the superclass.

The method get_starttag_text returns the text of the most recently opened tag. The method setnomoretags tells the parser to stop processing tags. Similarly, the method setliteral tells the parser to treat the following text literally (ignoring tags).

Handling tags

To handle a particular tag, define start_xxx and end_xxx methods in your class, where xxx is the tag (in lowercase). A start_xxx method takes one parameter — a list of name-value pairs corresponding to the HTML tag's arguments. An end_xxx method takes no arguments.

You can also handle a tag with a method of the form do_xxx(arguments). The do method is called only if start and end methods are not defined.

For example, the following method prints the name of any background image for the page, as defined in a <BODY> tag:

```
def do_body(self,args):
    for ValTuple in args:
        # convert arg-name to upper-case
        if string.upper(ValTuple[0])=="BACKGROUND":
            print "Page background image:",ValTuple[1]
```

Other parsing methods

The method handle_data(data) is called to handle standard text that is not part of a tag. Note that handle_data may be called one or several times for one contiguous "block" of data.

The method anchor_bgn(href, name, type) is called for the start of an anchor tag, <a>. The method anchor_end is called at the end of an anchor. By default, these methods build up a list of links in the member anchorlist.

The method `handle_image(source,alt[,ismap[,align[,width[,height]]]])` is called when an image is encountered. The default implementation simply hands the string *alt* over to `handle_data`.

The method `save_bgn` starts storing data, instead of sending it to the formatter via `handle_data`. The method `save_end` returns all the data buffered since the call to `save_bgn`. These calls may not be nested, and `save_end` may not be called before `save_bgn`.

If a tag handler (of the form `start_xxx` or `do_xxx`) is defined for a tag, the method `handle_starttag(tag,method,arguments)` is called. The parameter *tag* is the tag name (in lowercase), and *method* is the `start` or `do` method for the tag. By default, `handle_starttag` calls *method*, passing *arguments*.

Similarly, the method `handle_endtag(tag,method)` is called for a tag if you have defined an end method for that tag.

The method `handle_charref(ref)` processes character references of the form &#ref. By default, *ref* is interpreted as an ASCII character value from 0 to 255, and handed over to `handle_data`.

The method `handle_entityref(ref)` processes entity references of the form &ref. By default, it looks at the attribute `entitydefs`, which should be a dictionary mapping from entity names to meanings. The variable `htmlentitydefs.entitydefs` defines the default entity definitions for HTMLParser. For example, the codes &amp, &apos, &gt, &lt, and &quot translate into the characters & ' > < ".

The method `handle_comment(commenttext)` is called when a comment of the form `<!-commenttext->` is encountered.

The attribute `nofill` is a flag governing the handling of whitespace. Normally, nofill is false, which causes whitespace to be collapsed. It affects the behavior of `handle_data` and `save_end`.

Handling unknown or bogus elements

The HTMLParser defines methods to handle unknown HTML elements. By default, these methods do nothing; you may want to override them (to report an error, for example).

The method `unknown_starttag(tag, attributes)` is called when a tag with no `start` method is encountered. (For a given tag, either `handle_starttag` or `unknown_starttag` is called.) The method `unknown_endtag(tag)` is called for unknown end tags. The methods `unknown_charref(ref)` and `unknown_entityref(ref)` handle unknown character and entity references, respectively.

The method `report_unbalanced(tag)` is called if the parser encounters a closing tag *tag* with no corresponding opening tag.

Example: Bold Only

Listing 18-1 illustrates a simple subclass of HTMLParser that filters out only bold text from an HTML stream. Listing 18-2 shows sample output from the parser.

Listing 18-1: **BoldOnly.py**

```
import htmllib
import formatter

TEST_HMTL_STRING="""<html>
<title>A poem</title>
There once was a <b>poet named Dan</b><br>
Who could not make <b>limericks</b> scan<br>
He'd be doing just fine<br>
Till the <b>very last line</b>
Then he'd squeeze in <b>too many syllables</b>
and it wouldn't even rhyme<br>
</html>"""

class PrintBoldOnly(htmllib.HTMLParser):
    def __init__(self):
        # AbstractFormatter hands off text to the writer.
        htmllib.HTMLParser.__init__(self,
            formatter.AbstractFormatter(formatter.DumbWriter()))
        self.Printing=0 # don't print until we see bold
        # Note: The bold tag <b> takes no attributes, so the
        # attributes parameter for start_b will always be an
        # empty list)
    def start_b(self,attributes):
        self.Printing=1
    def end_b(self):
        self.Printing=0
    def handle_data(self,text):
        if (self.Printing):
            # Call superclass method, pass text to formatter:
            htmllib.HTMLParser.handle_data(self,text)

if (__name__=="__main__"):
    Test=PrintBoldOnly()
    Test.feed(TEST_HMTL_STRING)
    Test.close()
```

Listing 18-2: **BoldOnly output**

```
poet named Dan
limericks
very last line too many syllables
```

Example: Web Robot

A *robot* is a program that browses the World Wide Web automatically. Listing 18-3 is a simple robot. It follows links between pages, and saves pages to the local disk. It overrides several methods of the HTMLParser in order to follow various links.

Listing 18-3: **Robot.py**

```python
import htmllib
import formatter
import urlparse
import re
import os
import string
import urllib

# Redefine this to a directory where you want to put files
ROOT_DIR = "c:\\python20\\robotfiles\\"

# Web page file extensions that usually return HTML
HTML_EXTENSION_DICT={"":1,"HTM":1,"HTML":1,"PHTML":1,"SHTML":1,
"PHP":1,"PHP3":1,"HTS":1,"ASP":1,"PL":1,"JSP":1,"CGI":1}

# Use this string to limit the robot to one site—only URLs
# that contain this string will be retrieved. If this is null,
# the robot will attempt to pull down the whole WWW.
REQUIRED_URL_STRING="kibo.com"
# Compile a regular expression for case-insensitive matching of
# the required string
RequiredUrlRE = re.compile(re.escape(REQUIRED_URL_STRING),
                           re.IGNORECASE)

# Keep track of all the pages we have visited in a dictionary,
# so that we don't hit the same page repeatedly.
VisitedURLs={}

# Queue of target URLs
TargetURLList=["http://www.kibo.com/index.html"]
```

Continued

Listing 18-3 *(continued)*

```
def AddURLToList(NewURL):
    # Skip duplicate URLs
    if (VisitedURLs.has_key(NewURL)): return
    # Skip URLs that don't contain the proper substring
    if (not RequiredUrlRE.search(NewURL)): return
    # Add URL to the target list
    TargetURLList.append(NewURL)

# Chop file-extension from the end of a URL
def GetExtensionFromString(FileString):
    DotChunks=string.split(FileString,".")
    if len(DotChunks)==1: return ""
    LastBlock=DotChunks[-1] # Take stuff after the last .
    if string.find(LastBlock,"/")!=-1:
        return ""
    if string.find(LastBlock,"\\")!=-1:
        return ""
    return string.upper(LastBlock)

class HTMLRobot(htmllib.HTMLParser):
    def StartNewPage(self,BaseURL):
        self.BaseURL=BaseURL
    def __init__(self):
        # Initialize the master class
        htmllib.HTMLParser.__init__(
            self,formatter.NullFormatter())
    def do_body(self,args):
        # Retrieve background image, if any
        for ValTuple in args:
            if string.upper(ValTuple[0])=="BACKGROUND":
                ImageURL = urlparse.urljoin(
                    self.BaseURL, ValTuple[1])
                AddURLToList(ImageURL)
    def do_embed(self,args):
        # Handle embedded content
        for ValTuple in args:
            if string.upper(ValTuple[0])=="SRC":
                self.HandleAnchor(ValTuple[1])
    def do_area(self,args):
        # Handle areas inside an imagemap
        for ValTuple in args:
            if string.upper(ValTuple[0])=="HREF":
                self.HandleAnchor(ValTuple[1])
    def handle_image(self, source, alt, ismap,
                     align, width, height):
        # Retrieve images
        ImageURL = urlparse.urljoin(self.BaseURL, source)
        AddURLToList(ImageURL)
    def anchor_bgn(self,TempURL,name,type):
        # Anchors (links). Skip mailto links.
```

```
                if TempURL[0:7].upper() == "MAILTO:": return
                NewURL=urlparse.urljoin(self.BaseURL,TempURL)
                AddURLToList(NewURL)
        def do_frame(self,args):
            # Handle a sub-frame as a link
            for ValTuple in args:
                if string.upper(ValTuple[0])=="SRC":
                    self.anchor_bgn(ValTuple[1],"","")
        def do_option(self,args):
            for ValTuple in args:
                if string.upper(ValTuple[0])=="VALUE":
                    # This might be a Webpage...
                    TheExtension = \
                        GetExtensionFromString(ValTuple[1])
                    if HTML_EXTENSION_DICT.has_key(TheExtension):
                        self.anchor_bgn(ValTuple[1],"","")

if (__name__=="__main__"):
    Parser = HTMLRobot()
    while (len(TargetURLList)>0):
        # Take the next URL off the list
        NextURL = TargetURLList[0]
        del TargetURLList[0]
        VisitedURLs[NextURL]=1 # flag as visited
        print "Retrieving:",NextURL
        # Parse the URL, and decide whether
        # we think it's HTML or not:
        URLTuple=urlparse.urlparse(NextURL,"http",0)
        TheExtension=GetExtensionFromString(URLTuple[2])
        # Get a local filename; make directories as needed
        TargetPath=os.path.normpath(ROOT_DIR+URLTuple[2])
        # If no extension, assume it's a directory and
        # retrieve index.html.
        if (TheExtension==""):
            TargetDir=TargetPath
            TargetPath=os.path.normpath(
                TargetPath+"/index.html")
        else:
            (TargetDir,TargetFile)=os.path.split(TargetPath)
        try:
            os.makedirs(TargetDir)
        except:
            pass # Ignore exception if directory exists
        if HTML_EXTENSION_DICT.has_key(TheExtension):
            # This is HTML - retrieve it to disk and then
            # feed it to the parser
            URLFile=urllib.urlopen(NextURL)
            HTMLText = URLFile.read()
            URLFile.close()
            HTMLFile=open(TargetPath,"w")
            HTMLFile.write(HTMLText)
```

Continued

Listing 18-3 *(continued)*

```
        HTMLFile.close()
        Parser.StartNewPage(NextURL)
        Parser.feed(HTMLText)
        Parser.close()
    else:
        # This isn't HTML - save to disk
        urllib.urlretrieve(NextURL,TargetPath)
```

Parsing XML with SAX

SAX is a standard interface for event-driven XML parsing. Parsers that implement SAX are available in Java, C++, and (of course) Python. The module xml.sax is the overseer of SAX parsers.

The method xml.sax.parse(xmlfile,contenthandler[,errorhandler]) creates a SAX parser and parses the specified XML. The parameter *xmlfile* can be either a file or the name of a file to read from. The parameter *contenthandler* must be a ContentHandler object. If specified, *errorhandler* must be a SAX ErrorHandler object. If no error handler is provided and an error occurs, the parser will raise a SAXParseException if it encounters errors. Similarly, the method parseString(xmlstring,contenthandler[,errorhandler]) parses XML from the supplied string *xmlstring*.

Parsing XML with SAX generally requires you to create your own ContentHandler, by subclassing xml.sax.ContentHandler. Your ContentHandler handles the particular tags and attributes of your flavor(s) of XML.

Using a ContentHandler

A ContentHandler object provides methods to handle various parsing events. Its owning parser calls ContentHandler methods as it parses the XML file. The method setDocumentLocator(locator) is normally called first. The methods startDocument and endDocument are called at the start and the end of the XML file. The method characters(text) is passed character data of the XML file via the parameter *text*.

The ContentHandler is called at the start and end of each element. If the parser is *not* in namespace mode, the methods startElement(tag, attributes) and endElement(tag) are called; otherwise, the corresponding methods startElementNS and endElementNS are called. Here, *tag* is the element tag, and *attributes* is an Attributes object.

The methods `startPrefixMapping(prefix,URI)` and `endPrefixMapping(prefix)` are called for each namespace mapping; normally, namespace processing is handled by the XMLReader itself. For a given prefix, `endPrefixMethod` will be called *after* the corresponding call to `startPrefixMapping`, but otherwise the order of calls is not guaranteed.

The method `ignorableWhitespace(spaces)` is called for a string *spaces* of whitespace. The method `processingInstruction(target,text)` is called when a processing instruction (other than an XML declaration) is encountered. The method `skippedEntity(entityname)` is called when the parser skips any entity.

A ContentHandler receives an Attributes object in calls to the `startElement` method. The Attributes object wraps a dictionary of attributes (keys) and their values. The method `getLength` returns the number of attributes. The methods `items`, `keys`, `kas_key`, and `values` wrap the corresponding dictionary methods. The method `getValue(name)` returns the value for an attribute name; if namespaces are active, the method `getValueByQName(name)` returns the value for a qualified attribute name.

Example: blood-type extractor

Listing 18-4 uses a SAX parser to extract a patient's blood type from the same exam data XML uses in Listing 18-5 and Listing 18-6.

Listing 18-4: **BloodTypeSax.py**

```
import xml.sax
import cStringIO

SAMPLE_DATA = """<?xml version="1.0"?>
<exam date="12/11/99">
<patient>Pat</patient>
<bloodtype>B</bloodtype>
</exam >"""

class ExamHandler(xml.sax.ContentHandler):
    def __init__(self):
        self.CurrentData=""
        self.BloodType=""
    def characters(self,text):
        if self.CurrentData=="bloodtype":
            self.BloodType+=text
    # We use the non-namespace-aware element handlers:
    def startElement(self,tag,attributes):
        self.CurrentData=tag
    def endElement(self,tag):
```

Continued

Listing 18-4 *(continued)*

```
        if self.CurrentData=="bloodtype":
            print "Blood type:",self.BloodType
        self.CurrentData=""

if (__name__=="__main__"):
    # create an XMLReader
    MyParser = xml.sax.make_parser()
    # turn off namepsaces
    MyParser.setFeature(xml.sax.handler.feature_namespaces, 0)
    # override the default ContextHandler
    Handler=ExamHandler()
    MyParser.setContentHandler(Handler)
    # Build and parse an InputSource
    StringFile=cStringIO.StringIO(SAMPLE_DATA)
    MySource = xml.sax.InputSource("1")
    MySource.setByteStream(StringFile)
    MyParser.parse(MySource)
```

Using parser (XMLReader) objects

The base parser class is xml.sax.xmlreader.XMLReader. It is normally not necessary to instantiate parser objects directly. However, you can access a parser to exercise tighter control on XML parsing.

The method xml.sax.make_parser([parserlist]) creates and returns an XML parser. If you want to use a specific SAX parser (such as Expat), pass the name of its module in the *parserlist* sequence. The module in question must define a create_parser function.

Once you have an XML parser, you can call its method parse(source), where *source* is a filelike object, a URL, or a file name.

An XML parser has properties and features, which can be set and queried by name. For example, the following lines check and toggle namespace mode for a parser:

```
>>> MyParser=xml.sax.make_parser()
>>> MyParser.getFeature(\
        "http://xml.org/sax/features/namespaces")
0
>>> # Activate namespace processing
>>> MyParser.setFeature(\
        "http://xml.org/sax/features/namespaces",1)
```

The features and properties available vary from parser to parser.

An XMLReader has several helper classes. You can access the parser's ContentHandler with the methods `getContentHandler` and `setContentHandler(Handler)`. Similarly, you can access the parser's ErrorHandler (with `getErrorHandler` and `setErrorHandler`), its EntityResolver, and its DTDHandler. The helper classes let you customize the parser's behavior further.

ErrorHandler

An ErrorHandler implements three methods to handle errors: `error`, `fatalError`, and `warning`. Each method takes a SAXParseException as its single parameter.

DTDHandler

A DTDHandler handles only notation declarations and unparsed entity declarations. The method `notationDecl(name,PublicID,SystemID)` is called when a notation declaration is encountered. The method `unparsedEntityDecl(name,PublicID,SystemID,text)` is called when an unparsed entity declaration is encountered.

EntityResolver

The XMLReader calls the EntityResolver to handle external entity references. The method `resolveEntity(PublicID,SystemID)` is called for each such reference — it returns either the system identifier (as a string), or an InputSource.

Locator

Most XMLReaders supply a locator to their ContentHandler by calling its `setDocumentLocator` method. The locator should only be called by the ContentHandler in the context of a parsing method (such as `characters`). The locator provides the current location, via methods `getColumnNumber`, `getLineNumber`, `getPublicId`, and `getSystemId`.

SAX exceptions

The base exception is `SAXException`. It is extended by `SAXParseException`, `SAXNotRecognizedException`, and `SAXNotSupportedException`. The constructors for `SAXNotSupportedException` and `SAXNotRecognizedException` take two parameters: an error string and (optionally) an additional exception object. The `SAXParseException` constructor requires these parameters, as well as a locator.

The message and exception associated with a `SAXException` can be retrieved by the methods `getMessage` and `getException`, respectively.

Parsing XML with DOM

The DOM API parses an entire XML document, and stores a DOM (a tree representation of the document) in memory. It is a very convenient way to parse, although it does require more memory than SAX. In addition, you can manipulate the DOM itself, and then write out the new XML document. This is a relatively painless way to make changes to XML documents.

A DOM is made up of *nodes*. Each element, each attribute, and even each comment is a node. The most important node is the *document node*, which represents the document as a whole.

The module xml.dom.minidom provides a simple version of the DOM interface. It provides two functions, parse(file[,parser]) or parseString(XML[,parser]), to parse XML and return a DOM. (Here *parser*, if supplied, must be a SAX parser object — minidom uses SAX internally to generate its DOM.)

DOM nodes

A node object has a type, represented by the integer attribute nodeType. The valid node types are available as members of xml.dom.minidom.Node, and include DOCUMENT_NODE, ELEMENT_NODE, ATTRIBUTE_NODE, and TEXT_NODE.

A node can have a parent (given by its parentNode member), and a list of children (stored in its childNodes member). You can add child nodes by calling appendChild(NewChild), or insertBefore(NewChild,OldChild). You can also remove children by calling removeChild(OldChild). For example:

```
>>> DOM=xml.dom.minidom.parse("Mystic Mafia.xml") # Build DOM
>>> print DOM.parentNode # The document node has no parent
None
>>> print DOM.childNodes
[<DOM Element: rdf at 10070740>]
>>> print DOM.childNodes[0].childNodes
[<DOM Text node "\n">, <DOM Text node "\n">, <DOM Text node "
">, <DOM Element: rdf:Description at 10052084>, <DOM Text node
"\n">]
```

Elements, attributes, and text

An element has a name, given by its member tagName. If the element is part of a namespace, prefix holds its namespace's name, localName within the namespace, and namespaceURI is the URL of the namespace definition. You can retrieve an element's attribute values with the method getAttribute(AttributeName), set attribute values with setAttribute(AttributeName, Value), and remove attributes with the method removeAttribute(AttributeName).

The text of an element is stored in a child node of type TEXT_NODE. A text node has an attribute, data, containing its text as a string.

For example, this code examines and edits an element:

```
>>> print TagNode.tagName,TagNode.prefix
rdf:Description rdf
>>> print TagNode.localName,TagNode.namespaceURI
Description http://www.w3.org/1999/02/22-rdf-syntax-ns#
>>> TagNode.getAttribute("type") # Value is Unicode
u'catalog'
>>> CNode.setAttribute("arglebargle","test")
>>> CNode.getAttribute("arglebargle")
'test'
>>> CNode.removeAttribute("arglebargle")
>>> # Getting a nonexistent attribute returns ""
>>> CNode.getAttribute("arglebargle")
''
```

The document node (DOM)

A document node, or DOM, provides a handy method, getElementsByTagName(Name), which returns a list of all the element nodes with the specified name. This is a quick way to find the elements you care about, without ever iterating through the other nodes in the document.

A DOM also provides methods to create new nodes. The method createElement(TagName) creates a new element node, createTextNode(Text) creates a new text node, etc. The method toxml returns the DOM as an XML string.

When you are finished with a DOM, call its method unlink to clean it up. Otherwise, the memory used by the DOM may not get garbage-collected until your program terminates.

Example: data import and export with DOM

XML is great for data interchange. Listing 18-5 is an example of XML's power: It exports data from a relational database to an XML file, and imports XML back into the database. It uses the mxODBC module for database access. This test code assumes the existence of an EMPLOYEE table (see Chapter 14 for the table's definition, and more information on the Python DB API).

Listing 18-5: **XMLDB.py**

```python
import xml.dom.minidom
import ODBC.Windows # Replace for your OS as needed
import sys
import traceback
IMPORTABLE_XML = """<?xml version="1.0"?><tabledata><row>
<EMPLOYEE_ID>55</EMPLOYEE_ID><FIRST_NAME>Bertie</FIRST_NAME>
<LAST_NAME>Jenkins</LAST_NAME><MANAGER_ID></MANAGER_ID>
</row></tabledata>"""

def ExportXMLFromTable(Cursor):
    # We build up a DOM tree programatically, then
    # convert the DOM to XML.  We never have to process
    # the XML string directly (Hooray for DOM!)
    DOM=xml.dom.minidom.Document()
    TableElement=DOM.createElement("tabledata")
    DOM.appendChild(TableElement)
    while (1):
        DataRow=Cursor.fetchone()
        if DataRow==None: break # There is no more data
        RowElement=DOM.createElement("row")
        TableElement.appendChild(RowElement)
        for Index in range(len(Cursor.description)):
            ColumnName=Cursor.description[Index][0]
            ColumnElement=DOM.createElement(ColumnName)
            RowElement.appendChild(ColumnElement)
            ColumnValue=DataRow[Index]
            if (ColumnValue):
                TextNode=DOM.createTextNode(\
                    str(DataRow[Index]))
                ColumnElement.appendChild(TextNode)
    print DOM.toxml()

def ImportXMLToTable(Cursor,XML,TableName):
    # Build up the SQL statement corresponding to the XML
    DOM=xml.dom.minidom.parseString(XML)
    DataRows=DOM.getElementsByTagName("row")
    for RowElement in DataRows:
        InsertSQL="INSERT INTO %s ("%TableName
        for ChildNode in RowElement.childNodes:
            if ChildNode.nodeType==\
                xml.dom.minidom.Node.ELEMENT_NODE:
                InsertSQL+="%s,"%ChildNode.tagName
        InsertSQL=InsertSQL[:-1] # Remove trailing comma
        InsertSQL+=") values ("
        for ChildNode in RowElement.childNodes:
            if ChildNode.nodeType==\
                xml.dom.minidom.Node.ELEMENT_NODE:
                ColumnValue=GetNodeText(ChildNode)
                InsertSQL+="%s,"%SQLEscape(ColumnValue)
```

```
            InsertSQL=InsertSQL[:-1] # Remove trailing comma
            InsertSQL+=")"
            Cursor.execute(str(InsertSQL))

    def SQLEscape(Value):
        if (Value in [None,""]):
            return "Null"
        else:
            return "'%s'"%Value.replace("'","''")

    def GetNodeText(ElementNode):
        # Concatenate all text child-nodes into one large string.
        # (The normalize() method, available in version 2.1, makes
        # this a little easier by conglomerating adjacent
        # text nodes for us)
        NodeText=""
        for ChildNode in ElementNode.childNodes:
            if ChildNode.nodeType==xml.dom.minidom.Node.TEXT_NODE:
                NodeText+=ChildNode.data
        return NodeText

    if (__name__=="__main__"):
        print "Testing XML export..."
        # Replace this line with your database connection info:
        Conn=ODBC.Windows.connect("AQUA","aqua","aqua")
        Cursor=Conn.cursor()
        Cursor.execute("select * from EMPLOYEE")
        print ExportXMLFromTable(Cursor)
        # Delete employee 55 so that we can import him again
        Cursor.execute("DELETE FROM EMPLOYEE WHERE\
            EMPLOYEE_ID = 55")
        print "Testing XML import..."
        ImportXMLToTable(Cursor,IMPORTABLE_XML,"EMPLOYEE")
        # Remove this line if your database does not have
        # transaction support:
        Conn.commit()
```

Parsing XML with xmllib

The module xmllib defines a single class, XMLParser, whose methods are similar to that of htmllib.HTMLParser. You can define start and end handlers for any tag. Listing 18-6 is a simple example that parses a patient's blood type from examination data.

Caution Unlike xml.sax and xml.dom, xmllib doesn't require any extra modules to be built. Also, it is quite simple, and similar to htmllib. However, it is not a fast parser, and is deprecated as of Version 2.0.

Note This example stores the blood type using one or more calls to `handle_data`. Strings may be passed to `handle_data` all at once or in several pieces.

Listing 18-6: **BloodType.py**

```
import xmllib
SAMPLE_DATA = """<?xml version="1.0"?>
<exam date="5/13/99">
<patient>Pat</patient>
<bloodtype>B</bloodtype>
</exam >"""

class ExamParser(xmllib.XMLParser):
    def __init__(self):
        xmllib.XMLParser.__init__(self)
        self.CurrentData="" # Track current data item
        self.BloodType=""
    def start_bloodtype(self,args):
        self.CurrentData="blood"
    def end_bloodtype(self):
        if (self.CurrentData=="blood"):
            print "Blood type:",self.BloodType
        self.CurrentData=""
    def handle_data(self,text):
        if (self.CurrentData=="blood"):
            self.BloodType+=text

if (__name__=="__main__"):
    MyParser = ExamParser()
    MyParser.feed(SAMPLE_DATA)
    MyParser.close()
```

Elements and attributes

The XMLParser attribute `elements` is a dictionary of known tags. If you subclass XMLParser with a parser that handles a particular tag, then that tag should exist as a key in `elements`. The corresponding value is a tuple (StartHandler,EndHandler), where StartHandler and EndHandler are functions for handling the start and end of that tag. Normally, you don't need to access `elements` directly, as handlers of the form `start_xxx` and `end_xxx` are inserted automatically.

The attribute `attributes` is a dictionary tracking the valid attributes for tags. The keys in `attributes` are known tags. The values are dictionaries that map all valid attributes for the tag to a default value (or to None, if there is no default value). If any other attribute is encountered in parsing, the method `syntax_error` is called. By default, `attributes` is an empty dictionary, and any attributes are permitted for any tag.

XML handlers

XMLParser defines various methods to handle XML elements. These methods do nothing by default, and are intended to be overridden in a subclass.

The method `handle_xml(encoding,standalone)` is called when the `<?xml?>` tag is parsed. The parameters *encoding* and *standalone* equal the corresponding attributes in the tag.

The method `handle_doctype(root_tag,public_id,sys_id,data)` is called when the <!DOCTYPE> tag is parsed. The parameters *root_tag*, *public_id*, *sys_id*, and *data* are the root tag name, the DTD public identifier, the system identifier, and the unparsed DTD contents, respectively.

The method `handle_cdata(text)` is called when a CDATA tag of the form `<!CDATA[text]>` is encountered. (Normal data is passed to `handle_data`.)

The method `handle_proc(name,text)` is called when a processing instruction of the form `<?name text?>` is encountered.

The method `handle_special(text)` is called for declarations of the form `<!text>`.

Other XMLParser members

The method `syntax_error(errormessage)` is called when unparsable XML is encountered. By default, this method raises a RuntimeError exception.

The method `translate_references(text)` translates all entity and character references in *text*, and returns the resulting string.

The method `getnamespace` returns a dictionary mapping abbreviation from the current namespace to URIs.

Summary

You can easily parse HTML by subclassing the standard parser. There are several varieties of parsers for XML, which you can customize to handle any kind of document. In this chapter, you:

✦ Parsed HTML with and without an output-formatter.

✦ Built a robot to automatically retrieve Web pages.

✦ Parsed and generated XML files for data exchange.

In the next chapter, you'll meet Tkinter, Python's de facto standard library for user interfaces.

✦   ✦   ✦

User Interfaces and Multimedia

P A R T

IV

◆   ◆   ◆   ◆

Chapter 19
Tinkering with Tkinter

Chapter 20
Using Advanced
Tkinter Widgets

Chapter 21
Building User
Interfaces with
wxPython

Chapter 22
Using Curses

Chapter 23
Building Simple
Command
Interpreters

Chapter 24
Playing Sound

◆   ◆   ◆   ◆

Tinkering with Tkinter

✦ ✦ ✦ ✦

In This Chapter

Creating a GUI

Using common options

Gathering user input

Using text widgets

Building menus

Using Tkinter dialogs

Handling colors and fonts

Drawing graphics

Using timers

✦ ✦ ✦ ✦

Tkinter is a package used for building a graphical user interface (GUI) in Python. It runs on many operating systems, including UNIX, Windows, and Macintosh. Tkinter is the de-facto standard GUI library for Python, and is often bundled with it.

Tkinter is very easy to use; it is built on top of the high-level scripting language Tcl.

Getting Your Feet Wet

If you're dying to see Tkinter in action, the program shown in Listing 19-1 should provide some instant gratification. It displays some text in a window. Notice how little code it takes — such are the joys of Tkinter!

Listing 19-1: **HelloWorld.py**

```
import Tkinter
# Create the root window:
root=Tkinter.Tk()
# Put a label widget in the window:
LabelText="Ekky-ekky-ekky-ekky-z'Bang, zoom-
Boing,\
z'nourrrwringmm"
LabelWidget=Tkinter.Label(RootWindow,text=Labe
lText)
# Pack the label (position and display it):
LabelWidget.pack()
# Start the event loop. This call won't return
# until the program ends:
RootWindow.mainloop()
```

Run the code, and you'll see something resembling the screenshot shown in Figure 19-1.

```
C:\winnt\System32\cmd.exe                                    _ □ ×
Directory of C:\Python20\Bible20                                ▲

01/28/2001  12:29p   <DIR>          .
01/28/2001  12:29p   <DIR>          ..
01/28/2001  02:23p          7,601  ColorChooser.py
01/28/2001  01:33p          5,235  colch.bak
01/28/2001  02:24p            254  TkinterColors.ini
01/28/2001  02:14p          7,513  ColorChooser.bak
01/28/2001  04:06p            899  Events.py
01/28/2001  11:07p            955  WaitCursor.py
01/28/2001  11:04p              0  PlayList.m3u
01/28/2001  11:04p   <DIR>          poo
01/28/2001  11:04p   <DIR>          foo
01/28/2001  11:41p            855  Complaint.py
01/29/2001                         p.py
01/29/2001   ┌─ tk ──────── _ □ × ─┐ r.py
             │ Ekky-ekky-ekky-ekky-z'Bang, zoom-Boing, z'nourrrwringmm │ e
             └────────────────────┘
C:\Python20\Bible20>cd ..

C:\Python20>cd bible19

C:\Python20\Bible19>helloworld.py

C:\Python20\Bible19>copy helloworld.py helloworld.pyw
        1 file(s) copied.

C:\Python20\Bible19>helloworld.pyw

C:\Python20\Bible19>                                            ▼
◄                                                              ►
```

Figure 19-1: Greetings from Tkinter

 Note   On Windows, Tkinter applications look more professional when you run them with pythonw.exe instead of python.exe. Giving a script a .pyw extension sends it to pythonw instead of python. Pythonw does not create a console window; the disadvantage of this is that you can't see anything printed to sys.stdout and sys.stderr.

Creating a GUI

To use Tkinter, import the Tkinter module. Many programmers import it into the local namespace (from Tkinter import *); this is less explicit, but it does save some typing. This chapter's examples *don't* import Tkinter into the local namespace, in order to make it obvious when they use Tkinter.

Building an interface with widgets

A user interface contains various widgets. A *widget* is an object displayed onscreen with which the user can interact. (Java calls such things *components,* and Microsoft calls them *controls.*) Tkinter provides a button widget (Tkinter.Button), a label widget (Tkinter.Label), and so on. Most widgets are displayed on a *parent* widget, or owner. The first argument to a widget's constructor is its parent widget.

A Toplevel widget is a special widget with no parent; it is a top-level window in its own right. Most applications need only one Toplevel widget — the root widget created when you call `Tkinter.Tk()`.

For example, a *frame* is a widget whose purpose in life is to contain other widgets. Putting related widgets in one frame is a great way to group them onscreen:

```
MainWindow=Tkinter.Tk() # Create a top-level window
UpperFrame=Tkinter.Frame(MainWindow)
# The label and the button both live inside UpperFrame:
UpperLabel=Tkinter.Label(Frame)
UpperButton=Tkinter.Button(Frame)
```

Widget options

Widgets have *options* (or *attributes*) that control their look and behavior. Some options are used by many widgets. For example, most widgets have a `background` option, specifying the widget's normal background color. Other options are specific to a particular kind of widget. For example, a button widget has a `command` option, whose value is a function to call (without arguments) when the button is clicked.

You can access options in various ways:

```
# You can set options in the constructor:
NewLabel=Tkinter.Label(ParentFrame,background="gray50")
# You can access options dictionary-style (my favorite!)
NewLabel["background"]="#FFFFFF"
# You can set options with the config method:
NewLabel.config(background="blue")
# You can retrieve an option's current value:
CurrentColor=NewLabel["background"]
# Another way to get the current value:
CurrentColor=NewLabel.cget("background")
```

A few option names are, coincidentally, reserved words in Python. When necessary, append an underscore to such option names:

```
# "from" is a reserved word. Use from_ in code:
VolumeWidget=Tkinter.Scale(ParentFrame,from_=0,to=200)
# Use "from" when passing the option name as a string:
VolumeWidget["from"]=20 # "from_" is *not* ok here
```

See "Using Common Options" for an overview of the most useful widget options.

Laying Out Widgets

The *geometry manager* is responsible for positioning widgets onscreen. The simplest geometry manager is the *packer*. The packer can position a widget on the left

(Tkinter.LEFT), right, top, or bottom side of its parents. You invoke the packer by calling the pack method on a widget.

The *grid* geometry manager divides the parent widget into a grid, and places each child widget on a square of the grid. You invoke the grid geometry manager by calling the grid(row=x,column=y) method on a widget. Grid square numbering starts with 0.

You can also position a widget precisely using place. However, using place is recommended only for perfectionists and masochists! If you use the placer, then whenever you add a widget to your design, you'll need to reposition *all* the other widgets.

Different geometry managers don't get along well — if you pack one child widget and grid another, Tkinter may enter a catatonic state. You can use pack and grid in the same program, but not within the same parent widget!

Note   Remember to call pack, grid, or place on every widget. Otherwise, the widget will never be displayed, making it rather difficult to click on!

Packer options

Following are options you can pass to the pack method. These options override the default packing. The default packing lays widgets out from top to bottom within their parent (side=TOP). Each widget is centered within the available space (anchor=CENTER). It does not expand to fill its space (expand=NO), and it has no extra padding on the sides (padx=pady=0).

side

Passing a *side* option to pack places the widget on the specified side of its parent. Valid values are LEFT, RIGHT, TOP, and BOTTOM. The default is TOP. If two widgets are both packed on one side of a parent, the first widget packed is the closest to the edge:

```
Label1=Tkinter.Label(root,text="PackedLast")
Label2=Tkinter.Label(root,text="PackedFirst")
Label2.pack(side=Tkinter.LEFT) # leftmost!
Label1.pack(side=Tkinter.LEFT) # Placed to the right of label2
```

Mixing LEFT/RIGHT with TOP/BOTTOM in one parent widget often yields creepy-looking results. When packing many widgets, it's generally best to use intermediate frame widgets, or use the grid geometry manager.

fill, expand

Pass a value of YES for *expand* to let a widget expand to fill all available space. Pass either X, Y, or BOTH for *fill* to specify which dimensions will expand. These options are especially useful when a user resizes the window. For example, the following code creates a canvas that stretches to the edges of the window, and a status bar (at the bottom) that stretches horizontally:

```
DrawingArea=Tkinter.Canvas(root)
DrawingArea.pack(expand=Tkinter.YES,fill=Tkinter.BOTH)
StatusBar=Tkinter.Label(root,text="Ready.")
StatusBar.pack(side=Tkinter.BOTTOM,expand=\
    Tkinter.YES,fill=Tkinter.X)
```

anchor

If the widget has more screen space than it needs, the *anchor* option determines where the widget sits, within its allotted space. This does not affect widgets with fill=BOTH. Valid values are compass directions (N, NW, W, SW, S, SE, E, NE) and CENTER.

padx,pady

These options give a widget some additional horizontal or vertical "elbow room." Putting a little space between buttons makes them more readable, and makes it harder to click the wrong one:

```
Button1=Tkinter.Button(root,text="Fire death ray",
    command=FireDeathRay)
# 10 empty pixels on both sides:
Button1.pack(side=Tkinter.LEFT,padx=10)
Button2=Tkinter.Button(root,text="Send flowers",
    command=PatTheBunny)
# 10+10=20 pixels between buttons:
Button2.pack(side=Tkinter.LEFT,padx=10)
```

Grid options

Following are options to pass to the grid method. You should specify a row and a column for every widget; otherwise, things get confusing.

row, column

Pass *row* and *column* options to specify which grid square your widget should live in. The numbering starts at 0; you can always add new rows and columns. For example, the following code lays out some buttons to look like a telephone's dial pad:

```
for Digit in range(9):
    Tkinter.Button(root,text= Digit+1).grid(row=Digit/3,\
        column=Digit%3)
```

sticky

This option specifies which side of the square the widget should "stick to." It is similar to *anchor* (for the packer). Valid values are compass directions and CENTER. You can combine values to stretch the widget within its cell. For example, the following button fills its grid cell:

```
BigButton=Tkinter.Button(root,text="X")
# Using "from Tkinter import *" would let this next line
# be much less messy:
BigButton.grid(row=0,column=0,sticky=Tkinter.W+Tkinter.E+\
    Tkinter.N+Tkinter.S)
```

columnspan,rowspan

These options let you create a big widget (one that spans multiple rows or columns).

Example: Breakfast Buttons

Listing 19-2 presents a beefier Tkinter program. It provides a food menu, with several buttons you can click to build up a complete breakfast. Your selection is displayed on a multiline label. Figure 19-2 shows the resulting user interface.

This example initializes widgets in several different ways. In practice, you'll want to do it the same way every time. (Personally, I like the pattern for the "Spam" button, and I hate the pattern for the "Beans" button.)

Listing 19-2: **FoodChoice.py**

```
import Tkinter

# In Tkinter, a common practice is to subclass Tkinter.Frame, and make
# the subclass represent "the application itself". This is
# convenient (although, in some cases, the separation
# between logic and UI should be clearer). FoodWindow is our application:
class FoodWindow(Tkinter.Frame):
    def __init__(self):
        # Call the superclass constructor explicitly:
        Tkinter.Frame.__init__(self)
        self.FoodItems=[]
        self.CreateChildWidgets()
    def CreateChildWidgets(self):
        ButtonFrame=Tkinter.Frame(self)
        # The fill parameter tells the Packer that this widget should
        # stretch horizontally to fill its parent widget:
        ButtonFrame.pack(side=Tkinter.TOP,fill=Tkinter.X)

        # Create a button, on the button frame:
        SpamButton=Tkinter.Button(ButtonFrame)
        # Button["text"] is the button label:
        SpamButton["text"]="Spam"
        # Button["command"] is the function to execute (without arguments)
        # when someone clicks the button:
        SpamButton["command"]=self.BuildButtonAction("Spam")
        SpamButton.pack(side=Tkinter.LEFT)
```

```python
        # You can specify most options by passing keyword-arguments
        # to the widget's constructor:
        EggsAction=self.BuildButtonAction("Eggs")
        EggsButton=Tkinter.Button(ButtonFrame,text="Eggs",command=EggsAction)
        # This is the second widget packed on the LEFT side of ButtonFrame, so
        # it goes to the right of the "Spam" button:
        EggsButton.pack(side=Tkinter.LEFT)

        # Some people like to do everything all in one go:
        Tkinter.Button(ButtonFrame,text="Beans",\
                command=self.BuildButtonAction("Beans")).pack(side=Tkinter.LEFT)

        # You can also set widget options with the "config" method:
        SausageButton=Tkinter.Button(ButtonFrame)
        SausageAction=self.BuildButtonAction("Sausage")
        SausageButton.config(text="Sausage",command=SausageAction)
        SausageButton.pack(side=Tkinter.LEFT)

        # It's often good for parent widgets to keep references to their
        # children. Here, we keep a reference (self.FoodLabel) to the label, so
        # we can change it later:
        self.FoodLabel=Tkinter.Label(self, wraplength=190,\
                relief=Tkinter.SUNKEN,borderwidth=2,text="")
        self.FoodLabel.pack(side=Tkinter.BOTTOM,pady=10,fill=Tkinter.X)

        # Packing top-level widgets last often saves some repainting:
        self.pack()
    def ChooseFood(self,FoodItem):
        # Add FoodItem to our list of foods, and build a nice
        # string listing all the food choices:
        self.FoodItems.append(FoodItem)
        LabelText=""
        TotalItems=len(self.FoodItems)
        for Index in range(TotalItems):
            if (Index>0):
                LabelText+=", "
            if (TotalItems>1 and Index==TotalItems-1):
                LabelText+="and "
            LabelText+=self.FoodItems[Index]
        self.FoodLabel["text"]=LabelText
    # Lambda forms are a convenient way to define commands, especially when
    # several buttons do similar things. I put the lambda-construction in its
    # own function, to prevent duplicated code for each button:
    def BuildButtonAction(self,Label):
        # Note: Inside a lambda definition, you can't see any names
        # from the enclosing scope. So, we must pass in self and Label:
        Action=lambda Food=self,Text=Label: Food.ChooseFood(Text)
        return Action

if (__name__=="__main__"):
    MainWindow=FoodWindow()
    MainWindow.mainloop()
```

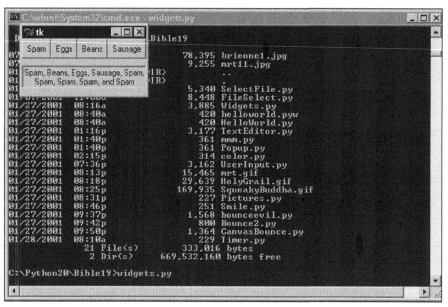

Figure 19-2: Responding to buttons

Using Common Options

The following sections provide an overview of the most commonly used widget options, organized by category. Those options that apply to button widgets also apply to check button and radio button widgets.

Color options

The following options control the colors of a widget:

background, foreground	Background and foreground colors. A synonym for `background` is `bg`; a synonym for `foreground` is `fg`.
activebackground, activeforeground	For a button or menu, these options provide colors used when the widget is active.
disabledforeground	Alternative foreground color for a disabled button or menu.
selectforeground, selectbackground	Alternative colors for the selected element(s) of a `Canvas`, `Entry`, `Text`, or `Listbox` widget.
highlightcolor, highlightbackground	Colors for the rectangle around a menu.

Size options

The following options govern the size and shape of a widget.

width
: Widget width, as measured in average-sized characters of the widget's font. A value of 0 (the default) makes the widget just large enough to hold its current text.

height
: Widget height, as measured in average-sized characters.

padx, pady
: Amount of extra internal horizontal or vertical padding, in pixels. Generally ignored if the widget is displaying a bitmap or image.

Appearance options

The following options, together with the color and size options, control a widget's appearance:

text
: Text to display in the widget.

image
: Image for display in a button or label. If an image is supplied, any `text` option is ignored. Pass an empty string for `image` to remove an image.

relief
: Specifies a 3-D border for the widget. Valid values are `FLAT`, `GROOVE`, `RAISED`, `RIDGED`, `SOLID`, and `SUNKEN`.

borderwidth
: Width of the widget's 3-D border, in pixels.

font
: The font to use for text drawn inside the widget.

Behavior options

The following options affect the behavior of a widget:

command
: Specifies a function to be called, without parameters, when the widget is clicked. Applies to buttons, scales, and scrollbars.

state
: Sets a widget state to `NORMAL`, `ACTIVE`, or `DISABLED`. A `DISABLED` widget ignores user input, and (usually) appears grayed-out. The `ACTIVE` state changes the widget's color (using the activebackground and activeforeground colors).

underline
: Widgets can use keyboard shortcuts. The `underline` option is the index of a letter in the widget's text; this letter becomes the "hot key" for using the widget.

takefocus
: If true, the widget is part of the "tab order" — when you cycle through widgets by hitting Tab, this widget will get the focus.

Gathering User Input

Many widgets collect input from the user. For example, the `Entry` widget enables the user to enter a line of text and the `Checkbox` widget can be switched on and off. Most such widgets store their value in a Tkinter variable. Tkinter variable classes include `StringVar`, `IntVar`, `DoubleVar`, and `BooleanVar`. Each Tkinter variable class provides `set` and `get` methods to access its value:

```
>>> Text=Tkinter.StringVar()
>>> Text.get()
''
>>> Text.set("Howdy!")
>>> Text.get()
'Howdy!'
```

You hook a widget to a variable by setting one of the widget's options. A check button generally uses a `BooleanVar`, attached using the `variable` option:

```
SmokingFlag=BooleanVar()
B1=Checkbutton(ParentFrame,text="Smoking",variable=SmokingFlag)
# This line sets the variable *and* checks the Checkbutton:
SmokingFlag.set(1)
```

The `Entry` and `OptionMenu` widgets generally use a `StringVar`, attached using a `textvariable` option:

```
# PetBunnyName.get() and NameEntry.get() will both
# return the contents of the entry widget:
PetBunnyName=StringVar()
NameEntry=Entry(ParentFrame,text="Bubbles",
    textvariable=PetBunnyName)
ChocolateName=StringVar()
FoodChoice=OptionMenu(ParentFrame,ChocolateName,
    "Crunchy Frog","Spring Surprise","Anthrax Ripple")
```

Several `Radiobutton` widgets can share one variable, attached to the `variable` option. The `value` option stores that button's value; I like to make the value the same as the radio button's label:

```
Flavor=StringVar()
Chocolate=Radiobutton(ParentFrame,variable=Flavor,
    text="Chocolate",value="Chocolate")
Strawberry=Radiobutton(ParentFrame,variable=Flavor,
    text="Strawberry",value="Strawberry")
Albatross=Radiobutton(ParentFrame,variable=Flavor,
    text="Albatross",value="Albatross")
```

Some widgets, such as Listbox and Text, use custom methods (*not* Tkinter variables) to access their contents. Accessors for these widgets are described together with the widgets.

Example: Printing Fancy Text

The program in Listing 19-3 can print text in various colors and sizes. It uses various widgets, attached to Tkinter variables, to collect user input. Figure 19-3 shows the program in action.

Listing 19-3: **UserInput.py**

```
import Tkinter
import tkFont # the Font class lives here!

class MainWindow(Tkinter.Frame):
    def __init__(self):
        Tkinter.Frame.__init__(self)
        # Use Tkinter variables to hold user input:
        self.Text=Tkinter.StringVar()
        self.ColorName=Tkinter.StringVar()
        self.BoldFlag=Tkinter.BooleanVar()
        self.UnderlineFlag=Tkinter.BooleanVar()
        self.FontSize=Tkinter.IntVar()
        # Set some default values:
        self.Text.set("Ni!  Ni!  Ni!")
        self.FontSize.set(12)
        self.ColorName.set("black")
        self.TextItem=None
        # Create all the widgets:
        self.CreateWidgets()
    def CreateWidgets(self):
        # Let the user specify text:
        TextFrame=Tkinter.Frame(self)
        Tkinter.Label(TextFrame,text="Text:").pack(side=Tkinter.LEFT)
        Tkinter.Entry(TextFrame,textvariable=self.Text).pack(side=Tkinter.LEFT)
        TextFrame.pack()
        # Let the user select a color:
        ColorFrame=Tkinter.Frame(self)
        Colors=["black","red","green","blue","deeppink"]
        Tkinter.Label(ColorFrame,text="Color:").pack(side=Tkinter.LEFT)
        Tkinter.OptionMenu(ColorFrame,self.ColorName,"white",*Colors).pack(\
            side=Tkinter.LEFT)
        ColorFrame.pack()
```

Continued

Listing 19-3 *(continued)*

```python
        # Let the user select a font size:
        SizeFrame=Tkinter.Frame(self)
        Tkinter.Radiobutton(SizeFrame,text="Small",variable=self.FontSize,
            value=12).pack(side=Tkinter.LEFT)
        Tkinter.Radiobutton(SizeFrame,text="Medium",variable=self.FontSize,
            value=24).pack(side=Tkinter.LEFT)
        Tkinter.Radiobutton(SizeFrame,text="Large",variable=self.FontSize,
            value=48).pack(side=Tkinter.LEFT)
        SizeFrame.pack()
        # Let the user turn Bold and Underline on and off:
        StyleFrame=Tkinter.Frame(self)
        Tkinter.Checkbutton(StyleFrame,text="Bold",variable=\
            self.BoldFlag).pack(side=Tkinter.LEFT)
        Tkinter.Checkbutton(StyleFrame,text="Underline",variable=\
            self.UnderlineFlag).pack(side=Tkinter.LEFT)
        StyleFrame.pack()
        # Add a button to repaint the text:
        GoFrame=Tkinter.Frame(self)
        Tkinter.Button(GoFrame,text="Go!",command=self.PaintText).pack()
        GoFrame.pack(anchor=Tkinter.W,fill=Tkinter.X)
        # Add a canvas to display the text:
        self.TextCanvas=Tkinter.Canvas(self,height=100,width=300)
        self.TextCanvas.pack(side=Tkinter.BOTTOM)
        # Pack parent-most widget last:
        self.pack()
    def PaintText(self):
        # Erase the old text, if any:
        if (self.TextItem!=None):
            self.TextCanvas.delete(self.TextItem)
        # Set font weight:
        if (self.BoldFlag.get()):
            FontWeight=tkFont.BOLD
        else:
            FontWeight=tkFont.NORMAL
        # Create and configure a Font object.
        # (Use tkFont.families(self) to get a list of available font-families)
        TextFont=tkFont.Font(self,"Courier")
        TextFont.configure(size=self.FontSize.get(),
            underline=self.UnderlineFlag.get(), weight=FontWeight)

        self.TextItem=self.TextCanvas.create_text(5,5,anchor=Tkinter.NW,
            text=self.Text.get(),fill=self.ColorName.get(),font=TextFont)

if (__name__=="__main__"):
    App=MainWindow()
    App.mainloop()
```

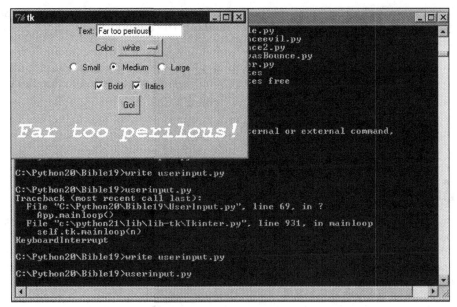

Figure 19-3: Printing fancy text

Using Text Widgets

The text widget (Tkinter.Text) is a fancy, multiline text-editing widget. It can even contain embedded windows and graphics. It is an Entry widget on steroids!

The contents of a text widget are indexed by line and column. A typical index has the form n.m, denoting character *m* in line *n*. For example, 5.8 would be character 8 from line 5. The first line of text is line 1, but the first character in a line has column 0. Therefore, the beginning of a text widget has index 1.0. You can also use the special indices END, INSERT (the insertion cursor's location), and CURRENT (the mouse pointer's location).

You can retrieve text from a text widget via its method get(start[,end]). This returns the text from index *start* up to (but not including!) index *end*. If *end* is omitted, get returns the single character at index *start*:

```
TextWidget.get("1.0",Tkinter.END) # Get ALL of the text
TextWidget.get("3.0","4.0") # Get line 3
TextWidget.get("1.5") # get the 6th character only
```

The method delete(start[,end]) deletes text from the widget. The indexes *start* and *end* function as they do for the get method. The method insert(pos,str) inserts the string *str* just before the index *pos*:

```
TextWidget.insert("1.0","Bob") # Prepend Bob to the text
TextWidget.insert(Tkinter.END,"Bob") # Append Bob to the text
# insert Bob wherever the mouse is pointing:
TextWidget.insert(Tkinter.CURRENT,"Bob")
# Clear the widget (remove all text):
TextWidget.delete("1.0",Tkinter.END)
```

Building Menus

To build a menu in Tkinter, you use a menu widget (Tkinter.Menu). You then flesh out the menu by adding entries. The method add_command(label=?,command=?) adds a menu line with the specified label. When the user chooses the menu line, the specified command is executed. add_separator adds a separator line to a menu, suitable for grouping commands.

A call to add_cascade(label=?,menu=?) attaches the specified menu as a sub-menu of the current menu. And add_checkbutton(label=?[,...]) adds a check button to the menu. You can pass other options for the new Checkbutton widget (such as variable) to add_checkbutton.

Create one instance of Menu to represent the menu bar itself, and then create one Menu instance for each "real" menu. Unlike most widgets, a menu is never packed. Instead, you attach it to a window using the menu option of a TopLevel widget, as shown in the following example:

```
root=Tkinter.Tk()
MenuBar=Tkinter.Menu(root) # Menu bar must be child of Toplevel
root["menu"]=MenuBar # attach menubar to window!
FileMenu=Tkinter.Menu(MenuBar) # Submenu is child of menubar
FileMenu.add_command(label="Load",command=LoadFile)
FileMenu.add_command(label="Save",command=SaveFile)
HelpMenu=Tkinter.Menu(MenuBar)
HelpMenu.add_command(label="Contents",command=HelpIndex)
# Attach menus to menubar:
MenuBar.add_cascade(label="File",menu=FileMenu)
MenuBar.add_cascade(label="Help",menu=HelpMenu)
```

You can create pop-up menus in Tkinter. Call the menu method tk_popup(x,y[,default]) to bring a menu up as a pop-up. The pop-up is positioned at *(x,y)*. If *default* is supplied, the pop-up menu starts with the specified label selected, as shown in Listing 19-4:

Listing 19-4: **Popup.py**

```
import Tkinter
def MenuCommand():
    print "Howdy!"
def ShowMenu():
    PopupMenu.tk_popup(*root.winfo_pointerxy())
root=Tkinter.Tk()
PopupMenu=Tkinter.Menu(root)
PopupMenu.add_command(label="X",command=MenuCommand)
PopupMenu.add_command(label="Y",command=MenuCommand)
Tkinter.Button(root,text="Popup",command=ShowMenu).pack()
root.mainloop()
```

Using Tkinter Dialogs

The module `tkMessageBox` provides several functions that display a pop-up message box. Each takes *title* and *message* parameters to control the window's title and the message displayed.

Table 19-1
Message Boxes

Function	Description
showinfo	Shows an informational message.
showwarning	Displays a warning message.
showerror	Displays an error message.
Askyesno	Displays Yes and No buttons. Returns true if the user chose Yes.
Askokcancel	Displays OK and Cancel buttons. Returns true if the user chose OK.
Askretrycancel	Displays Retry and Cancel buttons. Returns true if the user chose Retry.
Askquestion	Same as askyesno, but returns Yes or No as a string.

This snippet of code uses `tkMessageBox` to get user confirmation before quitting:

```
def Quit(self):
    if self.FileModified:
        if (not tkMessageBox.askyesno("Confirm",\
            "File modified. Really quit?")):
                return # don't quit!
    sys.exit()
```

File dialogs

The module `tkFileDialog` provides functions to bring up file-selection dialogs. The function `askopenfile` lets the user choose an existing file. The function `asksaveasfilename` lets the user choose an existing file or provide a new file name. Both functions return the full path to the selected file (or an empty string, if the user cancels out).

Optionally, pass a *filetypes* parameter to either function, to limit the search to particular file types. The parameter should be a list of tuples, where each tuple has the form (description,extension):

```
MusicFileName=tkFileDialog.askopenfilename(
    filetypes=[("Music files","mp3")])
```

Example: Text Editor

The example in Listing 19-5 is a simple text editor. With it, you can open, save, and edit text files. The code illustrates the use of the text widget, Tkinter menus, and some of Tkinter's standard dialog boxes. Figure 19-4 shows what the text editor looks like.

Listing 19-5: TextEditor.py

```python
import Tkinter
import tkFileDialog
import tkMessageBox
import os
import sys

# Filetype selections for askopenfilename and asksaveasfilename:
TEXT_FILE_TYPES=[("Text files","txt"),("All files","*")]

class TextEditor:
    def __init__(self):
        self.FileName=None
        self.CreateWidgets()
    def CreateWidgets(self):
        self.root=Tkinter.Tk()
        self.root.title("New file")
        MainFrame=Tkinter.Frame(self.root)
        # Create the File menu:
        MenuFrame=Tkinter.Frame(self.root)
```

```
        MenuFrame.pack(side=Tkinter.TOP,fill=Tkinter.X)
        FileMenuButton=Tkinter.Menubutton(MenuFrame,
            text="File",underline=0)
        FileMenuButton.pack(side=Tkinter.LEFT,anchor=Tkinter.W)
        FileMenu=Tkinter.Menu(FileMenuButton,tearoff=0)
        FileMenu.add_command(label="New",underline=0,
            command=self.ClearText)
        FileMenu.add_command(label="Open",underline=0,command=self.Open)
        FileMenu.add_command(label="Save",underline=0,command=self.Save)
        FileMenu.add_command(label="Save as...",underline=5,
            command=self.SaveAs)
        FileMenu.add_separator()
        self.FixedWidthFlag=Tkinter.BooleanVar()
        FileMenu.add_checkbutton(label="Fixed-width",
            variable=self.FixedWidthFlag,command=self.SetFont)
        FileMenu.add_separator()

        FileMenu.add_command(label="Exit",underline=1,command=sys.exit)
        FileMenuButton["menu"]=FileMenu
        # Create Help menu:
        HelpMenuButton=Tkinter.Menubutton(MenuFrame,text="Help",underline=0)
        HelpMenu=Tkinter.Menu(HelpMenuButton,tearoff=0)
        HelpMenu.add_command(label="About",underline=0,command=self.About)
        HelpMenuButton["menu"]=HelpMenu
        HelpMenuButton.pack(side=Tkinter.LEFT,anchor=Tkinter.W)
        # Create the main text field:
        self.TextBox=Tkinter.Text(MainFrame)
        self.TextBox.pack(fill=Tkinter.BOTH,expand=Tkinter.YES)
        # Pack the top-level widget:
        MainFrame.pack(fill=Tkinter.BOTH,expand=Tkinter.YES)
    def SetFont(self):
        if (self.FixedWidthFlag.get()):
            self.TextBox["font"]="Courier"
        else:
            self.TextBox["font"]="Helvetica"
    def About(self):
        tkMessageBox.showinfo("About textpad...","Hi, I'm a textpad!")
    def ClearText(self):
        self.TextBox.delete("1.0",Tkinter.END)
    def Open(self):
        FileName=tkFileDialog.askopenfilename(filetypes=TEXT_FILE_TYPES)
        if (FileName==None or FileName==""):
            return
        try:
            File=open(FileName,"r")
            NewText=File.read()
            File.close()
            self.FileName=FileName
            self.root.title(FileName)
```

Continued

Listing 19-5 *(continued)*

```
        except IOError:
            tkMessageBox.showerror("Read error...",
                "Could not read from '%s'"%FileName)
            return
        self.ClearText()
        self.TextBox.insert(Tkinter.END,NewText)
    def Save(self):
        if (self.FileName==None or self.FileName==""):
            self.SaveAs()
        else:
            self.SaveToFile(self.FileName)
    def SaveAs(self):
        FileName=tkFileDialog.asksaveasfilename(filetypes=TEXT_FILE_TYPES)
        if (FileName==None or FileName==""):
            return
        self.SaveToFile(FileName)
    def SaveToFile(self,FileName):
        try:
            File=open(FileName,"w")
            NewText=self.TextBox.get("1.0",Tkinter.END)
            File.write(NewText)
            File.close()
            self.FileName=FileName
            self.root.title(FileName)
        except IOError:
            tkMessageBox.showerror("Save error...",
                "Could not save to '%s'"%FileName)
            return
    def Run(self):
        self.root.mainloop()

if (__name__=="__main__"):
    TextEditor().Run()
```

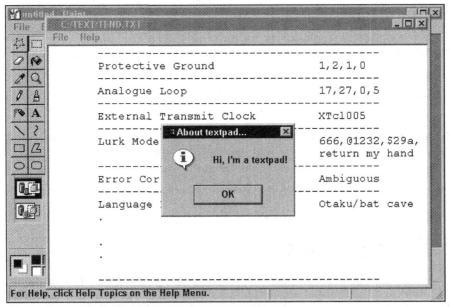

Figure 19-4: A text editor with dialogs

Handling Colors and Fonts

You can customize the color (or colors) of your widgets, as well as the font used to paint widget text.

Colors

Colors are defined using three numbers. The three numbers specify the intensity of red, green, and blue. Tkinter accepts colors in the form of a string of the form #RGB, or #RRGGBB, or #RRRGGGBBB. For example, #FFFFFF is white, #000000 is black, and #FF00FF is purple. The longer the string, the more precisely one can specify colors.

Tkinter also provides many predefined colors — for example, red and green are valid color names. The list also includes some exotic colors, such as thistle3 and burlywood2.

Fonts

Font descriptors are tuples of the form (family,size[,styles]). For example, the following lines display a button whose label is in Helvetica 24-point italics:

```
root=Tkinter.Tk()
Tkinter.Button(root,text="Fancy",
    font=("Helvetica",24,"italic")).pack()
```

If the name of a font family does not contain spaces, a string of the form "family size styles" is an equivalent font descriptor. You can also use X font descriptors:

```
Tkinter.Button(root,text="Fixed-width",
    font="-*-Courier-bold-r-*-*-12-*-*-*-*-*-*-*').pack()
```

Drawing Graphics

The PhotoImage class enables you to add images to your user interface. Images in GIF, PPM, and PGM format are supported. The constructor enables you (optionally) to name the image. You can also specify a file to read the image from, or pass in raw image data:

```
MisterT=PhotoImage("Mr. T",file="mrt.gif")
# Another way to get the same image:
ImageFile=open("mrt.gif")
ImageData=ImageFile.read()
ImageFile.close()
MisterT=PhotoImage(data=ImageData) # no name
```

Once you have a PhotoImage object, you can attach it to a label or button using the image option:

```
MisterT=Tkinter.PhotoImage(file="mrt.gif")
Tkinter.Button(root,image=MisterT).pack()
```

You can query the size of a PhotoImage using the width and height methods.

Note   You can construct PhotoImage objects only after you instantiate a TopLevel instance.

The canvas widget

The canvas widget (Tkinter.Canvas) is a window in which you can programmatically draw ovals, rectangles, lines, and so on. For example, the following code draws a smiley-face:

```
Figure=Tkinter.Canvas(root,width=50,height=50)
Figure.pack()
```

```
Figure.create_line(10,10,10,20)
Figure.create_line(40,10,40,20)
Figure.create_arc(5,15,45,45,start=200,extent=140,
    style=Tkinter.ARC)
```

Several different canvas items are available for your drawing pleasure:

create_line(x1,y1,x2, y2,...,xn,yn)	Draws lines connecting the points (x1,y1) through (xn,yn), in order. The lines are normally straight; set the *smooth* option to true to draw smooth lines.
create_polygon(x1,y2, x2,y2,...,xn,yn)	Similar to create_line. Fills the area spanned by the lines with the color supplied for the *fill* option (by default, "transparent"). Pass a color for the *outline* option to control the line color. Set the *smooth* option to true to draw smooth lines.
create_image(x,y, image=?[,anchor=?]) (x,y).	Draw the specified image on the canvas at The *image* option can be either a PhotoImage instance or the name of a previously created PhotoImage. The *anchor* option, which defaults to CENTER, specifies which portion of the image lies at (x,y).
create_oval(x1,y1,x2,y2)	Draw an oval inside the rectangle defined by the points (x1,y1) and (x2,y2). Pass a color in the *outline* option to control the outline's color. Pass a color in the *fill* option to fill the oval with that color. You can control the outline's width (in pixels) with the *width* option.
create_rectangle (x1,y2,x2,y2)	Draw a rectangle. The *fill, outline,* and *width* options have the same effect as for create_oval.
create_text(x,y,text=? [,font=?])	Draw the specified text on the canvas. Uses the supplied font, if any.

Manipulating canvas items

The items drawn on a canvas are widgets in their own right — they can be moved around, have events bound to them, and so on. The create_* methods return an ID for the canvas item. You can use that ID to manipulate the canvas item, using the canvas's methods. For example, the canvas method delete(ID) deletes the specified item. The method move(ID, DeltaX, DeltaY) moves the canvas item horizontally by *DeltaX* units, and vertically by *DeltaY* units.

Using Timers

Tkinter also provides a timer mechanism. Call the method `after(wait,function)` on a TopLevel widget to make the specified function execute after *wait* milliseconds. To make a timed action recur (for example, once every five minutes), make another call to `after` at the end of *function*. For example, the code in Listing 19-6 calls a function every ten seconds:

Listing 19-6: Timer.py

```
import Tkinter

def MinuteElapsed():
    print "Ding!"
    root.after(1000*60,MinuteElapsed)

root=Tkinter.Tk()
root.after(10000,MinuteElapsed)
root.mainloop()
```

Example: A Bouncing Picture

The program in Listing 19-7 displays a picture that moves around, bouncing off the sides of the window, as shown in Figure 19-5. It uses a PhotoImage object and a canvas to handle the display and the TopLevel `after` method to schedule calls to `MoveImage`.

Listing 19-7: CanvasBounce.py

```
import Tkinter
class Bouncer:
    def __init__(self,Master):
        self.Master=Master
        self.X=0
        self.Y=0
        self.DeltaX=5
        self.DeltaY=5
        self.Figure=Tkinter.Canvas(self.Master)
        self.GrailWidth=GrailPicture.width()
        self.GrailHeight=GrailPicture.height()
        self.GrailID=self.Figure.create_image(
            0,0,anchor=Tkinter.NW,image=GrailPicture)
        self.Figure.pack(fill=Tkinter.BOTH,expand=Tkinter.YES)
        # Move the image after 100 milliseconds:
        root.after(100,self.MoveImage)
```

```
    def MoveImage(self):
        # Move the image:
        self.X+=self.DeltaX
        self.Y+=self.DeltaY
        self.Figure.coords(self.GrailID,self.X,self.Y)
        # Bounce off the sides:
        if (self.X<0):
            self.DeltaX=abs(self.DeltaX)
        if (self.Y<0):
            self.DeltaY=abs(self.DeltaY)
        if (self.X+self.GrailWidth>self.Figure.winfo_width()):
            self.DeltaX=-abs(self.DeltaX)
        if (self.Y+self.GrailHeight >\
            self.Figure.winfo_height()):
            self.DeltaY=-abs(self.DeltaY)
        # Do it again after 100 milliseconds:
        self.Master.after(100,self.MoveImage)

if (__name__=="__main__"):
    root=Tkinter.Tk()
    GrailPicture=Tkinter.PhotoImage(file="HolyGrail.gif")
    Bouncer(root)
    root.mainloop()
```

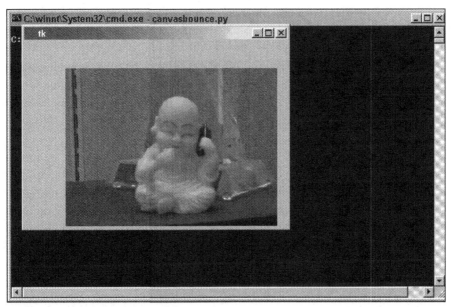

Figure 19-5: A bouncing picture

Summary

After working with Tkinter, you will understand why it is so popular. Creating and customizing an interface is simple. In this chapter, you:

✦ Created a GUI with buttons, labels, menus, and other Tkinter widgets.

✦ Used Tkinter's standard dialogs.

✦ Set up timers.

✦ Drew pictures on a canvas.

The next chapter delves into Tkinter in more detail. It covers events, drag-and-drop operations, and some more widgets.

✦   ✦   ✦

Using Advanced Tkinter Widgets

In This Chapter

Handling events

Advanced widgets

Creating dialogs

Supporting drag-and-drop operations

Using cursors

Designing new widgets

Further Tkinter adventures

This chapter introduces some of Tkinter's fancier features — custom event handlers, advanced widgets, and more. Tkinter scales up painlessly from quick-and-dirty interfaces to sophisticated, full-featured applications.

Handling Events

A GUI program spends most of its time waiting for something to happen. When something does happen — the user clicking the mouse, for example — *events* are sent to the affected widget(s). Events are sometimes called *messages* or *notifications*. A widget responds to an event using a function called an *event handler*.

Creating event handlers

Often, Tkinter's standard event handlers are good enough. As you saw in the last chapter, you can create an interesting UI without ever writing event handlers. However, you can always define a custom event handler for a widget. To define a custom handler, call the widget method bind(EventCode, Handler[,Add=None]). Here, *EventCode* is a string identifying the event, and *Handler* is a function to handle the event. Passing a value of + for *Add* causes the new handler to be added to any existing event binding.

You can also bind event handlers for a particular widget class with a call to bind_class(ClassName,EventCode, Handler[,Add]), or bind event handlers for application-level events with bind_all(EventCode,Handler[,Add]).

When the widget receives a matching event, *Handler* is called, and passed one argument — an event object. For example, the following code creates a label that beeps when you click it:

```
BeepLabel=Tkinter.Label(root,text="Click me!")
BeepHandler=lambda Event,Root=root:Root.bell()
BeepLabel.bind("<Button-1>",BeepHandler)
BeepLabel.pack()
```

Binding mouse events

Mouse buttons are numbered — 1 is the left button, 2 is the middle button (if any), and 3 is the right button. Table 20-1 lists the available mouse event codes.

<table>
<tr><td colspan="2" align="center">Table 20-1
Mouse Events</td></tr>
<tr><td>*Event code*</td><td>*Description*</td></tr>
<tr><td><Button-1></td><td>Button 1 was pressed on the widget. Similarly for <Button-2> and <Button-3>.</td></tr>
<tr><td><B1-Motion></td><td>The mouse pointer was dragged over the widget, with button 1 pressed.</td></tr>
<tr><td><ButtonRelease-1></td><td>Button 1 was released over the widget.</td></tr>
<tr><td><Double-Button-1></td><td>Button 1 was double-clicked over the widget.</td></tr>
</table>

Binding keyboard events

The event code <Key> matches any keypress. You can also match a particular key, generally by using that key's character as an event code. For example, the event code x matches a press of the x key. Some keystrokes have special event codes. Table 20-2 lists the event codes for some of the most common special keystrokes.

<table>
<tr><td colspan="2" align="center">Table 20-2
Common Special Keystrokes</td></tr>
<tr><td>*Event code*</td><td>*Keystroke*</td></tr>
<tr><td><Up></td><td>Up arrow key</td></tr>
<tr><td><Down></td><td>Down arrow key</td></tr>
<tr><td><Left></td><td>Left arrow key</td></tr>
<tr><td><Right></td><td>Right arrow key</td></tr>
</table>

Event code	Keystroke
<F1>	Function key 1
<Shift_L>,<Shift_R>	Left and right Shift key
<Control_L>,<Control_R>	Left and right Control key
<space>	Spacebar

Event objects

An event object, as passed to an event handler, has various attributes that specify just what happened. The attribute widget is a reference to the affected widget.

For mouse events, the attributes x and y are the coordinates of the mouse pointer, in pixels, as measured from the top-left corner of the widget. The attributes x_root and y_root are mouse pointer coordinates, as measured from the top-left corner of the screen.

For keyboard events, the attribute char is the character code, as a string.

Example: A Drawing Canvas

The program in Listing 20-1 provides a canvas on which you can draw shapes by left- and right-clicking. In addition, you can move the Quit button around by using the arrow keys. Figure 20-1 shows the program in action.

Listing 20-1: **Events.py**

```
import Tkinter
import sys

def DrawOval(Event):
    # Event.widget will be the main canvas:
    Event.widget.create_oval(Event.x-5,Event.y-5,
        Event.x+5,Event.y+5)
def DrawRectangle(Event):
    Event.widget.create_rectangle(Event.x-5,Event.y-5,
        Event.x+5,Event.y+5)
def MoveButton(Side):
    # The methods pack_forget() and grid_forget() unpack
    # a widget, but (unlike the destroy() method)
```

Continued

Listing 20-1 *(continued)*

```
        # do not destroy it; it can be re-displayed later.
        QuitButton.pack_forget()
        QuitButton.pack(side=Side)
root=Tkinter.Tk()
MainCanvas=Tkinter.Canvas(root)
MainCanvas.bind("<Button-1>",DrawOval)
MainCanvas.bind("<Button-3>",DrawRectangle)
MainCanvas.pack(fill=Tkinter.BOTH,expand=Tkinter.YES)
QuitButton=Tkinter.Button(MainCanvas,text="Quit",
        command=sys.exit)
QuitButton.pack(side=Tkinter.BOTTOM)
root.bind("<Up>",lambda e:MoveButton(Tkinter.TOP))
root.bind("<Down>",lambda e:MoveButton(Tkinter.BOTTOM))
root.bind("<Left>",lambda e:MoveButton(Tkinter.LEFT))
root.bind("<Right>",lambda e:MoveButton(Tkinter.RIGHT))
root.geometry("300x300") # Set minimum window size
root.mainloop()
```

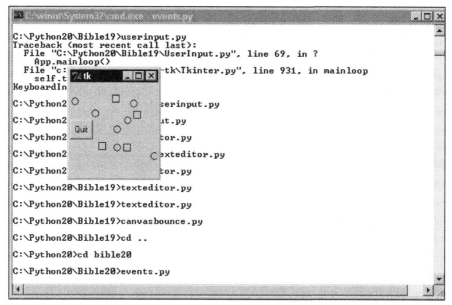

Figure 20-1: A canvas with custom mouse and keyboard event handlers

Advanced Widgets

This section introduces three more widgets for your Tkinter widget toolbox: listbox, scale, and scrollbar.

Listbox

A listbox (Tkinter.Listbox) displays a list of options. Each option is a string, and each takes up one row in the listbox. Each item is assigned an index (starting from 0).

The option selectmode governs what kind of selections the user can make. SINGLE allows one row to be selected at a time; MULTIPLE permits the user to select many rows at once. BROWSE (the default) is similar to SINGLE, but allows the user to drag the mouse cursor across rows. EXTENDED is similar to MULTIPLE, but allows fancier selections to be made by Control- and Shift-clicking.

The option *height*, which defaults to 10, specifies how many rows a listbox displays at once. If a listbox contains more rows than it can display at once, you should attach a scrollbar — see the section "Scrollbar" for details.

Editing listbox contents

To populate the listbox, call the method insert(before,element[,...]). This inserts one or more elements (which must be strings!) prior to index *before*. Use the special index Tkinter.END to append the new item(s) to the end of the listbox.

The method delete(first[,last]) deletes all items from index *first* to index *last*, inclusive. If *last* is not specified, the single item with index *first* is deleted.

Checking listbox contents

The method size returns the number of items in the listbox.

The method get(first[,last]) retrieves the items from index *first* to index *last*, inclusive. Normally, get returns a list of strings; if *last* is omitted, the single item with index *first* is returned.

The method nearest(y) returns the index of the row closest to the specified y-coordinate. This is useful for determining what row a user is clicking.

Checking and changing the selection

The method curselection returns the current selection, in the form of a list of indices. If no row is selected, curselection returns an empty string. The method selection_includes(index) returns true if the item with the specified index is selected.

The method `selection_set(first[,last])` selects the items from index *first* to index *last*, inclusive. The method `selection_clear(first[,last])` deselects the specified items.

Note When you specify a range of listbox indices, the list is inclusive, not exclusive. For example, MyList.selection_set(2,3) selects the items with index 2 and 3.

Scale

A scale widget (`Tkinter.Scale`) looks like a sliding knob. The user drags the slider to set a numeric value. You can attach a scale to a Tkinter variable (using the *variable* option), or use its `get` and `set` methods to access its value directly.

Range and precision

The options *from* and *to* specify the numeric range available; the default is the range from 0 to 100. The option *resolution* is the smallest possible change the user can make in the numeric value. By default, *resolution* is 1 (so that the scale's value is always an integer).

Note Remember to use from_, not from, when passing the "from" option as a keyword argument.

Widget size

The option *orient* determines the direction in which the scale is laid out; valid values are HORIZONTAL and VERTICAL. The option *length* specifies the length (in pixels) of the scale; it defaults to 100. The option *sliderlength* determines the length of the sliding knob; it defaults to 30.

Labeling

By default, a scale displays the current numeric value above (or to the left of) the sliding scale. Set the *showvalue* option to false to disable this display.

You can label the axis with several tick-marks. To do so, pass the distance between ticks in the option *tickinterval*.

Scrollbar

A scrollbar widget (`Tkinter.Scrollbar`) is used in conjunction with another widget when that widget has more to show than it can display all at once. The scrollbar enables the user to scroll through the available information.

The *orient* option determines the scrollbar's orientation; valid values are VERTICAL and HORIZONTAL.

To attach a vertical scrollbar to a Listbox, Canvas, or Text widget, set the scroll-bar's *command* option to the *yview* method of the widget. Then, set the widget's *yscrollcommand* option to the scrollbar's *set* method. (To attach a horizontal scrollbar, perform a similar procedure, but use *xview* and *xscrollcommand*.)

For example, the following two lines "hook together" a scrollbar (MyScrollbar) and a listbox (MyListbox):

```
MyScrollbar["command"]= MyListbox.yview
MyListbox["yscrollcommand"]= MyScrollbar.set
```

Example: Color Scheme Customizer

Tkinter allows you to use a predefined color scheme. These colors are used as defaults for the *foreground* and *background* options of widgets. The TopLevel method option_readfile(filename) reads in default colors and fonts from a file. You should call option_readfile as early in your program as possible, because it doesn't affect any widgets already displayed onscreen.

A typical line in the file has the form *Widget*foreground: Color, where *Widget* is a widget class and *Color* is the default color for that sort of widget. The line *foreground: Color sets a default foreground for all other widgets. Similar lines set the default background colors.

The example shown in Listing 20-2 lets you define a new color scheme. It uses a list-box, a scrollbar, and three sliding scales (for setting red, green, and blue levels). See Figure 20-2 for an example.

Listing 20-2: **ColorChooser.py**

```
import Tkinter
import os
import sys

WIDGET_NAMES = ["Entry","Label","Menu","Text","Button","Listbox","Scale",
                "Scrollbar","Canvas"]
OPTION_FILE_NAME="TkinterColors.ini"
COLOR_COMPONENTS=["Red","Green","Blue"]

class ColorChooser:
    def __init__(self):
        self.root = Tkinter.Tk()
        # Dictionary of options and values - corresponds to
        # the option database (TkinterColors.ini):
        self.Options={}
```

Continued

Listing 20-2 *(continued)*

```
        # Flag linked to the "Option set?" checkbox:
        self.OptionSetFlag=Tkinter.BooleanVar()
        self.GetOptionsFromFile()
        self.BuildWidgets()
        self.SelectedColorItem=None
        self.SelectNewColorItem(0)
    def SaveCurrentColorValues(self):
        "Use Scale-widget values to set internal color value"
        if (self.SelectedColorItem!=None):
            if (self.OptionSetFlag.get()):
                ColorString="#"
                for ColorComponent in COLOR_COMPONENTS:
                    ColorString+="%02X"%self.ColorValues[ColorComponent].get()
                self.Options[self.SelectedColorItem]=ColorString
            else:
                # The user un-checked the "option set" box:
                if (self.Options.has_key(self.SelectedColorItem)):
                    del self.Options[self.SelectedColorItem]
    def UpdateControlsFromColorValue(self):
        "Use internal color value to update Scale widgets"
        if (self.SelectedColorItem!=None and self.OptionSetFlag.get()):
            ColorString=self.Options.get(self.SelectedColorItem,"")
            if len(ColorString)!=7:
                ColorString="#000000" # default
        else:
            ColorString="#000000"
        RedValue=int(ColorString[1:3],16)
        self.ColorValues["Red"].set(RedValue)
        GreenValue=int(ColorString[3:5],16)
        self.ColorValues["Green"].set(GreenValue)
        BlueValue=int(ColorString[5:],16)
        self.ColorValues["Blue"].set(BlueValue)
    def OptionChecked(self):
        """Callback for clicking the "Option set" checkbox"""
        if (self.OptionSetFlag.get()):
            self.EnableColorScales()
        else:
            self.DisableColorScales()
    def EnableColorScales(self):
        for ColorComponent in COLOR_COMPONENTS:
            self.ColorScales[ColorComponent]["state"]=Tkinter.NORMAL
    def DisableColorScales(self):
        for ColorComponent in COLOR_COMPONENTS:
            self.ColorScales[ColorComponent]["state"]=Tkinter.DISABLED
    def SelectNewColorItem(self,NewIndex):
        """Choose a new color item - save the current item, select the
        new entry in the listbox, and update the scale-widgets from the
        new entry"""
```

```
            self.SaveCurrentColorValues()
            self.SelectedColorItem=self.ItemList.get(NewIndex)
            self.ItemList.activate(NewIndex)
            self.ItemList.selection_set(NewIndex)
            print "sel:",self.SelectedColorItem
            print self.Options.has_key(self.SelectedColorItem)
            self.OptionSetFlag.set(self.Options.has_key(self.SelectedColorItem))
            print self.OptionSetFlag.get()
            self.OptionChecked()
            self.UpdateControlsFromColorValue()
        def ListboxClicked(self,ClickEvent):
            "Event handler for choosing a new Listbox entry"
            NewIndex=self.ItemList.nearest(ClickEvent.y)
            self.SelectNewColorItem(NewIndex)
        def BuildWidgets(self):
            """Set up all the application widgets"""
            self.LeftPane=Tkinter.Frame(self.root)
            self.RightPane=Tkinter.Frame(self.root)
            self.ItemList=Tkinter.Listbox(self.LeftPane,
                selectmode=Tkinter.SINGLE)
            self.ItemList.pack(side=Tkinter.LEFT,expand=Tkinter.YES,
                fill=Tkinter.Y)
            self.ListBoxScroller=Tkinter.Scrollbar(self.LeftPane)
            self.ListBoxScroller.pack(side=Tkinter.RIGHT,expand=Tkinter.YES,
                fill=Tkinter.Y)
            # Add entries to listbox:
            self.ItemList.insert(Tkinter.END,"*foreground")
            self.ItemList.insert(Tkinter.END,"*background")
            for WidgetName in WIDGET_NAMES:
                self.ItemList.insert(Tkinter.END,"*%s*foreground"%WidgetName)
                self.ItemList.insert(Tkinter.END,"*%s*background"%WidgetName)
            # Attach scrollbar to listbox:
            self.ListBoxScroller["command"]=self.ItemList.yview
            self.ItemList["yscrollcommand"]=self.ListBoxScroller.set
            # Handle listbox selection events specially:
            self.ItemList.bind("<Button-1>",self.ListboxClicked)
            # Add checkbox for setting and un-setting the option:
            ColorSetCheck=Tkinter.Checkbutton(self.RightPane,
                text="Option set", variable=self.OptionSetFlag,
                command=self.OptionChecked)
            ColorSetCheck.pack(side=Tkinter.TOP,anchor=Tkinter.W)
            # Build red, green, and blue scales for setting colors:
            self.ColorValues={}
            self.ColorScales={}
            for ColorComponent in COLOR_COMPONENTS:
                ColorValue=Tkinter.IntVar()
                self.ColorValues[ColorComponent]=ColorValue
                NewScale=Tkinter.Scale(self.RightPane,
                    orient=Tkinter.HORIZONTAL,from_=0,to=255,
                    variable=ColorValue)
                self.ColorScales[ColorComponent]=NewScale
```

Continued

Listing 20-2 *(continued)*

```
            Tkinter.Label(self.RightPane,text=ColorComponent).pack\
                (side=Tkinter.TOP)
            NewScale.pack(side=Tkinter.TOP,pady=10)
        # Add "SAVE" and "QUIT" buttons:
        ButtonFrame=Tkinter.Frame(self.RightPane)
        ButtonFrame.pack()
        Tkinter.Button(ButtonFrame,text="Save",
            command=self.SaveOptionsToFile).pack(side=Tkinter.LEFT)
        Tkinter.Button(ButtonFrame,text="Quit",
            command=sys.exit).pack(side=Tkinter.LEFT)
        # Pack the parentmost widgets:
        self.LeftPane.pack(side=Tkinter.LEFT,expand=Tkinter.YES,
            fill=Tkinter.BOTH)
        self.RightPane.pack(side=Tkinter.RIGHT,expand=Tkinter.YES,
            fill=Tkinter.BOTH)
    def Run(self):
        self.root.mainloop()
    def SaveOptionsToFile(self):
        # Update internal color-settings from scale-widgets:
        self.SaveCurrentColorValues()
        File=open(OPTION_FILE_NAME,"w")
        # Save *foreground and *background first:
        if self.Options.has_key("*foreground"):
            File.write("*foreground: %s\n"%self.Options["*foreground"])
            del self.Options["*foreground"]
        if self.Options.has_key("*background"):
            File.write("*background: %s\n"%self.Options["*background"])
            del self.Options["*background"]
        for Key in self.Options.keys():
            File.write("%s: %s\n"%(Key,self.Options[Key]))
        File.close()
        print "Saved!"
    def GetOptionsFromFile(self):
        if os.path.exists(OPTION_FILE_NAME):
            # Read the colors in:
            File=open(OPTION_FILE_NAME,"r")
            for Line in File.readlines():
                LineHalves=Line.split(":")
                if len(LineHalves)!=2:
                    # Not a proper setting
                    continue
                Value = LineHalves[1].strip()
                Index = LineHalves[0].strip()
                self.Options[Index] = Value
            File.close()
            # Tell Tkinter to use these colors, too!
            self.root.option_readfile(OPTION_FILE_NAME)

if (__name__=="__main__"):
    ColorChooser().Run()
```

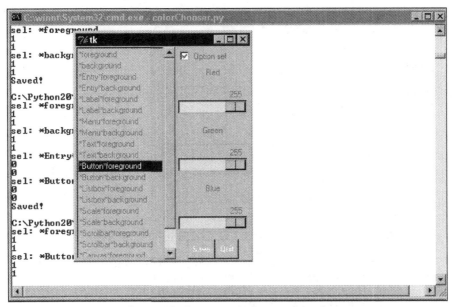

Figure 20-2: Using scales and listboxes to design a color scheme

Creating Dialogs

Instead of using the standard dialogs (as described in Chapter 19), you can create dialog boxes of your own. The module tkSimpleDialog provides a class, Dialog, that you can subclass to create any dialog box. When you construct a Dialog instance, the dialog is (synchronously) displayed, and the user can click OK or Cancel. The constructor has the syntax Dialog(master[,title]).

Override the method body(master) with a method that creates the widgets in the dialog body. If the body method returns a widget, that widget receives the initial focus when the dialog is displayed. Override the apply method with a function to be called when the user clicks OK.

In addition, you can create custom buttons by overriding the buttonbox method. The buttons should call the ok and cancel methods. In addition, binding <Return> to OK, and <Escape> to Cancel, is generally a good idea.

The example in Listing 20-3 displays a simple dialog when the user presses a button.

Listing 20-3: Complaint.py

```
import Tkinter
import tkSimpleDialog

class ComplaintDialog(tkSimpleDialog.Dialog):
    def body(self,Master):
        Tkinter.Label(self,
            text="Enter your complaint here:").pack()
        self.Complaint=Tkinter.Entry(self)
        self.Complaint.pack()
        return self.Complaint # set initial focus here!
    def apply(self):
        self.ComplaintString=self.Complaint.get()

def Complain():
    # This next line doesn't return until the user
    # clicks "Ok" or "Cancel":
    UserDialog=ComplaintDialog(root,"Enter your complaint")
    if hasattr(UserDialog,"ComplaintString"):
        # They must have clicked "Ok", since
        # apply() got called.
        print "Complaint:",UserDialog.ComplaintString

root=Tkinter.Tk()
Tkinter.Button(root,text="I wish to register a complaint",
               command=Complain).pack()
root.mainloop()
```

Supporting Drag-and-Drop Operations

The module Tkdnd provides simple drag-and-drop support for your Tkinter applications. To implement drag-and-drop, you need to have suitable draggable objects, and suitable targets. A draggable object (which can be a widget) should implement a dnd_end method. A target can be any widget that implements the methods dnd_accept, dnd_motion, dnd_enter, dnd_leave, and dnd_commit.

To support drag-and-drop, bind a handler for <ButtonPress> in the widget from which you can drag. In the event handler, call Tkdnd.dnd_start(draggable, event), where *draggable* is a draggable object and *event* is the event you are handling. The call to dnd_start returns a drag-and-drop object. You can call this object's cancel method to cancel an in-progress drag; otherwise, you don't use the drag-and-drop object.

As the user drags the object around, Tkdnd constantly looks for a new target widget. It checks the widget under the mouse cursor, then that parent's widget, and so on. When it sees a widget with a dnd_accept method, it calls dnd_accept(draggable, event), where *draggable* is the object being dragged. If the call to dnd_accept returns anything but None, that widget becomes the new target.

Whenever the dragged object moves, one of the following happens:

✦ If the old target and the new target are both None, nothing happens.

✦ If the old and new targets are the same widget, its method dnd_motion (draggable,event) is called.

✦ If the old target is None and the new target is not, its method dnd_enter(draggable,event) is called.

✦ If the new target is None and the old target is not, its method dnd_leave(draggable, event) is called.

✦ If the old and new targets are not None and are different, dnd_leave is called on the old one and then dnd_enter is called on the new one.

If the draggable object is dropped on a valid target, dnd_commit(draggable,event) is called on that target. If the draggable object is *not* dropped on a valid target, dnd_leave is called on the previous target (if any). In either case, a call to dnd_end(target,event) is made on the draggable object when the user drops it.

The program in Listing 20-4 illustrates drag-and-drop through the use of two custom listboxes. Entries can be dragged around within a listbox, or dragged between listboxes. Figure 20-3 shows what the program looks like.

Listing 20-4: **DragAndDrop.py**

```
import Tkinter
import Tkdnd

class DraggableRow:
    def __init__(self,Index,ItemStr,Widget):
        self.Index=Index
        self.ItemStr=ItemStr
        self.Widget=Widget
        self.PreviousWidget=Widget
    def dnd_end(self,Target,Event):
        if Target==None:
            # Put the item back in its original widget!
            self.PreviousWidget.insert(Tkinter.END,
                self.ItemStr)
```

Continued

Listing 20-4 *(continued)*

```
class DragAndDropListbox(Tkinter.Listbox):
    def __init__(self,Master,cnf={},**kw):
        Tkinter.Listbox.__init__(self,Master,cnf)
        self.bind("<ButtonPress>",self.StartDrag)
    def StartDrag(self,Event):
        Index=self.nearest(Event.y)
        ItemStr=self.get(Index)
        Tkdnd.dnd_start(DraggableRow(Index,ItemStr,self),Event)
    def dnd_accept(self,Item,Event):
        return self
    def dnd_leave(self,Item,Event):
        self.delete(Item.Index)
        Item.PreviousWidget=self
        Item.Widget=None
        Item.Index=None
    def dnd_enter(self,Item,Event):
        if (Item.Widget==self and Item.Index!=None):
            self.delete(Item.Index)
        Item.Widget=self
        NewIndex=self.nearest(Event.y)
        NewIndex=max(NewIndex,0)
        self.insert(NewIndex,Item.ItemStr)
        Item.Index=NewIndex
    def dnd_commit(self,Item,Event):
        pass
    def dnd_motion(self,Item,Event):
        if (Item.Index!=None):
            self.delete(Item.Index)
        NewIndex=self.nearest(Event.y)
        NewIndex=max(NewIndex,0)
        Item.Index=NewIndex
        self.insert(NewIndex,Item.ItemStr)

root=Tkinter.Tk()
LeftList=DragAndDropListbox(root)
LeftList.pack(side=Tkinter.LEFT,fill=Tkinter.BOTH,
    expand=Tkinter.YES)
RightList=DragAndDropListbox(root)
RightList.pack(side=Tkinter.RIGHT,fill=Tkinter.BOTH,
    expand=Tkinter.YES)
# Add some elements to the listbox, for testing:
for Name in ["Nene","Syvia","Linna","Priscilla"]:
    LeftList.insert(Tkinter.END,Name)
root.mainloop()
```

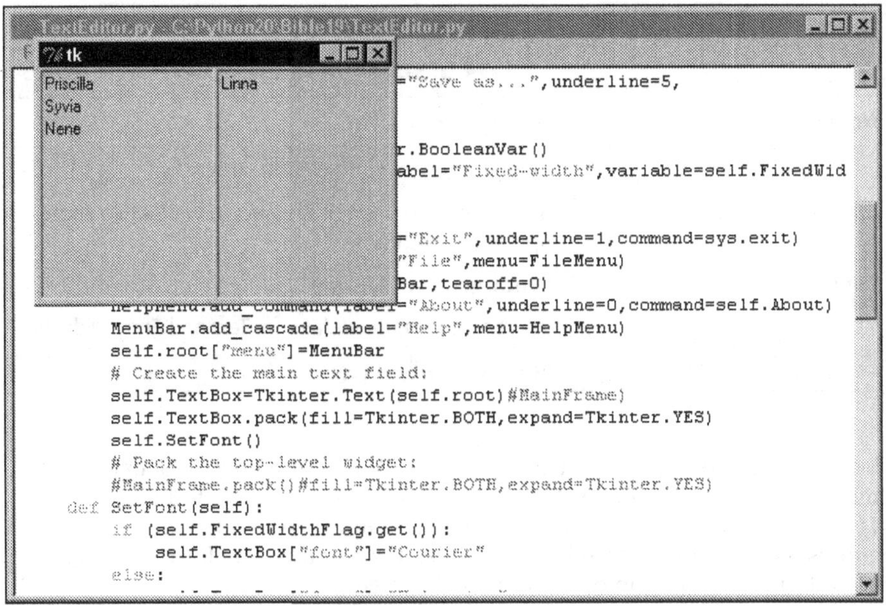

Figure 20-3: Dragging and dropping elements between two listboxes

Using Cursors

The standard widget option *cursor* specifies the name of a cursor image to use when the mouse is positioned over the widget. Setting *cursor* to an empty string uses the standard system cursor. For example, the following code creates a Quit button, and changes the cursor to a skull-and-crossbones when it is positioned over the button:

```
Tkinter.Button(root,text="Quit",command=sys.exit,
    cursor="pirate").pack()
```

Many cursors are available, which range from the useful to the silly. Table 20-3 describes some useful cursors.

<table>
<tr><td colspan="2" align="center">Table 20-3
Cursors</td></tr>
<tr><td>***Name***</td><td>***Description***</td></tr>
<tr><td>left_ptr</td><td>Pointer arrow; a good default cursor</td></tr>
<tr><td>watch</td><td>Stopwatch; used to tell the user to wait while some operation finishes</td></tr>
<tr><td>pencil</td><td>Pencil; good for drawing</td></tr>
<tr><td>xterm</td><td>Insertion cursor; the default for Text and Entry widgets</td></tr>
<tr><td>trek, gumby, box_spiral</td><td>Some cute, silly cursors</td></tr>
</table>

The TopLevel method `after` executes a function after a specified amount of time has passed. (See "Using Timers" in Chapter 19). The related method `after_idle(function)` executes a specified function as soon as Tkinter empties its event queue and becomes idle. It is a handy way for restoring the cursor to normal after an operation has finished.

The example in Listing 20-5 finds .mp3 files in the current directory and all its subdirectories, and adds them to a playlist. It displays a busy cursor while it is searching the directories. (A fancier approach would be to spawn a child thread to do the search.)

Listing 20-5: **WaitCursor.py**

```
import Tkinter
import os
OldCursor=""
def DoStuff():
    # Save the old cursor, so we can restore it later.
    # (In this example, we know the old cursor is just "")
    OldCursor=root["cursor"]
    # Change the cursor:
    root["cursor"]="watch"
    # Wait for Tkinter to empty the event loop. We must do
    # this, in order to see the new cursor:
    root.update()
    # Tell Tkinter to RestoreCursor the next time it's idle:
    root.after_idle(RestoreCursor)
    File=open("PlayList.m3u","w")
    os.path.walk(os.path.abspath(os.curdir),CheckDir,File)
    File.close()

def CheckDir(File,DirName,FileNames):
    # Write all the MP3 files in the directory to our playlist:
    for FileName in FileNames:
```

```
        if os.path.splitext(FileName)[1].upper()==".MP3":
            File.write(os.path.join(DirName,FileName)+"\n")

def RestoreCursor():
    root["cursor"]=OldCursor

root=Tkinter.Tk()
Tkinter.Button(text="Find files!",command=DoStuff).pack()
root.mainloop()
```

Designing New Widgets

You can create new widgets by combining or subclassing existing ones. However, before you do, do a quick search online — any widget you can imagine has probably been created already!

Listing 20-6 shows a simple example — a progress bar, which keeps track of progress as a percentage from 0 to 100. Figure 20-4 shows the program partway through its run.

Listing 20-6: **ProgressBar.py**

```
import Tkinter
import time
import sys

class ProgressBar:
    def __init__(self, Parent, Height=10, Width=100,

ForegroundColor=None,BackgroundColor=None,Progress=0):
        self.Height=Height
        self.Width=Width
        self.BarCanvas = Tkinter.Canvas(Parent,
            width=Width,height=Height,
            background=BackgroundColor,borderwidth=1,
            relief=Tkinter.SUNKEN)
        if (BackgroundColor):
            self.BarCanvas["backgroundcolor"]=BackgroundColor
        self.BarCanvas.pack(padx=5,pady=2)
        self.RectangleID=self.BarCanvas.create_rectangle(\
            0,0,0,Height)
        if (ForegroundColor==None):
            ForegroundColor="black"
        self.BarCanvas.itemconfigure(\
                self.RectangleID,fill=ForegroundColor)
        self.SetProgressPercent(Progress)
    def SetProgressPercent(self,NewLevel):
```

Continued

Listing 20-6 *(continued)*

```
        self.Progress=NewLevel
        self.Progress=min(100,self.Progress)
        self.Progress=max(0,self.Progress)
        self.DrawProgress()
    def DrawProgress(self):
        ProgressPixel=(self.Progress/100.0)*self.Width
        self.BarCanvas.coords(self.RectangleID,
            0,0,ProgressPixel,self.Height)
    def GetProgressPercent(self):
        return self.Progress

# Simple demonstration:
def IncrememtProgress():
    OldLevel=Bar.GetProgressPercent()
    if (OldLevel>99): sys.exit()
    Bar.SetProgressPercent(OldLevel+1)
    root.after(20,IncrememtProgress)
root=Tkinter.Tk()
root.title("Progress bar!")
Bar=ProgressBar(root)
root.after(20,IncrememtProgress)
root.mainloop()
```

Figure 20-4: A custom widget for displaying a progress bar

Further Tkinter Adventures

There are many more widgets, options, and tricks in Tkinter than are covered here. Following are some places to learn more.

Additional widgets

Python MegaWidgets (Pmw) is a large collection of Tkinter widgets. Examples include Notebook (a tabbed display) and Balloon (a class for adding popup help). Pmw is a nice way to develop fancier interfaces without becoming a Tk Jedi Master. Visit `http://www.dscpl.com.au/pmw/` to check it out.

There are other collections of Tk widgets — such as Tix and BLT — that may help you save time developing a GUI.

Learning more

The Tkinter distribution is lacking in documentation, but there are several good Tkinter references out there:

✦ *An Introduction to Tkinter,* by Fredrik Lundh. Comprehensive, with many good examples.

`http://www.pythonware.com/library/tkinter/introduction/index.htm`

✦ *Python and Tkinter Programming,* by John E. Grayson. Many interesting examples. Covers Pmw in great detail. The book's Web site is at

`http://www.manning.com/Grayson/`

✦ The Tkinter topic guide — a good starting point for all things Tkinter.

`http://www.python.org/topics/tkinter/doc.html`

✦ *The Tkinter Life Preserver,* by Matt Conway.

`http://www.python.org/doc/life-preserver/index.html`

When all else fails, read up on Tk. The correspondence between Tkinter and Tk is straightforward, so anything you learn about Tk will carry over to Tkinter too.

Summary

Tkinter can handle sophisticated GUIs without much trouble. You can use the layout managers and event handler to get your program's appearance and behavior just right. In this chapter, you:

✦ Handled various events.

✦ Created advanced widgets and dialogs.

✦ Used custom mouse cursors.

In the next chapter, you learn all about the Curses module — a good user interface choice for terminals on which graphics (and hence Tkinter) aren't available.

✦   ✦   ✦

Building User Interfaces with wxPython

♦ ♦ ♦ ♦

In This Chapter

Introducing wxPython

Creating simple
wxPython programs

Choosing different
window types

Using wxPython
controls

Controlling layout

Using built-in dialogs

Drawing with device
contexts

Adding menus and
keyboard shortcuts

Accessing mouse and
keyboard input

Other wxPython
features

♦ ♦ ♦ ♦

Although it is not Python's official user interface library, wxPython is becoming an increasingly popular set of tools for building graphical user interfaces. Like Tkinter, it is powerful, easy to use, and works on several platforms. This chapter gives you a jump start on using wxPython in your own applications.

Introducing wxPython

wxPython (http://wxpython.org) is an extension module that wraps a C++ framework called wxWindows (http://wxwindows.org). Both wxPython and wxWindows provide cross-platform support and are free for private as well as commercial use. This chapter focuses on the cross-platform GUI support provided by wxPython, but wxWindows also gives you cross-platform APIs for multithreading, database access, and so on.

Tip   Visit the wxPython Web site for straightforward download-ing and installing instructions, as well as the latest news and support. You can also join the wxPython community by subscribing to a free mailing list for questions, answers, and announcements. Visit http://wxpros.com for infor-mation about professional support and training.

The full feature set of wxPython deserves an entire book of its own, and a single chapter will all but scratch the surface. The purpose of this chapter, therefore, is to give you a high-level picture of what it supports, and to get you started on writing some wxPython programs of your own. You'll still want to later sift through the documentation for additional options and features. Because wxPython is so easy to use, however, by the end of this chapter you'll be able to write some very functional programs, and with very little effort.

In addition to its built-in features, wxPython can also detect and use some popular Python extension modules such as Numerical Python (NumPy) and PyOpenGL, the OpenGL bindings for Python.

 Cross-Reference See Chapter 32 for an introduction to `NumPy`.

wxPython often outperforms Tkinter, both with large amounts of data and overall responsiveness; it comes with a good set of high-level controls and dialogs; and it does a pretty good job of giving applications a native look and feel (which isn't necessarily a goal of Tkinter anyway). For these reasons, and because I find using wxPython very straightforward and intuitive, I personally prefer wxPython over Tkinter even though it doesn't ship as a standard part of the Python distribution.

Creating Simple wxPython Programs

Most wxPython programs have a similar structure, so once you have that under your belt, you can quickly move on to programs that are more complex. Listing 21-1 is a simple program that opens up a main window with a giant button in it. Clicking the button pops up a dialog box, as shown in Figure 21-1.

Listing 21-1: wxclickme.py — A wxPython application with buttons

```
from wxPython.wx import *

class ButtonFrame(wxFrame):
    'Creates a frame with a single button in the center'
    def __init__(self):
        wxFrame.__init__(self, NULL, -1, 'wxPython',
                         wxDefaultPosition, (200, 100))

        button = wxButton(self, 111, 'Click Me!')
        EVT_BUTTON(self, 111, self.onButton)

    def onButton(self, event):
        'Create a message dialog when the button is clicked'
        dlg = wxMessageDialog(self, 'Ow, quit it.', \
                              'Whine', wxOK)
        dlg.ShowModal()
        dlg.Destroy()
```

```
class App(wxApp):
    def OnInit(self):
        'Create the main window and insert the custom frame'
        frame = ButtonFrame()
        frame.Show(true)
        return true # Yes, continue processing

# Create the app and start processing messages
app = App(0)
app.MainLoop()
```

Figure 21-1: The program in Listing 21-1 opens the dialog box on the button click event.

To understand this program, start at the end and work your way back. All wxPython programs instantiate a wxApp (or subclass) object and call its MainLoop method to start the message handling (MainLoop doesn't return until the application window is closed). The wxApp subclass in the example, App, overloads the OnInit method that is called during initialization. OnInit creates a custom frame, ButtonFrame, makes it visible, and returns true (actually, wx.true) to signal success. These lines of code will be nearly identical for almost all your wxPython programs; for each new program, I usually cut and paste them from the previous program I wrote, changing only the name of the frame class to use.

A frame is a top-level window like the main window in most applications (it usually has a title bar, is resizable, and so forth). The __init__ method of the ButtonFrame class calls the parent (wxFrame) constructor to set the title to "wxPython" and the size to 200 pixels wide and 100 tall. It adds a button with the label Click Me!, and tells wxPython to route button-click messages for that button to ButtonFrame's onButton method. Notice how trivial it is to set up event routing. The line

```
EVT_BUTTON(self, 111, self.onButton)
```

tells wxPython to take all button-click events generated in the current window (self) with an ID of 111 (a random number I chose and assigned to the button) and send them to the onButton method. The only requirement for the onButton method is that it take an event argument. You can use a method such as onButton as the handler for many different events (if it makes sense to do so) because it receives as an argument the event to process. Each event is derived from the wxEvent class and has methods that identify the event source, type, and so on. For example, if you registered onButton to handle events from several different buttons, onButton could call the event's GetId() method to determine which button was clicked.

Tip   Use the wxNewId() function to generate unique ID numbers.

The onButton method pops open a standard message dialog, waits for you to click OK, and closes it.

Fiddle around with the program until the basic structure makes sense and you're comfortable with what's happening. Conceptually, that's the bulk of programming in wxPython—now you can just learn about other widgets besides buttons, and other events besides button-clicks. There's plenty more to learn, of course, but the designers of wxPython have done an excellent job of insulating us from a lot of nasty details.

Choosing Different Window Types

The wxWindow class is the base class of all other windows (everything from the main application window to a button or a text label is considered a window). Of the window types that can contain child windows, there are two types: managed and nonmanaged.

Tip   Repeat ten times out loud: "A button is a window." Nearly everything is a descendent of wxWindow; therefore, for example, if the documentation tells you that you can call some method to add a child window to a parent, bear in mind that the child window can be a panel, a button, a scrollbar, and so on.

Managed windows

A *managed window* is one that is directly controlled by the operating system's window manager. The first type is one you've already seen, wxFrame, which often has a title bar, menus, and a status bar, and is usually resizable and movable by the user. wxMiniFrame is a wxFrame subclass that creates a tiny frame suitable for floating toolbars.

A wxDialog window is similar to a wxFrame window and is usually used to request input or display a message. When created with the wxDIALOG_MODAL style, the calling program can't receive any user input until the dialog box is closed.

Managed window constructors are generally like wxWindow(parent, id, title[, position][, size][, style]), where parent can be None for managed windows, id can be –1 for a default ID, and style is a bitwise OR combination of several class-specific flags:

```
>>> from wxPython.wx import *
>>> f = wxFrame(None,-1,'', size=(200,100),
                style=wxRESIZE_BORDER)
>>> f.Center(); f.Show(1) # Later, use f.Show(0) to kill it
```

Nonmanaged windows

Nonmanaged windows are controlled by wxPython, and you use them by placing them inside other windows. For example, the following creates a window with a resizable vertical split like the one shown in Figure 21-2:

```
>>> f = wxFrame(None,-1,'SplitterWindow',size=(200,100))
>>> s = wxSplitterWindow(f,-1)
>>> s.SplitVertically(wxWindow(s,-1),wxWindow(s,-1))
1
>>> f.Show(1)
1
```

Figure 21-2: A user-resizable splitter window

Notice that wxSplitterWindow's SplitVertically method takes as parameters the two windows it splits; for simplicity, I just created two plain windows. A wxPanel window is like a dialog box in that you place controls (buttons, text entry fields, and so on) in it, except that a panel lives inside another window such as a frame. The wxHtmlWindow class displays HTML files; you can even embed any wxPython widget *within* an HTML page and have it respond to events normally.

Tip Consult demo.py in the wxPython distribution for information about embedding widgets in HTML pages. The demo also contains terrific examples of many other wxPython features.

You can add scrolling to any window by first placing it inside a wxScrolledWindow instance. Be sure to call its SetScrollBars method to initialize the size of the scrollbars. Some windows, such as wxHtmlWindow, are derived from wxScrolledWindow, or already have scrolling support to save you the trouble.

The wxGrid class gives your application a spreadsheet-like table with rows and columns. It has plenty of standard helpers for controlling user input or displaying data in certain ways, or you can implement your own grid cell renderers.

The wxStatusBar and wxToolBar classes enable you to add a status bar and a toolbar to any frame (call the frame's SetStatusBar and SetToolBar methods, respectively). In the wxPython.lib.floatbar module, you'll find wxFloatBar, a wxToolBar subclass implemented in Python that provides "dockable" toolbars that users can pull out of the frame and move elsewhere.

Applications such as Microsoft Visual Studio enable you to open several files at a time, each in a separate child window that can't leave the boundaries of a single parent window. wxPython enables you to create applications with this style of interface using the wxMDIChildFrame, wxMDIClientWindow, and wxMDIParentFrame classes.

The program in Listing 21-2 creates a viewer for HTML files stored locally. Notice in Figure 21-3 that it uses a wxNotebook window to enable you to open several HTML files simultaneously, and the toolbar has buttons for adding and removing pages as well as quitting the application.

Listing 21-2: **grayul.py — A local HTML file viewer**

```
from wxPython.wx import *
from wxPython.html import *
from wxPython.lib.floatbar import *
import time,os

class BrowserFrame(wxFrame):
    'Creates a multi-pane viewer for local HTML files'
    ID_ADD = 5000
    ID_REMOVE = 5001
    ID_QUIT = 5002

    # Load support for viewing GIF files
    wxImage_AddHandler(wxGIFHandler())

    def __init__(self):
        wxFrame.__init__(self, NULL, -1, 'Grayul')

        # Create a toolbar with Add, Remove, and Quit buttons
        tb = wxFloatBar(self,-1)
        addWin = wxButton(tb,self.ID_ADD,'Add new window')
        removeWin = wxButton(tb,self.ID_REMOVE,
                             'Remove current window')
        quit = wxButton(tb,self.ID_QUIT,'Quit')

        # Tie button clicks to some event handlers
        EVT_BUTTON(tb,self.ID_ADD,self.OnAdd)
        EVT_BUTTON(tb,self.ID_REMOVE,self.OnRemove)
        EVT_BUTTON(tb,self.ID_QUIT,self.OnQuit)

        # Add the buttons to the toolbar
        tb.AddControl(addWin)
```

```
            tb.AddControl(removeWin)
            tb.AddSeparator()
            tb.AddControl(quit)
            tb.Realize()

            self.SetToolBar(tb)
            tb.SetFloatable(1)

            # Create a notebook to hold each window
            self.note = wxNotebook(self,-1)

    def GetFileName(self):
        'Gets the name of an HTML file from the user'
        types = 'HTML files|*.html;*.htm' # Limit types to view
        dlg = wxFileDialog(self,style=wxOPEN|wxFILE_MUST_EXIST,
                           wildcard=types)
        dlg.ShowModal()
        file = dlg.GetFilename()
        dlg.Destroy()
        return file

    def OnAdd(self,event):
        'Adds a new HTML window'
        file = self.GetFileName()
        if file:
            newWin = wxHtmlWindow(self.note,-1)
            self.note.AddPage(newWin,os.path.split(file)[1],1)
            newWin.LoadPage(file)

    def OnRemove(self,event):
        'Removes the current HTML window'
        page = self.note.GetSelection()
        if page != -1:
            self.note.DeletePage(page)
            self.note.AdvanceSelection()

    def OnQuit(self,event):
        self.Destroy()

class App(wxApp):
    def OnInit(self):
        'Create the main window and insert the custom frame'
        frame = BrowserFrame()
        frame.Show(true)
        return true

# Create an app and go!
app = App(0)
app.MainLoop()
```

Figure 21-3: Build this simple viewer to display the documentation that ships with Python.

This application uses an instance of the wxFloatBar class (a wxToolbar child) to create a floating toolbar. (Try it out — click on the toolbar and drag it around the screen. Close it or move it back over its original location to dock it.) Although I just added some normal buttons, you can use the AddTool method to add icons like the ones you find on toolbars in many applications.

Using the wxNotebook class is straightforward; for each tab, create a new window that is a child of the notebook, and add it with a call to AddPage or InsertPage. Likewise, the wxHtmlWindow class is an easy way to display HTML pages. The BrowserFrame class definition contains a call to wxImage_AddHandler so that it can view CompuServe GIF files.

A PyShellWindow enables users to access a Python interpreter running in interactive mode:

```
from wxPython.wx import *
from wxPython.lib.pyshell import PyShellWindow

class App(wxApp):
    def OnInit(self):
        frame = wxFrame(None,-1,'MyPyShell')
        PyShellWindow(frame,-1)
        frame.Show(true)
        return true

app = App(0)
app.MainLoop()
```

Using wxPython Controls

wxPython ships with a comprehensive set of high-level controls, or widgets. Most often, you place them in a `wxPanel` or `wxDialog`, but they can be used elsewhere, such as in a status bar or toolbar. This section shows you what controls are available and how to use some of them; the process of controlling their layout is covered in the Controlling Layout section.

Common controls

Figure 21-4 shows most of the common controls available to you in wxPython.

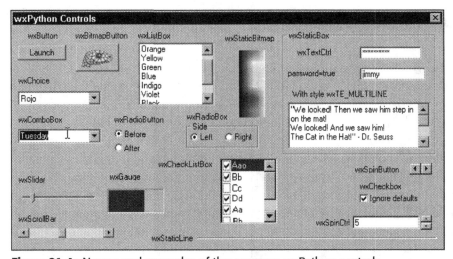

Figure 21-4: Names and examples of the common wxPython controls

You can use `wxButton` and `wxBitmapButton` to trigger an event; use the `EVT_BUTTON(id, func)` function to link a button ID and an event handler. The `FileBrowseButton` button combines a button, a file dialog, and a text entry widget so that when clicked, the user browses for a file and the chosen file name ends up in the text entry field. `FileBrowseButtonWithHistory`'s text entry field has a drop-down list in which you can store previous choices. The `wxGenButton` class is a button class that is implemented by wxPython (and not natively) so that you can customize how the button behaves and how it looks when pressed. See the `wxGenBitmapButton`, `wxGenToggleButton`, and `wxGenBitmapToggleButton` for additional variations.

Most controls let you attach event handlers when the user modifies the control's state. For example, by using the `EVT_CHECKBOX(id, func)` function, your handler function will be called anytime the checkbox is toggled.

Controls with a user-defined value (such as a text entry widget) usually have one or more Get methods to retrieve the user's input. wxSlider.GetValue(), for example, returns the current position of the slider. Controls that let users choose from a predefined set of values usually have methods such as GetSelection. wxChoice.GetSelection() returns the 0-based index of the currently selected string. Each Get method of a control usually has a corresponding Set method that you can use to programmatically set the control's state.

Tree controls

wxTreeCtrl is the standard tree control in wxPython. Use the code in Listing 21-3 to create the tree shown in Figure 21-5.

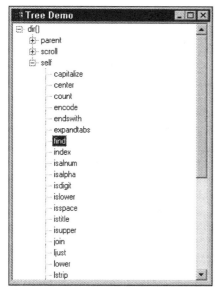

Figure 21-5: wxPython's tree control showing the results of nested dir() calls

---

Listing 21-3: **treedemo.py — Sample using wxTreeCtrl**

```
from wxPython.wx import *

class TreeFrame(wxFrame):
    def __init__(self):
        wxFrame.__init__(self, NULL, -1,
                         'Tree Demo',size=(300,400))
        # Make it a scrolled window so all data fits
        scroll = wxScrolledWindow(self,-1)
        self.tree = wxTreeCtrl(scroll)
        EVT_SIZE(scroll,self.OnSize)
```

```
        # Populate a small tree
        parent = self.tree.AddRoot('dir()')
        for i in dir():
            child = self.tree.AppendItem(parent,i)
            for j in dir(i):
                grandchild = self.tree.AppendItem(child,j)

    def OnSize(self, event):
        # Make the tree control the size of the client area
        self.tree.SetSize(self.GetClientSizeTuple())

class App(wxApp):
    def OnInit(self):
        'Create the main window and insert the custom frame'
        frame = TreeFrame()
        frame.Show(true)
        return true

app = App(0)
app.MainLoop()
```

Apart from the usual initialization work, there is code to populate the tree and to ensure that the tree control fills the entire client area of the frame (using the EVT_SIZE event function). You create a root node with a call to AddRoot, and then add children with AppendItem calls. Refer to the documentation for information about other features, including support for event notification, editing items, and using icons in the tree.

wxPython.lib.mvctree has the wxMVCTree class, which is a tree control that uses a model-view-control architecture in which code to display the information is largely independent of the code to store the data. Such a model enables you to change one with little or no change to the other.

Editor controls

The wxEditor and wxPyEditor classes (in wxPython.lib.editor) are rudimentary text editor controls (wxPyEditor is a wxEditor subclass that adds syntax highlighting). A more heavyweight and advanced edit control is wxStyledTextCtrl (in wxPython.stc). It enables you to mix different fonts and font attributes much like a word processor, and it has built-in syntax highlighting for a few languages, including Python.

Controlling Layout

When you put more than one control into a panel, dialog box, or other container, you have to decide how you want to lay out, or organize, them. In some cases, you can get by with specifying exact *x* and *y* coordinates for the controls. Other times, you need to correctly handle layout if there is a change in window size, default font (vision-impaired users often use a larger default font, for example), or platform (this *is* Python, after all). wxPython gives you several mechanisms to control the layout.

Tip It's important to learn what layout options are available to you, but if you plan to build a lot of user interfaces, consider acquiring a tool such as wxDesigner, Boa Constructor, or wxStudio to help you out.

As you learn about the different types of layout mechanisms, don't be fooled into thinking that you always have to choose one to the exclusion of another. You should use whatever works best for your particular situation, and that may mean mixing them together. You can't combine them within the same container (a panel, window, and so on), but you can have child containers use different methods. For example, your GUI could have two panels, one that uses sizers and one that uses layout constraints; and then you can lay them both out in the main window using hard-coded coordinates.

Specifying coordinates

The simplest way is occasionally the best. The constructor for every control takes two optional parameters, size and pos, that specify the control's size and position, respectively:

```
>>> from wxPython.wx import *
>>> dlg = wxDialog(None,-1,'Hey',size=(200,200))
>>> dlg.Show(1)
1
>>> dlg.SetSize((200,200))
>>> wxButton(dlg,-1,'Quit',pos=(10,100),size=(100,25))
```

Using size and pos, you can manually control the exact size and position of each control. It can be pretty tedious, however, so if this is the route you choose, build your GUI in an interactive Python session so that you can fine-tune it without having to re-run your program.

Tip After you've added a control to a container, you can adjust its size and position by calling its SetSize and SetPosition methods:

```
myButton.SetSize((200,100)) # Both methods take a tuple
```

wxWindows ships with a simple dialog editor (and documentation) that creates a WXR file describing the layout of your dialog box, and you can use WXR files in wxWindows or wxPython programs. For example, if you have a file called sample.wxr and it contains the definition for a dialog box named 'myDialog', you could open the dialog as follows:

```
...
wxResourceParseFile('sample.wxr')
dlg = wxDialog(parent, -1, '')
```

```
dlg.LoadFromResource(parent,'MyDialog')
dlg.ShowModal()
...
```

The call to `wxResourceParseFile` needs to happen only once, so you could call it during initialization.

Tip   If your dialog box looks great in wxPython's dialog editor, but looks compressed or otherwise messed up in your program, toggle the `useDialogUnits` flag in the dialog box's properties in the editor.

The downside to using fixed coordinates is that, well, they're fixed. A well-organized dialog box on one platform may look lousy on another, and if you have to change something later, you might end up doing a lot of extra work. One alternative is to create a different version of the resource file for each platform, and load the appropriate one on startup. Despite these potential problems, precise widget layout sometimes requires less effort than wxPython's other layout mechanisms, so you'll have to judge for yourself. One approach that has helped me is to sketch out on paper the GUI I plan to build and then divide it up into small groups of controls. Implement each group with a `wxPanel` that has its controls laid out at specific coordinates, and then use sizers (see the next section) to add the different groups to the window.

Sizers

Sizers are objects that help control window layout by dividing a window into subwindows that are laid out according to sizer rules. A sizer talks to all of its child objects to determine its own minimum size, which it reports to its parent. You can nest sizers inside other sizers to form an arbitrarily complex and deep nesting. The sizers you'll use are children classes of `wxSizer`, but if you want to create your own sizer type, you should derive it from `wxPySizer`.

Box sizers

`wxBoxSizer` and `wxStaticBoxSizer` are the simplest forms of sizers, and the two are the same except that `wxStaticBoxSizer` includes a `wxStaticBox` control around the outside of all of its children objects. A box sizer lays out controls to form either a row or a column, which you choose when you create the sizer:

```
sizer = wxBoxSizer(wxVERTICAL) # A sizer that creates a column

box = wxStaticBox(myFrame, -1, 'Stuff')
sizer = wxStaticBoxSizer(box, wxHORIZONTAL) # A row with border
```

The direction you choose is called its *primary orientation,* so a `wxBoxSizer` with `wxVERTICAL` has a vertical primary orientation. Once you have your sizer, you add objects to it using its `Add` or `Prepend` methods (`Add` puts the new object at the end of the group, `Prepend` at the beginning), which have the following forms:

```
sizer.Add(window, option, flag, border) # Add window or widget
sizer.Add(sizer, option, flag, border) # Add a child sizer
sizer.Add(w, h, option, flag, border) # Add a spacer
```

When you add a window or control, keep in mind that when you create the control, it is still a child of a window, *not* a sizer (so don't try to use the sizer as the parent argument in the control's constructor). You can pass to Add (or Prepend) a control or window, a child sizer (which may in turn contain other sizers), or the width and height of an invisible spacer object to pad between two items.

When the sizer is laying out its items and has extra space along its primary orientation, it looks at the option argument to determine how much extra space to give to each one. A value of 0 means that that item does not change size. If one item has an option value of 1 and another has a value of 2, the second item will get twice as much space as the first.

The flag argument is a bitwise OR of several values that tell the sizer the border type to use around the item and what it should do with extra space along the opposite, or *secondary*, orientation. The border can be any combination of wxTOP, wxBOTTOM, wxLEFT, or wxRIGHT (wxALL puts them all together for you). For example, if you want a blank border around the top and left sides of your widget, you could use a flag of wxTOP | wxLEFT.

If the flag value contains wxGROW (or wxEXPAND), the item will grow to fill the available extra space. A value of wxSHAPED means that it will grow proportionally so that it always maintains the original aspect (width-to-height) ratio. Instead of growing, the item can remain aligned against a side (by using wxALIGN_LEFT, wxALIGN_CENTER, wxALIGN_RIGHT, wxALIGN_TOP, or wxALIGN_BOTTOM).

The border argument is the number of pixels of padding around the item, and it makes sense only if the flag argument specifies one or more borders (such as wxTOP).

Tip   The sizers also have an AddMany method that you can use to combine multiple Add calls.

Call the parent window's SetSizer(sizer) method to tell it to use your new sizer. When the window's Layout() method is called, the window will lay out its contents with help from the sizer. An alternative is to call the window's SetAutoLayout(1) method so that it automatically calls Layout anytime the window size changes.

The sizer.Fit(window) method resizes the parent window to the minimum acceptable size of its contents. If you then call sizer.SetSizeHints(window), the sizer will remember the current size as the minimum and prevent the user from ever making the window smaller than that minimum.

Before all of this seeps out of your brain, try the following code so you can see a wxBoxSizer in action:

```
>>> from wxPython.wx import *
>>> f = wxFrame(None,-1,'Sizer Test')
>>> f.Show(1)
>>> sizer = wxBoxSizer(wxVERTICAL)
>>> sizer.Add(wxButton(f,-1,'One'),1,wxALL|wxALIGN_LEFT,3)
>>> sizer.Add(wxButton(f,-1,'Two'),2,wxALIGN_RIGHT)
>>> sizer.Add(wxButton(f,-1,'Three'),2,wxALL|wxALIGN_CENTER,3)
>>> sizer.Add(10,10,2,wxALL,3)
>>> sizer.Add(wxButton(f,-1,'Four'),4,wxALL|wxGROW,3)
>>> sizer.Add(wxButton(f,-1,'Five'),4,wxALL,3)
>>> f.SetAutoLayout(1)
>>> f.SetSizer(sizer)
>>> sizer.Fit(f)
>>> sizer.SetSizeHints(f)
```

Resize the window in each direction, and once you're done playing, use `f.Show(0)` to make the window go away. As shown in Figure 21-6, vertically (the primary orientation) the buttons grow according to the `option` value used (for example, button Five is four times as tall as button One). Most of the buttons have a three-pixel border on all sides, and their horizontal alignment, or stretching, follows the `flag` values.

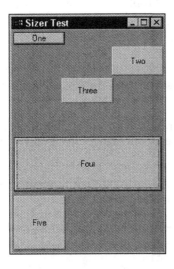

Figure 21-6: Buttons resize and align according to the rules of the box sizer.

A good exercise for you to try now would be to replace one of the buttons with a horizontal `wxBoxSizer` that also contains buttons of its own. This forms a row of buttons that are treated as a single unit by the parent sizer, but are laid out individually by the child sizer. This will help you see how you can use a hierarchy of nested sizers to achieve a complex layout.

Grid sizers

`wxGridSizer` lays out objects in a table. The width of each column is the width of the widest item in the grid; and the height of each row is that of the tallest item. You create this sizer by calling `wxGridSizer([rows|cols]=n)`, where n is the number of rows or columns you want. You choose either `rows` or `cols` to limit the number of rows or columns, and `wxGridSizer` figures out the correct value for the other dimension. For example, if you set a limit of two rows and then added seven buttons to the sizer, the first row would have the first four buttons, and then second row would have the last three buttons.

`wxFlexGridSizer` is like `wxGridSizer` except that instead of having uniform column and row sizes, each column is the width of the widest item in that column only; and the height of each row is that of the tallest item in that row only.

Layout constraints

Layout constraints define the size and position of an item in terms of its siblings or parents. Each item has eight constraints that you can define: four for the edges (left, right, top, and bottom), two for the size (width and height), and two for its center (*x*, *y*). For example, you might constrain a button by specifying that its height should be left unchanged, its left edge should be aligned with that of some other button, its width should be half that of the parent panel, and its center *y* coordinate should match that of some other widget's top:

```
wc = wxLayoutConstraints()
wc.height.AsIs() # "Don't change it"
wc.left.SameAs(someButton, wxLeft)
wc.width.PercentOf(parentPanel, 50)
wc.centerY.SameAs(someOtherWidget, wxTop)
myButton.SetConstraints(wc)
```

You usually have to specify four of the eight constraints in order for the widget to be *fully constrained*. Once it is fully constrained, the layout algorithm can deduce the remaining constraints on its own.

The constraint names are `left`, `right`, `top`, `bottom`, `width`, `height`, `centerX`, and `centerY`. You can call the following methods for each constraint:

`Above(win[, margin])`, `Below(win[, margin])`, `LeftOf(win[, margin])`, `RightOf(win[,margin])`	Sets the constraint to be above, below, to the left of, or to the right of the window `win`, with an optional `margin`
`Absolute(value)`	Sets the constraint to this value. For example, `wc.left.Absolute(10)` gives the left edge an *x* coordinate of 10.
`AsIs()`	Does not change the constraint's current value
`Unconstrained()`	Returns this constraint to its default state

| PercentOf
(win,edge,percent) | Makes the current constraint a percentage of the given edge of the given window |
| SameAs
(win, edge[, margin]) | Makes the current constraint the same as the given edge of the given window |

As with sizers, you can call a window's Layout() method to perform the layout, or you can call SetAutoLayout(1) so that Layout is called each time the parent window is resized.

Layout algorithms

For MDI or SDI applications, you can use the wxLayoutAlgorithm class to lay out subwindows. Study the wxLayoutAlgorithm and wxSashLayoutWindow documentation for more information.

Using Built-in Dialogs

One of wxPython's strengths is its rich set of built-in dialogs that you can use to get user input. In general, the way you use each dialog follows this pattern (the example here uses a dialog that has the user choose a directory name):

```
dlg = wxDirDialog(None)            # Create it
if dlg.ShowModal() == wxID_OK:     # Check the return code
        path = dlg.GetPath()       # Read user's input
dlg.Destroy()                      # Destroy it
```

The dialog's ShowModal method usually returns wxID_OK or wxID_CANCEL, and each dialog has its own set of methods you use to retrieve the user's input.

Table 21-1 describes some of wxPython's useful built-in dialogs.

Table 21-1
Useful wxPython Dialogs

Class	Use the Dialog To
wxDirDialog	Browse for a directory name
wxFileDialog	Browse for a file name
wxFontDialog	Choose a font, point size, color, and so on
wxColourDialog	Choose a color
wxPrintDialog	Select a printer

Continued

Table 21-1 *(continued)*	
Class	**Use the Dialog To**
wxPageSetupDialog	Modify page orientation and margins
wxProgressDialog	Display a moving progress meter
wxMessageDialog	Display a simple message
wxScrolledMessageDialog	Display a longer message in a scrollable window
wxSingleChoiceDialog	Choose an item from a list
wxMultipleChoiceDialog	Choose one or more items from a list
wxTextEntryDialog	Enter a line of text
wxBusyInfo	Notify the user that the program is temporarily busy

The wxBusyInfo dialog is unique in that the dialog appears as soon as you create it, and it disappears when the object goes out of scope:

```
def rollbackChanges(self):
    wxBusyInfo('Reverting to previous state...')
    # Do some work, dialog destroyed automagically when done
```

Drawing with Device Contexts

Like some other GUI frameworks, wxPython uses *device contexts* as an abstraction for displaying information on some output device. All device contexts are descendents of the wxDC class, so code that outputs to a device context automatically works whether the output device is the screen, a printer, or just a file. Table 21-2 lists some common device context classes.

Table 21-2 wxPython Device Context Classes	
Class	**Outputs To**
wxWindowDC	An entire window, including title bars and borders
wxClientDC	Window client area outside of the OnPaint method
wxPaintDC	Window client area during a call to OnPaint
wxPrinterDC	A Microsoft Windows printer
wxPostScriptDC	A PostScript file or printer
wxMemoryDC	A bitmap
wxMetaFileDC	A Microsoft Windows metafile

Device contexts give you a large number of methods to perform all sorts of actions, including clipping; writing text; converting between different units; and drawing graphics primitives, including lines, arcs, and splines.

Tip   To ensure that your programs work on Microsoft Windows, before drawing, call the device context's `BeginDrawing()` method; and call its `EndDrawing()` method when you're done.

The device context uses the current *pen* to draw lines and outlines; pens (wxPen) have attributes such as line thickness and color. Text color is not affected by pen color. To fill in regions, it uses the current *brush* (wxBrush), which can have both a color and a pattern that it uses when filling.

The program in Listing 21-4 shows you how to use a device context to paint on the screen, and generates output as shown in Figure 21-7.

Listing 21-4: **wxcanvas.py – An example of drawing with device contexts**

```
from wxPython.wx import *
import whrandom

class CanvasFrame(wxFrame):
    # A list of stock brushes we can use instead of
    # creating our own
    brushes = [wxBLACK_BRUSH,wxBLUE_BRUSH,
               wxCYAN_BRUSH,wxGREEN_BRUSH,
               wxGREY_BRUSH,wxRED_BRUSH,wxWHITE_BRUSH]

    def __init__(self):
        wxFrame.__init__(self,None,-1,
                         'CanvasFrame',size=(550,350))
        self.SetBackgroundColour (wxNamedColor("WHITE"))

        # Capture the paint message
        EVT_PAINT(self, self.OnPaint)

    def OnPaint(self, event):
        dc = wxPaintDC(self)
        dc.BeginDrawing()

        # Draw a grid of randomly colored boxes
        for y in range(15):
            for x in range(10):
                dc.SetBrush(whrandom.choice(self.brushes))
                dc.DrawRectangle(x*20,y*20,20,20)

        # Draw a random polygon over the boxes
        # (Outline is in blue, but fill color is that
```

Continued

Listing 21-4 *(continued)*

```
            # of the last box it drew)
            dc.SetPen(wxPen(wxNamedColour ('BLUE')))
            pts = []
            for i in range(20):
                pts.append((whrandom.randint(0,200),
                            whrandom.randint(0,300)))
            dc.DrawPolygon(pts)

            # Draw some rotated text
            font = wxFont(20, wxNORMAL, wxNORMAL, wxNORMAL)
            font.SetFaceName('Jokerman LET')
            dc.SetFont(font)
            for a in range(0, 360, 20):
                c = a * 0.71 # 360/255, fit angle into color range
                dc.SetTextForeground(wxColour (c,c,c))
                dc.DrawRotatedText("      wxPython", 350, 150, a)

            dc.EndDrawing()

class App(wxApp):
    def OnInit(self):
        'Create the main window and insert the custom frame'
        frame = CanvasFrame()
        frame.Show(true)
        return true

app = App(0)
app.MainLoop()
```

Figure 21-7: Using device contexts to draw graphics

The __init__ function calls EVT_PAINT so that the OnPaint method will be called each time the screen needs to be redrawn. Notice that OnPaint creates a wxPaintDC for drawing, and that it begins and ends with calls to BeginDrawing and EndDrawing.

Adding Menus and Keyboard Shortcuts

Your wxPython application can have popup menus or groups of menus on a menu bar at the top of a frame. Individual menu items can be disabled or grayed out, and each can have an associated line of help text.

A menu consists of one or more menu items, each of which has a unique numerical identifier. Create a menu by calling wxMenu([title]), and add items with its Append(id, name) method:

```
menu = wxMenu()
menu.Append(10, 'Load')
menu.Append(11, 'Save')
menu.Append(12, 'Quit')
```

The menu title is displayed as part of the menu's contents. Create a menu bar by calling wxMenuBar(). Attach a menu to a menu bar by calling the menu bar's Append(menu, title) method:

```
mb = wxMenuBar()
mb.Append(menu, 'File')
```

Finally, call a frame's SetMenuBar(bar) method to attach the menu bar to the frame:

```
frame.SetMenuBar(mb)
```

Tip   By creating menu items separately as wxMenuItems, you can create more powerful menu items, such as menu items with bitmaps.

Accelerators are keyboard shortcuts for commands users would normally have to generate with the mouse (clicking a menu item, for example). By calling a window's SetAcceleratorTable(table) method, you can assign a group of shortcuts to that window. You create an accelerator table by calling the wxAcceleratorTable(list) constructor, where list is a list of accelerator entry tuples of the form (flag, code, command). flag is a bitwise-OR combination of keypress modifiers such as wxACCEL_ALT and wxACCEL_SHIFT, and code is the ASCII code of the keypress or one of wxPython's many special key variables, such as WXF_10 (for the F10 key) or WXK_END (the End key). command is the menu item identifier. For example:

```
accel = [(wxACCEL_CTRL,WXK_ESCAPE,10),
         (wxACCEL_NORMAL,WXK_ESCAPE,11),
         (wxACCEL_CTRL|wxACCEL_SHIFT,WXK_F1,12)]
frame.SetAcceleratorTable(wxAcceleratorTable(accel))
```

enables Ctrl-Esc, Esc, and Ctrl-Shift-F1 as accelerators for menu commands 10 through 12.

Accessing Mouse and Keyboard Input

Most input events are handled by wxPython directly. When a user clicks a button, for example, the window automatically processes the clicking and releasing of the mouse button. If necessary, however, you can intercept and handle this lower-level input.

When you call EVT_CHAR(win, func), future keystrokes ("normal" keys, but not modifiers such as Ctrl or Shift) directed to win will cause wxKeyEvents to be sent to func. Use EVT_CHAR_HOOK to catch modifier keypresses, and EVT_KEY_UP and EVT_KEY_DOWN to be notified when keys are pressed or released.

Tip   Only one window has keyboard focus at any time, so your window will receive keystroke notifications only if it has the focus. Use the window's SetFocus() method to acquire keyboard focus.

If you want only to intercept some input but let wxPython handle the rest, your handler function can pass the input on to the window's normal handler. For example, if you want a keypress to be interpreted using the normal behavior, your handler should call the window's OnChar method.

For catching mouse button click events, use EVT_LEFT_DOWN, EVT_LEFT_UP, and EVT_DCLICK to capture mouse left button presses, releases, and double-clicks, respectively. There are corresponding functions for the middle and right buttons as well.

EVT_MOTION causes each mouse movement to be reported, and use EVT_ENTER_WINDOW and EVT_LEAVE_WINDOW to be notified when the window has mouse focus. If you want to process all mouse events, just use EVT_MOUSE_EVENTS to capture them all.

Other wxPython Features

As mentioned before, wxPython has far more features than can adequately be covered in one chapter. This final section is here to pique your interest enough to do some investigating on your own, and to ensure that you don't invest a lot of time implementing something that wxPython already has.

Clipboard, drag and drop, and cursors

You can create and change mouse cursors and tool tips with the `wxCursor` and `wxToolTip` classes and their children.

The `wxClipboard`, `wxDataFormat`, and `wxDataObject` class hierarchies implement support for transferring data to and from the clipboard and converting it between different formats. The `wxDragImage` class is useful for implementing your own visual representation of dragging a file or other object in your application. See the `wxDropSource` and `wxDropTarget` classes too.

By calling a window's `SetCursor(cursor)` method, the mouse cursor will change to the given cursor any time it enters the window. You can create your own cursor or use one of the built-in cursors:

```
myFrame.SetCursor(wxStockCursor(wxCURSOR_BULLSEYE))
```

Graphics

The Object Graphics Library (OGL) is a library for creating and easily manipulating flowcharts and other graphs. See the `wxShapeCanvas`, `wxShape`, and `wxDiagram` classes for more information.

`wxBitmap`, `wxImage`, and `wxIcon` all deal with loading and displaying images in different ways. For each file type you use, you must load a `wxImageHandler` instance that handles decoding the image data (wxPython comes with several, such as `wxJPEGHandler` and `wxGIFHandler`). See also the `wxMask` and `wxPalette` classes.

If you have installed the PyOpenGL extension module, you can use `wxGLCanvas` to include an OpenGL window in your application.

Date and time

wxPython has powerful date and time support (covering dates even hundreds of millions of years in the future). `wxDateTime` represents a specific point in time, whereas `wxDateSpan` and `wxTimeSpan` represent intervals.

The `wxCalendarCtrl` is a control that looks like a wall calendar and is useful for both displaying and inputting dates.

Fonts

`wxFont` objects hold information about fonts, and `wxFontData` objects hold information about the dialogs users use to choose fonts and set font properties.

HTML

The wxPython.html module contains classes for parsing, printing, and displaying HTML pages in a window or a device context.

Printing

wxPrintDialog and wxPageSetupDialog wrap two dialogs used for configuring the printer and page in preparation for printing, and wxPrinter and wxPrintout take care of the actual printing. There are also the wxPrintPreview and wxPreviewFrames classes for supporting print preview.

Other

Finally, if you're using Windows and want to use COM, you can dynamically create a wxWindows-like class to embed any ActiveX control in your application by using wxPython.lib.activexwrapper.MakeActiveXClass.

Summary

wxPython is a powerful library for creating cross-platform GUI applications. It has a full set of simple and high-level controls, including built-in support for trees and tables; and it is very easy to use. In this chapter you:

✦ Learned the basic structure of most wxPython applications.

✦ Created powerful and functional GUI-based applications in very few lines of code.

✦ Used wxPython's built-in dialogs for browsing for files, choosing colors, and so on.

✦ Reviewed the different types of windows, controls, and features that wxPython provides.

The next chapter shows you how to use the *curses* (not the spoken kind) library to create text-based user interfaces.

✦   ✦   ✦

Using Curses

◆ ◆ ◆ ◆

In This Chapter

A Curses overview

Starting up and
shutting down

Displaying and
erasing text

Moving the cursor

Getting user input

Managing windows

Editing text

Using color

Example: a simple
maze game

◆ ◆ ◆ ◆

Curses is a library for handling a text-based display terminal. It is widely used on UNIX. It can handle text windows,
colors, and keyboard input. Moreover, it saves you the trouble
of learning the control codes for every kind of terminal.

A Curses Overview

In ancient days of yore, there was not a computer in every
office. People used terminals like the VT100 to connect to a
central system. These terminals displayed a grid on which
each square contained a text character. Sending control codes
to the terminal could change the color, move the cursor, and
so on. However, the magical control codes varied between
systems. Therefore, a program that produced cute output on a
Tektronix 4105 terminal might have produced bizarre symbol
salad on a VT230.

The *curses* library was born as a portable tool for text display.
It has been eclipsed by *ncurses*, which adds some features.
The Python module curses is a thin wrapper for the ncurses
API. The various functions in the curses API have some overlap — for example, the window methods addch, addstr, and
addnstr all print text. For purposes of brevity, this chapter
omits many redundant items.

Curses provides a class, WindowObject, for display. You can
use one or more windows, resize them, move them, and so
forth.

Note   In curses, the top-left corner square of the screen has coordinates (0,0). Screen coordinates in curses are given with
vertical position first — (y, x). This is the opposite of the
usual ordering, so be careful not to get your coordinates
reversed!

Listing 22-1 provides a simple curses program. Run it to get
some quick gratification (and to make sure that curses is
installed on your system!)

Listing 22-1: CurseWorld.py

```
import curses
try:
    MainWindow=curses.initscr() # initialize curses
    MainWindow.addstr("Hello, damn it!")
    MainWindow.refresh()
    MainWindow.getch() # Read a keystroke
finally:
    curses.endwin() # de-initialize curses
```

Starting Up and Shutting Down

The function initscr initializes curses and returns a Window object representing the whole screen. The function endwin de-initializes curses. The function isendwin returns true if endwin has been called.

The module function wrapper(mainfunc,*args) handles typical setup and shutdown for you. Calling wrapper sets up curses, creates a window, and calls mainfunc(window,*args). It also restores the terminal to normal when your main function completes, even if it terminates abnormally. This is important, because a curses program that doesn't call endwin may leave the shell in a highly weird state! For reference, wrapper does (and later undoes) the following things:

✦ Creates a window (curses.initscr())

✦ Turns off echo (curses.noecho())

✦ Turns off keyboard buffering (curses.cbreak())

✦ Activates color, where available (curses.start_color())

Caution   The functions filter and use_env, which must be called before initscr, do not work (as of Python 2.0 and 2.1).

Displaying and Erasing Text

The window method addstr([y,x,]text[,attributes]) prints the string *text* at screen position (*y, x*) — by default, at the current cursor position. You can specify attributes to control the appearance of the text. Attributes can be combined by bit-wise-OR. See Table 22-1 for a list of available text attributes:

Table 22-1
Text Attributes

Attribute	Meaning
A_BLINK	Blinking text
A_BOLD	Bold text
A_DIM	Dim text
A_NORMAL	Ordinary text
A_STANDOUT	Highlighted text
A_UNDERLINE	Underlined text

For example, the following code prints a bold, blinking "Howdy!" at column 50 of row 5:

```
MainWindow.addstr(5,50,"Howdy!",curses.A_BLINK | curses.A_BOLD)
```

Inserting

addstr overwrites any text that was already on the window. To insert text, call insstr([y,x,]str[,attributes]). Any characters on the line are moved to the right; characters moved off the right edge of the screen are lost. A call to insertln inserts a blank row under the cursor; all following rows move down by one.

Default attributes

The method attrset(attributes) sets the default attributes for all subsequent calls to addstr. The methods attron(attribute) and attroff(attribute) toggle one default attribute.

Reading from the window (screen-scraping)

The method inch(y,x) returns the character at the given window position. Actually, it returns the character as a number in the lower eight bits, and the attributes in the upper twenty-four bits. Therefore, the following code would check for a bold X at row 3, column 10:

```
Character= MainWindow.inch(3,10)
Letter = chr(Character & 0xFF)
Attributes = Character & (~0xFF)
return ((Attributes & curses.A_BOLD) and (Letter=="X"))
```

The method instr([y,x,]n) returns a string of *n* characters, extracted from the specified screen position. It ignores attribute information.

Erasing

The method `erase` clears the window. `clrtoeol` erases from the current cursor position to the end of the line; `clrtobot` also clears all lines below the cursor. The method `delch([y,x])` erases a single character (by default, the one under the cursor) — characters to its right move left by one square. `deleteln` deletes the line under the cursor — any following lines move up by one row.

Refreshing

After changing the contents of a window, call its `refresh` method to repaint the actual screen. If you get tired of calling `refresh`, call `immedok(flag)` to set the "immediate refresh" flag — if the flag is set, the window will be repainted after every change. However, note that this can result in reduced speed and/or flickering.

If you are using several windows at once, the most efficient way to repaint is to call the `noutrefresh` method of a window (instead of `refresh`), and then call the `doupdate` function.

You can flag a window as "dirty" to ensure that it will be redrawn at the next refresh call. The methods `touchwin` and `untouchwin` mark the entire window as dirty or clean, respectively. `touchline(y,count)` marks *count* lines as dirty, starting with line *y*. The methods `is_linetouched(y)` and `is_wintouched` return true if the specified line, or the window itself, is dirty.

Boxes and lines

The method `border` draws a border around the window's edges. The border is made up of individual characters. If you like, you can specify the characters to display, by passing them (as integers) to `border(W,E,N,S,NW,NE,SW,SE)`. Here, *S* is the character to use for the bottom edge, *NE* is the character to use for the top-right corner, and so forth. Pass 0 as a character to use the default.

You can draw an arbitrary box by calling `curses.textpad.rectangle(window,Top,Left,Bottom,Right)`. The box uses line-drawing characters where available. Otherwise, it will fall back to standard ASCII-art pluses, pipes, and dashes.

The window background

Windows have a background. The method `bkgdset(character[,attributes])` changes the window's background. When the window (or a portion of it) is erased, it is painted with *character*, with the specified attributes. Furthermore, the specified attributes are combined with any nonblank characters drawn on the window. The similar method `bkgd(character[,attributes])` immediately paints blank squares of the window with *character*.

Example: masking a box

Listing 22-2 illustrates a simple Mask class, for temporarily covering a part of the screen. A mask can cover a rectangular block of a window with a call to cover, and then restore the original text with a call to reveal.

Listing 22-2: Mask.py

```
import curses
class Mask:
    def __init__(self,Window,Top,Bottom,Left,Right):
        self.Window=Window
        self.Top=Top
        self.Bottom=Bottom
        self.Left=Left
        self.Right=Right
        self.OldText=None
    def Cover(self,Character="X",Attributes=curses.A_DIM):
        # Cover the current screen contents. Store
        # them in OldText[RowIndex][ColumnIndex] for later:
        self.OldText=[]
        for Row in range(self.Top,self.Bottom+1):
            self.OldText.append([])
            for Col in range(self.Left, self.Right+1):
                self.OldText[-1].append(\
                    self.Window.inch(Row,Col))
                self.Window.addstr(Row,Col,
                    Character,Attributes)
    def Reveal(self):
        if (self.OldText==None): return
        for Row in range(self.Top,self.Bottom+1):
            CurrentLine=self.OldText[Row-self.Top]
            for Col in range(self.Left, self.Right+1):
                CurrentCol=(Col-self.Left)
                Character=chr(CurrentLine[CurrentCol] & 0xFF)
                Attributes=CurrentLine[CurrentCol] & (~0xFF)
                self.Window.addstr(Row,Col,
                    Character,Attributes)

def Main(MainWindow):
    MainWindow.addstr(10,10,"Yes it is!")
    MainWindow.addstr(11,10,"No it isn't!",curses.A_BOLD)
    MainWindow.addstr(12,10,"Yes it is!",curses.A_UNDERLINE)
    MainWindow.addstr(13,10,"No it isn't!",curses.A_STANDOUT)
    MainWindow.addstr(14,10,"YES IT IS!",curses.A_BOLD)
    MyMask=Mask(MainWindow,10,20,10,40)
    MainWindow.refresh()
    MainWindow.getch()
```

Continued

Listing 22-2 *(continued)*

```
        MyMask.Cover()
        MainWindow.refresh()
        MainWindow.getch()
        MyMask.Reveal()
        MainWindow.refresh()
        MainWindow.getch()

if (__name__=="__main__"):
    curses.wrapper(Main)
```

Moving the Cursor

The function getsyx returns the cursor's screen position in the form of a tuple (*y*, *x*). The function setsyx(y,x) moves the cursor to the specified position.

The window methods getyx and move(y,x) check and set the cursor position within a window. If the window fills the screen (as the window returned by a call to initscr does), window positioning is the same as screen positioning.

The window method getparyx returns the window's coordinates relative to its parent window. These coordinates are the location (in the parent) of the window's top-left corner. If the window has no parent, getparyx returns (-1, -1). Note that cursor position is tracked independently by every window.

The window method getmaxyx returns the size of the window in a tuple of the form (height, width). Note that getmaxyx()[0] is *not* a valid *y*-coordinate, as row numbering is 0-based; the last row of the screen has *y*-coordinate getmaxyx()[0]-1. The same is true for *x*-coordinates.

The window method leaveok (flag) toggles the "Leave-the-cursor-where-it-is-after-repainting-the screen" flag. Calling leaveok(1) is a good idea if a blinking cursor won't convey useful information to the user. If the flag is set, getsyx returns (-1, -1); calling setsyx(-1,-1) sets the flag to true.

The function curs_set(visibility) sets the cursor visibility to 0 (invisible); 1 (visible — often an underline); or 2 (very visible — often a block). The return value of curs_set is the old visibility level.

Listing 22-3 paints a spiral pattern on the window, using cursor positioning.

Listing 22-3: **Spiral.py**

```
import curses
import math

def DrawSpiral(Window,CenterY,CenterX,Height,Width):
    ScalingFactor=1.0
    Angle=0
    HalfHeight = float(Height)/2
    HalfWidth = float(Width)/2
    while (ScalingFactor>0):
        Y = CenterY +
            (HalfHeight*math.sin(Angle)*ScalingFactor)
        X = CenterX + (HalfWidth*math.cos(Angle)*ScalingFactor)
        Window.move(int(Y),int(X))
        Window.addstr("*")
        Angle+=0.05
        ScalingFactor=ScalingFactor - 0.001
        Window.refresh()

def Main(Window):
    (Height,Width)=Window.getmaxyx()
    Height-=1 # Don't make the spiral too big
    Width-=1
    CenterY=Height/2
    CenterX=Width/2
    DrawSpiral(Window,CenterY,CenterX,Height,Width)
    Window.getch()

if __name__=="__main__":
    curses.wrapper(Main)
```

Getting User Input

Curses starts out in *cooked* mode — the user's keyboard input is buffered and pro-cessed one line at a time. In *raw* mode, buffering is turned off, and keys are pro-cessed as they are pressed. Call the functions raw and noraw to toggle between modes.

In addition, you can call cbreak and nocbreak to switch cbreak mode (also known as "rare" mode) on and off. The difference between cbreak and raw is that special characters (such as suspend) lose their normal effects in raw mode. The four modes (raw, noraw, cbreak, and nocbreak) are mutually exclusive.

The window method keypad(flag) toggles keypad mode for a window. If keypad mode is *not* set, special character codes are not interpreted by curses. This means that special keystrokes such as function keys will put several special characters into the keyboard buffer, extended keystrokes will not be available, and mouse events will not be available. In general, you want keypad mode on!

Call echo and noecho to toggle the automatic echoing of user input to the screen. By default, echoing is on; curses.wrapper turns echoing off and switches to cbreak mode.

Reading keys

The window method getch reads a character and returns it as an integer. For an ASCII character, the value returned is the character's ASCII value (as returned by ord); other characters (such as function keys) may return non-ASCII values. The method getkey reads a character, returning it as a string.

Both getch and getkey are normally synchronous; they wait until the user presses a key. The method nodelay(flag) makes them synchronous if *flag* is true. In synchronous mode, if no keypress is available, the methods return getch and getkey which return -1 and "-1", respectively.

The method getstr reads a string from the user, handling things such as backspacing in the process. Note that getstr doesn't play well with nodelay or noecho. In fact, getstr is quite primitive; see "Editing Text" for a more pleasant way to extract input from your users.

Other keyboard-related functions

You can throw a character onto the keyboard buffer by calling the function ungetch(character). The next call to getch will return *character*. You can only "un-get" one character at a time.

A call to the function flushinp clears out the input buffers, throwing away any pending input that you haven't processed yet.

Fancy characters

When keypad mode is active, control characters are interpreted for you by curses. Most of these characters have corresponding constants. For example, the following code fragment checks whether the user pressed F5:

```
Char=Window.getch()
if Char==curses.KEY_F5:
    # do stuff!
```

Arrow keys (where available) are represented by KEY_UP, KEY_LEFT, KEY_RIGHT, and KEY_DOWN. See the curses documentation for a complete list of these constants.

In addition, the module curses.ascii provides constants and functions for cleanly handling ASCII characters. For example, curses.ascii.SP is equal to 32 (the ASCII value for a space); curses.ascii.BEL is 7 (the bell-character; Ctrl-G on most systems).

Reading mouse input

In order to detect mouse events, you must call the function mousemask(mask), where mask represents the mouse events you want to see. The return value has the form (available,old). Here, *available* is a mask of the events that will be reported (hopefully, the same as mask), and *old* is the old event mask. For example, the following code tries to watch for clicks and double-clicks of button 1 (the left button):

```
(available,old) = curses.mousemask(curses.BUTTON1_PRESSED |
                              curses.BUTTON2_PRESSED)
if (available & curses.BUTTON1_PRESSED):
    CanSeeClick=1
else:
    CanSeeClick=0
```

You also need to turn keypad mode on; otherwise, mouse events are not visible.

Mouse events are first signaled by a value of KEY_MOUSE passed to getch. At this point, you can examine the mouse input with a call to the function getmouse. The return value is a tuple of the form (id, x, y, z, state). Here, *x* and *y* are the coordinates of the mouse click, *state* is the event type, and *id* and *z* can be safely ignored.

Table 22-2 describes all the available mouse events. A particular event (or event mask) may be a bitwise-OR or several of them. The pound sign (#) represents a number from 1 to 4.

Table 22-2
Mouse Events

Name	Meaning
BUTTON#_PRESSED	Button # was pressed
BUTTON#_RELEASED	Button # was released
BUTTON#_CLICKED	Button # was clicked
BUTTON#_DOUBLE_CLICKED	Button # was double-clicked
BUTTON#_TRIPLE_CLICKED	Button # was triple-clicked
BUTTON_SHIFT	Button was Shift-clicked
BUTTON_CTRL	Button was Control-clicked
BUTTON_ALT	Button was Alt-clicked

The function ungetmouse(id,x,y,z,state), **similar to** ungetch, **pushes a mouse** event back onto the buffer.

Example: yes, no, or maybe

The program shown in Listing 22-4 provides three options, and lets the user choose one either by clicking it or by pressing a key.

Listing 22-4: **Deathray.py**

```
import curses
import curses.textpad
import whrandom

class CursesButton:
    def __init__(self,Window,Y,X,Label,Hotkey=0):
        self.Y=Y
        self.X=X
        self.Label=Label
        self.Width=len(Label)+2 # label, plus lines on side
        self.Underline=Underline
        # Draw the button:
        curses.textpad.rectangle(Window,Y,X,Y+2,X+self.Width)
        # Draw the button label:
        Window.addstr(Y+1,X+1,Label,curses.A_BOLD)
        # Make the hotkey stand out:
        Window.addstr(Y+1,X+Underline+1,Label[Underline]
            ,curses.A_REVERSE)
        Window.refresh()
    def KeyPressed(self,Char):
        if (Char>255): return 0 # skip control-characters
        if chr(Char).upper()==self.Label[self.Underline]:
            return 1
        else:
            return 0
    def MouseClicked(self,MouseEvent):
        (id,x,y,z,event)=MouseEvent
        if (self.Y <= y <= self.Y+2) and \
           (self.X <= x < self.X+self.Width):
            return 1
        else:
            return 0

def ShowDialog(Window):
    curses.mousemask(curses.BUTTON1_PRESSED)
    Window.addstr(5,0,"Really, REALLY fire death ray?")
    YesButton=CursesButton(Window,8,10,"Yes")
    NoButton=CursesButton(Window,8,20,"No")
    MaybeButton=CursesButton(Window,8,30,"Maybe")
    Buttons=[YesButton,NoButton,MaybeButton]
    Window.nodelay(1)
```

```
        Action=""
        while 1:
            Key=Window.getch()
            if (Key==-1):
                continue
            for Button in Buttons:
                if Button.KeyPressed(Key):
                    Action=Button.Label
            # Handle mouse-events:
            if (Key==curses.KEY_MOUSE):
                MouseEvent=curses.getmouse()
                for Button in Buttons:
                    if Button.MouseClicked(MouseEvent):
                        Action=Button.Label
            if Action!="": break
        # Handle the actions
        if (Action=="Yes"):
            FireDeathRay(Window)
        if (Action=="No"):
            pass
        if (Action=="Maybe" and whrandom.random() > 0.5):
            FireDeathRay(Window)

    def FireDeathRay(Window):
        Window.clear()
        # Kra-ppoowwww!  Frrrraapppp!!
        Window.bkgd("X")
        Window.nodelay(0)
        Window.getch()

    if __name__=="__main__":
        curses.wrapper(ShowDialog)
```

Managing Windows

You can create a new, parentless window by calling the function
newwin([lines,columns,]y,x). The new window's top-left corner will be at
(*y*, *x*). It will have *height* lines and *width* columns — by default, it will stretch to the
bottom-right edge of the screen. Similarly, you can create a subwindow within an
existing window by calling the method subwin([lines,columns,]y,x).

The method mvwin(y,x) moves a window so that its upper-left corner is at (*y*, *x*).

Pads

A *pad* is similar to a window, except that it can be larger than the screen. It is a convenient way to make more data available than you can show all at once. It supports
all the methods of a window, but has a different refresh method.

The function `newpad(rows, columns)` creates a pad of the given size. To draw the pad's contents, call `refresh(screenY,screenX,padTop,padLeft,padBottom, padRight)`. A region within the pad will be displayed, with its top-left corner at (*screenY,screenX*). The pad contents displayed lie in the rectangle with corners (*padTop,padLeft*) and (*padBottom,padRight*).

Stacking windows

The module curses.panel allows you to cleanly "stack" windows on top of each other so that only the visible portion of each window is displayed. The function `new_panel(Window)` returns a panel that wraps the specified window. You can change the panel's stacking position by calling its methods `bottom` and `top`. You can hide and reveal panels by calling `hide` and `show`. After changing patterns, call the function `update_panels` to update the virtual screen, then `curses.doupdate` to repaint the screen. The function `bottom_panel` returns the bottom-most panel, and `top_panel` returns the topmost panel.

Editing Text

The module `curses.textpad` provides a class, Textbox, for convenient text editing. The constructor takes one argument: the window in which to place the Textbox.

Once you have a Textbox, you can call `edit([validator])` to let the user enter data, and call `gather` to retrieve the Textbox's contents (as a string). The user can type text, scroll around the Textbox, and finish input by pressing Ctrl-G (or Enter, if the window has only one line). Because `gather` returns the *entire* window's contents, you generally want to create a special window for use by only your Textbox.

Table 22-3 describes the commands available within a Textbox.

Table 22-3 Textbox Commands	
Keystroke	**Action**
Ctrl-A	Go to left edge of window
Ctrl-B	Cursor left, wrapping to previous line if appropriate
Ctrl-D	Delete character under cursor
Ctrl-E	Go to right edge (stripspaces off) or end of line (stripspaces on)
Ctrl-F	Cursor right, wrapping to next line when appropriate

Keystroke	Action
Ctrl-G	Terminate, returning the window contents
Ctrl-H	Delete character backward
Ctrl-J	Terminate if the window is one line; otherwise, insert newline
Ctrl-K	If line is blank, delete it; otherwise, clear to end of line
Ctrl-L	Refresh screen
Ctrl-N	Cursor down; move down one line
Ctrl-O	Insert a blank line at cursor location
Ctrl-P	Cursor up; move up one line

You can, optionally, pass a callback function to edit([validator]). This function is called whenever the user presses a key, and the keystroke is passed as a parameter. The return value of *validator,* if any, is passed along to the Textbox. For instance, use the following if you want Esc to finish input in your Textbox:

```
def Validator(Ch):
    if Ch==curses.ascii.ESC:
        return curses.ascii.BEL
    else:
        return Ch
```

Using Color

The function has_colors returns true if the terminal can display colors. The method start_color initializes color display; it should be called immediately after initscr.

Numbering

Colors come in two forms: color *numbers* and color *pairs*. Color numbers range from 0 to COLORS; they identify a color in the curses palette. Color pairs are valid attributes to pass to Window.addstr; they identify a foreground color number and a background color number. Therefore, each color pair is basically a pair of color numbers.

Just to make things more interesting, color pairs are also numbered. Try not to confuse pair numbers with color numbers. (Go on, I dare you — try! Actually, the whole system starts to make sense after a while.)

The function `color_pair(number)` returns the color pair corresponding to the given pair number; the opposite function, `pair_number(pair)`, returns the pair number of a color pair.

Setting colors

Color pair 0 is always white on black. You can change the colors of the other pairs by calling `init_pair(pair_number, foreground, background)`. Here *background* and *foreground* are color numbers. The function `pair_content(pair_number)` returns the pair's current colors as a tuple of the form (foreground,background).

The constants COLOR_BLACK, COLOR_RED, COLOR_GREEN, COLOR_YELLOW, COLOR_BLUE, COLOR_MAGENTA, COLOR_CYAN and COLOR_WHITE are available to denote the corresponding color numbers. For example, the following code draws a simple German flag:

```
# In the next line, 1 is the number of a
# color-pair, while curses.WHITE is a
# color-number:
curses.init_pair(1,curses.WHITE,curses.BLACK)
curses.init_pair(2,curses.WHITE,curses.RED)
curses.init_pair(3,curses.WHITE,curses.YELLOW)
Window.addstr(0,0," "*10,curses.color_pair(1))
Window.addstr(1,0," "*10,curses.color_pair(2))
Window.addstr(2,0," "*10,curses.color_pair(3))
```

Tweaking the colors

Defining colors is not possible on most terminals. The function `can_change_color` returns true on those terminals where it is. A call to `init_color(number, red, green, blue)` redefines color number to have the specified intensities of red, green, and blue. Intensity ranges from 0 to 1,000. The function `color_content(number)` returns the current definition of color *number* as a tuple of the form (red, green, blue).

Example: A Simple Maze Game

I have a soft spot in my heart for curses because I have spent more time than I care to admit playing ASCII-based games such as Angband and Nethack. The program shown in Listing 22-5 is far simpler, but it does use several curses features. It uses a pad to hold a large maze, which the user can move around in.

Listing 22-5: **Maze.py**

```
import curses
import curses.ascii
import whrandom
# Possible contents of maze-squares:
MAZE_WALL="X"
MAZE_ENTRANCE="*"
MAZE_HALLWAY="."
# Attributes for displaying maze squares:
MAZE_ATTRIBUTE={MAZE_WALL:curses.A_NORMAL,
                MAZE_ENTRANCE:curses.A_BOLD,
                MAZE_HALLWAY:curses.A_DIM,}
# Simple class representing a compass direction:
class Direction:
    def __init__(self,Name,XDelta,YDelta):
        self.Name=Name
        self.XDelta=XDelta
        self.YDelta=YDelta
        self.Marker=Name[0]
    def SetOpposite(self,Dir):
        self.Opposite=Dir
        Dir.Opposite=self
NORTH=Direction("North",0,-1)
SOUTH=Direction("South",0,1)
EAST=Direction("East",1,0)
WEST=Direction("West",-1,0)
NORTH.SetOpposite(SOUTH)
EAST.SetOpposite(WEST)
VALID_DIRECTIONS=[NORTH,SOUTH,EAST,WEST]
# Maze creation uses direction "markers" to indicate how we got
# to a square, so that we can (later) backtrack:
MARKED_DIRECTIONS={NORTH.Marker:NORTH,SOUTH.Marker:SOUTH,
            EAST.Marker:EAST,WEST.Marker:WEST}
# Map keystrokes to compass directions:
KEY_DIRECTIONS={curses.KEY_UP:NORTH,curses.KEY_DOWN:SOUTH,
                curses.KEY_LEFT:WEST,curses.KEY_RIGHT:EAST}
class Maze:
    def __init__(self,Size=11):
        # Maze size must be an odd number:
        if (Size%2==0):
            Size+=1
        self.Size=Size
        self.Pad=curses.newpad(self.Size+1,self.Size+1)
        self.FillWithWalls()
    def FillWithWalls(self):
        for Y in range(0,self.Size):
            self.Pad.addstr(Y,0,MAZE_WALL*self.Size,MAZE_ATTRIBUTE[MAZE_WALL])
    def Set(self,X,Y,Char):
        self.Pad.addstr(Y,X,Char,MAZE_ATTRIBUTE.get(Char,curses.A_NORMAL))
```

Continued

Listing 22-5 *(continued)*

```python
def Get(self,X,Y):
    return self.Pad.instr(Y,X,1)
def BuildRandomMaze(self):
    self.FillWithWalls()
    CurrentX=1
    CurrentY=1
    self.Set(CurrentX,CurrentY,MAZE_ENTRANCE)
    while (1):
        Direction=self.GetValidDirection(CurrentX,CurrentY)
        if (Direction!=None):
            # Take one step forward
            self.Set(CurrentX+Direction.XDelta,
                CurrentY+Direction.YDelta,MAZE_HALLWAY)
            CurrentX+=Direction.XDelta*2
            CurrentY+=Direction.YDelta*2
            self.Set(CurrentX,CurrentY,Direction.Marker)
        else:
            # Backtrack one step
            BackDirectionMarker=self.Get(CurrentX,CurrentY)
            BackDirection=MARKED_DIRECTIONS[BackDirectionMarker].Opposite
            CurrentX+=BackDirection.XDelta*2
            CurrentY+=BackDirection.YDelta*2
            # If we backtracked to the entrance, the maze is done!
            if self.Get(CurrentX,CurrentY)==MAZE_ENTRANCE:
                break
    # Fix up the maze:
    for X in range(0,self.Size):
        for Y in range(0,self.Size):
            if self.Get(X,Y) not in [MAZE_HALLWAY,MAZE_WALL, MAZE_ENTRANCE]:
                self.Set(X,Y,MAZE_HALLWAY)
def GetValidDirection(self,X,Y):
    DirectionIndex=whrandom.randint(0,len(VALID_DIRECTIONS)-1)
    FirstIndex=DirectionIndex
    while (1):
        Direction=VALID_DIRECTIONS[DirectionIndex]
        NextSquare=(X+Direction.XDelta*2,Y+Direction.YDelta*2)
        if ((0 < NextSquare[0] < self.Size) and
            (0 < NextSquare[1] < self.Size) and
            self.Get(NextSquare[0],NextSquare[1])==MAZE_WALL):
                return Direction
        DirectionIndex+=1
        if (DirectionIndex>=len(VALID_DIRECTIONS)):
            DirectionIndex=0
        if (DirectionIndex==FirstIndex):
            return None
def ShowSelf(self,ScreenLeft,ScreenTop,PlayerX,PlayerY,Radius):
    Top=PlayerY-Radius
    Bottom=PlayerY+Radius
    Left=PlayerX-Radius
```

```
                Right=PlayerX+Radius
                ScreenRight=ScreenLeft+Radius*2+1
                ScreenBottom=ScreenTop+Radius*2+1
                if (Top<0):
                    ScreenTop -= Top
                    Top=0
                if (Left<0):
                    ScreenLeft -= Left
                    Left=0
                if (Right>self.Size-1):
                    ScreenRight-=(self.Size-1-Right)
                    Right=self.Size-1
                if (Bottom>self.Size-1):
                    ScreenBottom-=(self.Size-1-Bottom)
                    Bottom=self.Size-1
                self.Pad.refresh(Top,Left,ScreenTop,ScreenLeft,ScreenBottom,ScreenRight)

        def Main(Window):
            # Set up colors:
            curses.init_pair(1,curses.COLOR_GREEN,curses.COLOR_BLACK)
            curses.init_pair(2,curses.COLOR_BLUE,curses.COLOR_BLACK)
            curses.init_pair(3,curses.COLOR_RED,curses.COLOR_BLACK)
            MAZE_ATTRIBUTE[MAZE_HALLWAY] |= curses.color_pair(1)
            MAZE_ATTRIBUTE[MAZE_ENTRANCE] |= curses.color_pair(2)
            MAZE_ATTRIBUTE[MAZE_WALL] |= curses.color_pair(3)
            curses.curs_set(0) # invisible cursor
            MyMaze=Maze(20)
            MyMaze.BuildRandomMaze()
            PlayerX=19
            PlayerY=19
            LightRadius=3
            MazeWindow=curses.newwin(10,10,10+LightRadius*2+1,10+LightRadius*2+1)
            while 1:
                MazeWindow.erase()
                MyMaze.ShowSelf(10,10,PlayerX,PlayerY,LightRadius)
                Window.addch(10+LightRadius,10+LightRadius,"@",
                    curses.color_pair(2) & curses.A_STANDOUT)
                Window.refresh()
                Key=Window.getch()
                if (Key==ord('q') or Key==curses.ascii.ESC):
                    break
                Direction=KEY_DIRECTIONS.get(Key,None)
                if (Direction):
                    TargetSquare=MyMaze.Get(PlayerX+Direction.XDelta,
                        PlayerY+Direction.YDelta)
                    if TargetSquare==MAZE_ENTRANCE:
                        MazeFinished(Window)
                        break
                    if TargetSquare==MAZE_HALLWAY:
                        PlayerX += Direction.XDelta
                        PlayerY += Direction.YDelta
```

Continued

Listing 22-5 *(continued)*

```
def MazeFinished(Window):
    Window.clear()
    Window.addstr(5,5,"CONGRATULATION!",curses.color_pair(2))
    Window.addstr(6,5,"A WINNER IS YOU!",curses.color_pair(3))
    Window.getch()
    pass

if (__name__=="__main__"):
    curses.wrapper(Main)
    print "Bye!"
```

Summary

The curses library is an easy, portable way to create a text-mode user interface. In this chapter, you used curses to:

✦ Display and read text onscreen.

✦ Handle mouse and keyboard input.

✦ Use Textboxes for easy input.

✦ Draw colorful text.

The next chapter demonstrates various ways to create a command interpreter in Python, including the spiffy graphics language Lepto.

Building Simple Command Interpreters

◆　◆　◆　◆

In This Chapter

Beginning with the end in mind

Understanding the Lepto language

Creating a Lepto Lexical analyzer

Adding interactive-mode features

Executing Lepto commands

◆　◆　◆　◆

When someone says "user interface," I usually think of a GUI with nice buttons and menus, but sometimes a more appropriate and powerful interface uses a custom mini-language in which your users write small programs or scripts. This chapter introduces Python's support for such a user interface and walks you through the process of creating a graphical plotting application that is driven by a small, custom scripting language called *Lepto*.

Beginning with the End in Mind

The Python libraries covered in this chapter are the `shlex` and `cmd` modules. The nature of these two modules makes it difficult to cover each feature in isolation, so each section of this chapter builds a portion of a single application. Once you've seen the modules in that larger context, rereading the explanations of the modules' features will make more sense.

The application that you will build is a simple plotter (sort of like the turtle graphics you find in languages like LOGO). It is controlled by user-provided scripts, and the scripting language provides basic movement commands and support for creating subroutines (procedures).

If you imagine a spectrum on which you position programming languages according to their power and flexibility, the high end would contain Python, and the low end would contain this chapter's language. Because one of the world's largest snakes is a type of Python (around 10 meters long), I named this new language *Lepto*, short for *Leptotyphlopidae*, a type of blind snake that ranks as one of the world's smallest, around 13 centimeters.

The following is a sample Lepto program, and Figure 23-1 shows the result of running it through the finished application from this chapter:

Listing 23-1: **leptogui.py – A sample Lepto program**

```
C:\temp>leptogui.py
Welcome to Lepto!
Enter a command or type 'help'
: color blue
: scale 30
: sub kochedge # A subroutine to draw an edge
..    f 1 l 60  # f = forward
..    f 1 r 120 # l and r = turn
..    f 1 l 60
..    f 1
..    r 120
..    end
: repeat 3 kochedge
: scale 0.5
: repeat 3 kochedge
: scale 0.5
: repeat 3 kochedge
: scale 0.5
: repeat 3 kochedge
```

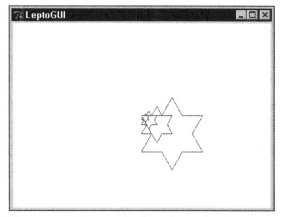

Figure 23-1: The result of running a simple Lepto program

Understanding the Lepto Language

Lepto programs are very simple; each line of a Lepto script contains one or more complete statements. Blank lines and other whitespace are ignored, and comments will be like Python's and consist of a pound symbol (#) and everything after it on the same line.

Table 23-1 explains the statements Lepto supports.

Table 23-1 Valid Lepto Statements	
Statement	**Description**
`f amnt`	Move forward (in the current direction) `amnt` units
`b amnt`	Move backward (away from the current direction) `amnt` units
`l amnt`	Turn left `amnt` degrees
`r amnt`	Turn right `amnt` degrees
`scale amnt`	Multiply the current scale by `amnt`. Initially the scale is 1, meaning one pixel for each unit of movement.
`color name`	Change the current drawing color to `name`. A color name is any valid `Tkinter` color.
`push arg`	Save a state attribute to its own stack for later retrieval. `arg` can be one of `color`, `direction`, `scale`, or `position`.
`pop arg`	Restore a previously saved state attribute. `arg` is one of `color`, `direction`, `scale`, or `position`. No effect results if the stack is empty.
`reset arg`	Restore a state attribute to its original value. `arg` can be one of `direction`, `color`, `screen`, `scale`, `position`, or `all`.
`include file`	Read and execute the contents of the file named `file` as if the contents had been entered from the console.
`sub name`	Begin the creation of a new subroutine called `name`. Overwrites any previous subroutine of the same name.
`end`	Finish creating a new subroutine
`call name`	Execute the subroutine called `name`
`repeat count sub`	Repeatedly execute the subroutine called `sub count` times

The features of this language are obviously limited so that the example isn't too cumbersome, but it has enough functionality to be interesting.

Creating a Lepto Lexical Analyzer

Users will create Lepto programs using a text editor or by entering them in via an interactive console. Either way, their input will be plain text, so the first step toward a finished application is parsing the text input and spitting out Lepto commands in some internal format that the rest of the program can understand. During this conversion, the parser will also verify that the Lepto commands are valid according to the simple grammar explained in the previous section.

The shlex module

Python's `shlex` module provides basic lexical analysis for simple shell-like languages. It defines the `shlex` class, which you can use as is or through your own subclass. You create a `shlex` object by calling `shlex([instream[, infile]])`, where `instream` is an open filelike object and `infile` is the file's name (printed with error messages). If you provide neither, then `shlex` uses `stdin`. `shlex` breaks the input down into individual words, or *tokens*.

A `shlex` object has several members, which you can modify to affect how it interprets the input stream. The `commenters` member is a string of all valid comment characters (defaulting to '#'), and `quotes` is a string with all valid quote characters (defaulting to single and double quotes). If a comment character is in the middle of a token (with no surrounding whitespace), it counts as a single token that just so happens to contain the comment character.

The `whitespace` member is a string of token separators (by default, whitespace is any combination of tabs, spaces, carriage returns, and linefeeds). `wordchars` defaults to alphanumeric characters (letters and numbers) and the underscore; it represents all valid token characters. Any character not in `whitespace`, `wordchars`, `quotes`, or `commenters` is returned as a single-character token.

`source` is a string holding the keyword `shlex` uses as the "import" or "include" equivalent found in Python or C, telling `shlex` to read and parse the contents of a file. Setting it to a value of `beable`, for example, means a user can use the following command to include the contents of the file `foofoo.txt`:

```
beable "foofoo.txt"
```

`infile` is the name of the current file (the original input file name, or the name of the file currently being included), and `instream` has the filelike object from which data is being read. The `lineno` member is the current source line number. For debugging purposes, you can set the `debug` member to 1 or more to have `shlex` generate more verbose output.

With your `shlex` object configured the way you want, all you need to do is repeatedly call its `get_token()` method to retrieve the next token from the stream. When all the input has been read, `get_token` returns an empty string. `push_token(str)` pushes `str` onto the token stack (so that the next call to `get_token` returns `str`).

When a user includes a file's contents (using the keyword stored in source), the sourcehook(path) method is called to locate and open the file called path. You can override this method to implement your own file location algorithm; source-hook returns a 2-tuple (file name, open file object).

If you need to print out an error message, prefix your message with the string returned from the object's error_leader([file[, line]]) method. Unless you indicate otherwise, it uses the current file name and line number to return a message header string that is friendly to editors such as Emacs. For example:

```
>>> print s.error_leader()+'Expected a number'
"foofoo.txt", line 17: Expected a number
```

Putting shlex to work

The parser in Listing 23-2 understands the simple Lepto language as described earlier in this chapter. At the highest level, it repeatedly calls shlex.get_token to get a command and then calls a corresponding parse_<command> method to read and verify that command's arguments. Each finished command is stored in a LeptoCmd object (a simple container), all of which are buffered and eventually returned as a list of commands.

Listing 23-2: **leptoparser.py – Coverts tokens to LeptoCmd objects**

```
import shlex,sys

class LeptoCmd:
    'Simple container class'
    def __init__(self,cmd,**kwargs):
        self.cmd = cmd
        self.__dict__.update(kwargs)

    def __repr__(self):
        s = 'LeptoCmd %s(' % self.cmd
        for item in self.__dict__.items():
            if item[0] != 'cmd':
                s += ' %s=%s' % item
        return s + ' )'
class LeptoParser:
    def __init__(self,stopOnError=1):
        self.stopOnError = stopOnError
def err(self,msg,dest=sys.stderr):
        dest.write(self.lexer.error_leader()+msg+'\n')
```

Continued

Listing 23-2 *(continued)*

```
def next_token(self):
    'Returns the next token or None on error'
    tok = self.lexer.get_token()
    if tok == '':
        self.err('Unexpected end of file')
    return tok

def next_number(self,func=float):
    'Returns the next token as a number'
    tok = self.next_token()
    if tok:
        try: tok = func(tok)
        except ValueError:
            return self.err('Expected a number, not '+tok)
    return tok

def parse_reset(self):
    tok = self.next_token()
    if tok:
        if not tok in ['all','direction','color',\
                       'screen','scale','position',\
                       'stacks']:
            return self.err('Invalid reset argument')
        return LeptoCmd('reset',arg=tok)

def parse_push(self):
    tok = self.next_token()
    if tok:
        if not tok in ['color','direction',\
                       'scale','position']:
            return self.err('Invalid push argument')
        return LeptoCmd('push',arg=tok)

def parse_pop(self):
    tok = self.next_token()
    if tok:
        if not tok in ['color','direction',\
                       'scale','position']:
            return self.err('Invalid push argument')
        return LeptoCmd('pop',arg=tok)

def amntcmd(self,cmd):
    'Util for commands with a single numerical arg'
    num = self.next_number()
    if num: return LeptoCmd(cmd,amnt=num)

# These are all nearly identical
def parse_f(self): return self.amntcmd('f')
def parse_b(self): return self.amntcmd('b')
def parse_l(self): return self.amntcmd('l')
```

```
    def parse_r(self): return self.amntcmd('r')
    def parse_scale(self): return self.amntcmd('scale')

    def namecmd(self,cmd):
        'Util for commands with a single string arg'
        tok = self.next_token()
        if tok: return LeptoCmd(cmd,name=tok)

    # More nearly identical stuff
    def parse_color(self): return self.namecmd('color')
    def parse_sub(self): return self.namecmd('sub')
    def parse_call(self): return self.namecmd('call')

    def parse_end(self): return LeptoCmd('end')

    def parse_repeat(self):
        num = self.next_number()
        if num:
            n = self.next_token()
            if n:
                return LeptoCmd('repeat',count=num,name=n)

    def parse(self, stream=None, name=None):
        'Returns a list of LeptoCmd objects'
        lexer = shlex.shlex(stream,name)
        lexer.source = 'include'
        lexer.wordchars += '.,-' # For numbers
        self.lexer = lexer
        cmds = []
        while 1:
            tok = lexer.get_token()
            if tok == '': # End of the file
                break

            # See if there's a parser for this token
            parser = 'parse_'+tok
            if not hasattr(self,parser):
                self.err('Unknown command: '+tok)
                if self.stopOnError:
                    break
                else:
                    continue

            # Call the parser to convert to a LeptoCmd object
            cmd = getattr(self,parser)()
            if cmd is None:
                if self.stopOnError: break
                else: continue

            cmds.append(cmd)

        return cmds
```

Basically, you create a `LeptoParser` object, pass it a stream, and it returns to you a list of `LeptoCmd` objects, checking for errors along the way. Later sections will make use of the `LeptoParser` class, but you can already verify that it works correctly:

```
>>> import leptoparser
>>> p = leptoparser.LeptoParser()
>>> p.parse()
color red                   # You enter this
f 10 l 20 f 10 l 5 f 5      # You enter this
^Z                          # Hit Ctrl-Z (Win) or Ctrl-D (Unix)
[LeptoCmd color( name=red ),
 LeptoCmd f( amnt=10.0 ),  LeptoCmd l( amnt=20.0 ),
 LeptoCmd f( amnt=10.0 ),  LeptoCmd l( amnt=5.0 ),
 LeptoCmd f( amnt=5.0 )]
```

Adding Interactive-Mode Features

The next step toward a finished application is the addition of a "shell" similar to when you use Python in interactive mode. The shell passes the commands through to the parser, and also provides online help.

Using the cmd module

The `cmd` module defines the `Cmd` class that provides some scaffolding for building an interactive, command-line interpreter. Because it is just scaffolding, you normally don't use it directly, but instead create a subclass. If the `readline` module is present, `cmd` automatically uses its editing and history features.

Cross-Reference   The `readline` module is an optional UNIX module, covered in Chapter 38.

The `Cmd` constructor takes no arguments, but once you have a `Cmd` object (or an object of your subclass), you can use the following members to customize it.

The `prompt` member is the input prompt displayed while the user enters a command. `identchars` is a string containing all acceptable characters in a command prefix (defaulting to letters, numbers, and underscores). By default the prompt is `'(Cmd) '`.

For each line of input from a user, `Cmd` considers the first token to be a *command prefix*, and it uses that prefix to dispatch the input to a handler method. For example, if the first word on the line of input is the string reverse, then `Cmd` sends the remainder of the line to its `do_reverse(line)` method, if present. If no handler is present, the line is sent to the `default(line)` method.

Cmd comes with a few special commands. If a user enters help reverse or just ? reverse, a built-in do_help method calls help_reverse(), if present, which you can implement to print online help (just print it to stdout using one or more print statements). A command prefix of just an exclamation point sends the remaining arguments to a do_shell(line) method if it exists. If the input is just a blank line, the emptyline() method is called, which by default repeats the previous input (by calling self.onecmd(self.lastcmd)). Finally, when the end of user input is reached, the do_EOF() method is called.

onecmd(line) takes an entire line of input and processes it as if it had been entered by the user.

The cmdloop([intro]) method makes Cmd repeatedly prompt the user for input and then dispatches it. intro is a message to display before entering the loop; if omitted, Cmd displays the message in self.intro, which is empty by default. You can implement the preloop() and postloop() methods to do work immediately before and after Cmd goes into its loop (i.e., they will both be called once per call to the cmdloop method).

For each line of input, Cmd performs a series of calls like the following:

```
stop = None
line = raw_input(self.prompt)
line = self.precmd(line)
stop = self.onecmd(line)
stop = self.postcmd(stop, line)
```

It receives user input, sends it to precmd (where you can modify it if you want), and then passes it off to onecmd, where the correct do_<command> method is called. If, at the end of the loop, stop has a value besides None, cmdloop calls postloop and then returns.

If a user enters **help** with no other argument, do_help displays a sort of table of contents of available help topics:

```
print self.doc_header
print self.ruler * len(self.doc_header)
print <all do_ methods that have a help_ method>
print self.misc_header
print self.ruler * len(self.misc_header)
print <all help_ methods that don't have a do_ method>
print self.undoc_header
print self.ruler * self.undoc_header
print <all do_ methods without a help_ method>
```

Sample output might look something like the following:

```
Documented commands (type help <topic>):
========================================
go          stop          add          subtract
delete

Miscellaneous help topics:
==========================
overview              rules

Undocumented commands:
======================
quit
```

Subclassing cmd.Cmd

Listing 23-3 contains the next piece of the Lepto application, and it's a good way to see a Cmd object in action; it defines LeptoCon, a Cmd subclass that wraps the Lepto parser so that users have online help and readline support, if present.

Listing 23-3: **leptocon.py — Lepto interactive console**

```python
import cmd, leptoparser, cStringIO

def defaultHandler(cmds):
    'Simple handler for testing'
    for cmd in cmds:
        print cmd

class LeptoCon(cmd.Cmd):
    normalPrompt = ': '
    subPrompt = '..    '

    def __init__(self,handler=defaultHandler):
        cmd.Cmd.__init__(self)
        self.timeToQuit = 0
        self.prompt = self.normalPrompt
        self.parser = leptoparser.LeptoParser()
        self.doc_header = "Type 'help <topic>' for info on:"
        self.intro = 'Welcome to Lepto!\n'\
                     "Enter a command or type 'help'"
        self.misc_header = ''
        self.undoc_header = ''
        self.handler = handler

    def do_sub(self,line):
        'Change the prompt for subroutines'
        self.prompt = self.subPrompt
        self.default('sub '+line) # Now process normally
```

```
def do_end(self,line):
    'Change the prompt back after subroutines'
    self.prompt = self.normalPrompt
    self.default('end '+line) # Now process normally

def default(self,line):
    'Called on normal commands'
    sio = cStringIO.StringIO(line)
    cmds = self.parser.parse(sio,'Console')
    self.handler(cmds)

def do_quit(self,line):
    self.timeToQuit = 1

def postcmd(self,stop,line):
    if self.timeToQuit:
        return 1
    return stop

# Now come all the online documentation functions
def help_help(self): print 'I need help!'
def help_quit(self): print 'Duh.'

def help_reset(self):
    print 'reset <all | direction | color | '\
          'screen | scale | position | stacks>'
    print 'Reverts to default settings'

def help_color(self):
    print 'color <name | None>'
    print 'Changes current color to <name> or no color'\
          ' for invisible movement'

def help_push(self):
    print 'push <color | direction | scale | position>'
    print 'Saves an attribute to its own stack'

def help_pop(self):
    print 'pop <color | direction | scale | position>'
    print 'Retrieves a previously pushed attribute'

def help_f(self):
    print 'f <amnt>'
    print 'Moves forward in the current direction'

def help_b(self):
    print 'b <amnt>'
    print 'Moves opposite of the current direction'

def help_l(self):
    print 'l <amnt>'
    print 'Turns left the specified number of degrees'
```

Continued

Listing 23-3 *(continued)*

```
        def help_r(self):
            print 'r <amnt>'
            print 'Turns right the specified number of degrees'

        def help_scale(self):
            print 'scale <amnt>'
            print 'Multiplies the current scaling factor by amnt'

        def help_sub(self):
            print 'sub <name>'
            print 'Creates a new subroutine called name'
            print 'Be sure to terminate it using the end command'

        def help_end(self):
            print 'end\nEnds a subroutine definition'

        def help_call(self):
            print 'call <name>\nCalls a subroutine'

        def help_include(self):
            print 'include "file"\nExecutes the contents of a file'

        def help_repeat(self):
            print 'repeat <count> <name>'
            print 'Calls a subroutine several times'

if __name__ == '__main__':
    c = LeptoCon()
    c.cmdloop()
```

Because the parser handles entire commands, most commands are routed to the `default` method, which passes the whole line on to the parser. Once again, this is part of a still larger program, but you can test this portion of it to make sure everything's working. Here's an example session from a Windows command line (text in bold is what I typed):

```
C:\temp>python leptocon.py
Welcome to Lepto!
Enter a command or type 'help'
: help

Type 'help <topic>' for info on:
==================================
help       quit
sub        include       b          r            push
pop        l             scale      color        f
end        repeat        call       reset
```

```
: help call
call <name>
Calls a subroutine
: color red
LeptoCmd color( name=red )
: f 10 r 20 f 10
LeptoCmd f( amnt=10.0 )
LeptoCmd r( amnt=20.0 )
LeptoCmd f( amnt=10.0 )
: quit

C:\temp>
```

Notice that you can enter more than one command per line as long as the entire command is on that line. The default command handler does nothing but print the commands to stdout, but it at least lets you see what's happening.

It may seem like overkill to use both shlex and cmd because there is some overlap in what they do (I could have just implemented methods such as do_color, do_reset, and so on, for example). But as you've seen, using both made it easy to test these first two parts independently, which could be important for languages with more complex grammars. It also makes it easy to later re-use LeptoParser for handling input directly from a file. Furthermore, it enables you to easily add interactive-mode features (such as online help and using a different prompt when the user is defining a subroutine) without cluttering the parsing code.

Executing Lepto Commands

Now that you have a Lepto parser and a user-friendly interface, all you need is something to act on those commands. The code in Listing 23-4 builds upon the previous two sections and creates a graphical display showing the results of the Lepto scripts (the display is nothing more than a Tkinter window with a single canvas widget).

Listing 23-4: **leptgui.py – Plots Lepto commands**

```
from Tkinter import *
import leptocon, threading, math

deg2rad = math.pi * 2.0 / 360.0

class LeptoGUI:
    def __init__(self,canvas):
        self.canvas = canvas
        self.subs = {}
        self.newSub = None
        self.firstCmd = 1
```

Continued

Listing 23-4 *(continued)*

```python
def do_reset_direction(self): self.direction = 0
def do_reset_color(self): self.color = 'black'
def do_reset_scale(self): self.scale = 1.0

def do_reset_position(self):
    # Move to center of canvas
    x = self.canvas.winfo_width() / 2
    y = self.canvas.winfo_height() / 2
    self.position = (x,y)

def do_reset_screen(self):
    ids = self.canvas.find_all()
    self.canvas.delete(*ids)

def do_reset_stacks(self):
    self.direction_stk = []
    self.color_stk = []
    self.scale_stk = []
    self.position_stk = []

def do_reset_all(self):
    self.do_reset_direction()
    self.do_reset_color()
    self.do_reset_scale()
    self.do_reset_position()
    self.do_reset_screen()
    self.do_reset_stacks()

def do_reset(self,cmd):
    'Reset color, position, etc'
    getattr(self,'do_reset_'+cmd.arg)()

def do_color(self,cmd):
    'Change color'
    self.color = None
    if cmd.name.lower() != 'none':
        self.color = cmd.name

def do_push(self,cmd):
    'Push a color, position, etc'
    arg = cmd.arg
    getattr(self,arg+'_stk').append(getattr(self,arg))

def do_pop(self,cmd):
    'Pop a color, position, etc'
    stk = getattr(self,cmd.arg+'_stk')
    if len(stk):
        setattr(self,cmd.arg,stk.pop())
```

```
    def do_f(self,cmd):
        'Move forward'
        x,y = self.position
        dir = self.direction * deg2rad
        amnt = self.scale * cmd.amnt
        nx = x + amnt * math.cos(dir)
        ny = y - amnt * math.sin(dir)
        if self.color:
            self.canvas.create_line(x, y, nx, ny, width=1,\
                                    fill=self.color)
        self.position = (nx,ny)

    def do_b(self,cmd):
        'Move backward'
        self.direction = (self.direction + 180) % 360
        self.do_f(cmd)
        self.direction = (self.direction - 180) % 360

    def do_l(self,cmd):
        'Turn left'
        self.direction = (self.direction + cmd.amnt) % 360

    def do_r(self,cmd):
        'Turn right'
        self.direction = (self.direction - cmd.amnt) % 360

    def do_scale(self,cmd):
        'Change scale'
        self.scale *= cmd.amnt

    def do_sub(self,cmd):
        'Create a new subroutine'
        if self.newSub:
            print "Can't create nested subroutines"
            return
        self.newSub = cmd.name
        self.subs[cmd.name] = []

    def do_end(self,cmd):
        'Finish creating a subroutine'
        if not self.newSub:
            print 'No subroutine to end'
            return
        self.newSub = None

    def do_call(self,cmd):
        'Invoke a subroutine'
        sub = cmd.name
        if self.subs.has_key(sub):
            self.cmdHandler(self.subs[sub])
        else:
            print 'Unknown subroutine',sub
```

Continued

Listing 23-4 *(continued)*

```
        def do_repeat(self,cmd):
            'repeat - Just do_call <count> times'
            c = leptocon.leptoparser.LeptoCmd('call',name=cmd.name)
            for i in range(cmd.count):
                self.do_call(c)

        def cmdHandler(self,cmds):
            'Called for each command object'
            if self.firstCmd:
                # Widget info (w,h) won't be ready in the
                # constructor, but it will be ready by now
                self.firstCmd = 0
                self.do_reset_all()

            for cmd in cmds:
                if self.newSub and cmd.cmd != 'end':
                    self.subs[self.newSub].append(cmd)
                else:
                    getattr(self,'do_'+cmd.cmd)(cmd)

if __name__ == '__main__':
    # Create a Tk window with a canvas
    root = Tk()
    root.title('LeptoGUI')
    canvas = Canvas(root,bg='White')
    canvas.pack()

    gui = LeptoGUI(canvas)

    # Let Tkinter run in the background
    threading.Thread(target=root.mainloop).start()

    # Repeatedly get commands and process them
    c = leptocon.LeptoCon(gui.cmdHandler)
    c.cmdloop()
    root.quit()
```

leptogui.py uses the usual trick of dispatching commands by taking a command name (such as scale), converting it to a method name (do_scale), and then invoking it. Because so much work was taken care of by the parser, the final pieces of the graphical application ended up being quite simple and straightforward.

Launch leptogui.py to give Lepto a try. Following is a sample session; the resulting output is shown in Figure 23-2.

```
C:\temp>leptogui.py
Welcome to Lepto!
Enter a command or type 'help'
: color blue f 40 r 90
: color green f 40 r 90
: color red f 40 r 90
: color brown f 40 r 90
: l 90 color none f 20 # Please step away from the box
: color black
: sub rayrot # Draws a ray and then rotates left
..    push position
..    f 100
..    pop position
..    l 5
..    end
: repeat 10 rayrot
```

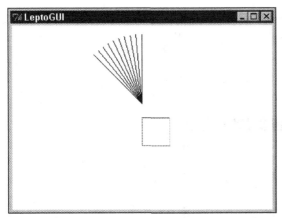

Figure 23-2: Sample output from a program written in the custom language called Lepto

You can store useful subroutines in a separate file and import them using the include command. For example, save the Lepto code that follows in Listing 23-5 to a file called shapes.lep, and try the following (the output is shown in Figure 23-3):

```
C:\temp>leptogui.py
Welcome to Lepto!
Enter a command or type 'help'
: include "shapes.lep"
: color blue
: call circle
: color black
: scale 10
: call tri
```

```
: r 180
: color green
: call box
: sub cirrot # draw a circle and rotate a little
..    push color push position
..    color none
..    f 50
..    pop color
..    call circle
..    pop position
..    r 20
..    end
: reset scale reset position reset color
: repeat 18 cirrot
```

Listing 23-5: shapes.lep – Sample Lepto include file

```
sub circedge f 10 r 15 end
sub circle repeat 24 circedge end
sub box f 10 r 90 f 10 r 90 f 10 r 90 f 10 r 90 end
sub tri f 10 r 120 f 10 r 120 f 10 r 120 end
```

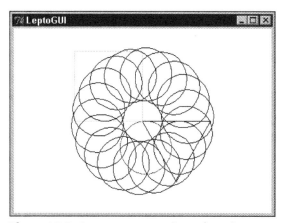

Figure 23-3: Lepto program using subroutines stored in a separate file

Lepto is a simple, yet realistic, example of how you can benefit from the shlex and cmd modules. A good exercise to try now would be to expand the grammar of Lepto to make it more powerful. For example, you could add support for variables and expressions (let Python do the work of evaluation via the eval function), or you could let the repeat statement accept a sequence of commands instead of forcing users to define a subroutine first.

Summary

A scripting interface to a program gives your users powerful tools to work with. Python's `shlex` module makes lexical analysis a lot less tedious, and `cmd` gives you a base upon which you can build a flexible command-line interface. In this chapter, you:

✦ Created a parser for a simple scripting language.

✦ Wrapped the parser in a command-line interface complete with built-in online help.

✦ Built an interpreter for the parser output that plots drawings graphically.

The next chapter covers Python's support for processing and playing sound files in various formats.

✦   ✦   ✦

Playing Sound

Sound is stored in a bewildering range of formats. Fortunately, Python's standard libraries can read, write, and convert a wide range of audio files. You can also play back sounds on a variety of platforms.

Sound File Basics

Sound is basically vibration in the air. The louder the sound, the more forceful the vibration. The higher the sound, the faster the vibration.

To store sound digitally, a microphone or other recorder measures (or *samples*) the analog sound waveform many times per second. Each sample takes the form of a number, and this number measures the amplitude of the sound waves at an instant in time. A speaker can later translate digitized sound (this long list of integers) back into sound waves.

There are many, many ways to digitize and store sound. They can differ in several ways:

◆ Sample rate — How many times per second the amplitude of the sound waves is measured. A common sample rate is 44100 Hz (samples per second), the rate used on audio compact discs.

◆ Sample encoding — The simplest (and most common) is *linear encoding,* where each sample is a linear measurement of amplitude. Other encoding types include u-LAW, in which measurement is performed on a logarithmic scale.

◆ Sample width — A sample can be an 8-bit, 16-bit, or 32-bit integer.

◆ Channels — Sound can be recorded with one, two, or more channels. This boils down to the storage of one or more audio streams together in one file. The corresponding samples from each channel are normally stored together in one frame.

In This Chapter

Sound file basics

Playing sounds

Examining audio files

Reading and writing audio files

Handling raw audio data

All sound formats make some trade-offs between sound quality (how much information is lost in digitizing the sound) and file size (the better the sound quality, the more data needs to be stored). For example, one second of sound could be stored in 8-bit mono at a sample rate of 22050; the total space used would be 22050 bytes. Storing the same sound in 16-bit stereo at a sampling rate of 44100 would require 44100 frames at 4 bytes per frame, for a total of 176400 bytes (8 times as much space).

Playing Sounds

Because playing sound is tied to the operating system (OS), the libraries for playing sound are also OS-specific.

Playing sound on Windows

The module `winsound` plays sound on a Windows system. The function `Beep(frequency,duration)` uses the computer's internal speaker to play a sound at pitch *frequency* for *duration* milliseconds. The frequency can range from 37 to 32767. If `Beep` can't play the sound, it raises a `RuntimeError`. For example, the following code plays a tinny-sounding major scale, starting from middle C. Each note lasts half a second:

```
ScalePitches=[262,294,330,349,392,440,494,523]
for Pitch in ScalePitches:
    winsound.Beep(Pitch,500)
```

The function `PlaySound(sound,flags)` plays a WAV file, using any available sound card. The parameter *sound* can be a file name, an alias, an audio stream, or None. The parameter *flags* should equal one or more constants, combined using bitwise-OR.

Specify one (and only one) flag to indicate where the sound should come from:

✦ SND_FILENAME indicates that the *sound* is the path to a WAV file.

✦ SND_ALIAS indicates that *sound* is the name of a control panel sound-association.

✦ SND_MEMORY indicates that *sound* is the contents of a WAV file.

For example:

```
# Play a sound file from disk:
SoundFileName="JudyGarlandKraftCheese.wav"
winsound.PlaySound(SoundFileName,winsound.SND_FILENAME)
```

```
# Play the "Exclamation" sound, as set up in Control Panel:
winsound.PlaySound("Exclamation",winsound.SND_ALIAS)
# Read sound file from disk, then play it:
SoundFile=open(SoundFileName,"rb")
winsound.PlaySound(SoundFile.read(),winsound.SND_MEMORY)
```

Other flags let you tweak behavior:

SND_ASYNC	Start playing the sound and return immediately. Otherwise, the call to PlaySound doesn't return until the sound has finished playing.
SND_LOOP	Keep playing the sound indefinitely. (This flag should be combined with SND_ASYNC.)
SND_PURGE	Stop the specified sound.
SND_NOSTOP	Don't stop currently playing sounds. (Raise RuntimeError if a sound is playing.)
SND_NOWAIT	Return immediately if the sound driver is busy.
SND_NODEFAULT	If the sound is not found, don't play a default beep.

Playing and recording sound on SunOS

The Sun audio hardware can play audio data in u-LAW format, with a sample rate of 8000 Hz. The module sunaudiodev enables you to manipulate the Sun audio hardware using a filelike object. The related module SUNAUDIODEV provides various constants for use with sunaudiodev.

The function open(mode) returns an audio device object. The parameter *mode* can be r for recording, w for playback, rw for both, or control for control access.

Playing sound

The method write(samples) plays sound, where *samples* is audio data as a string. A call to write adds the audio data into the audio device's buffer. If the buffer doesn't have enough room to contain *samples*, write will not return immediately.

The method obufcount returns the number of samples currently buffered for playback.

The method flush stops any currently playing sound, and clears the audio output buffer. The method drain waits until playback is complete, and then returns.

Recording sound

The method read(size) reads exactly *size* samples from the audio input, and returns them as a string. It blocks until enough data is available.

The method ibufcount returns the number of samples buffered for recording; you can read up to this many samples without blocking.

Controlling the audio device

The audio device provides a status object. The object has no methods, but has attributes as described in the audio man page. The device object provides accessors getinfo and setinfo for the status object.

The method fileno returns the file descriptor for the audio device.

Examining Audio Files

Because there are so many file formats for storing sound, it is sometimes difficult to know which format a particular file uses. The module sndhdr provides a function, what(filename), that examines the file *filename* and returns its storage format. (The function whathdr is a synonym for what.)

The return value of what is a 5-tuple of the form (type, SampleRate, channels, frames, BitsPerSample). Here, *type* is the data type; its possible values are aifc, aiff, au, hcom, sndr, sndt, voc, wav, 8svx, sb, ub, and ul. The value *BitsPerSample* is A for A-LAW encoding, U for u-LAW encoding, or the number of bits for standard encoding.

The values *SampleRate* and *channels* are 0 if they cannot be determined. The value *frames* is -1 if it cannot be determined. If what is completely stumped (for example, if the file isn't a sound file at all), it returns None.

For example, the following code examines a .wav file. The file has a sampling rate of 11024. It is in mono, and uses 8 bits per sample:

```
>>> print sndhdr.what("bond.wav")
('wav', 11025, 1, -1, 8)
```

This file is in SunAudio format, in mono, with 188874 frames in all:

```
>>> params=sndhdr.what("fallofthephoton.au")
>>> params
('au', 8012, 1, 188874, 'U')
>>> float(params[3])/params[1] # sound length (in seconds)
23.573889166250623
```

Reading and Writing Audio Files

The modules aifc, wave, and sunau handle AIFF, WAV, and AU files, respectively. The interfaces for the modules are almost identical. The aifc module is documented first, followed by an accounting of the differences.

Reading and writing AIFF files with aifc

The method open(file[, mode]) returns an audiofile object. The parameter *file* is either a file name or an open filelike object. If *file* is a file name, use the *mode* parameter to control how the file is opened.

File format

An audiofile object provides accessors for the file format. You can access each component of the file format on any audiofile. You can also set the file format on a new audiofile, but only before writing any frames:

✦ getnchannels, setnchannels(channels) — Access the number of channels.

✦ getsampwidth, setsampwidth(size) — Access the size, in bytes, of each sample.

✦ getframerate, setframerate(frames) — Access the number of frames per second.

✦ getnframes, setnframes(frames) — Access the number of frames in the entire file.

✦ getcomptype, getcompname, setcomptype(type,name) — Access the compression scheme. getcomptype returns the compression scheme as a code: NONE, ALAW, ULAW, or G722. getcompname returns the compression scheme as a human-readable string. Of the parameters to setcomptype, *type* should be a code (as returned by getcomptype), and *name* should be a human-readable name (as returned by getcompname).

The method setparams sets all five components at once. Its argument is a tuple of the form (Channels,SampleWidth,FrameRate,CompType,CompName). The method getparams returns the parameters in the same order.

Note | Usually, you need not call setnframes to write out a new file, because the number of frames is written to the file's header when you call close. However, if you open a filelike object that does not support seeking, then you must call setnframes before writing out audio data.

Input

The method readframes(count) reads *count* frames of audio data from the file, returning them (decompressed) in a string.

Output

The method writeframes(data) writes the audio data *data* to the file. The method writeframesraw(data) writes audio data without updating the header; it is useful for writing to a filelike object with no seek method.

Frame numbers

When reading, the method `setpos(framenumber)` jumps to frame *framenumber*, and the method `rewind` jumps to the beginning of the file (frame 0).

When writing, the method `tell` returns the current frame number.

Using markers

An AIFF file can have one or more *markers*. A marker has an id number, a position (frame number), and a name. To create a marker when writing a file, call `setmark(id,position,name)`. When reading a file, you can access a list of markers by calling `getmarkers`. Each list element is a tuple of the form (id,position,name). You can also access a particular marker with `getmark(id)`.

Reading and writing AU files with sunau

The interface of the `sunau` module is basically the same as that of `aifc`, with the following two exceptions:

✦ The available compression types are limited to ALAW, ULAW, and NONE.

✦ Markers are not available. Stub marker methods are provided for compatibility with `aifc`.

Reading and writing WAV files with wave

The interface of the `wave` module is basically the same as that of `aifc`, with these two exceptions:

✦ Compression is not available; the only supported scheme is NONE.

✦ Markers are not available. Stub marker methods are provided for compatibility with `aifc`.

Example: Reversing an audio file

Listing 24-1 reads in an audio file, and then writes out the same sound played backwards. Note that this could also be accomplished by one call to `audioop.reverse` (see "Handling Raw Audio Data," later in this chapter). This example does things the long way for purposes of exposition.

Listing 24-1: **ReverseSound.py**

```
"""Reverse a sound file. Handy for finding subliminal
messages."""
import sndhdr
import aifc
import sunau
import wave

def ReverseAudioStream(AudioFileIn,AudioFileOut):
    """
    Reverse an audio file (takes two opened audiofiles
    as arguments)
    """
    # Get header info from the input file; write it out to
    # the output file.
    Params=AudioFileIn.getparams()
    AudioFileOut.setparams(Params)
    # Collect all the frames into a list, then write them out
    # in reversed order:
    FrameCount=AudioFileIn.getnframes()
    FrameDataList=[]
    for FrameIndex in range(FrameCount):
        FrameDataList.append(AudioFileIn.readframes(1))
    for FrameIndex in range(FrameCount-1,-1,-1):
        AudioFileOut.writeframes(FrameDataList[FrameIndex])
    # We're done!  Close the files.
    AudioFileIn.close()
    AudioFileOut.close()


def ReverseAudioFile(InputFileName,OutputFileName):
    """
    Reverse an audio file (takes two file names as arguments)
    """
    # First, check to see what kind of file it is:
    FileInfo=sndhdr.what(InputFileName)
    if (FileInfo==None):
        print "Unkown sound format - can't reverse:",
            InputFileName
        return
    FileType=FileInfo[0]
    try:
        if FileType=="aifc" or FileType=="aiff":
            # aiff/aifc: use aifc module
            InFile=aifc.open(InputFileName,"rb")
            OutFile=aifc.open(OutputFileName,"wb")
        elif FileType=="au":
            # Sun Audio format: use sunau module
            InFile=sunau.open(InputFileName,"rb")
            OutFile=sunau.open(OutputFileName,"wb")
```

Continued

Listing 24-1 *(continued)*

```
        elif FileType=="wav":
            # Wave format: use wave module
            InFile=wave.open(InputFileName,"rb")
            OutFile=wave.open(OutputFileName,"wb")
        else:
            print "Sorry, can't reverse type",FileType
            return
        ReverseAudioStream(InFile,OutFile)
    except IOError:
        print "Unable to open file!"
    return

if (__name__=="__main__"):
    # Reverse a file. Then reverse it again, to get
    # (hopefully) the same thing we started with:
    ReverseAudioFile("test.wav","backwards.wav")
    ReverseAudioFile("backwards.wav","forwards.wav")
    # Try another audio format, too:
    ReverseAudioFile("test.au","backwards.au")
    ReverseAudioFile("backwards.au","forwards.au")
```

Reading IFF chunked data

Some sound files are divided into chunks, including AIFF files and Real Media File Format (RMFF) files. The chunk module provides a class, Chunk, to make it easier to read these files.

Each chunk consists of an ID (4 bytes), a length (4 bytes), data (many bytes), and possibly one byte of padding to make the next chunk start on a 2-byte boundary. The length generally does not include the 8 header bytes. The length is normally stored in big-endian format (most-significant bit first).

The constructor has the following syntax:
Chunk(file[,align[,bigendian[,inclheader]]]). Here, *file* is an opened file-like object that contains chunked data. The flag *align* indicates whether chunks are aligned. The flag *bigendian* indicates whether the chunk length is a big-endian number. And the flag *inclheader* indicates whether the length includes the 8 header bytes. Parameters *align* and *bigendian* default to true; *inclheader* defaults to false.

The methods getname and getsize return the ID and the size of the chunk, respectively. The method close skips to the end of the current chunk, but does not close the underlying file. After calling close on a chunk, you can no longer read or seek it.

The method read([size]) reads up to *size* bytes of data from the chunk, and returns them as a string. If *size* is omitted or is negative, it reads the entire chunk. If no data is left in the chunk, it returns a blank string.

The method tell returns the current offset into the chunk. The method skip jumps to the end of the current chunk. And the method seek(pos[,whence]) jumps to the position *pos*. If *whence* is 0 (the default), *pos* is measured from the start of the file. If *whence* is 1, *pos* is measured relative to the current file position. And if *whence* is 2, *pos* is measured relative to the start of the chunk. In addition, the method isatty is defined and returns 0 (for compatibility with normal file objects).

Normally, one iterates over chunks of a file by creating, reading, and closing several chunk instances, as follows:

```
def PrintChunkInfo(ChunkedFile):
    try:
        while (1):
            CurrentChunk=Chunk(ChunkedFile)
            print "ID:",CurrentChunk.getname()
            print "Size:",CurrentChunk.getsize()
            Chunk.close()
    except EOFError:
        # Constructing a chunk failed, because we
        # finished reading the file. Exit loop:
        break
```

Handling Raw Audio Data

The module audioop is a big box of handy functions for working with audio data. It is implemented in C, for speed. Each function takes audio data as a *fragment*, a sequence of linear-encoded samples, stored as a string. Most functions can handle 1-byte, 2-byte, or 4-byte sample widths, and they take the sample width as an argument; a few can only handle 2-byte samples.

Examining a fragment

These following functions each take two arguments — a fragment and a sample width:

avg returns the average of all the samples in the fragment. avgpp returns the average peak-peak (with no filtering done). max returns the largest sample value. maxpp returns the largest peak-peak value. minmax returns a tuple of the minimum and maximum samples. cross returns the number of zero-crossings in the fragment. To measure the power of the fragment audio signal, call rms (root-mean-square).

The function `getsample(fragment,width,n)` returns the *n*th sample from a fragment. The sample is frame number *index* if *fragment* is in mono.

Searching and matching

The function `findfactor(target,fragment)` attempts to match *fragment* with *target*. It returns a float X such that *fragment* multiplied by X is as similar to *target* as possible. The samples *target* and *fragment* should be 2-byte samples of the same length:

```
>>> QuietData=audioop.mul(Data,2,0.5) # half as loud
>>> audioop.findfactor(Data,QuietData)
2.0001516619075197
```

The function `findfit(target,fragment)` searches for *fragment* in *target*. It returns a tuple of the form (offset,X). The closest match found starts at frame *offset*, and is scaled by a factor of X. Here, *target* and *fragment* are 2-byte samples, where *fragment* is no longer than *target*.

The function `findmax(fragment,length)` looks for the loudest part of a sound. It finds a slice *length* samples long for which the audio signal (as measured by `rms`) is as large as possible. It returns the offset of the start of the slice.

Translating between storage formats

The `audioop` module can handle linear encoding, u-LAW, and Intel/DVI ADPCM. It provides several functions for converting between these schemes, as shown in Table 24-1.

<table>
<tr><th colspan="2">Table 24-1
Audio Format Conversion Functions</th></tr>
<tr><th>Function</th><th>Effect</th></tr>
<tr><td>lin2lin(fragment, width, NewWidth)</td><td>Converts a linear-encoded sample to a new sample width; returns the converted sample. Decreasing sample width lowers sound quality but saves space; increasing sample width just uses up more space.</td></tr>
<tr><td>lin2adpcm(fragment, width,state)</td><td>Converts a linear-encoded sample to 4-bit ADPCM encoding. The value state represents the encoder's internal state. The return value is (newfragment,newstate), where newstate should be passed for state to the next call to lin2adpcm. Pass None for state in the first call. lin2adpcm3 is a variant of lin2adpcm, using only 3 (not 4) bits per sample-difference.</td></tr>
</table>

Function	Effect
`adpcm2lin(fragment, width,state)`	Converts an ADPCM-encoded fragment to linear encoding. Returns a tuple of the form (NewFragment,NewState). adpcm32lin is a variant of adpcm2lin, for conversion from 3-bit ADPCM.
`lin2ulaw (fragment,width)`	Converts a linear-encoded sound fragment to u-LAW encoding
`ulaw2lin (fragment,width)`	Converts a u-LAW encoded fragment to linear encoding. (u-LAW encoding always uses 1-byte samples, so *width* affects only the output fragment.)

In addition, you can convert linear-encoded fragments between mono and stereo. `tomono(fragment,width,lfactor,rfactor)` converts a stereo fragment to a mono fragment by multiplying the left channel by *lfactor*, the right channel by *rfactor*, and adding the two channels. `tostereo(fragment,width,lfactor,rfactor)` converts a mono fragment to stereo. The left channel of the new fragment is the original fragment multiplied by *lfactor*, and similarly on the right.

Most `audioop` functions do not differentiate between the left and right channels of stereo audio. Consider using `tostereo` and `tomono`:

```
>>> audioop.max(Data,2) # max over both channels
26155
>>> LeftChannel=audioop.tomono(Data,2,1,0) # left*1,right*0
>>> RightChannel=audioop.tomono(Data,2,0,1)
>>> audioop.max(RightChannel,2)
26155
>>> audioop.max(LeftChannel,2)
25556
>>> LoudLeftChannel=audioop.mul(LeftChannel,2,2)
>>> QuietRightChannel=audioop.mul(RightChannel,2,0.5)
>>> # Add the two channels back together:
>>> NewData=audioop.add(audioop.tostereo(LeftChannel,2,1,0),
                        audioop.tostereo(RightChannel,2,0,1),
                        2)
```

Manipulating fragments

The function `add(fragment1, fragment2, width)` combines two fragments of the same length and sample width by adding each pair of samples.

The function `reverse(fragment,width)` reverses a sound fragment.

The function `mul(fragment,width,factor)` multiplies each sample in *fragment* by *factor*, truncating any overflow. This has the effect of making the sound louder or softer.

The function `bias(fragment,width,bias)` adds *bias* to each sample in *fragment* and returns the result.

You can speed up or slow down a fragment by calling `ratecv(fragment,width,channels,inrate,outrate,state[,weightA[,weightB]])`. Here, *inrate* and *outrate* are the frame rates of the input and output fragments; what is important is the ratio between *inrate* and *outrate*. The parameter *state* represents the internal state of the converter. `ratecv` returns a tuple of the form (fragment,newstate), where the value *newstate* should be passed in as *state* for the next call to `ratecv`. You can pass None for *state* in your first call. Finally, the values `weightA` and `weightB` are used for a simple audio filter; weightA (which must be at least 1) is a weight for the current sample, and weightB (which must be at least 0) is a weight for the previous sample.

For example, the following code reads an audio file and slows it down to half-speed:

```
>>> WavFile=wave.open("green1.wav","rb")
>>> Params=WavFile.getparams()
>>> Data=WavFile.readframes(Params[3]) # Params[3]=framecount
>>> # outrate=2*inrate; twice as many frames per second means
>>> # the sound is half as fast:
>>> NewData=audioop.ratecv(Data,Params[1],Params[0],1,2,None)
>>> NewFile=wave.open("green2.wav","wb")
>>> (NewData,State)=audioop.ratecv(
        Data,Params[1],Params[0],1,2,None)
>>> NewFile.setparams(Params)
>>> NewFile.writeframes(NewData)
>>> NewFile.close()
>>> winsound.PlaySound("green2.wav",winsound.SND_FILENAME)
```

Summary

Sound can be stored in many file formats. Python's standard libraries can read and write most sound files, and perform low-level manipulation of audio data. They also enable you to play sound on many operating systems. In this chapter, you:

✦ Played a musical scale on a PC speaker.

✦ Parsed sound files in various formats, and stored sounds in reverse.

✦ Manipulated raw audio data.

In the next chapter, you learn how to create and manage multiple threads in your Python programs.

✦   ✦   ✦

Advanced Python Programming

◆ ◆ ◆ ◆

Chapter 25
Processing Images

Chapter 26
Multithreading

Chapter 27
Debugging, Profiling,
and Optimization

Chapter 28
Security and
Encryption

Chapter 29
Writing Extension
Modules

Chapter 30
Embedding the
Python Interpreter

Chapter 31
Number Crunching

Chapter 32
Using NumPy

Chapter 33
Parsing and
Interpreting
Python Code

◆ ◆ ◆ ◆

Processing Images

In This Chapter

Image basics

Identifying image file types

Converting between color systems

Handling raw image data

Using the Python imaging library

T his chapter describes the modules that help you work with graphics files. Python comes with modules that help you identify image file types, convert between different color systems, and handle raw image data.

Image Basics

Computer images are made up of a group of pixels, or picture elements, and an image's size is usually specified by its width and height in pixels.

There is a mind-boggling number of file formats that you can use to store images; fortunately, however, a few (such as GIF, JPEG, and PNG) are popular enough to be considered standard. Some image file formats limit the number of different colors you can have in the image (GIFs, for example, can be any 256 out of 16,777,217 different colors), and some represent each pixel by its index in a *palette* of color definitions.

Image file formats store the data in either *raw*, or uncompressed, form, or they apply some sort of compression to make the date smaller. Compression techniques fall into two categories: *Lossless* compression (as is used by GIF files) means that no data is lost and that when a viewer decompresses the image and displays it, it is identical to the original. *Lossy* compression (as is used by JPEG files) means some detail is thrown away in order to achieve better compression.

Some image file formats also support *transparency,* so that if you display the image over another image, the parts that were marked as transparent leave that part of the original image visible. Index-based formats tag a particular color as the transparent color (so that pixels having that index value are completely transparent), and other formats include an *alpha channel* that tells the degree of transparency of each pixel.

Identifying Image File Types

The imghdr module makes an educated guess as to the type of image stored in a file:

```
>>> import imghdr
>>> imghdr.what('c:\\temp\\jacobSwingSleep.jpg')
'jpeg'
```

It looks at the first few bytes of the header, not the entire file, so it doesn't guarantee file integrity, but it does serve to differentiate between valid types. Instead of passing in a file name, you can pass in a string that contains the first few bytes of a file:

```
>>> hdr = open('snake.bmp','rb').read(50) # Read a little
>>> imghdr.what('',h=hdr)
'bmp'
```

Table 25-1 lists the values that the what function returns and the different file types that imghdr recognizes.

Table 25-1 Image Types Recognized by imghdr	
Image Type	*Value Returned*
CompuServe Graphics Interchange	gif
JFIF Compliant JPEG	jpeg
Windows or OS/2 Bitmap	bmp
Portable Network Graphics	png
SGI Image Library (RGB)	rgb
Tagged Image File Format	tiff
Portable Bitmap	pbm
Portable Pixmap	ppm
Portable Graymap	pgm
Sun Raster Image	rast
X11 Bitmap	xbm

By adding to imghdr's tests list of functions, you can have it check for additional file types. The module is just testing for known file types; it is not doing anything specific to images. The following example looks for the special prefix at the beginning of all bytecode-compiled Python (.pyc) files:

```
>>> def test_pyc(h,f):
...     import imp
...     if h.startswith(imp.get_magic()):
...         return 'pyc'
>>> imghdr.tests.append(test_pyc)
>>> imghdr.what('leptolex.pyc')
'pyc'
```

Custom test functions like the one shown in the preceding example take two parameters. The first contains a string of bytes representing either the first few bytes of the file (if what was called with a file name) or the string of bytes the user passed in to what. If the user called what with a file name, the f parameter is an open filelike object positioned just past the read to retrieve the bytes for the h parameter.

Converting Between Color Systems

A *color system* is a model that represents the different colors that exist; color systems make it possible to refer to colors numerically. By converting a color to a number, things like television signals and computer graphics become possible. Each color system has its own set of advantages, and the colorsys module helps you convert colors from one system to another.

Color systems

colorsys supports conversion between four of the most popular color systems; and in each, a color is represented by a 3-tuple of numbers from 0.0 to 1.0.

RGB

If you've worked with computer graphics, then the *RGB* or *red-green-blue* color system is probably somewhat familiar; it's the color system used by most computer software and hardware. This model is derived from the *tristimulus theory of vision,* which states that there are three visual pigments in the cones in the retinas of our eyes. When they are stimulated, we perceive color. The pigments are red, green, and blue.

YIQ

The *YIQ* color system is the one used by the National Television System Committee (NTSC), the standards body for television signals in the United States. Unlike RGB, which has three distinct signals, TVs have only a single composite signal. To make matters more complicated, the same signal must work with both black-and-white and color televisions sets. The Y component in a YIQ color is the brightness (luminance) of the color. It is the only component used by black-and-white televisions, and is given the overwhelming majority of the TV signal bandwidth. The I component contains orange-cyan hue information, which provides the coloring used in flesh tones. The Q component has green-magenta hue information, and is given the least amount of signal bandwidth.

HLS

For people, the *HLS,* or *hue-lightness-saturation,* color system is more intuitive than RGB because you can specify a color by first choosing a pure hue (such as pure green) and then adding different amounts of black and white to produce tints, tones, and shades. The L component is the lightness, where 1.0 is white and 0.0 is black. S is the saturation level of the hue; 1.0 is fully saturated (the pure hue), whereas 0.0 is completely unsaturated, giving you just a shade of gray.

HSV

The *HSV,* or *hue-saturation-value,* system is very close to the HLS model except that the pure hues have a V (corresponding to L in HLS) component value of 0.5.

Converting from one system to another

`colorsys` contains functions for converting from RGB to any of the other systems, and from any of the others to RGB:

```
>>> import colorsys
>>> colorsys.hls_to_rgb(0.167,0.5,1.0) # Yellow
(0.998, 1.0, 0.0)
```

To convert from HLS to YIQ, for example, you use a two-step process — converting first to RGB and then from RGB to YIQ. Of course, if you were planning to do many such conversions, it would be worthwhile to write your own function to convert directly between the two.

Although these routines use color parameters in the range from 0.0 to 1.0, it's also common to see each parameter specified using an integer range from 0 to 255 (the values that fit in a single byte of memory). To convert to that format, just multiply each component by 255. This format reduces the number of unique colors you can specify (down to around 16.8 million), but don't worry: the human eye can't really distinguish between more than about 83,000 anyway.

Listing 25-1 is a color choosing utility. You choose a color using the HLS color system and it shows that color along with its RGB equivalent, as shown in Figure 25-1.

Listing 25-1: **choosecolor.py — A HLS-to-RGB color converter**

```
from Tkinter import *
import colorsys

def update(*args):
    'Get the scale values and change the canvas color'
    r,g,b = colorsys.hls_to_rgb(h.get()/255.0,
                                l.get()/255.0,s.get()/255.0)
    r,g,b = r*255,g*255,b*255
    rgb.configure(text='RGB:(%d,%d,%d)' % (r,g,b))
    c.configure(bg='#%02X%02X%02X' % (r,g,b))

# Create a window with 3 scales and a canvas
root = Tk()
hue = Label(root,text='Hue')
hue.grid(row=0,column=0)
light = Label(root,text='Lightness')
light.grid(row=0,column=1)
sat = Label(root,text='Saturation')
sat.grid(row=0,column=2)
rgb = Label(root,text='RGB:(0,0,0)')
rgb.grid(row=0,column=3)

h = Scale(root,from_=255,to=0,command=update)
h.grid(row=1,column=0)
l = Scale(root,from_=255,to=0,command=update)
l.grid(row=1,column=1)
s = Scale(root,from_=255,to=0,command=update)
s.grid(row=1,column=2)

c = Canvas(root,width=100,height=100,bg='Black')
c.grid(row=1,column=3)

root.mainloop()
```

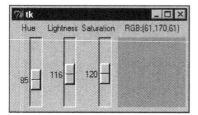

Figure 25-1: This utility converts colors
from the HLS system to the RGB system.

Handling Raw Image Data

Python works well as a general-purpose programming language, and often leaves
special-purpose functionality up to third-party developers. As such, Python's built-
in support for handling raw image data is meager at best.

The `imageop` module manipulates raw image data that you pass it as a Python
string of bytes. The data must be either 8-bit (each pixel is represented by one character in the string) or 32-bit (4 characters per pixel; each group of 4 characters represents red, green, blue, and alpha or transparency components for that pixel). How
you go about obtaining data in that format is up to you, but if you're on an SGI computer, you can use the `imgfile` module. In addition, if you have an SGI RGB file, you
can load it using the `rgbimg` module, and then pass its contents to `imageop`.

`imageop` has a few functions for cropping and scaling images, but the bulk of its
functions have to do with converting between grayscale images of different color
depths (for example, converting from a 2-bit grayscale image to an 8-bit grayscale
image).

For real image processing, see the next section for information about available
third-party modules.

Using the Python Imaging Library

If you plan to do a lot of image processing, check out the Python Imaging Library
(PIL) from Pythonware (www.pythonware.com). It is free for both private and commercial use, and Pythonware also has commercial support plans available. It's painless to install and is well worth the download.

PIL is fast, and its wide range of features enables you to perform a number of image
processing tasks, including converting between different file formats; processing
images (cropping, resizing, and so forth); annotating existing images with text; and
creating new images from scratch with its drawing functions.

The next few sections show you how to get started with PIL; consult its online documentation for even more features.

 Tip   Visit the Graphics section in the Vaults of Parnassus (www.vex.net/parnassus/) for plenty of other graphics and image processing utilities.

Retrieving image information

The main module in PIL is Image, and you use it to open and create images:

```
>>> import Image
>>> i = Image.open('shadowtest.bmp')
>>> i.mode
'RGB'
>>> i.size
(320, 240)
>>> i.format
'BMP'
>>> i.getbands()
('R', 'G', 'B')
>>> i.show() # Displays the image
```

An image's mode specifies its color depth and storage; some of the common values are listed in Table 25-2.

Table 25-2
PIL Mode Values

Mode	Description
1	1-bit pixels, black and white
L	8-bit pixels, black and white
P	8-bit pixels, using a 256-color palette
RGB	3 bytes per pixel, true color
RGBA	4 bytes per pixel, true color with alpha (transparency) band
I	32-bit integer pixels
F	32-bit floating point pixels

Images have one or more *bands,* or components, of data. For example, each pixel in an RGB image has a red, green, and blue component; that image is said to have three bands.

An image's show() method is a debugging facility that saves the image to a temporary file and launches the default viewer for that file type.

Note   Sometimes the show() command has trouble working from inside IDEs such as PythonWin.

One nice feature about PIL is that it waits to read and decode file data until it really needs to. This means, for example, that you can open an enormous image and read its size and type information very quickly.

Copying and converting images

The copy() method returns a new image object identical to the old one, so that you can make changes without modifying the original.

convert(mode) returns a new image in the given mode (there are also variations on this method that let you pass in a palette or even a conversion matrix). The following example loads a full-color JPEG image, converts it to a 1-bit black-and-white image, and displays it as shown in Figure 25-2:

```
>>> img = Image.open('binky.jpg')
>>> img.show() # Show the original
>>> img.convert('1').show() # Show the new version
```

The save(filename) method writes the contents of the current image to a file. PIL looks at the extension you give the file name, and converts it to the appropriate format. For example, if you have an image file named test.jpg, you can convert it to a GIF as follows:

```
>>> Image.open('test.jpg').save('test.gif')
```

Because JPEG files are true color, but GIF uses a 256-color palette, PIL takes care of the necessary conversion as it saves the file.

As mentioned earlier, PIL waits as long as possible before loading and decoding file data, so even if you open an image, its pixel data isn't read until you display it or apply some conversion. Therefore, you can use the draft(mode, (w,h)) method to instruct the image loader to convert the image *as it is loaded*. For example, if you have a huge 5,000 × 5,000–pixel, full-color image and you only want to work on a smaller, 256-color copy of it, you can use something like the following:

```
img = Image.open('huge.jpg').draft('P',(250,250))
```

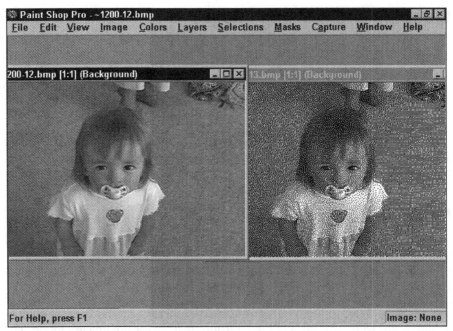

Figure 25-2: A true color image (on the left) and a 1-bit version (on the right) after using the convert() method

Using PIL with Tkinter

The ImageTk module provides two classes, BitmapImage and PhotoImage, that create Tkinter-compatible bitmaps and images that can be used anywhere Tkinter expects a bitmap (black-and-white image) or image (color image). Not only can you then use PIL's image processing features in any Tkinter program, you can also use it to load image formats that Tkinter doesn't understand.

Refer to Chapters 19 and 20 for coverage of Tkinter.

PIL also has functions for creating a Windows-compatible bitmap (DIB) that can be drawn into a Windows device context, and functionality for writing images out to PostScript files or printers.

Cropping and resizing images

The crop((left, top, right, bottom)) method returns a rectangle portion of an image.

resize((w, h)[, filter) returns a resized copy of an image. The filter argument controls what sort of sampling is used against the original image, and can be one of BILINEAR, BICUBIC, or NEAREST (the default).

One other useful method is thumbnail((w, h)), which resizes the object in place while maintaining the original aspect (width-to-height) ratio. Because of this, it may not use the exact size you pass in.

Modifying pixel data

You can access and change the value of any image pixel by its (*x,y*) coordinates, with (0,0) being the upper-left corner. Like Python slices, coordinates refer to the spaces *between* pixels, so a rectangle with its upper-left and lower-right corners at (0,0) and (20,10) would be 20 pixels wide and 10 tall.

The getpixel((x, y)) and putpixel((x, y), value) methods get and set individual pixels, where value is in the appropriate form for the image's mode. The following code opens an image, paints a black band across it, and displays the results (shown in Figure 25-3):

```
>>> i = Image.open('shadowtest.bmp')
>>> i.getpixel((10,25))
(156, 111, 56)
>>> for y in xrange(50,60):
...     for x in xrange(i.size[0]):
...         i.putpixel((x,y), (0,0,0))
>>> i.show()
```

Figure 25-3: Use getpixel and putpixel
to operate on individual pixel values.

`getdata()` returns a list of tuples representing each pixel in the image, and `putdata(data, [,scale][, offset])` places a sequence of tuples into the image (the `offset` defaults to the beginning of the image, and the `scale` defaults to 1.0).

PIL's `ImageDraw` module provides `Draw` objects that let you draw shapes and text on an image. The following example displays the image shown in Figure 25-4:

```
>>> import Image, ImageDraw
>>> from whrandom import randrange
>>> img = Image.open('happy.jpg')
>>> draw = ImageDraw.Draw(img)
>>> points = [] # Create a list of random points
>>> for i in xrange(10):
...     points.append((randrange(img.size[0]), # x
                        randrange(img.size[1]))) # y
>>> draw.line(points)
>>> img.show()
```

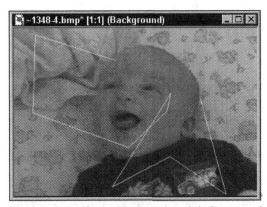

Figure 25-4: The ImageDraw module lets you draw shapes and text on images.

Listing 25-2 takes the current time and creates a GIF file containing an analog clock face image, as shown in Figure 25-5. On-the-fly image generation is often useful in creating dynamic content for Web pages (and if there's anything the world needs, it's yet another time display on a Web page).

Listing 25-2: clockgif.py — Generates a clock face showing the current time

```python
import time,Image,ImageDraw

def centerbox(rmax,perc):
    'Returns a coordinate box perc % of rmax'
    sub = rmax*perc/100.0
    return (rmax-sub,rmax-sub,rmax+sub,rmax+sub)

r = 100 # clock face radius
img = Image.new('RGB',(r*2,r*2),color=(128,128,128))
draw = ImageDraw.Draw(img)

# Make the clock body
draw.pieslice(centerbox(r,100),0,360,fill=(0,0,0))
draw.pieslice(centerbox(r,98),0,360,fill=(80,80,255))
draw.pieslice(centerbox(r,94),0,360,fill=(0,0,0))
draw.pieslice(centerbox(r,93),0,360,fill=(255,255,255))

# Draw the tick marks
for i in range(12):
    deg = i * 30
    draw.pieslice(centerbox(r,90),deg-1,deg+1,fill=(0,0,0))
draw.pieslice(centerbox(r,75),0,360,fill=(255,255,255))
# Get the current time
now = time.localtime(time.time())
hour = now[3] % 12
minute = now[4]

# Draw the hands
hdeg = hour * 30 + minute / 2
mdeg = minute * 6
draw.pieslice(centerbox(r,50),hdeg-4,hdeg+4,fill=(100,100,100))
draw.pieslice(centerbox(r,85),mdeg-2,mdeg+2,fill=(100,100,100))

#img.rotate(90).show() # For debugging
img.rotate(90).save('currenttime.gif')
```

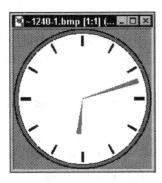

Figure 25-5: With PIL, it's easy to create on-the-fly images.

As you may have noticed, this example makes heavy use of Draw's `pieslice((left, top, right, bottom, startangle, stopangle[, fill][, outline])` method. In order to make it easy to use a different size clock, all measurements are calculated as percentages of the radius (therefore, changing the value of r is all you need to do). The `centerbox` function is a helper function that returns a square enclosing a circle of the right size.

One other thing to notice is that an angle of zero is directly to the right of center, and angle measurements are clockwise from there. Instead of working around that in the calculations for the placement of the clock hands, it was easier to just draw them as if the clock were on its side, and then rotate the entire image by 90 degrees (note that image rotation degrees are counterclockwise).

The following list contains the more common methods of a Draw object:

```
setink(ink)
setfill(onoff)
setfont(font)
arc((x1, y1, x2, y2), start, end[, fill])
bitmap((x, y), bitmap[, fill])
chord((x1, y1, x2, y2), start, end[, fill][, outline])
ellipse((x1, y1, x2, y2)[, fill][, outline])
line((x, y)[, fill])
pieslice((x1, y1, x2, y2), start, end[, fill][, outline])
point((x, y)[, fill])
polygon((x, y)[, fill][, outline])
rectangle((x1, y1, x2, y2)[, fill][, outline])
text((x, y), text[, fill][, font][, anchor])
```

Other PIL features

New versions of PIL continue to add powerful new features; check the Pythonware Web site (www.pythonware.com) for new versions and more documentation. Other interesting PIL modules and features include:

✦ ImageEnhance — Contains classes for adjusting the color, brightness, contrast, and sharpness of an image

✦ ImageChops — Provides arithmetic image operations (adding and subtracting images) as well as functions for lightening, darkening, and inverting images

✦ Support for creating animated (multiframe) GIF and FLI/FLC images

✦ Transformations, including rotating at arbitrary angles and applying a Python function to each pixel

✦ Image filters for blurring images or finding edges

✦ The capability to add your own decoders for new image types

Summary

Python offers helpful support for processing images, such as modules for identifying image file types. In this chapter, you:

✦ Learned about the information commonly stored in image files.

✦ Identified file types using the imghdr module.

✦ Converted colors between different color systems such as RGB and HLS.

✦ Modified images using the Python Imaging Library.

The next chapter shows you how to create multithreaded applications so that your programs can work on more than one task at a time.

✦   ✦   ✦

Multithreading

Running several threads is similar to running several different programs concurrently, but with the following benefits:

✦ Threads can easily share data, so writing threads that cooperate is simpler than making different programs work together.

✦ Threads do not require much memory overhead; they are cheaper than processes. (In the UNIX world, threads are often called *light-weight processes*.)

✦ ✦ ✦ ✦

In This Chapter

Understanding threads

Spawning, tracking, and killing threads

Avoiding concurrency issues

Preventing deadlock

Example: downloading from multiple URLs

Porting threaded code

Weaving threads together with Queue

✦ ✦ ✦ ✦

Understanding Threads

Threads are useful in many situations where your program needs to perform several tasks that aren't necessarily interdependent. Programs with a GUI, for example, often use two threads: one to handle user interface jobs such as repainting the window, and one to handle the "heavy lifting," such as talking to a database. Other times, threads are useful because it's more logical to divide work into distinct parts. For example, a game might have a separate thread for each computer-controlled player or object.

A thread may be interrupted by another thread at any time. After any line of code, the Python interpreter may switch to another thread.

 Note Some programmers call this interruption *timeslicing*. However, strictly speaking, timeslicing refers to the vaguely Communist notion of giving every thread equal amounts of CPU time.

The interpreter checks for thread switching once every few bytecode instructions; `sys.setcheckinterval` (which defaults to 10) is the number of bytecodes between switches.

The switching is transparent to you, and exactly when the switch happens is up to the Python interpreter, the operating system, and the phase of the moon: In a multi-threaded program, the order of execution may change from one run to the next.

This unpredictability is the reason why multithreading can be trickier than single-threaded programming: A buggy program might work nine times out of ten, and then crash the tenth time because the order of execution was different.

In general, you create all threads (other than the main thread) yourself. However, a C extension may create *dummy threads* to do its work. Talking to these threads from Python is difficult, so be forewarned if you want to communicate with dummy threads. A long-running calculation in an extension module effectively counts as one instruction, so be aware that other threads may have to wait a while for a dummy thread to take its turn!

Spawning, Tracking, and Killing Threads

Python features two multithreading modules, *thread* and *threading*. The modules overlap enough that you can choose the one you like best and use it exclusively. threading is a high-level module that calls thread for lower-level operations. threading includes a Thread class similar to Java's thread class, so it is a good choice for Java veterans. We included two versions of this chapter's example — one using thread and one using threading — to illustrate the workings of both.

Creating threads with the thread module

To spawn another thread, call

```
start_new_thread (function, args[, kwargs])
```

The function call returns immediately and the child thread starts and calls *function*; when *function* returns, the thread terminates. *function* can be an object method. *args* is a tuple of arguments; use an empty tuple to call *function* without passing any arguments. *kwargs* is an optional dictionary of keyword arguments.

Here are two ways of starting a new thread:

```
thread.start_new_thread(NewThread.run,())
thread.start_new_thread(CalcDigitsOfPi,(StartDigit,NumDigits))
```

Each thread has an ID number, which you can see by calling thread.get_ident(). The ID is unique at any given time, but if a thread dies, a new thread may re-use its ID.

If several threads print log messages, it can become hard to determine which thread said what; something like a party where everyone talks at once. The following example uses thread identifiers to indicate which thread is talking:

```
def PrintDebugMessage(ThreadNameDict,Message):
    CurrentThreadID = thread.get_ident()
    # Look up the thread name in the name dictionary. If
    # there is no name entry for this ID, use the ID.
    CurrentThreadName = ThreadNameDict.get(\
        CurrentThreadID, `CurrentThreadID`)
    print CurrentThreadName,Message
```

A thread terminates when its target function terminates, when it calls `thread.exit()`, or when an unhandled `SystemExit` exception is raised.

Python raises the exception `thread.error` if a threading error occurs.

Starting and stopping threads with the threading module

`threading` defines a `Thread` class to handle threads. To spawn a new thread, you first create a `Thread` object and then call its `start()` method. `start()` creates the actual thread and starts the target function; you should call `start` only once per thread.

The `Thread` constructor takes several keyword arguments, all of which are optional:

- ✦ target—Function to call when you `start()` the thread. Defaults to None. You should pass a value for *target* unless you override the `run()` method of `Thread` in a subclass; otherwise, your thread will not do anything.

- ✦ name—String name of this thread. The default name is of the form "Thread-n," where *n* is a small decimal number.

- ✦ args—A tuple of arguments to pass to the target function. Empty by default.

- ✦ kwargs—Keyword argument dictionary to pass to the target function. Empty by default.

- ✦ group—Currently unused. In the future, it will designate a thread group.

This code uses a `Thread` object to run the function CalcDigitsOfPi in a new thread:

```
PiThread = \
    Thread(target=CalcDigitsOfPi,args=(StartDigit,NumDigits))
PiThread.start()
```

You can create a subclass of the `Thread` class, and override the `run()` method to do what you want. This is a good approach if you are tracking thread-specific data. You should not override methods other than __init__() and run(). If you override __init__, you should call the __init__ method of the parent class in your constructor:

```
class SearchThread(threading.Thread):
    def __init__(self):
        threading.Thread.__init__(self)
        # Now carry on constructing...
        self.Matches={}
```

Threads can be flagged as *daemon threads*. The main thread (and therefore, your Python program) keeps running as long as there are non-daemon threads running; if only daemonic threads are running, the script exits. You set daemon status with setDaemon(*boolean*) and check it with isDaemon(). You must set a thread's daemon status before calling start(). Child threads inherit their daemonic status from their parents.

Note

> In a programming context, a *daemon* is a process or thread that silently handles some ongoing, invisible task. If you should encounter a daemon outside a programming context, we recommend you avoid signing anything.

Thread status and information under threading

You can check whether a Thread object is running with the method isAlive(). isAlive() returns true if someone has called start(), and the run() method has not returned yet.

Each thread has a name, an arbitrary string which you can access by getName() and setName(*newName*).

Finding threads under threading

threading.enumerate() returns a list of all active Thread objects. This includes dummy threads, daemon threads, and the main thread. Because the list contains the main thread, it is never empty. threading.activeCount() returns the number of active threads; this number is equal to the length of the list returned by threading.enumerate().

A call to threading.currentThread() returns an object corresponding to the current thread of control. (Even the main thread has a corresponding Thread object.)

Waiting for a thread to finish

To wait for a Thread to terminate, call its join method. join blocks until the thread dies; it returns immediately if the thread has not started, or has already terminated.

For example, the following lines of code (executed in the main thread) wait until all the other currently active threads have terminated:

```
ThisThread = threading.currentThread()
```

```
while (threading.activeCount()>1):
    CurrentActiveThreads = threading.enumerate()
    for WaitThread in CurrentActiveThreads:
        # Don't wait for myself:
        if (WaitThread != ThisThread):
            WaitThread.join()
# Now all those threads have finished. We are now the
# only running thread, unless someone spawned new threads
# while we were waiting. If that happened, we make
# another pass through the while loop. (If that can't
# happen, the whiling is superfluous)
```

Avoiding Concurrency Issues

"Oh, what a tangled web we weave, when first we practice to...implement multi-threaded database access."

—Sir Walter Scott, as reinterpreted by an unnamed programmer at 2 a.m.

Imagine a chalkboard on which three professors are each writing some information. The professors are so deep in thought that they are blissfully unaware of one another's presence. Each professor erases some chalk marks, writes on the board, pauses to think, and then continues. In the process, the professors erase bits of each other's writings, and the resulting blackboard is a mess of unrelated word salad.

Threads run in the same address space, so they can access the same data. Unfortunately, threads can also break other thread's data if they do not cooperate. The professors and the chalkboard illustrate what can go wrong. The phrase *concurrency issues* is a catchall term for all the ways in which two threads, working together, may put data into an unusable form. A program or object free of concurrency issues is called *thread-safe*.

Returning to the chalkboard example: Everything would have been fine if the professors had taken turns, and the second professor had waited until the first was done with the chalkboard. You can solve most concurrency issues by restricting data access to one thread at a time. A *lock*, or *mutex* (from "mutually exclusive"), is the way you make your threads take turns. A lock has two states: acquired and released. A thread must acquire the lock before it is allowed to access the data. When the thread is done, it releases the lock. If a lock has been acquired, other threads must wait, or *block*, until the lock is released before they can acquire it.

Locking with thread

To create a new lock, call thread.allocate_lock(), which returns a lock object.

To acquire the lock, call the method acquire([*waitflag*]). Call acquire(1) to wait for the lock as long as necessary. Call acquire(0) to return immediately if the lock isn't available. If you pass a value for *waitflag*, acquire() returns 1 if it acquired the lock, 0 if it didn't. If you don't pass a *waitflag*, acquire() waits for the lock, and returns None.

This code snippet uses locks to access some data in a thread-safe way:

```
# Acquire the employee lock. Block until acquired.
EmployeeLock.acquire(1)
# Try to acquire the Company lock, and return immediately.
if (CompanyLock.acquire(0)):
    # Do stuff with the company object, then release it
else:
    # Don't do stuff with the company object, because
    # you don't have its lock!
```

To release a lock, call its release() method. You can release a lock that was acquired by another thread. If you release a lock that isn't currently acquired, the exception thread.error is raised.

You can check whether a lock is acquired with the locked() method. When first created, the object is in its released state.

Use acquire(0), and not just a call to locked() if you don't want your code to wait for a lock. For example, the following code may block if another thread grabs the lock between our call to locked() and our call to acquire():

```
if (not RecordLock.locked()):
    RecordLock.acquire() # We may be here a while!
```

Locking with threading

The threading module offers several flavors of concurrency control. The Lock class is a simple wrapper for the lock class of the thread module; most of the other concurrency-control classes are variations on the Lock class.

Lock — simple locking

When you create a Lock object, it starts in the released state. The Lock object has two methods: acquire() and release(). These methods are wrappers for the acquire() and release() methods in the thread module; see the previous sections for details.

RLock — reentrant locking

RLock ("reentrant lock") is a variation on Lock, and its acquire() and release() methods have the same syntax. An RLock may be acquired multiple times by the same thread. The RLock keeps track of how many times it has been acquired. Other threads cannot acquire the `RLock` until the owning thread has called `release()` once for each call to `acquire()`. An `RLock` must be released by the same thread that acquired it.

Semaphore — n-at-a-time locking

A semaphore is also a kind of lock. The `Semaphore` class has `acquire()` and `release()` methods with the same syntax as `Lock`. However, whereas a lock restricts access to one thread at a time, a semaphore may permit access by several threads at a time. A semaphore keeps an internal counter of "available slots." Releasing the semaphore increases the counter; acquiring the semaphore decreases the counter. The counter is not allowed to go below zero. If the counter is at zero, no thread can acquire the semaphore until it has been released at least once, and so threads that try to acquire it will block until the semaphore has an available slot. Passing an integer to the `Semaphore` constructor gives the counter an initial value; it defaults to 1.

For example, assume several threads want to call a function that is memory-intensive. More than one thread can call it at once, but if too many calls happen at once, the system will run out of physical memory and slow down. You could limit the number of simultaneous calls with a semaphore:

```
# Create a semaphore, for later use:
MemorySemaphore = Semaphore(MAXIMUM_CALLERS)

# This is a safe wrapper for the function MemoryHog:
def SafeMemoryHog():
    MemorySemaphore.acquire(1)
    MemoryHog()
    MemorySemaphore.release()
```

Event — simple messages between threads

An `event` lets one thread block until triggered by another. The `Event` class has an internal true/false flag that is initially false. This flag is similar to a traffic light, where false means stop and true means go. You can check the flag's value with the `isSet()` method, set it to true with `set()`, and set it to false with `clear()`. Calling `clear()` is like a stop sign to other threads; calling `set()` is a go sign.

You can make a thread wait until the flag is true. Call the event's `wait()` method to block until the event's flag is set. You can pass a number to `wait()`, indicating a timeout. For example: If the flag is not set within 2.5 seconds, a call to `wait(2.5)` will return anyway.

For example, this code snippet is part of a script that munges data. The munging can be stopped and started by setting the global `Event` object, `MungeEvent`:

```
def StopMunging():
    MungeEvent.clear() # stop!
```

```
def StartMunging():
    MungeEvent.set() # go!

def MungeData():
    while (1):
        MungeEvent.wait() # wait until we get the green light
        MungeOneRecord()
```

Condition – wrapper for a lock

The `Condition` class wraps a lock. You can pass a `Lock` object to the `Condition` constructor; if not, it creates an `RLock` internally. A condition object has `acquire()` and `release()` methods, which wrap those of the underlying lock object.

Condition objects have other methods: `wait([timeout])`, `notify()`, and `notifyAll()`. A thread should `acquire` the lock before calling these methods.

A call to the `wait([timeout])` method immediately releases the lock, blocks until notification is received (when another thread calls `notify()` or `notifyAll()`), acquires the lock again, and then returns. If you supply a value for *timeout*, the call will return after that many seconds have passed, whether or not it was notified or reacquired the lock.

You call `notify` to wake up other threads that have called `wait` on the condition. If there are waiting threads, `notify` awakens at least one of them. (Currently, `notify` never awakens more than one, but this is not guaranteed for future versions.) `notifyAll` wakes up all the waiting threads.

A word of warning

When threads share data, examine every piece of data to ensure that thread interaction can't put the data into an invalid state. A program that is not thread-safe may work for months, waiting for a dramatic time to fail. Eternal vigilance is the price of multithreading!

Preventing Deadlock

Assume one thread acquires a lock, but hangs without releasing it. Now, no other threads can acquire that lock. If another thread waits for the lock (by calling the `acquire(1)` method), it will be frozen, waiting for the lock forever. This state is called *deadlock*. Deadlock is not as sneaky a bug as some concurrency issues, but it's definitely not good!

The section of code between acquiring a lock and releasing it is called a *critical section*. To guard against deadlock, there should be only one code path into the critical section, and only one way out. The critical section should be as short as possible, to prevent deadlock bugs from creeping in. In addition, the critical section should execute as quickly as possible — other threads may be waiting for the lock, and if they spend a long time waiting, nothing happens in parallel and the benefits of multithreading evaporate.

It is generally good practice to put a `try...finally` clause in a critical section, where the `finally` clause releases the lock. For example, here is a short function that tags a string with the current thread ID and writes the string to a file:

```
def LogThreadMessage(LogFile,Message):
    LogFileLock.acquire(1)
    try:
        LogFile.write(`thread.get_ident()`+Message+"\n")
    finally:
        # If we do not release the lock, then another thread
        # might wait forever to acquire it:
        LogFileLock.release()
```

Example: Downloading from Multiple URLs

The following code is a more complex example of some of the features covered in this chapter. The script retrieves files from a list of target URLs. It spawns several threads, each of which retrieves one file at once. Multithreading makes the whole process faster, because thread A can receive data while thread B is waiting for a response from the server.

See "Multitasking Without Threads" in Chapter 13 for an alternate solution to this problem using the `asyncore` and `select` modules.

We wrote two versions of the URLGrabber script — one using the `threading` module (see Listing 26-1), and one using `thread` (see Listing 26-2). Most of the code is the same; unique code is bolded in the source listing.

Listing 26-1: **URLGrabber — threading version**

```
# URLGrabber retrieves a list of target files from the network to
# the local disk. Each file has a particular URL, indicating where
# and how we should request it.
#
# This version of URLGrabber uses the threading module. It uses
# a Lock object to limit access to the URLList. (Without this lock,
# two threads might both grab the same URL)

import threading
import urllib
import urlparse
import os
```

Continued

Listing 26-1 *(continued)*

```
import sys
import traceback

# The optimal number of worker threads depends on one's bandwidth
WORKER_COUNT = 4

# Default filename of our url list
URL_FILE_NAME = "MyURLList.txt"

""" A WorkerThread downloads files from URLs to disk. Each
    WorkerThread object corresponds to a single flow of control.
    WorkerThread is a subclass of Thread, overriding the run()
    and __init__() methods. (Thread's other methods should
    not be overridden!) """
class WorkerThread(threading.Thread):
    def __init__(self, URLList, URLListLock):
        # Call the Thread constructor (Python subclasses do *not*
        # automatically invoke parent class constructors)
        threading.Thread.__init__(self)
        # Cache references...
        self.URLList=URLList
        self.URLListLock = URLListLock
    """ Acquire the URLList lock, grab the first URL from the list,
    cross the URL off the list, and release the URLList lock.
    (This code could be part of run(), but it's good to put critical
    sections in their own function) """
    def GrabNextURL(self):
        self.URLListLock.acquire(1) # 1 means we block
        if (len(self.URLList)<1):
            NextURL=None
        else:
            NextURL=self.URLList[0]
            del self.URLList[0]
        self.URLListLock.release()
        return NextURL
    """ We override Thread's run() method with one that does
    what we want. Namely: Take URLs from the list, and retrieve them.
    When we run out of URLs, the function returns, and the thread dies. """
    def run(self):
        while (1):
            NextURL = self.GrabNextURL()
            if (NextURL==None):
                # The URL list is empty! Exit the loop.
                break
            try:
                self.RetrieveURL(NextURL)
            except:
                self.LogError(NextURL)
    def RetrieveURL(self,NextURL):
        # urlparse splits a URL into pieces;
        # piece #2 is the file path
```

```
        FilePath=urlparse.urlparse(NextURL)[2]
        FilePath = FilePath[1:] # strip leading slash
        # If file name is blank, invent a name
        if (FilePath==""): FilePath="index.html"
        # Strip trailing newline, if we have one
        if (FilePath[-1]=="\n"): FilePath=FilePath[:-1]
        # Create subdirectories as necessary.
        (Directory,FileName)=os.path.split(FilePath)
        try:
            os.makedirs(Directory) # make directories as needed
        except:
            # os.makedirs raises an exception if the directory exists.
            # We ignore the exception.
            pass
        LocalPath = os.path.normpath(FilePath)
        urllib.urlretrieve(NextURL,FilePath)
    def LogError(self,URL):
        print "Error retrieving URL:",URL
        # Quick-and-dirty error logging: This code prints the
        # stack-trace that you see normally when an unhandled
        # exception crashes your script.
        (ErrorType,ErrorValue,ErrorTB)=sys.exc_info()
        print "\n\n***ERROR:"
        print sys.exc_info()
        traceback.print_exc(ErrorTB)


# Main function
if __name__ == '__main__':
    # Open the URL-list file. Take the first command-line
    # argument, or just use the hard-coded name.
    if (len(sys.argv)>=2):
        URLFileName = sys.argv[1]
    else:
        URLFileName=URL_FILE_NAME
    try:
        URLFile = open(URLFileName)
        URLList = URLFile.readlines()
        URLFile.close()
    except:
        print "Error reading URLs from:",URLFileName
        sys.exit()
    # Create some worker threads, and start them running
    URLListLock = threading.Lock()
    WorkerThreadList = []
    for X in range(0,WORKER_COUNT):
        NewThread = WorkerThread(URLList,URLListLock)
        NewThread.setName(`X`)
        WorkerThreadList.append(NewThread)
        # call start() to spawn a new thread (not run()!)
        NewThread.start()
    # Wait for each worker in turn, then exit.
    # join() is the "vulture method" - it waits until the thread dies
    for X in range(0,WORKER_COUNT):
        WorkerThreadList[X].join()
```

Listing 26-2: **URLGrabber — thread version**

```python
# URLGrabber retrieves a list of target files from the network to
# the local disk. Each file has a particular URL, indicating where
# and how we should request it. Several threads run in parallel,
# each downloading one file at once. Multithreading makes the
# whole process faster, since thread A can receive data while
# thread B is waiting on the server.
#
# This version of URLGrabber uses the thread module. It uses
# a lock to limit access to the URLList. (Without this lock,
# two threads might both grab the same URL)

import thread
import urllib
import urlparse
import os
import sys
import traceback

# The optimal number of worker threads depends on one's bandwidth
WORKER_COUNT = 4

# Default filename of our url list
URL_FILE_NAME = "MyURLList.txt"

""" A WorkerThread downloads files from URLs to disk. Each
    WorkerThread object corresponds to a single flow of control. """
class WorkerThread:
    def __init__(self, URLList, URLListLock):
        # Cache references...
        self.URLList=URLList
        self.URLListLock = URLListLock
    """ Acquire the URLList lock, grab the first URL from the list,
    cross the URL off the list, and release the URLList lock.
    (This code could be part of run(), but it's good to put critical
    sections in their own function) """
    def GrabNextURL(self):
        self.URLListLock.acquire(1) # 1 means we block
        if (len(self.URLList)<1):
            NextURL=None
        else:
            NextURL=self.URLList[0]
            del self.URLList[0]
        self.URLListLock.release()
        return NextURL
    """ run() is the target-function of our worker threads """
    def run(self):
        IncrementThreadCount()
        while (1):
            NextURL = self.GrabNextURL()
```

```
            if (NextURL==None):
                # The URL list is empty! Exit the loop.
                break
            try:
                self.RetrieveURL(NextURL)
            except:
                self.LogError(NextURL)
        DecrementThreadCount()
    def StartFirstWorker(self):
        MainThreadLock.acquire(1)
        self.run()
    def RetrieveURL(self,NextURL):
        # urlparse splits a URL into pieces;
        # piece #2 is the file path
        FilePath=urlparse.urlparse(NextURL)[2]
        FilePath=FilePath[1:] # strip leading slash
        # If file name is blank, invent a name
        if (FilePath==""): FilePath="index.html"
        # Strip trailing newline, if we have one
        if (FilePath[-1]=="\n"): FilePath=FilePath[:-1]
        # Create subdirectories as necessary.
        (Directory,FileName)=os.path.split(FilePath)
        try:
            os.makedirs(Directory) # make directories as needed
        except:
            # os.makedirs raises an exception if the directory exists.
            # We ignore the exception.
            pass
        LocalPath = os.path.normpath(FilePath)
        urllib.urlretrieve(NextURL,FilePath)
    def LogError(self,URL):
        print "Error retrieving URL:",URL
        # Quick-and-dirty error logging: This code prints the
        # stack-trace that you see normally when an unhandled
        # exception crashes your script.
        (ErrorType,ErrorValue,ErrorTB)=sys.exc_info()
        print "\n\n***ERROR:"
        print sys.exc_info()
        traceback.print_exc(ErrorTB)


def DecrementThreadCount():
    ThreadCountLock.acquire()
    global WorkerThreadCount
    WorkerThreadCount = WorkerThreadCount - 1
    if (WorkerThreadCount<1):
        MainThreadLock.release()
    ThreadCountLock.release()


def IncrementThreadCount():
    ThreadCountLock.acquire()
    global WorkerThreadCount
    WorkerThreadCount = WorkerThreadCount + 1
```

Continued

Listing 26-2 *(continued)*

```
        ThreadCountLock.release()

# Main function
if __name__ == '__main__':
    # Open the URL-list file. Take the first command-line
    # argument, or just use the hard-coded name.
    if (len(sys.argv)>=2):
        URLFileName = sys.argv[1]
    else:
        URLFileName=URL_FILE_NAME
    try:
        URLFile = open(URLFileName)
        URLList = URLFile.readlines()
        URLFile.close()
    except:
        print "Error reading URLs from:",URLFileName
        sys.exit()
    # Create some worker threads, and start them running
    URLListLock = thread.allocate_lock()
    ThreadCountLock = thread.allocate_lock()
    # We acquire the MainThreadLock. The last worker thread to exit
    # releases the lock, so that we can acquire it again (and exit)
    MainThreadLock = thread.allocate_lock()
    MainThreadLock.acquire()
    WorkerThreadCount = 0
    for X in range(0,WORKER_COUNT):
        NewThread = WorkerThread(URLList,URLListLock)
        thread.start_new_thread(NewThread.run,())
    # This call will block until the last thread releases the main
    # thread lock in DecrementThreadCount().
    MainThreadLock.acquire()
```

Porting Threaded Code

Not all operating systems include support for multithreading — an OS may multi-task without including native thread support. Note some minor differences in how threading works on different platforms:

✦ On most platforms, child threads are immediately killed (without executing object destructors or `try...finally` clauses) when the main thread exits. However, child threads keep running on SGI IRIX. We recommend terminating all threads before the main thread exits anyway, to ensure proper cleanup.

✦ Signals generally go to the main thread. Therefore, if your script handles signals, the main thread should not block. In particular, if you are using Tkinter, you should run `mainloop()` from the main thread. However, on platforms where the `signal` module is not available, signals go to an arbitrary thread.

Weaving Threads Together with Queues

The Queue module defines a thread-safe queue class (Queue.Queue). A queue is similar to a list. A queue handles concurrency control internally, which saves you the bother of handling it in your code.

Call the constructor Queue.Queue(*maxsize*) to create a queue. If *maxsize* is greater than zero, the queue will be limited to that many elements; otherwise, the length of the queue is unlimited.

To add an item to the queue, call put(*item, block*). The method get(*block*), returns the next item in the queue. Setting *block* to 1 makes these methods wait until they can successfully add or retrieve an item.

Setting *block* to 0 causes get and put to return immediately. You can also use the synonym methods get_nowait(item) and put_nowait(item). A nonblocking call to put raises the exception Queue.Full if the queue is full. (If the queue's length is not limited, put will always succeed.) A nonblocking call to get raises the exception Queue.Empty if no items are on the queue.

The Queue class includes some methods to inspect the queue. qsize() returns the queue length. isEmpty() returns 1 if the queue is empty, and 0 otherwise. isFull() returns 1 if the queue is full, and 0 if the queue is empty. Be careful: other threads may have touched the queue while you were inspecting it! Therefore, you must take the output of these methods with a grain of salt. For instance, the following code may raise a Queue.Empty exception:

```
if (not MyQueue.isEmpty()):
    FirstItem = MyQueue.get() # unsafe!
```

To safely modify a queue synchronously, use get_nowait() and put_nowait(), and catch any Full or Empty exceptions.

Technical Note: How Simultaneous Is Simultaneous?

A CPU can only handle one flow of control at a time. Computers switch between processes quickly, so in a single second, a processor may execute some instructions for thread A and thread B. To the user, the threads appear to run at the same time. We say that these programs are "simultaneous," although they are actually taking turns. On a multiprocessor machine, threads can be literally simultaneous — CPU 1 is running program A at the same instant that CPU 2 is running program B.

Currently, Python maintains a *global interpreter lock,* so that it executes only one Python thread at once. The disadvantage here is that a multiprocessor machine can devote only one processor to a particular Python program. This limitation doesn't matter much (especially if you're using a single processor machine!), but you may want to work around it for performance reasons. A C extension can create parallel dummy threads, as long as those threads do not manipulate Python objects directly. Alternatively, you can run separate processes if your program's work can be cleanly split.

For More Information

The Python threading SIG is a group working to document and improve the state of threading in Python; mailing list archives are available. See the Python SIG page at `http://www.python.org/sigs/`.

Stackless Python is an alternate implementation of the Python interpreter that supports, among other things, *microthreads*, or ultra-lightweight processes, which enables your program to handle hundreds or even thousands of threads without getting bogged down just switching between them. Visit `www.stackless.org` for more information.

Summary

Threads enable your programs to perform multiple tasks at once. Untamed threads can break one another's data, but Python's locking mechanisms let you direct threads to work together. In this chapter, you:

✦ Created threads with the `thread` and `threading` modules.

✦ Controlled data access with locks and semaphores.

✦ Built easy thread-safe code with the `Queue` class.

In the next chapter, you'll learn tools and techniques to help you debug and profile your Python applications.

✦   ✦   ✦

Debugging, Profiling, and Optimization

◆ ◆ ◆ ◆

In This Chapter

Debugging Python code

Working with docstrings

Automating tests

Finding bottlenecks

Common optimization tricks

Taking out the trash — the Garbage Collector

◆ ◆ ◆ ◆

Bugs can surface in the best of code — often at the worst possible times. Fortunately, Python features a debugger to help squash bugs. You can also use Python's profiler to identify bottlenecks in your code. A few optimization tricks can go a long way toward speeding up a sluggish script.

Debugging Python Code

Adding `print` statements is no substitute for stepping through code. The Python debugger, pdb, lets you set breakpoints, examine and set variables, and view source code. pdb is similar to the C/C++ debugger gdb (which, in turn, was based on xdb), so the gdb veterans in the audience will recognize most commands. Most commands can be written in a long way or a short way. For reference, this chapter lists them in the following form: `Long way (abbreviation)`. For example: `continue (c)`. A list of commands is also available within pdb by typing `help (h)`.

Cross-Reference See Appendix B for a guide to debugging under IDLE and PythonWin. Both provide excellent debuggers that are more powerful than pdb.

Starting and stopping the debugger

To use the debugger, import the module `pdb`. Then, you can start the debugger by calling `pdb.run(statement[,globals[,locals]])`. Here, *statement* is code to execute (as a string). You can run in a particular context by passing global and local namespace-dictionaries for *globals* and *locals*. The debugger will stop and wait for input before actually running the code; this is a handy time to set breakpoints:

```
>>> import pdb
>>> pdb.run("import DebugMe")
> C:\PYTHON20\<string>(0)?()
(Pdb) print "I can execute arbitrary commands at this prompt!"
I can execute arbitrary commands at this prompt!
(Pdb) fred=25
(Pdb) fred
25
```

You can do whatever you want from the pdb prompt. However, it provides some useful special commands, described next.

The function runeval is the same as run, except that runeval returns the value of the statement executed in the debugger. The function runcall(function[, arguments...]) executes the function *function* in the debugger, passing along any arguments to the function. It returns the return-value of *function*.

The function post_mortem(traceback) enters post-mortem debugging of a particular traceback. The function pm starts debugging the most recent traceback; it is a synonym for post_mortem(sys.last_traceback).

The function set_trace enters the debugger immediately. It is a useful function to put in code that encounters (or raises) an AssertionError.

To get back out of the debugger, use the command quit (q).

Examining the state of things

The all-important command list (l) shows the source code you are debugging. Use list FirstLine LastLine to list a range of lines (by default, pdb shows up to five lines above and five lines below the current line).

The command where (w) shows the current stack trace, while up (u) and down (d) move through the stack. (Note that running w under an IDLE shell shows about 10 extra stack frames, because IDLE is running above your code.)

You can display a variable's value with print (p).

For example, here is a simple debugging session. Looking at the code, plus some variables in context, gives me a pretty good idea what went wrong:

```
>>> FancyPrimeFinder.FindPrimes(100)
Traceback (innermost last):
  File "<pyshell#19>", line 1, in ?
    FancyPrimeFinder.FindPrimes(100)
  File "C:\PYTHON20\FancyPrimeFinder.py", line 9, in FindPrimes
    NumList=filter(lambda y,x=NumList[Index]:
```

```
IndexError: list index out of range
>>> import pdb
>>> pdb.pm()  # Post mortem!
> C:\PYTHON20\FancyPrimeFinder.py(9)FindPrimes()
-> NumList=filter(lambda y,x=NumList[Index]:
(Pdb) l
  4             NumList = range(2,EndNumber)
  5             Index=0
  6             while (Index<len(NumList)):
  7                     Index += 1
  8  ->                 NumList=filter(lambda y,x=NumList[Index]:
  9                                    (y<=x or y%x!=0), NumList)
 10             return NumList
[EOF]
(Pdb) p NumList
[2, 3, 4, 5, 7, 11, 13, 17, 19, 23, 29, 31, 37, 41, 43, 47, 53,
59, 61, 67, 71, 73, 79, 83, 89, 97]
(Pdb) Index
26
(Pdb) p len(NumList)
26
(Pdb) p NumList[Index]
*** IndexError: <exceptions.IndexError instance at 0098E714>
```

Setting breakpoints

The break (b) command handles breakpoints. You set breakpoints in two ways: break [name:]index sets a breakpoint on line *index* of file *name*. break function[, condition] sets a breakpoint on the specified function, but only when *condition* is true. Breakpoints are given sequential ID numbers, starting with 1. Running break (b) with no arguments prints a list of the current breakpoints:

```
(Pdb) b
 (Pdb) b FancyPrimeFinder.py:9
Breakpoint 1 at C:\PYTHON20\FancyPrimeFinder.py:9
(Pdb) b
Num Type           Disp Enb   Where
1   breakpoint     keep yes   at C:\PYTHON20\FancyPrimeFinder.py:9
```

Use clear (cl) to clear breakpoints. Pass their ID numbers, or just type cl to clear them all. Similarly, use disable to disable breakpoints. You can re-enable a break-point with enable (but a cleared breakpoint is gone forever).

The command ignore id [count] ignores breakpoint *id* up to *count* times. The command tbreak, with the same arguments as break, sets a temporary break-point, which is automatically cleared the first time it is hit. Finally, the command condition id [expr] attaches the condition *expr* to breakpoint *id*; if *expr* is omit-ted, the breakpoint becomes unconditional.

Running

The command `continue` (c) tells pdb to start running the program again. The command `return` (r) keeps running until the current function returns. The commands `next` (n) and `step` (s) execute only the current statement. The difference between the two is that `step` "steps into" functions (it breaks inside the function call), and `next` "steps over" function calls (it runs the whole function call, and then breaks on the next line of the current source file).

Aliases

The command `alias [name [command]]` creates an alias, *name*, which executes *command*. The alias can take arguments. These arguments replace %1, %2, and so on, in *command*, while %* is replaced by all the arguments. Calling `alias` without passing a command shows the current command for *name*; calling `alias` with no arguments lists the current aliases. Aliases can be nested. They only apply to the first word typed at the pdb command line.

For example, here is an alias to print an object's members, and a shortcut for printing the members of `self`:

```
(Pdb) alias pi for k in %1.__dict__.keys(): print "%1."+k+"="+%1.__dict__[k]
(Pdb) alias ps pi self
(Pdb) pi TempFile
TempFile.BackupFileName=C:\DOCUME~1\ADMINI~1\LOCALS~1\Temp\~3400-1
TempFile.File=<open file 'fred.txt', mode 'w' at 008053D8>
TempFile.FileName=fred.txt
```

You can put alias definitions (or any other pdb commands) into a file named .pdbrc in your home directory or the current directory. pdb will execute the commands from .pdbrc on startup. If .pdbrc files exist in your home directory and the current directory, the home directory's .pdbrc executes first, followed by the local file.

Debugging tips

Bugs in destructors can be especially hard to track down. Any exceptions thrown in a destructor are spewed to `stderr` and ignored. Therefore, destructors are a great place to call `pdb.set_trace`:

```
def __del__(self):
    try:
        self.cleanup()
    except:
        # If we don't catch it, NO ONE CAN!
        pdb.set_trace()
```

If an object is still around when the program finishes running, its destructor may execute *after* the Python interpreter has freed any imported modules. Therefore, an innocent-looking call to os.remove may result in the error "'None' object has no attribute 'remove'". A trick that sometimes works is to prefix a module-level variable with an underscore; such items are destroyed before other members. Safest of all is not to do anything too clever in destructors, unless you carefully get rid of objects as you go.

Working with docstrings

Documentation helps people use each other's Python modules. But documentation often becomes out-of-date, which is sometimes worse than no documentation at all! By using docstrings, you can maintain code and documentation in one place. You can also use the pydoc module to extract your code's docstrings into professional-looking text or HTML documentation, so that people can use your modules without ever needing to read code.

You can use pydoc interactively. Call pydoc.help(object) to view Python documentation for an object. This can be much more convenient than leaving the interpreter to read documentation. For example:

```
>>> pydoc.help(string.strip)
Help on function strip in module string:

strip(s)
    strip(s) -> string

    Return a copy of the string s with leading and trailing
    whitespace removed.
```

You can also use pydoc from the command line. To view module documentation as text, pass the module name as an argument, like this:

```
python pydoc.py urllib
```

Or, use the -w argument to write out documentation to an HTML file. For example, this commend writes HTML documentation of urllib to the file urllib.html:

```
python pydoc.py -w urllib
```

The pydoc module has one more trick up its sleeve: Run it with no command line arguments, and it will run as a documentation Web server. You can read documentation for all the modules in your PYTHONPATH, all from the comfort of your browser!

 New Feature   The pydoc module is new in Python 2.1. (However, it runs on versions 1.5 and up.)

Automating Tests

Testing code is not as fun as writing code. But testing is essential to avoid poor-quality code. Luckily, Python comes with tools to help you build automated tests. The unittest module (also known as PyUnit) is a framework for testing your code. The doctest module helps you keep documentation and code in synch.

New Feature   Both doctest and unittest are new in Python 2.1.

Synching docstrings with code

The doctest module helps you defend against out-of-date documentation. To use doctest, copy the text of a successful interpreter session and then paste it into your code's docstrings. Later, run doctest.testmod(module) to re-run that interpreter session, and make sure that the output is the same.

For example, suppose I am parsing some comma-delimited files that I exported from Microsoft Excel. Normally, I could use string.split to split a line into fields. But Excel uses some special rules to deal with commas within data. So, I write a function called SplitCommaFields to split fields, and test it in the interpreter. It works — so far, so good. To make sure my code's documentation doesn't become out-of-date, I copy my interpreter session into the docstring. Listing 27-1 shows the resulting file:

Listing 27-1: CSV.py

```
import doctest
import CSV # Import ourselves!
def SplitCommaFields(Line):
    """
    SplitCommaFields breaks up a comma-delimited .csv file into
    fields:
    >>> SplitCommaFields('a,b,c')
    ['a', 'b', 'c']

    It handles commas within fields:
    >>> SplitCommaFields('Atlas shrugged,"Rand,Ayn",1957')
    ['Atlas shrugged', 'Rand,Ayn', '1957']

    Also, it handles double-quotes within fields:
    >>> SplitCommaFields('"Are ""you"" happy?","Stuff,is,fun"')
    ['Are "you" happy?', 'Stuff,is,fun']
    """
    Fields=Line.split(",")
    RealFields=[]
    InsideQuotes=0
    BigField=""
```

```
    for Field in Fields:
        if InsideQuotes:
            BigField+=","+Field
            if BigField[-1]=='"':
                BigField=BigField[:-1] # kill trailing "
                RealFields.append(BigField)
                InsideQuotes=0
        elif len(Field)==0 or Field[0]!='"':
            RealFields.append(Field)
        else: # we saw a start-quote
            if (Field[-1]=='"'):
                RealFields.append(Field[1:-1])
            else:
                BigField=Field[1:]
                InsideQuotes=1
    return map(lambda x:x.replace('""','"'), RealFields)

if __name__=="__main__":
    doctest.testmod(CSV) # Test this module
```

When I run CSV.py from the command line, I get no output, indicating that my function still runs as documented. As a sanity check, I can pass the -v argument to see doctest do its work:

```
C:\source\test>python CSV.py -v
Running CSV.__doc__
0 of 0 examples failed in CSV.__doc__
Running CSV.SplitCommaFields.__doc__
Trying: SplitCommaFields('Atlas shrugged,"Rand,Ayn",1957')
Expecting: ['Atlas shrugged', 'Rand,Ayn', '1957']
ok
[...deleted for brevity...]
3 passed and 0 failed.
Test passed.
```

Unit testing

The unittest module is a Python version of Kent Beck's unit testing framework. It belongs to the same illustrious lineage as JUnit and CppUnit. You can use it to build one or more *test cases* for a class or module and group test cases into *test suites*.

To build an automated test, create a subclass of unittest.TestCase. Your class should override the runTest method to perform some test, using the assert to flag errors. For example, this class tests the SplitCommaFields function defined earlier:

```
class CommaContentsTestCase(unittest.TestCase):
    def runTest(self):
        Line='one,two,"three,three,thr,ee","fo,ur",five'
        assert SplitCommaFields(Line)==\
            ['one','two','three,three,thr,ee','fo,ur','five']
```

You can run the test interactively by calling the run method of a TestRunner object, such as the TextTestRunner:

```
>>> TestRunner=unittest.TextTestRunner()
>>> TestRunner.run(CSV.CommaContentsTestCase())
.
- - - - - - - - - - - - - - - - - - - - - - - - - - - - - - - - - - - - - - - - -
Ran 1 tests in 0.000s

OK
<unittest._TextTestResult run=1 errors=0 failures=0>
```

You can also run tests from the command line. One method is to change your script to call unittest.main():

```
if __name__=="__main__":
    unittest.main()
```

Then, calling your script from the command line will run all its test cases.

Test suites

The TestSuite class is a handy way to group related test cases. It provides a method, addTest(TestCase), for adding test cases to a list. For example, this function returns a suite of test cases:

```
def CSVSuite():
    Suite=unittest.TestSuite()
    Suite.add(CommaContentsTestCase())
    Suite.add(QuoteCommentsTestCase())
    return Suite
```

If you define a function (such as CSVSuite previously) to return a TestCase or TestSuite object, you can invoke your unit test(s) from the command line like this:

```
python unittest.py CSV.CSVSuite
```

Repeated testing tasks

The TestCase class provides setUp and tearDown methods, called before and after the main runTest method. These methods help you build test cases without repeating the same setup and cleanup steps in your test code. For example, suppose you have several tests that must create a temporary file. This base class takes care of file creation and cleanup, so that your test cases can freely write to `self.File` in the `runTest` method:

```
class FileTestCase(unittest.TestCase):
    def setUp(self):
        self.FileName=tempfile.mktemp()
        self.File=open(self.FileName,"w")
    def tearDown(self):
        self.File.close()
        os.remove(self.FileName)
```

Finding Bottlenecks

Python is a high-level language, often used in situations where speed is not crucial. Programmer time is usually more expensive than processor time. However, it is sometimes important to *optimize* your Python program — to make them conserve time, memory, or some other resource, such as database cursors.

Note some rules of thumb for optimization:

1. Optimize last. Life is too short to spend time optimizing code that may be rewritten or scrapped.

2. Test your optimizations by timing them on realistic runs. Optimization often means some sacrifice of simplicity, readability, or maintainability; it's best to make sure the sacrifice is worth the gains.

3. Comment all but the most glaringly obvious optimizations. This helps innocent bystanders understand your code, and (it is hoped) ensures that no one will undo the optimizations for the sake of readability.

Profiling code

To quickly profile a statement, import the `profile` module, and then call `profile.run(statement)`. For example, the following code profiles a script that sorts MP3 files by artist:

```
>>> profile.run("SortMP3s()")

        30289 function calls (30166 primitive calls) in 10.560 CPU seconds

   Ordered by: standard name

   ncalls  tottime  percall  cumtime  percall filename:lineno(function)
        1    0.029    0.029    9.685    9.685 <string>:1(?)
      271    0.020    0.000    0.020    0.000 ID3Tag.py:105(__init__)
```

```
        9    0.000    0.000    0.000    0.000 ID3Tag.py:130(theTitle)
        9    0.000    0.000    0.000    0.000 ID3Tag.py:137(theArtist)
        1    0.292    0.292    0.704    0.704 ID3Tag.py:20(?)
        1    0.000    0.000    0.000    0.000 ID3Tag.py:23(ID3Tag)
      271    0.151    0.001    0.168    0.001 ID3Tag.py:304(Read)
       45    0.016    0.000    0.016    0.000 ID3Tag.py:333(RemovePadding)
[...truncated for brevity...]
```

Each line of the output corresponds to a function. The columns show the following:

✦ ncalls — How many times the function was called. If a function recurses, two numbers are shown: total calls, and then total primitive calls. For instance, the script made one call to `os.path.walk`, which resulted in 123 other calls:

```
124/1    0.500    0.004    8.862    8.862 ntpath.py:255(walk)
```

✦ tottime — Total CPU time spent in the function.

✦ percall — Average CPU time. Equal to tottime divided by ncalls.

✦ cumtime — Cumulative CPU time spent in the function and its subfunctions.

✦ percall — Average cumulative time. Equal to cumtime divided by ncalls.

✦ filename:lineno(function) — Source file name, line number, and function name. The first line of output corresponds to the code passed to `run`; its filename is listed as "<string>".

Note When profiling from a Python shell window in IDLE or PythonWin, any code that prints to stdout will trigger function calls within the IDE's framework. These function calls will show up in the profiler's output! Running Python from the command line works around this problem.

Using Profile objects

The Profile class provides a `run(command)` method to profile the specified command. Normally, the command runs in the current namespace. To run the command in a particular namespace context, pass the global and local dictionaries (as returned by built-in functions globals and locals) to `runctx(command, globals, locals)`. To profile a function call, you can call `runcall(functionname[,arguments...])`.

After running a command, call the `print_stats` method to print statistics, or the `dump_stats(filename)` to write out stats (in nonreadable format) to the specified file.

A call to `profile.run(command[,filename])` creates a Profile object, calls `run(command)`, and then calls either `print_stats` or `dump_stats(filename)`.

The `Profile` class can be subclassed. For example, the class `HotProfile` is a subclass of `Profile`. It calculates less data (ignores caller-callee relationships), but runs faster.

Calibrating the profiler

There is a small time lag between the time that an event happens and the time that profiler records. The call to time.clock is not free. This lag adds up over the course of many function calls, and can make timing information less accurate.

Calibrating the profiler compensates for this lag by adding a "fudge factor." This makes the profiler's statistics more accurate. To calibrate the profiler, call its calibrate method:

```
>>> import profile
>>> Prof=profile.Profile()
>>> "%f" % Prof.calibrate(100000)
'0.000017'
```

The number returned is your fudge factor. To use it, you must edit the library code (in lib\profile.py). In the trace_dispatch method, replace the line

```
t = t[0] + t[1] - self.t          # No Calibration constant
```

with this line:

```
t = t[0] + t[1] - self.t - (your calibration constant)
```

Note

> Profiling with calibration is more accurate overall. However, the profiler may occasionally report that a negative amount of time was spent in a function. This results from the imperfection of the fudge factor, and is not a cause for panic.

Customizing statistics

The module pstats provides a class, Stats, for storing and printing statistics gathered in a profiling run.

The Stats constructor takes either a file name or a Profile object. You can either pass in a Profile object (after calling run), or pass the name of a stats file created by the profiler. You can also pass one (or more) file names or Profile instances to Stats.add.

For example, the following code runs the same command several times, and combines the statistics, on the assumption that behavior may vary from one run to the next:

```
def ProfileSeveralRuns(Command,Times):
    if (Times<1): return
    StatsFiles=[]
    for RunIndex in range(Times):
        FileName="stats%d"%(RunIndex)
        profile.run(Command, FileName)
```

```
        StatsFiles.append(FileName)
# Pass one filename to the constructor:
AggregateStats=pstats.Stats(StatsFiles[0])
# Pass along all other filenames:
if len(StatsFiles)>1:
        AggregateStats.add(*(StatsFiles[1:]))
AggregateStats.print_stats()
```

It is generally a good idea to call `strip_dirs` to trim the path to each function's file name.

You can change the ordering of statistics by calling the method `sort_stats` (field[,...]). Here, *field* is the name of a field to sort on. You can pass several field names. In this case, subsequent fields are used to sort if values of the first field are equal. Alphabetic fields are sorted in ascending order; numeric fields are sorted in descending order. (The method `reverse_order` reverses the ordering.) Table 27-1 lists the available fields.

Table 27-1
Stats Field Names

Name	Meaning
cumulative	Cumulative time spent in a function
calls	Total calls to a function
time	Time spent in a function (not including subfunctions)
name	Function name
file	Source filename
module	Source filename (same meaning as file)
line	Source line number
nfl	Name/File/Line. `sort_stats("nfl")` is the same as `sort_stats("name","file","line")`
pcalls	Total primitive (nonrecursive) calls to a function
stdname	Standard name

The method `print_stats([restrictions...])` prints the statistics. You can pass one or more arguments to filter which lines are printed. Pass an integer, n, to print only the first n lines. Pass a decimal between 0 and 1 to print that percentage of the lines. Or, pass a regular expression (as a string) to print only lines whose file name matches the regular expression.

This example runs some code and then prints statistics for the most time-consuming functions:

```
>>> Prof=profile.Profile()
>>> Prof.run("import FancyPrimeFinder")
<profile.Profile instance at 00854E54>
>>> MyStats=pstats.Stats(Prof)
>>> MyStats.sort_stats("time") # expensive functions first
<pstats.Stats instance at 007E48DC>
>>> MyStats.strip_dirs().print_Stats(10) # top 10 only
```

Note that most methods of Profile and Stats return the object itself; this makes it easy to chain several method calls in one line, as the last line of the preceding code does.

The method print_callers([restrictions...]) shows all the callers for each function. On the left is the called function; on the right is its caller, with the number of calls in parentheses. Similarly, print_callees([restrictions...]) shows each function on the left column; functions it called are on the right.

Common Optimization Tricks

The following sections outline some ways to speed up Python code. Use these on bottleneck code, after you have identified the bottlenecks using the profile module. Keep in mind that sometimes the best way to speed up a function is simply to write it as an extension module in C.

 See Chapter 29 for more information about how you can create C libraries usable from your Python programs.

Sorting

Sorting a sequence with the sort method is very fast for numbers and strings. If you need to perform custom sorting (e.g., a comparison of two objects), you can pass a comparison function to sort. You can also customize sorting for a class by defining a __cmp__ method. However, passing a function to sort is faster than implicit use of the __cmp__ method. Compare the following two lines:

```
PointList.sort(Point) # Uses Point.__cmp__ implicitly
PointList.sort(Point.__cmp__) # Trickier, but faster!
```

When sorting a list of objects, one trick is to find a "key" that you can sort on. The key values should be an easy-to-sort type (for example, numbers); and they should be mostly unique across list entries. The following function provides an example:

```
def SortByKey(List,KeyMaker):
    """Sort a list. The parameter KeyMaker is a function that
    returns a key for the list element. The keys are used
    sort the list."""
    # Replace each element x with (KeyMaker(x),x):
    TempList=map(lambda x,f=KeyMaker: (f(x),x), List)
    # Tuples sorted by comparing just the first elements:
    # If the first elements match, the second elements
    # are compared; so if KeyMaker(x)==KeyMaker(y), then we
    # *will* end up comparing x and y directly.
    TempList.sort()
    # Get rid of the keys - replace (KeyMaker(x),x) with x:
    return map(lambda(key,x):x, TempList)
```

For instance, I wrote code to sort a list of points according to their distance from the origin. Using SortByKey (instead of passing a function to sort) made the code roughly three times faster.

Looping

Use xrange for looping across long ranges; it uses much less memory than range, and may save time as well. Both versions are likely to be faster than a while loop:

```
for x in range(10000): pass # memory hog
for x in xrange(10000): pass # good!
```

You can often eliminate a loop by calling map instead.

I/O

Each call to a file's readline method is quite slow. It is much faster to read the entire file into memory by calling readlines; however, this uses up a lot of RAM. Another approach is to read blocks of lines. Best of all — in Python 2.1 — is to use the xreadlines method of a file:

```
# 1 - Slow:
while 1:
    FileLine=file.readline()
    if (FileLine==""): break # EOF
    DoStuff(FileLine)
# 2 - Fast, but possibly memory-intensive:
FileLines=file.readlines()
for FileLine in FileLines:
    DoStuff(FileLine)
# 3 - Faster than 1, without hogging too much memory:
# (Use this for filelike objects without an
# xreadlines() method)
while 1:
    FileLines=file.readlines(100)
```

```
        if len(FileLines)==0: break # EOF
        for FileLine in FileLines:
            DoStuff(FileLine)
# 4 - Fast and simple; requires version 2.1:
for FileLine in file.xreadlines():
    DoStuff(FileLine)
```

Strings

Building up strings with the concatenation operator + can be slow, because it often involves copying strings several times. Formatting using the % operator is generally faster, and uses less memory. For example:

```
HTMLString=HTMLHeader+HTMLBody+HTMLFooter # slow!
HTMLString="%s%s%s"%(HTMLHeader,HTMLBody,HTMLFooter) # fast!
```

If you are building up a string with an unknown number of components, consider using string.join to combine them all, instead of concatenating them as you go:

```
# Slow way:
Str=""
for X in range(10000):
    Str+=`X`
# Fast way (10 times as fast on my machine):
List=[]
for X in range(10000):
    List.append(`X`)
Str=string.join(List,"")
```

When using regular expressions, create a reusable regular expression object using re.compile instead of re.search and re.match directly. This saves time, because the regular expression doesn't have to be repeatedly parsed. Following is a contrived example:

```
PATTERN=r"^[0-9]+(\.[0-9]+)*$" # Match valid version numbers
ValidDottedDecimal=re.compile(PATTERN)
for Index in range(100):
  re.search(PATTERN,"2.4.5.3") # slow way!
for Index in range(100):
  ValidDottedDecimal.search("2.4.5.3") # fast way!
```

Threads

If your script uses only one thread, you can save time by forcing the interpreter to check for other threads less often. The method sys.setcheckinterval(codes) tells Python to consider switching threads after *codes* bytecodes. The default check-interval is 10; setting it to something large (like 1,000) may improve your performance. On my Windows machine, the gain is negligible.

Taking out the Trash—the Garbage Collector

Python doesn't require you to explicitly allocate and free memory. When you need more memory to hold some data, the Python interpreter allocates it for you. When you are finished with data, the interpreter usually gets rid of it.

Python cleans up memory by using *reference counting*: For each chunk of memory you use, Python keeps track of how many references to the object exist. When you assign a reference to an object, its reference count increases; when you get rid of a reference, the object's reference count decreases. When there are no more references to an object, Python frees the object's memory:

```
>>> class Thingy:
...     def __init__(self,Name):
...         self.Name=Name
...     def __del__(self):
...         print "Deleting:",self.Name
...
>>> A=Thingy("X") # The variable A holds only reference
>>> A="Crunchy frog" # Refcount goes to 0 -> object is freed!
Deleting: X
>>> A=Thingy("X")
>>> B=Thingy("Y")
>>> A.ref=B # Y's Refcount goes from 1 to 2
>>> B=None # Y's Refcount goes from 2 to 1
>>> # This takes X's refcount to 0, so X is deleted. Deleting
>>> # X takes Y's refcount to 0, so Y is deleted too:
>>> A=None
Deleting: X
Deleting: Y
```

Note that the built-in function del does not (necessarily) delete an object; it deletes a variable (and thus decrements the object's reference count):

```
>>> A=Thingy("X")
>>> B=Thingy("Y")
>>> A.ref=B
>>> del B # Variable B is gone, but object Y still exists
>>> A. ref.Name # See!  Object Y is still there!
'Y'
```

Reference counts and Python code

Reference counting is different from automatic garbage collection (as seen in Java). For example, as long as two objects hold references to each other, Python won't free them. If an object is no longer usable by a program, but its memory is not freed, the object is *leaked*. Leaked memory normally gets cleaned up when the program terminates. However, a program that runs for a long time can leak many megabytes of memory, a few bytes at a time. For example, after you run the following statements, the two objects each have a reference count of 1, and so will stick around until you exit the interpreter:

```
>>> A=Thingy("X")
>>> B=Thingy("Y")
>>> A.ref=B # Y's refcount is now 2
>>> B.ref=A # X's refcount is now 2
>>> del A
>>> del B
>>> # Congratulations! You just leaked memory!
```

Normally, these memory leaks are not big or common enough to worry about. If you find yourself running low on memory, however, you may need to start worrying. In order to rid yourself of an object, you must get rid of all references to it — and to do that, you must keep track of all the references.

Reference counts and C/C++ code

Shooting yourself in the foot is downright difficult in Python, but very easy in C. When writing C extensions, you must keep track of the reference counts of each Python object. Losing track of reference counts can lead to memory hemorrhaging (as opposed to mere memory leaks), and even core dumps.

The macros `Py_INCREF(x)` and `Py_DECREF(x)` increment and decrement the reference counts of a Python object x. At any given time, each reference is considered to be owned by some function. When that function exits, it must transfer ownership of the reference, or else get rid of the reference with a call to `Py_DECREF`. A function can also *borrow* a reference — the borrower uses the reference, never touches the reference count, and lets go of the reference before the owner does. Owning and borrowing are not explicit in the code, but the comments generally indicate to whom a reference belongs.

When writing C extensions, it is important to track reference counts properly. Linking Python with `Py_REF_DEBUG` and `Py_TRACE_REFS` turned on provides extra information for debugging reference counts. In addition, you can call `_Py_PrintReferences` to print out all the objects and their refcounts.

Summary

Debugging is never a painless process, but pdb helps make it as easy as possible. In addition, IDEs like PythonWin provide debugging with a snappier interface. The Python profiler helps you find bottlenecks in your code. In addition, a review of Python's garbage collector can save a lot of memory. In this chapter, you:

✦ Debugged Python programs using pdb.

✦ Profiled code to find the most expensive functions.

✦ Optimized various types of code.

✦ Learned how to leak memory (and how *not* to leak memory).

In the next chapter, you learn how to combine the speed of C with the power of Python by writing C extensions.

✦   ✦   ✦

Security and Encryption

◆ ◆ ◆ ◆

In This Chapter

Checking passwords

Running in a
restricted environment

Creating message
fingerprints

Using 1940s-era
encryption

◆ ◆ ◆ ◆

With the explosive growth of the Internet and with countries shifting to more global economies, the issue of security is increasingly important. Banks, businesses, governments, and consumers routinely transfer sensitive information; and computers attached to the Internet are potentially accessible by anyone. This chapter describes Python's modules for creating digital fingerprints of messages, running Python code in a safe *sandbox,* and using basic encryption and decryption. Online, you can also find strong encryption extension modules for triple DES, Blowfish, and the like.

Checking Passwords

The most basic and common form of security is restricting access until the user enters a valid username and password. When you prompt a user for his or her password, however, you don't want the password to be displayed on the screen, lest a "neighbor" with wandering eyes sees the password too. For these situations, use the getpass module.

There really isn't a safe and platform-independent way to have the user enter a password, so getpass has a different implementation for UNIX, Windows, and Macintosh systems. If for some reason it can't use any of the special implementations, it will at least warn the user that the password might accidentally be displayed on the screen.

Caution The Windows version uses getch() in the msvcrt module, which doesn't behave quite how you'd expect in some IDEs, such as IDLE or PythonWin, so if you want to try getpass out, run it in an interpreter started on the command line.

Use the `getpass([prompt])` function to request the user's password. The following function queries the user for a name and password and then returns them as a tuple:

```
>>> import getpass
>>> def getLogin():
...     name = raw_input('Name:')
...     passwd = getpass.getpass('Password:')
...     return name,passwd
...
>>> getLogin()
Name:robinhood
Password:              # Characters typed are not echoed
('robinhood', 'littlejohn')
```

`getpass` also has the `getuser()` function, which returns the login name of the user:

```
>>> getpass.getuser()
'dave'
```

`getuser` checks the values of the `LOGNAME`, `USER`, `LNAME`, and `USERNAME` environment variables, returning the value of the first one that is present and not empty. If all fail and the system has the `pwd` module (UNIX), then that is used; otherwise, an exception is raised.

Chapter 38 provides the `pwd` module, which you can use for accessing the UNIX user account database. You can also use the `crypt` module to check whether the password a user entered is correct (i.e., matches their login password).

Most GUI toolkits have their own method for prompting a user for a password. For example, in wxPython, you can set a flag in the text entry field that holds a password, so that anything typed is displayed with asterisks.

UNIX users that have the `readline` module activated need not worry that after entering their password it will show up in the command history. `getpass` uses its own implementation of `raw_input` in order to avoid that security hole.

Running in a Restricted Environment

Imagine that you decided to create an online game in which players from all over the world would upload virtual robots to traverse a maze and destroy one another. Not only did you decide to implement most of the game in Python, you chose to let the players program their robots using Python too. One problem, though, is that a malicious entrant could include code to erase files on your computer, install a Trojan horse, or cause damage in any number of other ways. How could you deal with that danger?

The rexec sandbox

The rexec module helps prevent such a scenario. It enables you to run Python code in a *sandbox*, a restricted environment in which you control what resources it can access — just as a child in a sandbox imagines it to be the entire world when in reality it's quite isolated and small. You can, for example, enable Python programs to do whatever they want as long as they don't try to create any socket connections, or enable them to create files only in a particular directory. With rexec, you can more safely run Python programs that didn't necessarily come from a trusted source.

To create an execution sandbox, you call RExec([hooks][verbose]) to create an RExec object (or call the constructor of a subclass you've created in order to override or add to its access policies). hooks is an instance of the RHooks class (or a subclass), which is itself a subclass of the Hooks class in the ihooks module; and is what is called when it's time to import a module. By providing your own import hooks, you can monitor or log what modules are loaded, or even load them from a different source. The verbose argument is passed to the Hooks constructor and, if 1, prints extra debugging information.

 Refer to Chapter 34 for information about the ihooks module and implementing your own module import behavior.

Before creating your RExec instance object, you can change some of its class variables to tailor what modules and functions will be available to the executing code. (Changing these class variables does not affect instances already created — only those subsequent to your changes will see the effects.) For security reasons, you should be careful about what values you change. If you want to change the list of prohibited built-in functions, for example, consider adding to the list instead of completely replacing it, so that you don't inadvertently create a security hole.

ok_path is a tuple containing the paths to search when importing a module. By default, it matches the value of sys.path.

ok_builtin_modules is a tuple of built-in (not implemented in Python) modules that are safe to import. The default value contains the names of the following modules:

audioop	imageop	parser	strop
array	marshal	regex	struct
binascii	math	pcre	time
cmath	md5	rotor	
errno	operator	select	

ok_posix_names is a tuple of allowed functions from the os module (if present in the current platform's implementation of os). The default value contains the names of the following modules:

```
error        readlink      getpid        getgid
fstat        stat          getppid       geteuid
listdir      times         getcwd        getegid
lstat        uname         getuid
```

`ok_sys_names` is a tuple of variables and functions from the `sys` module that restricted access programs can use. The default value contains the following:

```
ps1          copyright     platform      maxint
ps2          version       exit
```

`nok_builtin_names` is a tuple of built-in function names that programs are *not* allowed to use. By default, the list contains `'open'`, `'reload'`, and `'__import__'`, so functions such as `map` are still allowed (most built-in functions are relatively safe).

`RExec` intercepts calls from the restricted program to `import`, `reload`, and `unload` and routes the calls through the internal module loader and importer (which makes use of the custom import hooks). You can override `RExec`'s `r_reload(module)`, `r_unload(module)`, and `r_import(modulename[, globals[, locals], fromlist]]])` methods to provide custom behavior. If a module isn't safe to be loaded, `r_import` should raise in `ImportError` exception.

Calls to `open` are sent to `RExec`'s `r_open(filename[, mode[, bufsize]])`. By default, files can be opened for reading only, but you can override this with different behavior if needed.

Once you (finally!) have your `RExec` object, you can actually execute Python code in a restricted object by calling its `r_eval(code)`, `r_exec(code)`, or `r_exec-file(filename)` methods, all of which run the code in the __main__ module of your new sandbox. `r_eval` takes as an argument either a Python expression as a string or a compiled code object, and returns the value of the expression:

```
>>> import rexec
>>> r = rexec.RExec()
>>> r.r_eval('2 + 2')
4
```

`r_exec` can take a string containing one or more lines of Python code or a compiled code object:

```
>>> s = """
... print 'My name is George'
... q = range(10)
... print q
... """
>>> r.r_exec(s)
My name is George
[0, 1, 2, 3, 4, 5, 6, 7, 8, 9]
```

Cross-Reference Chapter 33 has information about code objects and Python introspection capabilities.

`r_execfile` executes the contents of a Python file in the restricted environment. For example, first save the code in Listing 28-1 to a file called bad.py.

Listing 28-1: **bad.py — "Untrusted" code to test in the rexec sandbox**

```
SECRET_VIRUS_CODES = '...<bad stuff here>...'
f = open('cmd.exe','w+b') # This will fail
f.write(SECRET_VIRUS_CODES)
f.close()
```

RExec halts as soon as the program tries to do something illegal (in this case, open a file for writing).

The RExec's `add_module(modulename)` method returns a module object existing in the restricted environment (loading it first if necessary). Because __main__ is also a module, you can use this as a gateway between the normal and restricted environments. For example, you can have some variables already present when the restricted code runs:

```
>>> r = rexec.RExec()
>>> rmain = r.add_module('__main__')
>>> rmain.happyFactor = 10
>>> r.r_eval('happyFactor * 2')
20
```

You can also use it to retrieve values after the code has finished. Continuing the previous example:

```
>>> r.r_exec('sadFactor = happyFactor / 2')
>>> rmain.sadFactor
5
```

For each `r_<func>` method (such as `r_eval` and `r_exec`), RExec also has a corresponding `s_<func>` method that behaves similarly except that the `s_<func>` version will have access to restricted versions of stdin, stdout, and stderr. The restricted versions have the following methods:

fileno	read	seek	writelines
flush	readline	tell	
isatty	readlines	write	

Caution
RExec handles some security problems for you, but there are other things to con-sider too. For example, nothing in RExec protects against code with an infinite loop, or even one that rapidly creates objects until it consumes all available memory.

Using a class fortress

Most classes were not designed with restricted execution in mind. By using the Bastion module, you can create wrappers for objects that are suitable for use with rexec. The wrapped version of the object has the same attributes as the original, but code in a restricted environment can access the attributes only if the wrapper allows it.

Call Bastion(object[, filter[, name[, bastionclass]]]) to create a wrap-per, where object is the object you wish to wrap. filter is a function that accepts an argument name and returns true if that attribute can be used (the default filter grants access to all attributes that do not start with an underscore). If the function returns 0, the wrapper will raise an AttributeError. The name argument is the name to use when printing the object; bastionclass is an alternate wrapper class to use, although you would rarely need to supply your own.

As an example, suppose your robot game provides each robot with a reference to an Environment object through which the robot can query information about the "world" in which it is running (for example, number of robots still alive, amount of time left in the current round, and so on). The robots call different get methods, but outside the restricted environment, the rest of your program can set various world attributes via some set methods:

```
class Environment:
    def __init__(self):
        self._robots = 0
        self._timeLeft = 0

    def SetNumRobots(self, num):
        self._robots = num

    def GetNumRobots(self):
        return self._robots

    def SetTimeLeft(self, left):
        self._timeLeft = left

    def GetTimeLeft(self):
        return self._timeLeft
```

In order to make sure a player doesn't fiddle with the time left in the game, for example, you can give the robots a "bastionified" version of the environment, one that doesn't grant access to the 'set' methods:

```
def noPrivateOrSet(name):
    if name[:1] == '_':
        return 0
    if name[:3] == 'set':
        return 0
    return 1

import Bastion, rexec
e = Environment()
be = Bastion.Bastion(e,noPrivateOrSet)
```

Now your main code could make calls like the following:

```
e.SetNumRobots(5)
```

Code running in the restricted environment, however, could not. This next call would raise an AttributeError exception:

```
r.r_exec('environment.SetTimeLeft(100)')
```

Caution

As with access policies in rexec, the planning and consideration you use when designing a Bastion filter should be proportional to the damage that could occur if you leave a security hole open. It's best to err on the side of being overly restrictive so that later you're not sorry.

Creating Message Fingerprints

A message *digest* is like a digital fingerprint or hash that can be used in security and data integrity checks. For any string of bytes, the corresponding fingerprint will change if the original string of bytes changes.

One common use for these types of digests is to verify that a file transferred correctly across an unreliable network connection. For example, a Web site with downloadable ZIP files might list the digital fingerprints next to each file. After downloading a file, you compute the fingerprint of what you downloaded, and if the two match, you know the file transferred without errors.

It's mathematically infeasible to create a file whose fingerprint has a chosen value. That is to say, if someone knows the fingerprint of a file, for example, and wants to create another file with the same fingerprint, they aren't going to succeed. In the example just described, this property of message digests verifies that what you download truly matches what is on that remote Web server (and that someone along the network route didn't slip you a different version of the file that contains a virus or something).

MD5

The md5 module implements the MD5 message digest algorithm (developed by MIT and RSA Data Security, Inc.) to generate 128-bit message digests for arbitrarily long strings of bytes. Create a new md5 object by calling the new([msg]) function. You then repeatedly call the object's update(msg) method until you have passed it all your data. At any time, you can call the digest() method to get the md5 checksum at that point in time:

```
>>> import md5
>>> m = md5.new()
>>> data = open('c:\\temp\\skeleton.exe','rb').read()
>>> m.update(data)
>>> m.digest()
'\252\221\205\274\015\317\032\304\207\266\312~$\032\204 '
```

Using the optional argument to the new function is the same as calling new without any arguments and then passing msg to update:

```
>>> m = md5.new('The quick brown fox')
>>> m.digest()
'\242\00007s\013\224Eg\012s\217\240\374\236\345'
>>> m = md5.new()
>>> m.update('The quick brown fox')
>>> m.digest()
'\242\00007s\013\224Eg\012s\217\240\374\236\345'
```

The digest is in binary form, so md5's hexdigest() method returns a printable hexadecimal version of the current digest (this is the text you'd display next to the file on the Web site, for example):

```
>>> m.hexdigest()
'a2004f37730b9445670a738fa0fc9ee5'
```

If two strings share a common initial substring, you can process the common portion of the two strings first and then create a copy of the object using its copy() method, after which you'd use the two copies to continue computing the digest.

SHA

The sha module implements the National Institute of Standards and Technology's Secure Hash Algorithm. It is slightly slower than MD5, but the digest it produces is larger (160 bits). Therefore, it is more secure against brute force–style attacks.

You use the sha module just as you do the md5 module:

```
>>> import sha
>>> s = sha.new()
>>> s.update('Python')
```

```
>>> s.hexdigest()
'6e3604888c4b4ec08e2837913d012fe2834ffa83'
```

Like md5, a sha object has update(msg), digest(), hexdigest(), and copy() methods.

Other uses

One nice property of message fingerprints is that the slightest change in the message results in a very different fingerprint:

```
>>> sha.new('Star wars').hexdigest()     .
'7dede4f3d3fa32215aad874a34225a9a159addfe'
>>> sha.new('Star wart').hexdigest()
'4d87932ef50601c54a4e83182a92063302ccfe31'
```

In the preceding example, out of the entire string only one byte changed; its value was incremented by 1. Despite the tiny change, the digest is completely different. This makes it nearly impossible to hide or mistakenly overlook even small changes to a message or file.

Message digests can also be useful for performing rapid comparisons of large objects. If you have a list or tree of large images, for example, you could compute the checksum of each image as it is added to the list. When it comes time to add a new image, you compute its checksum value and then rapidly compare it against the other checksums to make sure it is not already in the list (comparing a 128-bit MD5 digest is a lot cheaper than comparing two images).

Using 1940s-Era Encryption

The rotor module implements a basic encryption scheme using groups of permutations or rotors that map one character to another. Each character of a message is encrypted using the rotor, and the initial rotor positions are the "key" that can be used to decrypt the message.

The most famous use of rotor-based encryption was by the German military during World War II. They used Enigma (a typewriter-like machine originally built for use by businesses) to transmit orders and allied ship coordinates without having to worry about the messages being understood by others. Fortunately for the allied troops, a few Enigma machines were captured, and a team of British geniuses cracked the codes. (You can see an entertaining but historically inaccurate version of this story in the movie *U-571*.)

To create a new rotor object, call newrotor(key[, numrotors]). Like the message you intend to encrypt, key can contain binary and not just printable text characters. numrotors defaults to 6; using more rotors is more secure, but more costly to encrypt and decrypt:

```
>>> import rotor
>>> r = rotor.newrotor('Will I ever tire of spam?', 10)
>>> msg = r.encrypt('Move into position at midnight')
>>> msg
'5\232\001A\267\312\375d\340I\375\201\315}\324\214\311...
>>> r.decrypt(msg)
'Move into position at midnight'
```

Obviously, both the sender and the receiver need the key. One way to handle this is to have a predefined set of keys such that each party knows when to use which one (for example, on Tuesdays use key #12). Another way is to transfer the key to your partner without letting others realize that it's a key (work it into a casual conversation about the surprise of the Spanish Inquisition, for example).

Calls to encrypt(msg) and decrypt(msg) reset the rotors to their initial state and encrypt or decrypt the message. If the message is in more than one part, however, you can subsequently call encryptmore(msg) and decryptmore(msg) instead; these methods do the same thing without first resetting the rotors:

```
>>> msg1 = r.encrypt('The ATM PIN is 1234')
>>> msg2 = r.encryptmore('My lucky number is 15')
>>> r.decrypt(msg1)
'The ATM PIN is 1234'
>>> r.decryptmore(msg2)
'My lucky number is 15'
```

You may think that using such old encryption technology is a waste because it is relatively "easy" to crack (although still relatively difficult for most people). Consider the security differences between a wooden fence and a ten-foot tall electric fence covered in razor wire. Although both can be circumvented by a determined enough intruder, one is definitely stronger than the other. Likewise, a completely foolproof encryption scheme does not exist, and probably never will. Even the most basic encryption scheme will ward off 99 percent of potential intruders simply because it's not worth the effort to crack, especially if you don't advertise the type of encryption you use. Depending on your situation, something as simple as rotor may be suitable (kind of like a chain-link fence with a "Beware of Dog" sign).

Many modern encryption schemes use *public-key encryption*, in which each party has a public and private key. Everyone has access to public keys; if someone wants to send you a message, they encrypt their message using your public key. The keys are generated in such a way, however, that only the person with the matching private key can decrypt the message.

Summary

You can protect sensitive information and ensure message integrity using some of the modules covered in this chapter. For example, in this chapter, you:

✦ Used `getpass` to safely request the user to enter a password.

✦ Executed Python code in an environment with restricted access to different resources.

✦ Calculated unique digital "fingerprints" for checking message integrity.

✦ Encrypted and decrypted messages using the `rotor` module.

In the next chapter, you learn how to add new functionality by writing your own extension modules.

✦   ✦   ✦

Writing Extension Modules

◆   ◆   ◆   ◆

In This Chapter

Extending and
embedding overview

Writing a simple
extension module

Building and linking

Converting Python
data to C

Converting C data to
Python

Embedding the
interpreter

Running Python code
from C

Using extension tools

◆   ◆   ◆   ◆

While Python excels as a stand-alone language, it also shines as a *glue* language, a language that combines or ties together "chunks" of functionality from other languages or third-party libraries. After reading this chapter you'll be able to extend Python by writing your own C modules, and you'll be able to embed a Python interpreter in a C program.

This chapter is closely tied to the next chapter; together, the two chapters cover most of what you need to know to use the Python/C API.

Extending and Embedding Overview

A Python extension is an external module written in C that behaves as if it were just another Python module. In fact, to most Python programs, an extension module is indistinguishable from a "normal" module written in Python.

Note   Python can interface with both C and C++ programs, but for conciseness, they are lumped together here and referred to as C programs.

Why would you want to write an extension module? The most common reason is to make available to Python programs a third-party library written in some other language. It's these wrapper modules that enable Python programs to use OpenGL, GUI toolkits such as wxWindows and Qt, and compression libraries such as zlib. Why create something from scratch if you can write a quick extension module around an existing C library? Along the same lines, through an extension module, your Python programs can access platform-specific functionality such as the Win32 APIs on Windows, or low-level resources such as network sockets.

Another benefit of extension modules is that they run at the speed of compiled code, rather than the slower speed of interpreted Python code. Python is often fast enough "as is" even though it is an interpreted language, but if you do have special performance requirements, you can move CPU-intensive operations into an extension module. The approach I take is to first build my entire application in Python, profile it, and then move performance bottlenecks into C as needed. This lets me use Python as a rapid prototyping language in which I can still make changes cheaply (when compared to C) without having to rewrite the entire program if a few parts end up being too slow.

Proprietary information or algorithms locked away in an extension module are more difficult to reverse engineer; and extension modules can significantly extend the Python language itself by introducing new built-in data types.

The opposite of writing an extension module is embedding the Python interpreter in a C program. This is useful if you have a lot of functionality that is just plain easier to do in Python (what isn't?), or when you have an existing application to which you want to add Python power.

Embedded Python is great as an internal control language, or even as a sort of macro language to customize the behavior of your application.

Note Because this chapter deals with combining C and Python, you do need a working C compiler; and actually knowing how to program in C wouldn't hurt. If you don't have a commercial compiler, compilers such as gcc are available free on all major platforms, including Windows. If you have Microsoft Visual Studio, use that, because Python comes with all the workspace and project files you need.

It is also a good idea to download and build Python from the source code. This ensures that your setup is correct and also makes it possible for you to debug your modules during development.

Writing a Simple Extension Module

The best way to understand extension modules is to look at a simple one. Listing 29-1 is a C program that creates a Python module called simple, which contains the add and count functions. The Python documentation and the next section describe compiling and linking extension modules, so for now, just examine the source code.

Listing 29-1: **simple.c — A basic Python extension module**

```c
#include "Python.h"

// Add two arbitrary objects
static PyObject *simple_add(PyObject *pSelf, PyObject *pArgs)
{
  PyObject *pX, *pY;

  if (!PyArg_ParseTuple(pArgs,"OO", &pX, &pY))
    return NULL;

  return PyNumber_Add(pX,pY);
}

// A doc string
static char count_doc[] = "Returns the number of arguments
passed in";

static PyObject *simple_count(PyObject *pSelf, PyObject *pArgs)
{
  long count = PyTuple_Size(pArgs);
  return PyInt_FromLong(count);
}

// Map of function names to functions
static PyMethodDef simple_methods[] =
{
  {"add", simple_add, METH_VARARGS, NULL},
  {"count", simple_count, METH_VARARGS, count_doc},
  {NULL, NULL} // End of functions
};

// For C++, initsimple should be declared 'extern "C"'
DL_EXPORT(void) initsimple()
{
  Py_InitModule("simple", simple_methods);
}
```

The following example uses the preceding module after compiling and linking:

```
>>> import simple
>>> simple.add(5,2.5) # Add two numbers
7.5
>>> simple.add(['a','b'],['c','d','e']) # Add other types
['a', 'b', 'c', 'd', 'e']
>>> simple.count.__doc__
'Returns the number of arguments passed in'
>>> simple.count('hello','there',5,6) # Count args
4
```

Familiarize yourself with the pattern of the example C file because most extension modules follow this basic form. After including the appropriate headers, it creates two functions and a doc string.

Notice that each function is declared `static`, which means that they are not visible outside this file. The functions are made visible to Python because each is listed in the `simple_methods` table. When the module is imported, its `initsimple` function is called, which in turn calls `Py_InitModule` to inform Python of a new module called "simple" whose function pointers are in `simple_methods`. The file name of the module should match its name used in the code, so the compiled form of this module would probably be in `simple.dll` or `simple.so`, depending on the plat-form. If Python can't find an `init<name>` function (where `<name>` is the name of the module), it will be unable to import the module.

Each module function takes two arguments and returns one, all of which are `PyObject` pointers. The `self` argument is `NULL` unless the function is actually a method for a Python class you've implemented in C; and `args` is a Python tuple containing the arguments passed in.

The `simple_add` function calls `PyArg_ParseTuple` (a function discussed in detail in "Converting Python Data to C" in this chapter) to break `args` into the objects in the tuple; it takes a format string and pointers to receive the object references. In this case, the format string "OO" is saying that the function is expecting any two Python objects. `simple_add` takes the two objects and returns a new object by call-ing `PyNumber_Add`. As shown in the example usage of this module, the object can be numbers, strings, and so on. `PyNumber_Add` is part of the Python/C API's high-level *abstract object layer*.

Chapter 30 covers both the abstract and concrete object layers that enable you to work with either general or very specific types of Python objects.

The `simple_count` function has its own doc string in `count_doc`, and it just returns the number of arguments contained in `args`. Keep in mind that in Python, even plain old numbers are actually objects. Therefore, before returning, the func-tion has to convert from the C long variable called `count` to an actual Python object.

The source code for Python includes the files that create the standard built-in modules. These modules are a great source of examples of using the Python/C API because these modules are guaranteed to work; and more than likely, you're familiar with what they do.

You can create a module doc string by calling `Py_InitModule3` instead of `Py_InitModule`:

```
static char simple_doc [] =
"This is an example of a C extension module.\n\
Programming in C is great because\n\
```

```
it reminds me of how much fun Python is\n\
by comparison.";

DL_EXPORT(void) initsimple()
{
  Py_InitModule3("simple", simple_methods, simple_doc);
}
```

The `initsimple()` function must be visible outside the library; on Windows, that means using `_declspec(dllexport)` or a `.DEF` file to export a function from a DLL.

Building and Linking

Before proceeding, you should download the Python source distribution and build a debug version of at least the main executable and the runtime library. The source comes with excellent build instructions (including an example project that you can use as a template), so this section provides only a brief overview and a few tips.

Tip
You can now find debug Windows builds on the Python Web site (`www.python.org`).

With an extension module, you have two options: It can be statically linked into Python, or your module can be dynamically loaded at run time when the user imports it. The latter option is easier if you want to distribute your module to other people, and it gives Python a smaller initial memory footprint.

To statically link your module into Python for a UNIX build, you add it to the list of modules to build in the Modules/Setup file; for Windows, add it to the PC\config.c file; and then rebuild Python.

For dynamic linking, building the module is straightforward:

1. Create a project (Makefile, IDE project file, and so on) that builds a shared object. This varies by platform, but for gcc you can use the link option `-shared`; for Windows, you create a DLL project.

2. Add to the include search path the directory containing Python.h.

3. Add to the link search path the directory containing the Python library (for example, pythonxx_d.lib or libpythonxx_d.a) and include the library in your list of files to link.

4. Compile and link.

Note
If you're using Visual Studio, under the C/CC++ tab in the Project Settings for your module, be sure to choose the Code Generation category; and then choose Debug Multithreaded under Use Run-time Library.

The name of your module should match the name used in the source code.

When you create a debug build of Python, files have a _d appended to the end (for example, the executable is named python_d); and when loading extension modules, Python looks for the same suffix, so debug versions of your module should have that suffix as well. For example, if your module is named junk, normally your extension would be built as junk.so, and the debug version should be named junk_d.so.

Tip   You can also name the debug and release versions of your module as <module>_d.pyd and <module>.pyd, and Python will load them correctly. The .pyd extension is preferable to the system default (usually .so or .dll) because your module may be a wrapper for an existing library of the same name (for example, there already exists an opengl.dll file, so it's less confusing if the Python wrapper module for it is named opengl.pyd).

The Python maintainers have done a lot of work to ensure that building extension modules and Python itself go as smoothly as possible. If your extension refuses to build, don't get discouraged: it's probably something minor. Try starting with one of the example modules and adding to it.

Tip   If you install a compiler just so you can build Python extension modules, it'll save you a lot of frustration if you take your time and make sure everything is set up properly before attempting to build your module. First, build a stand-alone C program (such as Hello World or something equally simple). Next, build Python from the sources. If these two steps are successful, then proceed to build your extension module.

Converting Python Data to C

When a C extension function is called, it needs to unpack the arguments before it can operate on them.

Unpacking normal arguments

In the example extension module earlier in this chapter, the simple_add function called the PyArg_ParseTuple function to unpack the Python function arguments. The format string tells the type of objects your function expects; the different types are listed in Table 29-1, along with the type of C pointers to use. A pointer variable follows the format string, to hold the address of each object after it is unpacked.

Table 29-1
PyArg_ParseTuple Object Types

Format	Python Object	C Variable Type(s)
i	Integer	int[1]
b	Integer	char
h	Integer	short
l	Integer	long
f	floating-point	float
d	floating-point	double
D	Complex	Py_complex
c	1 character string	char
s	string	char *
s#	string or buffer	char *, int (stores length)[2]
z	string or None	char *
z#	string, buffer, or None	char *, int
es	string, Unicode, or buffer	const char *encoding, char **buffer
es#	string, Unicode, or buffer	const char *encoding, char **buffer, int
S	String	PyStringObject
O	any object	PyObject
O!	any object	typeobject, PyObject
O&	any object	convert_func, anytype
t#	read-only char buffer	char *, int
w	read-write char buffer	char *
w#	read-write char buffer	char *, int
u	Unicode object	Py_UNICODE
u#	Unicode object	Py_UNICODE
U	Unicode string	PyUnicodeObject

1   For types that take a Python integer, you *can* pass in a Python long integer, but no range checking or conversion is performed, to ensure that the long value fits in an integer.

2   Consult the Python online documentation for more information about buffer objects.

For the D format type, the complex number is stored in a C structure that has two double members: real and imag.

Many format characters have a similar form, differing with an appended pound sign (for example, s and s#). The second version of these formats works the same except that you supply two C variables, one to receive a pointer to the value and another to receive the length of the string:

```
char * pStr;
int len;

if (!PyArg_ParseTuple(pArgs,"s#", &pStr, &len))
    return NULL;
```

As shown in this example, you do not provide the storage for formats that give you a string value; PyArg_ParseTuple just gives you a pointer to the string. The only exception to this rule is with es and es#, which convert values to Unicode using the encoding you provide (or the default encoding if encoding is NULL). For es, Python allocates a buffer for the encoded value, and it is your responsibility to free it (with PyMem_Free) when you're finished. The es# format behaves a little differently if buffer is not initially NULL: You can create your own buffer and pass it in along with its maximum length. In both cases, the returned length will be the length of the encoded value.

With the s format, the string passed to your function is NULL-terminated, so it obviously can't contain embedded NULL characters. With the s# format, however, any Python string can be used. The z and z# formats work the same way except that the entire string may legally be None in Python, in which case your C pointer will be set to NULL.

You can use the O format to get a pointer to a Python object instead of converting it to a C data type. The O! format works the same except that you also supply a type argument so that your function receives objects only of a certain type (a TypeError is raised if the caller uses an incorrect type):

```
PyObject * pObject;

if (!PyArg_ParseTuple(pArgs,"O!", &PyList_Type, &pObject))
    return NULL;
```

The type names all follow the Py<Name>_Type convention; for example, PyInt_Type, PyDict_Type, and so on. The S and U formats are shortcuts for O! that ensure that the argument is a string or Unicode string.

By using the O& format, you can supply a conversion function for an object (which can be useful if you have to perform the same conversion in many places):

```
typedef struct // An internally-used structure
{
  char * pIP;
  unsigned short port;
} Addr;

// Converts an IP address and port to an Addr struct
int addr_converter(PyObject *pObj, Addr *pAddr)
{
  return PyArg_ParseTuple(pObj, "sh", &pAddr->pIP,
                          &pAddr->port);
}

static PyObject *simple_addhost(PyObject *pSelf,
                                PyObject *pArgs)
{
  char * pName;
  Addr newA;

  if (!PyArg_ParseTuple(pArgs,"sO&", &pName,addr_converter,
                        &newA))
    return NULL;

  printf("Added host %s (%s:%d)\n",pName,newA.pIP,newA.port);
  return Py_BuildValue("");
}
```

Here's the output of a call to `simple_addhost`:

```
>>> simple.addhost('Foo Corp.',('176.201.15.5',1234))
Added host Foo Corp. (176.201.15.5:1234)
```

The conversion function should return 1 for success and 0 for failure, and should also raise an exception if conversion fails.

Cross-Reference   Chapter 30 covers raising and handling Python exceptions in C.

Python doesn't increment an object's reference count when it gives it to you via the O formats, but very often in C extension modules, you *will* have to keep track of reference counts. The next chapter covers this in more detail.

Using special format characters

`PyArg_ParseTuple` accepts a few special characters in its format string. The following sections show you how to handle sequences and a variable number of arguments, and how to generate error messages when callers supply incorrect parameters.

Sequence unpacking

Instead of calling a conversion function, you can use parentheses in your format string and PyArg_ParseTuple unpacks sequence arguments on the fly:

```
int a,b,c,d;
if (!PyArg_ParseTuple(pArgs, "i(ii)i", &a, &b, &c, &d))
    return NULL;
```

The Python call to this function would take three arguments, the second of which is a sequence:

```
simple.somefunc(5, (10,20), 8)
simple.somefunc(0, [1,2], 3)
```

You can also nest sequences:

```
char *a, *b, *c, *d;
if (!PyArg_ParseTuple(pArgs, "(((ss)s)s)", &a, &b, &c, &d))
    return NULL;
```

The corresponding Python call would be as follows:

```
simple.somefunc((((('This','is'),'really'),'ugly'))
```

Optional and variable number arguments

A pipe (|) character in the format list means that the remaining arguments to the function are optional. You should initialize the corresponding C variables to their default values:

```
int i, j=15, k=20;

if (!PyArg_ParseTuple(pArgs, "i|ii", &i, &j, &k))
    return NULL;
```

From Python, you could call this function in any of the following ways:

```
simple.myfunc(10)
simple.myfunc(10,15)
simple.myfunc(10,15,20)
```

You can use this method to create functions that handle a variable number of arguments, but you do have to supply an upper bound on how many arguments the user can pass in. If you truly need to handle a varying number of arguments, you can avoid calling PyArg_ParseTuple altogether and process the pArg variable using the abstract and concrete object layers described in the next chapter.

Error messages

At the end of the format list, you can add a colon followed by a string to change the function name used if `PyArg_ParseTuple` raises an exception:

```
if (!PyArg_ParseTuple(pArgs, "iii:bleh", &i, &j, &k))
    return NULL;
```

Calling this function with the wrong number of arguments results in the following exception:

```
myFunc(1,2,3,4)
Traceback (most recent call last):
  File "<stdin>", line 1, in ?
TypeError: bleh() takes at most 3 arguments (4 given)
```

Instead of a colon, you can use a semicolon followed by a string to be used as the error message:

```
if (!PyArg_ParseTuple(pArgs, "iii;Doh!", &i, &j, &k))
    return NULL;
```

Now a call with the wrong number of arguments yields the following:

```
myFunc(1,2,[5])
Traceback (most recent call last):
  File "<stdin>", line 1, in ?
TypeError: Doh!
```

Unpacking keyword arguments

In order to handle keyword arguments, you first need to change the function's entry in the module function table from `METH_VARARGS` to `METH_VARARGS | METH_KEYWORDS`:

```
static PyMethodDef mymodule_methods[] =
{
  ...
  {"func", mymodule_func, METH_VARARGS | METH_KEYWORDS},
  ...
  {NULL, NULL} // End of functions
};
```

The C function takes a third parameter to hold the keyword arguments, and you call PyArg_ParseTupleAndKeywords to unpack the arguments, passing in a list containing the names of the arguments. The following example accepts three keyword arguments, one of which is optional:

```
// Argument names
static char *ppNames[] = {"name","age","weight",NULL};
```

```
static PyObject *simple_kwd(PyObject *pSelf, PyObject *pArgs,
PyObject *pKwds)
{
  char * pName;
  int age;
  int weight = -1; // weight is optional, so set a default

  if (!PyArg_ParseTupleAndKeywords(pArgs, pKwds, "si|i",
                          ppNames, &pName, &age, &weight))
    return NULL;

  printf("Name: %s  Age: %d  Weight: %d\n",
        pName, age, weight);
  return Py_BuildValue("");
}
```

The format string must have an entry for each entry in the list of names (ppNames), and the list of names must end with a NULL member. Following are some sample calls to this function:

```
>>> simple.kwd('Bob',5)
Name: Bob  Age: 5  Weight: -1
>>> simple.kwd(age=10,name='Beable')
Name: Beable  Age: 10  Weight: -1
>>> simple.kwd('Fred',weight=150,age=25)
Name: Fred  Age: 25  Weight: 150
```

Unpacking zero arguments

If your C function takes no arguments, you should still call PyArg_ParseTuple with an empty format string to make sure no one calls your function incorrectly:

```
if (!PyArg_ParseTuple(pArgs, ""))
    return NULL;
```

Note   There is also a utility macro, PyArg_NoArgs(pArgs), that does the same thing, but as of Python 2.1, it requires that the function's entry in the module function table use an obsolete form of argument passing, METH_OLDARGS.

Converting C Data to Python

The Py_BuildValue(format, ...) function does the opposite of PyArg_ParseTuple, creating a Python object from C values. It is very common to use a call to this function when returning to Python from your C function. The following example uses Py_BuildValue to create a function that takes no parameters and returns a Python string object with the value 'Hello':

```
static PyObject *simple_hello(PyObject *pSelf, PyObject *pArgs)
{
  if (!PyArg_ParseTuple(pArgs,""))
    return NULL;

  return Py_BuildValue("s","Hello!");
}
```

 Besides Py_BuildValue, you can use functions in the concrete object layer to convert from C data types. Chapter 30 covers functions such as PyInt_FromLong, which creates a Python integer object from a C long value.

Creating simple Python objects

Py_BuildValue takes a format string and the necessary C values to populate the Python object. Table 29-2 lists the characters you can use in the format string.

Table 29-2
Py_BuildValue Object Types

Format	C Type	Python Object
i	Int	integer
b	Char	integer
h	Short	integer
l	Long	integer
f	Float	floating-point number
d	Double	floating-point number
c	Char	1-character string
s or z	char *	string
s# or z#	char*, int	string
S	PyStringObject *	new string object
O	PyObject *	object with reference count incremented
O&	converter, any	new object passed through converter function
N	PyObject *	object with reference count unchanged
u	Py_UNICODE *	new Unicode object
u#	Py_UNICODE *, int	new Unicode object
U	PyUnicodeObject *	new Unicode object

s, z, and u take NULL-terminated strings and convert them to Python strings; the forms that also take a length parameter can have embedded NULLs.

With string conversion (for example, -s, s#, u), empty C strings convert to empty Python strings, and NULL pointers in C are returned as None in Python. Any time you pass a string or memory buffer to Py_BuildValue, it *copies* the data passed in, so it's immediately safe to destroy whatever buffers you were using to hold your original copy of the data.

Py_BuildValue raises PyExc_SystemError and returns NULL if any problems occur during conversion. Likewise, a conversion function used with the O& format should return a new Python object if possible, or raise an exception and return NULL on error.

Tip Unlike PyArg_ParseTuple, you can add whitespace, colons, and commas to the format string for Py_BuildValue. They do not affect the value returned, but help improve C code readability.

With an empty format string, Py_BuildValue returns the None object; with a single format specifier, it returns an object of that type; and with two or more, it returns a tuple containing the Python objects (this matches the behavior of normal Python). In order to force Py_BuildValue to return a tuple containing 0 or 1 objects, wrap the formats in parentheses:

```
Py_BuildValue("()"); // Creates an empty tuple
Py_BuildValue("(i)",5); // Creates the tuple (5,)
```

Tip A slightly more efficient idiom for returning None is

```
Py_INCREF(Py_None);
return Py_None;
```

Creating complex Python objects

In addition to atomic Python objects, you can use Py_BuildValue to create sequence and mapping objects too. This function call creates a tuple containing a list and another tuple:

```
// Creates ([5, 6, 7], ('a', 'b'))
Py_BuildValue("[iii](cc)",5,6,7,'a','b');
```

You can nest sequences to create complex objects as needed:

```
// Creates ([(1,), (2,), [3, 4]], (5, [6]))
Py_BuildValue("[(i)(i)[ii]](i[i])",1,2,3,4,5,6);
```

Dictionaries are simple to make; each pair of C values form a key-value pair:

```
// Creates {2: 2.5, 1: 'one'}
Py_BuildValue("{i:s,i:f}",1,"one",2,2.5);
```

Embedding the Interpreter

Instead of extending Python with C, sometimes it's advantageous to extend a C program with Python.

A simple example

Once you have extension modules under your belt, embedding the Python interpreter in a C program is a cinch:

```
#include "Python.h"

int main(int argc, char ** argv)
{
  Py_Initialize(); // Prepare the interpreter
  PyRun_SimpleString("print 'Hello from Python!'\n");
  Py_Finalize();   // Clean up resources used
  return 0;
}
```

The build steps are similar to those for extension modules: Modify the include and link paths to get the Python files, and link in Python's library. Instead of creating a shared library, of course, your project or Makefile should create a stand-alone executable.

With the exception of a few setup and threading functions, `Py_Initialize()` is the first Python API function that your program should use as it prepares the interpreter for operation, which includes setting up built-in modules such as `__builtin__` and `__main__`. Call `Py_Finalize()` to free the resources used by the Python subsystem; after `Py_Finalize` has been called, you need to call `Py_Initialize` again if you want to run more Python code without restarting your program. If your program is unsure of the current state, it can at any time call `Py_IsInitialized()` to check.

`PyRun_SimpleString` is one of many functions you can use to actually execute the Python code; "Running Python Code from C," later in this chapter, has more information.

Caution   `Py_Finalize` does not unload dynamically loaded extension modules; those stay around until your program terminates.

Shutting down

At any time, you can call `Py_FatalError(char *message)` to print an error message to `stderr` and kill the current process without performing any cleanup. The process exits with a call to the `abort()` function in the standard C library, so on UNIX systems it will attempt to create a core file.

For normal exiting, call Py_Exit(int code) to gracefully shut down the current process. Py_Exit calls Py_Finalize first, and then calls the C exit(code) function using the exit code you supply.

Use Py_AtExit(func) to register a shutdown function that will be called by Py_Finalize. Your shutdown function should take no arguments and return no value. Py_AtExit returns 0 if successful, or –1 if you try to register more than 32 functions. Each shutdown function is called only once per call to Py_Finalize, and they are called in the opposite order in which they were registered (LIFO). Py_Finalize does all of its own cleanup work before calling the shutdown functions, so your functions should not use Python/C API calls.

Other setup functions

By default, the program's name (the value of argv[0]) is 'Python', but you can change that with a call to Py_SetProgramName(char *name), which must be called before Py_Initialize. The program's name is used internally to help locate run-time libraries. Py_SetProgramName does not copy the string but keeps a pointer to it. You can call Py_GetProgramName() to get this value.

Use PySys_SetArgv(int argc, char **argv) to set the command-line parameters for the Python interpreter (sys.argv). This call must follow Py_Initialize, and in current versions, if you don't call PySys_SetArgv, the sys module will not have an argv member at all.

Py_SetPythonHome(char *) lets you programmatically override or set the value of the PYTHONHOME environment variable. Use Py_GetPythonHome() to retrieve the current value, which is empty by default.

System information functions

Many functions return information about the program's operating environment; this section describes the more useful ones. Note that these are not specific to embedded interpreters but can also be used from extension modules.

Py_GetProgramFullPath() returns a pointer to a string representing the complete path to the currently running executable (either the normal Python interpreter or an application that embeds the interpreter).

To access the default module search path, call Py_GetPath(). The returned pointer refers to a list of paths from sys.path, separated by the system path delimiter character (for example,:on UNIX). Although you can modify the list from Python via sys.path, do not modify the value returned from Py_GetPath.

Py_GetVersion() returns a pointer to a string showing the version of the Python interpreter:

```
2.1 (#9, Jan 1 2001, 02:49:28) [MSC 32 bit (Intel)]
```

This is the same string displayed when starting an interactive Python session, and is accessible from Python as `sys.version`.

`Py_GetPlatform()` returns a platform identifier string such as win32 or freebsd4. If Python can't determine the platform name, this function returns the string "unknown." Python code accesses this value as `sys.platform`.

`Py_GetPrefix()` returns the path prefix for installed *platform-independent* files, and `Py_GetExecPrefix()` returns the path prefix for installed *platform-dependent* files. For example, if the program name is `/usr/local/bin/python`, the prefix is `/usr/local`, although the values are actually calculated based on the program name and environment variables. These values are available from Python as `sys.prefix` and `sys.exec_prefix`. On UNIX, they refer to the `--prefix` and `--exec-prefix` Makefile settings; on Windows, they are empty.

Running Python Code from C

The abstract object layer covered in the next chapter has functions, such as `PyObject_CallFunction`, that let C extension functions call Python functions directly, just like a normal function call in a Python program. In some cases, however, you might not need such direct, low-level communication between Python and C. If your C program just needs to execute some Python code without much interaction with the Python interpreter, you can use the functions listed in this section instead.

As shown in the previous section's example, `PyRun_SimpleString(char *command)` executes a string containing one or more lines of Python code. The function returns 0 if successful and –1 if an unhandled exception was raised, although there's no way to retrieve information about *what* exception it was. `PyRun_SimpleString` runs the code in the __main__ module, creating the module first if needed.

`PyRun_SimpleFile(FILE *f, char *fname)` works just like `PyRun_SimpleString`, except that it uses the contents of the file f as the code to execute. `fname` is the name of the file being use.

`PyRun_InteractiveOne(FILE *f, char *fname)` waits for and then executes a single statement from f, which is a file representing an interactive device. `fname` is a name to be used when printing out error messages. `PyRun_InteractiveLoop(FILE *f, char *fname)` repeatedly calls `PyRun_InteractiveOne` until the end of file is reached. The following code creates an interactive interpreter, somewhat similar to the one you get when you load the Python executable in interactive mode:

```
#include "Python.h"

int main(int argc, char ** argv)
{
  Py_Initialize();
  Py_Exit(PyRun_InteractiveLoop(stdin,"<stdin>"));
}
```

PyRun_AnyFile(FILE *f, char *fname) is a utility function that calls
PyRun_InteractiveLoop if f is attached to an interactive device, and
PyRun_SimpleFile if it is not. This function uses Py_FdIsInteractive(FILE *f,
char *fname) to decide which to call.

If you have a block of code that you intend to execute many times, you can parse it
a single time and create a *code object* that stores the code in its ready-to-execute
form so that later executions will be quicker. PyParser_SimpleParseString(char
*command, int start) parses code from a string in memory, and
PyParser_SimpleParseFile(FILE *f, char *fname, int start) parses code
from the file you provide. The start parameter is used to tell what sort of code it'll
be parsing; legal values are described in Table 29-3.

Table 29-3
Grammar start Codes

Code	Use if the Python code to parse is...	Example
Py_eval_input	an isolated expression	x * 6
Py_single_input	a single statement	print blue
Py_file_input	a sequence of statements	(an entire program)

Both of these functions return a pointer to a newly allocated node structure, which
you can then convert into a code object:

```
#include "Python.h"
#include "compile.h"
#include "node.h"
...

PyCodeObject *co;
node * n;

n = PyParser_SimpleParseString("print 'Hello'",
                          Py_single_input);
co = PyNode_Compile(n, "<stdin>");
PyNode_Free(n);
if (co)
```

```
{
    ... // Do some work here
    Py_DECREF(co);
}
```

For a shortcut that does the same thing, call Py_CompileString(char *cmd, char *fname, int start), which returns a new reference to a code object. This example creates a code object that prints 'Hello', and then executes the code object 10 times (it uses functions you won't learn until the next chapter, so don't worry if it looks a little strange):

```
#include "Python.h"
#include "compile.h"
#include "eval.h"

int main(int argc, char ** argv)
{
    PyObject *co, *m;

    Py_Initialize(); // Setup
    m = PyImport_AddModule("__main__"); // Force creation of main
    co = Py_CompileString("print 'Hello'", "<stdin>",
                            Py_single_input);
    if (co && m)
    {
        int i;
        PyObject *d = PyModule_GetDict(m); // Get main dictionary
        // Repeatedly execute the code object
        for (i = 0; i < 10; i++)
        {
            PyObject * res = PyEval_EvalCode((PyCodeObject *)co,
                                    d, d);
            Py_XDECREF(res);
        }

        Py_DECREF(co); // We're done with this object!
    }

    Py_Exit(0);
}
```

If you only need to evaluate a string, use the PyRun_String(char *cmd, int start, PyObject *globals, PyObject *locals) function, which returns a new reference to a Python object containing the result of running the code. globals and locals are Python objects that reference the global and local dictionaries in which to run the code. The following example takes a Python expression as a string, evaluates it, and converts the result to a C integer:

```
#include "Python.h"

int main(int argc, char ** argv)
{
```

```
PyObject *m, *d, *result;
char * cmd = "2 * 11";

Py_Initialize();  // Set up
m = PyImport_AddModule("__main__");
d = PyModule_GetDict(m); // Get dictionary to use

// Evaluate it and get a PyObject back
result = PyRun_String(cmd, Py_eval_input, d, d);

// Convert the PyObject to something chicken and print it
printf("%s is %d\n",cmd,(int)PyInt_AsLong(result));

Py_Exit(0);
}
```

The result is printed on `stdout`:

```
2 * 11 is 22
```

Finally, if your input is coming from a file, you can do the same thing with `PyRun_File`
(`FILE *f, char *fname, int start, PyObject *globals, PyObject *locals`).

Tip   `PyRun_AnyFile`, `PyRun_SimpleFile`, and `PyRun_File` all have extended versions (for example, `PyRun_AnyFileEx`) that take an integer third parameter,
which, if non-zero, tells the function to close the file descriptor when finished.

Using Extension Tools

Writing code to create the interface between Python and C is generally very
straightforward and, therefore, often boring. After you've been spoiled by development in Python, you may find that your extension modules have bugs because you
have to manually manage object reference counts. Fortunately, several popular
tools are available to help you automate these tasks.

Tip   In addition to the tools mentioned here, the Vaults of Parnassus have others that
you can try too. Visit the Python Tools/Extensions section at `http://www.vex.`
`net/parnassus`.

SWIG

The Simplified Wrapper and Interface Generator (SWIG) is a development tool
designed to connect C and C++ programs with high-level languages, including, but
not limited to, Python, Perl, and Tcl/Tk. It is especially useful for creating an extension module from an existing C or C++ library. In some cases, it can generate all the
interface code *automatically*. SWIG is free for commercial and private use and is
available from `www.swig.org`.

Some areas in which SWIG shines include the following:

✦ Wrapping existing libraries (your own or third-party libraries)

✦ Rapid prototyping and application development

✦ Interactive debugging (use your library in an interactive Python session)

✦ Regression testing (Python scripts that test your C/C++ code)

✦ Creating a GUI front-end in Python for an underlying C program

Using SWIG

To use SWIG, you create an *interface file* that lists the variables and functions you want to be available to Python. The format of the file is very C-like (it's read by a C preprocessor), and in some cases you can even use your source code as the interface file itself.

Once the interface file is ready, you run SWIG to generate the wrapper code. You then compile the wrapper code and link in your original C code, and you end up with a ready-to-use Python module.

A SWIG example

SWIG has many features, but the following simple example gives you an idea of what it does. Suppose I want to create (or have already created) a C library called useless and I want to be able to access its powerful features from Python. The source code is in useless.c:

```
#include "stdio.h"

int getnum()
{
  return 42;
}

void message()
{
  printf("Hello, SWIG!\n");
}

int addem(int j, int k)
{
  return j + k;
}
```

The next step is to create the interface file called useless.i:

```
%module useless
%include useless.c
```

The %module directive says that the finished module will be called useless. The rest of the file contains C variable and function declarations; because the original source code is clean, I decide to pass it all to SWIG verbatim. Alternatively, I could have used the following:

```
%module useless
int getnum();
void message();
int addem(int j, int k);
```

Often, the second form is what you'll use, because you might not want every library function exported to Python, and the interface file lets you add features specific to the Python version of your library.

The next step is to run SWIG and generate the wrappers:

```
/home/dave/swig> swig -python useless.i
Generating wrappers for Python
```

SWIG creates useless_wrap.c and useless_wrap.doc (a documentation file). The -python argument selects Python as the output language. Now it's time to build the module:

```
home/dave/swig> gcc -shared useless.c useless_wrap.c -o \
  uselessmodule.so -I/usr/local/include/python2.0 \
  -DHAVE_CONFIG -I/usr/local/lib/python2.0/config
```

If you do this more than once, you'll obviously want to wrap this into a Makefile. The SWIG Web site also has instructions for using Microsoft Developer Studio.

The new module is complete. Here's a test:

```
>>> import useless
>>> dir(useless)
['__doc__', '__file__', '__name__', 'addem',
 'getnum', 'message']
>>> useless.addem(10,5)
15
>>> useless.message()
Hello, SWIG!
>>> useless.getnum()
42
```

Other nifty features

SWIG works with both C++ classes and templates; but for some C++ features, you have to put forth a little extra effort to get them to work (it's all well documented, but a little less intuitive). SWIG does a great job of making the common case fast (the creators of SWIG cite the example of creating a Python module for OpenGL in 15 minutes or so); more complex C++ features require more work to make them callable from Python.

With structures and classes, the Python equivalents become `Classname_method-name`. The `print(msg)` method in a `List` class would be `List_print(instance, msg)`, which is sort of klunky, but SWIG's `-shadow` command line option has it create a *shadow class* that makes the Python version easier to use; for example, `myList.print(msg)`.

Your interface file can also implement the special methods that Python classes use. For example, you could implement in C a `__getitem__` method to handle attribute access.

One final feature worth mentioning here is a *typemap*, which automatically handles conversion to and from Python data types when calling your C functions. For example, if you have a C `writeToFile` function that takes a C `FILE` pointer, you can create a typemap that converts to and from `FILE` pointers and Python file objects. Then, without changing the original C code, Python routines can pass in file objects to any C functions that expect `FILE`s.

CXX

CXX is a set of C++ facilities that helps you write Python extensions easily and with fewer bugs. You can download CXX from `http://cxx.sourceforge.net`. CXX has two main parts: CXX_Objects and CXX_Extensions.

Note   SCXX (Simplified CXX) is another Python/C++ API library that is also free to use for commercial and private applications. Its main purpose is to wrap Python objects and manage reference counts, and it stays away from C++ features found only in newer compilers. Visit `http://www.mcmillan-inc.com` for more information.

CXX_Objects

The main idea behind CXX_Objects is that too much of the work of writing Python extension modules deals with checking return codes for errors and managing reference counts, and that using the standard Python/C API is too low-level.

CXX_Objects is a set of high-level C++ classes (named Float, Tuple, String, Dict, and so on) that wrap their Python counterparts. Their constructors and destructors keep track of reference count details; and as a group, they use C++ exceptions to signify error conditions and as a cleanup mechanism. In short, it makes writing C++ extension modules cleaner by using the features that make C++ a higher-level language than C.

Because you rarely use `PyObject` pointers directly, and instead use high-level wrapper objects, your extension module code is more "Pythonic," less buggy, and easier to maintain.

Unhandled Python API errors or uncaught CXX exceptions are automatically converted to Python exceptions and passed back to the caller, although you always have the option of handling the exceptions yourself.

CXX_Extensions

CXX_Extensions is a more recent addition to CXX. As with CXX_Objects, the motivation behind it is that the Python/C API way of doing things can be improved upon by using the features of C++.

A garden-variety C extension module has numerous static functions and a single public initialization function that is called when the module is imported. The `init` function passes back to Python a table that has pointers to the various functions implemented by the module.

The CXX_Extensions approach is that all extension modules are actually C++ classes that are derived from ExtensionModule (a base class template). Each function in your module is implemented as a method of that class.

CXX_Extensions also includes PythonExtension, a C++ class from which you derive new Python extension types. Unlike other objects, PythonExtension objects can be created either on the Python heap or in automatic (stack) storage. Creating and destroying objects on the heap can be relatively expensive, so programs that can create and use PythonExtension objects created on the stack enjoy better performance.

Extension classes

Although you can create new Python types in a C extension module, Python types in general aren't very object-oriented (you can't directly subclass floating point numbers, for example). Digital Creations (the maker of Zope) has created *extension classes*, which are Python extension types that look and act as if they were really classes.

With extension classes, you can create an extension base class in C or C++ and then subclass it in Python. As with normal classes, it is trivial to create new instances of them, and they even work with multiple inheritance (for example, a Python subclass is derived from both a C extension class and a Python class).

One advantage of extension classes is that instance data can be stored in a dictionary as usual, as instance data in a C++ object, or some combination of the two. You could have a few special members stored in a C struct for performance reasons, for example, and let the other object attributes remain in the instance dictionary.

Extension classes also enable you to invoke unbound methods (unlike normal Python classes, for which you need an instance object in order to use them).

You can download extension classes from `www.digicool.com`.

Summary

This chapter introduced what you need to know to begin using Python with C. By reading this chapter, you learned how to:

✦ Write a complete C extension module.

✦ Pass data from Python and convert it to C data types.

✦ Return data from a C extension to a Python program.

✦ Use popular third-party packages to automatically generate Python-C interface code.

✦ Embed the interpreter in a C program.

Chapter 30 finishes our coverage of the Python/C API. In it, you'll learn about the different object layers available and how you can properly handle and report errors from C.

✦　　✦　　✦

Embedding the Python Interpreter

♦ ♦ ♦ ♦

In This Chapter

Tracking reference counts

Using the abstract and concrete object layers

Working with number objects

Working with sequence objects

Working with mapping objects

Using other object types

Creating threads and sub-interpreters

Handling errors and exceptions

Managing memory

♦ ♦ ♦ ♦

This chapter is the second of a two-part look at the Python/C API. Whereas the previous chapter introduced the concepts of using Python and C/C++ together, this chapter is a reference for the functions used to manipulate Python objects from C. It also deals with other issues, such as error handling and C memory management.

Tracking Reference Counts

Each Python object always knows how many variables reference it; and when there are no remaining variables, the object magically goes away. To remind you how much you enjoy programming in Python, when using the C API, you have to do some of the reference counting yourself. Each time you use a PyObject pointer (or one of its subtypes), you need to track the type of reference ownership that goes along with that object pointer. There's nothing in the code itself that contains this information; the Python/C API has a few documented terms and conventions that act as guidelines.

Types of reference ownership

Suppose you have a PyObject pointer named x. You use the Py_INCREF(x) macro to tell Python, "Hey, I'm using the object pointed to by x; I need a new reference to it"; and you use Py_DECREF(x) to say, "I'm done with (my reference to) x." If you don't do this, it's quite possible that somewhere else the last reference to x is released, the object is cleaned up, and you're left with a pointer to memory that has already been freed. Your well-behaved C extension module suddenly becomes the cause of strange crashes and other evils.

The first type of reference is an *owned* reference. If your block of code owns a reference to an object, then it's safe to store the object pointer, for example, because the object won't be destroyed at least until you release your reference to it. One way to gain a reference is to call `Py_INCREF`, another is when a function returns to you a new reference.

You can cease to own a reference by calling `Py_DECREF` or by *transferring* the reference to someone else. When you own a reference and call a function that assumes ownership of that reference, that function is said to *steal* the reference from you.

The second type of reference is a *borrowed reference*. Because you're using C pointers to Python objects, it's possible to pass objects to another function that doesn't modify the reference counts at all. If this is intentional, such a function is said to *borrow* references to objects (otherwise, it's a bug). One case in which this is safe is in a function that uses the object pointer to perform some operation and then returns control to the caller without storing the pointer or modifying the reference count. If the caller owns a reference, then the object is guaranteed to exist until program control is returned to the caller. The rule here is that the borrower can't use the reference any longer than the true owner does. To change a borrowed reference to an owned reference, simply call `Py_INCREF`.

Note   Although these references are called *borrowed references,* they aren't really borrowed at all, as the caller still owns the reference. Another way to think of it is that the reference owner gives permission to another function to access the object temporarily.

To sum it up, you become an owner of a reference by calling `Py_INCREF` or by receiving a new reference from someone else. There are two legal ways to rid yourself of an owned reference: decrease the reference count or give the reference to someone else. Anything else is a reference leak and, in turn, a memory leak (and potentially a leak of other resources).

Tip   `Py_XINCREF` and `Py_XDECREF` modify reference counts, but first check to make sure the object is non-`NULL`.

Reference conventions

The Python/C API documentation specifies whether references are borrowed or owned (although occasionally it doesn't hurt to look at the function source code just to convince yourself).

As a general rule of thumb, the API functions that return some type of `PyObject` pointer return a new reference to that Python object. For example, many C extension functions return with a call to `Py_BuildValue`; it returns a new reference to you, which you pass on to the caller of your function. The main exceptions to this rule (we'll remind you again later) are `PyTuple_GetItem` and `PyList_GetItem`, which return borrowed references to tuple and list items.

When you pass object references to functions, those functions generally borrow the references (if they want a reference, they'll call `Py_INCREF`). The main exceptions are `PyTuple_SetItem` and `PyList_SetItem`, which steal references from their callers.

Along the same lines, C functions called from Python borrow references to their arguments because the objects are basically guaranteed to exist until the function returns. If you need to store a pointer to an object, however, be sure to grab your own reference to it.

Common pitfalls

Usually, tracking reference counts isn't too much hassle, but two very common but subtle bugs are confusing enough to warrant mention here. Don't be surprised if you run into these exact bugs or close variants.

One common mistake occurs in multithreaded programs. There is a global lock (discussed in the "Creating Threads and Sub-Interpreters" section later in this chapter) that the current thread must hold in order to operate on Python objects. Before potentially long operations (a blocking socket call, for example), it is customary to release this lock so that other threads can do work. Problems arise if the other threads end up deleting the last reference to an object to which you have only a borrowed reference. In this case, when you regain control of the global lock, your once valid object has now been deleted. The solution is to increment the reference count before releasing the lock and decrement it on return — even if no other references remain, your owned reference will still exist.

A similar problem occurs when an object's reference count is implicitly decremented. Calling `PyList_SetItem`, for example, puts an object in a list (such as the Python code `a[5] = 'hello'`). The object originally in that position is replaced, its reference count is decremented by 1, and, if that was the last reference, the object is deleted. Any borrowed references you have to that object (perhaps from a call to `PyList_GetItem`) may now be bogus. Again, the solution is to explicitly get a new reference to the object so that you can guarantee that it is not destroyed too soon.

Using the Abstract and Concrete Object Layers

The Python/C API contains functions to perform all possible operations on Python objects. The functions used to manipulate objects are organized hierarchically according to object type, and it has two main layers: abstract and concrete.

Object layers

The *abstract object layer* is an API layer that enables you to work with general categories of objects. For example, you can call `PyNumber_Add` to add two numbers without worrying too much about their exact type. The abstract layer also has functions for dealing with sequence types and mapping types.

The *concrete object layer* has functions specific to each type of object. `PyFloat_Check` checks to see if an object is a floating-point number, for example; and `PyComplex_FromDoubles` creates a complex number object from two C numbers.

> In general, API functions that return a pointer use NULL to denote an error, and those that return an integer use −1 for errors. In both cases, the functions also set an error condition so that the Python caller ends up with an exception. See "Handling Errors and Exceptions" later in this chapter for more information about error handling.

If you have a choice between functions in the abstract and concrete object layers, use the more general abstract functions, for greater flexibility.

Working with generic objects

At the top of the hierarchy is a group of general-purpose functions for working with any Python object. Table 30-1 lists common object operations in Python and their corresponding C function call. Calls that return `PyObject` pointers return a new reference unless otherwise noted.

Table 30-1 General Object Functions	
Python	**Equivalent C Function Call**
repr(o) or `o`	PyObject *PyObject_Repr(PyObject *o)
str(o)	PyObject *PyObject_Str(PyObject *o)
	PyObject *PyObject_Unicode(PyObject *o)
len(o)	int PyObject_Length(PyObject *o)
hasattr(o, name)	int PyObject_HasAttrString(PyObject *o, char *name)
	int PyObject_HasAttr(PyObject *o, PyObject *name)
getattr(o, name)	PyObject *PyObject_GetAttrString(PyObject *o, char *name)
	PyObject *PyObject_GetAttr(PyObject *o, PyObject *name)

Python	Equivalent C Function Call
o.name = v	int PyObject_SetAttrString(PyObject *o, char *name,PyObject *v)
	int PyObject_SetAttr(PyObject *o, PyObject *name, PyObject *v)
del o.name	int PyObject_DelAttrStr(PyObject *o, char *name)
	int PyObject_DelAttr(PyObject *o, PyObject *name)
cmp(o1, o2)	int PyObject_Compare(PyObject *o1, PyObject *o2)
	int PyObject_Cmp(PyObject *o1, PyObject *o2, int *result)
	int PyObject_RichCompare(PyObject *o1, PyObject *o2, int op)
o[key]	PyObject *PyObject_GetItem(PyObject *o, PyObject *key)
o[key] = val	int PyObject_SetItem(PyObject *o, PyObject *key, PyObject *val)
del o[key]	int PyObject_DelItem(PyObject *o, PyObject *key)
print >> fp, `o`	int PyObject_Print(PyObject *o, FILE *fp, 0)
print >> fp, o	int PyObject_Print(PyObject *o, FILE *fp, Py_PRINT_RAW)
type(o)	PyObject *PyObject_Type(PyObject *o)
hash(o)	int PyObject_Hash(PyObject *o)
not not o (is o true?)	int PyObject_IsTrue(PyObject *o)
callable(o)	int PyCallable_Check(PyObject *o)

The PyObject_RichCompare function compares two objects using the comparison you specify in the op parameter. If neither object supports the necessary comparison function, Python compares them using its own methods. The op parameter can be any of the following global variables that correspond to the rich comparison function names:

```
Py_LT
Py_LE
Py_EQ
Py_NE
Py_GT
Py_GE
```

To compare using an object's __lt__ function, for example, you'd call PyObject_RichCompare with an op of Py_LT. As of Python 2.1, the PyObject_Compare function checks for the presence of rich comparison functions before using Python's default comparison functionality.

New Feature   PyObject_RichCompare is new in Python 2.1.

Cross-Reference   You can read more about the rich comparison functions in Chapter 7.

The equivalent of apply(o, args) or o(*args) is PyObject_CallObject (PyObject *o, PyObject *args), where args can be NULL if a function takes no arguments. PyObject_CallObject returns a new reference to an object containing the function call result.

PyObject_CallFunction(PyObject *o, char *format, ...) works the same way except that you use a Py_BuildValue-like format string to specify the argument types, or a NULL format string to denote no arguments. When calling methods of instance objects, use PyObject_CallMethod(PyObject *o, char *method, char *format, ...). Note that you can't call special methods (for example, __add__) this way; the API provides individual functions for calling those methods (for example, PyNumber_Add).

Tip   Even if there isn't a public C API for a particular Python method, you can still call it using these functions. For example, mapping objects (for example, dictionaries) have an items() method to return a list of key-value pairs, so you could invoke it as follows:

```
PyObject_CallMethod(O,"items",NULL)
```

PyObject_AsFileDescriptor(PyObject *o) is a utility function for getting an integer file descriptor from an object. If the Python object is an integer or long number, it returns its value. Otherwise, it returns the result from calling the object's fileno() method, if present.

Working with Number Objects

The abstract object layer has the PyNumber family of functions for dealing with any numerical object; and the concrete layer has functions specific to integers, long integers, floating-point numbers, and complex numbers.

Any numerical type

Use PyNumber_Check(PyObject *o) to determine whether a particular Python object supports numerical operations.

Table 30-2 lists numerical operations in Python and their Python/C API equivalents. As usual, `PyObject` pointers returned from functions represent a new reference to a Python object, or are `NULL` to indicate an error.

Table 30-2 Numerical Functions	
Python	**Equivalent C Function Call**
`a + b`	`PyObject *PyNumber_Add(PyObject *a, PyObject *b)`
`a - b`	`PyObject *PyNumber_Subtract(PyObject *a, PyObject *b)`
`a * b`	`PyObject *PyNumber_Multiply(PyObject *a, PyObject *b)`
`a / b`	`PyObject *PyNumber_Divide(PyObject *a, PyObject *b)`
`a % b`	`PyObject *PyNumber_Remainder(PyObject *a, PyObject *b)`
`divmod(a, b)`	`PyObject *PyNumber_Divmod(PyObject *a, PyObject *b)`
`-a`	`PyObject *PyNumber_Negative(PyObject *a)`
`+a`	`PyObject *PyNumber_Positive(PyObject *a)`
`~a`	`PyObject *PyNumber_Invert(PyObject *a)`
`abs(a)`	`PyObject *PyNumber_Absolute(PyObject *a)`
`a << b`	`PyObject *PyNumber_Lshift(PyObject *a, PyObject *b)`
`a >> b`	`PyObject *PyNumber_Rshift(PyObject *a, PyObject *b)`
`a & b`	`PyObject *PyNumber_And(PyObject *a, PyObject *b)`
`a	b`	`PyObject *PyNumber_Or(PyObject *a, PyObject *b)`
`a ^ b`	`PyObject *PyNumber_Xor(PyObject *a, PyObject *b)`
`int(a)`	`PyObject *PyNumber_Int(PyObject *a)`
`long(a)`	`PyObject *PyNumber_Long(PyObject *a)`
`float(a)`	`PyObject *PyNumber_Float(PyObject *a)`
`a,b = coerce(a,b)`	`int PyNumber_Coerce(PyObject **a, PyObject **b)`

The Python `pow(a,b,c)` function is accessible as `PyNumber_Power(PyObject *a, PyObject *b, PyObject *c)`. The third parameter, c, can be a Python number object or `Py_None`.

For many of the functions in Table 30-2, there are corresponding functions for the in-place version of the same operation. For example, `PyObject*` `PyNumber_InPlaceLshift (PyObject *a, PyObject *b)` is the C way of doing a `<<= b` in Python.

Integers

Python integer objects are represented in C by the `PyIntObject` structure. `PyInt_Check(PyObject *o)` returns 1 if the given object is an integer object (it has the type `PyInt_Type`).

`PyInt_FromLong(long val)` takes a C `long` integer and returns a new reference to a Python integer object. `PyInt_AsLong(PyObject *o)` converts an integer object back to a C `long`, coercing the object to a Python integer object first if needed. If you already know that it is an integer, you can use the `PyInt_AS_LONG(PyOBject *o)` macro to do the same thing, but without coercion and error checking.

The largest value that can be stored in an integer object is defined as `LONG_MAX` in the header files; you can use `PyInt_GetMax()` to retrieve this value.

Longs

Python long integers are stored in `PyLongObject` structures, their type is `PyLong_Type` (this is the same as `types.LongType` in Python), and you can call `PyLong_Check(PyObject *o)` to test whether an object is a long number object.

`PyLong_FromLong(long val)`, `PyLong_FromUnsignedLong(unsigned long val)`, and `PyLong_FromDouble(double val)` return a new reference to a long integer object having the given value.

One other way to create a new Python long object is by passing a character string to `PyLong_FromString(char *str, char **end, int base)`. The base or radix of the number is specified by the `base` argument; values can be in the range from 2 to 36, or 0, which means that the function should look at the string itself to determine the base. It will use base 16 if the string starts with 0x or 0X, base 8 if it starts with 0, and base 10 otherwise. `PyLong_FromString` ignores leading spaces, and stores the position of the first character after the end of the number in `end` if it is not `NULL`.

`PyLong_AsLong(PyObject *o)` and `PyLong_AsUnsignedLong(PyObject *o)` convert long integer objects to C `long` and `unsigned long` variables. Because Python long integers can be any size, values that cannot be converted to C cause an `OverflowError` exception to be raised. `PyLong_AsDouble(PyObject *o)` returns the value of a long integer in a C `double`.

Floating-point numbers

Floating-point numbers are stored in `PyFloatObject` structures; their type is `PyFloat_Type` and you can ensure that an object is a floating-point number by calling `PyFloat_Check(PyObject *o)`.

`PyFloat_FromDouble(double val)` returns a new reference to a Python floating-point number object.

Given a Python floating-point number, you can convert it to a C `double` by calling `PyFloat_AsDouble(PyObject *o)`. This function has some overhead due to error checking, so if you are already sure your object is a floating-point number, you can just call `PyFloat_AS_DOUBLE(PyObject *o)`.

Complex numbers

Python complex numbers live in `PyComplexObject` structures and have the type `PyComplex_Type` (equivalent to `types.ComplexType` in Python). `PyComplex_Check(PyObject *o)` returns 1 if the given object is a Python complex number.

To create a complex number object, call `PyComplex_FromDoubles(double real, double imag)` to specify its real and imaginary components. You can also use `PyComplex_FromCComplex(Py_complex *c)`. `Py_complex` is a C structure declared as follows:

```
typedef struct {
    double real;
    double imag;
} Py_complex;
```

Given a Python complex number object, you can extract its real and imaginary parts by calling `PyComplex_RealAsDouble(PyObject *o)` and `PyComplex_ImagAsDouble(PyComplex *o)`. Both functions return a C `double`. You can also call `PyComplex_AsCComplex(PyObject *o)` to place the values into a `Py_complex` structure.

Working with Sequence Objects

The functions in this section enable you to manipulate Python objects that are lists, tuples, and strings.

When using functions that return slices, keep in mind that generally what is returned to you is a new reference, and that each item in it had its reference count incremented before it was sent back to you.

Any sequence type

These functions are part of Python's abstract object layer and work on any sequence object. PySequence_Check(PyObject *o) returns a nonzero value if the object supports sequence functions.

Table 30-3 lists C function calls for corresponding sequence operations in Python. Functions that return a PyObject pointer return a new reference of that object or NULL if an error occurs. Those that return integers use a value of -1 to denote failure.

Table 30-3 C Sequence Functions	
Python	**Equivalent C Function Call**
len(s)	int PySequence_Length(PyObject *s)
s[i]	PyObject *PySequence_GetItem(PyObject *s, int i)
s[a:b]	PyObject *PySequence_GetSlice(PyObject *s, int a, int b)
s[i] = v	int PySequence_SetItem(PyObject *s, int i, PyObject *v)
s[a:b] = v	int PySequence_SetSlice(PyObject *s, int a, int b, PyObject *v)
del s[i]	int PySequence_DelItem(PyObject *s, int i)
del s[a:b]	int PySequence_DelSlice(PyObject *s, int a, int b)
s1 + s2	PyObject *PySequence_Concat(PyObject *s1, PyObject *s2)
s1 += s2	PyObject *PySequence_InPlaceConcat(PyObject *s1, PyObject *s2)
s * count	PyObject *PySequence_Repeat(PyObject *s, int count)
s *= count	PyObject *PySequence_InPlaceRepeat(PyOBject *s, int count)
s.count(v)	int PySequence_Count(PyObject *s, PyObject *v)
v in s	int PySequence_Contains(PyObject *s, PyObject *v)
s.index(v)	int PySequence_Index(PyObject *s, PyObject *v)
tuple(s)	PyObject *PySequence_Tuple(PyObject *s)
list(s)	PyObject *PySequence_List(PyObject *s)

Two sequence functions perform less error checking to increase performance. PySequence_Fast (PyObject *o, const char *m) returns a new reference to o after converting it to a tuple, leaving it unchanged (except for the reference count) if it is already a tuple or a list. If the object o can't be converted to a sequence, the function returns NULL and raises a TypeError with m as the message text. You can then pass the returned object to PySequence_Fast_GET_ITEM(PyObject *o, int index) to get borrowed references to sequence members.

Caution   PySequence_Fast_GET_ITEM assumes that the index values you pass in are valid and doesn't check for errors.

Strings

A PyStringObject is a specific type of sequence used to hold Python strings. PyString_Check(PyObject *o) returns 1 if the given object is a string object; it verifies that o's type is PyString_Type (equivalent to types.StringType in Python).

You create a new string object from a null-terminated C string by calling PyString_FromString(const char *s). It returns a PyObject pointer that is a new reference to a string object of that value. For strings that might have embedded null characters, use PyString_FromStringAndSize(const char *s, int len).

PyString_Format(PyObject *format, PyObject *args) returns a new reference to a string object created using a format string and a tuple of arguments, equivalent to the Python format % args.

After creating a new string object, you can call PyString_Resize(PyObject **s, int newsize) to change its size to newsize. To Python, strings are immutable, so it is safe to call this function only if no other part of the program knows about the string yet (for example, when you just created it).

Going the other direction, PyString_AsString(PyObject *s) returns a char pointer to the string data, converting the object to a string first if needed. PyString_AsStringAndSize(PyObject *s, char **buffer, int *len) sets buffer to point at a string representation of the object, returns the string length in len (len can be NULL as long as the string has no embedded null characters), and returns -1 on failure. Both functions return pointers to internal buffers that you shouldn't modify or de-allocate.

Tip   PyString_AsStringAndSize works on both string and Unicode string objects.

PyString_Size(PyObject *s) returns the length of the string. If the object is not already a string, the function first calls PyString_AsStringAndSize and then returns the size.

In cases where you know the object really is a string object, you can call PyString_AS_STRING(PyObject *s) and PyString_GET_SIZE(PyObject *s) for better performance.

`PyString_Concat(PyObject **s, PyObject *new)` concatenates new onto the end of s. The function itself returns no value; s contains a new reference to the concatenated string object, or `NULL` on failure. `PyString_Concat` calls `Py_DECREF` on the s object you pass in; in effect, you are *transferring* your reference to it and it gives you a new reference back. `PyString_ConcatAndDel(PyObject **s, PyObject *new)` is a utility function that calls `PyString_Concat` and then calls `Py_XDECREF` on new so you don't have to.

`PyString_InternInPlace(PyObject **s)` is equivalent to the Python intern function. When you call this function, you transfer ownership of the reference and receive back a new reference. The object that you receive will be either the original object or a previously interned string of the same value. `PyString_InternFromString (const char *s)` is a utility function that converts a C string to a Python string object, interns it, and returns to you a new reference of the result.

`PyString_Encode(Py_UNICODE *s, int size, char *encoding, char *errors)` returns a new reference to an encoded string object. The encoding and errors arguments are the same as those for the encode Python function (for example, errors can have values strict, ignore, and replace). `PyString_AsEncodedString (PyObject *unicode, const char *encoding, const char *errors)` works the same way, but takes a PyUnicodeObject.

`PyString_Decode(char *s, int size, char *encoding, char *errors)` returns a new reference to a decoded string object, like the Python unicode function.

Cross-Reference
See "Unicode strings" later in this chapter for more functions to handle Unicode objects.

Lists

A `PyListObject` holds a Python list; it has the type `PyList_Type` (equivalent to Python's types.ListType). `PyList_Check(PyObject *p)` returns 1 if the given object is a list.

Table 30-4 lists Python list operations and their equivalent C function calls. Unless returning an actual numeric value, functions returning integers return 0 to denote success.

Table 30-4	
C List Functions	
Python	**Equivalent C Function Call**
len(t)	int PyList_Size(PyObject *t)
t[i]	PyObject *PyList_GetItem(PyObject *t, int i)
t[i] = o	int PyList_SetItem(PyObject *t, int i, PyObject *o)

Python	Equivalent C Function Call
t.insert(i, o)	int PyList_Insert(PyObject *t, int i, PyObject *o)
t.append(o)	int PyList_Append(PyObject *t, PyObject *o)
t[a:b]	PyObject *PyList_GetSlice(PyObject *t, int a, int b)
t[a:b] = t2	int PyList_SetSlice(PyObject *t, int a, int b, PyObject *t2)
t.sort()	int PyList_Srt(PyObject *t)
t.reverse()	int PyList_Reverse(PyObject *t)
tuple(t)	PyObject *PyList_AsTuple(PyObject *t)

The list functions that take an index parameter assume that the index you supply is valid. PyList_GetItem returns a borrowed reference to an item; and with PyList_SetItem, you give up (transfer) ownership of the reference, but PyList_Insert behaves "normally" (it increments the reference count of the object passed in). Don't forget that setting a list item replaces another item, causing its reference count to be decremented (which could in turn call its destructor).

PyList_GetSlice returns a new reference to a list object containing the requested objects; those objects are also new references to the originals. PyList_SetSlice requires that both arguments (t and t2) be list objects. PyList_AsTuple returns a new reference to a tuple object, and each member of the tuple is a new reference as well.

PyList_New(*int len*) returns a new reference to a list object that has an initial length of len.

PyList_GET_SIZE(PyObject *t) is a slightly faster way to retrieve a list's size; it doesn't verify that the object t is really a list. The same is true for PyList_GET_ITEM(PyObject *t, int i) and PyList_SET_ITEM(PyObject *t, int i, PyObject *o).

Tuples

A PyTupleObject is the C version of a Python tuple; it has the type PyTuple_Type, which is the same as Python's types.TupleType. Call PyTuple_Check(PyObject *o) to determine whether an object is a tuple.

PyTuple_New(int len) returns a new reference to a tuple object of length len. PyTuple_Resize(PyObject *o, int newsize, 0) resizes a given tuple; as with the list resize function, it is safe to call only if no other references to this object exist. This function returns 0 on success.

Table 30-5 lists the C function calls for common tuple operations.

	Table 30-5
	C Tuple Functions

Python	Equivalent C Function Call
len(t)	int PyTuple_Size(PyObject *t)
t[i]	PyObject *PyTuple_GetItem(PyObject *t, int i)
t[i] = o	int PyTuple_SetItem(PyObject *t, int i, PyObject *o)
t[a:b]	PyObject *PyTuple_GetSlice(PyObject *t, int a, int b)

PyTuple_GET_ITEM(PyObject *t, int i) and PyTuple_SET_ITEM(PyObject *t, int i, PyObject *o) are faster versions of PyTuple_GetItem and PyTuple_SetItem; they assume you're honest and pass in tuple objects.

The same rules apply here as for lists: index values are assumed to be valid, PyTuple_GetItem returns a borrowed reference, and PyTuple_GetSlice increments the reference count for each object in the slice. In addition, PyTuple_SetItem transfers ownership of the reference to the tuple, and the reference count of the item being replaced is decremented by 1.

Buffers

Python objects in C can implement a *buffer interface,* which is a group of functions that let an object expose the memory where it stores its data. Buffer interfaces are often low-level or performance-conscious functions that want to access data in its raw byte format without having to copy the data.

The C PyBufferObject structure is used to represent a Python buffer. These objects have a type of PyBuffer_Type. As usual, you can call PyBuffer_Check(PyObject *o) to determine whether an object is a buffer.

Given an object that has an internal buffer, PyBuffer_FromObject(PyObject *o, int offset, int size) creates a read-only buffer object to access the data starting at the given offset. If the object allows reading and writing of its buffer data, using PyBuffer_FromReadWriteObject(PyOBject *o, int offset, int size) creates a buffer object that supports writing too. Both functions return a new reference to a buffer object, and for size you can use the constant Py_END_OF_BUFFER to include all data from the given offset to the end of the object.

You can wrap a block of memory into a read-only buffer object by calling PyBuffer_FromMemory(void *p, int size). Py_Buffer_FromReadWriteMemory (void *p, int size) does the same thing but allows writing to the buffer as well. Of course, for both of these functions you need to ensure the block of memory is valid for as long as the buffer object exists. An alternative is to let the buffer own and manage the block of memory itself; call `PyBuffer_New(int size)` to create a memory buffer of the given size.

`PyObject_AsReadBuffer(PyObject *o, const void **buffer, int *size)` returns a pointer and a size value for a given object's internal buffer. For objects that support it, `PyObject_AsWriteBuffer(PyObject *o, void **buffer, int *size)` returns the same information for a writeable buffer.

Unicode strings

Unicode strings have the type `PyUnicode_Type` and are stored in a `PyUnicodeObject` structure. Call `PyUnicode_Check(PyObject *o)` to determine whether an object is a Unicode string. The actual characters of the string are stored in a member of this structure having the type `Py_UNICODE`, which is a C typedef for 16-bit values.

> **Note**   On platforms such as Windows, which provide a usable wide character type (`wchar_t`), Python uses this type and its supporting functions for better performance and compatibility.

`PyUnicode_GET_SIZE(PyObject *o)` returns the number of characters in the string, and `PyUnicode_GET_DATA_SIZE(PyObject *o)` returns the number of bytes used to store the string (string length * size of each character). `PyUnicode_GetSize(PyObject *o)` returns the string's length after verifying that the object is a Unicode string.

Converting to and from Unicode

`PyUnicode_AS_UNICODE(PyObject *o)` returns a read-only pointer to the structure's internal `Py_UNICODE` member, and `PyUnicode_AS_DATA(PyObject *o)` does the same but casts the return pointer to `char *`. `PyUnicode_AsUnicode(PyObject *o)` returns a pointer to the internal data but first ensures that the object really is a Unicode string. `PyUnicode_AsWideChar(PyUnicodeObject *o, wchar_t *buff, int length)` copies the Unicode string into the given buffer, copying at most `length` characters, and returns the number of characters copied.

`PyUnicode_FromUnicode(const Py_UNICODE *buff, int length)` returns a new reference to a Unicode string object of the given length whose contents were copied from `buff` if it was not `NULL`. `PyUnicode_FromWideChar(const wchar_t *buff, int length)` does the same but copies from a wide character buffer pointer that must not be `NULL`.

`PyUnicode_FromEncodedObject(PyObject *obj, const char *encoding, const char *errors)` uses `encoding` and `errors` to coerce an encoded object to a Unicode object if needed, and returns a new reference to the Unicode object. Set `encoding` and `errors` to `NULL` to use the defaults.

`PyUnicode_FromObject(PyObject *obj)` is a utility function that calls `PyUnicode_FromEncodedObject` with `encoding` set to `NULL`, and `errors` set to `"strict"`.

`PyUnicode_Decode(const char *s, int length, const char *encoding, const char *errors)` takes a string `length` bytes long that uses the given encoding and converts it to Unicode, returning to you a new reference to the Unicode object. `PyUnicode_Encode (const Py_UNICODE *s, int length, const char * encoding, const char *errors)` encodes a `Py_UNICODE` buffer and returns a Python string object.

> **Note**
>
> The API also provides shortcut routines for encoding and decoding strings using standard encodings such as 7-bit ASCII, UTF8, UTF16, Latin-1, and so on. See `unicodeobject.h` for details.

Checking and converting individual characters

`Py_UNICODE_ISSPACE(Py_UNICODE ch)` returns 1 if the given Unicode character is whitespace. Additionally, you can use the following to perform other similar checks:

```
Py_UNICODE_ISLOWER          Py_UNICODE_ISUPPER
Py_UNICODE_ISTITLE          Py_UNICODE_ISLINEBREAK
Py_UNICODE_ISDECIMAL        Py_UNICODE_ISDIGIT
Py_UNICODE_ISNUMERIC        Py_UNICODE_ISALPHA
Py_UNICODE_ISALNUM
```

`Py_UNICODE_TOLOWER(Py_UNICODE ch)`, `Py_UNICODE_TOUPPER`, and `Py_UNICODE_TOTITLE` return the given character converted to lowercase, uppercase, and titlecase, respectively.

`Py_UNICODE_TODECIMAL(Py_UNICODE ch)` and `Py_UNICODE_TODIGIT` return the given character converted to an integer decimal and an integer digit (usually the same thing). `Py_UNICODE_TONUMERIC(Py_UNICODE ch)` returns a `double` holding the numeric value of the given character (for example, given the single-character symbol for one-half, it would return the number 0.5).

Using string manipulation functions

The following `PyUnicode` functions work like their `PySequence` and `PyString` counterparts:

```
PyObject *PyUnicode_Concat(PyObject *a, PyObject *b)
PyObject *PyUnicode_Split(PyObject *s, PyObject *sep, int
                          maxsplit)
PyObject *PyUnicode_Join(PyObject *sep, PyObject *sequence)
int PyUnicode_Count(PyObject *str, PyObject *substr, int
                    start, int end)
```

```
int PyUnicode_Contains(PyObject *container, PyObject *element)
int PyUnicode_Compare(PyObject *left, PyObject *right)
PyObject* PyUnicode_Format(PyObject *format, PyObject *args)
```

PyUnicode_Replace(PyObject *str, PyObject *substr, PyObject *replstr, int maxcount) works like the normal string replace function; maxcount is the maximum number of replacements to perform.

PyUnicode_Find(PyObject *str, PyObject *substr, int start, int end, int direction) returns the index of the first match of substr in str[start:end], searching left-to-right if direction is 1, and right-to-left if direction is -1.

PyUnicode_Splitlines (PyObject *s, int maxsplit) returns a list of strings split at line breaks (the line break characters are removed), stopping after all text has been processed or maxsplit splits have occurred.

PyUnicode_Tailmatch (PyObject *str, PyObject *substr, int start, int end, int direction) checks whether substr matches a portion of str. If direction is -1, the function returns 1 if str[start:end] starts with substr. If direction is greater than or equal to 0, the function returns 1 if str[start:end] ends with substr.

PyUnicode_Translate (PyObject *str, PyObject *table, const char *errors) maps characters to new values using a lookup table. The table object can be a dictionary or sequence (or anything that has a __getitem__ method). For each character in str, the function looks up its entry in table and inserts the new value in the result (a Unicode object returned to you as a new reference). If the character's entry in the table has a value of None, the character is deleted in the result (not copied); and if there is no entry in the table (the lookup causes a LookupError), the character is copied as is.

Working with Mapping Objects

Although Python currently has only one mapping object type, the Python/C API still makes a distinction between the abstract and concrete object layers.

Functions for any mapping type

PyMapping_Check(PyObject *o) returns 1 if the object is a mapping object. Table 30-6 lists Python code for common mapping object operations and the corresponding C function calls.

	Table 30-6 **C Mapping Functions**
Python	***Equivalent C Function Call***
len(o)	PyMapping_Length(PyObject *o)
o[key]	PyMapping_GetItemString(PyObject *o, char *key)
o[key]=val	PyMapping_SetItemString(PyObject *o, char *key, PyObject *val)
del o[key]	PyMapping_DelItem(PyObject *o, PyObject *key)
	PyMapping_DelItemString(PyObject *o, char *key)
o.has_key(k)	PyMapping_HasKey(PyObject *o, PyObject *k)
	PyMapping_HasKeyString(PyObject *o, char *key)
o.keys()	PyMapping_Keys(PyObject *o)
o.values()	PyMapping_Values(PyObject *o)
o.items()	PyMapping_Items(PyObject *o)

Dictionaries

Dictionaries are represented by PyDictObject structures, and they have the type PyDict_Type (types.DictionaryType in Python). PyDict_Check(PyObject *o) returns 1 if the given object is a dictionary.

Table 30-7 lists dictionary operations in Python and C.

	Table 30-7 **C Dictionary Functions**
Python	***Equivalent C Function Call***
d = {}	PyDict_New()
d.clear()	PyDict_Clear(PyObject *d)
len(d)	PyDict_Size(PyObject *d)
d[key]	PyDict_GetItem(PyObject *d, PyObject *key) ¥ PyDict_GetItemString(PyObject *d, char *key) ¥
d[key] = val	PyDict_SetItem(PyObject *d, PyObject *key, PyObject *val) PyDict_SetItemString(PyObject *d, char *key, PyObject *val)

Python	Equivalent C Function Call
del d[key]	PyDict_DelItem(PyObject *d, PyObject *key) PyDict_DelItemString(PyObject *d, char *key)
d.keys()	PyDict_Keys(PyObject *d)
d.values()	PyDict_Values(PyObject *d)
d.items()	PyDict_Items(PyObject *d)
d.copy()	PyDict_Copy(PyObject *d)

ᵛ Returns a borrowed reference to the value object

Using Other Object Types

The following sections describe a few other miscellaneous object types available in the Python/C API.

Type

PyTypeObject structures describe Python's built-in types. These objects have the type PyTypeObject, and PyType_Check(PyObject *o) returns 1 if the given object is a type object.

None

Py_None is the C equivalent of Python's None. Use this anyplace to denote a lack of value instead of using NULL, because the Python/C API uses NULL to indicate an error.

Note Py_None is an actual object, so treat it like any other with respect to reference counting. For example, when a C extension module function has no return value, it should use the following idiom:

```
Py_INCREF(Py_None);
return Py_None;
```

File

Python file objects are thin wrappers around FILE objects in the standard C libraries. The Python/C API uses a PyFileObject structure to represent a file object; these structures have the type PyFile_Type, and you can call PyFile_Check(PyObject *o) to verify that an object is a file.

`PyFile_FromFile(FILE *f, char *name, char *mode, int (close*)(FILE*))` creates a Python file object from a C file of the given name and mode. The file pointer f must be an already open file or `NULL` (although you should fill in a valid `FILE` structure before letting any other code use it). The `close` argument is the function to call to close the file; you can pass in the standard C `fclose` function if you don't need anything special.

`PyFile_FromString(char *fname, char *mode)` uses mode to open (or create, depending on the mode) a file named fname. Like `PyFile_FromFile`, it returns a new reference to a Python file object.

You can access the `FILE` pointer of a Python file object using `PyFile_AsFile(PyObject *f)`, and `PyFile_Name(PyObject *f)` returns a borrowed reference to a string object containing the file's name.

To simulate `f.readline(n)`, call `PyFile_GetLine (PyObject *f, int n)`. If the end of file has been reached, the function still returns a string object (but of length 0). If n is 0, the function reads one line, and if n is greater than 0, the function will read up to n bytes. If n is less than 0, the function reads one line of data but raises `EOFError` if the end of file has been reached already.

You can set or clear the `softspace` flag of a file or filelike object by calling `PyFile_SoftSpace(PyObject *f, int flag)`. A value of 1 means that a space will be output before the next data is written to the file.

`PyFile_WriteString(char *s, PyObject *f)` writes a string to an open file.

`PyFile_WriteObject(PyObject *o, PyObject *f, int flags)` writes a string representation of the given object o to the file f. By default, it gets the output by calling `repr`; use a `flags` value of `Py_PRINT_RAW` to have it call `str` instead.

Module

The Python/C API has functions for working with module objects and importing them, as described in the following sections.

Module objects

`PyModuleObject` structures have the type `PyModule_Type`, and `PyModule_Check(PyObject *o)` returns 1 if the object o is a module.

`PyModule_New(char *name)` returns a new reference to a new module object and creates the module's namespace dictionary. The module's __name__ member is set to name, and its __doc__ member is set to an empty string. Before letting other parts of the program use the new module, you should at least set its __file__ member.

`PyModule_GetDict(PyObject *m)` returns a borrowed reference to the module's dictionary (__dict__). `PyModule_GetName(PyObject *m)` returns a char pointer

to the value of the module's __name__ member, and
PyModule_GetFilename(PyObject *m) returns a char pointer to the value of its
__file__ member.

 **New
Feature** The following functions were introduced in Python 2.0.

PyModule_AddObject(PyObject *m, char *name, PyObject *value) adds the
object value to the module m. This function steals a reference to value.

PyModule_AddIntConstant(PyObject *m, char *name, int value) is a utility
function that creates an integer object with the given value and adds it to the module. PyModule_AddStringConstant(PyObject *m, char *name, char *value)
does the same for a string variable.

Importing modules

PyImport_ImportModule(char *name) loads the requested module and returns a
new reference to it. Internally, PyImport_ImportModule calls
PyImport_ImportModuleEx (char *name, PyObject *globals, PyObject
*locals, PyObject *fromlist), which loads a module with the given global and
local dictionaries, which may be NULL. Python's __import__ function calls
PyImport_ImportModuleEx.

PyImport_Import(PyObject *name) also loads a module, but it uses the current
import hooks to do the loading.

**Cross-
Reference** Chapter 35 shows you how to override importing behavior using import hooks.

PyImport_ReloadModule (PyObject *m) reloads the given module (just like the
Python reload() function) and returns a new reference to it.

PyImport_AddModule(char *name) returns a borrowed reference to a module
called name, creating an empty module object if necessary.
PyImport_GetModuleDict() returns a borrowed reference to the module dictionary (stored in sys.modules).

PyImport_ExecCodeModule(char *name, PyObject *co) returns a new reference
to a module object. The module is created and imported using co, which is a code
object (obtained from a call to compile or read in from a .pyc file). If the module
already exists, it is reloaded using the given code object.
PyImport_GetMagicNumber() returns a C long containing the little-endian, 4-byte
magic number at the start of all .pyc and .pyo files.

Before a call to Py_Initialize, you can add your module to the list of built-in modules by calling PyImport_AppendInittab(char *name, void (*initfunc)
(void)), passing in the module name and initialization function to call. To add

several modules, call `PyImport_ExtendInittab(struct _inittab *newtab)`, where `newtab` is an array of entries for each module, with an extra entry on the end with a `NULL` name to denote the end of the list. The `_inittab` structure has the following format:

```
struct _inittab {
    char *name;
    void (*initfunc)(void);
};
```

`PyImport_ImportFrozenModule(char *name)` loads a *frozen* module (created with the Freeze utility). This function only loads the module; you still need to call `PyImport_ImportModule` to import it.

Cross-Reference   The Freeze utility is covered in Chapter 36.

CObjects

Occasionally, it's necessary to pass a C object (well, a pointer) from a function through Python code and back into C again. The `PyCObject` structure is the Python/C API equivalent of a `void` pointer for just this purpose. Your code can call `PyCObject_Check(PyObject *o)` to determine whether an object is of this type.

To create a PyCObject, call `PyCObject_FromVoidPtr (void* cobj, void (*destr)(void *))`, which returns a new reference to the object. `destr` is a function that will be called when Python is about to destroy the object. If you don't need to do any cleanup, this argument can be `NULL`.

`PyCObject`s can also contain some extra information called a *description*. Call `PyCObject_FromVoidPtrAndDesc (void* cobj, void* desc, void (*destr)(void *, void *))` to create an object with a description. Note that the destructor function receives both the object and its description when called.

`PyCObject_GetDesc(PyObject *o)` returns a pointer to the description data, and `PyCObjcet_AsVoidPtr(PyObject *o)` returns the original C pointer used to create the `PyCObject`.

Creating Threads and Sub-Interpreters

One application can have multiple interpreters running, and each interpreter can have multiple threads, but they all share the Global Interpreter Lock (GIL). In order to operate on a Python object, a thread must have control of the GIL or it risks corrupting memory.

The interpreter releases and reacquires the lock often to ensure that each thread gets a chance to run; you can set how many bytecode instructions it processes before releasing the lock by calling `sys.setcheckinterval(n)`; the current default is 10 instructions.

Before potentially blocking I/O routines or long computations that don't require working with Python objects, your code should manually release the lock and then reacquire it when the work is complete.

Threads

Each thread has some state information stored in a `PyThreadState` structure, and a global variable holds a pointer to the current thread's state. To release and reacquire the GIL, use the standard Python macros:

```
Py_BEGIN_ALLOW_THREADS
... // Some work
Py_END_ALLOW_THREADS
```

Among other things, these macros call `PyEval_ReleaseLock` and `PyEval_AcquireLock` on the global lock.

 Caution When working with the global interpreter lock, pay close attention to when you release it and acquire it. Trying to acquire it once you already have it (through a recursive call, for example) is an excellent way to cause deadlock and bring your program to a screeching halt.

`PyEval_InitThreads()` initializes the thread subsystem and acquires the GIL (creating it if necessary). It's safe to call this before `Py_Initialize`, although this is normally called automatically so that you don't need to.

Before a new thread created in C can access Python objects, it has to manually create its own thread state, acquire the GIL, and then set the current thread state to point to the new thread's state. When finished, it needs to reset the old thread state and release the lock. The Python/C API has several pairs of functions for working with the GIL and the current thread state.

`PyThreadState_New(PyInterpreterState *interp)` creates a new thread state structure. The `interp` argument is the current interpreter's state, which is accessible as the `interp` variable of any thread state structure. Call `PyThreadState_Get()` to get a pointer to the current thread state. Although you must have the GIL to get the current state, you do not need to have it to create a new thread state structure.

Call `PyThreadState_Clear(PyThreadState *state)` to clear a thread's state before calling `PyThreadState_Delete(PythreadState *state)` to free the thread state memory. You must have the GIL to clear a thread state structure, but not to delete it.

PyEval_AcquireLock() and PyEvalReleaseLock() acquire and release the global interpreter lock, respectively.

PyEval_AcquireThread(PyThreadState *state) acquires the GIL and sets the current state to state. PyEval_ReleaseThread(PyThreadState *state) sets the current thread state to NULL and releases the GIL. You have to pass in your thread state as a safety check to ensure that the correct thread is releasing the lock.

PyThreadState_Swap(PyThreadState *state) swaps the current thread state with state, which can be NULL (leaving the thread state selection up to the interpreter). You must have the GIL to call this function.

Sub-interpreters

The global state for the interpreter is stored in a PyInterpreterState structure. PyInterpreterState_New() creates a new state structure, PyInterpreterState_Clear(PyInterpreterState *state) clears it before you release it, and PyInterpreterState_Delete(PyInterpreterState *state) frees its associated memory. You don't need to have the GIL to create or destroy an interpreter state structure, but you do need to hold it to clear one.

Py_NewInterpreter() creates a new sub-interpreter that is almost completely independent of other interpreters (it still shares the global interpreter lock, however). The function returns a PyThreadState pointer that represents the now-current thread state in the new interpreter. Do not call this function until after you've called Py_Initialize and you have the GIL. Although the thread state has been created, you still need to create a new thread.

Py_EndInterpreter(PyThreadState *state) destroys the sub-interpreter to which the given thread state belongs. All thread states for that interpreter are also destroyed; and on return, the current thread state is NULL. You must hold the global lock to call this function.

Tip   Py_Finalize automatically destroys all sub-interpreters.

Handling Errors and Exceptions

The general error convention used in the Python/C API is that when a function fails, it returns an error value (usually NULL) and sets an error flag to indicate that an exception has been raised. Other functions shouldn't also raise an exception, only the "source" of the problem.

Checking for errors

In addition to checking return codes, you can call `PyErr_Occurred()`. If an exception has been raised, this function returns a borrowed reference to the exception object, and `NULL` otherwise. `PyErr_Print()` prints the stack traceback for the exception that was raised and then clears the error flag. You can also call `PyErr_Clear()` to clear the error flag; use this if you don't want a raised exception to make it back to the rest of the program.

After an error occurs, you can see if it matches a specific type by calling `PyErr_ExceptionMatches(PyObject *e)`, which returns 1 to indicate a match. The value e is a pointer to an exception object. Exceptions in C are named the same as in Python, but with a "`PyExc_`" prefix. For example, if a function returned `NULL` to indicate an error and you want to see if it was an `ImportError`, you'd use something like the following:

```
if (PyErr_ExceptionMatches(PyExc_MemoryError))
    . . .
```

`PyErr_GivenExceptionMatches(PyObject *given, PyObject *e)` returns 1 if the two exceptions match.

Tip

> Both of these functions let you perform multiple checks with a single call. The object e can be a Python tuple containing a sequence of exceptions (or other tuples too) to compare against.

Signaling error conditions

`PyErr_SetString(PyExc *e, char *info)` signals that the exception e has occurred (where e is one of Python's exception objects as explained above). `info` is an extra message to be displayed with the exception name.
`PyErr_Format(PyObject *e, const char *format, ...)` sets the error indicator and displays a formatted message using printf-style formatting. The recognized format codes are c (character), d (decimal), x (hex), and s (string).

Instead of a string, you can set the extra information to be any Python object with `PyErr_SetObject(PyObject *e, PyObject *value)`. If you don't want to provide any extra information with your error, just call `PyErr_SetNone(PyObjcet *e)`.

Many C library calls fail and set the per-thread error variable `errno`. Use `PyErr_SetFromErrno()` to raise an exception, and use the value in `errno` to come up with an appropriate informational message.

Note

> You do not need to increment reference counts on any of the Python objects passed to the error functions listed above.

If you need to temporarily save and restore the current error state, call `PyErr_Fetch(PyObject **type, PyObject **value, PyObject **traceback)` to save it, and call `PyErr_Restore(PyOBject *type, PyObject *value, PyObject *traceback)` to restore it.

Several functions raise exceptions for common problems. For example, if a direct call to one of Python's memory manager routines fails, you should call `PyErr_NoMemory()`. If one of your functions is called with a wrong argument type, call `PyErr_BadArgument()` to raise a `TypeError`.

Sometimes an error occurs but an exception cannot be raised (inside an object destructor, for example). In this case, `PyErr_WriteUnraisable(PyObject *obj)` can be called to write a warning to `stderr`. It also prints the `repr` representation of `obj`.

Tip   When an error occurs, don't forget to release owned references before your function exits. In addition, when raising exceptions, use the exception type that best matches the type of error that occurred.

Creating custom exceptions

It's pretty easy to create a new exception type in C. For example, suppose you are writing a caching extension module called `cache` and need to create an exception that will be known in Python as `cache.error`. Use the following steps to create an exception type:

1. Declare a static PyObject pointer for the error:

```
static PyObject *Cache_Error;
```

2. In the module's initialization function, create the error object:

```
Cache_Error = PyErr_NewException("cache.error", NULL, NULL);
```

3. Using the module's dictionary object, add the exception to its namespace:

```
PyDict_SetItemString(d, "error", Cache_Error);
```

Raising warnings

The `PyErr_Warn(PyObject *category, char *message)` function sends the warning pointed to by `message` to the user, which Python by default displays on standard error. The `category` parameter can be any of the following global warning variables:

```
PyExc_Warning
PyExc_DeprecationWarning
```

```
PyExc_RuntimeWarning
PyExc_SyntaxWarning
PyExc_UserWarning
```

Under normal circumstances `PyErr_Warn` returns 0, but if the user configures Python to escalate warnings to errors, then the function returns -1 to indicate that it raised an exception. If it does raise an exception, be sure to treat it like any other exception by releasing owned references and returning an error code from the current function.

New Feature

Warnings are new in Python 2.1.

`PyErr_WarnExplicit(PyObject *category, char *message, char *filename, int lineno, char *module, PyObject *registry)` **lets you raise a warning and have complete control over all warning attributes. This function calls the** `warn_explicit` **function in the Python** `warnings` **module.**

Cross-Reference

Chapter 5 covers the `warning` module through which you can control how Python handles warning messages.

Managing Memory

Python has its own private memory pool, or heap, in which it stores all Python objects and their data. Because it has its own memory allocation and de-allocation routines, you shouldn't use `malloc`, `free`, `new`, and `delete` on Python objects. In fact, although it's safe for you to use the normal C memory allocators for your own private memory usage, it doesn't hurt to always use the Python memory manager.

`PyMem_MALLOC(size_t n)` **returns a** `void` **pointer to a block of memory, and** `PyMem_FREE(void *p)` **frees a pointer p if it is not** `NULL`.

`PyMem_NEW(TYPE, size_t n)` **allocates enough memory to store n items of type** `TYPE`, **where** `TYPE` **is any C data type (that is, it allocates** `sizeof(TYPE) * n` **bytes of memory). It returns a pointer of the same type.** `PyMem_DEL(p)` **frees the memory associated with p.**

`PyObject_NEW(TYPE, PyTypeObject *t)` **creates a new Python object using the given C structure type and its corresponding Python type object:**

```
PyObject_NEW(dictobject, &PyDict_Type) // Create a dictionary
```

`PyObject_DEL(p)` **frees an object's memory.**

Summary

The Python/C API must be full-featured because it's the same set of functions used to create the built-in modules and much of the interpreter itself. While not as easy to use as Python, the API makes working with Python objects in C at least tolerable. In this chapter, you learned about:

- ✦ Tracking the reference counts of Python objects.
- ✦ Using the abstract and concrete object layers to manipulate objects.
- ✦ Raising and handling Python exceptions in C.
- ✦ Managing memory using Python's memory heap functions.

In the next chapter, you learn to use NumPy, a set of numerical extensions for Python that let you do things such as efficiently handle large arrays of data.

✦   ✦   ✦

Number Crunching

♦ ♦ ♦ ♦

In This Chapter

Using math routines

Computing with complex numbers

Generating random numbers

Using arbitrary-precision integers

♦ ♦ ♦ ♦

Python can crunch numbers with the best of them. It offers built-in complex numbers, functions to handle advanced mathematics, random number generators, and more. This chapter covers Python's number-crunching abilities.

Using Math Routines

The `math` module provides various higher-math functions. The functions raise a `ValueError` if passed an input not in their domain.

The `math` module also provides constants `pi` and `e`:

```
def Circumference(Radius):
    return Radius*2*math.pi

def
ContinuousCompounding(Principal,InterestRate,Y
ears):
    # Find the balance in a bank account,
after some time
    # earning the specified interest rate (for
example, .05),
    # compounded continuously.
    return Principal * math.pow(math.e,
InterestRate*Years)
```

Rounding and fractional parts

The function `ceil(x)` returns the smallest integer >=x. `floor(x)` returns the largest integer <=x. To round to the nearest integer, use the built-in function `round`. For instance:

```
>>> math.ceil(2.2),math.floor(2.2),round(2.5)
(3.0, 2.0, 3.0)
>>> math.ceil(-2.5),math.floor(-3)
(-2.0, -3.0)
```

The function `modf(x)` returns a tuple of the form (Frac,Int), where *Int* is the integral part of x, and *Frac* is the fractional part:

```
>>> math.modf(3)
(0.0, 3.0)
>>> math.modf(-2.22)
(-0.2200000000000002, -2.0)
```

General math routines

The function `sqrt(x)` returns the square root of a non-negative number x.

The function `hypot(x,y)` returns the hypotenuse of a triangle with sides of length *x* and *y*—that is, it returns `math.sqrt(x*x + y*y)`.

The function `fmod(x,y)` returns the remainder when *x* is divided by *y*. It uses the platform C library, which normally (but not always) returns the same answer as `x%y`.

Logarithms and exponentiation

The function `exp(x)` returns e to the power of *x*, while `log(x)` returns the natural logarithm of *x*. The function `log10(x)` returns the base-10 logarithm of *x*. The function `pow(x,y)` returns *x* raised to the power of *y*.

Note that `5**-1` (an integer to a negative power) is illegal, but `math.pow(5,-1)` is legal (and equals 0.2, as you would expect). `math.pow(-5,0.5)` is still illegal—for that, you need to use the `cmath` module. (See "Computing with Complex Numbers" later in this chapter.)

The function `ldexp(x,y)` (short for "load exponent") returns `x * (2**y)`. The function `frexp(x)` returns the mantissa and exponent of *x*—a tuple (a,b) such that x == a * (2**b). The exponent, *b*, is an integer. The mantissa, *a*, is such that `0.5<=a<1`, unless *x* is 0, in which case, `frexp(x)==(0.0,0)`.

Trigonometric functions

The functions `sin(x)`, `cos(x)`, and `tan(x)` return the sine, cosine, and tangent (respectively) of an angle x, measured in radians:

```
>>> math.cos(math.pi)
-1.0
>>> DEGREES_TO_RADIANS = math.pi/180
>>> math.tan(45*DEGREES_TO_RADIANS) #Convert degrees to radians
0.99999999999999989
```

The functions `sinh(x)`, `cosh(x)`, and `tanh(x)` compute hyperbolic sine, cosine, and tangent, respectively.

The inverse trigonometric functions `asin(x)`, `acos(x)`, and `atan(x)` return the arc sine, arc cosine, and arc tangent of x, respectively. The values of `asin(x)` and `atan(x)` are chosen between -pi/2 and pi/2. The value of `acos(x)` is chosen between 0 and pi.

Computing with Complex Numbers

Recall that in Python, the imaginary part of a complex number is indicated by a j (not an i). The function `complex(real[,imag])` creates a complex number. The attributes `real` and `imag` of a complex number return its real and imaginary part, respectively; and the `conjugate` method returns its complex conjugate, as shown in the following example:

```
>>> (1 - 1j) * (1 + 1j)
(2+0j)
>>> complex(-5) + 3J # j or J, case doesn't matter
(-5+3j)
>>> x = (2+3j)
>>> x.real,x.imag,x.conjugate()
(2.0, 3.0, (2-3j))
>>> abs(x) # magnitude of x = hypot(x.real,x.imag)
3.6055512754639896
```

The `math` functions operate only on real numbers; for instance, `math.sqrt(-4)` raises a `ValueError` exception, because -4 has no real roots. `math`'s sister-module, `cmath`, provides functions for working with complex numbers. These `cmath` functions accept complex input, but are otherwise the same as the corresponding math functions: `acos`, `asin`, `atan`, `cos`, `exp`, `log`, `log10`, `sin`, `sinh`, `tan`, and `tanh`.

In addition, `cmath` provides the inverse hyperbolic trigonometric functions: `asinh(x)`, `acosh(x)`, and `atanh(x)`.

Generating Random Numbers

The `random` module provides a pseudo-random number generator.

Random numbers

Several functions are available to produce random numbers; you can also instantiate your own random number generator.

Note Prior to Version 2.1, the `random` module used the `whrandom` module — which provides much of the same functionality — however, the `whrandom` module is now deprecated.

Random integers

The function `randrange([start,]stop[,step])` provides a random number chosen from the corresponding range. `randrange` is now the preferred way to get a random integer, but you can also call `randint(min,max)`.

Random floating-point numbers

The function `random` provides a floating-point number x such that 0<=x<1. The function `uniform(a,b)` provides a floating-point number x such that a<=x<b.

Random selections

The function `choice(sequence)` returns a randomly selected element of the specified sequence. The function `shuffle(sequence)` shuffles a sequence in place. (Note that the sequence must be mutable — to shuffle a tuple or string, first convert it to a list.)

Seeding the RNG

The random number generator is not actually random, merely hard to predict. It is deterministic, and its output is determined by its seed values. By default, `random` seeds the generator with numbers derived from the current system time. But you can seed it yourself by calling `seed(x)`, where *x* is a hashable object. This example seeds and re-seeds the generator:

```
>>> random.seed(123)
>>> random.random()
0.54140954469092906
>>> random.seed(123) # do it again!
>>> random.random()
0.54140954469092906
```

The functions in `random` are actually methods of the class `random.Random`. The module automatically creates one instance of the class for you. If you like, you can instantiate one or more `Random` instances yourself, to produce independent streams of pseudo-random numbers. This is highly recommended for multi-threaded programs, as two threads using the same random number generator may receive the same numbers.

Generator state

The random number generator keeps an internal state, which changes each time it supplies a new random number. The function `getstate` returns a snapshot of its current state, which you can restore using `setstate(state)`. You can also call `jumpahead(n)` to skip forward *n* steps in the stream of random numbers.

New Feature   The methods `getstate`, `setstate`, and `jumpahead` are new in Version 2.1.

Example: shuffling a deck

The example shown in Listing 31-1 prints out a deck of playing cards in random order.

Listing 31-1: **Cards.py**

```
import random

# Represent a card as a tuple of the form (Value,Suit):
CARD_VALUES=["A",2,3,4,5,6,7,8,9,10,"J","Q","K"]
CARD_SUITS=["Clubs","Hearts","Diamonds","Spades"]

Cards=[]
for Suit in CARD_SUITS:
    for Value in CARD_VALUES:
        NewCard=tuple((Value,Suit))
        Cards.append(NewCard)

random.shuffle(Cards)

for Card in Cards:
    print Card
```

Random distributions

Then random module provides functions to provide random numbers distributed according to various formulae, such as the normal distribution. The following statistics functions are available:

✦ **betavariable(a,b)** — The beta distribution. Probability density is $x^{a-1}(1 - x)^{b-1}$ / $B(\alpha,b)$, where $B(a, b) = \Gamma(a) \Gamma(b) / \Gamma(a+b)$. Both a and b must be greater than -1.

✦ **cunifvariate(mean,arc)** — Circular uniform distribution. Both mean and arc must be an angle (in radians) from 0 to pi.

✦ **expovariate(lambda)** — The exponential distribution. Probability density is $\lambda e^{-\lambda x}$.

✦ **gammavariate(a,lambda)** — The gamma distribution. Probability density is $\lambda^{\alpha} x^{(\alpha-1)} e^{-x/b} / \Gamma(\alpha)$. must be larger than -1, and b must be larger than 0.

✦ **gauss(mu,sigma)** — The Gaussian (normal) distribution with mean *mu* and standard deviation *sigma*. This is slightly faster than normalvariate.

✦ **lognormvariate(mu,sigma)** — The log normal distribution. The natural logarithm of this distribution has mean *mu* and standard deviation *sigma*.

✦ **normalvariate(mu,sigma)** — The normal distribution. Mean is *mu,* and the standard deviation is *sigma.*

✦ **paretovariate(a)** — The Pareto distribution. Probability density is a / x^{a+1} for x >=1

✦ **vonmisesvariate(mu,kappa)** — The Von Mises distribution. Mean angle (in radians) is *mu*, and *kappa* is the concentration parameter.

✦ **weibullvariate(a,b)** — The Weibull distribution. Probability density is $\alpha\beta x^{\beta-1} esp(-\alpha x^{\beta-1})$. a must be greater than 0; b must be at least 1. Same as the exponential distribution if b=1.

Example: plotting distributions using Monte Carlo sampling

Listing 31-2 plots different random distribution with a text graph. It uses a trick called *Monte Carlo sampling*: It samples the distribution many times, and graphs the sample results. These results approximate the actual random distribution.

Listing 31-2: **Plotter.py**

```
import random

def MonteCarloSampler(DistributionFunction,Min,Max,
                     Step,Times=1000):
    """
    Call the Distribution function the specified number
    of times. Divide the range [Min,Max] into intervals
    (buckets), each with width Step. Keep track of how
    many values fall into each bucket.
    """
    Buckets=[]
    BucketLeft=Min
    while BucketLeft<Max:
        Buckets.append(0)
        BucketLeft+=Step
    for Sample in range(Times):
        Value=DistributionFunction()
        BucketIndex = int((Value-Min)/Step)
        if (BucketIndex>0 and BucketIndex<len(Buckets)):
            Buckets[BucketIndex]+=1
    return Buckets

def PlotValues(Buckets, Height):
    """
    Plot a collection of values, scaling them to the specified
    height (in rows).
    """
```

```
        MaxValue = max(Buckets)
        ScaledBuckets=[]
        for Value in Buckets:
            ScaledBuckets.append(Value*Height/MaxValue)
        for RowNumber in range(Height,0,-1):
            for Value in ScaledBuckets:
                if Value>=RowNumber:
                    print "*",
                else:
                    print " ",
            print


NormalCaller = lambda : random.normalvariate(100,5)
Values=MonteCarloSampler(NormalCaller,80,120,1)
PlotValues(Values,20)

GammaCaller = lambda : random.gammavariate(0.5,5)
Values=MonteCarloSampler(GammaCaller,0,5,0.15)
PlotValues(Values,20)
```

Using Arbitrary-Precision Numbers

The mpz module provides an interface to the integer functionality of the GNU
Multiple Precision Arithmetic Library (GMP). mpz is an optional module, and
requires GMP to work. Visit GMP's homepage at http://www.swox.com/gmp to
learn about installing and building GMP.

The mpz module enables you to do arithmetic using high-precision integers, or
mpz-numbers. You can construct an mpz-number with the function mpz(Number),
where Number is an integer, a long, another mpz-number, or an mpz-string. An mpz-
string is a binary representation of an mpz-number; it consists of an array of radix-
256 digits, with the least significant digit first. The method binary returns an
mpz-string for an mpz-number:

```
>>> SmallNumber = mpz.mpz(5)
>>> SmallNumber # string representation has form mpz(#):
mpz(5)
>>> BigNumber = mpz.mpz(50000L)
>>> BigNumber.binary()
'P\303'
>>> BigNumber % 256 # should equal ord(P), or 80:
80
>>> type(BigNumber)==mpz.MPZType # MPZType is for type-checking
1
```

An mpz-number has no other methods. It supports all the usual arithmetic operators, as well as built-in functions such as `abs`, `int`, and so on.

The `mpz` module provides several extra functions for manipulating mpz-numbers. Each function takes mpz-number for its argument(s), converting ints and longs if necessary.

The function `gcd(X,Y)` returns the greatest common divisor of X and Y. The function `gcdext(X,Y)` provides a tuple of the form (GCD, S,T) such that $X*S + Y*T ==$ GCD, and GCD is the greatest common divisor of X and Y.

The function `sqrt(X)` returns the square root of X, rounding the result (if necessary) toward zero. The function `sqrtrem(X)` returns a tuple (Root,Remainder) such that `Root*Root + Remainder == X`; the tuple is chosen such that Remainder is as small as possible.

The function `powm(Base,Exponent,Modulus)` raises *Base* to the power *Exponent*, and then returns the result modulo *Modulus*. It is a shortcut for `(Base**Exponent)%Modulus`.

The function `divm(Numerator,Denominator,Modulus)` computes the quotient of *Numerator* and *Denominator* modulo *Modulus* — a number Q such that `(Q*Denominator)%Modulus == Numerator`. *Modulus* and *Denominator* must be relatively prime, as shown here:

```
>>> mpz.divm(10,20,99) # 10/20 is equal to 50, modulo 99.
mpz(50)
```

Summary

Python can do complex arithmetic, trigonometric functions, and even some statistics. Moreover, it can do it all very precisely. In this chapter, you:

+ Did complex arithmetic and some simple trigonometry.

+ Shuffled a deck of cards, with the help of `random`.

+ Did high-precision integer arithmetic.

In the next chapter, you'll learn all about Numeric Python — NumPy: powerful extension modules for fast computation matrix arithmetic and much more.

Using NumPy

The NumPy extension modules introduce a new sequence type: the *array*. Arrays are fast — much faster than lists or tuples for "heavy lifting" such as image processing. Arrays also have many powerful methods and functions associated with them, so they are often handy, even when speed isn't an issue.

Introducing Numeric Python

Numeric Python (also known as NumPy) is a collection of extension modules for number crunching. The core module, `Numeric`, defines the array class and various helper functions. This chapter focuses on the Numeric module. NumPy's other optional modules include the following:

+ **MA** — Masked arrays. These are arrays that may have some missing or invalid elements.

+ **FFT** — Fast Fourier transforms

+ **LinearAlgebra** — Linear algebra routines (calculation of determinants, eigenvalues, and so on)

+ **RandomArray, RNG** — Interface to random number generators. These may be useful if the `random` module doesn't have what you need.

Installing NumPy

Because NumPy is not part of the standard Python distribution, the first order of business is to install it. The NumPy project is hosted at SourceForge (`http://sourceforge.net/projects/numpy`). Here, you can download the NumPy source code, or (for Windows) a binary distribution. I recommend downloading the source tarball, in any case, as it includes a nice tutorial (in Demo\NumTut) and some examples.

✦ ✦ ✦ ✦

In This Chapter

Introducing Numeric
Python

Accessing and slicing
arrays

Calling universal
functions

Creating arrays

Using element types

Reshaping and
resizing arrays

Using other array
functions

Array example:
analyzing price
trends

✦ ✦ ✦ ✦

Some quick definitions

An *array* is a sequence — a collection of elements all of a particular type (usually numeric). A universal function, or *ufunc*, is a function that takes an array (or other sequence), acts on each element individually, and returns an array of results. The size of an array (the total number of elements) is fixed. However, its shape may vary freely; for example, a linear array of 12 elements may be reshaped into a 3×4 grid, a $2 \times 2 \times 3$ cube, and so on. These shapes can be represented in Python as tuples of the form (12,), (3,4), or (2,2,3). An array can have several dimensions, or *axes*.

Meet the array

You can construct an array by calling `array(sequence)`. Here, *sequence* is a collection of values for the array. For example:

```
>>> import Numeric
>>> Sample=Numeric.array([1,2,3,4,5])
>>> Sample # Print the array:
array([1, 2, 3, 4, 5])
>>> # Remember not to do this:
>>> BadSample=Numeric.array(1,2,3,4,5) # Too many arguments!
Traceback (innermost last):
  File "<pyshell#236>", line 1, in ?
    BadSample=Numeric.array(1,2,3,4,5)
TypeError: function requires at most 4 arguments; 5 given
```

A nested *sequence* results in a multi-dimensional array. However, note that the source sequence must form a valid shape:

```
>>> Numeric.array([[1,2],[3,4],[5,6]]) # 3x2 array
array([[1, 2],
       [3, 4],
       [5, 6]])
>>> Numeric.array([[1,2],[3,4,5]]) # Not rectangular!
Traceback (innermost last):
  File "<pyshell#14>", line 1, in ?
    Numeric.array([[1,2],[3,4,5]]) # not rectangular!
TypeError: an integer is required
```

Accessing and Slicing Arrays

You can access an array's elements by index or by slice:

```
>>> Fibonacci=Numeric.array((1,1,2,3,5,8,13))
>>> Fibonacci[4] # An element
5
>>> Fibonacci[:-1] # A slice (giving a sub-array)
array([1, 1, 2, 3, 5, 8])
```

```
>>> Fibonacci[0]=44 # Arrays are mutable (but not resizable)
>>> Fibonacci # (We broke the Fibonacci series)
array([44, 1, 2, 3, 5, 8, 13])
>>> MagicSquare=Numeric.array([[6,1,8],[7,5,3],[2,9,4]])
>>> MagicSquare[0] # The first row
array([6, 1, 8])
>>> MagicSquare[0][2] # A single element
8
```

Arrays can be sliced along any axis, or along multiple axes at once. You provide the slicing information for each axis, one by one. For example, following are some slices on a 4 × 4 array:

```
>>> # Produce an array of the numbers 0 to 15:
>>> Sixteen=Numeric.arrayrange(16)
>>> # Re-shape the array into a 4x4 grid:
>>> FourByFour=Numeric.reshape(Sixteen,(4,4))
>>> FourByFour
[[ 0, 1, 2, 3,]
 [ 4, 5, 6, 7,]
 [ 8, 9,10,11,]
 [12,13,14,15,]]
>>> FourByFour[1:3,1:3] # rows 1 and 2, columns 1 and 2
[[ 5, 6,]
 [ 9,10,]]
>>> FourByFour[:,0] # Every row, but only the first column
[ 0, 4, 8,12,]
```

The array returned by a slice is *not* a copy of the old array, but a reference to the old array's data. Note that this is different from the behavior of the slice operator on lists. Compare the results of the following two operations:

```
>>> FirstList=[1,2,3,4,5]
>>> SecondList=FirstList[1:4] # Normal slice copies data
>>> SecondList[0]=25 # FirstList is unchanged!
>>> FirstList
[1, 2, 3, 4, 5]
>>> FirstArray=Numeric.array(FirstList)
>>> SecondArray=FirstArray[1:4] # Array slice doesn't copy data
>>> SecondArray[0]=25 # FirstArray is changed!
>>> FirstArray
[ 1,25, 3, 4, 5,]
```

Note   Some array manipulations make a copy of array data, while others provide a new reference to the same data. Make sure that you know which you are doing — otherwise, you may end up with two array variables that "step on each others' toes"!

Optionally, you can provide a third "step" parameter for an array slice. This enables you to take every nth element within a slice, or to reverse the order of a slice:

```
>>> Sixteen[1:10:2] # Every other element from the slice
[1,3,5,7,9,]
```

```
>>> Sixteen[::-1] # Reverse the order of the slice
[15,14,13,12,11,10, 9, 8, 7, 6, 5, 4, 3, 2, 1, 0,]
```

Contiguous arrays

An ordinary array is *contiguous* — its entries all live next to one another in memory. Passing a slice-step is one way to get a noncontiguous array. The iscontiguous method of an array returns true if the array is contiguous. Most functions don't care whether an array is contiguous or not, but some (such as the flat attribute) do:

```
>>> SomeNumbers=Numeric.arange(10)
>>> OddNumbers=SomeNumbers[::2]
>>> OddNumbers.iscontiguous()
0
>>> OddNumbers.flat
Traceback (innermost last):
  File "<pyshell#84>", line 1, in ?
    Fred.flat
ValueError: flattened indexing only available for contiguous
array
```

The function ravel(array) returns a one-dimensional, contiguous copy of an array.

Converting arrays to lists and strings

You can extract array contents as a list (by calling the array's tolist method) or as a string (by calling tostring). For example, in the following 4 × 4 array, the letters of each row and column form a word:

```
>>> MyArray=Numeric.array(["HORN","OBOE","ROSE","NEED"])
>>> MyArray
[[H,O,R,N,]
 [O,B,O,E,]
 [R,O,S,E,]
 [N,E,E,D,]]]
>>> MyArray[3] # The letters of row 3 form a word:
[R,O,S,E,]
>>> MyArray[:,2] # The letters of column 3 form the same word:
[R,O,S,E,]
```

I cannot compare one slice to another directly, because comparison operators are not defined for arrays. However, by converting slices to lists, I can verify that the column words are the same as the row words:

```
>>> MyArray[2]==MyArray[:,2] # == is not available for arrays
Traceback (innermost last):
  File "<pyshell#315>", line 1, in ?
    MyArray[2]==MyArray[:,2]
TypeError: Comparison of multiarray objects other than rank-0
arrays is not implemented.
```

```
>>> MyArray[2].tolist()==MyArray[:,2].tolist()
1
```

Calling Universal Functions

Universal functions, or ufuncs, are performed *elementwise* — they affect each element individually:

```
>>> A=Numeric.array([[1,2],[3,4]]) # 2x2 array
>>> Numeric.add(A,5) # Add 5 to each element
array([[6, 7],
       [8, 9]])
>>> A+5 # Operators are overloaded to ufuncs
array([[6, 7],
       [8, 9]])
```

Two arrays of compatible shape and size can be added, multiplied, and so on. These operations are also done element by element; therefore, multiplying two arrays does *not* perform the matrix multiplication of linear algebra. (For that, call the `matrixmultiply` function, or use the `Matrix` module.) For instance:

```
>>> B=Numeric.array([[5,6],[7,8]])
>>> A*B # Elementwise multiplication
array([[ 5, 12],
       [21, 32]])
```

A ufunc can operate on any sequence, not just an array. However, its output is always an array. The Numeric module provides many ufuncs, whose names are fairly self-explanatory (see Table 32-1):

Table 32-1
Universal Functions

Category	Ufuncs
Arithmetic	add, subtract, multiply, divide, remainder
Powers and Logs	power, exp, log
Comparison	equal, not_equal, greater, greater_equal, less, less_equal, minimum, maximum
Logic	logical_and, logical_or, logical_xor, logical_not
Trigonometry	sin, cos, tan, sinh, cosh, tanh, arcsin, arccos, arctan, arcsinh, arccosh, arctanh
Bitwise	bitwise_and, bitwise_or, bitwise_xor, bitwise_not

Ufunc destinations

By default, a ufunc creates a brand-new array to store its results. An optional last argument to a ufunc is the destination array. The output of a ufunc can be stored in any appropriately sized array with compatible typecode. If the destination is the same as the source array, an operation can be performed in place, as it is here:

```
>>> Numbers=Numeric.array((4,9,16),Numeric.Float)
>>> Numeric.sqrt(Numbers) # Elementwise square-root
array([ 2.,  3.,  4.])
>>> Numbers # Original array is unchanged
array([  4.,   9.,  16.])
>>> Numeric.sqrt(Numbers,Numbers) # Take roots in place
array([ 2.,  3.,  4.])
>>> Numbers # The original array WAS changed!
array([ 2.,  3.,  4.])
```

Performing operations in place is more efficient than creating new arrays left and right. However, the destination must be compatible with the ufunc's output, both in size and in typecode. For instance, the preceding square root example used a float array, because an in-place square root operation is not allowed on an int array:

```
>>> Numbers=Numeric.array((4,9,16)) # (NOT a float array)
>>> Numeric.sqrt(Numbers,Numbers)
Traceback (innermost last):
  File "<pyshell#33>", line 1, in ?
    Numeric.sqrt(Numbers,Numbers)
TypeError: return array has incorrect type
```

Example: editing an audio stream

Listing 32-1 provides an example of the power of the array class. We read in a stream of audio data as an array of numbers. The left and right channels of the stereo sound are mixed together — every other number represents sound on the left channel. We shrink the numbers corresponding to the left channel, and thereby make the left channel quieter without affecting the right channel.

 Cross-Reference   See Chapter 24 for more information on audio operations in Python, including an explanation of the wave module.

Listing 32-1: **Quiet.py**

```
import Numeric
import wave

BUFFER_SIZE=5000
# NB: This is an 8-bit stereo .wav file. If it had a different
```

```
# sample size, such as 16-bits, we would need to convert the
# sequence of bytes into an array of 16-bit integers by
# calling Numeric.fromstring(Data,Numeric.Int16)
InFile=wave.open("LoudLeft.wav","rb")
OutFile=wave.open("QuietLeft.wav","wb")
OutFile.setparams(InFile.getparams())
while 1:
    # Read audio data as a string of bytes:
    Data=InFile.readframes(BUFFER_SIZE)
    if len(Data)==0:
        break
    # Create an array based on the string:
    Frames=Numeric.array(Data,
        typecode=Numeric.UnsignedInt8,savespace=1)
    # Take every other frame to get just the left side. And,
    # divide each one by 2. (We would like to use
    # Numeric.divide(Frames[::2],2), but we can't,
    # because the returned array would have float type).
    Frames[::2] = Frames[::2]/2
    OutFile.writeframes(Frames.tostring())
InFile.close()
OutFile.close()
```

Repeating ufuncs

Each binary ufunc provides a `reduce` method. The `reduce` method of a ufunc is similar to the built-in function `reduce`. It iterates over a sequence of array elements. At each stage, it passes in (as arguments) the new value and the most recent output. For example, `multiply.reduce` multiplies a sequence of numbers:

```
>>> Factors=Numeric.array((2,2,3,5))
>>> Numeric.multiply.reduce(Factors)
60
```

The `reduce` method takes a second, optional parameter — the axis to reduce over. (By default, reduce combines values along the first axis.) For instance, suppose I want to test whether a matrix is a magic square, wherein each row and column of numbers has the same sum. I can call `add.reduce` to calculate all these sums:

```
>>> Square=Numeric.array([[1,15,14,4],[12,6,7,9],
    [8,10,11,5],[13,3,2,16]])
>>> Numeric.add.reduce(Square) # Sum over each column
array([34, 34, 34, 34])
>>> Numeric.add.reduce(Square,1) # Sum over each row
array([34, 34, 34, 34])
```

I can verify that the sums are all the same by checking whether `minimum.reduce` and `maximum.reduce` give the same value, as that can only happen if the sequence elements are all identical. With a few more lines of code, I have a function to find magic squares, magic rectangles, magic cubes, or even magic hypercubes, as shown in Listing 32-2:

Listing 32-2: MagicSquare.py

```
import Numeric

def IsMagic(Array):
    TargetSum=None
    for Axis in range(len(Array.shape)):
        AxisSums=Numeric.add.reduce(Array,Axis)
        MinEntry=Numeric.minimum.reduce(AxisSums)
        MaxEntry=Numeric.maximum.reduce(AxisSums)
        # For 3 dimensions and up, MinEntry and MaxEntry
        # are still arrays, so keep taking minima and maxima
        # until they become ordinals:
        while type(MinEntry)==Numeric.ArrayType:
            MinEntry=Numeric.minimum.reduce(MinEntry)
            MaxEntry=Numeric.maximum.reduce(MaxEntry)
        if (MinEntry!=MaxEntry):
            return 0
        if (TargetSum==None):
            TargetSum=MinEntry
        elif TargetSum!=MinEntry:
            return 0
    return 1

if __name__=="__main__":
    Square=Numeric.array([[1,15,14,4],[12,6,7,9],
                          [8,10,11,5],[13,3,2,16]])
    print IsMagic(Square)

    Cube=Numeric.array([[[10,26,6],[24,1,17],[8,15,19]],
                        [[23,3,16],[7,14,21],[12,25,5]],
                        [[9,13,20],[11,27,4],[22,2,18]]])
    print IsMagic(Cube)
```

In addition to reduce, each binary ufunc has an accumulate method. A call to accumulate retains all the intermediate results of the function. For example, I could determine where a running total became negative:

```
>>> Numbers=Numeric.array((5,10,20,-4,-2,-10,-5,-3,-10,-2))
>>> Numeric.add.accumulate(Numbers)
array([ 5, 15, 35, 31, 29, 19, 14, 11,  1, -1])
```

Finally, each binary ufunc has an outer method. This method calls the ufunc many times — once for each pair of elements from the two arrays. If A is an n-dimensional array and B is an m-dimensional array, then outer(A,B) is an (n+m)-dimensional array, where the element with coordinates (a1,a2,...,an,b1,b2,...,bm) is the output of ufunc(A[a1][a2]...[an],B[b1][b2]...[bm]). For example, here is the effect of outer multiplication:

```
>>> Numeric.multiply.outer([1,2,3],[4,5,6])
array([[ 4,  5,  6],
       [ 8, 10, 12],
       [12, 15, 18]])
>>> Numeric.multiply.outer([[1,2,3],[4,5,6]],(1,2))
array([[[ 1,  2],
        [ 2,  4],
        [ 3,  6]],
       [[ 4,  8],
        [ 5, 10],
        [ 6, 12]]])
```

Creating Arrays

The array constructor has syntax array(sequence[,typecode[,copy=1[, savespace=0]]]). Here, *sequence* is (as you have seen) a source of data for the array. The element *typecode* is an element type (as described in the next section). If *savespace* is true, the array element's type will not increase in precision:

```
>>> Squares=Numeric.array((4,9,16))
>>> SpaceSaverSquares=Numeric.array((4,9,16),savespace=1)
>>> Squares/float(5) # elements are all upcast to float
[ 0.8, 1.8, 3.2,]
>>> SpaceSaverSquares/float(5) # elements are NOT upcast!
[0,1,3,]
```

If *CopyFlag* is false and *sequence* is an array, the new array will be a reference into the old array. This saves space and processing time, but remember that altering either array will affect the other! This code creates two arrays that point to the same block of memory:

```
>>> Array1=Numeric.array((1,2,3,4,5))
>>> # Next line has same effect as Array2=Array1[:]
>>> Array2=Numeric.array(Array1,copy=0)
>>> Array2[2]=0
>>> Array1
[1,2,0,4,5,]
```

Array creation functions

The function arrayrange([start,]stop[,step]) returns an array consisting of a range of numbers; it is a shortcut for calling array(range(...)). The function zeros(shape[,typecode[,savespace=0]]) creates a zero-filled matrix with the specified shape. The function ones is similar:

```
>>> Numeric.zeros(5)
[0,0,0,0,0,]
>>> Numeric.ones((3,3))
[[1,1,1,]
 [1,1,1,]
 [1,1,1,]]
```

You may encounter the word `zeros` if you create an empty array. For example, if I take an empty slice of an array, the result is a 0-dimensional array of zeroes:

```
>>> bob=Numeric.array((1,2,3))
>>> bob[2:2] # Empty slice
zeros((0,), 'l')
```

The function `identity(n)` returns the identity matrix with rank *n* as an array:

```
>>> identity(3)
[[1,0,0,]
 [0,1,0,]
 [0,0,1,]]
```

You can combine several arrays into one big array with a call to `concatenate ((arrays)[,glueaxis=0])`. The arrays provided are "glued together" along the specified axis. The arrays can have any size along axis *glueaxis*, but their sizes along all other axes must match.

The function `indices(shape)` provides a tuple of "index arrays" of the given shape. The tuple has one element for each axis of *shape*, and the nth tuple corresponds to the nth axis. Each tuple element is an array of the specified shape, such that each entry's value is equal to the index of its nth element. Confused? Here is an example:

```
>>> Coords=Numeric.indices(2,3) # a 2x3 box
>>> Coords[0] # First coordinates for each element
[[0,0,0,]
 [1,1,1,]]
>>> Coords[1] # Second coordinates for each element
[[0,1,2,]
 [0,1,2,]]
>>> Coords[0][1][2] # What's the first coordinate of (1,2)?
1
>>> Coords[1][1][2] # What's the second coordinate of (1,2)?
2
```

Seeding arrays with functions

You can create an array from the output of an arbitrary function. The function `fromfunction(Generator,Shape)` creates an array of the specified shape. The value stored in each array element is produced by a single call to *Generator*. The arguments passed to *Generator* are the contents of `indices(Shape)`, as shown in the following example:

```
>>> Numeric.fromfunction(lambda X,Y: X+Y, (3,3))
[[0,1,2,]
 [1,2,3,]
 [2,3,4,]]
```

When coding a call to `fromfunction`, one can often ignore the fact that *Generator* is acting on arrays, and rely on elementwise array operations to do the work. However, keep in mind that some operations (such as comparison) do not work well with arrays. The example shown in Listing 32-3 calls the universal function `Numeric.minimum`, because the built-in function `min` does not work on arrays. This example prints, for each array entry, the remainder obtained by dividing the entry's two coordinates. Listing 32-4 shows the script's output.

Listing 32-3: **Remainder.py**

```
import Numeric

def Remainder(X,Y):
    # Avoid division by 0 by adding 1 to the coordinates:
    X=X+1
    Y=Y+1
    Small=Numeric.minimum(X,Y)
    Large=Numeric.maximum(X,Y)
    return (Large%Small)
print Numeric.fromfunction(Remainder,(25,25))
```

Listing 32-4: **Remainder.py output**

```
[[ 0  0  0  0  0  0  0  0  0  0  0  0  0  0  0  0  0  0  0  0  0  0  0  0  0]
 [ 0  0  1  0  1  0  1  0  1  0  1  0  1  0  1  0  1  0  1  0  1  0  1  0  1]
 [ 0  1  0  1  2  0  1  2  0  1  2  0  1  2  0  1  2  0  1  2  0  1  2  0  1]
 [ 0  0  1  0  1  2  3  0  1  2  3  0  1  2  3  0  1  2  3  0  1  2  3  0  1]
 [ 0  1  2  1  0  1  2  3  4  0  1  2  3  4  0  1  2  3  4  0  1  2  3  4  0]
 [ 0  0  0  2  1  0  1  2  3  4  5  0  1  2  3  4  5  0  1  2  3  4  5  0  1]
 [ 0  1  1  3  2  1  0  1  2  3  4  5  6  0  1  2  3  4  5  6  0  1  2  3  4]
 [ 0  0  2  0  3  2  1  0  1  2  3  4  5  6  7  0  1  2  3  4  5  6  7  0  1]
 [ 0  1  0  1  4  3  2  1  0  1  2  3  4  5  6  7  8  0  1  2  3  4  5  6  7]
 [ 0  0  1  2  0  4  3  2  1  0  1  2  3  4  5  6  7  8  9  0  1  2  3  4  5]
 [ 0  1  2  3  1  5  4  3  2  1  0  1  2  3  4  5  6  7  8  9 10  0  1  2  3]
 [ 0  0  0  0  2  0  5  4  3  2  1  0  1  2  3  4  5  6  7  8  9 10 11  0  1]
 [ 0  1  1  1  3  1  6  5  4  3  2  1  0  1  2  3  4  5  6  7  8  9 10 11 12]
 [ 0  0  2  2  4  2  0  6  5  4  3  2  1  0  1  2  3  4  5  6  7  8  9 10 11]
 [ 0  1  0  3  0  3  1  7  6  5  4  3  2  1  0  1  2  3  4  5  6  7  8  9 10]
 [ 0  0  1  0  1  4  2  0  7  6  5  4  3  2  1  0  1  2  3  4  5  6  7  8  9]
 [ 0  1  2  1  2  5  3  1  8  7  6  5  4  3  2  1  0  1  2  3  4  5  6  7  8]
 [ 0  0  0  2  3  0  4  2  0  8  7  6  5  4  3  2  1  0  1  2  3  4  5  6  7]
```

Continued

Listing 32-4 *(continued)*

```
[ 0  1  1  3  4  1  5  3  1  9  8  7  6  5  4  3  2  1  0  1  2  3  4  5  6]
[ 0  0  2  0  0  2  6  4  2  0  9  8  7  6  5  4  3  2  1  0  1  2  3  4  5]
[ 0  1  0  1  1  3  0  5  3  1 10  9  8  7  6  5  4  3  2  1  0  1  2  3  4]
[ 0  0  1  2  2  4  1  6  4  2  0 10  9  8  7  6  5  4  3  2  1  0  1  2  3]
[ 0  1  2  3  3  5  2  7  5  3  1 11 10  9  8  7  6  5  4  3  2  1  0  1  2]
[ 0  0  0  0  4  0  3  0  6  4  2  0 11 10  9  8  7  6  5  4  3  2  1  0  1]
[ 0  1  1  1  0  1  4  1  7  5  3  1 12 11 10  9  8  7  6  5  4  3  2  1  0]]
```

Using Element Types

Array elements can have one of several types. Each type has a *type code,* a single character that uniquely identifies it. The Numeric module provides constants for most type codes. These constants do not vary by platform, although the corresponding character may.

Type codes can be used as arguments to the array constructor; they can also be retrieved from an array by calling its typecode method, as shown in the following example:

```
>>> Word=Numeric.array("Blancmange") # An array of characters
>>> Word
[B,l,a,n,c,m,a,n,g,e,]
>>> Word.typecode() # Characters have typecode "c"
'c'
>>> Word=Numeric.array("Blancmange",Numeric.Int)
>>> Word # By overriding typecode, we made an array of ints:
[ 66,108, 97,110, 99,109, 97,110,103,101,]
```

The most common typecodes are the numeric ones: Int, Float, and Complex. In addition, these numeric typecodes have sized variants. For example, Int16 is (usually) a 16-bit integer. If the operating system does not provide 16-bit integers, then Int16 is the smallest integer type whose size is at least 16 bits. The typecodes Int0, Int8, Int16, Int32, and (on some platforms) Int64 and Int128 are all available. Analogous typecodes exist for Float and Complex (for example, Float32).

The other available typecodes are UnsignedInt8 (for numbers between 0 and 255), and PyObject (for arrays of Python objects).

Reshaping and Resizing Arrays

The array attribute shape holds an array's current shape as a tuple. The function reshape(OldArray,Shape) returns an array with the specified shape. No data is copied—the new array holds references to the values in OldArray. The new shape must have the same size as the old:

```
>>> Shapely=Numeric.array((1,2,3,4,5,6))
>>> Shapely.shape
(6,)
>>> Numeric.reshape(Shapely,(2,3))
[[1,2,3,]
 [4,5,6,]]
```

A one-dimensional version of any contiguous array is always available as the member `flat`; an array's total size is always equal to `len(ArrayName.flat)`.

The function `resize(OldArray,Shape)` also returns an array with a new shape—however, the new shape need not be the same size as the old. The old array will be repeated or truncated as necessary to fill the new shape. The new array is a copy; it does not hold references to the original data:

```
>>> Numeric.resize(Shapely,(3,3))
[[1,2,3,]
 [4,5,6,]
 [1,2,3,]]
>>> Numeric.resize(Shapely,(2,2))
[[1,2,]
 [3,4,]]
```

Using Other Array Functions

In addition to the universal functions previously described, the Numeric module provides several other array-manipulation functions. The following sections describe some of the most useful ones.

sort(array,[axis=-1])

This function returns a copy of the given array, sorted along the given axis:

```
>>> People
array([[6, 7, 2],
       [8, 3, 5],
       [1, 9, 4]])
>>> Numeric.sort(People,0)
array([[1, 3, 2],
       [6, 7, 4],
       [8, 9, 5]])
>>> Numeric.sort(People,1)
array([[2, 6, 7],
       [3, 5, 8],
       [1, 4, 9]])
```

where(condition,X,Y)

The where function treats the array *condition* as a mask for creating a new array. It returns an array of the same shape and size as *condition*. Each element of the new array is either X or Y. The new array element is X if the corresponding element of *condition* is true; it is Y if the corresponding element of *condition* is false:

```
>>> Checkerboard=Numeric.resize((0,1),(5,5))
>>> Checkerboard
array([[0, 1, 0, 1, 0],
       [1, 0, 1, 0, 1],
       [0, 1, 0, 1, 0],
       [1, 0, 1, 0, 1],
       [0, 1, 0, 1, 0]])
>>> Numeric.where(Checkerboard,"Y","N")
array([[N, Y, N, Y, N],
       [Y, N, Y, N, Y],
       [N, Y, N, Y, N],
       [Y, N, Y, N, Y],
       [N, Y, N, Y, N]],'c')
```

swapaxes(array,axis1,axis2)

This returns a new array that shares the data of the old, but with the specified axes swapped. This is different from a call to reshape — it actually transposes an array:

```
>>> TwoByThree=Numeric.array([[1,2,3],[4,5,6]])
>>> ThreeByTwo=Numeric.swapaxes(TwoByThree,0,1)
>>> ThreeByTwo
array([[1, 4],
       [2, 5],
       [3, 6]])
>>> ThreeByTwo[2][1]==TwoByThree[1][2]
1
>>> Numeric.reshape(TwoByThree,(3,2)) # Different!
array([[1, 2],
       [3, 4],
       [5, 6]])
```

Matrix operations

The function matrixmultiply(A,B) performs matrix (not elementwise!) multiplication on A and B and returns the result. The function dotm(A,B) returns the dot product of two arrays.

The optional LinearAlgebra module provides several linear algebra functions that operate on arrays. These include determinant(a), inverse(a), eigenvalues(a), and solve_linear_equations(a,b). This example multiplies two matrices:

```
>>> Matrix=Numeric.array([[1,2,3],[4,5,6],[7,8,10]])
>>> Inv=LinearAlgebra.inverse(Matrix)
>>> Numeric.matrixmultiply(Matrix,Inv)
array([[ 1.00000000e+000,  8.88178420e-016, -4.44089210e-016],
       [ 0.00000000e+000,  1.00000000e+000, -1.77635684e-015],
       [ 0.00000000e+000,  0.00000000e+000,  1.00000000e+000]])
```

Because LinearAlgebra does its work using floating-point numbers, multiplying the matrix by its inverse does not yield the identity matrix exactly; however, the error is extremely tiny. Note that `LinearAlgebra.inverse` will happily try (and fail!) to provide an inverse for a non-invertible matrix.

Array Example: Analyzing Price Trends

The script in Listing 32-5 uses an array of imaginary stock prices to compute *moving averages*. A moving average is a computation, for each day, of the average stock price for the last few days. The moving average can "smooth out" volatile changes in a stock price to a greater or lesser extent. For example, a five-day moving average is a relatively short-term measurement, whereas a 200-day moving average takes a more long-term view.

Technical analysts use moving averages to help decide how to trade everything from stocks to pork bellies. This script will probably never beat the market, but it illustrates how easy it is to do number crunching with array functions. Listing 32-6 shows the script's output.

Listing 32-5: **MovingAverage.py**

```
import Numeric

Prices=Numeric.array([10,12,15,18,20,22,22,19,20,
                      23,24,28,30,25,23,20,18,15,
                      13,8,7,7,8,])

# NB: The MA (Masked Array) provides an average function.
# Since it's a one-liner, we define it ourselves here:
def Average(Array):
    return Numeric.add.reduce(Array)/float(len(Array.flat))

def ProduceMovingAverage(StockPrices,Days):
    Slices=[]
    for LastDay in range(1,len(StockPrices)):
        SliceStart=max(0,LastDay-Days)
        Slices.append(StockPrices[SliceStart:LastDay])
    return map(Average, Slices)
```

Continued

Listing 32-5 *(continued)*

```
# When the 5-day average crosses above the 11-day average,
# it may be a good idea to buy the stock. When the 5-day
# average drops below the 11-day average, it may be a good
# time to sell. (The correct day-lengths to use,
# and the effectiveness of the strategy, vary widely between
# markets)
FiveDay=ProduceMovingAverage(Prices,5)
ElevenDay=ProduceMovingAverage(Prices,11)
print Numeric.greater(FiveDay,ElevenDay)
```

Listing 32-6: **MovingAverage output**

```
[0 0 0 0 0 1 1 1 1 1 1 1 1 1 1 1 1 0 0 0 0 0]
```

Summary

NumPy's arrays are fast and flexible; and they mesh well with Python's standard structures, such as lists and tuples. If you need to handle many numbers at once, arrays are probably a good choice — especially if efficiency is important. In this chapter, you:

✦ Created, resized, and manipulated arrays of hundreds of numbers.

✦ Discovered magic squares and magic cubes.

✦ Analyzed the stock market with moving averages.

In the next chapter, you'll examine Python's parsing, tokenizing, and reflection capabilities.

✦   ✦   ✦

Parsing and Interpreting Python Code

◆ ◆ ◆ ◆

In This Chapter

Examining
tracebacks

Introspection

Checking indentation

Tokenizing Python
code

Example: syntax-
highlighting printer

Inspecting Python
parse trees

Low-level object
creation

Disassembling Python
code

◆ ◆ ◆ ◆

Python provides powerful introspection features — even more powerful with the addition of function attributes in Version 2.1. With programmatic access to the Python interpreter's parser and disassembler, documentation, debugging, and development become much easier.

Examining Tracebacks

If your program throws an uncaught exception, it exits, and the Python interpreter prints a traceback, or stack trace. However, your program need not crash to use traceback objects — the `traceback` module provides a suite of functions to work with them.

One usually grabs a traceback with a call to `sys.exc_info()`, which returns a tuple of the form (Exception,Exception, Traceback). In an interactive session, meeting an unhandled exception populates the values `sys.last_type`, `sys.last_value`, and `sys.last_traceback`; one often makes use of these with a call to `pdb.pm()`.

Cross-Reference See Chapter 27, on debugging, for more information about how to use tracebacks with pdb.

Printing a traceback — print_exc and friends

The function `print_exc([limit[,file]])` prints a traceback for the most recent exception (as stored in `sys.exc_info()`). The optional parameter *limit* provides an upper limit on how many stack frames to print. Normally, the exception is printed to `sys.stderr`. Passing a *file* parameter causes the exception to be printed to a file.

You can also call `print_last([,limit[,file]])` to print the traceback for the last uncaught exception in an interpreter session. A more general function is `print_exception(type, value, traceback[,limit[,file]])`, which prints the specified traceback for the specified exception. A call to `print_tb(traceback [,limit[,file]])` prints just a traceback (without exception info).

Extracting and formatting exceptions

The function `extract_stack` grabs a stack trace from the current stack frame. The function `extract_tb(traceback[,limit])` grabs a stack trace from the specified traceback. The return value of each function takes the form of a list of tuples. Each element corresponds to a stack frame — the last element is the current stack frame. Each element is a 4-tuple of the form (Filename, LineNumber, FunctionName, LineText). For instance, this (excessively) recursive code (Listings 33-1 and 33-2) prints a stack trace:

Listing 33-1: **StackPrint.py**

```
import traceback

def Factorial(n):
    if (n<2):
        print traceback.extract_stack()
        return 1
    return n*Factorial(n-1)

print Factorial(3)
```

Listing 33-2: **Output of StackPrint.py**

```
[('C:\\StackPrint.py', 9, '?', 'print Factorial(3)'),
('C:\\StackPrint.py',7, 'Factorial', 'return n*Factorial(n-
1)'),
('C:\\StackPrint.py', 7, 'Factorial', 'return n*Factorial(n-
1)'),
('C:\\StackPrint.py', 5, 'Factorial', 'print
traceback.extract_stack()')]
6
```

You can format traceback tuples however you want. To use the standard formatting, call `format_exception(Type,Value,StackTrace[,limit])`. A formatted exception is a list of one or more newline-terminated strings. You can format just a stack trace with `format_list(StackTrace)`, or just an exception with `format_exception_only(Type,Value)`. As a shortcut, call `format_tb (traceback[,limit])` to format a traceback directly, or call `format_stack` to format the current call stack.

 Caution If optimization (the -O switch) is active, the line numbers reported by a traceback may be slightly off. The function `tb_lineno(Traceback)` computes the actual line number for a traceback.

Example: reporting exceptions in a GUI

Normally, printing tracebacks to a log file is sufficient. However, when debugging a GUI, it can be nice to see the traceback onscreen. The code in Listing 33-3 shows a simple way to report exceptions in a Tkinter window.

Listing 33-3: **GUIErrors.py**

```python
import Tkinter
import traceback
import sys

def LogError():
    TBStrings=traceback.format_exception(*sys.exc_info())
    for Line in TBStrings:
        TraceText.insert(Tkinter.END,Line)

def DoBadThings():
    try:
        smurflicious # bogus name
    except:
        LogError()

root=Tkinter.Tk()
TraceText=Tkinter.Text(root)
TraceText.pack()
BadButton=Tkinter.Button(root,text="DoBadThings",
    command=DoBadThings)
BadButton.pack()
root.mainloop()
```

Eating arbitrary exceptions is bad for you

Code that catches an exception and does nothing (the `except: pass` pattern) is sometimes said to "swallow" the exception. This is often sensible. For example, a call to `os.mkdirs` raises an exception if the directory already exists. This `OSError` is eminently edible. On the other hand, when one catches an arbitrary exception, it's best not to swallow it. Unforeseen problems may remain lurking in the program.

For instance, the exception could be a `NameError` due to a typo in your code. Perform some minimal error handling, even in a quick-and-dirty script such as the following:

```
try:
    DoLotsOfStuff()  # This should never fail.
except:
    # Oh no!  I don't know what to do. But I'd better
    # not just pass, or debugging will hurt.
    traceback.print_exc()
```

The time you spend typing that last line is your insurance against long, distracting interludes spent debugging.

Introspection

Omphaloskepsis is a fancy word meaning "contemplating one's navel." The programming equivalent, *introspection* (also called *reflection*), is a fancy word for code that can examine itself. With Python, you can programmatically browse information such as function and class definitions. It is a handy way to generate documentation, perform type checking, and more.

Review: basic introspection

The built-in function `hasattr(Object, MemberName)` returns true if an object has a member with the specified name. The function `getattr(Object,AttributeName[,Default])` returns the specified object member, or *Default* if the object has no such member. And the function `dir(Object)` returns a list of member names for an arbitrary object.

For example, suppose the Master object has various members. Some of the members should be explicitly cleaned up (with a call to the `cleanup` method). The following code would clean up each member:

```
for Entry in dir(MainApp):
    if hasattr(Entry,"cleanup"):
        getattr(Entry,"cleanup")()
```

The built-in function `issubclass(Child,Parent)` returns true if *Child* is a subclass of *Parent*. A class is considered a subclass of itself. The function `isinstance(Object,ClassOrType)` returns true if the specified object is an instance of the specified class, or has the specified type.

For example, a commonly used pattern is to check whether a variable *X* is a string by testing `type(X)==type("")`. The problem with this is that *X* may be a unicode string! The following function is a better test for most purposes:

```
def IsString(X):
    return (isinstance(X,types.StringType) or
            isinstance(X,types.UnicodeType))
```

Browsing classes

The module `pyclbr` provides a PYthon CLass BRowser (hence the name). It browses Python source code directly—therefore, it can browse a module without importing it, but it can't browse a C extension module. The main function `readmodule(ModuleName[,Path])` parses the classes in the specified module file. The optional parameter *Path* is a list of directories to add to the module search path `sys.path`. The return value of `readmodule` is a dictionary, where each key is a class name, and each value is a *class descriptor*.

A class descriptor has several data members. The members `name`, `module`, `file`, and `lineno` provide the class name, module name, module file name, and definition line number, respectively. The following examines the FTP class from ftplib:

```
>>> FTPDescriptor=pyclbr.readmodule("ftplib")["FTP"]
>>> FTPDescriptor.name
'FTP'
>>> FTPDescriptor.lineno
75
```

The member `methods` is a dictionary, mapping the name of each method to the line number on which it is defined. The member `super` is a list of class descriptors for the class's base classes; `super` has length 1 for single inheritance. If `readmodule` doesn't have a class descriptor for a base class, the corresponding entry in `super` is the base class name (as a string) instead.

Browsing function information

A function (or method) has attributes. Several built-in attributes are available for every function, as shown in Table 33-1.

Table 33-1
Built-in Function Attributes

Name	Description
func_name	Function name (as a string)
func_doc	Function's docstring; same as the __doc__ member
func_dict	Dictionary of user-defined attribute names and values
func_globals	Global namespace of the function; same as m.__dict__, where m is the module defining the function

Continued

<table>
<tr><td colspan="2" align="center">Table 33-1 (continued)</td></tr>
</table>

Name	Description
func_defaults	Default function parameters, as a tuple
func_code	The function, as a code object; suitable for passing to exec or eval
func_defaults	Default parameters

You can also set arbitrary attributes on any Python function (but not on a built-in function).

New Feature   Function attributes are a new feature in Python 2.1

For example, the function in Listing 33-4 checks a software version number (as a string) to ensure that it is a valid dotted-decimal. It uses function attributes to track the number of calls and the number of successes. Listing 33-5 shows the output.

Listing 33-4: **FunctionAttributes.py**

```
import re
DottedDecimalRegExp=re.compile(r"^[0-9]+(\.[0-9]+)*$")

def CheckVersionNumber(Str):
    # One way to handle function attributes is to assume
    # they are uninitialized until proven otherwise:
    OldCount = getattr(CheckVersionNumber,"CallCount",0)
    CheckVersionNumber.CallCount = OldCount+1
    if (DottedDecimalRegExp.search(Str)):
        CheckVersionNumber.SuccessCount+=1
        return 1
    return 0
# One way to handle function attributes is to
# initialize them up-front. (Unlike this example,
# you will want to choose one pattern and stick with it)
CheckVersionNumber.SuccessCount=1

print CheckVersionNumber("3.5")
print CheckVersionNumber("2")
print CheckVersionNumber("3.4.5.")
print CheckVersionNumber("35.")

print "Total calls:",CheckVersionNumber.CallCount
print "Valid version numbers:",CheckVersionNumber.SuccessCount
```

Listing 33-5: Output of FunctionAttributes.py

```
0
0
0
1
Total calls: 4
Valid version numbers: 2
```

Checking Indentation

The module `tabnanny` is a safeguard against ambiguous indentation in Python code. To quote the docstring: "The Tab Nanny despises ambiguous indentation. She knows no mercy." Run the module from the command line to check a file. For example, suppose you created a source file in which one line is indented with tabs, and another is indented with spaces. (This sort of mismatched whitespace usually happens when people with different text editors are sharing and editing the same source files.) The Tab Nanny will not be pleased:

```
> tabnanny.py -v parsing.py
'parsing.py': *** Line 8: trouble in tab city! ***
offending line: '     print "testing!"\012'
indent not equal e.g. at tab sizes 1, 2, 3, 4, 5, 6, 7
```

Tokenizing Python Code

Parsing source code can be a bit of a chore. Fortunately, Python's standard libraries can parse code for you.

The function `tokenize.tokenize(Readline[,Processor])` reads from an input stream, tokenizes code, and passes each token along to a processor. The *Readline* parameter is generally the `readline` method of a filelike object. It should return one line of input per call, and return an empty string when no data remains. The *Processor* parameter is called once for each token, and passed a tuple of the form (TokenType, TokenString, (StartRow,StartColumn), (EndRow,EndColumn), LineNumber). Here, *TokenType* is a numeric code, and *TokenString* is the token itself. *LineNumber* is the logical line where the token began. The default processor prints out the token information:

```
>>> Code=StringIO.StringIO("str = 'hi there'")
>>> tokenize.tokenize(Code.readline)
1,0-1,3:    NAME        'str'
1,3-1,4:    OP          '='
1,4-1,14:   STRING      "'hi there'"
2,0-2,0:    ENDMARKER   ''
```

The `token` module provides various token-type constants (such as `STRING` and `ENDMARKER`, as shown in the preceding printout). It provides a dictionary, `tok_name`, which maps from token types to token-name strings. It also provides the function `ISEOF(TokenType)`, which returns true if the token is an end-of-file marker. The `tokenize` module exports all of the TokenType constants of `token`, as well as one additional one: `COMMENT` (the TokenType of a Python comment).

A useful parsing-related module is `keyword`. It provides one function, `iskeyword(str)`, which returns true if *str* is a Python keyword.

Example: Syntax-Highlighting Printer

Listing 33-6 uses the tokenizer to provide a syntax-highlighted HTML version of Python source code. It uses the keyword module to look up Python keywords.

Listing 33-6: **SyntaxHighlighter.py**

```
import tokenize
import cgi
import keyword

KEYWORD="Keyword"

# Use a dictionary to keep track of what HTML tags we
# will put before and after each token.
TOKEN_START_HTML={tokenize.NAME:"<font color=BLUE>",
                  tokenize.COMMENT:"<font color=RED>",
                  tokenize.STRING:"<font color=GREEN>",
                  KEYWORD:"<font color=ORANGE>",
                  }
TOKEN_END_HTML={tokenize.NAME:"</font>",
               tokenize.COMMENT:"</font>",
               tokenize.STRING:"</font>",
               KEYWORD:"</font>",
               }

class SyntaxHighlighter:
    def __init__(self,Input,Output):
        self.Input=Input
        self.Output=Output
        self.OldColumn=0
        self.OldRow=0
    def ProcessToken(self,TokenType,TokenString,StartTuple,
                     EndTuple,LineNumber):
        # If this token starts after the last one ended,
        # then maintain the whitespace:
        if StartTuple[0]>self.OldRow:
            self.OldColumn=0
```

```
        Whitespace = " "*(StartTuple[1]-self.OldColumn)
        self.Output.write(Whitespace)
        # Special case: Variable names and Python keywords
        # both have token type NAME, but we'd like the keywords
        # to show up in a different color. So, we switch the
        # token type to suit our needs:
        if (TokenType==tokenize.NAME and
            keyword.iskeyword(TokenString)):
            TokenType=KEYWORD
        # Pre-token tags:
        PreToken = TOKEN_START_HTML.get(TokenType,"")
        self.Output.write(PreToken)
        # The token itself:
        self.Output.write(cgi.escape(TokenString))
        # Post-token tags:
        PostToken = TOKEN_END_HTML.get(TokenType,"")
        self.Output.write(PostToken)
        # Track where this token ended:
        self.OldRow=EndTuple[0]
        self.OldColumn=EndTuple[1]
    def PrintHighlightedCode(self):
        self.Output.write("<HTML><PRE>")
        tokenize.tokenize(self.Input.readline,
                          self.ProcessToken)
        self.Output.write("</PRE></HTML>")

Input=open("SyntaxHighlight.py","r") # highlight ourself!
Output=open("SyntaxHighlight.html","w")
Highlighter=SyntaxHighlighter(Input, Output)
Highlighter.PrintHighlightedCode()
```

Inspecting Python Parse Trees

When Python code is parsed, it is stored internally in an Abstract Syntax Tree (AST). The parser module provides you with access to AST objects. You can convert back and forth between sequences and AST objects, in order to manipulate an expression.

Caution   Manipulating ASTs is not for the faint of heart — they are low-level beasts that may vary from one release of Python to the next.

Creating an AST

The function parser.expr(source) parses the provided expression, and returns the resulting AST. It parses a single expression, in the same way that compile(source, "file.py", "eval") would. The function parser.suite(source) parses a suite of statements, in the same way that `compile(source, "file.py", "exec")` would. Both functions raise a `ParserError` if they cannot parse the code.

ASTs and sequences

The AST method `totuple([LineInfo])` returns a tuple representation of the AST. The tuple contains many deeply nested subtuples. Each tuple is either a terminal element (a token) or a nonterminal element (a symbol).

Each terminal element of the source is represented by a tuple of the form (TokenType,TokenString[,LineNumber]). Here, *LineNumber* is provided only if the LineInfo parameter (passed to `totuple`) was true. The constants in the token module provide readable names for terminal element types.

Each nonterminal element of the source is represented by a tuple of the form (SymbolType,SubElement[,SubElement...]). Here, *SymbolType* is one of the symbol constants provided in the symbol module, and each *SubElement* is a child element (either terminal or nonterminal).

Similarly, the AST method `tolist([LineInfo])` returns a list representation of the AST. You can produce an AST from a sequence by calling the function `sequence2ast(Sequence)`.

Using ASTs

An AST object has several methods. The method `isexpr` returns true if the AST corresponds to a single expression; conversely, `issuite` returns true if the AST corresponds to a block of code. The member `compile([filename])` compiles the AST into a code object, suitable for passing to `exec` (if `issuite` is true) or to `eval` (if `isexpr` is true). The dummy file name defaults to <ast>.

Low-Level Object Creation

The `new` module provides functions to create a new instance, class, function, module, or method.

The function `instance(Class,Members)` creates and returns an instance of *Class* with the specified member dictionary (i.e., the new object's __dict__ attribute will be *Members*).

The function `instancemethod(function,instance,class)` returns a new method object. If *instance* is none, the new method is an unbound (class) method.

The function `function(code, globals[,name[,defaults]])` creates a function with the specified code (as a code object) and the specified globals (as a dictionary). If specified, *defaults* should be a tuple of default arguments for the function.

The function module(name) creates a new module with the specified name.

The function classobj(name,BaseClasses,NameSpace) creates a new class with the specified name. *BaseClasses* is a tuple (possibly empty) of base classes, and *NameSpace* is the class's namespace dictionary.

The normal way of creating things is usually the right way, but occasionally the low-level power of new is useful. For example, suppose that Employee and Person are classes with similar data members. You could create a Person from an Employee by using new, as shown in Listing 33-7:

Listing 33-7: **UsingNew.py**

```
import new

class Employee:
    pass

class Person:
    pass

Bob=Employee()
Bob.Name="Bob"
Bob.SSN="123-45-6789"
Bob.ManagerName="Earl"
# Passing Bob.__dict__ gives rise to some unnatural behavior
# later on; passing Bob.__dict__.copy() would be healthier!
BobThePerson=new.instance(Person,Bob.__dict__)
print BobThePerson.Name
BobThePerson.SSN="987-65-4321"
print Bob.SSN # It has changed!!!
```

Disassembling Python Code

Python code is compiled into byte code before execution, for improved efficiency. This byte-compiled code is stored on disk in .pyc files. The dis module enables you to disassemble and examine this byte code. The main function, dis([Source]), disassembles byte code and prints the results. The parameter *Source* may be a function or method, a code object, or a class. The function distb([tb]) disassembles the top function of a traceback object. By default, both dis and distb disassemble the last traceback.

Each line of output contains the instruction address, the opcode name, the operation parameters, and the interpretation of the operation parameters:

```
>>> def Tip(Bill):
    return Bill * 0.15
>>> dis.dis(Tip)
          0 SET_LINENO              1

          3 SET_LINENO              2
          6 LOAD_FAST               0 (Bill)
          9 LOAD_CONST              1 (0.14999999999999999)
         12 BINARY_MULTIPLY
         13 RETURN_VALUE
         14 LOAD_CONST              0 (None)
         17 RETURN_VALUE
```

The instructions at 6 and 9 push the two values onto the stack; the instructions at 12 and 13 multiply them and return the result. Notice that the instructions at 14 and 17 (which return None) will never actually execute. (Experiments have been done with an optimizing Python compiler; such a compiler might well omit these extraneous instructions!)

The attribute dis.opname is a sequence of operation code names; the index of each opcode is its byte code. The dis module provides several sequences for keeping track of the available opcodes. For example, haslocal is a sequence of byte codes that accesses a local variable:

```
>>> dis.haslocal
[124, 125, 126]
>>> dis.opname[125] # Look up the opcode for this byte code
'STORE_FAST'
```

Consult the Python documentation for a full list of the operation codes and their behavior.

Summary

When it is feeling introspective, Python can parse itself, compile itself, tokenize itself, and even disassemble itself. All this flexibility makes programming Python easier. In this chapter, you:

- ✦ Reported errors in a graphical user interface.
- ✦ Used function attributes to track some simple statistics.
- ✦ Created an HTML page of Python code, complete with syntax highlighting.
- ✦ Parsed and disassembled source code.

The next chapter deals with internationalizing applications. This is where Unicode starts to really come in handy!

✦   ✦   ✦

Deploying
Python
Applications

◆   ◆   ◆   ◆

Chapter 34
Creating Worldwide
Applications

Chapter 35
Customizing Import
Behavior

Chapter 36
Distributing Modules
and Applications

◆   ◆   ◆   ◆

Creating Worldwide Applications

In This Chapter

Internationalization
and localization

Preparing
applications for
multiple languages

Formatting locale-
specific output

The modules covered in this chapter help you create programs that are easily adaptable to different languages and countries. These tools extract language- and region-specific information so that, without additional programming, your program will work well with users who speak different languages or have different local customs than your own.

Internationalization and Localization

Internationalization is the process by which a program is prepared for using a different language than that of the programmer. *Localization* is the process by which an internationalized program is adapted to the end-user's choice of language and customs. Together they make up what is known as *native language support*, or *NLS*.

Note Due to the annoying length of the words *internationalization* and *localization*, a popular abbreviated form is to write the first and last letters and place between them the *number* of remaining letters. Thus internationalization becomes i18n and localization becomes l10n.

Internationalization isn't usually difficult. If you write your program with the idea that you will be running it in different languages, then adding internationalization support requires little effort. If you are retrofitting an existing application, the work isn't hard but merely tedious. The internationalization techniques in this chapter deal with marking strings in your application as ones that need to be translated. Special tools then extract these strings and lump them together in a human-readable file that you pass to a translator.

With a little effort, localization can happen almost automatically. Given the file containing translations for the marked strings in your program, Python's tools will look up the translated version before displaying textual messages to the user. Additionally, there are functions that help you format numbers, currencies, dates, and so forth, without requiring you to know the different formats for every single region in the world. Each set of region-specific settings is known as a *locale,* and there are pre-built libraries of common locales throughout the world.

 Note   Python's native language support routines are largely based on GNU's native language support project. Visit the gettext section on `www.gnu.org` for interesting links and more information.

Preparing Applications for Multiple Languages

This section walks you through the process of preparing a tiny program for using different languages. For a real application, you'll follow these steps in a different order, but the order given here is better for a first-time look at the process. At first, it may seem like a lot of work, but after you've been through it all once, you'll see that it's actually quite simple.

An NLS example

Not all strings in an application need to be localizable (translatable). File names, development error messages, and other strings that aren't visible to the user can remain in your native language. Mark the strings that do need to be translated by sending them to a dummy function named _(s):

```
def _(s): return s
print _('What do you want to do today?')
print '1 -', _('Bake something')
print '2 -', _('Play with food')
i = raw_input( _('Enter 1 or 2: '))
if i == '1':
  print _('Oh boy! Baking!')
else:
  print _('Food is fun!')
```

The function name can be anything, but the single underscore character is the conventional choice because it doesn't pollute your source code too much, it doesn't take too much extra effort to include it, and it's very unlikely that you're already using a function of the same name. Moreover, some processing tools may be expecting that you follow the herd and use the same convention.

In Python's `Tools/i18n` directory lives `pygettext.py`, a tool that extracts strings tagged for translation and places them into a human-readable file. Using the preceding example program (saved as `chef.py`), you extract the tagged strings as follows:

```
d:\Python20\Tools\i18n\pygettext.py chef.py
```

Normally, you won't see any output from running this (unless you use –h for help), but it generates a `messages.pot` file such as the following:

```
# SOME DESCRIPTIVE TITLE.
# Copyright (C) YEAR ORGANIZATION
# FIRST AUTHOR <EMAIL@ADDRESS>, YEAR.
#
msgid ""
msgstr ""
"Project-Id-Version: PACKAGE VERSION\n"
"PO-Revision-Date: Wed Feb 14 20:31:20 2001\n"
"Last-Translator: FULL NAME <EMAIL@ADDRESS>\n"
"Language-Team: LANGUAGE <LL@li.org>\n"
"MIME-Version: 1.0\n"
"Content-Type: text/plain; charset=CHARSET\n"
"Content-Transfer-Encoding: ENCODING\n"
"Generated-By: pygettext.py 1.1\n"

#: chef.py:5
msgid "What do you want to do today?"
msgstr ""

#: chef.py:6
msgid "Bake something"
msgstr ""

#: chef.py:7
msgid "Play with food"
msgstr ""

#: chef.py:10
msgid "Oh boy! Baking!"
msgstr ""

#: chef.py:12
msgid "Food is fun!"
msgstr ""

#: chef.py:8
msgid "Enter 1 or 2: "
msgstr ""
```

This template file can then be copied and edited to form a language-specific version. For the following example, we downloaded an *echeferizer*, a program that translates text into the language spoken by the Swedish chef from the Muppets.

I took `messages.pot`, added translations, and saved it as `messages.po` (the following text shows only the lines that changed):

```
#: chef.py:5
msgid "What do you want to do today?"
msgstr "Vhet du yuoo vunt tu du tudey?"

#: chef.py:6
msgid "Bake something"
msgstr "Beke-a sumetheeng"

#: chef.py:7
msgid "Play with food"
msgstr "Pley veet fuud"

#: chef.py:10
msgid "Oh boy! Baking!"
msgstr "Ooh buy! Bekeeng!"

#: chef.py:12
msgid "Food is fun!"
msgstr "Fuud is foon!"

#: chef.py:8
msgid "Enter 1 or 2: "
msgstr "Inter 1 oor 2: "
```

The `gettext` module understands translation files in the `.mo` format, so use the `msgfmt.py` tool (also in Python's `Tools/i18n` directory) to convert from the `.po` format:

```
d:\Python20\Tools\i18n\msgfmt.py messages.po
```

Once again, no output message means success, although you should now find a `messages.mo` file in the current directory. Make a directory off your current directory called `chef`, and in it create another directory called `LC_MESSAGES`. Now move `messages.po` into that `LC_MESSAGES` directory (I'll explain why in a minute).

The final step is to replace the underscore function with a *translator* function from Python's `gettext` module. (Of course, you could have skipped using the dummy function altogether and used `gettext` from the get-go, but I wanted to keep it simple.) Replace the old underscore function with the following:

```
import gettext
_ = gettext.translation('messages','.').gettext
```

Tip   Instead of using the translation object's `gettext` method, you can use `ugettext` to have it return the string as a Unicode string.

Back on the command line, set the environment variable `LANGUAGE` to `chef` and run the program:

```
C:\temp>set LANGUAGE=chef
C:\temp>chef.py
Vhet du yuoo vunt tu du tudey?
1 - Beke-a sumetheeng
2 - Pley veet fuud
Inter 1 oor 2: 1
Ooh buy! Bekeeng!
```

What it all means

Now that you've seen an example, you can better understand the process. The underscore function acts as a lookup function that receives an original string and returns a translated string. The work of extracting the strings, translating them, and converting the file to the `.po` format is pretty straightforward. (Python uses the `.po` format because that's what GNU uses and there are third-party tools that use the same format.)

The `gettext.translation(domain[, localdir[, languages[, class]]])` function returns an instance of the `Translation` class that handles lookups for you. `domain` is useful if you want to group strings by module or category, and `localdir` is the base path from which to search for translation files (if omitted, it looks in the default system locale directory). If the `languages` parameter is omitted, the function searches through the environment variables `LANGUAGE`, `LC_ALL`, `LC_MESSAGES`, and `LANG` to decide which language to use. `class` lets you supply your own class to parse the translation file; if omitted, the `GNUTranslations` class is used.

Tip

`gettext.install(domain[, localdir[, unicode]]))` installs the underscore function in Python's built-in namespace so that all modules will be able to access it. Use this only when you want to force the entire application to use the same language.

Based on the argument and environment information, `gettext` looks in `localdir/language/LC_MESSAGES/domain.mo` for a translation file, and opens and processes it, although it first passes the `language` to `gettext._expand_lang` to get a list of directory names it will check for:

```
>>> import gettext
>>> gettext._expand_lang('french')
['fr_FR.ISO8859-1', 'fr_FR', 'fr.ISO8859-1', 'fr']
>>> gettext._expand_lang('american')
['en_US.ISO8859-1', 'en_US', 'en.ISO8859-1', 'en']
>>> gettext._expand_lang('chef')
['chef'] # Unknown locale returned as-is
```

You could place a single English translation in an `en` directory so that all English-speaking users would get that one translation; or you could provide translations that differ for Australia and the United States, for example.

When you ship your program, you would include .mo files for each language you wish to support. Based on the user's environment variables, your program automatically displays itself in the correct language.

Note

The gettext module also has a set of APIs that closely mirror the GNU C APIs, but using the class-based APIs discussed in this section is the method of choice; it's flexible and much more Pythonic. For example, you can create your own translation class, and you can localize each module separately, instead of the entire application.

Formatting Locale-Specific Output

The locale module helps you localize program output by formatting numbers and strings according to the rules of an end-user's locale. The following sections show you how to query and set various properties of the current locale.

Changing the locale

The default locale is called the C locale, but you can change the locale with setlocale(category[, value]). Each locale is a set of rules for formatting currencies, dates, and so on, and you can use the category argument to specify what part of the locale you want to switch. Table 34-1 lists the different categories you can use. If value is omitted, the current locale for the given category is returned.

<table>
<tr><td colspan="2" align="center">Table 34-1
Locale Categories</td></tr>
<tr><td>*Category*</td><td>*Affects rules dealing with . . .*</td></tr>
<tr><td>LC_ALL</td><td>All subcategories</td></tr>
<tr><td>LC_TIME</td><td>Time formatting</td></tr>
<tr><td>LC_MESSAGES</td><td>Operating system-generated messages</td></tr>
<tr><td>LC_NUMERIC</td><td>Number formatting</td></tr>
<tr><td>LC_MONETARY</td><td>Currency formatting</td></tr>
<tr><td>LC_COLLATE</td><td>String sorting</td></tr>
<tr><td>LC_CTYPE</td><td>Character functions</td></tr>
</table>

In general, you switch all categories at the same time:

```
>>> import locale
>>> locale.setlocale(locale.LC_ALL,'german')
'German_Germany.1252'
```

Calling `setlocale` with an empty string for the `value` argument switches to the user's default locale (which is discovered by looking in environment variables such as `LANGUAGE`, `LC_ALL`, `LC_CTYPE`, and `LANG` or by querying the operating system).

Note   Many users set their locale in `site.py`, which is loaded when Python starts up, so before setting the locale, you should first verify that it isn't already something other than the default C locale.

`setlocale` is not generally thread-safe, so if you do call it, be sure to do so near the beginning of the program if possible. Programs running in embedded Python interpreters should not set the locale, but if the embedding application sets the locale before the interpreter starts, Python will use the new locale setting.

Locale-specific formatting

`str(f)` formats a floating-point number using the user's locale settings to decide what decimal character to use:

```
>>> import locale
>>> locale.setlocale(locale.LC_ALL,'german')
'German_Germany.1252'
>>> locale.str(5.21)
'5,21'
```

The `format(format, val[, grouping])` function formats a number just as the normal % operator would, except that it also takes into account the user's numerical separator characters. If `grouping` is 1 instead of the default of 0, a grouping character (such as a thousand's separator) is used:

```
>>> locale.format('%5.2f',12345.23)
'12345,23'
>>> locale.format('%5.2f',12345.23,1)
'12.345,23'
```

`atof(str)` and `atoi(str)` convert a string to a floating-point number or integer, taking into account the user's grouping and decimal characters. The following uses the preceding locale settings:

```
>>> locale.atof('1.000.002,5')
1000002.5
```

`strcoll(s1, s2)` compares two strings using the lexicographic rules of the user's locale:

```
>>> locale.setlocale(locale.LC_ALL,'us')
'English_United States.1252'
>>> locale.strcoll('chump','coward') # 'ch' < 'co' in English
-1
>>> locale.setlocale(locale.LC_ALL,'sp')
'Spanish_Spain.1252'
>>> locale.strcoll('chump','coward') # In Spanish, 'ch' > 'c'
1
```

In order to compare strings using non-native lexicographic rules, strcoll first transforms the strings in such a way that a normal string compare yields the correct result. If you will be performing many comparisons of the same string (sorting, for example), you can instead call strxfrm(s) to get the transformed format. This would calculate it only once, after which you can use Python's normal comparisons, such as cmp and the equality operators.

Properties of locales

Each locale has a set of attributes describing its various rules. The localeconv() function returns a dictionary containing the rules for the current locale. The keys of this dictionary and their meanings are listed in Table 34-2.

Table 34-2
Keys for the localeconv Dictionary

Key	Meaning	U.S. English Example
decimal_point	Decimal-point character	.
mon_decimal_point	Monetary decimal point	.
thousands_sep	Number grouping character	,
mon_thousands_sep	Monetary grouping character	,
currency_symbol	Local currency symbol	$
int_curr_symbol	International currency symbol	USD
positive_sign	Sign for positive money values	<blank>
negative_sign	Sign for negative money values	-
frac_digits	Number of fractional digits used in local monetary values	2
int_frac_digits	Number of fractional digits used in international values	2
p_cs_precedes	1 if currency symbol precedes value for positive monetary values	1

Key	Meaning	U.S. English Example
n_cs_precedes	1 if currency symbol precedes value for negative values	1
p_sep_by_space	1 if space between positive value and currency symbol	0
n_sep_by_space	1 if space between positive value and currency symbol for negative values	0
p_sign_posn	Sign position, positive money values	3
n_sign_posn	Sign position, negative money values	0
grouping	List of separator positions	[3, 0]
mon_grouping	List of separator positions, for monetary values	[3, 0]

For p_sign_posn and n_sign_posn, a value of 0 means that the currency and the value are enclosed in parentheses; 1 means that the sign comes before the value and the currency symbol; and 2 means that the sign follows the value and the currency symbol. A value of 3 means that the sign immediately precedes the value, and 4 means that the sign immediately follows the value. A value of LC_MAX means nothing is specified for this locale.

The grouping and mon_grouping attributes have lists of numbers specifying the positions where "thousands" (numerical grouping) separators should be put. If the last entry is CHAR_MAX, no further grouping is performed after the next-to-last position has been used. If the last entry is 0, the last group is repeated, so [3, 0] means place the separator character every three digits.

Summary

Adding native language support to your application makes it possible for your programs to adapt themselves to the locale of the end-user, without requiring you to know the customs of every single region in the world. In this chapter, you:

✦ Flagged translatable strings in your program and extracted them with Python's tools.

✦ Created a translation table for your application and ran it in a different language.

✦ Formatted numeric output according to the rules of the end-user's locale.

The next chapter shows you how to take control of and modify the standard module import behavior.

✦   ✦   ✦

Customizing Import Behavior

♦ ♦ ♦ ♦

In This Chapter

Understanding
module importing

Finding and loading
modules with imp

Importing encrypted
modules

Retrieving modules
from a remote source

♦ ♦ ♦ ♦

In most cases, the normal behavior for importing modules is just what you need: You give Python a module name and it finds and loads the module code and adds a new module object to the current namespace. Occasionally, however, you may need to change the way the import process works. This chapter covers the several mechanisms Python provides for easily creating custom module import behavior.

Understanding Module Importing

When the Python interpreter processes the `import` statement, it calls the function `__import__(name[, globals[, locals[, fromlist]]])`, which in turn locates the module called `name`, retrieving its byte code so that a new module object can be created. The `globals` and `locals` parameters hold the global and local dictionaries so that `__import__` can determine the context in which the import is taking place. `fromlist` is a list of items to import from the module when the `from x import y` form of `import` is used.

Cross-Reference Chapter 6 describes modules, packages, and the `import` statement.

The primary reason `__import__` exists in Python (as opposed to being accessible only via the Python/C API) is so that you can modify or track module imports. For example, the following code replaces the normal importer with a function that informs you of each module being loaded:

```
oldimp = __import__    # Save a reference to the
original
```

```
def newimp(name, globals=None, locals=None, fromlist=None):
    # Display info about the import request
    if not fromlist:
        print ':: import',name
    else:
        print ':: from',name,'import',', '.join(fromlist)

    # Now call the original function
    return oldimp(name,globals,locals,fromlist)

__builtins__.__import__ = newimp
```

After running the preceding code, you can see that import calls are indeed routed
to the new function, including imports that other modules request on their own:

```
>>> import os
:: import os
>>> os = reload(os)
:: import sys
:: from nt import *
:: from nt import _exit
:: import ntpath
:: import UserDict
```

Tip
The knee module in the standard Python distribution is an example of replacing
the built-in __import__ function. It doesn't add new functionality, but it *is* useful
for seeing how things work.

Another use of __import__ is to modify the module before returning it to the caller.
For example, the following code adds a timestamp to each module, marking when it
was originally loaded:

```
import sys, time

oldimp = __import__

def newimp(name, globals=None, locals=None, fromlist=None):
    try:
        mod = sys.modules[name]
        first_load = mod.first_load
    except (AttributeError, KeyError):
        first_load = time.time()

    mod = oldimp(name,globals,locals,fromlist)
    mod.first_load = first_load
    return mod

__builtins__.__import__ = newimp
```

The module maintains its original timestamp, even if reloaded:

```
>>> import md5
>>> md5.first_load
982444108.24399996
>>> md5 = reload(md5)
>>> md5.first_load
982444108.24399996
```

 Note Some modules will have already been loaded by the time your import hook is called, so they won't have a timestamp unless they are loaded again later.

Instead of completely replacing Python's import behavior, other modules let you replace or extend only parts of it. The following sections cover the `imp` and `imputil` modules.

 Note The `ihooks` module is another way to modify module import behavior; it is currently used by `rexec` (restricted execution). New programs should avoid using `ihooks`, and use `imp` and `imputil` instead.

Finding and Loading Modules with imp

The `imp` module gives you access to some of the behind-the-scenes functionality associated with module importing. It's useful if you're creating your own module importer or working with Python module files.

Each byte-compiled (.pyc) file has a special header identifying it as Python byte-code; this header can vary from one version of Python to the next to signify a change in bytecode format. `get_magic()` returns the header for the current version:

```
>>> import imp
>>> imp.get_magic()
'\207\306\015\012'
```

`get_suffixes()` returns a list of module suffixes that Python uses when searching for modules. The list contains tuples of the form (`suffix`, `mode`, `type`):

```
>>> imp.get_suffixes()
[('.pyd', 'rb', 3), ('.dll', 'rb', 3), ('.py', 'r', 1),
 ('.pyc', 'rb', 2)]
```

The `mode` tells what mode should be passed to the `open` function to read the file contents, and `type` tells the type of the module. `imp` defines a variable to name each type, as listed in Table 35-1.

Table 35-1
Module Type Values

Value	Type Name	Module is . . .
1	PY_SOURCE	Source code
2	PY_COMPILED	Bytecode
3	C_EXTENSION	Dynamically-loaded C extension
4	PY_RESOURCE	Source code as a program resource (Mac)
5	PKG_DIRECTORY	A package directory
6	C_BUILTIN	Statically-linked C extension
7	PY_FROZEN	Bytecode generated by the Freeze utility (see Chapter 36)
8	PY_CODERESOURCE	Bytecode as a program resource (Mac)

find_module(name[, pathlist]) locates a module with the given name or raises ImportError if it can't find the module. pathlist is a list of directories in which find_module will look, returning the first match it can find. If you don't supply a list of paths, find_module first checks to see if the module exists as a built-in or frozen module. Next, it searches in special platform-specific locations (the system registry on Windows and as a program resource on Macintosh). Finally, it will look through the paths listed in sys.path. When searching for a module, find_module finds files that have the same name as the name argument and that have any of the extensions in the list returned by get_suffixes.

The value returned from find_module is a 3-tuple of the form (file, path, description). file is an open file object for the module file (ready for reading the file contents), path is the full path to the file on disk, and description is a tuple like the ones get_suffixes uses:

```
>>> imp.find_module('asynchat')
(<open file 'D:\Py20\lib\asynchat.py', mode 'r' at  0172E900>,
'D:\\Python20\\lib\\asynchat.py',
('.py', 'r', 1)) # 1 is PY_SOURCE
```

If the module isn't a file on disk, the file and path are empty:

```
>>> imp.find_module('md5')
(None, 'md5', ('', '', 6)) # 6 is C_BUILTIN
```

Note that find_module doesn't handle hierarchical names; locating such modules is a multi-step process:

```
>>> imp.find_module('wxPython')
(None, 'D:\\Python20\\wxPython', ('', '', 5))
>>> imp.find_module('wx',['d:\\python20\\wxPython'])
(<open file 'd:\python20\wxPython\wx.py', mode 'r' at
017D07C8>, 'd:\\python20\\wxPython\\wx.py', ('.py', 'r', 1))
```

`load_module(name, file, filename, description)` loads the module called
name (reloading it if it was already loaded). The `file`, `filename`, and `description`
arguments are the same as the values returned from `find_module`, but name is the
full module name (for example, wxPython.wx). `load_module` returns a module
object or raises `ImportError`.

Note `load_module` does not close the file object after it reads in the module. Be sure
to close it yourself, especially if the load fails and an exception is raised.

You can create a new, empty module object by calling `new_module(name)`. The
module object returned is not inserted into `sys.modules` and has two members:
`__name__` (set to the name value passed in to `new_module`) and `__doct__` (set to
the empty string).

Importing Encrypted Modules

The `imputil` module makes it easy to modify importing behavior while reusing as
much of the current import functionality as possible (so you don't have to rewrite
the whole thing yourself). This section uses `imputil` to read Python modules
stored in an encrypted format.

Tip `importers.py` (in Python's `Demo/imputil` directory) contains examples of
using `imputil` in different ways.

`ImportManager` is a class in `imputil` that takes care of locating and loading Python
modules. The `install([namespace])` method installs the `ImportManager`
instance into the given namespace dictionary, defaulting to `__builtin__` so that all
modules use it (`namespace` can be a module or a module dictionary):

```
>>> import imputil
>>> im = imputil.ImportManager()
>>> im.install()
```

Caution As of Python 2.0, `imputil` and the PythonWin IDE have problems working
together. Try the examples of this section from a different IDE or from the command line.

Note The `ImportManager` constructor can optionally take an instance of the
`imputil.Importer` class; see the next section for details.

Once the `ImportManager` is installed, you can add to its list of recognized suffixes for Python modules by calling its `add_suffix(suffix, importFunc)` method. When the `import` statement is used, the `ImportManager` searches through known module locations (for example, `sys.path`) for files that have the requested module name and an extension that matches one in `ImportManager`'s internal suffix list. When found, it calls the `importFunc` to import that module.

The code in Listing 35-1 puts the `ImportManager` to work by adding the new file suffix `.pye`, which for now will contain only normal Python source code (in a later example, it will contain encrypted bytecode). Basically, no functionality is added, except that you can now store Python code in .pye files.

Listing 35-1: **importpye.py – Adds.pye as valid Python module files**

```
import imputil

def handle_pye(fullpath, fileinfo, name):
    # Print a debugging message
    print 'Importing "%s" from "%s"' % (name,fullpath)

    data = open(fullpath).read()
    return 0, compile(data,fullpath,'exec'),{}

im = imputil.ImportManager()
im.add_suffix('.pye',handle_pye)
im.install()
```

Now create a `.pye` Python module. For example, save the following code to a file called `stuff.pye`:

```
print 'I am being imported!'
a = 10
b = 'Hello'
```

After importing `importpye`, any other module can automatically import `.pye` modules:

```
>>> import stuff # This fails - doesn't check .pye files yet
Traceback (most recent call last):
  File "<stdin>", line 1, in ?
ImportError: No module named stuff
>>> import importpye
>>> import stuff # Now .pye files are checked and loaded
Importing "stuff" from "stuff.pye"
I am being imported!
>>> stuff.a, stuff.b
(10, 'Hello')
```

The `importFunc` passed to `add_suffix` takes three arguments: the full path to the module file, a file information tuple (from a call to `os.stat`), and the name of the module being imported. If the function doesn't return a value, `ImportManager` continues looking in other locations and with other suffixes until it loads a module, finally raising `ImportError` if unsuccessful, so your `importFunc` could choose to ignore some import requests because the `ImportManager` will continue looking if needed.

Your `importFunc` should either not return anything or return a 3-tuple (`isPkg`, `code`, `initialDict`). `isPkg` is 1 if the module is actually a package directory, `code` is a code object for the module (which will be executed in the namespace of the new module), and `initialDict` is a dictionary containing any initial values you want present in the new module's dictionary before the code object is executed.

With the import hook working, you can add in support to decrypt the module as it is being imported. Listing 35-2 expands the previous version of `importpye.py` to decrypt the file contents before returning it to the `ImportManager`. It also adds a utility function, `encrypt`, to take a `.py` file and create a `.pye` file containing compiled and encrypted bytecode.

Listing 35-2: **importpye.py – Imports-encrypted Python modules**

```
import imputil, rotor, os, marshal

SECRET_CODE = 'bitakhon'
rot = rotor.newrotor(SECRET_CODE)

def encrypt(name):
    # Compiles and encrypts a Python file
    data = compile(open(name).read(), name, 'exec')

    base, ext = os.path.splitext(name)
    data = rot.encrypt(marshal.dumps(data))
    open(base+'.pye', 'wb').write(data)

def handle_pye(fullpath, fileinfo, name):
    # Print a debugging message
    print 'Importing "%s" from "%s"' % (name,fullpath)

    data = marshal.load(fullpath)
    return 0, rot.decrypt(data),{}

im = imputil.ImportManager()
im.add_suffix('.pye',handle_pye)
im.install()
```

To test it, rename `stuff.pye` to just `stuff.py` (or use any other Python source file) and use the `encrypt` function to create a `.pye` file:

```
>>> import importpye
>>> importpye.encrypt('stuff.py')
```

Now you can distribute the `stuff.pye` file, and programs can load it without needing to handle the details of decryption:

```
>>> import importpye
>>> import stuff
I am being imported!
>>> stuff.a, stuff.b
(10, 'Hello')
```

With a little extra work, you can use this method to distribute Python modules whose contents are relatively secure. Using the Python/C API, you can create a small C program that embeds the Python interpreter and takes care of setting up the rotor (or whatever other decryption engine you use) so that it's not overly trivial for someone else to decrypt the files. Furthermore, by not advertising the fact that your program is actually Python, and by grouping all the modules together into a single archive file (perhaps as a pickled dictionary), you can prevent all but the nosiest of people from obtaining your program source.

Chapters 29 and 30 cover extending and embedding Python with C, and Chapter 12 teaches you how to serialize Python objects using the `pickle` and `marshal` modules.

Retrieving Modules from a Remote Source

The `imputil.Importer` class is a base class from which you derive custom import subclasses. In this section, you'll create a subclass that retrieves Python modules from a remote module repository.

Subclassing Importer

Most subclasses of `Importer` override only one method, `get_code(parent, name, fqname)`. If not `None`, `parent` is a parent module in a module hierarchy. `name` is the name of the module, and `fqname` is the fully qualified name (from the root of the module namespace down to this module).

If `get_code` can't find the module or doesn't want to handle the request, it shouldn't return anything. If it does load the module, the return value should be a 3-tuple of the form (`isPkg`, `code`, `initialDict`), as with the `importFunc` in the previous section.

The easiest way to use an `Importer` is to add it to `sys.path`. Normally, `sys.path` holds directory names, but with the `ImportManager` installed, it can contain directory names or `Importer`s. Listing 35-3 creates a dummy `Importer` and installs it.

Listing 35-3: dumbimp.py – A dummy custom Importer

```
import imputil, sys

# Create an install the ImportManager
ier = imputil.ImportManager()
ier.install()

class DummyImp(imputil.Importer):
    def get_code(self, *args):
        print 'Importing',args

# Install at the front of the list
sys.path.insert(0,imputil.BuiltinImporter())
sys.path.insert(0,DummyImp())

# Test it
import Tkinter
```

Running the program yields the following output:

```
C:\temp>dumbimp.py
Importing (None, 'Tkinter', 'Tkinter')
Importing (None, 'FixTk', 'FixTk')          # Indirect imports
Importing (None, '_tkinter', '_tkinter')
Importing (None, 'types', 'types')
Importing (None, 'Tkconstants', 'Tkconstants')
Importing (None, 'string', 'string')
Importing (None, 'MacOS', 'MacOS')
```

Right behind the new importer is also an instance of `BuiltinImporter` to handle normal imports. When downloading modules from a remote source, the custom importer should probably come last in the list so that all other importing techniques are exhausted before an attempt is made to download it over the relatively slow network connection.

Creating the remote Importer

The server side of the network connection is as simple as possible: it accepts incoming connections, reads a request for a single module, and returns the Python source code or an empty string if the module doesn't exist on the remote side. In real-world applications, it's a good idea to add security, message compression, the ability to handle multiple requests on a single socket, and lots of error checking.

Listing 35-4 shows the remote importer implementation.

Listing 35-4: **rimp.py – Remote module importer**

```python
import struct, SocketServer, imp, imputil
from socket import *

# Simple message layer - adds length prefix to each
# message so remote side knows how much data to read
MSG_HDR = '!I'
MSG_HDR_LEN = struct.calcsize(MSG_HDR)

def MsgSend(sock, msg):
    'Sends a message with a length prefix'

    # Add length prefix
    msg = struct.pack(MSG_HDR, len(msg)) + msg

    # Send until all is sent
    while msg:
        count = sock.send(msg)
        if count > 0:
            msg = msg[count:]

def MsgRecv(sock):
    'Reads and returns a message'

    # Read the prefix
    pre = sock.recv(MSG_HDR_LEN)
    if not pre:
        return
    count = struct.unpack(MSG_HDR, pre)[0]

    # Read the message
    msg = ''
    while 1:
        leftToRead = count - len(msg)
        if not leftToRead:
            break
        msg += sock.recv(leftToRead)
    return msg

# Server side
PORT = 55555
ADDRESS = '127.0.0.1'

class ImportHandler(SocketServer.BaseRequestHandler):
    def handle(self):
        print 'Received new connection'
        msg = MsgRecv(self.request)
        print 'Remote side requests module',msg
```

```
            file = None
            try:
                file, name, info = imp.find_module(msg)
                source = file.read()
            except ImportError:
                source = ''
            if file:
                file.close()
            print 'Sending %d bytes' % len(source)
            MsgSend(self.request, source)
            print 'Done'

def StartServer():
    print '[Starting server]'
    serverClass = SocketServer.ThreadingTCPServer
    listenAddress = (ADDRESS, PORT)
    serverClass(listenAddress, ImportHandler).serve_forever()

# Client side
class RemoteImporter(imputil.Importer):
    def get_code(self, parent, name, fqname):
        print 'Checking remote host for module',name
        s = socket(AF_INET, SOCK_STREAM)
        s.connect((ADDRESS, PORT))
        MsgSend(s, name)
        code = MsgRecv(s)
        if not code:
            return

        # Save the module for next time
        open(name+'.py','wt').write(code)
        print 'Saved %s.py to disk' % name

        # Now return the code for this time
        return 0, compile(code, name+'.py', 'exec'), {}

if __name__ == '__main__':
    StartServer()
else:
    # The module is being imported, so install the
    # custom importer
    import imputil, sys

    # Install an ImportManager only if one has not
    # already been installed globally
    if __import__.__name__ != '_import_hook':
        ier = imputil.ImportManager()
        ier.install()
        sys.path.append(imputil.BuiltinImporter())

    # Install it at the end of the list
    sys.path.append(RemoteImporter())
```

Cross-Reference   Chapter 15 covers sockets and `SocketServers`.

The first part of the program creates a simple messaging layer that adds a message length prefix to messages so that the receiving side knows how many bytes to read.

The server side of the importer subclasses `SocketServer.BaseRequestHandler` to repeatedly receive a request, find it with `imp.find_module`, and send back the Python source code (because bytecode might be incompatible if the client and server sides have different versions of Python). The server listens on a local address so that you can run both sides of the example on a single computer.

The client side connects to the server, sends a request, and reads a response. If the server sends back an empty string, it couldn't find the module either, but if found, the client side writes the module to disk so that future imports won't require the network transfer.

Depending on how the module is loaded (as a standalone program or imported by another module), the `rimp` module starts the listening server or installs the custom importer.

Testing the remote Importer

To see the remote importer work, first run it as a standalone program in a directory that contains at least one other module (I ran it in the directory that had the `stuff.py` module from previous sections.):

```
C:\temp>rimp.py
[Starting server]
```

Now copy `rimp.py` to another directory (so that the "client" side doesn't have access to the same modules) and start up a Python interpreter. Import `rimp` and then import the module that the server side has:

```
>>> import rimp
>>> import stuff
Checking remote host for module stuff
Saved stuff.py to disk
I am being imported!
```

The server side shows that it processed the request successfully:

```
Received new connection
Remote side requests module stuff
Sending 49 bytes
Done
```

Now try a module that doesn't exist anywhere:

```
>>> import borkborkbork
Checking remote host for module borkborkbork
Traceback (most recent call last):
  File "<stdin>", line 1, in ?
  File "D:\Python20\lib\imputil.py", line 91, in _import_hook
    raise ImportError, 'No module named ' + fqname
ImportError: No module named borkborkbork
```

The normal (and correct!) ImportError is raised, even though the server tried to locate the module on its side:

```
Received new connection
Remote side requests module borkborkbork
Sending 0 bytes
Done
```

Finally, look in the client-side directory and note that the module that was transferred successfully has been cached so that next time no network transfer will be needed:

```
C:\temp\t>dir /b
rimp.py
rimp.pyc
stuff.py   # Yay!
```

In addition to the enhancements mentioned earlier, a more useful solution might include versioning information so that the client automatically gets newer versions from the server as needed.

The nicest part about the import hooks discussed in this chapter is that nothing needs to change in any other modules in order for them to work. Only the initial startup module needs to install the hooks; all other modules are completely unaware that a module is being decrypted or transferred halfway around the world via the Internet.

Summary

In this chapter, you:

✦ Learned how to replace the normal Python import function with a custom function.

✦ Created an import function to handle encrypted modules.

✦ Retrieved Python modules from a remote server via a network connection.

The next chapter covers Python's module and application distribution tools and describes how you can bundle your entire program into a standalone executable that works even if users don't already have Python installed.

✦   ✦   ✦

Distributing Modules and Applications

◆ ◆ ◆ ◆

In This Chapter

Understanding
distutils

Other distutils
features

Distributing extension
modules

Creating source and
binary distributions

Building standalone
executables

◆ ◆ ◆ ◆

Once you've created your Python masterpiece, how do you get it into users' hands? This chapter answers that question by introducing distutils — the tools you use to distribute individual modules or entire applications.

Instead of providing an exhaustive and tedious review of the distutils package, in writing this chapter I tried to focus on what you need to know for 95 percent of the situations you might encounter when distributing Python applications. Rest assured, however, that the standard Python documentation probably lists a special option or feature to cover each case in the obscure 5 percent, and if anything is missing beyond that, you can customize and extend the tools even further.

Understanding distutils

The distutils package was introduced in Python 1.6 to standardize the process of building and installing third-party Python libraries.

The main work when using distutils is creating the setup script, which, by convention, is called setup.py. This small Python program describes to distutils the files that need to be in the distribution and gives additional information like version numbers, author name, and so on.

The setup script tells distutils to bundle the necessary files (which might be Python code, C source files, or other data files) and generate whatever kind of distribution package you want. Your distribution type can range from an ordinary ZIP file to a full-blown Linux RPM or Windows installer.

Creating a simple distribution

The following is a simple example so you can see distutils in action. Listing 36-1 shows a small example library that I want to make available to other people.

Listing 36-1: timeutil.py – Time Utilities to Be Packaged by distutils

```
import time as _time

def _getnow():
    'Returns current time tuple'
    return _time.localtime(_time.time())

def time():
    'Returns current time as string'
    return _time.strftime('%I:%M %p',_getnow())

def date():
    'Returns current date as string'
    return _time.strftime('%b %d, %Y',_getnow())
```

With my application ready, it's time to create the setup script, shown in Listing 36-2.

Listing 36-2: setup.py – Setup Script for timeutil Distribution

```
from distutils.core import setup

setup(name='timeutil',
      version='0.9',
      author = 'pokey',
      author_email = 'pokey@yellow5.com',
      url = 'www.yellow5.com/pokey',
      py_modules = ['timeutil'])
```

The setup script is very simple—it imports `distutils` and calls the `setup` function with a bunch of keyword arguments that give basic information about your software (other standard arguments you can use include `maintainer`, `maintainer_email`, `license`, `description`, and `long_description`).

The `py_modules` argument names a list of Python modules to include in the distribution; this simple example has only one. You can specify modules that are part of a package as `'packagename.modulename'` (this assumes that `packagename/__init__.py` really exists) or as files in other directories as `'directory/modulename'`.

Note   The setup script is meant to be cross-platform compatible, so always use forward (UNIX-style) slashes in directory names—`distutils` takes care of converting them as needed on each different platform.

Keep in mind that the setup script is just a Python program, so any valid Python code works in your setup script. When you run the setup script you supply a command argument telling `distutils` what you want it to do. In this case I want to create a Windows installer, so I run the command like this:

```
C:\temp>setup.py bdist_wininst
```

This command and others are covered in "Creating Source and Binary Distributions" later in this chapter. Assuming all went well, in the `dist` directory you will find a file called `timeutil-0.9.win32.exe` (Version 0.9 was the version I chose in the setup script). Because I chose a platform-specific distribution format, the file name also includes the platform required to run it (Win32).

That's it! My module is now ready for distribution.

Installing the simple distribution

Now imagine that you're one of the lucky few to have gained possession of the powerful `timeutil` library and that you want to install and begin using it. Running the program displays a screen like the one shown in Figure 36-1.

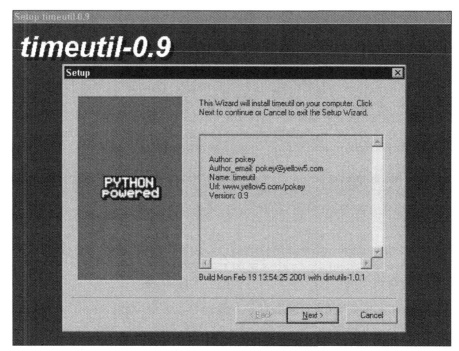

Figure 36-1: The main screen of the distutils-generated installer for Windows

To install the timeutil module, click Next a few times; now the module is in a location on your system where all Python programs can find it. For example, after starting up a Python interpreter from any directory:

```
>>> import timeutil
>>> timeutil.time(), timeutil.date()
('02:07 PM', 'Feb 19, 2001')
```

Tip   The distutils package chooses the correct default location for third-party modules based on the current platform. On UNIX, for example, the default directory is usually /usr/local/lib/pythonx.y/site-packages and on Windows, it's c:\pythonxy, where x and y are major and minor version numbers.

Another distribution method is to give the source files and the setup script to the user as-is (or in a ZIP file or compressed tarball from which the user first extracts the files). The setup script also acts as the installation script. To install the timeutil module, you simply run:

```
setup.py install
```

Once again, distutils installs the module where all programs can find it.

 Tip You should also create a file called README or README.txt that gives a brief description of your distribution and maybe a little help on how to install it. distutils automatically includes these README files in the distribution, if present.

 Tip The -home=<dir> command-line argument tells the install command to place the modules in a different directory than the default. This option can be useful on systems where normal users don't have write access to the default directory.

Other distutils Features

As I mentioned before, distutils has features to handle just about any sort of situation you might encounter. In this section I cover a few of the most useful features.

Distributing packages

If you install more than one or two modules in the default directory, that directory starts to become pretty cluttered. Worse, if you want to uninstall a particular distribution, you have a tough time determining which files go with which third-party library (because, by default, they all end up in the same directory).

A better approach is to distribute your modules as a package (which in turn could include other packages too). This method is much more organized and requires very little extra work from you. It is also less prone to errors: distutils automatically includes all the Python files that are part of a package so you don't have to list each file individually.

So, as an advocate of clean directory structures, suppose I decide to go back and distribute my timeutil module as a package. In fact, envisioning it to be part of some future suite of utilities, I rename it to be the datetime module in the daveutil package. The conversion is easy: create a daveutil directory and copy timeutil.py into it, renaming it to datetime.py. Inside the daveutil directory, I create a __init__.py file (which can simply be empty or contain a comment) to identify daveutil as a package.

Listing 36-3 shows the slightly modified setup script that uses the packages keyword argument to list the packages it will include. (Once again, like py_modules, this is a list, so it could include several package names.)

Listing 36-3: **setup.py – A Setup Script That Distributes an Entire Package**

```
from distutils.core import setup

setup(name='daveutil',
      version='0.9',
      author = 'pokey',
      author_email = 'pokey@yellow5.com',
      url = 'www.yellow5.com/pokey',
      packages = ['daveutil'])
```

Now the resulting distribution from setup.py installs the daveutil package, leaving the main default install directory clutter free. Users can still access the new daveutil.datetime module from any program:

```
>>> from daveutil import datetime
>>> datetime.date()
'Feb 19, 2001'
```

The package_dir keyword argument enables you to use a different directory scheme if you don't want to use the default one. Its value is a dictionary whose keys are package names and whose values are directory names. To change the directory for modules that aren't part of any package, use a key of an empty string. For example, if src is the base directory of all your source code, you could use the following portion of a setup script:

```
package_dir = {'' : 'src'}
py_modules = ['mod1', 'mod2']
```

This code causes distutils to look for the modules src/mod1.py and src/mod2.py.

Including other files

If you need to include additional, non-Python files in your distribution, you can use the data_files keyword argument to setup:

```
...
data_files = ['dialog.res', 'splash.jpg'],
...
```

Each item in the list can also be a tuple containing a destination directory name and a list of files. For example, to have the installer put `dialog.res` and `splash.jpg` into the `resource` directory, use:

```
...
data_files = [('resource', ['dialog.res', 'splash.jpg'])],
...
```

If you want total control over which files end up in a source distribution, create a file called `MANIFEST` in the same directory as your setup script. The file should contain one file name per line. If specifying each file is too much of a pain, create a *manifest template* file (call it `MANIFEST.in`) that `distutils` uses to generate the list of files to include. Each line of the file contains a rule describing a group of files. For example, to include any text files in the current directory and any Python files in the current or child subdirectories that start with 'd', the `MANIFEST.in` file looks like:

```
include *.txt
recursive-include d*.py
```

Table 36-1 lists the rules you can use in the manifest template file.

Table 36-1
Manifest Template File Rules

Rule	Description
Include p1 p2 ...	Include any files matching any of the patterns.
Recursive-include p1 p2 ...	Same, but search only in child directories.
Global-include p1 p2 ...	Same, but search current *and* child directories.
Graft dir	Include all files in `dir` and its children.
Exclude p1 p2 ...	Exclude any files matching any of the patterns.
Recursive-exclude p1 p2 ...	Same, but search only in child directories.
Global-exclude p1 p2 ...	Same, but search current *and* child directories.
Prune dir	Exclude all files in `dir` and its children.

Python applies the rules in order, so you can arrange them to specify any list of files. In addition to valid file name characters, patterns can include asterisks (*) to match any sequence of characters, question marks (?) to match any single character, and `[range]` to match a range of characters, like `[a-f0-9]` and `[b-f]`.

Note As of Python 2.0, the `data_files` argument works only with binary distributions and source distributions that have a manifest file.

Customizing setup

Python checks for a file called `setup.cfg` for additional configuration options. These options override any corresponding settings from the setup script, but they themselves are overridden by corresponding settings specified on the command line. This configuration file is useful if you need to let users customize setup or if there are some settings you always need to specify.

The format of the configuration file is

```
[command]
variable=value
```

where `command` is one of the standard commands like `bdist` (for a complete list, run `setup.py --help-commands`). Each `variable` is a setting for that command (you can get a list of settings for a command by running `setup.py <command> --help`). To continue a value onto the next line, just indent the next line's value.

Note If the command-line version of a setting has a dash in it, use an underscore character in the configuration file instead. Also, if a setting is normally an "on-off" type flag (for example, `--quiet`), write it as `setting=1` in the configuration file.

Some settings you may wish to always use, even across all projects. In this case you can create a `pydistutils.cfg` file in the directory specified by `sys.prefix`, and `distutils` will read settings from it before reading from a project's `setup.cfg`, if any.

Tip On UNIX systems, each user can also create a `.pydistutils.cfg` file in his or her home directory for user-specific custom settings.

Distributing Extension Modules

The `distutils` package doesn't just work with Python files: it is quite happy to distribute C extension modules too. Pass the `ext_modules` keyword argument to the `setup` function to specify which extensions to include, for example:

```
...
ext_modules = [ext1, ext2]
...
```

Each extension you list is actually an instance of the Extension class. Here's a more complete setup script that includes one extension module called trade that is built from two source files, stock.c and option.c:

```
from distutils.core import setup, Extension # nota bene!

trade_ext = Extension('trade', ['stock.c', 'option.c'])

setup(name = 'trader', ext_modules = [trade_ext])
```

The first argument to the Extension constructor is the module name including the package name, if any. If you plan on listing several extensions belonging to the same package, you can use the ext_package keyword argument before ext_modules.

The Extension constructor also takes some optional keyword arguments of its own. include_dirs is a list of directories in which the compiler should look for include files, and library_dirs is a list of directories to include as link paths. libraries is a list of files to include in the link.

The define_macros and undef_macros keyword arguments are lists of preprocessor definitions to use when compiling:

```
trade_ext = Extension('trade', ['stock.c', 'option.c'],
                 define_macros=[('DEBUG_LOGGING',None),
                                ('MAX_COUNT','100')]
                 undef_macros=['TRACE'])
```

The preceding code is equivalent to having the following code at the top of every source file:

```
#define DEBUG_LOGGING
#define MAX_COUNT 100
#undef TRACE
```

See the following section for information on how C extension modules are handled with different distribution types.

Creating Source and Binary Distributions

You can create distributions containing just source code or binary distributions too. In this section I show you how to generate each type of distribution using the same setup script so you can easily compare the results. The setup script is as follows:

```
from distutils.core import setup, Extension
```

```
ext = Extension('ext',['extension.c'])

setup(name='daveutil',
      version='0.9',
      author = 'pokey',
      author_email = 'pokey@yellow5.com',
      url = 'www.yellow5.com/pokey',
      py_modules = ['pymod'],
      ext_modules = [ext])
```

In the preceding example, extension.c is a simple C extension module and pymod.py is a small Python file with a single function in it; both files are in the same directory as the setup.py listed above.

Chapters 29 and 30 show you how to create C extension modules in Python.

Source distributions

A source distribution contains Python and C source files (no bytecode or compiled C files). This type of distribution is the quickest to generate and you can use it on any platform. The following command creates a source distribution:

```
python setup.py sdist
```

The output file ends up in the dist directory, and its default type depends on your platform (for example, a ZIP file on Windows). On my machine, the finished file was daveutil-0.9.zip and it contained these files:

```
extension.c      pymod.py       README.txt
```

You can choose the output file type with the -formats=f1, f2, ... argument. Use the following command to see the output formats available:

```
C:\temp>setup.py sdist --help-formats
List of available source distribution formats:
  --formats=bztar   bzip2'ed tar-file
  --formats=gztar   gzip'ed tar-file
  --formats=tar     uncompressed tar file
  --formats=zip     ZIP file
  --formats=ztar    compressed tar file
```

The availability of different formats also depends on other libraries you have installed (such as zlib for compression).

Users who download your distribution archive use a command similar to the following to install it:

```
setup.py install
```

The setup script installs the files in the correct place for the end user's machine, and it builds extension modules automatically. Of course, if the user doesn't have a compiler installed, he or she can't build the C extension modules using this kind of distribution.

Binary distributions

Binary distributions include the Python source code, byte-compiled versions of each file, and the compiled versions of any C extension modules. The C source code is not included, making binary distributions suitable for users who don't have compilers or in cases where you don't want to distribute the C source. The drawback is that C extension modules you provide in the distribution work only on compatible platforms, so if you want to make it available on both Windows and Linux platforms, for example, you need to create two different distribution packages.

Use the following command to create a binary distribution:

```
setup.py bdist
```

distutils kindly builds your extension modules for you and places the compiled modules into the archive. On my machine, the finished file was daveutil.0.9.win32.zip and it contained these files:

```
pymod.pyc       ext.pyd       pymod.py
```

Once again, you can use the --formats and --help-formats commands to choose and list output formats. Users install your distribution the same way as before, only this time they don't need a compiler.

Installers

One other form of binary distribution is an *installer*, like the one I used in the first section of this chapter. These work the same way as normal binary distributions except that they have an installation program familiar to users of the target system.

Most Windows users are familiar with downloading an executable program that they run to install the program for them. To create such an executable, run this command:

```
setup.py bdist_wininst
```

On my computer, this command created the file daveutil-0.9.win32-py2.0.exe. When you run it, you see a few dialogs letting you know what it's going to install and where.

Linux folk are used to downloading and installing RPM files, which perform essentially the same function but without the glitzy user interface. To generate an RPM file, use:

```
setup.py bdist_rpm
```

You can optionally add a --source-only parameter to build just a source RPM or --binary-only to build only a binary RPM. RPMs also have a .spec file that describes them; distutils generates this file automatically for you using the information from the setup script, command-line, and configuration files. You can specify other .spec options that aren't part of a normal Python distribution using the parameters listed in Table 36-2.

Table 36-2
Linux RPM SPEC Options

Option	Meaning
--distribution-name	Name of the *Linux* distribution for this RPM
--release	RPM release number
--serial	RPM serial number
--vendor	Vendor or author (defaults to author or maintainer in setup.py)
--packager	RPM packager (defaults to vendor)
--group	Package classification (defaults to Development/Libraries)
--icon	Icon file to use
--doc-files	Comma-separated list of documentation files
--changelog	Path to RPM change log
--provides	Capabilities provided by this RPM
--requires	Capabilities required by this RPM (dependencies)
--build-requires	Capabilities required to build the RPM
--conflicts	Capabilities that conflict with this RPM
--obsoletes	Capabilities made obsolete by this RPM

The type of distribution you choose to create depends on who you think will use it. When possible, it doesn't hurt to create several different types so that users can choose whichever they find most convenient.

Building Standalone Executables

Despite all the wonderful things about Python, most people do not have it installed on their computers. Worse, those that do have it may have a version that conflicts with the version you used to create your program. The tools in this section show you how to create a self-contained executable that has the Python interpreter, your Python modules, and everything else needed to run your program with no other dependencies.

py2exe

My favorite tool for building standalone Windows applications is Thomas Heller's py2exe (available at `http://py2exe.sourceforge.net`). It extends the `distutils` package so it fits in nicely with the topics covered so far in this chapter, and it is very simple to use.

For an example, I'll use this small program saved as `hello.py`:

```
import sys

print sys.version
print 'Hello!'
```

Here's the setup script, `setup.py`:

```
from distutils.core import setup
import py2exe

setup(name='hello', scripts = ['hello.py'])
```

The differences are in italic bold: import `py2exe` before calling `setup`, list your module name in the `scripts` list, and include the extension. The command to use with the setup script is `py2exe`:

```
setup.py py2exe
```

The preceding command creates `hello.exe` in `dist\hello`. Also in that directory is `python20.dll` and `msvcrt.dll` (a supporting library). The program runs like any other executable:

```
C:\temp\dist\hello>hello
2.0 (#8, Oct 19 2000, 11:30:05) [MSC 32 bit (Intel)]
Hello!
```

The py2exe program figures out what other libraries and files it needs to include in order to make your program truly self-contained; you can create executables even for something complex like a GUI application using wxPython.

> **Note**   You may be alarmed at the size of the files for the simple hello program (about 1 MB). Don't worry—most of that is fixed-sized overhead, so a program with 10 times as many lines of Python code is still very small.

Use setup.py py2exe --help to see a list of optional arguments you can use on the command line or in the setup configuration file. For example, --debug generates an executable with debug information and --icon enables you to specify an icon file that the application should use. --includes lets you add other modules to those that py2exe detects that it should include, and --force-imports adds the given modules to sys.modules before your script begins to run.

> **Tip**   The current version of py2exe can't detect imports made by calls to the __import__ function (as opposed to the import statement), to PyImport_ImportModule (instead of PyImport_Import), or to modules whose names aren't known until runtime. Force py2exe to include these modules by using the --includes option. For PyImport_ImportModule calls, you should use --force-imports so that the modules will already be in sys.modules by the time the C code calls for them.

Freeze

The freeze utility is a nice alternative for creating standalone programs because it comes as part of the standard Python distribution, and it is not limited to Windows computers. You do, however, need to have a compiler installed. freeze determines the modules your program needs, compiles them to bytecode, and stores ("freezes") the bytecode in huge C byte arrays. A small embedding application starts up a Python interpreter and notifies the import mechanisms of the frozen modules it has so that imports don't require external Python files to be present.

The freeze utility predates Python's distutils, so you don't write a setup script like you do for py2exe. Instead, just type:

```
python freeze.py hello.py
```

Of course, you may have to specify the location of freeze.py. On my FreeBSD system, it lives in /usr/local/lib/python2.0/Tools/freeze. freeze creates a bunch of C files and a Makefile; usually all you need to do now is type make to build the executable.

> **Note**   In order to use freeze, you need to have built Python from the source distribution.

Other tools

Gordon McMillan has developed a small suite of tools for creating standalone executables for Windows and Linux; you can download them from `http://mcmillan-inc.com`.

Archives

Archives work like the `freeze` utility except that archives store the bytecode in a compressed archive to take up less space. One nice side effect that archives and `freeze` executables enjoy is reduced disk I/O because all the modules are in a single compressed file; these applications tend to load up quicker because the interpreter doesn't have to hunt through `sys.path` to locate the modules to load.

Standalones

Standalones store the compressed bytecode in an embedding application, but also link in as many of the binary dependencies as possible so that the result is a single executable that users can easily run, copy, or delete.

Installer

Gordon's tools also come with a simple installer that generates self-extracting (and self-cleaning when finished) installation programs. Once nice feature is that they can even detect if they are being run from a read-only media source such as a CD-ROM and still run correctly (using an alternate location for temporary decompression storage).

This set of tools is very flexible and has many options to customize its behavior. Its different pieces are kept as separate as possible while still remaining interoperable so that you can mix and match (or extend) different pieces to suit your specific needs.

Summary

Once you've written your program, you still have the task of delivering it to your users. Fortunately, Python's `distutils` package makes this process relatively painless. In this chapter you:

✦ Created distribution packages that automatically install files in the correct place on end users' computers.

✦ Built distributions that included just the source code.

✦ Built distributions that included precompiled C extension modules.

✦ Wrapped your application in an easy-to-use installer for Windows or Linux.

✦ Created self-contained Windows applications that don't require a preexisting Python installation, or don't conflict with other versions of Python.

The next chapter shows you how to make the most of the Windows-specific modules that come with Python.

✦   ✦   ✦

Platform-
Specific Support

Chapter 37
Windows

Chapter 38
UNIX-Compatible
Modules

♦ ♦ ♦ ♦

Windows

Most of Python's libraries are portable. However, sometimes the need arises to take advantage of OS-specific services, such as the Windows registry. Accordingly, Python's standard libraries provide some Windows-specific support. In addition, the Python Extensions for Windows (win32all) wrap most of the Win32 API, so you can do plenty of Windows programming without even having to write a C extension.

Using win32all

The Python Extensions for Windows, also known as win32all, include wrappers for much of the Windows API. If you've done Windows programming before, you should feel right at home with win32all! Currently, win32all is hosted at ActiveState (www.activestate.com), and is part of the ActivePython distribution.

I keep a copy of Visual Studio running when I program with win32all so that I can consult MSDN as needed. The win32all package includes some documentation, but at some point you'll probably want to have a comprehensive reference on the win32 API.

Data types

In places where the Windows API would use a struct, win32all often uses a dictionary. The dictionary's keys are the names of the struct's data members; its values are the corresponding values. For example, the Windows API NetUserGetInfo can return information about a user in the form of a struct:

```
typedef struct _USER_INFO_10 {
  LPWSTR    usri10_name;
  LPWSTR    usri10_comment;
  LPWSTR    usri10_usr_comment;
  LPWSTR    usri10_full_name;
} USER_INFO_10;
```

In This Chapter

Using win32all

Example: using some Windows APIs

Accessing the Windows registry

Using msvcrt goodies

When you use win32all to manipulate user info, you use the corresponding dictionary:

```
>>> win32net.NetUserGetInfo(None,"Administrator",10)
{'full_name': u'', 'name': u'Administrator', 'usr_comment':
u'', 'comment': u'Built-in account for administering the
computer/domain'}
```

Error handling

The win32api modules translate any API errors into the exception
win32api.error. This error has a member, args, which takes the form (ErrorCode, FunctionName, Info). For example:

```
>>> win32net.NetUserGetInfo(None,"Doctor Frungy",10)
Traceback (innermost last):
  File "<pyshell#51>", line 1, in ?
    win32net.NetUserGetInfo(None,"Doctor Frungy",10)
api_error: (2221, 'NetUserGetInfo', 'The user name could not be
found.')
```

Finding what you need

The Windows API is a large beast, and could easily fill a book larger than this one. And so, finding a function that does what you want can take some sifting. I generally search MSDN for online help. The book *Programming Windows,* by Charles Petzold (Microsoft Press 1998), is also an excellent (and readable) reference on the Windows API. And if you want to read up on win32all itself — particularly the COM extensions — *Python Programming on Win32,* by Mark Hammond and Andy Robinson (O'Reilly and Associates 2000), is a good reference.

You may discover that win32all does not yet expose the API you want. If so, your best recourse is to create a C extension to wrap the API. If you do, the source code for win32all is a good reference to borrow ideas from. See Chapter 29 for an introduction to C extensions.

Example: Using Some Windows APIs

Listing 37-1 illustrates some of the APIs that win32all provides. The program is a simple text editor. It uses some predefined constants from the win32con module (which provides about 4000 different constants!). It uses Tkinter to put up a simple GUI (see Chapter 19 for more information on Tkinter). And it uses the win32help and win32clipboard modules, to access the Windows help system, and the clipboard.

Listing 37-1: TextEditor.py

```python
import Tkinter
import sys
import win32help # Launching .hlp files
import win32con # Constants used by the other win32 modules
import win32clipboard # Clipboard APIs

class TextEditor:
    def __init__(self,root):
        self.root=root
        # Create the menus:
        MenuBar=Tkinter.Menu(root)
        FileMenu=Tkinter.Menu(MenuBar,tearoff=0)
        FileMenu.add_command(label="Quit",command=sys.exit)
        MenuBar.add_cascade(label="File",menu=FileMenu)
        EditMenu=Tkinter.Menu(MenuBar,tearoff=0)
        EditMenu.add_command(label="Copy",command=self.DoCopy)
        EditMenu.add_command(label="Paste",
            command=self.DoPaste)
        MenuBar.add_cascade(label="Edit",menu=EditMenu)
        HelpMenu=Tkinter.Menu(MenuBar,tearoff=0)
        HelpMenu.add_command(label="Index",command=self.DoHelp)
        MenuBar.add_cascade(label="Help",menu=HelpMenu)
        root.config(menu=MenuBar)
        # Create the main text window:
        self.TextWindow=Tkinter.Text(root)
        self.TextWindow.pack(expand=Tkinter.YES,
            fill=Tkinter.BOTH)
    def DoCopy(self):
        Selection=self.TextWindow.tag_ranges(Tkinter.SEL)
        if len(Selection)>0:
            SelectedText =\
                self.TextWindow.get(Selection[0],Selection[1])
            # One must open (and lock) the clipboard before
            # using it, then close (and lock) the clipboard
            # afterwards:
            win32clipboard.OpenClipboard(0)
            # SetClipboardText is a shortcut for
            # SetClipboardData(test, CF_TEXT):
            win32clipboard.SetClipboardText(SelectedText)
            win32clipboard.CloseClipboard()
    def DoPaste(self):
        win32clipboard.OpenClipboard(0)
        PasteText=win32clipboard.GetClipboardData(\
            win32con.CF_TEXT)
        win32clipboard.CloseClipboard()
        self.TextWindow.insert(Tkinter.INSERT,PasteText)
    def DoHelp(self):
```

Continued

```
# win32help includes a single function, WinHelp, that
# wraps the WinHelp API. Here, we open the help file
# "Editor.hlp" to its index.
win32help.WinHelp(0,"Editor.hlp",win32con.HELP_INDEX)

# Main code:
root=Tkinter.Tk()
TextEditor(root)
root.mainloop()
```

Accessing the Windows Registry

The Windows *registry* is a repository of system information. It keeps track of users, program settings, port information, and more. The registry takes the form of a tree, where each node of the tree is called a *key*. Each key can have one or more named *values*. Each top-level key is called a *hive*. The usual way to access the registry by hand is by running the program regedit; another good registry browser is regedt32.exe.

For example, Windows stores your system's Internet Explorer version number in the value Version in the key Software\Microsoft\Internet Explorer in the HKEY_LOCAL_MACHINE hive.

Caution   Breaking the registry can have very weird, very bad effects. *Always* back up the registry before running any code that tweaks it. Otherwise, a single typo might break your system!

Accessing the registry with win32all

To examine an existing key, call win32api.RegOpenKeyEx(Hive,Subkey,0[, Sam]). Here *Hive* is the key to open; it is generally one of the win32con constants HKEY_CLASSES_ROOT, HKEY_CURRENT_USER, HKEY_LOCAL_MACHINE, or HKEY_USERS. *Subkey* is the subkey to open, as a string. And *Sam* is a combination of flags indicating the level of key access we want. I generally use win32con.KEY_ALL_ACCESS, but KEY_READ (the default value) is safer if you don't want to risk breaking the registry. Table 37-1 lists the available access levels.

The first argument to RegOpenKeyEx need not be a hive; it can be any registry key handle. In this case, the subkey name should be the path to the subkey from the specified key, instead of from the hive.

Table 37-1
Registry Access Constants (from win32con)

Constant	Ability Granted
KEY_ALL_ACCESS	Full access
KEY_READ	Read access
KEY_WRITE	Write access
KEY_CREATE_LINK	Create symbolic links
KEY_CREATE_SUB_KEY	Create Subkeys (included in KEY_WRITE)
KEY_ENUMERATE_SUB_KEYS	Iterate over subkeys (included in KEY_READ)
KEY_EXECUTE	Read access
KEY_NOTIFY	Change notification (included in KEY_READ)
KEY_QUERY_VALUE	Subkey read access (included in KEY_READ)
KEY_SET_VALUE	Modify subkey values (included in KEY_WRITE)

A call to RegOpenKeyEx returns a key handle. Once you have this handle, you can call RegQueryValueEx(KeyHandle, Name) to retrieve a key value. Here *Name* is the name of the value (or "", to query the key's default/unnamed value). RegQueryValueEx returns a tuple of the form (Value,ValueType). You can also set values by calling RegSetValueEx(KeyHandle,Name,0,ValueType,Value). Here *ValueType* is a constant, indicating the data type of *Value*. Table 37-2 shows the most common value types.

When you are finished with a registry key, you should close it, with a call to RegCloseKey(KeyHandle).

You can access the registry on a remote Windows system, if that system's security settings permit this. To obtain a key handle for the remote registry, call RegConnectRegistry(SystemName, Hive). Here *Hive* is one of the hive constants from win32con, except for HKEY_CLASSES_ROOT or HKEY_CURRENT_USER. The parameter *SystemName* is a string of the form \\computername.

Table 37-2 Common Registry Value Types (from win32con)	
Constant	**Meaning**
REG_SZ	String
REG_DWORD	A 32-bit integer
REG_BINARY	Binary data
REG_MULTI_SZ	Array of strings

Example: setting the Internet Explorer home page

Internet Explorer has a home page, or "start page," that appears when you start the application. Windows stores the URL of the home page in the registry. Listing 37-2 examines, and then tweaks, the home page URL:

Listing 37-2: **HomePage.py**

```
import win32api
import win32con

SubKey="SOFTWARE\\Microsoft\\Internet Explorer\\Main"
StartPageKey=win32api.RegOpenKeyEx(win32con.HKEY_CURRENT_USER,
    SubKey,0,win32con.KEY_ALL_ACCESS)
(OldURL, ValueType)=win32api.RegQueryValueEx(StartPageKey,
    "Start Page")
print OldURL
NewURL="http://www.google.com"
win32api.RegSetValueEx(StartPageKey,"Start Page",0,
    win32con.REG_SZ,NewURL)
win32api.RegCloseKey(StartPageKey)
```

Creating, deleting, and navigating keys

The win32api function RegCreateKey(Hive,Subkey) creates a subkey in the specified hive, and returns a handle to the new key. The function RegDeleteKey(Hive, SubkeyName) deletes the specified key, and RegDeleteValue(KeyHandle,Name) deletes the specified value from a key. Note that RegDeleteKey *cannot* delete a key that has any subkeys.

The function `RegEnumKey(KeyHandle, Index)` retrieves the names of the subkeys of the specified key. It raises an exception (`win32api.error`) if the key has no subkey with the specified Index. For example, this code prints the immediate subkeys of the HKEY_LOCAL_MACHINE hive:

```
try:
    SubKeyIndex=0
    while 1:
        print win32api.RegEnumKey(
            win32con.HKEY_LOCAL_MACHINE, SubKeyIndex)
        SubKeyIndex += 1
except win32api.error:
    pass # (We ran out of subkeys.)
```

The function `RegEnumValue(KeyHandle,Index)` retrieves values for the specified key. Its return value is a tuple of the form (ValueName, Value, ValueType).

Often programmers keep calling the enumerator functions until they raise an exception. However, one can also call `RegQueryInfoKey` (see "Other registry functions" later in this chapter), and iterate over subkeys and values without ever triggering exceptions.

Example: recursive deletion of a key

Listing 37-3 provides a function to delete a registry key. Unlike `RegDeleteKey`, it can kill off a key with subkeys.

Listing 37-3: **KillKey.py**

```
import win32api
import win32con

def KillKey(ParentKeyHandle,KeyName):
    KeyHandle = win32api.RegOpenKeyEx(ParentKeyHandle,KeyName,
        win32con.KEY_ALL_ACCESS)
    while 1:
        try:
            # We always retrieve subkey number 0, because
            # when we delete a subkey, the old subkey #1
            # becomes #0:
            SubKeyName = win32api.RegEnumKey(KeyHandle,0)
        except:
            break
        KillKey(KeyHandle,SubKeyName)
    print "Deleting",KeyName
    win32api.RegDeleteKey(ParentKeyHandle, KeyName)
```

Continued

Listing 37-3 *(continued)*

```
# Create some keys:
RootKey=win32api.RegOpenKeyEx(win32con.HKEY_LOCAL_MACHINE,
    "SYSTEM",win32con.KEY_ALL_ACCESS)
win32api.RegCreateKey(RootKey,"Junk")
win32api.RegCreateKey(RootKey,"Junk\\Stuff")
win32api.RegCreateKey(RootKey,"Junk\\Stuff\\Wooble")
win32api.RegCreateKey(RootKey,"Junk\\Stuff\\Weeble")
win32api.RegCreateKey(RootKey,"Junk\\More stuff")
# Delete all the keys:
KillKey(RootKey,"Junk")
```

Other registry functions

The function `RegQueryInfoKey(KeyHandle)` returns key metadata, in a tuple of the form (SubKeyCount, ValueCount, ModifiedTime). Here *SubKeyCount* and *ValueCount* are the key's total subkeys and values, respectively. *ModifiedTime,* if nonzero, is the key's last modification date, in 100's of nanoseconds since 1/1/1600.

Changes made to the registry do not take effect immediately—they take effect sometime soon after you close the registry key handle. You can commit registry changes immediately with a call to `RegFlushKey(KeyHandle)`.

You can save a registry key (and all its subkeys) to a file by calling `RegSaveKey(KeyHandle,FileName)`. Later, you can restore registry settings from disk with a call to `RegLoadKey(Hive,Subkey,FileName)`. These operations require special privileges that you must activate programmatically; see the `win32security` API documentation for details.

Accessing the registry with _winreg

The standard library `_winreg` also exposes the Windows registry API. Since the underlying API is the same, the functions in `_winreg` are very similar to the registry API in win32api. Table 37-3 shows the correspondence:

Table 37-3	
_winreg and win32api Functions	
_winreg Function	**win32api Function**
CloseKey	RegCloseKey
ConnectRegistry	RegConnectRegistry

_winreg Function	win32api Function
CreateKey	RegCreateKeyEx
DeleteKey	RegDeleteKey
DeleteValue	RegDeleteValue
EnumKey	RegEnumKey
EnumValue	RegEnumValue
FlushKey	RegFlushKey
LoadKey	RegLoadKey
OpenKey	RegOpenKeyEx
QueryInfoKey	RegQueryInfoKey
QueryValueEx	RegQueryValueEx
SaveKey	RegSaveKey
SetValueEx	RegSetValueEx

Using msvcrt Goodies

The msvcrt module, part of the Python distribution on Windows, exposes some useful Windows-specific services from the VC++ runtime library.

Console I/O

You can read a line of input from the user with a call to sys.stdin.readline, and you can handle single-character input with Curses, available on most UNIX systems. But what if you want to handle one character at a time on Windows? msvcrt provides the functions you need.

The function getch reads one keystroke from the user, and returns the resulting character. The call to getch is synchronous: it does not return until the user hits a key. For example, this code prints the characters you type until you press Control-Break (which is *not* handled by getch):

```
import msvcrt
while 1:
    print msvcrt.getch()
```

Hitting a special key (such as F1) puts two characters on the keystroke buffer. The first is an escape character (either chr(0) or chr(224)). The two characters, together, encode the special key.

The function `ungetch(char)` is the opposite of `getch`; it puts a character back onto the keystroke buffer. You can only un-get *one* character at a time. The function `kbhit()` returns true if any characters are waiting on the keystroke buffer. And the function `putch(char)` writes the specified character to the console without buffering. For example, this code writes out some text s-l-o-w-l-y:

```
for Char in "Hello there!":
    time.sleep(0.1)
    msvcrt.putch(Char)
```

Other functions

The function `setmode(FileDescriptor, Flag)` sets the line-end translation mode for the specified file. Here *FileDescriptor* is the file's descriptor (as returned by `os.open`), and *Flag* should be `os.O_TEXT` or `os.O_BINARY`.

The function `locking(FileDescriptor, Mode, Bytes)` wraps the C runtime function `_locking`, enabling you to lock specified bytes of a file.

You can translate between file handles and file descriptors. The function `open_osfhandle(File, Flags)` produces a file descriptor for the specified file handle. The available flags to set are `os.O_TEXT`, `os.O_APPEND`, and `os.O_RDONLY`. The function `get_osfhandle(FileDescriptor)` provides a file handle for the specified file descriptor.

The function `heapmin` tidies up the heap, freeing unused blocks for use. It is available on Windows NT/2000, but not 95 or 98.

Summary

If you're like me (and I know I am), you use Windows systems often. So it's a good thing that Python supports Windows programming. In this chapter, you:

✦ Tried out the Python Extensions for Windows (win32all).

✦ Tweaked the Windows registry.

✦ Handled single-character input with msvcrt.

The next chapter moves from the Windows side of the fence to UNIX.

✦   ✦   ✦

UNIX- Compatible Modules

♦ ♦ ♦ ♦

In This Chapter

Checking UNIX passwords and groups

Accessing the system logger

Calling shared library functions

Providing identifier and keyword completion

Retrieving file system and resource information

Controlling file descriptors

Handling terminals and pseudo-terminals

Interfacing with Sun's NIS "Yellow Pages"

♦ ♦ ♦ ♦

Most Python programs you write automatically work on any platform that supports Python. Sometimes, however, you need to write a platform-specific program but still want to use Python because of its easier maintenance, quicker development time, and so on.

This chapter shows you the modules that come with Python that are specific to UNIX-compatible platforms. Many of the functions are nearly identical to similarly named functions in C; although I try to give an introductory explanation to all of them, some are complex or system-dependent enough that you need to spend time reading through their UNIX man pages.

Checking UNIX Passwords and Groups

The pwd module has functions for retrieving entries from the UNIX account and password database (usually stored in /etc/passwd). getpwnam(name) returns the entry for the person with the given login name, and getpwuid(uid) returns the same information but instead you provide the user's unique ID:

```
>>> import pwd
>>> pwd.getpwnam('dave')
('dave', '*', 1000, 1000, 'Dave Brueck',
'/home/dave',
 '/usr/local/bin/tcsh')
>>> pwd.getpwuid(1000)
('dave', '*', 1000, 1000, 'Dave Brueck',
'/home/dave',
 '/usr/local/bin/tcsh')
```

Both functions return a seven-tuple of the form

```
(name, password, user ID, group ID, fullname, home path, shell)
```

Note   The password field is encrypted and contains just an asterisk or 'x' if the actual encrypted password is in the shadow password file (/etc/shadow).

The getpwall() function returns a list (in random order) of all entries in the user database.

You can use the crypt module to see if a password value is correct for a given user (if your program requires that a user "sign in," for example):

```
import crypt, pwd
def checkPass(username, password):
    'returns 1 if the password is correct'
    try:
        epass = pwd.getpwnam(username)[1]
    except KeyError:
        epass = 'BLAH'
    return epass == crypt.crypt(password,  epass)
```

Tip   For non-GUI programs, the getpass() function in the getpass module is a safe way to request that the user input his or her password because it returns the string the user enters without echoing the characters to the screen. Most GUI toolkits such as wxPython have similar functions for safely requesting passwords.

The grp module is similar to pwd except that it returns entries from the groups database. getgrnam(name) returns the entry for the group of the given name and getgrgid(gid) returns the same information except that you supply the group ID:

```
>>> import grp
>>> grp.getgrnam('operator')
('operator', '*', 5, ['root'])
>>> grp.getgrgid(5)
('operator', '*', 5, ['root'])
```

The information returned is a four-tuple of the form

```
(group name, group password, group ID, list of group members)
```

Note   The group password is often blank (or an asterisk), and the member list usually doesn't include the group entries from the password database (so you need to look in both databases for a complete list of group members).

The getgrall() function returns an unordered list containing all entries in the groups database.

Accessing the System Logger

UNIX systems have a systemwide logging facility for programs to use. Various settings in `syslog` module let you send messages and alter their priorities and destinations.

In the simplest case, you can send a message to the system logging daemon by calling `syslog([priority], message)`. The optional `priority` can be any of the values listed in Table 38-1 (listed from highest to lowest).

```
>>> import syslog
>>> syslog.syslog(syslog.LOG_EMERG,
                'UPS loses power in 2 minutes!')
```

After the above call, all users on my FreeBSD machine see:

```
Message from syslogd@ at Wed Dec  6 02:50:43 2000 ...
python: UPS loses power in 2 minutes!
```

Table 38-1
syslog Priority Values

Value	Meaning
LOG_EMERG	Panic condition (normally sent to all users)
LOG_ALERT	Condition that needs immediate correction
LOG_CRIT	Critical conditions like hard device errors
LOG_ERR	Errors
LOG_WARNING	Warnings
LOG_NOTICE	Nonerrors that might still warrant special handling
LOG_INFO	Informational messages (this is the default priority)
LOG_DEBUG	Debugging messages

The system logger maintains an internal mask of message priorities that it should log; it ignores messages with priorities that are not in its mask. `setlogmask(mask)` sets the internal mask to `mask` and returns the previous value. `LOG_MASK(pri)` calculates the mask value for the given priority, and `LOG_UPTO(pri)` calculates a log mask that includes priorities from `LOG_EMERG` down to (and including) the priority `pri`:

```
>>> from syslog import *
>>> setlogmask(LOG_ALERT) # Only LOG_ALERT messages get logged.
>>> setlogmask(LOG_UPTO(LOG_ALERT)) # Allows EMERG and ALERT.
```

For greater control over message logging, call openlog(ident[, logopt[, facility]]). ident is an identifier prefix to include in every message, and logopt is a bit field that chooses one or more options from Table 38-2.

Table 38-2
openlog Logging Option Flags

Flag	Meaning
LOG_CONS	Messages go to the console if sending to logging daemon fails.
LOG_NDELAY	Connect to the logging daemon immediately (instead of waiting until you log the first message).
LOG_PERROR	Write the message to stderr as well as the system log.
LOG_PID	Include the process ID with the log message.

The facility parameter to openlog is to assign a default *facility* or classification to messages that don't have a facility due to their priority. Table 38-3 lists the possible values.

Table 38-3
openlog Facility Values

Value	Meaning
LOG_AUTH	Authorization system (from login, su, and so forth)
LOG_AUTHPRIV	Same, but logged to a nonworld readable file
LOG_CRON	From the cron daemon
LOG_DAEMON	System daemons
LOG_FTP	The ftp daemons
LOG_KERN	Kernel-generated messages
LOG_LPR	The line printer spooling system
LOG_MAIL	Mail system
LOG_NEWS	Network news system
LOG_SYSLOG	Internal syslog messages
LOG_USER	Messages from any user process (this facility is the default)
LOG_UUCP	The UUCP system
LOG_LOCAL0	Reserved for local use (also LOG_LOCAL1 through 7)

The `closelog()` function closes the log file.

Calling Shared Library Functions

The `dl` module lets you dynamically load and call functions that exist in C shared libraries.

Caution As much as possible, avoid using this module. It is inherently platform-specific, and makes it much easier to crash your programs.

Before you can call a shared library function, you have to open the library by calling `open(name[, mode])`. The `mode` can be `RTLD_LAZY` (the default) or `RTLD_NOW` to denote late or immediate binding, although some platforms do not provide `RTLD_NOW` (in which case the module won't even have `RTLD_NOW`).

Upon success, `open` returns a `dl` object. To see if the object has a specific function, call its `sym(name)` method:

```
>>> import dl
>>> dlo = dl.open('/usr/lib/libc.so')
>>> dlo.sym('getpid')
673070304
>>> dlo.sym('destroyworld')
>>>
```

A `dl` object's `call(name[, arg1, args...])` calls a function in the library. You can pass in up to 10 arguments; they can be integers, strings, or `None` for `NULL`. The function you call should return no value or an integer:

```
>>> import dl, os
>>> dlo = dl.open('/usr/lib/libc.so')
>>> dlo.call('getpid')
3539  # The "bad" way
>>> os.getpid()
3539  # The "good" way
>>> dlo.call('daemon',1,0) # Make the process a daemon process.
```

When you're finished with a `dl` object, call its `close()` method to free its resources. On most systems, however, the memory taken up by the library won't be freed until the main program shuts down.

Providing Identifier and Keyword Completion

The `readline` and `rlcompleter` modules work together to add useful editing functionality to Python's user input routines (including how the interpreter works in interactive mode).

Note The Python `readline` module calls the rather large GNU readline library. This section covers only some of its features; for a complete list of the features available through the `readline` module, you should visit the readline section of the GNU Web site (`www.gnu.org`).

Use the following code to try out tab-completion support:

```
>>> import rlcompleter
>>> import readline
>>> readline.parse_and_bind('tab: complete')
>>> rea # Now hit the tab key!
```

Pressing the tab key completes the impartial identifier. If there exists more than one completion possibility, you'll hear a beep. Pressing tab a second time lists the possible completions:

```
>>> r # Press tab twice!
raise     raw_input      reduce repr   rlcompleter
range     readline       reload return round
```

With `readline` installed, you can use the keys listed in Table 38-4 for cursor navigation and editing.

Note `C-x` means *press and hold Ctrl while you press x*. `M-x` means the same but with the Meta key. On systems that do not have a Meta key, the Esc key works by default instead, although you should not press and hold Esc. In this case, `M-x` means *press and release Esc, then press and release x*.

Table 38-4
readline Key Bindings

Key Sequence	Action
C-b	Move back one character
M-b	Move back one word
C-f	Move forward one character
M-f	Move forward one word
C-a	Move to the start of the line
C-e	Move to the end of the line
DEL	Delete the character to the left of the cursor
C-d	Delete the character under the cursor
C-_	Undo
C-l	Clear the screen, reprinting current line at top

In readline terms, cutting and pasting text are *killing* and *yanking*, respectively. Cutting, or killing, text saves it to a *kill-ring* from which it can later be "yanked back." Consecutive kills get saved to the same buffer (so that a single yank brings it all back at once). Table 38-5 lists the kill and yank keystrokes.

Table 38-5
readline Kill and Yank Key Bindings

Key Sequence	Action
C-k	Kill to end of line
M-d	Kill to end of word
M-DEL	Kill to start of word
C-w	Kill to previous whitespace
C-y	Yank most recently killed text
M-y	Rotate the kill ring buffer and yank the new top

You can use M-y only right after you yank text (with C-y). It cycles through the kill ring buffer, showing you the available text.

The readline module also lets you save keystrokes as a *macro* that you can later play back as if you had retyped them. C-x ((left parentheses) starts recording keystrokes and C-x) (right parentheses) stops. From then on you can use C-x e to replay the saved keystrokes.

The *command history* stores each command you type. C-p and C-n cycle through the previous and next entries in the history (these functions are often bound to the up and down arrow keys too). Call readline's get_history_length() function to see how many commands the list can hold (a negative value means an unlimited number) and set_history_length(newlen) to set the maximum history length. write_history_file([file]) writes the history to a file and read_history_file([file]) reads a previously saved file (both use ~/.history if you don't supply a file).

Retrieving File System and Resource Information

The os module contains two functions for retrieving file system information: statvfs(path) returns information for the file system that contains the given path, and fstatvfs(fd) does the same thing except that you provide a file descriptor.

File system information

The statvfs module contains constants for interpreting the tuples returned by the statvfs and fstatvfs functions. Table 38-6 describes the different values available.

Table 38-6
statvfs Identifiers

Identifier	Meaning
F_FILES	Total number of file nodes
F_FFREE	Total number of free file nodes
F_FAVAIL	Number of free nodes available to nonsuper users
F_NAME_MAX	Maximum file name length
F_BLOCKS	Total number of blocks
F_BFREE	Total number of free blocks
F_BAVAIL	Number of free blocks available to nonsuper users
F_BSIZE	Preferred file system block size
F_FRSIZE	Fundamental file system block size
F_FLAG	System dependent flags

For example, the following code calculates what percentage of file blocks are not in use:

```
>>> import os, statvfs
>>> info = os.statvfs('/tmp')
>>> print '%.2f %% of blocks are free' % \
        (info[statvfs.F_BFREE] * 1.0/ info[statvfs.F_BLOCKS])
0.94 % of blocks are free
```

Resource usage

The resource module is useful for tracking resource usage. getrusage(who) returns a tuple of values described in Table 38-7. The who parameter can be RUSAGE_SELF (to request information about the current process only), RUSAGE_CHILDREN (for information about child processes), or RUSAGE_BOTH (for information about the current process and its children).

Table 38-7 getrusage Tuple Values	
Index	**Value**
0	Time spent executing in user mode
1	Time spent in the system executing on behalf of the process(es)
2	Maximum resident set size used
3	Shared memory used in the text segment
4	Unshared memory used in the data segment
5	Unshared memory in the stack segment
6	Page faults serviced without any I/O activity
7	Page faults serviced that required I/O activity
8	Times the process was swapped out of main memory
9	Times the file system had to perform input
10	Times the file system had to perform output
11	Number of IPC messages sent
12	Number of IPC messages received
13	Number of signals delivered
14	Number of voluntary (early) context switches
15	Number of forced context switches

```
>>> import resource
>>> resource.getrusage(resource.RUSAGE_SELF)
(0.077617, 0.181107, 1588, 3300, 2292, 1280, 140, 0, 0, 0,
 0, 0, 0, 0, 50, 3)
```

Tip
The resource.getpagesize() function returns the system page size (the number of bytes in a memory page). Multiply this value by the number of pages in use to get how many bytes of memory a process is using. Note that the system page size is not necessarily the same as the underlying hardware's page size.

Resource limits

You can also use the resource module to get and set resource limits. Each controllable resource has a *soft limit* and a *hard limit*. When a process's resource usage crosses a soft limit, it receives a signal indicating that it has crossed that boundary. A process can never exceed a hard limit, however. Attempting to do so usually results in the termination of the process.

Note Only superusers can alter the hard limits.

The `getrlimit(resource)` function returns a tuple (`soft, hard`) containing the limit values for that resource. `setrlimit(resource, (soft, hard))` sets new limits for `resource` (you can use limit values of -1 to specify the maximum allowable value). Table 38-8 lists the resource names and their meanings (sizes are in bytes); if a particular platform does not support a resource then it will not be in the `resource` module.

Table 38-8
Resource Names and Meanings

Name	Maximum Value of
RLIMIT_AS	Address space area
RLIMIT_CORE	Size that a core file can have
RLIMIT_CPU	Number of seconds to be used by each process
RLIMIT_DATA	Size of a process's data segment
RLIMIT_FSIZE	File size
RLIMIT_MEMLOCK	Address space you can lock into memory
RLIMIT_NOFILE	Number of open files per process
RLIMIT_NPROC	Number of simultaneous processes for this user
RLIMIT_RSS	Resident set size
RLIMIT_STACK	Stack segment size
RLIMIT_VMEM	Mapped memory occupied by the process

To see the soft and hard limits on the maximum number of open files per process, for example, you can use the following code:

```
>>> import resource
>>> resource.getrlimit(resource.RLIMIT_NOFILE)
(1064L, 1064L)
```

Controlling File Descriptors

The functions in the `fcntl` module operate on file descriptors, which you can access by calling a file or socket object's `fileno()` method. The options for these functions vary by platform; see your system's man pages for details.

The fcntl(fd, op[, arg]) and ioctl(fd, op[, arg]) functions perform the operation op on the file descriptor fd. If arg is an integer, the functions return integers. If the particular operation requires a C structure, you can pass in a string object created using struct.pack; in this case the functions return a string representing the modified buffer you passed in.

> **Tip**
>
> The FCNTL module defines names for many of the operations you'd pass to fcntl. For example, fcntl.fcntl(file.fileno(), FCNTL.F_GETFD) returns the close-on-exec flag for the given file descriptor.

The flock(fd, op) function performs a locking operation on a file descriptor. This operation lets multiple processes cooperatively have simultaneous access to an open file (although some other rogue process might still access the file without using locks — see the flock man pages for details). Valid operations are LOCK_SH (shared lock), LOCK_EX (exclusive lock), LOCK_NB (don't block when locking), and LOCK_UN (release a lock).

Handling Terminals and Pseudo-Terminals

The termios and TERMIOS modules implement POSIX-style terminal (tty) control. termios defines a few functions to use, and TERMIOS defines "constants" (equivalent to their C counterparts) that you pass to those functions.

The tcgetattr(fd) function gets the terminal state referenced by the file descriptor fd and returns it in a list defined as:

```
[input flags, output flags, control flags, localflags,
 input speed, output speed, control characters]
```

The control characters entry is a list of one-character strings. You can set a tty's attributes using tcsetattr(fd, when, attributes). attributes is in the same form as returned by tcgetattr, and when tells you when the attribute changes should take place. It can be any of the following constants (defined in TERMIOS): TCSANOW (make the changes immediately), TCSADRAIN (wait for the system to transmit to the terminal all data you've written to fd and then make the changes), or TCSAFLUSH (same, but also discard any unread input).

The tcdrain(fd) function waits for the system to transmit to the terminal the output you've written to fd. tcflush(fd, queue) discards queued data on fd. If queue is TCIFLUSH, it discards the input queue data; if TCOFLUSH, it flushes the output queue; and if TCIOFLUSH, it flushes both queues.

The tcflow(fd, action) function suspends or resumes I/O on fd. Actions TCIOFF and TCION suspend and resume input, and TCOOFF and TCOON suspend and resume output.

The tcsendbreak(fd, duration) function sends a stream of 0 (break) bytes on fd. If duration is 0, it sends the bytes for about half a second; the behavior of nonzero values varies by platform (many systems ignore the value anyway).

The tty module has two convenience functions for controlling terminals; internally they call tcsetattr. Its setraw(fd[, when]) function changes fd into raw mode (the system performs no I/O processing so I/O data is "raw"). when can be any of the same values you pass to tcsetattr (for example, TCSANOW). setcbreak(fd[, when]) switches the terminal to a cbreak mode.

The pty module enables you to create and control pseudo-terminals: you create a separate process but can read and write to the process's controlling terminal programmatically. This module works on at least Linux; but it hasn't had as much testing on other platforms.

The pty's spawn(argv) function spawns a child process and connects its controlling terminal to the parent process's standard I/O. openpty() creates and returns a pseudo-terminal pair of file descriptors in a two-tuple of the form (master, slave). fork() forks the current process and connects the child's controlling terminal to a pseudo-terminal. The return value from fork is a two-tuple of the form (pid, fd). On the parent side, pid is the child's process ID and fd is a file descriptor for the pseudo-terminal. In the child process, pid is 0.

Note The os module has forkpty and openpty functions that do the same thing, but the pty version is the preferred one because it uses a more platform-independent implementation.

Interfacing with Sun's NIS "Yellow Pages"

NIS is an RPC-based client/server service that allows a group of computers to share a set of configuration files. It helps system administrators by enabling them to update information in a central location (the NIS master server) and have that information get propagated automatically to all NIS clients that are part of the same group or *domain*.

Sun Microsystems originally designed NIS, but implementations are now available on just about every UNIX derivative. Python's nis module wraps a few of the more useful NIS functions, but this module is really useful only if you already know something about NIS and have it up and running on your system.

The NIS master server maintains databases of information called *maps*; they basically map keys to values much like a Python dictionary. The maps() function returns a list of all map names in the domain, and match(key, mapname) returns the value associated with the given key in the map called mapname. cat(mapname) returns a dictionary of key-value mappings for the given map.

Note NIS keys and values are arbitrary strings of bytes and not limited to just normal ASCII characters.

Summary

This chapter covered the standard Python modules that work only on UNIX-specific platforms. In this chapter you learned to:

✦ Access the UNIX password and group databases.

✦ Write messages to the system-wide logger.

✦ Control file descriptors and pseudo-terminals.

✦ Call shared library functions and retrieve system information.

This chapter concludes the "Platform-Specific Support" part of the book. The appendixes that follow cover some of the online resources available and show you how to use popular Python development environments.

✦ ✦ ✦

Online Resources

T he Internet holds a wealth of information about Python, as well as Python programs to do all sorts of things. This appendix covers some of the key Internet resources for Python.

Visiting This Book's Web Site

We, the authors, maintain the Python Bible's Web site at www.pythonapocrypha.com. The site includes source code printed in this book, extras that were too big to fit in, and errata for any problems that (heaven forbid) made their way into print. It also includes updated links to other Python stuff. We hope that you find it a useful companion to the book itself.

Installing Software

You can download the standard Python distribution from the Python Language Web site (www.python.org), or directly from SourceForge (http://sourceforge.net/projects/python/). SourceForge is also the place to report bugs in Python itself. (SourceForge is a good place to search for open-source software in general, whether Python-related or not.)

You may prefer to download ActivePython, the Python distribution by ActiveState. It is available for Linux, Solaris, and Windows. ActivePython includes extras such as the Python extensions for windows. Visit www.activestate.com/Products/ActivePython/ to check it out.

PythonWare publishes another Python distribution. It extends the standard distribution with the PythonWare Image Library (PIL), PythonWare Sound Toolkit, and support for the commercial IDE PythonWorks.

If you often glue Python to Java, you may prefer JPython, an implementation of Python written entirely in Java. Visit `www.jpython.org` for more information.

The Vaults of Parnassus (`http://www.vex.net/parnassus/`) are a general repository of Python programs, organized by topic.

The Python Extensions for Windows, also known as `win32all`, are great resources if you want to call the Windows API from Python. `win32all` also includes PythonWin, a free Windows IDE for Python. Mark Hammond maintains `win32all` at `starship.python.net/crew/mhammond/`.

If you plan to use Python for Web development, consider downloading Zope (`www.zope.org`). Zope has a steep learning curve, but is a powerful program, comparable in abilities to most commercial application servers.

Finding Answers to Questions

The Python FAQ is a good place for general questions — it lives at `www.python.org/doc/FAQ.html`.

The FAQTs knowledge base includes a large, searchable collection of Python questions and answers. It covers a much broader range of topics than the main Python FAQ. Visit `python.faqts.com` to check it out.

The main Python Web site includes topic guides — good starting places for tackling specialized areas like databases, plotting, and so on (`http://www.python.org/topics/`). Also available are HOWTOs — detailed guides to very specific topics, like configuring your favorite editor for Python (`http://www.python.org/doc/howto/`).

Also, the archives of the Special Interest Group (SIG) mailing lists or the Python newsgroups (see below) may be a good place to search for specific topics.

Subscribing to Newsgroups and Mailing Lists

Two USENET newsgroups are of interest to Python users: `comp.lang.python` is an open newsgroup for Python-related discussions. It is a fairly high-volume group, carrying dozens of new posts each day. The summary group `comp.lang.python. announce` is a moderated, low-volume newsgroup (about a dozen posts a week) providing announcements of general interest. It is available as a mailing list — visit `http://mail.python.org/mailman/listinfo/python-announce-list` to sign up.

Archives of old USENET posts are often a good place to search for information, although you'll have to sift through some noise. One searchable archive of old newsgroup postings lives at `http://groups.google.com/`.

Python users have formed several Special Interest Groups to discuss various Python topics. For example, you can find an XML processing SIG, an international-ization SIG, and a threading SIG. Visit `http://www.python.org/sigs/` to sub-scribe to the SIG mailing lists or view the archives.

Understanding PEPs: Python Enhancement Proposals

New features for Python are first proposed in PEPs (Python Enhancement Proposals). To get an idea of what new features are coming to Python, you can browse the list of PEPs online at `http://python.sourceforge.net/peps/`. In par-ticular, PEP number 1 is a description of PEPs, and how to go about creating and submitting them.

✦ ✦ ✦

Python Development Environments

Several good editors are available for writing Python programs. In addition, you can find some integrated development environments (IDEs) for Python that combine an editor with a debugger, a class browser, and more. This appendix provides an overview of some of the available software, plus a detailed look at IDLE.

Overview of Python IDEs

Interactive DeveLopment Environment (IDLE) is a free development environment for Python, written in Python. It includes a syntax-highlighting editor, a debugger, and a class browser. It is part of the standard Python distribution, and uses Tkinter for its user-interface.

Home page:	`http://www.python.org/idle/`
Pros:	Comes with Python; runs on many operating systems
Cons:	No layout designer for GUI programs

PythonWin is a free Python IDE for Windows. It offers the same features of IDLE, with somewhat spiffier packaging. PythonWin is part of the Python extensions for Windows (win32all), which are included in the ActivePython distribution. It can integrate with Microsoft Visual Source Safe (VSS).

Home page:	http://www.activestate.com/Products/ActivePython/win32all.html
Pros:	Excellent for COM applications; very easy to learn if you know Microsoft Visual Studio
Cons:	Platform-specific

PythonWorks is a commercial Python IDE for Windows, Linux, and Solaris. It includes a layout editor for graphical development of Tkinter GUIs. It includes a deployment tool, which packages projects for distribution. In addition, it integrates with the Perforce version control system.

Home page:	http://www.pythonware.com/products/works/
Pros:	Easy to create Tkinter layouts; version control integration; slick-looking
Cons:	The price tag—currently around $400 for an individual license

Wing IDE is a commercial Python IDE for Linux. It provides a customizable graphical interface for development.

Home page:	http://archaeopteryx.com/wingide
Pros:	Ease of customization—Wing IDE can behave like Emacs or more like a standard Windows application
Cons:	Currently platform-specific

Boa Constructor is a free IDE for building GUI programs using the wxPython toolkit.

Home page:	http://boa-constructor.sourceforge.net/
Pros:	Fast and precise GUI layout
Cons:	Debugger not fully implemented

BlackAdder is a commercial Python IDE for Linux and Windows. It includes support for the Qt windowing toolkit, a library similar to wxWindows.

Home page:	http://www.thekompany.com/products/blackadder/
Pros:	Nice Qt support
Cons:	Still in beta; requires a Qt installation

Configuring Editors for Python Source

Note: In the following section, C-X means "Hold down the Control key and press X" and M-X means "Hold down the Meta (or Alt) key and press X." The notation may string keystrokes together — for example, C-X C-B means "Type **Control-X** and then **Control-B**." (This is the usual notation for Emacs commands.)

A Python mode for Emacs is available — it makes editing Python code in Emacs much easier. Your copy of Emacs may already have Python mode available. If not, first visit http://www.python.org/emacs/python-mode/ to download it. Install python-mode.el into the correct directory (probably lisp/progmodes, below the main emacs directory).

Next, for improved speed, byte-compile the file. Within Emacs, type **M-X**, and then **byte-compile-file**. Then give the full path to python-mode.el. Emacs will create python-mode.elc, and spit up some warnings that you can ignore.

Next, add some lines to the bottom of your .emacs file, to ensure that files with a .py extension are opened in Python mode. If you don't have an .emacs file, create a new file named ".emacs" in your home directory, and paste the following lines into it (Emacs executes the Lisp code from the .emacs file when it starts up. You can put all sorts of stuff into the .emacs file, to customize Emacs behavior.):

```
(setq auto-mode-alist
    (cons '("\\.py$" . python-mode) auto-mode-alist))
(setq interpreter-mode-alist
(cons '("python" . python-mode)
    interpreter-mode-alist))
```

Now, open up some Python source code in Emacs. (Type **C-X C-F**, and then type the path to the source file.) The file should show up in color — one color for identifiers, another for comments, and so on. If not, you need to turn on syntax highlighting (or font-lock, as Emacs calls it). Put the following lines at the bottom of your .emacs file to activate global font-lock:

```
(cond ((fboundp 'global-font-lock-mode)
       (global-font-lock-mode t)
       (setq font-lock-maximum-decoration t)))
```

Start Emacs again, load the file, and enjoy the pretty colors.

Using Python mode

You (probably) have two new menus available when you open a Python source file. The Python menu enables access to all the Python-mode commands. The IM-Python menu lets you jump to any class, function, or method definition (very useful!). If you don't have these menus, you can get them by installing the easymenu.el package. Or just install a newer version of Emacs that includes easymenu.

From a buffer in Python mode, type **C-X m**. The online help for Python mode appears. Plenty of commands are available; following are some of the most useful ones to get you started.

Type `C-c` ! to open a Python shell. Type `C-c C-c` to execute the current buffer.

You can indent and un-indent a region with **C-C >** and **C-C <**. (You can, mark a region with the mouse, or press **C-<space>** to start marking a region and move the cursor around.) Type **C-c #** to comment out a region. Python mode doesn't have a keyboard command to uncomment a region (although it is available in the menu). Therefore, you may want to use the "delete rectangle" command. Consider the start and end of the current selection as two corners of a rectangle; typing **C-X R D** will delete that rectangle.

Pythonizing other editors

Python syntax-highlighting is available for Vim (VI iMproved). See `http://www.vim.org/syntax/python.vim` for one specification file. In addition, if you compile Vim with the +python feature, you can execute Python statements from within Vim. See `http://www.vim.org/html/if_python.html` for an explanation.

If you have another favorite source-code editor, you may be able to make it "Python-aware" with proper indentation rules, syntax highlighting, and so forth. The editor HOWTO (`http://www.python.org/doc/howto/editor/editor.html`) offers some useful pointers.

Editing with IDLE

I use IDLE for much of my Python development, and I've been quite happy with it. This tutorial will get you up and running with most of IDLE's features. If you like, follow along in IDLE as you read to get a feel for the available editor commands. (I know that I always need to try out new commands, to teach them to my fingers.)

Exploring the IDLE Python shell

The first window IDLE opens is a Python shell. Here, you can explore Python commands interactively, just as if you had run Python from the command line. IDLE also provides some shortcuts to make your work easier.

For example, suppose I am writing code to retrieve Web pages, and I decide to try out some functions from `urllib`. First I press Alt-F2, to make the IDLE window expand (vertically) to fill the screen. Next, from within the shell, I import the `urllib` module. To remind myself what the function `urllib.urlopen` does, I print its docstring — but make a typo. Oops! IDLE won't force me to retype the command, though. To repeat the last command, I press Alt-P. Pressing Alt-P repeatedly cycles through older commands; pressing Alt-N cycles through newer commands (useful if you press Alt-P too many times!). Next, to scroll back to the typo quickly, I can press Ctrl-Left-Arrow to move the cursor back, one word at a time.

Next, I start to call the function. Once I type the open-paren, IDLE pops up balloon help to show the function signature and docstring. Figure B-1 shows my current situation.

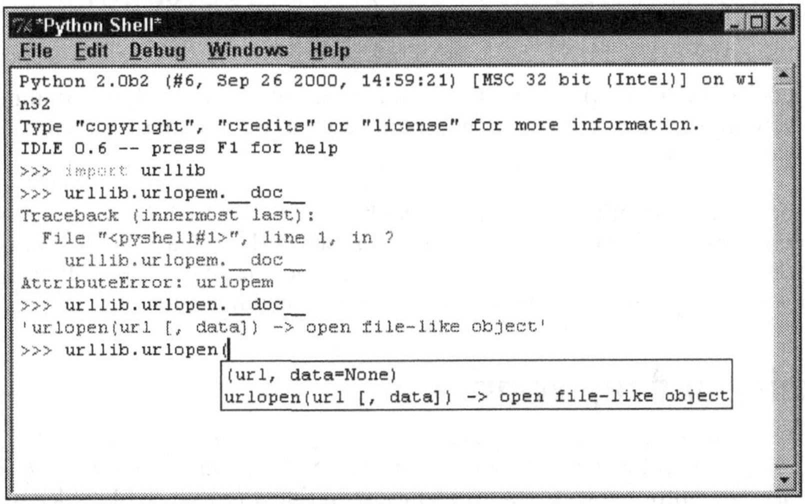

Figure B-1: IDLE with function signature displayed

At this point, I remember there was another function in `urllib`, one that grabbed a Web page to disk in one line. What was it called? Something starting with url . . . I'm feeling too lazy to look it up in the documentation. I could always type **print dir (urllib)** (or **urllib.__dict__.keys ()**) to jog my memory, but instead I type **urllib.url** and press Alt-/. The Alt-/ command completes typing half-finished names — when I press it more than once, it cycles through each possibility. In this case, it takes me to `urllib.urllib, urllib.urlopen, urllib.urlretrieve` — ah, yes, that's the function I want!

By the way, if IDLE ever finds itself without a Python shell open, you can summon a new one by choosing Python Shell from the File menu.

Navigating source code

You can cruise around in the source code with the arrow keys (or the mouse), Page Up, and Page Down. You can move to the start of the line with Home (or Ctrl-A), or the end of the line with End (or Ctrl-E). Ctrl-Home and Ctrl-End take you to the top and bottom of the file, respectively. To jump to a line, press Alt-G and type the line number.

Ctrl-Left and Ctrl-Right move around the file one word at a time. Ctrl-Up and Ctrl-Down move up and down one paragraph at a time. In addition, you can hold down the Shift key while moving around to select a block of source.

Block commands

Once you select a block of text, you can copy (Ctrl-C), cut (Ctrl-X), and later paste it (Ctrl-V).

Select a block of code and press Alt-3 to comment it out; press Alt-4 to uncomment it again. Note that comment lines do not count as un-indented lines for purposes of control block structure.

You can indent and un-indent (outdent) a block of code with Ctrl-] and Ctrl-[, respectively. You can also tabify and untabify a block with Alt-5 and Alt-6, respectively. I prefer to untabify (convert tabs to spaces) code mercilessly, and turn Tab mode off with Alt-T, because different editors treat tabs differently.

Searching and replacing

Press Ctrl-F to search for text in a file, and F3 to repeat a search. Press Ctrl-H to search and replace. Alt-F3 lets you search for text in files (such as running the UNIX utility grep). The output goes to its own window. In that window, right-click a line, and choose "Go to file/line" to jump to the file from which the line came.

More IDLE shortcuts

IDLE's class browser lets you jump to a class or function definition with minimal legwork. Press Alt-C to bring it up, poke around in the tree-browser of the current module's members, and double-click on an entry to jump to that line of code. (You'll probably want to keep the class browser's window handy, as pressing Alt-C repeatedly can leave numerous orphaned class browsers lying around.)

The Help menu includes a very useful link to the local Python documentation.

The path browser enables you to easily browse all the directories in your Python path. I don't use it often, but if (for example) you ever find yourself importing the wrong copy of a module or .pyd file, the path browser can show you where the bogus one is coming from.

Debugging with IDLE

Suppose you want to test some code. First do a quick save (Ctrl-S), and then press F5 to run the program within IDLE. Listing B-1 illustrates some buggy code, for practice:

Listing B-1: **Buggy.py**

```
import os

def FindSourceFiles(Directory,Results=[]): # Bug 2
    for FileName in os.listdir(Directory):
        Extension=os.path.splitextension(FileName) # Bug 1
        if Extension==".py":
            Results.append(FileName)
    return Results

print FindSourceFiles(os.curdir)
Path=os.path.join(os.curdir,"Lib")
print FindSourceFiles(Path)
```

When I run the program, Python quickly complains (and rightly so!) that there is no such thing as os.splitextension. I bring up IDLE's stack viewer by choosing Stack Viewer from the Debug window. (Actually, I cheated—I checked the Auto-Open Stack Viewer button in the Debug window, to save myself some time.) Note that the Debug window is available on the Python shell window, and not on source listing windows. From the stack viewer, I can jump to a source-code line by double-clicking it. I can right-click a stack-trace line in the shell, and choose Go to File/line. Figure B-2 shows IDLE's stack viewer.

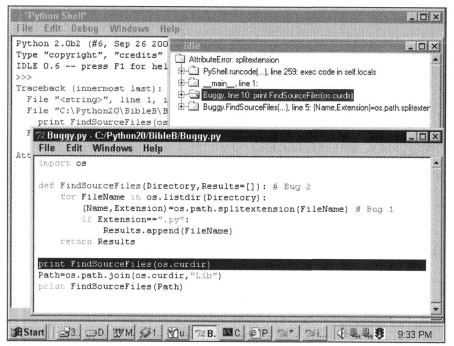

Figure B-2: Examining a call stack in IDLE

I replace os.splitextension with os.splitext. One bug squashed [cue victory chord]. But there's another bug in this code — it runs (as long as the current directory has a subdirectory named lib), but it doesn't give me what I want. I have three files in the current directory, and another file in the Lib subdirectory. My program's second list of source files seems to include all the entries from the first list, as seen in Listing B-2:

Listing B-2: **Sample Buggy Output**

```
['Buggy.py', 'LessBuggy.py', 'NotBuggy.py']
['Buggy.py', 'LessBuggy.py', 'NotBuggy.py',
 'FancyPrimeFinder.py']
```

How did those extra file names get in there? This looks like a job for the IDLE debugger. From the Debug menu, I choose Debugger, to open the debugger window. This time, when I press F5 to run my script, execution pauses, and I can step through it more carefully. (See Figure B-3.) The Step button executes the current source line, stepping into any Python function calls. The Over button executes the source line without stepping into subfunctions. The Out button keeps executing until the current stack frame finishes. The Go button keeps executing until the program finishes (or crashes), and the Quit button stops the program.

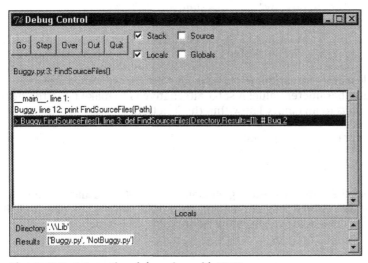

Figure B-3: Interactive debugging with IDLE

In this case, I notice that in my second function call, Results, is full of data right from the start. How did this happen? Ah, yes — the local variable Results is still a reference to the same old list, and the list still has data in it! I print out id(Results) within the function. The same object ID each time — the villainous bug is exposed, as seen in Listings B-3 and B-4:

Listing B-3: **LessBuggy.py**

```
import os

def FindSourceFiles(Directory,Results=[]): # Bug 2
    print id(Results)
    for FileName in os.listdir(Directory):
        (Name,Extension)=os.path.splitext(FileName)
        if Extension==".py":
            Results.append(FileName)
    return Results

print FindSourceFiles(os.curdir)
Path=os.path.join(os.curdir,"Lib")
print FindSourceFiles(Path)
```

Listing B-4: **Less buggy output**

```
9747060
['Buggy.py', 'NotBuggy.py', 'LessBuggy.py']
9747060
['Buggy.py', 'NotBuggy.py', 'LessBuggy.py',
'FancyPrimeFinder.py']
```

I've learned my lesson — be careful when passing a list (or any other mutable object) as a default parameter value! A safer alternative is to make None the default value, and set *Results* to an empty list within the function:

```
def FindSourceFiles(Directory,Results=None):
    if (Results==None):
        Results=[]
```

Caution   You can break the currently executing program with Ctrl-C . . . usually. Sometimes, there is no way to stop a program running under IDLE without stopping IDLE. Be sure to save your work in *every* window before using IDLE to debug!

Editing with PythonWin

The Python shell in PythonWin behaves much like it does in IDLE. Use Ctrl-Up and Ctrl-Down to cycle through old commands. Use Ctrl-Space to prompt PythonWin to suggest completions for names. In addition, PythonWin provides a list of available members when you type an object's name; use the arrow keys (or the mouse) to scroll through the possibilities, and then press Tab (or double-click a member name) to insert the name.

To toggle between source code and the Python shell, press Alt-I. You can also cycle through windows with Ctrl-F6 and Shift-Ctrl-F6.

Editing source in PythonWin

PythonWin can collapse blocks of code into a single line. This is a nice way to focus on the code you're interested in. Use the + and - from the numeric keypad to expand and collapse a block; use the * from the numeric keypad to expand and collapse the whole file at once. A block's status is indicated to the left of the source line with a + or -; you can also click these to open and close the block. I recommend turning Num-Lock off, and using the keypad arrows to scroll — this keeps your hand right next to the "tree-keys."

To go to a specific line number, press Ctrl-G and then type the line number.

To comment block in PythonWin, press Alt-3; to uncomment, press either Shift-Alt-3 or Alt-4. Block indent and un-indent are simply Tab and Shift-Tab.

Debugging with PythonWin

To get some practice using PythonWin's debugger, let's fix some buggy code. Listing B-5 is an example of some code with bugs:

Listing B-5: **Buggy.py**

```
import os
import string
import random

LegalChars=string.letters+string.digits

# Create a temp file
LetterIndex=0
while LetterIndex<20:
    FileName=FileName+random.choice(LegalChars)

File=open(FileName)
File.write("Test")
File.close
os.remove(FileName)
```

To run this code in PythonWin, I press F5. PythonWin complains about the missing variable name FileName. If the source window is maximized, the Python shell (where the stack trace is displayed) won't be visible; press Alt-I to jump to it.

I double-click on the error, in the shell window, to jump to the corresponding source code. (This is very useful when debugging a project with many files.) Then I add code to initialize *FileName* to "" above the `while` loop, and press F5 to run again.

I notice that my program is taking its own sweet time to execute. It looks like I may have an infinite loop. To stop executing the program, I look to my system tray (in my taskbar), right-click the PythonWin icon, and choose Break into Running Code. A quick glance at my code shows that the `while` statement will never finish, because *LetterIndex* will never be incremented.

Now the code runs, but the line `os.remove(FileName)` raises an `IOError` with the message "Permission denied." It seems there is another bug in the code. (You've probably spotted it by now, but bear with me.)

To prepare for my debugging session, I set a breakpoint on the line that tries to remove the file. To set a breakpoint, press F9, or click the breakpoint hand icon on the toolbar. Next, I press F5 to run. When execution stops, I go to the Watch window (if it's not showing, I click the glasses icon on the debugging toolbar to bring it up). I watch the expression FileName, and I watch the expression File. (See Figure B-4.)

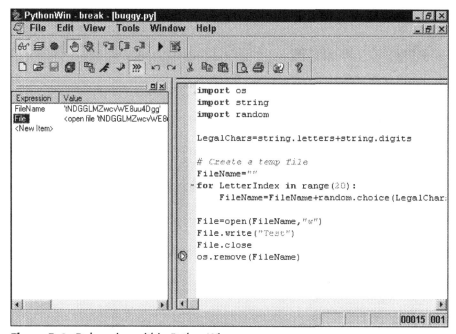

Figure B-4: Debugging within PythonWin

The line highlighted in Figure B-4 ought to delete the file. Aha! My file is still open — no wonder I can't delete it! The statement `File.close` is simply a reference to the `close` method of my file. I need to call `File.close()`.

Following are some other keys to keep in mind when debugging in PythonWin:

F5	Continue running
F11	Execute the next statement, stepping into any subfunctions
F10	Execute the next statement, without stepping into subfunctions
Shift-F11	Finish executing the current stack frame

✦   ✦   ✦

Index

Symbols & Numbers

– character, 23
   in string formatting, 41
! character, 141
!= characters, 30
# characters, 5
$ character, 141
% character, 7, 23
   in division operations, 7
   in string formatting, 40–41
() characters
   in calculations, 4
   in complex expressions, 32–33
   in regular expressions, 141
* character, 23
   with fnmatch() function, 164
   in regular expressions, 140
   repeating strings using, 37–38
   in string width fields, 42
** characters, 23
  character
   in regular expressions, 140
   in string formatting, 42
/ character, 23
? character, 141
[] characters, 30
   in regular expressions, 140
\ character
   in regular expressions, 141–143
   in string literals, 35
^ character, 23
   in regular expressions, 141
_ character, 20
{} characters, 141
| character, 23, 32
~ character, 23
+ character
   as arithmetic operator, 23
   concatenating strings using, 37
   overloading, 108
   in regular expressions, 141
   in string formatting, 41

< character, 30
<< characters, 24
<= characters, 30
== characters, 30
> character, 30
>= characters, 30

A

abort() function, 184
abs() function, 24
abs() method, 112
absolute paths, 155
absolute value, calculating, 24
abspath() function, 162
abstract object layer (Python/C API), 556
Abstract Syntax Trees (ASTs), 613–614
AbstractFormatter, 306
accelerators (wxPython), 411–412
accept() method, 252
access() function, 156
acquire() method, locking using, 485–486
ActiveX controls, embedding in xwPython, 414
add() method, 112
addheader() method, 313
adding attributes, 101–102
addition operator (+), 23
addresses, e-mail, 310–311
AddressList class, 310
addstr() method (curses module), 416–417
adler32() function, 211
after() function, 368
after() method, with Tkinter, 386
aifc module, 456
AIFF sound files
   handling chunked data, 460–461
   reading/writing, 456-461
   reversing (reverseSound.py), 459-460
alarm() function, 192
alias command (pdb module), 500
alignment modifiers (struct module), 206
allocate_lock() method, 485–486
alpha channels, in graphics files, 467

Alpha.py (module-tester), 93
and() method, 114
AND operator (&), 23, 31–32
anonymous (lambda) functions, defining, 90–91
anydbm dictionary, 229–230
Apache server CGI scripts, 299
appearance options (Tkinter widgets), 354
append() method, 58
    with arrays, 71
    with IMAP mailboxes, 288
    with wxPython, 411–412
apply() function, 90
arbitrary precision numbers, 587–588
archives utility, 657
arguments
    in exceptions, 81–82
    in functions/tuples, 89–90
arithmetic operators, 4
    date arithmetic, 220
    joins using, 52–53
arrays (array objects), 68–71
    array elements, 600
    attribute options, 600–601
    audio-editing program (quiet.py), 594–595
    converting to lists/strings, 592–593
    managing using Numeric Python, 597–600
    matrix arithmetic using (MovingAverage.py),
        603–604
article() method, 294
articles, in newsgroups, 293–295
ASCII values
    encoding binary data as, 317–319
    encoding in URLs, 276–277
asctime() function, 222
assert() function, 83
assertions, 83–84
assignment statements, 26–28
    using with lists, 57–58
AST objects, 613–614
asterisk character (*)
    with fnmatch() function, 164
    in regular expressions, 140
    in string width fields, 42
asynchronous HTML page retriever
        (asyncget.py), 272–273

asynchronous signals, handling, functions
        for, 191–193
asyncore module, 271–273
atexit module, 184
atof()/atoi()/atol() functions, 139
attributes. See also values
    in classes, managing, 101–102
    of functions, built in, 609–611
    of markup language tags, 326
attron()/attroff() methods (curses), 417
attrset() method (curses), 417
AU sound files
    reading/writing, 458
    reversing (ReverseSound.py), 459–460
audio files. See sound files
audio streams, editing (Quiet.py), 594–595
audioop module, handling audio fragments,
        461–464
auditing tables, 238–240
augmented assignment statements, 38
authentication, 278
avg() function (audioop module), 461–462

B

b amnt statement (Lepto), 435
backgrounds, terminal displays, creating, 418–419
backslash character (\)
    in regular expressions, 141–143
    in string literals, 35
bad.py_ (security test code), 519
base classes
    extending, 104–106
    overloading, 109
Base64 encoding (e-mail), 318–319
BaseHTTPRequestHandler, 264–265
BaseHTTPServer module, 264
Bastion module/object, 520–521
BeginDrawing() method, 409
behavior options (Tkinter widgets), 354
bkgd()/bkgdset() methods (curses module), 418
bidirectional() function, 153
binary data
    encoding as ASCII, 317–319
    reading/writing (struct module), 207
    storing, 195
binary distributions/installers, 653–654

binary mode data storage, 195

binary operations, 23

bind() method, 251

    with widgets, 372

bisect module, with sorted lists, 60

BitmapImage class (Tkinter module), using with Python Imaging Library, 475–476

bitwise operators, 114–115

BlackAdder development program, 690

blocking, by sockets, 253–254

BloodType.py, 342

BloodTypeSax.py (Sax module), 335–336

Boa Constructor development program, 690

body() method, overriding in Tkinter dialogs, 381

BoldOnly.py, 329–330

Boolean operators, 31–32

border() method (curses module), 418

bottlenecks, locating, 505–509

box sizers (wxPython), 403–405

boxes/borders (curses module), 418

brackets ([]), 30

    in regular expressions, 140

break statements, 8

    with looping statements, 77–79

breakfast buttons (FoodChoice.py), 352–354

breakpoints, setting (pdb module), 499

browsing, newsgroups, 293. See also Web browsers

BSD data objects, 233–234

bsddb module, 233–234

buffer interface, 566–567

buffer_info() method, 71

Buggy.py (error-filled code), 695

built-in data types/sequences, 49

built-in functions

    attributes (table), 609–611

    globals, 96

    locals, 96

    open(), 122

    in Python/C API, 571

buttonbox() method, 381

byte orders, 196

    converting, 71

byteswap() method, 71

C

C/C++ code. See also Python/C API

    converting from Python code, 538–541

    converting Python data to, 532–538

dictionary functions, 570–571

embedding Python in, 541–543

file objects, 571–572

general object functions, 559

handling empty values, 571

handling Unicode strings, 567–569

list functions, 564–565

mapping functions, 569–570

module objects, 572–574

number functions, 559

Python extension modules, 527–531

reference counting, 513

running Python code, 543–546

sequence functions, 562

tuple functions, 565–566

type object function, 571

C locale. See localization

C socket library, 248

C structures, converting to/from, 204–207

calculations. See operators

calendar() function, 225

calendar module, 224

call() method, 109–110

call name statement (Lepto), 435

callability, testing for, 110

call-by-values, 88

can_change_color() function (curses module), 428

canvas widgets (Tkinter module), 366–367.

        See also widgets

capitalization, methods for, 134–135

capwords() function, 139

cards.py (random number generator), 585

caret symbol (^), 23

    in regular expressions, 141

case-sensitivity, 5

    of identifiers, 19

category() function, 153

center() method, 134

cgi module, 298–302

CGI scripts

    Python support for, 267–269

    writing/managing, 298–302

CGIDebug.py, 301–302

CGIHTTPRequestHandler class, 267

CGIHTTPServer module, 264

channels (sound files), 453

character categories (string module), 138–139

character data type, 40

character groups, in regular expressions, 143

character sets, 150

characters

    accessing in strings, 38–40

    reading individual characters, 121

    special, in terminal displays, 422–423

chdir() function, 165

check() method (IMAP4), 287

checksum, computing, 211

child classes, 14, 102–104

child processes, running, 181–183

chmod() function, 157

choosecolor.py (color system conversions), 471–472

chr() function, 45

chunked data, reading/handling in sound files, 460–461

circular references, 65

class data type, 107

classes, class objects. *See also specific classes and objects*

    accessing members of, 15–16

    base, extending, 104–106

    base, overloading methods, 109

    browsing, 609

    child classes, 102–103

    class data type, 107

    class statements, 100

    class variables, 100

    creating, 100–101

    customizing/extending, 104–106

    defining, 15, 100, 107

    as exceptions, 82

    hiding data in, 106–107

    instance objects, 101

    managing attributes in, 101–102

    parent/child classes, 14

    protecting, 520–521

    retrieving string name, 108

    special members, 101

    variables, 100

ClassType data type, 68

clearcache() function, 174–175

clipboard, with wxPython, 413

clock() function, 220–221

clockgif.py (PIL Draw object), 478–479

close(), 123

    with child processes, 181

    with file descriptors, 173

    with GzipFile, 215

    with mmap objects, 176

    with shelve object, 203

ClosestPoint.py, 77–78

closing. *See also* exiting

    file objects, 123

    processes, 183–185

    sockets, 251

Cmd class, 440

cmd module, 433, 440–445

cmdloop() method (cmd module)

cmp() function, 109

    with file comparisons, 171–172

    with string comparisons, 43

cmp() method, 109–111

CObjects, 574

code, debugging, 497–501

    code testing tools, 502–505

    error tracebacks, 605–608

    exceptions, 81–83

    Interactive DeveLopment Environment for, 695–698

    locating bottlenecks, 505–509

    pdb for, 497–501

code, executing

    assertions, 83–84

    exec statement, 97

    flow control (if-statements), 73–74

    for-statements, 74–75

    Game of Life example, 84–86

    looping statements, 74–79

    performance statistics for, 507–508

    reference counting, 512–513

    running from C, 543–546

    self-examining code (introspection), 608–611

    while-statements, 79

code, imported, setting aside, 14

code, Python

    browsing classes/functions, 609

    browsing functions, 609–611

    checking indentation, 611

    converting to C, 531–532

    disassembling, 615–616

editing tools, 692–699
tokenizing, 611–613
codec module, 151–152
coerce function(), 25
coerce method, 115
coercing numbers, 24–26, 115
color name statement (Lepto), 435
color options
    curses module, 427–428
    Tkinket widgets, 354, 365
color pairs (curses module), 427–428
color palettes, 467
color_pair() function (curses module), 428
color scheme customizer (ColorChooser.py),
    377–381
color system conversions, 469–472
ColorChooser.py, 377–381
colorsys module, 470–471
column types, in databases, 240–241
combining() function, with Unicode strings, 153
command-line interpreter, creating, 440–442
command-line parameters, viewing, 166
command prompt, 4
    running programs, 6
Common Gateway Interface. *See* CGI scripts
commonprefix() function, 164
communications, multicasting (multitest.py),
    257–261. *See also* e-mail; Internet
    communications
comparing
    comparison functions, 30–31
    comparison operators, 29–30
    files, 171–172
    identity references, 63–64
    rich comparison methods, 110–111
    sequence data types, 53
    strings, 42–43
compile() function, 97
compiling
    modules, 95
    regular expressions, 144–146
Complaint.py, 382
complex expressions, 32–33
complex() function, 45
complex() method, 115
complex numbers
    combining, 24
    in math module functions, 583

components. *See* widgets
compound expressions, 31–32
compress() function, 211
compressing data, 196
    graphics files, 467
    gzip module, 213–214
    PyZipFile class, 216
    zipfile module, 214–215
    ZipInfo class, 215–216
    zlip module, 211–213
concatenating
    data types, 52–53
    strings, 37
Conceal.py (file-hiding program), 318–319
concurrency control (thread module/threading
    module), 485–488
Condition class (concurrency control), 488
conditional statements, 7–8
ConfigParser module/object, 188–190
configuration files, managing, 188–190
connect() method, 234, 251
connection() method, 289
connection objects, in databases, 234
constraints, layout (wxPyton), 406–407
constructors, 15
containers, pickling, 198
contains() method, 113
ContentHandler object, 334–335
contiguous arrays, identifying, 592
continue statements, with loooping statements,
    77–79
control blocks, 6
control flow using if statements, 73–74
controls (wxPython module), 399–401.
    See also widgets
convert() method, with graphics, 474–475
cooked mode (curses module), 421
cookie dictionary, creating (httpreq.py), 149–150
cookies (cookie module)
    importer for (CookieMonster.py), 323–324
    managing/storing, 322-324
coordinates, in wxPython, 402–403
copy(), 63
    copying objects, 65–67
    with IMAP4 objects, 287
    path management, 168
    in Python Imaging Library, 474
copy module, 66–67

copyfile() function, 168
copyfileobj() functions, 168
copying, graphics/images, 474
copymode() function, 168
copytree() function, 168
count() method, 136
    with arrays, 71
    with lists, 58–59
counting references, object, 64–65
cPickle module, 198
crc32() function, 211
create() method, for mailboxes, 287
crop() method, resizing images using, 476
CSV.py (testing example), 502–503
curly brackets ({}), in regular expressions, 141
curselection() method, 375
curses module, 121
    color options, 427–428
    cursor options, 420–421
    handling terminal displays, 415–416
    managing text, 416–417
    maze game (maze.py), 429–432
    starting up/shutting down, 416
    text editing options, 426–427
    user input options, 421–425
    window/screen displays, 417–420
    windows management, 425–426
CurseWorld.py, 416
cursors
    on curse-based terminal displays, 420–421
    in databases, 235
    Tkinter module options, 385–387
    with wxPython, 413
customized exceptions (Pyton/C API), 578
CXX, SCXX (Simplified CXX), 549–550

D

data
    audio. 460–464
    graphics, 472
    hiding, 106–107
data storage
    byte order (endianness), 196
    compressing data, 196, 210-216
    destination issues, 196
    end user issues, 196
    object state, 196
    saving objects to disk (pickling), 197–200
    text versus binary mode, 196
    in XML, 195
data types
    adding pickling support, 199
    built-in, 67–68
    class, 107
    dictionaries for (win32all), 661–662
    instance, 107
    packing/unpacking, 208–210
    printing listing of, 67–68
    sequence, 49
    in win32all, 661–662
data types, numeric
    combining, 24
    comparison functions, 30–31
    comparison operators, 29–30
    converting from string data type, 44–45
    converting to string data type, 45–47
    floating point numbers, 22
    functions for, 24–26
    imaginary numbers, 22
    integers, 21
    long integers, 21–22
    using operators with, 23–24
data types, string
    accessing characters/substrings, 38–40
    character data type, 40
    converting from numeric data type, 45–47
    converting to numeric data types, 44–45
    formatting, 40–42
    length, 35
    string comparisons, 42–43
    string literals, 35
databases, relational
    accessing, concurrency issues, 485
    auditing tables, 238–240
    column types, 240–241
    connection objects, 234
    cursor objects, 235
    database libraries, viewing information about, 242
    dbm objects, 229–231
    error hierarchies/exceptions, 243–244
    input/output sizes, 241
    metadata, 237–240

saving objects into, 203–204

SQL statement parsers, 242

transactions, 234–235

viewing information about, 242

DatagramRequestHandler, 264

date arithmetic, 219–220

dates

formatting, 222–223

handling in wxPython, 413

searching for, 225

daylight savings time, handling, 226

DB API. *See* Python Database API

dbhash module, 229, 233

dbm module/dbm objects, 229–232

deadlock, preventing, 488–489

deathray.py (curses module), 424–425

debugging. *See also* error handling

destructors, 500–501

Interactive DeveLopment Environment for, 695–698

Python code, 497–501

decimal() function, 153

decode() function, 312

uuencode algorithm, 317–318

DecoderRing.py, 75–76

decomposition() function, 153

decompress() function, 211

deepcopy() function, 66–67

deep copying, 66

def FunctionName statements, 6

def statements, 87–88

defaults() method, 189

defining

exceptions, 82

functions, 5–6, 87–91

new classes, 15

del() method/function

with dictionaries, 61

limitations of, 512

with list items/slices, 58

with object references, 65

del() method, 109–110

with widget listboxes, 375

deleting. *See also* removing

file contents, 124–125

list items or slices, 58

delitem()/_delslice_() methods, 113

derived classes. *See* child classes

destructors, finding errors in, 500–501

development tools

BlackAdder, 690

Boa Constructor, 690

Emacs editing tools, 691–692

Interactive DeveLopment Environment (IDLE), 689–690, 692–695

PythonWorks, 690

WingIDE, 690

device context classes (wxPython), 408–411

dialog/message boxes (Tkinter module), 361

customizing, 381–382

text editor example, 362–365

dialogs, built-in (xwPython), 407–408

dictionaries, 10–11

accessing, 61

adding to/replacing, 61

disk-based, 229–231

environ, 165

formatting strings using, 41

namespaces, 95, 97

pickling, 198

updating, 62

dictionary objects (Python/C API), 570–571

dictionary operators, overloading, 112–113

digests, message fingerprints, 521–523

digit() function, 153

dir() function, viewing module contents, 92

dircmp class, 171–172

directories (os/os.path modules)

changing, 165–166

creating, 169–170

functions for, 163–164

viewing working directory, 165

dis() function, 616

dis module, 615–616

disassembling Python code, 615–616

disk-based dictionaries, 229–231

dispatcher class, 271–273

displays, terminal, handling (curses module), 415–432

distributing applications

binary distributions, 653

controlling files in, 648–649

customizing setups, 650

non-Python files in, 648–650

Continued

distributing applications *(continued)*
    package distributions, 647–648
    simple distributions, 643–647
    source distributions, 648–653
    standalone executables, 655–657
disutils module
    distributing extension modules, 650–651
    package distributions, 647–648
    simple distributions (timeutil.py/setup.py),
       643–647
    source/binary distributions, 651–653
div() methods, 112
division calculations
    modulo operator (%) in, 7
    function for, 23, 25
division operator (/), 23
divmod() function, 25
divmod() method, 112
dl module, with C shared libraries, 675
DNS (Domain Name System), 248
docstrings, 87, 501
doctest module, 502
Document Object Model API. *See* DOM API
Document Type Descriptors (XML format), 326
documentation, creating and maintaining, 501
eo_EOF() method (cmd module), 441
do_help() method (cmd module), 441
do_shell() method (cmd mdoule), 441
dollar sign ($), in expressions, 141
DOM (Document Object Model) API, 338
    data exchange using (XMLDB.py), 340–341
    DOM nodes, 338–339
    elements, attributes, text, 338–339
    parsing XML files, 327, 338
Domain Name Servers (DNS), 248
domain names, 248
    host name, address functions, 248–250
dotted notation, accessing packaged modules, 96
downloading files using FTP, 290–291
drag-and-drop operations
    Tkinter support, 382–385
    with wxPython, 413
drawing. *See also* graphics/image files
    boxes, in curses module, 418
    Draw objects, 477–479
    Tkinter module widgets, 366–367
    xwPython device contexts, 409–411

drawing canvas, creating (Events.py), 373–374
DTDHandler class (XMLReader), 337
DTDs (Document Type Descriptors), 326.
       See also XML format
dumbdbm module, 229–230
dumpimp.py (dummy Importer), 637
dumps() function, 197
dup() function, 173
dup2() function, 173
dynamic extension module linking, 531–532

E
e constant, in math module, 581
e-mail
    encoding/decoding, 317–319
    IMAP protocol for, 285–288
    parsing messages, 309–310
    POP3 protocol for, 281–283
    SMTP protocol for, 283–285
    viewing/storing addresses, 310–311
echo/no echo functions (curses module), 422
editing text
    curses module options, 426–427
    wxPython controls, 401
elements, in XML, 326
else-blocks (elif-blocks)
    with except clauses, 81
    with if statements, 73–74
else-clauses, else-statements, 8
    with for-loops, 77-78
    with while-loops, 79
embedded Python, 528
    embedding in C/C++ programs, 541–543
empty values, in Python/C API, 571
encode() function, 317–318
EncodedFile() function, with non-ASCII strings, 152
encoding
    e-mail messages, 317–318
    sound files, 453
    text files, 150
encrypted modules, importing, 633–636
encryption tools, 523–524
end() method, 148
end statement (Lepto), 435
EndDrawing() method, 409
endianness. *See* byte orders
endswith() method, 136

EntityResolver class (XMLReader), 337
environ dictionary, 165
environmental variables
    PythonPath, 94
    viewing, 165
epochs, 219
EpochSeconds, converting from/to, 221
_eq_() method, 109
equality operator (==), 30
erase() method (curses module), 418
errno module/error messages, 190–191
error handling
    assertions for, 83–86
    code debugging tools, 695–698, 699–700
    ConfigParser object, 189
    debugging CGI scripts, 301
    debugging code using pdb, 497–501
    exceptions, 81–83
    locating bottlenecks, 505–509
    ZipFile objects, 215
error messages (exceptions), 5, 80–82
    in C/C++ conversions, 537
    with ConfigParser object, 189
    databases, 243–244
    formatting, viewing, 606–607
    FTP object, 291
    handling in Python/C API, 576–579
    IMAP object, 288
    I/OErrors, 81–82
    NNTP object, 295
    os module errors, 190
    PicklingErrors, 200
    raising, 82
    SAX exceptions, 337
    shlex module, 437
    SMTP objects, 284
    socket connections, 251–252, 254
    swallowing, 607–608
    with syntax errors, 97
    tracebacks, 605–608
    in win32all, 662
ErrorHandler class (XMLReader), 337
escape() function, 147
escape sequences, in strings
    formatting strings using, 36–37
    valid, listing of, 36

eval() function, 97
Event class (concurrency control), 487–488
event handlers/objects, 371–373
    for curse-based terminal displays, 423–424
except clauses, 81
exceptions. See error messages
exclamation point (!) character, in regular
    expressions, 141
exec() functions, 180–181
exec statement, 97
executemany() method, 242
executing code. See code, executing
exiting
    from functions, 88
    from processes, 183–185
    from Python, 4
expandtab() method, 134
expanduser()/expandvars() functions, 163
exponentiation, functions for, 582
expressions, 29–33
expunge() method, 287
extend() method
    with arrays, 71
    with lists, 58
Extensible Markup Language. See XML format
extension classes, 550, 650–651
extension modules, 527–528
    add/count functions, 529–530
    distributing, 650–651
    linking into Python, 531–532
    Numeric Python (NumPy), 589
extension tools, Python-C interfaces
    CXX, SCXX (Simplified CXX), 549–550
    SWIG, 546–549
extensions, for regular expressions, 143–144

F

f amnt statement (Lepto), 435
FancyURLopener, 277–278
FAQs, answers to, 686
fcntl module for UNIX file descriptors, 680–681
fdopen() function, 173
feedback.py (CGI feedback form), 300–303
fetch() method, for IMAP4, 286
FieldStorage objects (CGI), 299–299
file descriptors, 173–174

file formats, 467
    converting between, 208–210
    of databases, incompatibility, 232
    graphics file, 467–469
    mapping to MIME types, 316
    .pyc files, 631
    sound files, 456–463
file systems (UNIX), viewing information about,
        677–678
file viewer, creating (wxPython), 396–398
filecmp module, 171–172
FileInput class, 176–177
filelike objects, 126–127
fileno() method, 123
    with sunaudiodev module, 455
files (file objects)
    closing, 123
    comparing, 171–172
    compiling, 95
    configuration files, 188–190
    creating/opening, 11
    filelike objects, 127–129
    hiding, 318–319
    navigating, 123–124
    non-Python, including in distributions, 648–650
    opening, 122
    printing to file, 120
    in Python/C API, 571–572
    reading contents of, 125–126
    softspace attribute, 124
    transferring using FTP, 290–291
    viewing filenames, 163
    viewing current positions in, 123
    writing to, 124–125
files, managing
    file descriptor functions, 173–174
    file input class, 176–177
    filecmp module functions, 171–172
    fnmatch module functions for, 164
    glob module functions, 165
    mmap objects, 175–176
    os/os.path modules functions, 163–164, 168–169
    tempfile module functions, 170–171
    viewing information about, 159–161
finally clauses, raising exceptions using, 82–83
find() methods, 136
    with mmap objects, 176
findall() method/function, 145, 147

findfactor() method (audioop module), 462
fingerprints, for messages, 521–523
finish() method, 263
fire() method, 103–104
fix() function, 153
flags, for file descriptors, 173
float class, 7
float() function, 7, 44
float() method, 115
floating point (decimal) numbers, 7, 22, 24
    managing, 154
flush() function, 176
flush() method, 125
    in curses module, 422
    with sunaudiodev module, 455
fnmatch module, file/directory management
        functions, 164
fnmatchcase() function, 164
Folder objects, 320–321
fonts
    Internet text options, 305–306
    Tkinket options, 366
    wxPython options, 413–414
FoodChoice.py, 352–354
for-statements, 8, 74–77. See also looping
    with list comprehension, 51
    with lists or tuples, 55
form fields, accessing, 299–300
form() function, 182–183
formatter module, 304–306, 327
formatting
    Internet text, 305–306
    locale-specific formatting, 625–626
    time, syntax for, 222
    using user input, 357–359
formatting strings
    escape sequences for, 36–37
    formatting characters (tables), 40
    methods for, 134–135
    preserving formatting in, 35
    struct module format characters, 204
fpformat module (floating point numbers), 154
fragments, audio (audioop module)
    converting between formats, 463
    managing, 463–464
frames, 349. 393
    audio, managing, 457
freeze utility, 656

from function, 250–251

from() methods 70

fromlist() method, 70

fromstring() method, 70

fstat() function, with file descriptors, 173

FTP object, creating/using, 289–291

ftplib module, 289–291

ftruncate() function, with file descriptors, 173

fully qualified domain names, retrieving, 250

func() function, 164

FunctionAttributes.py (checking version numbers), 610–611

functions. *See also specific classes and objects*
  arguments in, 89–90
  array objects, 68
  browsing attributes, 609–611
  defining in code, 5–6
  overloading, 108–111
  pickling, 198
  seeding arrays with, 598–599
  testing, 502–503
  writing in C/C++, 527–531

G

Game of Life example (LifeGame.py), 84–86

gdbm module, 229, 232

geometry managers, widget layout, 349–350

get() methods
  accessing dictionary mappings, 61
  with ConfigParser object, 189–190
  with e-mail messages, 309
  opening Web browsers using, 308
  with Telnet object, 297
  with widget listboxes, 375
  with wxPython controls, 400

get_() methods, 297
  with curse module cursors, 420–421

getatime() function, 158

getattr() function, 102

getattr() method, 109–110

getch()/ungetch() functions, 121, 669–670

getch() method (curses module), 422

getcwd() function, 165

getfqdn() function, 248–250

gethostbyaddr(), 248–259

gethostbyname() function, 248

gethostname() function, 248–250

getitem() method, 113

getkey() method, 422

getline() function, 174–175

getmtime() function, 158

getname() method, 460

getpass module/getpass() function, 516–517

getpeername() method, 253

getsample() method 9audioop module), 462

GetSelection() method, 400

getservbyname () function, 248–250

getsignal() function, 192

getsize() method, 460

getSocket() function, 117

getsockname() method, 253

getsockopt() methods, 254–255

getstr() method, 422

getuser() function, 516

getweakrefs() function, 116

getweakrefscount() function, 116

getwelcome() method, 289

glob() function, 165

glob module, 165

global interpreter lock, 496

global namespaces, 95

GlobalDict, 97

globals built-in function, 96

gmtime() function, 221

Gopher protocol, 291–292

gopherlib module, 291–292

graphical user interfaces. *See* GUIs

graphics/image files. *See also* drawing
  animating (CanvasBounce.py), 368–369
  converting to bitmaps, 475–476
  creating GIF images (clockgif.py), 477–479
  file formats for, 467, 474–475
  with GUIs, 366–367
  handling using Python Imaging Library, 472–475
  handling in wxPython, 413
  identifying file types, 468–469
  modifying pixel data in, 476–477
  resizing, 476

grayul.py (HTML file viewer), 396–398

greater than operator (>), 30

greater than, equal to operator (>=), 30

grid method options, 351–352

grid sizers (wxPython), 405–406

group(), 148
  accessing newsgroups using, 293

groups, checking in UNIX systems, 671–672

groups() method, 148

grp module, in UNIX systems, 672

_gt_() method, 109–110

guessing game program (NumberGuess.py), 73–74

guess_type() function, 316

GUI-based applications, file-like objecs in, 128–129

GUIs (graphical user interfaces). *See also* Tkinter; wxPython

    appearance/behavior options, 354

    color options, 354, 365

    color scheme customizer (ColorChooser.py), 377–381

    dialog/message boxes in, 361–365

    event handlers, 371–372

    font options, 366

    graphics/images in, 366–369

    incorporating user input, 356–359

    Lepto-based interfaces, 433–450

    menu widgets, 360–361

    printing exception tracebacks (GUIErrors.py), 607

    size options, 354

    text widgets, 359–360

GUIErrors.py, 606–607

gunzip module, 213

gzip module, 213–214

H

handle() method, 263

HandleForm.py (CGI script), 267

handlers, for asynchronous signals, customizing, 191

hasattr() function, introspection using, 608–609

has_colors function (curses module), 427

hash() function, 62

hash() method, 109–110

hash() method, 110

hashablity, 62

has_key() method, 61

header values, e-mail message, retrieving, 309–310

HelloWorld.py (CGI script), 298–302

help systems

    in cmd module, 441–442

    newsgroups, 687

    technical assistance Web sites, 686

    tutorials, 17

hex() method, 115

hexadecimal values, converting strings to, 75–76

hives, in Windows registry, 664

HLS (hue-lightness-saturation) color system, 470

    converting to RGB color system (ChooseColor.py), 471–472

HomePage.py, 666

host names, 248

HSV (hue-saturation-value) color system, 470

HTML files

    converting Python code to, 612–613

    filtering text in, 329–330

    handling in wxPython, 414

    parsing, 327–329

    viewing in wxPython (grayul.py), 396–398

HTML markup language, 325

html module (wxPython), 414

htmllib module, 327

HTMLParser class

    filtering HTML text (BoldOnly.py), 329–330

    handling bogus/unknown elements, 329

    parsing methods, 327–329

    Web Robot (Robot.py), 331–334

HTTP() method, 279

HTTP request file (httpreq.py), 149–150

HTTP requests, sending/receiving, 279–280

httplib module, 278

Hypertext Markup Language. *See* HTML files

hypotenuse, calculating, 582

I

iadd() method, 112

id() function, 64

identifiers

    reserved words, 20

    valid versus invalid identifiers, 19–20

identity references, comparing, 63–64

idiv() method, 112

IDLE. *See* Interactive DeveLopment Environment

if blocks, setting aside code using, 14

if-statements, 8

    else-blocks (elif-blocks) with, 73

    with list comprehension, 51

ignore() function, 172

ihave() method, 295

ilshift() method, 114

ImageDraw module (Python Imaging Library), 477–479

images, adding to GUIs, 366–367. *See also* graphics/images

ImageTk module (Tkinter module), using with Python Image Library, 475–476

imaginary numbers, 22

IMAP4 objects, 285–288

imaplib module, 285–288

imghdr module, identifying image types, 468–469

immutable data types, 10
strings as, 38, 133

imod() method, 112

imp module, 629–631
importing Python modules, 631–633

import() function
overrriding, 94
using, 629–631

import statements, 14, 93, 629

Importer class, dummy custom Importer (dumbimp.py), 637

importing
encrypted modules, 633–636
Python modules, 14, 92–93, 629–631

importpye.py (importing modules), 634–636

imputil module
with encrypted modules, 633–636
Importer class, 636–637

imul() method, 112

in operator (string comparisons), 43

inch() method (curses), 417

include file statement (Lepto), 435

indenting
code, conventions for, 6
function definitions, 611

index() method
with arrays, 71
with lists, 58
with strings, 136

index names, stat module, 160

indexes
accessing sublists using, 9–10
with lists, 9
support for by sequence types, 9–10

indexing, array elements, 590–592

inequality operator (!=), 30

inheritance
child classes, 102–103
multiple inheritance, 14, 103–104

initialization methods, 100, 109

initscr() function, 416

inodes, 158

input() function, 120
with FileInput objects, 176

input. *See also* GUIs; user input
audio files, reading, 457
functions for, reading, 120–121
redirected, detecting, 128
wxPython module options, 411–412

input/output sizes, in databases, 242

insert() method, 59
with arrays, 71
with widget listboxes, 375

installers, 653–654
for standalone applications, 657

instance data type, 107

instance variables, 101

instances of classes, 14

InstanceType data type, 68

instr() method (curses module)

int() function, 44

int() method, 115

integers, 21

interact() method, 296

Interactive DeveLopment Environment (IDLE), 4, 689–690
debugging using pdb, 695–698
editing code using, 692–695

interfaces. *See also* GUIs
to GNU Multiple Precision Arithmetic Library, 587–588
with NIS "Yellow Pages," 682–683
Python - C/C++, 546–550

internationalization, 619-624

Internet Explorer, as home page, 666

Internet communications
formatting text, 304–307
managing URLs, 303–304
protocols for, 275, 303-307

interweaving threads, 495

introspection, 608–611

invalid identifiers, examples of, 19

inversion operator (~), 23
invert() method, 112
I/O (input/output) calls, optimizing, 510–511
I/O sizes, in databases, 242
IOError exceptions, 81–82
IP addresses, 247
is operator, in reference comparisons, 64
isabs() function, 157–158
isalnum() method, 135
isalpha() method, 135
isatty() function, with file descriptors, 173
isatty() method, 123, 128
isdigit() method, 135
isdir() function, 158
isfile() function, 158
isinstance() function, 68, 107
isleap() function, 225–226
islink() function, 158
islower() method, 135
isspace() method, 135
issub() method, 112
issubclass() function, 68, 107–108
istitle() method, 135
isupper() method, 135

J

join() function, building paths, 161–162
join() method, 138
joinfields() function, 140
joining sequences, 52–53

K

Key Bindings (readline module), 676
key names, in string formatting, 41
key-value pairs, 10–11
keyboard event bindings, 371–372
keyboard input
    accessing, 120–121
    with curse-based terminal displays, 421–422
    in wxPython, 412
keyboard shortcuts, in xwPython, 411–412
keypad() method (curses module), 421
keys, 10–11
    in Windows registry, 664
keyword arguments, unpacking in C/C++
            conversions, 537–538
Kill and Yank Key Bindings, 677

killing (readline module), 677
KillKey.py, 667–668

L

l amnt statement (Lepto), 435
lambda (anonymous) functions, 90–91
languages, Lepto, 435. *See also* C/C++
last item on list, accessing, 9
layout (wxPython)
    algorithms, 407
    constraints on, 406–407
    options for, 401–406
_le_() method, 109
leap years, 226
left bit-shift operator (<<), 24
len() function, 35
    with arrays, 71
    with dictionaries, 62
len()method, 110, 113
Lepto-based interfaces
    graphical interface for, 445–450
    interactive console for (leptocon.py), 442–445
    Lepto language basics, 435
    Lepto Lexical Analyzer, 436–440
    parser for (leptoparser.py), 437–440
    simple example of (leptogui.py), 445–450
LeptoCon class (cmd module), 442–445
leptogui.py, 445-50
Leptoparser.py, 437–440
less than operator (<), 30
less than or equal to operator (<=), 30
LessBuggy.py, 697–698
lexical analyses, shlex module for, 436–440
libraries, C shared, using in UNIX systems, 675. *See
            also specific classes and objects*
limits, UNIX system resources, 679–680
linear encoding (sound files), 453
linecache module, 174–175
lineno() function, 177
link() function, 168–169
links
    for extension modules, 531–532
    managing, functions for, 158
    symbolic/hard system links, 168
Linux RPM SPEC options, 654
list command (pdb module), 498
list comprehensions, 51

list() function, 50
list() method, 10
    with e-mail, 281
listbox widget, 375–376
listdir() function, 163–164
listen() method, 251–252
listenThread() function, 203
lists (list objects)
    accessing last item on, 9
    C functions for, 563–564
    converting arrays to, 69–70, 592–593
    creating, functions for, 50–52
    in dbhash module, 233
    deleting items or slices from, 58
    for. . .in-statements with, 55
    index numbers for, 9
    methods for, 58–60
    performance issues, 68
    pickling, 198
    processing functions, 55–57
    replacing values in, 57
    sorted, managing items in, 60
    switching to tuples from, 10
ljust() method, 134
loads() function, 197
local namespaces, 95
LocalDict, 97
locale module
    formatting options, 625–626
    locale categories, 624–625
    locale properties, 626–627
locale-specific formatting. *See* localization
localhost addresses, 247
localization, 619, 624–625
    time formats, 221, 223–224
locals built-in function, 96
Locator class (XMLReader), 337
Lock class (concurrency control), 486
locking, global interpreter lock, 496
locking threads, 485–488
    preventing deadlock, 488–489
logarithms, calculating, 582
login()/logout() methods (IMAP), 285–288
long() function, 44
long() method, 115
long integers, 21–22, 24

looping statements, 7
    break-statements with, 77–78
    breaking out from, 8
    changing reference sequences in, 78–79
    continue-statements with, 77–78
    else-clauses with, 77–78
    optimizing, 510
    while-statements with, 8, 79
loose typing, 4–5
lossless compression, 467
lossy compression, 467
lower() method, 134
lseek() function, with file descriptors, 173
lshift() method, 114
lstat() function, 161
lstrig() method, 134
_lt_() method, 109–110

M

MagicSquare.py (using ufuncs), 596
MainLoop() method, 393
mailbox module, 320–321
mailboxes
    administering, 287–288
    managing/searching, 285–286
    MH, managing, 320–321
    UNIX, parsers for, 320
mailcap files, parsing, 317
mailcap module, 317
maillists about Python, joining, 687
makedirs() function, 169–170
maketrans() function, 139
managed windows (wxPython), 394–395
mapping() function, 117
mapping objects (Python/C API), 569–570
mappings, dictionary
    accessing, 61
    adding to/replacing, 61
    updating, 62
mappings, of MIME type file extensions, 316
marked parameters (SQL statements), 242
markup languages, 325. *See also* HTML files;
        XML format
marshal module, 200
Mask class (curses module), 419–420
masked arrays, 589
mask.py (terminal display screen mask), 419–420

match() function, with regular expressions, 147
match() method, 145
match objects, methods for, 148
matching
    nongreedy, 143
    regular expressions, 145
math module
    exponent calculations, 582
    logarithm calculations, 582
    rounding, 581–582
    trigonometric functions, 582–583
matrix operations, with arrays, 603–604
max() function, 31, 55
    with string comparisons, 43
maze game (maze.py, curses module), 429–432
MD5 message digits algorithm, 522
membership testing, sequence data types, 53
memory, managing, 512, 579
memory-mapped files, 175–176
menu widgets, 360–361
menus, adding to xwPython, 411–412
message fingerprints, 521–523
Message objects, 309, 320–321
messages, adding to mailboxes, 288. *See also* e-mail; networking
metadata
    auditing table example (mirrormaker.py), 238–240
    sequence pieces (table), 238
metatext, 326
methods. *See also* functions *and specific classes and objects*
    for array objects, summary of, 71
    base methods, 109
    initialization methods, 100
    overloading (table), 111–112
    self referencing, 15
MH mailboxes (MH objects), 320–321
MIME messages
    encoding/decoding, 312
    mailcap files, parsing, 317
    mapping to file extensions, 316
    multipart messages, 313–314
    parsing, 311–313
    testing, example file (MimeTest.py), 314–315
mimetools module, 312
mime.types file, 316

mimetypes module, 316–317
MimeWriter module, 313
mimify() function, 312
mimify module, 312
min() function, 31, 43, 55
minimum field width number (string formatting), 41
minus operator (–), 23
    in string formatting, 41
mirrored() function, 153
mirrormaker.py (audit tool), 238–240
mix-ins, multiple inheritance with, 104
mkdir() function, 169
mktemp() function, 170
mktime() function, 221
mmap module/objects, 175–176
mod() method, 112
mode method, values, 122–123
mode values, open() function, 122
modes, for paths, setting, 157
modifying attributes, 101–102
module objects (Python/C API), 572–574
module type values, 632
modules. *See also specific modules*
    compiling/storing, 95
    copying, 66
    customizing using mix-ins, 104
    distributing/installing, 644–647
    encrypted, importing, 633–636
    extension, distributing, 650–651
    grouping into packages, 96–97
    importing, 14, 92–93, 629–631
    layout, 91–92
    locating, 94
    reading lines from, 175
    reimporting, 93–94
    retrieving from remote locations, 636–641
modulo operator (%), 7, 23
    in string formatting, 40–41
Monkeys.py, 96
Monte Carlo sampling (Plotter.py), 586–587
month() function, 224–225
monthcalendar() function, 224
monthrange() function, 225
Morsel object, 322–323
morsels, storing cookies as, 322–323
mouse buttons, binding, 372

mouse cursors, customizing (wxPython), 413

mouse input, mouse events

detecting in curses module, 423–425

terminal displays, 423–424

in wxPython, 412

mousemask() function (curses module), 423–424

using (Deathray.py), 424—425

MovingAverage.py (matrix arithmetic), 603–604

mpz module, 586–587

msvcrt module, 121

Windows-specific services, 669–670

mul() method, 112

multi-process socket server classes, 104

multi-threaded socket server classes, 104

multicast communications, example code for, 256–261

MultiFile class, 313

multiple assignment statements, 27

multiple inheritance, 14, 103–104

multiplication operator (*), 23

repeating strings using, 37–38

multiplying array matrices, 602–604

Multipurpose Internet Mail Extensions. *See* MIME messages

multitest.py (multicasting), 257–260

multithreading. *See* threading

MutableString class, 105

mxODBC module, database searching using, 235–237

N

name() method/function, 123, 187

namelist() method, 215

names, of variables, 19–20

namespaces, 95, 97

lambda (anonymous) functions, 91

objects, 63

in XML, 327

native language support (NLS), 619–620

adding to applications, 620–624

ncurses API. *See* curses module

ndiff utility, 172

_ne_(), 109

neg() method, 112

nearest() method, 375

netrc files, handling, methods for, 291

Network News Transport Protocol (NNTP) object, 292–295

network orders, 256

networking, 247–248, 267

byte ordering settings, 256

CGI script handlers, 267–269

connection objects, 251–252

HTTP servers, 264–267

multicast communications, 256–261

non-threaded communications, 269–273

sending/receiving data, 251–252

socket module functions, 248–250

socket servers, 261–263

networks, moving objects between, 200–203

new module, 614–615

newnews() method, 293–294

NewObject statement, 15

newpad() function (curses module), 426

new_panel() function (curses module), 426

newsgroups

accessing, 292

browsing, 293

managing, methods for, 292–295

NewsSlurp.py, 294–295

nextfile() function, 177

NIS (Sun System) "Yellow Pages," UNIX interface with, 682–683

NLS. *See* native language support

NNTP object, 292–295

nntplib module, 292–295

non-ASCII strings, 150

non-managed windows (wxPython), 395–396

None value, 11

nonprintable characters, 34

nonzero() function, 109

noraw() function (curses module), 421

normcase() function, 162

normpath() function, 162

not in operator, 43

not operator, 32

NullWriter, 306–307

NumberGuess.py (exception handling script), 73–74

NumberGuess2.py, 80–81

numbers, pickling, 198

numeric data types
    combining, 24
    comparison functions, 23–24
    comparison operators, 29–31
    converting to/from string data type, 43–47
    floating point numbers, 22
    functions for, 24–26
    imaginary numbers, 22
    integers, 21
    long integers, 21–22
numeric() function, 153
numeric operators, 111–112
Numeric Python (NumPy), 589
    array elements, 600
    array-handling functions, 590–593, 597–601
    array matrices, 602–604
    universal functions, 593–596

O

Object Graphics Library (OGL), accessing in
    wxPython, 413
object-oriented programming (OOP), 15
    classes, creating, 100–101
    Python support for, 99
object references
    passing, 88
    variables as, 88
object state, 196
objects, 14. *See also specific classes and objects*
    class definitions, 100
    class variables, 100
    classes, 100–101
    copying, 65–67
    creating from C/C++ code, 539–540
    creating new objects, 15
    identify references, 63–65
    instance objects, 101
    instance variables, 101
    keys, 10–11
    low-level, creating, 614–615
    managing attributes in, 101–102
    moving across networks, 200–203
    pickling, 198–200
    proxy objects, 117–118
    sys module, 126–127
    values, 10–11
    weak references with, 115–116

objects, in Python/C API
    buffer interface, 566–567
    built-in types, 571
    dictionary functions, 570–571
    file objects, 571–572
    generic objects, 556–558
    list functions, 564–565
    mapping objects, 569–570
    module objects, 572–574
    number objects, 558–561
    tuple functions, 565–566
obufcount() method (sunaudiodev module), 455
oct() function, 46
oct() method, 115
OGL (Object Graphics Library), accessing in
    wxPython, 413
onButton() method, 393–394
onecomd() method (cmd module), 441
OOP. *See* object oriented programming
open() function, 11
    with arrays, 203–204
    with audio files, 457
    creating file descriptors, 173
    gzip module, 215
    with non-ASCII strings, 152
    opening files, 121–122
    with sunaudiodev module, 455
    with URLs, 278
openlog()/closelog() functions, 674–675
openpty() function, 173
operator module, overloadable functions, 108–111
operators
    arithmetic operators, 4
    augmented assignments, 28
    Boolean operators, 31–32
    comparison operators, 29–30
    listing of, 20
    modulo operator (%), 7
    with numeric data types, 23–24
    overloading, 111–114
    precedence rules for, 4, 33–34
    reference comparisons, 64
    string comparisons, 43
optimizing. *See* performance, optimizing
_or_() method, 114
OR operator (|), 23, 32
ord() function, 45

order modifiers, in struct module, 206
orientation, of controls, in wxPython, 403–404
os module, 156
    error exceptions, 190–191
    executing shell commands, 179–181
    exiting from processes, 183–184
    file descriptor functions, 173–174
    file management functions, 163–164, 168–169
    file-opening functions, 122
    path management functions, 156–160
    process information functions, 185–186
    running child processes, 181–183
    viewing environmental variables, 165
    viewing system information, 187
OSError class, 190–191
os.path module
    building/vreaking up pths, 161–162
    comparison with os.module, 156
    file/directory management, 164
    path management functions, 157–162
output. See also I/O; printing
    audio files, 457–458
    print statement, 119–120
    WordCount.py, 13
overloading
    bitwise operators, 114–115
    dictionary operators, 112–113
    functions, 108–111
    numeric operators, 111–112
    sequence operators, 112–113
    type conversion operators, 115

P
pack() methods, 208–209
    widget layout, 350–351
packages
    distributing/installing, 647–648
    grouping modules into, 96–97
Packer objects, creating, 208–209
packing data types, 208–209
pads (curses module), 425–426
palettes, 467
parameters, in functions, 88–89
parent classes, 14
    child classes from, 102–103
    multiple inheritance, 103–104

parentheses (( ))
    in calculations, 4
    in complex expressions, 32–33
    in regular expressions, 141
parsing
    HTML files, 327–329
    Lepto programs, 436–440
    Python data, 531–537
    Python code, parse trees for, 613–614
    XML documents, 327
passwords
    managing, 516–517
    in UNIX systems, 671–672
path type test function, 160
paths, 155
    accessing, 156–157
    locating, for modules, 94
    managing , 156–161, 168–169
paths. managing
    os module functions for, 156–157, 168–169
    os.path module functions for, 157–159, 161–163
    stat module functions for, 160–161
    statcache module functions for, 161
pause() function, 192
pdb module (debugger), 497–498
performance, optimizing
    I/O calls, 510–511
    locating bottlenecks, 505–509
    looping, 510
    managing memory, 512
    organizing if-statements, 74
    performance statistics, 507–508
    "simultaneous" code, 495–496
    sorting, 509
    sound files, 454
    string-handling, 511
    thread-handling, 511
periods (.)
    in regular expressions, 140
    in string formatting, 42
permissions, 157
phone list (database), 231–232
PhotoImage class (Tkinter module), 366–367
    with Python Imaging Library, 475–476
pi constant, in math module, 581

pickling, 197–198
  classes, 199–200
  swap module example, 200–203
pipe() function, 173
pipes, 173
pixel data, modifying, 476–477
playing/recording sound files
  SunOS, 455–456
  Windows systems, 454–455
PlaySound() function (winsound), 454–455
plotter program, creating using shlex module, 433
plus operator (+), 23
  concatenating strings using, 37
  overloading, 108
  in regular expressions, 141
  in string formatting, 41
pocket calculator, Python as, 4
point class (Point.py), 15–16
PoliteGet.py, 307
poll() function, 270
polling objects, 270
pos() method, 112
pow() method, 112
pop() method, 59–60
  with arrays, 71
pop arg statement (Lepto), 435
POP3 accounts, accessing, 281–283
popen() functions, 181–182
popitem() method, 63
poplib module, 281–283
popmail.py, 281–282
Popup.py (menu widget), 361
porting threaded code, 494
pos() method, 112
post() method, 295
POST requests, 280
pow() function, 25–26
pow() method, 112
power operator (**), 23
precedence rules, operators, 4, 33–34
primary orientations, in wxPython, 403–404
PrimeFinder.py (looping statements), 7–8
print statement/command
  in pdb module, 498
  printing to file, 120
printing, 119–120
  calendars, functions for, 224–225

tracebacks, 605–607
  with wxPython, 414
prmonth() function, 225
processes
  handling, functions for, 181–185
  viewing information about, 185–186
profile module/Profile class, 506–507
programs, running, 6, 179–181. See also code, executing
progress bar, creating, 387–388
properties, of locales, 626–627
protocols, communications, 248, 275
proxy objects, 117–118
proxy servers, 276
pseudoterminals (UNIX systems), 681–682
pstats module/Stats class, 507–508
public access, versus private, 15–16
push() method, 313
push arg statement (Lepto), 435
pwd() method (FTP server), 289–290
pwd module, using with UNIX systems, 671–672
py2exe utility, 655–657
PyArg_ParseTuple object types, 533
Py_BuildValue object types, 539–540
.pyc files, 631
pyclbr module, browsing classes, 609
pydoc module, 501
PyInterpreterState objects, 576
.pyo files, 95
PyObject pointer, 553
PyShellWindow module (wxPython), 398
Python/C API
  built-in types, 571
  C list functions, 564–565
  CObjects, 574
  dictionary functions, 570–571
  empty values, 571
  error messages/exceptions, 576–579
  extension tools, 546–550
  file objects, 571–572
  generic objects, 556–558
  managing memory, 579
  mapping functions, 569–570
  module objects, 572–574
  number objects, 558–561
  object layers, 556
  reference conventions, 554–555

reference ownership, 553–555
    sequence objects, 561
    sub-interpreters, 576
    threads, 574–576
    tuple functions, 564–565
    Unicode strings, 567–569
Python Database API, 234–244
Python distribution downloads, 685–686
Python Enhancement Proposals (PEPs), 687
Python Extensions for Window. *See* win32all
Python Imaging Library (PIL)
    features, 472–475
    image formatting, 480
Python interpreter, starting and exiting from, 3–4
Python MegaWidgets (Pmw), 389
Python mode for Emacs, 692–669
Python Threading SIG, 496
PythonPath variable, 94
PythonWin, 698–699
PythonWorks, 690
PyZipFile class, 216

Q

querying relational databases (soundex.py),
        235–237
question mark (?), in expressions, 141
Queue module/Queue class, interweaving threads
        using, 495
Quiet.py (audio editor), 594–595
quote() function, 276
quoted-printable encoding, 319
quotes, in string literals, 35

R

r amnt statement (Lepto), 435
radd() method, 112
raising exceptions, 82
random numbers, generating, 583–587
    deck shuffling example, 585
    distributions for, 585
    Monte Carlo sampler (Plotter.py), 586–587
range() function, 8, 50–51
    with looping statements, 76–77
ranges, in lists, managing, 50–51
raw() function, 421
raw mode (curses module), 421
raw_input() function, 120–121
rdiv() method, 112

rduvmod() method, 112
re module. *See* regular expressions
read() methods, 125
    with audio files, 461
    with ConfigParser object, 188
    with file descriptors, 173
    with mmap objects, 176
    with sunaudiodev module, 455
    with Telnet objects, 297
    with ZipFile objects, 215
read_byte() method, 176
readframes() method, with audio files, 457.
        See also chunked data
reading file contents
    chunked audio files, 460-461
    nonchunked audio files, 457
    text files, 125–126
readline() method, 125–126
    with mmap objects, 176
readline module, 121
    in UNIX systems, 675–678
readlines() methods, 126
Real Media File Format (RMFF) files, reading,
        460–461
recursive grep utility (rgrep.py), 166–167
recv()/recvfrom() methods. *See* networking
redirected input, detecting, 128
ref() function, weak referencing, 116
references, object
    comparing, 63–64
    counting, 64–65
    and memory management, 512–513
    tracking ownership of, 553-555
    weak references, 115–116
refresh() method (curses module)
    with pads, 426
    with windows, 418
register() function, 184
    with Web browsers, 308
regular expressions
    character groups, 142–143
    creating, 144–145
    extensions, 143–144
    nongreedy matching, 143
    syntax, 140–141
    using, 145–147
reimporting modules, 93–94

relational databases
    accessing, 234–235
    auditing tables, 238–240
    column types, 240–241
    database libraries, 242
    error hierarchies/exceptions, 243–244
    input/output sizes, 241
    metadata, 237–240
    SQL statement parsers, 242
relative paths, 155
reload() function, 93–94
Remainder.py, 599–600
remainders, calculating, 7
remote importer, 637–640
remote server access, 296–298
remove() function, 168–169
remove() method, 59
    with arrays, 71
removedirs() function, 170
removing. See also deleting; exiting
    attributes, 101–102
    files, 169
rename()/renames() function, 168–169
renaming paths, 168–169
repeat statement (Lepto), 450
repeat count sub statement (Lepto), 435
repeating sequences, 52–53
repeating strings, 37
replace() method, 137
replacing, substrings, 137
report() method, 172
repr() function, 46–47
repr() method, 109
request handlers, 262–264
Request objects, managing HTTP files/URLs using,
    278–279
reserved words, 19
reset arg statement (Lepto), 435
reshaping, array objects, 600–601
resizing objects, 476, 600-601
resource module
    resource limit settings, 679–680
    UNIX system usage information, 678–679
resource usage (UNIX systems), 677–678
retr() method, 281
retrieve() method, 278
return-statements, 88

reverse() method, 60
    with arrays, 71
ReverseSound.py, 459–460
rexec module/RExec object, 517–520
rfc822 module (e-mail handling)
    e-mail address lists, 310–311
    handling MIME messages, 311–312
    parsing e-mail headers, 309–310
RFCs (requests for comments), 275
rfind() method, 136
RGB (red-green-blue) color system, 469–470
    converting HLS system to (choosecolor.py),
        471–472
rgrep.py, 166–167
rich comparison methods, 110
right bit-shift operator (>), 24
rindex() method, 136
rjust() method, 134
rlcompleter module, 675–678
RLock class, concurrency control, 486–487
rlshift() method, 114
RMFF (Real Media Format) sound files, handling,
    460
rmod() method, 112
rmtree() function, 169
rmul() method, 112
robot programs, 307–308
    Web robot example (Robot.py), 331–334
RobotFileParser object, 307–308
robotparser module, 3–7-308
rotor module/rotor objects, 523–524
round() function, 26, 45
rounding, 7, 581–582
rpow() method, 112
rshift()/_rrshift_() methods, 114
rstrip() method, 134
rsub() method, 112
ruimp.py (remote Importer), 638–640
run() method, 483–484
running programs, 6, 500. See also code, executing

S

sample rates/widths (sound files), 453
sandboxes, 517–520
saving objects into databases, 203–203
SAX (Simple API for XML), using, 327, 334–337
scale amnt statement (Lepto), 435

scale widget, 376
sci() function, 153
scope rules, 95–96
screen-scraping (curses module), 417–418
scripting languages (Lepto), 433–450
scrollbars
    with widgets, 376–377
    with xwPython windows, 396
search() method, 145, 147, 286
searching
    databases, 235–237
    dates, calendars, 225–226
    files, grep utility for, 166–167
    match objects, 147–148
    newsgroup articles, 293–294
    regular expressions, 145
    robot programs for, 331–334
    sound fragments, 462
    strings, methods for, 135–136
    Web searches, 280
secondary orientations, in wxPython, 404
Secure Hash Algorithm (SHA), 522–523
security issues, CGI scripts, 302
security tools
    encryption, 523–524
    message fingerprints, 521–523
    passwords, 516–517
    restricted environments, 516–521
seek() method
    changing current position within file, 123–124
    with mmap objects, 176
select() method (IMAP4), 286
select module, non-threaded communications,
        270–273
selection_set() method, 376
self-examining code (introspection), 608–611
self references, 15, 100
Semaphore class (concurrency control), 487
send() method/function, 203, 252
sending/receiving e-mail, 291–285
sendmail() method, 283
sendto() method, 252
sequence data types, 9–10, 49
    accessing portions of using slices, 54
    accessing portions of using subscription, 53
    comparing, 53
    joining/repeating, 52–53
    membership testing, 53

processing functions, 55–57
    unpacking, 54
sequence operators, overloading, methods for,
        112–113
set_() methods
    with Telnet object, 297
    with wxPython controls. 402, 411
SetAcceleratorTable() method, 411
setattr() function, 102
setattr() method, 109–110
setblocking() method, 253–254
SetCursor() method, 413
setdefault() method, 61
setfirstweekday() function, 225–226
setinputsizes()/setoutputsizes() methods, 241
setitem()/_setslice_() methods, 113
setparams() method, using with audio files, 457
SetPosition() method, 402
SetScrollBars() method, 395
SetSize() method, 402
setsockopt() method, 254–255
SetStatusBar() method, 395
SetToolbar() method, 395
setup functions, embedding, 542–543
setup() method, 263
setup.py
    customizing, 650
    for package distributions, 648
    for simple distributions, 644
SGML (Standard General Markup Language), 325
shallow copies, 65–67
shared libraries (UNIX systems), 675
shell commands, executing, 179–181
shelve module storage functions, 203–204
shlex module/shlex class, 433, 436–437, 522–523
    Lepto parser program (leptoparser.py), 437–440
shutdown() method, 251
shutil module
    file management functions, 169
    path management functions, 168
signal handlers, customizing, 191–193
signal module, asynchronous signal handling,
        191–193
sig.py (signal handler), 192–193
Simple API for XML. See SAX
simple.c extension program, 529–530
SimpleCookie class, 322
SimpleHTTPRequestHandler class, 266

SimpleHTTPServer module, 264
Simplified Wrapper and Interface Generator. *See* SWIG
single underscore (_) character, 20
size() function, 176
size() method, with widget listboxes, 375
size modifiers, struct module, 206
size options (Tkinter widgets), 354
sizers (wxPython), 403
    box sizers, 403–405
    grid sizers, 405-406
sleep() function, 221
slice operators (slicing)
    with array elements, 590–592
    copying objects using, 65–66
    with sequence data types, 54
    with strings, 39–40
SMTP accounts, 283–285
smtplib module, 283–285
sndhdr module, 456
socket module/socket objects, 248–250
    asynchronous dispatcher class, 271–273
    binding/connecting, 251–252
    calling, 117
    communications options, 254–255
    copying, 66
    creating, 250–251
    message handling, 251–253
    managing, 250–251
    open sockets, viewing, 247
    ports/IP addresses for, 253–254
    socket function(), 250–252
socket servers, 261–263
SocketServer module
    modifying using mix-ins, 104
    TCP/UDP subclasses, 261–263
softspace attribute, in file objects, 124
sorting
    array objects, 601
    lists, managing items in, 60
    optimizing, 509–510
sound files
    AIFF files, 456–458
    AU files, 458
    components/features of, 453–454
    converting formats, 462–463

    managing sound in, 463–464
    playing/recording, 454–456
    reading/writing, 456–461
    reversing sound on, 459–460
    storing, 456
    WAV files, 458
soundex.py (database query), 235–237
source code editors, 691-695
    Emacs editing tools, 691–692
    Interactive DeveLopment Environment (IDLE), 692–695
    making Python-aware, 692
source distributions
    controlling files in, 648–649
    creating, 651–653
span() method, 148
spawn() functions, 182–183
special characters, unpacking in C/C++ conversions, 536
spiral.py, 421
splitfields() function, 140
splitlines() method, 137–138
splitting
    paths, 162
    regular expressions, 146–147
    substrings, 137–138, 140
    windows in wxPython, 395–396
SplitVertically() method, 395
SQL statement parsers, 242
square roots, calculating, 582
stack traces, printing, 606–607
stacking windows (curses module), 426
StackPrint.py, 606–607
standalone applications, building tools
    archives and standalones, 657
    freeze, 656
    py2exe, 655–656
standard I/O, accessing, 126–127
start() method, 148
    with Thread object, 483–484
startbody()method, 313
startfile() function, 180
starting Python interpreter, 3
startwith() method, 136
stat() function, 159–160
stat module, index names (table), 160

statcache module, 161
statements. *See also specific types of statements*
  class definitions, 15
  function definitions, 5–6
  grouping by indentation level, 6–7
  Lepto-supported, 435
  types of, 6–8
statements, assignment
  augmented, 27–28
  multiple, 27
  simple, 26–27
static extension module linking, 531
statistics, code performance, 507–508
status bars, adding to windows (wxPython), 395–396
status() method (IMAP), 288
statvfs module (UNIX system information), 678–679
stderr/stdin/stdout objects, 126–128
store() method (IMAP4), 286–287
storing
  modules, 95
  objects, 203–204
  sound files, 456
  ufuncs output, 594
str() function, 46
_str() method, 109
StreamRequestHandler, 264
strerror() function, 190
strftime() function, 222
string class, customizing, 105
string data type, 34
  accessing characters/substrings, 38–40
  converting from numeric data type, 45–47
  converting to numeric data types, 44–45
  escape sequences with, 36–37
  formatting, 40–42
  length, 35
  string comparisons, 42–43
string literals, 35
  escape sequences in, 36–37
  raw strings, 37
  Unicode strings, 43
string module, 133
  atof() function, 139
  atoi() function, 139
  atol() function, 139
  capwords() function, 139
  character categories, 138–139

join() function, 138
joinfields() function, 140
maketrans() function, 139
splitfields() function, 140
StringIO class, 149–150
strings (string objects)
  C functions for, 563–564
  characters/substrings in, 38–40
  comparing, 42–43
  concatenating, 37
  converting arrays to, 592–593
  converting to hexadecimal values, 75–76
  formatting, 40–42, 134–135
  handling as files, 149–150
  immutability of, 133
  non-ASCII, 151–152
  optimizing, 511
  pickling, 198
  regular expressions, 140–147
  repeating, 37–38
  searching, 135–136
  Unicode strings, 150
strip() method, 134
strptime() function, 222–223
struct module
  converting to/from C structures, 204–207
  format characters, 204
  order, alignment and size modifiers, 206
styles, with Internet text, 305–306
sub-interpreters, 576
sub() method/function, 146–147
sub() method, 112
sub name statement (Lepto), 435
sublists, accessing, 9–10
subn() method, 146
subscribe() method, 287
subscription operators, 38
  with sequence dta types, 53–54
substituting in expressions, 146
substrings, 9–10
  accessing, 38–40
  managing/editing, 137–138
  searching for, 136
subtraction operator (-), 23
sunau module, 456–458
sunaudiodev module, 455–456
SunOS, using sound files in, 455–456

swapaxes() function, with arrays, 603

swapcase() method, 135

swap.py (swap module), 200–203

SWIG (Simplified Wrapper and Interface Generator), 546–549

symlink() function, 168–169

syntax. *See also specific classes, functions, objects, and statements*
  case-sensitivity, 5
  class definitions, 15
  creating new objects, 15
  regular expressions, 140–141
  simple assignments, 26–27
  variables and expressions, 4–6

SyntaxHighlighter.py, 612–613

sys module
  stderr (standard error) object, 126
  stdin (standard input) object, 126
  stdout (standard output) object, 126

sys.argv variable, 166

sys.getrefcount() function, 64–65

syslog module
  openlog()/closelog() functions, 674–675
  priority values, 673

system() function, 179–181

system information
  functions for, embedding, 542
  viewing, 187

system logger (UNIX systems), 673–675

SystemExit exception, 184

T

tags, in markup language, 325–326. *See also XML format*
  HTML methods, 328–329
  rules for, 326–327

TCPServer class, 104, 261–263

technical assistance Web sites, 686

tell() method, 123, 176
  with mmap objects, 176

Telnet protocol/Telnet class, 296–298

telnetlib module, 296–298

tempfile module, 170–171

template file rules, adding, 648–649

tempnam() function, 171

temporary files, creating, 169–170

TemporaryFile class, 170

terminal displays
  curses module functions, 415–432
  screen masks for (mask.py), 419–420
  in UNIX systems, 681–682

termios/TERMIOS modules, 681–682

TestCase class, 504–505

testing code, tools for
  automating, tools for, 502
  doctest modules, 502–503
  rexec security access (bad.py_), 519
  unittest module, 503–505

testing, remote Importer, 640–641

TestSuite class, 504

testzip() method, 215

text
  displaying on terminals, 415–432
  editing, 426–427
  encoding, 150
  formatting, user input for (UserInput.py), 357–359
  Internet, formatting, 304–307
  string data type for, 34

text editors
  Tkinter module example, 362–365
  Windows API example, 663–664
  in wxPython, 401

text files, accessing lines in, 174–175

text mode
  data storage, 195
  opening files in, 123–124

text widgets, 359–360

TextBox class (curses module), commends for (table), 426–427

TextEditor.py, 362–365
  win32all example, 663–664

textpad module (curses module), 426–427

thread module
  creating new threads, 482–483
  locking using, 485–486
  URLGrabber script example, 492–494

threading module/Thread object, 482–491
  checking thread status, 484
  locating threads, 484–485
  locking using, 486–488
  starting/stopping threats, 483–484
  URLGrabber script example, 489–491

threading process, 481–482
  concurrency issues, 484
  interweaving threads, 495
  optimizing, 511
  porting threaded code, 494
  preventing deadlock, 488–489
  threading example, 489–494
ticks
  in calendar module, 224
  converting from/to, 221
  telling time using, 219
tilde (~) character (inversion operator), 23
time
  formats for, 221
  formatting, functions for, 222–223
  handling in wxPython, 413
  localizing, 223–224
  parsing, 222–223
time module/time() function, 159, 219
  date/time formatting, 222–224
  handling time zones, 226
  stopwatch functions, 220–221
Timer.py, 367–369
timestamps, creating, 222
TimeTuples, converting, 221, 223
timeutil module, setting up, 644–647
title() method, 135
titlecase, converting strings to, 135
Tkdnd module, 382–385
Tkinter module, 347–348, 354
  adding widgets, 387–388
  breakfast buttons example (FoodChoice.py),
    352–354
  color options, 354, 365
  color scheme customizer, 377–381
  cursor options, 385–387
  dialog/message boxes, 361–365, 381–382
  drag-and-drop support, 382–385
  drawing canvas, 373–374
  font options, 366
  geometry manager, 349–350
  graphics images in, 366–367
  interface-building widgets, 348–349
  in Lepto-based GUI, 445–450
  listbox widget, 375–376
  menu widgets, 360–361
  moving images, 368–369
    with Python Imaging Library, 475–476
  scale widget, 376
  scrollbar widget, 376–377
  size options, 354
  text editor example, 362–365
  text widgets, 359–360
  timers with, 367–369
  user input with, 356–359
tkMessageBox, 361–362
TkSimpleDialog module, 381–382
tmpfile() function, 171
tmpnam() function, 171
tofile() method, 70
tokenize module/function, 611–613
tolist() method, 69
  viewing contents of range objects, 77
toolbars, adding to windows (wxPython), 395–396
tostring() method, 70
traceback module, 603–604
  printing GUI exceptions, 607
  printing stack traces, 606–607
  printing tracebacks, 605–606
transactions, in databases, 234–235
translating substrings, 137
  maketrans() function, 139
  string module functions, 139–140
tree controls (wxPython), 400–401
treedemo.py (wxPython module), 400–401
trigonometric functions, 582–583
truncate() method, 124–125
ttyname() function, 173
tuples, 9
  ASTs, 614
  C functions for, 565–566
  creating, 52
  for. . .in-statements with, 55
  passing arguments from, 90
  pickling, 198
  processing functions, 55–57
  switching to lists from, 10
  TimeTuple, 220
  unpacking, 40
two-digit years, enabling, 227
type codes (array objects), 69
type conversion operators, 115
types module/type() function, 67–68
types, sequence vs. immutable, 9–10

U

UDPServer, 261–263
ufuncs (universal functions), in NumPy, 593–597
    audio editing program, 594–595
    repeating/iterating, 595–597
uid() method, 287
uidl() method, 281
unary operations, 23
Unicode strings, 43, 150
    managing, 153
    in Python/C API, 567–569
Uniform Resource Locators. *See* URLs
unittest module, 503–505
UNIX mailboxes, 320–321
UNIX systems
    accessing Python, 3–4
    accessing system logger, 673–675
    CGI scripts for, 299
    child processes, 183
    controlling resource use, 679–680
    epochs, 219
    exiting from processes, 184–185
    file descriptors, 680–681
    inodes, 158
    passwords, groups, 671–672
    proxy servers in, 276
    PythonPath variable, 94
    reading individual characters, 121
    running Python programs, 6
    signal handlers, 192
    system information, viewing, 187, 677–679
    temporary files, managing, 171
    terminals, pseudoterminals in, 173, 681–682
    wildcards in, 167
UnixDatagramServer, 261
UnixStreamServer, 261
unpacking data types, 54, 210
unquote() function, 276
unsubscribe() method, 287
uploading files (FTP), 290–291
upper() method, 134
urlcleanup() function, 276
URLGrabber scripts (threading), 489–494
urljoin() function, 303–304
urllib library, 276
urllib2 library, 278
URLopener, 277–278

urlparse module/function, 277, 303–304
urlretrieve() function, 276
URLs (Uniform Resource Locators)
    handling as files, 277
    managing, 276–277, 303–304
    opening/accessing, 277–278, 308
    retrieving, 276
user input
    in curse terminal displays, 421–425
    in GUIs, 356–359
    reading, 120–121
user interfaces. *See also* GUIs
    Internet formatter interface, 304–305
    Lepto-based, 433–450
UserDict module/UserDict class, 106
UserInput.py, 357–359
UserList module/class, 104–105
UserString module
    MutableString class, 105
    UserString class, 105
UsingNew.py, 615
utime() function, 159
uu module/uuencoding algorithm, 317–318

V

valid identifiers, examples of, 19
values, 10–11, 14
    built-in, 11
    hash values, retrieving, 62
    referencing in variables, 5
    in Windows registry, 664
variables, 88
    assignment statements, 26–28
    class variables, 100
    creating, 26
    defining, scope rules, 95–96
    environmental, 94
    instance variables, 101
    naming, 19–20
    value references in, 5
vectors, adding, 108
verify() method, 284
version numbers, of software, checking, 610–611
vertical slash [|], 141

W

wait status interpretation functions, 184–185
WaitCursor.py (Tkinter module), 386–387

walk() function, 164
warnings, in Python/C API, 578–579
WAV files
    reading/writing, 458
    reversing (ReverseSound.py), 459–460
weak references, handling, 65, 115–117
weakref module
    creating weak references, 116
    getweakrefcount() function, 116
    getweakrefs() function, 116
    mapping() function, 117
    proxy() function, 117
Web browsers
    creating/managing, 264–269
    viewing files in, 308
Web requests, sending/receiving, 279–280
Web Robot, 331–334
Web servers
    cookies, 321–323
    creating/managing, 264–269
    documentation Web server, 501
Web sites
    extension classes, 550
    Python MegaWidgets, 389
    Python downloads, 685–686
    Python Enhancement Proposals (PEPs), 687
    Python Imaging Library, 472, 480
    tutorials, 17
    wxPython for, 391
WebSearch.py, 280
weekday() function, 225
where command (pdb module), 498
where() function, with arrays, 602
while-statements, 79
    in looping statements, 8
widgets (Tkinter module), 349
    appearance options, 355
    behavior options, 355
    building GUI with, 348–349
    color options, 354, 365
    color scheme customizer , 377–381
    creating drawing canvas, 373–374
    cursor options, 385–387
    designing/customizing, 387–388
    dialog/message boxes, 361–365
    event handlers/objects, 371–373
    font options, 366

geometry managers, 349–350
grid method options, 351–352
graphics handling, 366–367
layout constraints, 406–407
listbox widget, 375–376
MegaWidgets Web site, 389
menu widgets, 360–361
packer methods, 350–351
scale widgets, 376
scrollbar widgets, 376–377
size options, 355
text widgets, 359–360
timers with, 367–369
user input, incorporating, 356–359
width fields, 42
_winreg functions, 668–669
win32all (Python Extensions for Windows)
    accessing Windows registry, 664–669
    data type dictionaries, 661–662
    error messages (exceptions), 662
    setting Internet Explorer home page, 666
    text editor, 663–664
win32api functions, 668–669
WindowObject class, 415
Windows API wrappers, 661–664
Windows Internet Information Server (IIS), CGI
        scripts for, 298–299
windows (curses module)
    managing, 425–426
    refreshing, 418
Windows registry, 661
    access constants (table), 665
    accessing, 664–669
    killing keys in (KillKey.py), 667–668
Windows systems
    accessing Python from, 3–4
    epochs, 219
    opening text mode files, 123–124
    playing sound files, 454–455
    proxy servers in, 276
    PythonPath variable, 94
    reading individual characters, 121
    running Python programs, 6, 180
WingIDE, 690
winsound module, 454–455
WordCount.py, 12–13
working directory, viewing, 165

wrapper() function (curses module), 416
write() method/function, 124
    with ConfigParser object, 190
    with file descriptors, 173
    with mmap objects, 176
    with sunaudiodev module, 455
    ZipInfo object, 215
write_byte() method, 176
writeframes() method, with audio files, 457
writelines() method, 124
writepy() method, 216
writing to files, methods for, 124
wxAcceleratorTalbe class
wxApp object, 393
wxBitmap class, 413
wxBoxSizer classes, 403
wxButton classes, 399
wxcanvas.py, 409–411
wxCalendar class, 413
wxChoice class, 400
wxClipboard class, 413
wxDataFormat/DataObject classes, 413
wxDate/wxDateTime classes, 413
wxDialog class, 394, 399
wxDragImage class, 413
wxDropSource/DropTarget classes, 413
wxEditor class, 401
wxEvent class, 394
wxFloatBar clas, 398
wxFont/wxFontData classes, 413–414
wxFrame class, 394
wxGrid class, 395
wxGridSizer class, 405–406
wxHTMLWindow class, 395
wxIcon class, 413
wxImage/wxImageHandler classes, 413
wxMask class, 413
wxMDIChildFrame/ParentFrame classes, 396
wxMDIClientWindow class, 396
wxMenu class, 411
wxMVCTree class, 401
wxNewId() function, 394
wxNotebook clas, 398
wxPalette class, 413
wxPanel class, 399
wxPrintDialog/wxPageSetUpDialog classes, 414

wxPrintPreview class, 414
wxPyEditor class, 401
wxPython module, 391–392
    built-in dialogs, 407–408
    common controls, 399–400
    cursors, drag-and-drop, 413
    device context classes, 408–411
    drawing in, 409–411
    editor controls, 401
    example program, 392–394
    formatting options, 413–414
    HTML handling options, 414
    keyboard input options, 412
    layout options, 401–407
    menus, keyboard features, 411–412
    mouse options, 412
    printing options, 414
    tree controls, 400–401
    window options, 394–398
wxResourceParseFile object, 403
wxScrolledWindow object, 395
wxSplitterWindow class, 395
wxStatusBar class, 395
wxTimeSpan class, 413
wxToolbar class, 395
wxWindow class options, 394–398

X

XDR (eXternal Data Representation) format,
        converting to/from, 208
xdrlib module, 208
xgtitle() method, 294
xhdr() method, , 294
XML format, 325
    DTDs, 326
    namespaces, 327
    parsing, 334–343
    processing functions, 327
    saving XML files, 210
XML handlers, 343
xmllib module, 327
    features, 341–342
    parsing XML, example (BloodType.py), 342
XMLParser class, 341–343
XMLReader class, 336–337
xml.sax module, 334

XOR (exclusive-or) operator (^), 23
xor() method, 114
xover() method, 294
xrange() function, 51
xrange objects, 77
xreadlines() function, 126

Y

yanking, 677
years, two-digit, enabling, 227
YIQ color system, 470

Z

zero arguments, unpacking in C/C++
    conversions, 538
zeros, leading, in strings, 41
zfill() function, 140
zipfile module, 214–215
ZipInfo class, 215–216
zlip module
zones, time, handling, 226